Platoon 3

Platoon 3
A National Serviceman's Story

Tim Ramsden

Published in 2018 by:

30° South Publishers (Pty) Ltd
16 Ivy Road
Pinetown 3610
South Africa
website: www.30degreessouth.co.za

Copyright © Tim Ramsden

Cover design and concept by Anthony Cuerden
Email: ant@flyingant.co.za
Page layout by Blair Couper

Printed by Pinetown Printers (Pty) Ltd; Pinetown, KwaZulu-Natal

ISBN 978-1-928359-09-8

All rights reserved. No part of this publication may be reproduced, stored, manipulated in any retrieval system, or transmitted in any mechanical, electronic form or by any other means, without the prior written authority of the publishers, except for short extracts in media reviews. Any person who engages in any unauthorized activity in relation to this publication shall be liable to criminal prosecution and claims for civil and criminal damages.

Warning - This book contains some graphic imagery and language that some might find offensive.

**Dedicated to my son Shaun
and to those who served with me.**

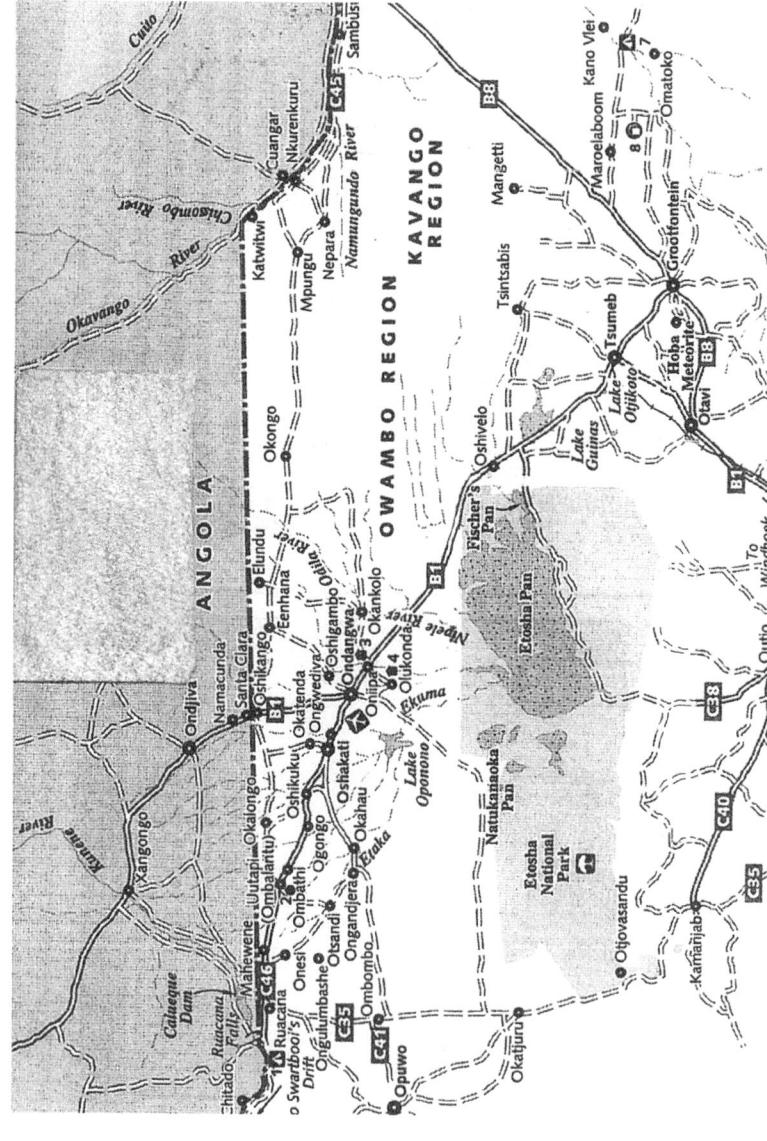

Map of the Border area.

Contents

Author's Note	8
Introduction	9
1. From Civvie to 'Roofie' (new recruit)	11
2. Our new company – Bravo Coy	33
3. De Brug: preparing for battle	44
4. A State of Emergency: in Tembisa Township	69
5. Bloemfontein: last days with 1-SAI	89
6. Middelburg – with 4-SAI	99
7. Our unknown history South-West African - Angolan border	109
8. Adjusting to a new setting	112
9. A long patrol and a dugout on the Yati	137
10. And the rains came	149
11. Etosha National Park: Ambushing the enemy	167
12. Patrols between beacons on the Yati	181
13. Our very own base camp	202
14. Actions of stupidity and more rain	222
15. An unforgettable scene	253
16. April fools	270
17. Going home at last	283
18. Guarding an ammo dump: An overdue pass	293
19. Mischief in the barracks: Life in the Intelligence house	303
20. Kostini Base: Kruger National Park	315
21. Leaderless: A dark shadow of doubt	326
22. Cause for celebration	334
23. Refugees: 40 days left to serve	346
24. Farewell to the Kruger	363
25. Farewell to National Service	387
26. Mozambique: A journey through hell	400
27. Soldiering on 1988	439
28. Operation Desert Fox	448
29. On the outside in Oshigambo	465
30. The frightening truth	479
31. After the war was over: Revisiting Namibia fifteen years on	490
Glossary	498
Bibliography	501
Credits	502

Author's Note

I have written this story in as much detail as I can truthfully and accurately remember. Painstakingly over three and a half years with patience, passion, and discipline I eventually unfolded my army life onto paper.

I want to thank all those who helped me in some way with this story, particularly Wayne who jogged my memory on certain details, and Grant, Dolf and Andrew who provided me with some photographs. I especially thank Laurence, who I know had to dig deep within himself as he reopened the door to his hellish capture in Mozambique. I have done my best to tell his side of the story, acquired through many long-distance telephone conversations, letters, as well as a journey with him into Mozambique, back to his prison, 20 years after the completion of our National Service. Last but not least, I want to say a big thank you to my mother who read my manuscript in all of about five days, catching the last mistakes before it went into print.

At the beginning of our National Service, we were merely young boys with our whole lives ahead of us – only to be conditioned with racial hatred through intense training, into a tight unit of soldiers with a hard, unwavering inner edge, ready to face whatever was thrown at us.

I apologise to any of those soldiers, especially from Platoon 3, whom I may have offended. It was certainly not my intention to do so, but to portray a true picture of life in 'browns' from one day to the next, I needed to express in detail how we actually lived – with actions, feelings, frustrations, and anger playing key roles. I apologise to the reader for the offensive language and racist slander, but unfortunately this is how we expressed ourselves at the time.

I am not proud of my racist thoughts, feelings and actions while living in a chaotic army world not of my choosing. I cannot change the past, but I can learn from it, move forward, and make myself a better person. I now live to embrace the diversity of cultures with an open mind, seeing people for who they are and what they represent, and I know my well-travelled life has helped me break down those barriers that divide. To see people as people, instead of just black and white, has been a miracle in itself.

Looking back, I am glad I served out my two years and faced the hardship head-on. It was a time I shall never forget, having grown through the experience, and to this day I am extremely proud to call myself South African. The friends, the fears, the highs and the lows will always be in my memory, and I thought it very important that my son know my whole story.

Introduction

This is my story written from the perspective of a young naive 18-year-old conscripted into the South African Army under the ruling apartheid government, under which every white male had to serve and protect his country as the 'call of duty.'

In 1984 I began the daunting task of becoming a soldier as I entered into a new and very scary world of strict discipline, confined to an army camp behind wire fences with concrete guard towers. As a new recruit, I was beaten down daily by loud, tormenting, and intimidating shouts of demeaning abuse, along with being forced to run agonizing miles with full military gear willed on by the sheer terror of not keeping up, despite blistered feet, aching limbs, and shattered spirits. For a year I was broken down, and then slowly built up, through intense infantry training – until I was a confident and highly-skilled, mechanized soldier capable of performing practice attacks with live ammunition. After ten months I had meshed into a tightly knit unit of young men from all walks of life, with stamina and endurance second to none and a depth of camaraderie that only a soldier can truly know.

After entering a black township as a show of force to restore peace, we were transferred to another infantry base. And then in 1985 my company was flown to the operational area, where South Africa had been at war with SWAPO (the South-West African People's Organization) since 1966. We served along the South-West African/Namibian border and into Angola, faced with real fears as we laid ambushes and patrolled the flat and arid land under scorching heat and heavy rainfall, adding to the daily torture of fatigue and thirst, while hating each suffering minute of being there.

Along this border-line our insanity set in, for we were plagued by the miseries of army life, surviving on dry rations, and pestered without end by mosquitoes and flies in a land ripe with malaria and far from home, with boredom and careless actions coming to the fore. It was in this land that one of our countless patrols led us into the aftermath of a bloodbath, wherein innocent women and children had been so brutally massacred.

The constant struggle through daily army life brought our platoon closer together, with drunken binges helping to suppress the raging anger and dreadful fear that came and went as we counted each day to the end of our mandatory two years of service.

Our platoon also served along the border of Swaziland and Mozambique, living in the Kruger National Park amongst the wildest of animals. There, in our last three months, three troops from my section were captured within shouting distance of our position. They were led away at gunpoint and imprisoned in Maputo, Mozambique, for three months – leaving them, and us, to suffer the anguish of the unknown.

Most of our time was spent in dirty clothes, sleeping on the ground, and cooking over an open fire. Our nerves were highly-strung and we always had a loaded rifle close at hand. One minute I would be scared out of my wits, and the next I could not care less – a make-believe shield of invincibility there to protect me. The infantry unit I served in was hardly ever granted leave home, and the money we were paid was a mere pittance for the hardship we endured' for that was the price all young white boys had to pay to live in South Africa.

After the completion of my two years, my Citizen Force call-ups began. On my third and last call-up in 1988, I was again placed in the operational area, being part of the largest massing of troops and armoury on foreign soil since the Second World War. I lived in fear of the seemingly inevitable attack deep into Angola.

We had all entered into the army as carefree young boys and lived out a distorted adventure as we made the most of our unpleasant situation, until we returned to our hometowns as tough, disciplined men with minds forever changed. I will always remember the long and hard journey for the unbreakable friendships forged within Platoon 3, amidst the agonizing sweat and deeply hidden fears of two-and-a-half challenging years.

This story follows my account of the events that unfolded – the sense of adventure, intrigue and boyish fun underlined with anger, resentment, tension, frustration and the determination to survive mixed with constant thoughts of civilian life, all of which willed me on until the bittersweet end.

1

From Civvie to 'Roofie' (new recruit)

The afternoon was sunny and humid, no different from any other day at that time of year. A cool breeze drifted off the Indian Ocean, casting a familiar salty aroma across the bustling city of Durban, South Africa.

12 January 1984, had dawned, and I reported to the Natal Command army base in Durban with my call-up papers and a carry bag, set to begin my mandatory two years of military service.

The ruling South African government had made it compulsory for all white males to join the military, in order that they might continue white minority rule with an iron fist. Being white South Africans, we felt ourselves to be rightful owners of this magical land, so rich in natural beauty. We did not even think to question otherwise. In our view, our forefathers had arrived first and built the country. With our white National Party government in control, we felt we would be spared the turmoil that faced the rest of Africa, with greed and corruption steering tribes to war and spiralling once-rich economies into worthless ruin.

One only had to look at the likes of the Belgian Congo, Kenya, Rhodesia, Angola, and Mozambique to see what had happened to these countries after they gained independence. Rejoicing in their new found 'freedom,' they emerged from their European-colonial past into societies traumatized with civil unrest – lawlessness and poverty becoming increasingly evident as the years passed, their economies getting poorer and poorer by the day.

Standing still, I looked up, beyond the buildings, into the depths of the powder-blue sky. I took a few deep breaths, inhaling lungfuls of fresh, sticky sea air into my hungry and nervous body. I savoured the moment' not knowing how many scary months would pass by until I could return to my familiar surroundings.

I did not want to run and hide, or show cowardice in fleeing the land of my birth, never to return' or to return only to the jail sentence that I would face if I chose not to serve. I did not want to find myself in a position where I could not get a job because I had not served my country. To live in the confines of our borders and remain firmly South African, I – along with thousands of school-leavers – had to take up the call of duty, to do what we had to do, to help continue the white rule that governed South Africa.

I waved a quick farewell to my mother, who had driven me to the base, before turning and making my way through the thick throng of grieving relatives and friends, hugging and holding their loved ones one last time before they would be changed forever.

I made it to the gates, guarded by uniformed soldiers clad in brown, and stepped past them into the unknown. In that fleeting step, I felt a change pass through me, my freedom as a civilian had been left on the other side of the gate. Two years sounded such an agonizingly long time.

I followed the line of people, who were as lost and disoriented as I, passing a makeshift sign that read Kroonstad. I hunted for one that read Bloemfontein – a place I knew absolutely nothing about, except that it was an Afrikaans city somewhere in the Orange Free State, which I knew was far away from Durban.

Clutching my army papers firmly in my hand, I stood and waited with hundreds of others by the Bloemfontein signpost. Then, looking at them, I confirmed my destination. I had been assigned to 1 South African Infantry Battalion. What that meant, I had absolutely no idea.

The soldiers, mainly corporals, hurriedly ordered us to unpack all our belongings onto the dry grass in front of us. Out of my brown bag came some unlikely items, all to soon prove their worth: Brasso, starch, cobra floor polish, brown boot polish, prestik, clothes pegs, cloths, stockings, padlocks, one and a half metres of chain, sun block, plasters, toiletries, and a steam iron. Soldiers from past and present had told me what to bring, and now I had a mountain of things in front of me, most of which I had never even used before.

To my surprise, I saw at least five Alsatians – German Shepherds, off their leashes, running madly with their noses to the ground, sniffing through our possessions. These dogs have a great sense of smell and are commonly used in the police force to sniff out bombs. They darted from one person to the next, hopping in an excited frenzy over our belongings, as if searching for well-hidden drugs.

Standing on my left, a short, stocky young man with long, blonde hair waited for his turn with the dogs. Among his belongings he had a cooked whole chicken, which attracted one of the dogs like a crazed Beagle on the scent of its chase. The dog would not leave his chicken, and barked and sniffed at it until one of the corporals arrived on the scene.

'Get the dog away' this is my food for the journey!' he cried, in pure desperation.

Eventually the dog was dragged away against his will, bringing relief to the round, suntanned face of the angry owner. Months later I would learn the real story behind the chicken that had been the centre of the commotion.

1. From Civvie to 'Roofie' (new recruit)

With shouts circling the camp, we got the order to pack up. Struggling to cram our belongings back into our bags, and looking as though we now had more than we came with, we stood ready and waiting for the next order – our crammed bags still unzipped. Finally we began to move, and walked out of the camp in two long lines under Military Police escort and without much talking. We walked for close to a kilometre, until we reached the drab, reddish-brown trains of the South African Railways.

We moved along in silence, with one bag held tightly in our hands. It gave me a cold appreciation for what the Jews under Hitler must have felt as they boarded trains into an uncertain future, cast off to out-of-the-way places, separation and fear playing havoc with their minds.

The majority of us had heard stories of physical and psychological battle scars' inflicted during intense training, border duty, and the unfortunate and untimely deaths of young National Servicemen. Accepting my call to duty, I could not help my rational thinking, knowing full well that some of us young boys would have to pay the ultimate price while serving our country.

Feeling nauseous and scared, but hiding it very well, I climbed onto a train for the very first time in my life. I weaved my way through the crowded but narrow corridor, past equally nervous 17 and 18 year-olds. Eventually I found a compartment with five others sitting quietly inside, waiting to be cast away to Bloemfontein.

Inside the small compartment was a small fold-out table below the window, and on either side of the compartment two fold-down bunks neatly rested. The six of us sat three to the bottom bed and introduced ourselves, asking each other what schools we had just matriculated from.

The six of us all had one thing in common: We were not looking forward to this compulsory experience and began wondering aloud when we would be granted our first pass.

Melvin was one of the six in my compartment and lived up to the image of being 'rough and tough from the Bluff' – a slogan that was given to those who lived on the Durban Bluff. He spoke very confidently and was not scared one bit of the hard road that lay ahead. I looked over to Alan and Colin and wished that I shared the same confidence that he aired unashamedly. Little did I know that in the very near future Alan and I would have the last laugh, at Melvin's unpleasant expense.

Ear-piercing whistles blew and anxious shouts followed as the train began to jerk its carriages forward, beginning an unforgettable two-year experience.

Sitting with all eyes on the window, we watched Durban disappear as the long troop train snaked its way out of the city, each one of us harbouring his own silent thoughts.

By the time late afternoon turned to darkness, we were far into the country but still wrestling with the claws of the unknown. Food was served in the meal carriage, a far walk down the long winding corridor and through many stiff train doors, but it served its purpose well.

On the walk back we passed our cubicle, walking through a couple of extra carriages until we realized our mistake. When we returned we began setting up for sleep, choosing our beds for the long night. Our minds raced a million miles an hour, and sleep did not come easy with the many stops that gathered more troops into the already-crowded train. Shouts in Afrikaans disrupted the cool night silence, and these were followed by a sharp, shrill from a whistle that signalled the driver to take up the route once again.

After nearly a full day's train ride, we eventually pulled into the Bloemfontein Station, looking forward to just getting out of the confined space and starting our service so we could work towards being one of 730 days closer to the end of our duty.

A dozen Samil 50s and old Bedford army trucks waited in welcome for us to board their empty metal hulls. Obeying the shouting from corporals and sergeants, we swarmed off the train and then clambered like a herd of cattle into the closest vehicle. Standing up, we held onto the metal bar beneath the sail cover. Our two hands clenched onto this bar for dear life, as the driver purposely swung hard left and then hard right, toying with our minds with each reckless swerve. I could envision a broad smile on the driver's face as he handed us what every new intake got – a 'roof ride.' This was just the beginning, warming us up for bigger and better things to come.

After a tense 15 minute drive, to the relief of all aboard we came to a halt on a rugby field in Tempe. We climbed off carefully, thankful to be standing on a surface that was not washing away beneath our weakened legs. Standing on the grass, I watched a guy climbing off the back of the open truck with a white cast mending his broken leg. How did he manage that ride? I wondered with admiration.

The corporals instructed us to sit in long lines, one behind the next, the boiling sun burning our exposed necks and faces. Slowly we inched forward as the lucky one in front of the line got up and vanished out of the burning heat and into the concrete building. After waiting for an hour, we realized what all this was about – we were each waiting our turn for a full medical examination. In less than five minutes with the army doctor, clad only in my underwear, I had a full physical and was pronounced G1K1 – the South African army code for a soldier that is 100 percent fighting-fit. This was a good sign for my own

1. From Civvie to 'Roofie' (new recruit)

personal health, but a bad sign for the hardship in infantry training that was destined to follow.

Climbing back into the Samils, we were driven through the high, black, steel-barred gates of 1 South African Infantry Battalion, into a new life that no level-headed person would freely choose. In this place, I just knew that our lives and our minds would forever be changed.

Feeling out of place and very lost, we were divided into platoons and assigned to a company. I was designated to Delta Company, whose insignia was a teardrop. Now attached to a company, my first three months of basic training had begun. Early the next morning we gathered into our platoons and answered roll call to the bark of our surnames.

'Present, Corporal!' we barked back. But it would not take long before we no longer answered to our name but rather to our army number – 81221285BT. '*Teenwoordig, Korporaal!*' soon became my new reply – countless times on any given day.

Still in our civilian clothes, we were marched off for haircuts – short back and sides, in true army fashion. Those with really long hair were punished for flouting the military order and had half their heads shaved, after which they were forced to the back of the line so their haircuts could be completed later. Looking at some of these people, half with long hair and half shaved, we could only laugh at their humiliation and be glad that we were spared it.

Our necks, exposed to the brutality of the midday sun, soon burned a very sore and uncomfortable red. Standing in formation, we would stare at the person's neck directly in front of us. We saw blisters, peeling, scabs, and watery pus oozing from red and tender burns – not the most appetizing scene one would want to see just before breakfast, even though that was not much better.

Still in a mismatch of clothing and bearing no resemblance to soldiers, we were marched to the stores, home to all the necessary kit we needed. Shedding clothes and shoes, we tried on our uniform and heavy boots. Satisfied that they fitted, we placed them into the cylinder-shaped kitbags known as *balsaks* in army lingo.

After being dragged from one giant storeroom to the next, our *balsaks* filled to the top and slung heavily over our shoulders, we returned overwhelmed and exhausted to our Delta line of bungalows.

Once there, we began to unpack our kit onto our beds and change into the brown overalls with our web belts and rock-hard, brown leather boots, which felt like lead weights on our feet. To top our *roofie* uniform, we yanked out the plastic that sat inside our metal helmets, called a *doibie* and placed them on our heads. This was paradise compared to running with the jarring weight and side-to-side movement of the infamous *staaldak*, or steel helmet.

Corporal Kruger, a big man, stood over six feet tall, as straight as a ruler, and in our eyes was built as solid as a brick shit house. He commanded us to attention with firm authority and marched us in pace up to a row of office buildings in the middle of the base. The usual wait was cast upon us as we stood in long lines, which snaked their way from the coolness of the roof overhang to the heat of the open, grey stony area between the buildings. On command, we entered through the doorway one at a time and were met with nurses dressed in pure white, who gently sat us down and got ready to siphon a few vials of blood from our outstretched arms.

'Where do you come from?' a nurse asked me softly, sensing my phobia of needles.

'Durban,' I said hastily, wanting to get the hell out of the chair.

'By the sea?' she asked, in a strong Afrikaans accent.

'No,' I said. 'About half an hour inland.'

A sharp scratch dug into my arm and I tensed and flinched. While my blood was drawn, I thought: Shit, I better not get shot' otherwise I will die of shock from the needle pumping blood back into me. Slightly pale-faced and light-headed, I exited the room and sought out the sun, which seemed to bring some colour back into my face.

When our blood results came back, our blood group was marked in permanent black ink onto the front of our web belts, worn religiously for all to see. I was A-negative and felt rare, as I spotted mainly O-positives, there being only a couple of other troops in my company who had the same blood type as me.

With a new day, another needle lay in store for us. Once assembled, Delta Coy was marched to the same medical building to await a tetanus shot. Our rank warned us to take the needle in the weaker of our arms, as it would stiffen and become temporarily unusable. Filing through in a long line, we took the injection in the shoulder. The nurse had been instructed to use one needle per three troops. Years later, after the AIDS outbreak, we became fearful of this action, though at the time it seemed safe and normal.

In another room, X-rays of our teeth were taken, to be used in a last resort to identify us if we were incinerated, as had been the case in *Operation Askari* when a Ratel armoured car was knocked out during an external raid into Angola. It sent shivers down my spine, for I knew full well that this was not a game of toy soldiers but a preparation for the identification of an unrecognizable body of charred remains.

Soon our shoulders began to tighten up and hurt like hell, leaving our limp arms to hang uselessly by our sides as we marched back to our bungalow.

All we needed now was a rifle, which would become our best friend and a curse at the same time. Our brand-new, brown R4 rifles were signed for, the six-digit serial number engraved in our minds along with our army numbers. 685139 and 81221285 were ingrained in my head as the two most important numbers in the world – my rifle and my name. This cold, five-kilogram piece of steel became our wives, and expected lots of tender care and respect from us. It could never be far from reach, and if it was out of sight we had to know damn well where it was. If lost, a troop was in shits creek.

Once I made the cardinal sin of dropping my rifle before the eyes and ears of a corporal. Before I could pick it up from the rock-hard earth, he was upon me like a cheetah on its kill.

'*Jou dom troep!*' – You dumb troop! – he screamed out in Afrikaans, angered at my stupidity.

All eyes were immediately cast in my direction, and knew exactly what I would be expected to do as punishment for my negligence. Under strict instruction from the corporal, and his cold, intimidating face, I had to stand dead straight with my rifle standing parallel to my right leg, and without bending my knees, fall backwards. I knew I had to do it right the first time, because if I did not I would be forced to repeat the action until I finally did.

I looked at him, fastened my helmet, straightened my arms, and let myself go. The back of my metal helmet hit the surface first, sending shockwaves ringing through my ears' and while I lay in the dust, I could only hope I had performed the way they wanted me to. With a few elbow grazes, and a very dusty overall, I was allowed to rejoin the squad for our daily, morning inspection.

The corporals walked between us as we stood at attention, and inspected us for neatness and presentation – checking for polished boots, clean and ironed overalls, and, most importantly, close-shaved faces. The corporal would run a cotton ball over our faces, and if it snagged on our growth we'd either get off very lightly by having to shave again or, more commonly, have to choose a stone with which to rub our growth. This unpleasant experience would be meted out to many of us, and we would be left with painfully red and angry faces.

The first few nights of sleep in a foreign, fast-paced environment gave us a lost and hollow feeling deep in the pit of our stomachs. Overwhelmed and hopelessly alone, without knowing a soul, we slept fitfully, for a million unanswerable questions plagued our alert minds and clouded our thoughts with worry.

With hidden fear and anxiety, a few hushed, whimpering cries flowed through the darkness of our barracks, followed by a couple of brave laughs sneering at those weaker than they. Having left home for boarding school at the age of 13, I was already used to fending for myself and adapting to change. That experience helped me somewhat in this heartless environment, in which I would have to be strong to survive. But nothing could really prepare us for the cold, uncaring life into which we had been plunged headfirst. At 17 and 18, we felt as though we had been cast out of society and dropped into a chaotic hell of ringing screams and whistles, every activity performed at an accelerated pace and controlled by the unrelenting hands of time.

This is how we imagined a jail sentence, with the freedom of a normal daily life ripped from us. With identical brown overalls and green helmets with the same short hair beneath them, and clutching a stainless steel, rectangular tray moulded to hold separate portions of food known as a *varkpan* – or pig pan – we filed past the food in lockstep and waited for it to be uncaringly slopped onto our *varkpans* like pig swill. Armed with our '*pikstels*' cutlery, we devoured the meal, not paying any attention to the taste but being more concerned with finishing within the allotted five-minute time frame – timed by the watchful eye of the rank.

'*Een minuut!*' – One minute! – the Corporal screamed as we raced like lightning to finish the meal that nearly had us vomiting from the taste and the sheer speed with which we had consumed it.

'*Eet nou en kou later!*' they screamed, telling us to 'eat now and chew later.' All too often we had to force-feed ourselves, sometimes closing our eyes to the disgusting sight of greenish-blue fried eggs, as rubbery as a bouncing ball. The toast was dry, hard, and cold and would have made a great frisbee.

We washed our meal away with a lukewarm, watered-down, and extremely sweet coffee, quite often with a skin on it. Then we washed our pans in dirty, greasy stainless steel sinks on the outside of the mess hall. Forming up, we waited for our friends – known as *maaitjies* in Afrikaans, a word that would become extremely important in our training to come. Running in pace as a squad we made it back to the bungalow still under the darkness of early morning.

Our day was only just beginning.

Each day brought forth a similar nightmare to the one just ended, each of us shuddering at the length of service we had remaining.

'How are we going to live through this?' I said.

Then, closing my eyes, I asked myself: Will I ever see the end? With more tossing and turning, I eventually succumbed to sleep. It seemed like I had just closed my eyes when I was screamed out of bed. I bolted out instantaneously, as though an explosion had awoken me.

'*Wakker word, wakker word!*' – Wake up, wake up! – the corporals bellowed.

'*Staan op, staan op!*' they roared again as they stormed into our bungalow, kicking beds with all the intimidation that their positions held. With fear of this strict military order now ingrained in us, we were up and dressed in a flash.

Rushing into the toilet area, we threw cold water onto our sleepy faces and readied ourselves for shaving, before dressing and charging outside with our stainless steel trays, taking our places in the squad in all of about ten minutes.

The worst of our nightmares came in the form of morning bungalow inspections, usually just before breakfast. These inspections wore us down mentally and reached their breaking point in all of us, lowering us to the level the rank wanted us to be at.

'*Eenvormig!*' – Uniform! – they shouted, like delirious, drunken men bullying us with guttural, demeaning chants. What they meant by this word was that each and every piece of army kit had to be identically laid out to match the troop on either side. Not a single piece could be out of place from that imaginary line that levelled everything, from beds to rifle parts, from one end of the bungalow to the other. Finger-spacing was used to accomplish this extremely hard-to-achieve, picture-perfect inspection, for which everything had to be the same no matter what.

Each bed in the bungalow had to be squared up, with the sides as square as a matchbox. This near-impossible task could only be achieved with starch, shaving cream, an iron, and a brush. Once our beds had been neatly made and pulled tight, we would apply shaving cream and starch to the sides. The hot iron would smooth over the sides, stiffening them, and the brush would meet up with the iron to form a perfect right angle.

On many occasions we had to chew the sides of the blanket to help with that mandatory sharp edge. When the bed was complete, it became a showpiece – so much so that we could not bring ourselves to sleep in them. There were many nights that we chose to sleep underneath our beds upon the cold tiled floor, rather than wake at 03:00 to begin the daunting task of squaring them.

Our clothes had to be clean and ironed at all times – another near impossible task, with us ironing our uniforms dry on many a late night. Late one evening a troop was rushing through his ironing, which he was doing completely naked. Well, the hot iron brushed too close to his manhood, causing him to shriek in pain and bring an abrupt end to an evening of ironing.

Every item of clothing we owned, from our underwear to our T-shirts, was brown, causing us to despise the colour, even though it hid the dirt so well.

Our rifles had to be stripped and the working parts laid out spotlessly clean, upon a brown towel, at the foot of our beds. Our round kit-back was folded neatly 12 centimetres high and squared in perfect position in our metal *trommels* – or trunks – at the side of our beds. These green trunks, along with our metal cupboards known as a *kas*, had to be picture-perfect, our clothes hanging neatly-ironed and folded as if it were a grand clothing store opening, looking as though they had never been worn before. If our rifles were not in our hands, they were religiously under lock and key, safely behind the sliding door of the metal cupboards.

The bungalow itself had to shine from tap to toilet, door to floor, and window to wall. The brown tiled floors were waxed with cobra floor polish and buffed to a mirror-like sheen by a rider and a driver who would pull a blanket up and down the length of the room – known as a taxi – and shout 'Who wants a ride?' to add weight upon the blanket and thus lift the wax, giving the floor tiles a beautiful, glossy shine. For the first and only time in my life, I was able to see my reflection in the floor, it was quite unbelievable.

Preparing for the daily inspection forced everyone to pull his weight and work together as a team-building exercise. But instead, we saw it as a mental breakdown that initiated us into the first three months of basic training – or 'basics,' as we called it – and gave us discipline at its best and torment at its worst.

In the toilet area, not a drop of water marked the stainless steel sinks that cast a reflection comparable to the mirror just above them. Out of the three toilets, only one could be used, and so the already-cleaned stalls were rendered out-of-order. Besides the one used toilet waiting for a quick clean, the bungalow was a showpiece of sparkling cleanliness that would make any mother proud. Day in and day out, we prepared the bungalow for our leaders, digging deep into our reserve to keep cool rather than crack under the enormous mental pressure.

One early morning I caught Rutledge sauntering out of one of the already-clean toilet stalls. He had only created more unnecessary work for the 60 man bungalow. I lost my cool and cracked, I had reached my breaking point.

'You fuckin' selfish bastard!' I screamed in a rage.

Before I knew what I had done, I rained three punches into his bewildered head and face, then turned and left him stunned and speechless. I was changing, and this place was doing it to me. It seemed to be survival of the toughest, and even though I was not the toughest I was sure going to survive, no matter what.

Day-by-day we had become more controlled, our leaders acting out their wishes and we obeying their orders handed down in fearful tones. Constantly

Corporal du Preez and Lieutenant Jordaan had told us to *'orientate jou maaitjie,'* and with so much anger in me I followed through and 'orientated my so-called friend' with no remorse.

In spite of our lack of sleep, constant mental drain, and physical hardship, the rank constantly looked for faults by which to break us down even further. When rank entered the bungalow, we were brought immediately to attention and stood dead still next to our beds, our unflinching eyes staring unblinkingly forward. With beds on either side, they walked slowly down the open passage with the air of Gestapo officers. I hoped that they were not going to stop in front of me.

Fault they would find, it was just a matter of when and where. When they found a lame excuse for fault, they laughed with scorn and great pleasure and then stripped our perfectly manicured beds, leaving anger to well up inside our frustrated minds. On their way out, a corporal threw a bucket of sand across our gleaming floors and then followed it with a bucket of water.

'Een uur, dan is alles reg,' he blurted out, giving us an hour to clean the mud from the floor and remake our beds before they returned.

It seemed an impossible task, but by pulling together as a team we had the bungalow almost exactly as it was before the slush of mud. They did not even bother to re-inspect it, but instead blew on their whistles, forming us into a squad and rushing us off to breakfast. This was pretty much how our inspections went over the next three treacherous months.

Some took these inspections to the extreme and applied silver polish to their *varkpans*, giving them a glinting, silver finish in their effort to impress the rank. Oosthuizen was one of these, and he showed off his brand-new-looking eating tray to us with such pride. To our sheer delight, after finishing his first meal eaten from this ultra-clean tray he was dealt a severe case of gippo guts – or diarrhoea – which had him running and us laughing for the rest of the day.

In the first week we had a mountain of papers to read and sign – and print our names out in full. This was the first and only time that I cursed my middle name, as I wrote out Timothy Geoffrey Frecheville Ramsden at least a hundred times. With our hands tired and our eyes sore, and being rushed against time by our corporals, we stopped reading and just signed. The most vivid document I signed was one stating that if I died in the army accidentally, or in the operational area, I would be given a full military funeral and my parents would receive R20 000 – our worth in death! But, on the other hand, if we were AWOL, or committed sewerage pipe – our lingo for suicide – our parents would receive nothing for our wasted lives.

When finished, we had signed our lives over to the government, thus becoming state property. We had been reminded many times that we were not being paid to think, but rather to do – if you can call R120 a month, pay. For damn sure it did not pay for our agony, but this was the call of duty to the land of our birth – no matter what.

Basic training included unforgettable kilometres of running under the weight of full kit, a heavy metal helmet that shifted from left to right with each stride, a cumbersome rifle five kilograms in weight, and heavy boots still stiff with new leather. The boots rubbed the skin into painful blisters and raw patches, which we dealt with by dousing our feet in hydrogen peroxide, which stung like hell but seemed to ease the pain somewhat, toughening our feet into leather. The short stockings under our socks came in handy, minimizing the friction as we tried desperately to break in our boots, which had inflicted such torture on our feet. We usually ran as a squad, drilled on by our leaders, following through on their shouts. While we waited on stragglers to rejoin the pack, we ran on the spot, with our knees waist-high and our rifles above our heads. The sweat poured off our faces under 33°C of heat, clouding our vision as we struggled to keep our wavering rifles above our heads and our jellied legs moving. Our mouths were as dry as a bone and our abused bodies were fighting to keep from shutting down.

This, although extremely hard, was part of the building process, whereby we were meshed into a unit that was only as strong as its weakest link and as fast as its slowest man. Many times slower troops were dragged, pulled, pushed, and even carried to beat our worst enemy – the unbeatable clock. To buckle under the weight of our packs, over harsh terrain and in scorching temperatures, gave us stamina and endurance and toughened us into a mental state lacking feeling and emotion.

Our forced hours of agony – better known to us as *opfoks* – came in many ways and drew immeasurable amounts of perspiration from our exhausted and run-down bodies. Our full kit and rifles added at least another ten to 12 kilograms, making us slower and clumsier with each step over the uneven terrain. We also used our rifles as a weight, and held them above our heads until our outstretched arms burned with excruciating pain and our tired legs felt as though they might just fall off.

After classes on the workings of our R4 rifle, we were told we were going for a ride, which amongst ourselves we thought would be quite exciting. They told us to extend our rifles straight out with our arms parallel to the ground and go for a ride, revving the barrel like a throttle – as if we were on a motorbike. In the beginning we laughed at the stupidity of riding our rifles, but we soon began struggling against the burning in our arms that forced our rifles to drop to our sides, only to be screamed back up, our arms seesawing back and forth.

Push-ups became yet another test of strength for our rapidly increasing stamina. Almost daily, we pushed our bodies up from the normal push-up position, rising up and down together as the count was shouted out. Many times we did these push-ups in our bungalow, our feet a metre off the ground, resting on top of our green, metal cupboards.

Some struggling voices pleaded for a reprieve.

'*Ek kan nie meer nie, Korporaal,*' they said. I cannot take any more.

'*Moenie moffie raak, jou dom rower. Vasbyt*!' they blasted back between whistles.

Translated into English, this statement did not share the same impact: 'Do not act like homosexuals, you stupid new recruit. Show willpower!'

Every order came down in Afrikaans, in which – it being my second language – I was not fluent, and I struggled to understand what they meant at times. But I realized over a short period of time that the loud voice and facial expression actually sounded the order and what came out of their mouths was a barrage of guttural insults. Such slander was constantly bombarded into us and we were called everything under the sun. We were no longer treated like normal people, with compassion and dignity' instead we were becoming soldiers, answering robotically to our eight-digit army numbers.

The verbal abuse was just another part of our mental training, and we quickly learned to take the vicious put-downs with a pinch of salt. It was extremely difficult to stand by helplessly and have our character demolished, many a tormenting time, by the sarcastic laughs of our superiors.

Roer jou gat, jou donderse does dief! was a very common saying, telling us to: Move your arse, you thundering cunt thief! – which we could not help but crack a smile over.

And to anyone wearing glasses: *Jou fokken kakhuis met vensters.* You fuckin' shit house with windows.

Over and over we had been referred to as *dom varkseuns* – dumb sons of pigs – which always sent waves of anger through me, giving me no option but to swallow the degradation and walk tall through it. The names and derogatory terms directed at us were endless, but nevertheless they succeeded in leathering our minds and allowing the severe words to bounce off as though we were bulletproof shields.

Out in the openness of our training area, we often got the order: '*Gaan kry n klip, jou dom troep*!' Go and a get a rock, you dumb troop! So we quickly looked for a suitable-sized rock that we knew we would have to carry for at least an hour. The rock had to be chosen wisely, so as to be neither too small nor too large.

Grant, another Durban boy in my platoon, made an extremely foolish mistake by choosing a rock twice the size of his head, and as a consequence he struggled under the cumbersome weight far more than the rest of our platoon. He paid a heavy price for his heroic act, his courage admired and his stupidity admonished, and his dirty, red, and blistered hands a lot worse for wear.

A valuable army lesson we quickly learned during an *opfok* was plain and simple – never to give more than we had to. Grant had gone against this rule for unknown reasons, and yet with his willpower and determination he had finished the *opfok* alongside us, which was a feat in itself.

'*Sien jy daai boom?*' Do you see that tree? Corporal du Preez asked us.

Looking far into the distance, we saw a tree standing alone on the horizon.

'*Fok weg, links om!*' he said.

So we fucked off in the direction of the tree, with instructions to go left around it, in the normal dress code of kit and rifle. Making sure we all followed the same path around it, we returned out of breath to our starting position one kilometre later.

'*Ek het gese, links om die boom, nie regs nie. Fokweer!*' Du Preez said. I told you to go left around the tree, not right. Fuck away again!

Again we made off for the lone tree, having failed in following through with the order, taking his left to be our right and therefore rounding the tree on the wrong side. This time we approached the tree on the right and circled left around it, and spread out in groups back to our waiting rank, thinking that we had accomplished our task. But unfortunately, we had not.

'*Gaan weer, en hierdie keer haal jou maaitjie!*' they shouted. Go again, and this time pull your friend along!

In disbelief we looked at them an extra second, wondering if we could manage it yet again.

'*Fokweg!*' they screamed in anger.

Immediately we turned and picked up our weary legs, keeping as a group this time as we ran over the reddish-brown and uneven ground. We navigated a path over the hard tufts of grass that, if stood on, shifted us off balance, knocking our fatigued bodies into the troop on our side. Troops fell, but were just as quickly picked up and carried forward under hard breathing through the shuffle of boot against the dry, dusty, unkind earth. The tree lured us towards it, but this time we converged on it as fast as our slowest man, constantly willing on the slower ones until we made it to the end as one big, beaten, and bedraggled group. Without a single thought further, the gelling and camaraderie had begun.

Inside the base of 1-SAI, marching became a daily routine and instilled further discipline into a rapidly advancing soldier. Our marching drills were practised on the red, stony earth of the parade ground, home to hours of perfected turns, halts, comings to attention, and standing at ease. Our right legs took all the abuse as we lifted our boots to knee-height and then stamped them together into the hard surface.

While standing at attention our corporals gave us the command: '*Maag in, bors uit, nek teen die kraag, pinkies teen die nate, voorwaarts mars*.'

With our stomachs in, our chests out, necks against the collar, fingers along the seams of our pants, we stepped forward and began marching. With our weapons shouldered, we marched with a swollen heart of pride, our right arms swinging back and forth at shoulder height in perfect time. It gave us a feeling of camaraderie, and we began to trust our fellow troops and build friendships with those united in our daily struggle and our new life.

During our drill on one very hot day, we saw a really exhausted troop wearing a yellow *staaldak* and sweating buckets, under the command of a sergeant from the Regimental Police. The yellow of the troop's helmet stood for cowardice, for he had run away from his base, and for this he had been handed two weeks CB drill and was confined to barracks.

With full kit, he was being drilled and was running on the spot with his knees reaching his waist. He also had to run and march at an accelerated step from sunrise to sunset. There was no doubt he was suffering and now paying the price for being AWOL.

Our corporals told us to openly laugh at him. While we laughed at his weakness, we began to feel stronger. His face was drawn and red with over-exhaustion, and as we looked at his eyes over a barrage of laughter, we saw that he was close to tears. I looked again and was dumbstruck to realise who it was. It was the confident and cocksure Melvin, with whom Alan and I had shared a compartment. Now I could laugh, knowing that I feared the uncertainty on the train and he had just bullshitted his bravado to us.

While we had been struggling with army life, he had been on the run. But now, for each day on AWOL he would have an extra day added to his two years. Seeing Melvin in this predicament just reinforced it the more – there was no escape from our hell, if you ran away, they would get you.

One important aspect of our basics was to become very familiar with our R4 rifles, which were South African made weapons with similar working parts to the AK-47. Nervously at first, we took our rifles apart and began to reassemble them, learning about each working part and the function it played. The five main working parts consisted of a body cover, a recoil spring, a piston grip, a rotating bolt, and a gas cylinder.

Almost daily, we were timed by a stopwatch while we stripped our rifles and put them back together. We averaged between ten and 15 seconds' our rifles cocked and ready to fire. The whole purpose of this exercise was to train us to, in the quickest possible time, free a bullet or shell that got jammed inside the chamber. Each vital second was a tick against your life. The more we practised, training for what we could be up against in pitch darkness, the easier it got, until we could strip and put our rifles back together blindfolded.

At the shooting range we were able to get a good feel for our rifles, shooting at targets from 100 to 500 metres away. Our shoulders soon got very sore from the kick and our ears rang from the deafening noise as we lay in a long line, taking careful aim on a target meant to represent a terrorist.

In our own time we squeezed each round, sometimes with empty shells plugged into our ears to muffle the sound of the shot. The hot, empty shells were expelled with every crack and bounced onto the person lying to our right, resulting more often than not in a minor burn that caused more shock than pain. Once we had finished firing, we took over from our fellow troops in the dugout and changed targets, enjoying the rest and listening to the cracking of bullets whizzing into and through the targets. Safety, especially on the shooting range, was drilled into us, and God forbid that anyone should put someone else's life at risk. They would be in for a serious *opfok*.

It did happen once, while a troop was making his rifle safe, firing a shot a few metres past an unsuspecting fellow troop. The rank was on him like a sore rash, snatching his rifle away and cursing him into deathly silence.

For his action, he was given a brown ammunition case of 5.56mm rounds and told to run with it. Grabbing the small metal handles on the side of the case, he slowly lifted it up, and hunched over it, he began to run around the shooting range, struggling against the weight that pulled him forward with each heavy step. His face was red with exertion and showed lines of pain, the handles cut marks into his weakened hands. He ran for at least half an hour as an example of what would come our way if we shot a stray bullet, which could so easily snatch a life.

An old Mercedes army truck met us on the range with at least ten warm, stainless steel boxes filled with our lunchtime meal. Digging into our webbings, we grabbed our dixies, which were two aluminum squares that fit as two halves into each other, making up a square box, both fitted with fold-out handles. Leaving our kit on the ground, we rushed forward, forming into a long line, and waited for the surprise that lay in the closed boxes.

Bowing our heads, we gave thanks for the food we were about to receive, and then five or six fellow troops were picked to dish out the food into our dixies. Shuffling down the line, kicking up dust as we went, and cleaning our dixies from grass, dirt, and an oil film from the previous meal, onto our dusty overalls, we extended our hand and gladly accepted the offering. The sides of the dixie prevented the meat doused in thick gravy from running off, and the next ladle of potatoes and vegetables was dumped right on top of it.

It helped to be friends with an *opskepper*, or server, as we were guaranteed to get slightly extra. All too often we only had one dixie, which gave us no choice but to have pudding placed on top of the meal. With jelly and long-life milk poured over the gravy and potatoes, I stirred it into a rubbery mix with a salty, sweet taste. Every meal included a piece of bread, which we always saved until last and used as a sponge to clean out the gravy and grease before it too was eaten. The taste did not worry me, but instead I enjoyed the feeling of a full belly, energised for whatever the rest of the day had in store.

While we sat on the ground, spread out in groups, and spooned in hungry mouthfuls with hands reeking of gunpowder, we watched the poor troop struggling with the ammo case. His mental punishment took him to new heights as he watched us eating, resting, and drinking. Soon his time came to an end, and when it did he had been pushed to the limit but had learned his lesson.

After the hurried meal, those who smoked lit up, sharing their precious cigarettes among close friends, and began to inhale lungful after lungful of Chesterfield and Camel tobacco and exhale the day's stress into the warm air in thick clouds of unwanted smoke. The few who smoked Lexington smoked it under the unwritten slogan 'Ten million Africans cannot be wrong,' for they had switched to a brand favoured more amongst the blacks in South Africa than the whites.

Beggars cannot be choosers, and smokers smoked what they could get their hands on, it did not matter what anyone thought – a cigarette in the army was a cigarette. The minority who did not smoke soon took it up out of boredom, and as a way to alleviate the mounting stress.

With the smokers smoking, I along with many others used the time to catch up on lost sleep. I had learned to sleep anywhere and in any position, from standing to lying on a cold concrete floor, in a moving truck, or on an uneven patch of dusty earth. Resting my head against my steel helmet, I stole some precious sleep, even if it was for only five minutes. When the shouts came, I was wide awake and we formed into a squad like the sheep we were and waited for a ride back to base.

Whether we were in the base or out in the bush, there were always those few who were too scared to bare their naked bodies in the showers, forcing the rest of us to fight off their foul body odour. When we complained to our leaders, they told us to 'sort them out!'

Armed with scrubbing brushes, the more ruthless among our platoon dragged the offenders fighting and kicking into the shower block. They knew full well the punishment that awaited them. After a long while they emerged very red, clean, and smelling like roses – a far cry from the old, stale sock smell.

The army had a term called *siff*. It means 'syphilis,' but we used it for anything that was disgustingly dirty, whether it was a body, a bungalow, or a vulgar joke. They had got the message and joined us in the showers from that moment forward, now cleansed of their *siff*.

Church soon began to play a big part in our army lives, with compulsory services every Wednesday and Sunday morning. As a company we were marched onto the parade ground, representing a proud Delta Company, and stood in formation along with Alpha, Bravo, Charlie, and Oscar Companies. The red ground was filled with over 1 000 troops.

The Regimental Sergeant Major brought us to attention and told us to stand at ease as he addressed his battalion. He stood like a dictator, iron-faced and expressionless, as he looked upon a sea of brown uniforms topped with the green beret of the infantry soldier, bearing the *bokkop* – buck-head – insignia.

Standing frozen to the spot, we dared not move, fearful of severe repercussions if we flinched. The sun beat down on us and soon began to burn at our feet, having been attracted by the beautiful sheen of our glossy, polished boots. Our toes began to squirm within our boots as the heat radiated down – as if it had been amplified through a magnifying glass – cooking our feet. Our muscles ached with the lack of movement and we itched to make the slightest shift in posture, but feared that if we did we would be removed from the parade ground and somehow find ourselves in the equivalent of a Russian prison camp, like Siberia.

RSM Stone cast fear into the pit of our stomachs, and for this reason we despised him. He waved his stick, which looked like a huge wooden divider, and then tucked it under his armpit, holding the end of it while he stood and screamed over the parade in his native Afrikaans.

After half an hour we started to see troops drop, suffering under the sun and sentry-like stillness, falling like stiff corpses onto the rock-hard ground. They lay where they fell asleep at our burning feet.

Colonel van Zyl finished his address to us after an hour of miserable paralysis. The RSM brought us to attention, but our brains were unable to transmit the order to our sleeping right legs, which were still glued to the stony earth. The first attempt failing horribly, a blood-curdling scream reverberated across the parade, and this time we came to attention with a sound of one stamp, and the Colonel departed.

Standing at ease, we stretched our aching muscles and moved our feet and our toes within our oven-like boots, waiting to be divided into our different church faiths. When the Dutch Reformed church, or N.G. Kerk, was called, there was a stampede as close to 700 Afrikaans troops sprinted across the parade ground like a herd of wildebeest. They ran to their formation, leaving behind a trail of dust hovering in the air, and broken ranks with a handful of English troops left behind.

The English-speaking South Africans – or *souties*, as our Afrikaans counterparts knew us – either went to the Anglican or Catholic Church, depending on which friends went where.

Separated into groups based on which church we had chosen, we were marched out of the main gates and down a long road, past the gates of 1-Special Services Battalion, 1-Parachute Battalion, and 3-Military Hospital, to our churches at the end of the tarred stretch of road. It was a great escape to be out of the unit, away from the tormenting shouts, and in the presence of a minister who showed us respect and some sympathy for the young people we were.

Sitting in the long pews, we closed our eyes, enjoying the peace away from the shouts, under the safety of the roof of the Lord. The ministers – or *dominees*, as they were known in Afrikaans – turned a blind eye and a deaf ear to our snoring through their sermon. Not only did we enjoy the sleep, but also it was a time to meet fellow troops from our neighbouring units and share similar stories of willpower.

After church, the rest of the day was granted to us as a day of rest. But we were still confined behind the high fences and guard towers surrounding the base. To us it certainly was not a day of rest, as we washed and ironed clothes, cleaned rifles, and readied ourselves for Monday's early-morning inspection.

When the corporals felt kind and were heading into town, they made lists of what we wanted and we gave them our money. It felt like Christmas when they returned with chips, chocolates, and 1.5 litre bottles of Coke – items we had not seen in well over a month. With the simple feast, we suddenly forgot about our changed lives, at least for the moment.

On Monday it all began again, starting with the loud angry shouts, the piercing shrill of whistles, the rushed meals, the inspections, the running until you wanted to curl up and die, the falling asleep during rifle lessons only to be screamed awake with: *Wakker word. Jou dom ding*! Wake up. You dumb thing! followed with a bucket of cold water, and finally the crashing dog-tired into bed – or underneath it.

Within the base there were many loudspeakers, posted on high wooden telephone poles, which often had military music playing on them. Whenever *Die Stem*, South Africa's national anthem, was played to the base, we had to come to an immediate halt, stand at attention, and salute in the direction of the sound. Hearing our anthem daily instilled us, out of fear, with conditioned patriotism, and we stood in silence with our thoughts swirling into the future, with many long and dark days ahead.

During our rifle stripping and practice session, Lieutenant Jordaan told us what had befallen our *ou manne* – being one year senior to us. At the end of 1983 and in January 1984, Delta Company was heavily involved in an operation inside Angola dubbed *Askari*. Twenty-one young lives were snuffed out during this operation, with one of Delta Company's platoons being the hardest hit.

Looking out of the window, he pointed with a solemn face to the bungalow in which we were housed and told us that was where they had slept. It sent a cold tingle down my spine, realizing that their fate could quite easily become ours. Our training was gearing us up for duty in South-West Africa and Angola, two places that most of us would have had trouble finding on a map, having little clue of its politics, or its colonial history. I had no idea that South Africa had been involved in a border war within South-West Africa since 1966, with continual cross border raids into Angola targeting the terrorist bases of the banned South-West African Peoples Organization known as SWAPO.

Our total focus was on our lieutenant as he recounted a story involving a platoon of Delta soldiers from his year of intake. During the operation a Ratel armoured car had become bogged down in a minefield and sat there as an open target for an advancing Russian T-54 tank. The Ratel was bombarded with shell after shell, and stood no chance against the onslaught. Some were incinerated where they sat, others left desperate claw marks on the closed metal hatches in a failed attempt to escape from a certain death, and the Ratel driver apparently shrunk to half his body size due to the heat of the explosion. Five soldiers from

1-SAI's Delta Company had to be identified through dental records and 'dog tags.' It was the battle's highest single loss and a dark day for the rest of Delta and 1-South African Infantry Battalion.

With a hushed silence, we looked up at our lieutenant as he fell silent, allowing the horror of the true story to sink in. They had been 1-SAI's Ratel soldiers' now here we were, as the next intake. What the hell lies ahead for us? was the only thought that shot through my brain. This was serious, young people our age had died, and tonight we would knowingly go to sleep on beds belonging to those soldiers who, only a few months ago, had slept in them but were now dead.

Sleeping that night gave some of us an eerie feeling, but we had to tell ourselves that it would not happen to us, even though it was always at the back of our minds.

With the first three months drawing to a close, we were starting to feel and look more like soldiers, for we had been moulded into men. The 12 weeks of 'mind fuck,' of being beaten down through *opfoks* and stretched thin through mental fatigue, the uncountable 2.4 kilometre runs, known as the dreaded two comma four, done in a blistering sprint were, for now, behind us. With three months down and 21 to go, the beginning was over, and we could only hope that the next three would be easier.

Upon completion of our basic training, I had seen the fat become leaner and the rake-like thin have muscle added to their slender frames. Having entered the army weighing 71 kilograms and being tall and thin, I could feel a change in my weight and in increase in my muscle. A guy we had nicknamed 'Bakery,' due to his love of sweets, was on the opposite end of the scale to me, and with no access to doughnuts and cakes, Bakery had no choice but to shed kilograms.

To be granted our first pass was like achieving a milestone, an achievement trapped within our dreams, being almost beyond our reach. Permission had been given to leave the base for five days and find our own way back to our hometowns to visit family and friends, to do what we wanted when we wanted and how we wanted.

With these thoughts, we felt almost normal as we exited the camp through the main black gates. To our left, on the far side of the gates, stood a small monument enclosed within a wire fence. It stood secluded and overgrown with long, dry grass, paying homage to the Afrikaner women and children who perished there in the concentration camps at the hands of the British during the Anglo-Boer War of 1899.

With our backs to the high barbed-wire fences and cold, concrete, cylinder-shaped guard towers, we breathed in the air, which seemed to be lighter and purer as we shrugged off the tension. In our minds we were free, at least for the moment, but in our uniforms and battalion insignia we were still bound to the state of South Africa.

Having been deprived of alcohol for three months, we longed for an ice-cold Castle beer and a nice, thick, juicy steak. Farewells to friendships formed were said as we dispersed in different directions – some to the airport or train station, others into waiting cars, and still others into army trucks to be dropped of on the side of the road.

Waiting on the roadside with an orange 'ride safe' glow in the dark, sash, worn over the right shoulder and across the body, it generally did not take very long to attract a driver to stop. The people who normally stopped to pick us up were either parents whose sons were doing their National Service or had completed it, or those who knew young conscripts in the line of duty.

One whole day of our pass was spent on the road in an urgent quest to reach our faraway destinations. The length of travel did not matter too much to us, after all, we would soon reach the comfort of our homes. I arrived in the dark in Pietermaritzburg and made my way to the city hall, where my brother John, in his brand-new Ford Escort XR3, met me. In it we completed the last leg of the journey to my hometown, Hillcrest, in record time.

To sleep past 05:00, eat tasty food, drink beer, and go out in any colour of clothing but brown was as though I had entered into paradise. After a quick but valued three days, it was time to shed the civilian clothes and mentality and button up into the browns for a day's travel back to the base at Bloem.

What a ghastly thought, to know full well the hell that was waiting to descend upon us as we entered through the gates.

2
Our new company – Bravo Coy

Arriving back at base, very down and dejected, we slept in the same bungalow in the Delta lines, knowing that the next day was going to bring about dramatic change.

In the morning, after a normal hurried breakfast, we marched onto the sports field and waited to be divided up like cattle under the auction block, into special military tasks. Junior leaders, gunners, medics, and signallers were all plucked from our ranks, leaving the rest of us standing, our destiny to be mechanized infantry soldiers.

Grant, Alan, Hodge, and I, along with a few other Durbanites, managed to cling together and move from Delta to Bravo Company. We were thankful to be with a few familiar faces, there being so many uncertainties under the new bungalow roof.

Laying claim to a bed with a newfound friend on either side, we began to unpack our kitbags and metal trunks. While we were adapting to our new surroundings, our new lieutenant and corporal entered in a cloud of thunder. Immediately we shot up to attention, complete silence spreading over the room. We were paralysed with a certain amount of fear as to how our new leaders would treat us.

Lieutenant Bennett sarcastically remarked on the high number of *souties* that were in his platoon. It did not take long before he educated us on this new word *soutie*, meaning an English-speaking South African.

'You have one foot in South Africa and the other in England,' he said, 'and your prick hangs in the ocean. That is why you are a bunch of salty pricks.'

He evinced a distinct loathing towards the English speakers in his new platoon.

Corporal Burger was no better, with a mouth like a sewer and a voice that could shake you in your boots. Right from day one he treated us like vermin. He was a short, ugly, pale-faced man with big, thick, red lips that slandered us with every conceivable Afrikaans word – so much so that our intense hatred for him grew by the day.

Instructing us to be ready for inspection in the morning, Bennett and Burger left us reeling with the certainty that we were in for a rough ride.

At 05:00 they arrived, blowing loudly on their whistles and panicking us rudely from sleep. In a matter of minutes, and without having to think twice, we were up, dressed, shaved, and beside our beds for the dreaded inspection. The outside of our quarters had to look just as neat as the inside. The grass had to be raked – which left us with a big dilemma, since there was not a blade of grass in sight but instead a million and one tiny grey stones. But soon we realized that these stones were our grass, which we raked daily removing all unwanted boot prints and replacing them with neat rows of raked lines.

Inspection was the time and place for our superiors to find fault and use it as an excuse to make us pay the price. All we could hope was that it would not require too much running. Our hopes were short-lived, we were given 60 seconds to sprint from our beds, down the 30 metre corridor, out of our bungalow door, once around the building, and back to attention at the side of our beds.

When the whistle blew we broke into a charge, coming to a near-standstill as we bottlenecked at the door, pushing and shoving our way out. Once out, we sidestepped the washing lines, upon which were still hanging uniforms frozen stiff in the cold, and dangling chains securing them from theft. Slipping and sliding on the gravel, we rounded the corners in our vain attempt to beat the stopwatch, and once we were back to attention at our beds, Lieutenant Bennett clicked the watch.

'*Peloton Drie julle maak dit net nie, fok weer*!' he sarcastically told us in Afrikaans.

Platoon 3 had not made it in the allotted time and so we had to go again. With anger pouring out of us, we repeated this exercise for half an hour, receiving the same news of failure each time, the lieutenant's words ringing through our minds and chiselling away at our sanity.

Eventually we were saved by the breakfast call. We passed by the food out of breath, sweating and with hardly an appetite left in us, before we took our first shaky mouthful.

In the very early days of Bravo, we got some unbelievable news concerning a troop from one of the other platoons within our company. This Afrikaans troop was an amateur boxer, and because he represented the unit in his sport he was granted a daily pass into Bloemfontein for training purposes. One disastrous day he was caught in bed with a married woman by the unforgiving husband, who was unable to curb his rage and shot and killed them both where they lay. It came as a shock to all of us, for we knew this troop by sight, and that made his death the more unbelievable.

Shortly after his death another shock hit our company, as word reached us that there had been a suicide. Bridger, from our platoon, had a friend in another

2. Our new company – Bravo Coy

platoon in our company who had been placed in DB – the Detention Barracks – for reasons unknown to us. While confined in the jail cell, he had removed a string a little thicker than a shoelace from the inside of his bush jacket, and tied it to the bars and around his neck. The next morning the Regimental Police found him dead. He became another statistic, and added to the climbing rate of suicide in the SADF.

There was no time for the shock to sink in, for we had become self-absorbed in our own survival, but we all knew that suicide plagued all units. At times it played on the minds of even the toughest of characters. There would always be a certain few who just could not keep up with the strict order of discipline, and they would pay by taking their own lives – their only bid to escape this torturous life forever. Not all of us conscripted into the military were of a mould to be fighting soldiers, and there was no room, in the eyes of our rank, for the weaker ones.

I knew Bridger's friend by sight, and I could see that he did not fit the mould of a soldier, and he too chose death as his final escape. Our platoon was very surprised at how well Bridger took the death of his friend, for he too was viewed by most of us as someone who would not be able to endure army life.

From the early days of Bravo, Platoon 3 began to grow together with a will to persevere through endless turmoil and an ability to shake off the hardships. This ability would prove its worth during our bush training, which was conducted at a training ground about 25 kilometres from Tempe.

The place we learned to hate, well before we stepped foot onto its sandy red soil, was called De Brug. It was an ugly, vast mass of dry, bare, open land stretching as far as vision would allow, surrounded by little hills known as koppies, with thorn bushes and trees dotted over the landscape. In some places the long, straight, dry grass grew above our knees, but for the most part the red soil was littered with hard tufts of brown grass thirsting for the next rainfall.

It was a fact that this land had cost young South Africans their lives, or serious bodily injury, due to the rigorous training and live ammunition. Bear in mind that it was only three months earlier that most of us had first fired a rifle – and that was on the shooting range, in a stationary position. The next phase of our training involved fire-and-movement, wherein we were trained to fire our rifles as we ran forward.

Entering into De Brug always gave me a lonely feeling, and pangs of anxiety in the pit of my stomach – for I knew quite well how quickly an accident could happen on this wasteland. I think that, for most of us, this hollowness embedded deep in our guts lasted seven or eight months, during which time we fired more live ammunition than we cared to remember and lived with hope and trust that we would all get through it in one piece.

With each deadly exercise, each of our lives was placed at high risk. We did what it took to become unwavering warriors within our platoons, capable of following through on an order without blinking an eye. With daily practice, our bush exercises became ingrained within us and we began to grow in confidence.

The art of camouflage was our initiation into the unforgiving bush, we began to blend into the rough terrain. Our brown uniform had been tailored to the drab and dry surroundings, and only the white of our skin remained to be covered. Our sleeves were always rolled down, so only our faces and hands needed to be blackened. For this we used an oily, black, creamy polish, which we referred to as 'black is beautiful.'

Our faces became as dark as the night and we became unrecognizable to our fellow troops. We could not help but break into fits of laughter at the sight of everyone's sudden ugliness. To top it off, our helmets had grass and small branches fed through the green netting, which broke the shape of the rounded metal and transformed us into walking, well-camouflaged, black Christmas trees with a rifle protruding from them.

After a few days of bush training it was virtually impossible to remove this thick film of polish from our sweaty faces, though we tried our best using cold water and sand as a scourer – but these resources removed it only partially. After a while we learned to smear our faces with cream beforehand and then apply the polish, which wiped off with ease compared to scrubbing our angry faces into a tender, blackened red.

In sections of ten men, we began training on fire-and-movement as we dashed over the open plains with our rifles, webbings, and helmets camouflaged into our surroundings. On command we fell flat on the ground, rolled away, and then crawled forward like a leopard using our elbows and the underneath of our arms, our rifles resting across our left arms. Once we had leopard-crawled a few metres, and still in the lying position, we raised our rifles and pretended to fire.

We performed this 'dash, down, roll, crawl' daily, uncountable times, with no live ammo, for at least five days, our bodies in excruciating pain from all the crashing down upon the rocky and uneven surface. With grazed and bleeding elbows and knees, we retired at the end of the day to our bivis, which was a groundsheet pegged out like a tent with two sticks propping up the middle, where we fell soundly asleep long before 20:00.

2. Our new company – Bravo Coy

With the freezing cold gnawing at us within our sleeping bags, and helped on by the echoing shouts of '*opstaan!*' and the whacks against the sides of our bivis that would knock the condensation onto our sleepy faces, our arms and legs aching from the previous day's fire-and-movement, we would drag ourselves, fully clothed, into the bitterly cold and crisp morning. Pulling on our boots, we leaned on our bivis, which were dripping wet from condensation, and became enveloped in the morning stillness, feeling as though we had been cast into a wilderness. This wilderness had seen much sweat and hidden tears, death and destruction all in the quest to make speedy, hard-core soldiers out of young teenagers. How we cursed this place silently and aloud.

A thick layer of mist hung a metre off the ground under the clear morning sky as dawn began to chase the darkness away. Shaking, we poured ice-cold water from our water bottles into our fire buckets – or canteen holders – and began to shave with the blades tearing at our skin. During our training, shaving was part of the discipline and had to be done under any conditions – bush or base, it did not matter.

After shaving, we lined up for roll call and then passed in front of the cold food and warm coffee. We stood and ate, too cold to sit on the freezing earth. Sipping from our fire buckets, which still tasted of lemon shaving cream with a floating film of short bristles, we washed away our unappetizing meals.

Slowly the sun came up, dissolving the fog and giving us the warmth we so desperately sought. Rubbing our gloveless hands together under the diluted warmth, we stood like statues in our paper-thin overalls with only a jersey beneath. We dared not move, fearing that the slightest shift in posture would force cold patches of clothing onto warmer parts of our skin, thus causing another cold shiver to shoot down our spines.

Live ammo was brought from the stationary Samil in a brown metal case and set before us, and then under orders we each filled a 35 round magazine with 30 rounds. Today we were going to perform fire-and-movement live, placing our lives in the hands of the person on either side of us.

One section at a time, we lined up and cocked our rifles, our nerves taut at the fear of being accidentally shot, or even worse shooting someone else. The first time would always be the hardest as we waited before throwing ourselves at the bush and firing through it.

While five of us dashed forward, another five gave cover from behind. We hit the deck, rolled and crawled, and began giving cover fire while our fellow troops ran a few metres past us and then fell. Then we got up and ran past them' and thus we continued, our adrenaline curbing all fear. The smell of gunpowder tickled our noses and our hands shook from the continual firing, and we enjoyed the feeling afterward of having successfully played a major part in the riflemen's job of fire-and-movement.

Thank God no one shot too far left or right, as had been the case in one of Charlie Company's sections when a troop took a bullet in the back and was paralysed in a split second.

During one of the section's attacks, a scruffy soldier from Cape Town, known to us as Snakehans, milled around as though he was in another world far from the one we were in. He had lost one rifle and broken the butt of his new one, and now the rank had confiscated it and given him a stick to use. It must have been humiliating for him, and yet it was comical for us as we watched him performing fire-and-movement shooting with his stick while the rest of the section unleashed live ammo all around him.

I often wondered if he had the last laugh on the army, for shortly after this he disappeared from within our ranks. Word later reached us that he been discharged from the army – a near-impossible feat.

Our trust and the respect in the person to the left and to the right of us was quickly won or lost in one live mock attack, wherein they passed within five to seven metres, chasing their live rounds. Accidents could happen so easily as we stumbled over the rough terrain' we had to hope and trust that all would end well.

Still living in the bush, we began training on platoon weapons – first in theory and then in earnest, with weapons we had seen only in war movies.

One by one we lay behind the MAG machine gun and sprayed blasts into the bushveld, our number two carefully feeding in the snake-like belts of 7.62mm rounds from the metal cases, trying hard to prevent a *stooring* – which occurred when the belt of rounds got entangled as they were being fed into the chamber, resulting in a jam that occurred all too often.

We shot and fed, learning quickly how to handle that beast the light machine gun, even though it was as heavy as hell. There was a close call as a troop lay behind it while it was not elevated high enough off its tripod. He began squeezing rounds, kicking up sand and dust only a metre in front of him. The chance of a ricochet from a nearby rock was high, but as luck would have it we were dealt no injuries.

'*Jou dom varkseun, fokweg*' You dumb son of a pig (fool), fuck away, was the livid remark from the irate rank.

The nervous troop was whisked up and away from the deadly machine gun.

'*Jou foken dom etter*!' You fuckin' stupid discharge of pus!.

2. Our new company – Bravo Coy

Again the verbal abuse was hurled at the troop as he looked up to his rank with a dazed look on his pale face, covered in embarrassment.

Recovering from the machine gun bursts, we moved onto the Bazooka, which looked like a harmless green cylinder open at both ends. Holding the handles firmly with one arm crossing the other, my legs apart, and my feet firmly planted on the ground, I waited for the bomb to be slid into the back of the tube that rested comfortably on my right shoulder. Once the loader had set the bomb in place, he hit me on the shoulder to give me the signal that the Bazooka was loaded and he was clear from the back blast.

Taking slow careful aim, I pointed the weapon into the openness before me. Imagining the many war movies of jeeps being blown sky high by these very weapons, I sent the projectile 100 metres. There followed, as my reward, a deafening explosion marked by black smoke and red dust, and a recoil that jerked the pipe upwards and forced me to take an unexpected step backwards.

Soon after, a troop was blown clean off his feet by the force of the recoil and landed in a pile of dust at the feet of our rank, his Bazooka smoking and pointing skyward.

Once most of us had taken a turn, we began learning about the *Snotneus*, which was a 40mm grenade launcher, short and stubby, with a barrel around four to five centimetres in diameter. It was loaded like a shotgun, and because of the severe recoil it could not be shot from the shoulder but rather from a 45° angle.

With all eyes on me, I took aim on a lonely tree, 200 to 300 metres away and gently squeezed on the trigger. It made a quiet pop as I expelled the round, and then a second later I saw a cloud of black smoke, followed immediately by a red flash, and then I heard the deep sound of the explosion as it landed plumb in the middle of the tree, shaking the hell out of it. I smiled inwardly, with glowing pleasure at having struck the target of my choice, and turning from the smoking tree, I was rewarded with the approval of my fellow troops.

Upon completion of our weapons training we returned very dirty to our bungalow at 1-SAI, looking forward to a hot shower, clean clothes, and a bed.

In the morning Staff Sergeant Nel, assembled us under the still, dark, and very cold winter sky, and we stood before our bungalows shivering with the chill. Brian, being the rebel he was, came sauntering out of the bungalow at his own time, dressed in a brown T-shirt.

'*Waar is jou foken hemp, troep?*' Staff Nel roared out, his six-foot-four tower of a frame dwarfing Brian. He had asked him where his fuckin' shirt was.

Brian looked up at him, meeting his evil stare, and casually replied, 'I washed my shirt. It is wet, staff.'

'*Ek voel fokall, jou slap gat, gaan haal hom en dra die donderse ding!*' – I feel fuck-all, you useless arse, go and get it and wear the thundering thing! Staff Nel bellowed his pitch-black moustache rising up to touch his nose with each word.

A few minutes later, Brian returned with a soaking wet shirt, which he wore in a temperature a few degrees above freezing. Shivering and shaking like a leaf, he joined our ranks as we were marched off for breakfast.

After our usual five-minute meal, we got the order to form up – *tree-aan*. We were never permitted to walk alone outside of our squad, which moved like a vehicle, smoothly and in pace over the dusty ground.

Exiting the base, we ran on the evenness of the paved road and made our way towards the junior leaders' sleeping area, where our driving courses were held. While we ran in perfect step, each boot making contact with the tar road at the same time, we followed our leader as he sang out '*Shosholoza*.' A couple of strides later we replied, '*Shosholoza*,' at least 100 voices echoing this well-known African mining chant that gave us newfound energy.

Our hearts began to swell with pride. We called this feeling the *nugget gevoel*, whereby our feet and bodies floated in unison as we sang, making us proud soldiers ready for a fight.

Another song that we sang over and over again, which gave us the ultimate *nugget gevoel*, went:

We are the 1-SAI Ratel soldiers!
We gonna march into Angola!
We gonna kill them, Sam Nujoma!

The words of this song came easily to us as we were being trained to kill, and hopefully not be killed, on the Angolan border. We had no idea who Sam Nujoma even was, or what implications the Angolan border held with South Africa.

Wet with sweat, we came to a halt in the confines of the buildings where the future corporals and lieutenants were being groomed. Our platoons were divided in half, one half attending driving classes on Ratels and the other half on Samils.

Sitting in the tiny classrooms, taking notes behind wooden desks, took us immediately back to our school days – which seemed like years ago, even though it had only been months. By now we were used to being active in the bush, not sitting in the confines of four dirty white walls. It had become a struggle to stay awake through hours of lectures on vehicles.

Our lunch was always a welcome break for fresh air from the 'brain drain,' and a good stretch from the hard, wooden seating. During one of our meals, a mean looking sergeant strolled past and screamed at all of the corporals to form into a squad, which they dutifully did. To our delight, he screamed the same obscenities at them that they would scream at us. Our rank stood still with shock, as they were being torn apart and degraded within earshot of us.

This new sergeant drilled them at an extremely fast pace and showered them with verbal abuse while they sweated in the dry heat of midday. Sitting on the ground just outside our classroom, we could not believe what we were seeing. It was almost as if the gods had answered our prayers and somehow reversed our roles. This was the greatest moment we had ever witnessed, and we relished every second, a smile drawn along each of our glowing faces. Now they knew how we felt under their strict orders as we ran and marched against time. After half an hour, the sergeant gave the order to dismiss, which the corporals gladly did. They drifted away from our sight, very sweaty and extremely angry.

This continued for almost two weeks, as we bore witness three times to our corporals' *opfok*. Eventually someone brave enough questioned the sergeant's rank, and the findings had the corporals screaming blue murder. The sergeant, it turned out, was just a civilian who had been a troop in 1-SAI a couple of years before and was seeking his revenge on the authority that had made his life a living hell during his time of service. He had stolen the stripes to impersonate the rank of sergeant, looking quite the part with his green beret and brown uniform and a face as tough as nails.

When the corporals found out, they were livid and wanted his head – which gave us even more satisfaction, as we realized how gullible they had been. We could only admire the balls this guy had, and to get away with it for two weeks was some accomplishment – it was a great pity that it was all over, as we would now have to suffer for their loss of face.

After the driving tests were written, we were told who was going to drive Ratels and who Samils. I had been selected to drive a Samil 50, which was a logistical vehicle capable of transporting 50 to 60 soldiers.

Under the guidance and watchful eye of Corporal Vincent, I began to get used to this beast on the long, open, sandy roads, where only I was leaving the dust trails. I towered over the terrain, sitting a good metre and a half above the ground, looking through the massive windscreen as I gripped the huge steering wheel, knowing that this would be an experience in itself. My right hand got used to the six gears and my left foot struggled with the stiff clutch' I worked my way up and down through the gears, watching the bushveld flash by. My body felt stiff and my left leg ached from all the clutch decompression, but I welcomed the end to my first day at the wheel.

From the dirt roads I moved on to the smooth tar roads, equally as quiet but easier to drive on. These quiet roads led me into the congestion of the city and I navigated my way through traffic, pedestrians, and the stop-and-go at each traffic signal, my hands and feet working overtime. I felt like King Kong in the concrete jungle as I moved like a giant through the hustle and bustle of tiny cars jockeying from one lane to the next, as I manoeuvred cautiously along with the stream.

Driving along the main streets of Bloemfontein went well, though with one very close call when I took a left turn too wide and nearly took out a car. If the looks I got from the occupants in the car could kill, then I would definitely be a dead man. I must have missed ramming the car by less than a coup0le of centimetres as I stood on the brake and waited for the sound of metal against metal. To my relief, all I got was angry stares, and I immediately followed Corporal Vincent's direction out of the slight traffic jam that I had initiated, and continued on, the remainder of the day being uneventful.

After three days of day driving, I began my night driving – which was even scarier, as I thundered down narrow trails of bush road under the beams of two lines of light. I watched many rabbits crisscross the rays of piercing light, only to be lost to the darkness in the flash of a second.

During my practical training with Corporal Vincent, a most horrific accident occurred involving Corporal Liebenberg, who had taken us through the classes on vehicle training. Most of us took a complete dislike to him and his arrogant treatment of us. Secretly we wished ill on him so that we might be spared the condescending words that made us feel useless. To make matters worse, he was also from Durban and yet showed no compassion to his fellow English-speaking comrades. I, for one, felt very bad when the news of his fate reached us as we stood in a group waiting to get behind the wheel of our vehicles.

Corporal 'Lieb' Liebenberg had taken out a new driver from Alpha Company in a Ratel and was standing in the section leaders turret relaying instruction via his headset. On an open stretch of dirt road, the driver floored the Ratel to a dangerously fast speed, causing a severe shaking as the 16 ton mass of metal jerked from side to side and went into a body roll. The driver began to panic and lose control, rolling the vehicle while Corporal Lieb was unable to pull the upper half of his body into the safety of the turret. The Ratel landed on top of him, pinning him hopelessly beneath. Apparently he remained alive for two hours, with half his face crushed, before he finally succumbed to the inevitable.

The driver was freed from the upturned vehicle, and on seeing the result of his driving catastrophe he lost his mind and went crazy, to a point of no return.

He was led past his dying instructor and taken away for questioning, never to be seen or heard of again. I often wondered if he was given a discharge for the accident that would haunt him for the rest of his life.

The news sent shockwaves through us. We had always thought that the Ratel was impossible to roll, but now that it had claimed a life we somehow looked at the monsters with renewed respect. The instructors became nervous, and they worried for their safety with their lives placed in our learning hands. I drove with the terrible accident in the back of my mind, and after five days I felt comfortable and confident in handling this massive vehicle. The downshifting – with the help of the exhaust brake and clutch work through six gears on a long shift stick had become second nature to me. The next step was to have my driving skills assessed in the hope of gaining a G3 licence, which was also valid in civilian life.

I returned the following day to the driving school and was met by a huge, round, red-faced man called Sergeant Ellis, who would take me for my driving test. This was the same instructor Grant had, who slapped him across the back of the head while he was driving. Sergeant Ellis had screamed to Grant to stop the vehicle and get out of the driving seat. The sergeant then took over the wheel, banishing Grant to the passenger seat while they returned to the base in uncomfortable silence. Grant unfortunately did not receive a licence.

I felt intimidated right from the get-go as I climbed into the Samil and took my position behind the huge steering wheel, waiting for his order to fire the diesel engine into life. Cautiously I exited the camp and made my way along the tarred roads towards Bloemfontein, while Sergeant Ellis sat and made ticks on his clipboard. Still I kept my nerve, navigating my course through the traffic-filled streets, halting at every cursed traffic light and downshifting to a stop. From the city, Sergeant Ellis took me into the bush for a brief drive before instructing me to return to base. I thought that, even if I had not passed, I had at least escaped from an open-handed slap across the back of my head from this giant of an Afrikaner.

'*Jy maak dit by n bal haar!*' You made it by a ball hair!, he said with an expressionless face.

He climbed out of the vehicle and disappearing into a building. A few minutes later he returned with a blue card, which we both signed. I was now officially a Samil driver, with five long days of driving behind me.

Close on six months into our service, we now had qualified drivers and riflemen capable of performing fire-and-movement – all that we needed now to round off a fighting platoon were Ratels, gunners, and section leaders.

3

De Brug: preparing for battle

Company by company we marched onto the parade ground, with the rank ordered to break the four companies into three fighting sections. They began with the drivers from Alpha, Bravo, and Charlie companies and then moved to the gunners from Staff Weisa's Oscar Company before adding one-liner section leaders from infantry school to each fighting section. There was a constant shaking of hands as troops were torn from the comfort zone of their old platoons and placed within a sea of new faces in more meaningful roles.

Drivers began stepping forward, bidding farewell to close friends before moving into another company or choosing to stay in 1-SAI as drivers for the following year's intake. I stood my ground while they repeatedly asked for all drivers to step forward. I had made up my mind that if we went into an operation and got hit, my best chance of survival would be as a smaller target on the ground.

I said goodbye to Hodge, who had slept in the bed alongside me for the last six months. There was also no way that I was going to spend my two years at 1-SAI, as Hodge had chosen. I wanted to stay with the bulk of friends I had come to know so well, and chose to be a rifleman rather than a driver.

The friends we lost to other companies were replaced with eight new faces taking up their roles as gunners and tail gunners. Toth, Stoop, and Kleinhans entered our platoon, and respectively, became the section leaders of Alpha, Bravo, and Charlie. Our platoon was now complete, with three fighting sections and a HQ section, along with our lieutenant and corporal.

Our new platoon was born in a melting pot, with a colourful mix from all walks of life, from drug addicts to young, hard-core drinkers, from hardened farm workers to clean-cut city boys to those who had done time in jail. Our platoon had come together, touching all four provinces in South Africa, to make a unit of *souties* and *dutchmen* – also known as rock spiders – with each culture generally sticking to those groups fluent in its own mother tongue.

Although most of us were born in South Africa, our parents' ancestries were British, Dutch, Portuguese, Hungarian, Polish, and Zimbabwean. Most of the English came from Cape Town and Durban, known by many as Durbs by the sea.

Good old Els had done time in a Durban prison, which explained to us why he was so handy with the broom, for it was a common scene to have man and broom sweeping the cell block clean. Tienie was fluent in both languages, and

3. De Brug: preparing for battle

had an ability with words, always being extremely descriptive as he spoke. As the saying went: He was rough and tough and smoked a lot of the stuff from the Bluff, which if Tienie was any example, was absolutely true.

One drunken night he stole the wheels off his friend's Mini, and during his getaway the Durban Police shot him, for he refused to stop after their shouts of warning. The bullet lodged precariously in his neck and could not be removed without putting him in risk of paralysis. He openly showed off his trophy to us – as the bullet sat in a round, reddish lump a fraction to the right of his spine. Johannes Jacobus Bernardus Christophilis Els became a character in our platoon, having the ability to make us laugh out loud in a tough situation.

Together as a platoon, we stood tall and short, clever and stupid, atheist and Christian, bold and timid, strong and weak, English and Afrikaans, together with two important factors we commonly shared: we did not want to be here, and we could only look forward to the day we would end our two years of service, still many months away. Thirty-nine soldiers made up the complement of our platoon, including Lieutenant Bennett and Corporal Burger, and we began to split into three fighting sections under the call signs of 23A, 23B and 23C.

With our specialised roles, we completed a fighting unit with myself assigned to 23A (Two Three Alpha – two was Bravo Coy, three was Platoon 3, and Alpha was my section). Toth, a tough looking, well-built troop from Kimberley, became our section leader, one new stripe on each arm. Born to a Hungarian family he was given the nickname '*Kommunis*' Communist. He had a fearless approach to leadership, and he guided our Ratel from his standing position in the turret.

Bennie, an Afrikaner from Kroonstad, took up reins behind the wheel and proved his worth as an exceptional driver on many occasions. Wayne, clad in his green asbestos overalls, manned the 20mm cannon from the gunner's turret adjacent to the section leader and quickly showed off his skill and superiority, his handling and accuracy second to none.

Nickol, who had left school early, had begun an apprenticeship as an electrician before receiving his call-up to the Tiffies in Pretoria. We became friends straight away along with the fact that our hometowns were only a ten to 15 minute drive apart. He had arrived at 1-SAI after completing his three-month basic training in Pretoria, at a time when the battalion was experiencing a food bug epidemic that severely weakened every soldier to the very core. It was also the time that a 17-year-old barefoot runner called Zola Budd from Bloemfontein broke the world record for the 5 000 metres, making a name for the city around the world.

Wayne soon won our admiration, as we could trust his ability under enormous pressure. Section leader, gunner, and driver were linked together by radio contact through the aid of brown headsets, which coordinated position and direction to the Ratels as they tore into the open bush. Fox, from Port Elizabeth, known to us as *Howuuu mannetjie*, the Leman or the Woo-man, joined our platoon with Wayne from Oscar Company and took up position as the tail gunner in the rear of the Ratel. Cloete was rifleman number one and became known in the platoon as 'JP,' after his first two initials. He was an Afrikaner fluent in English and came from Newcastle in Natal. Fourie came from Durban and had worked on the railways before his call-up. 'Foer,' as we called him, was a tall, quiet man with a strong Afrikaans accent who became nervous and flustered under pressure. He took up the seat next to me, as rifleman number two in the vehicle. I took the spot as rifleman number three, with a nickname of 'Ram' – a shortened form of my surname.

I maintained a dreadful worry about Foer and his ability with deadly ammunition. There was an empty place on my left, our Ratel being short a number four rifleman. Directly behind us sat Paul, who was second-in-command of the vehicle, with his machine gun group. Paul sat closest to the hydraulic door.

He got his name 'Sakkie' from a word that he used at the end of each sentence: How are you doing, Sakkie? What's up, Sakkie? Sakkie was a short, stocky, ginger-haired man with a smiling face, from Margate in Natal. He took his job very seriously and proved to be a reliable leader.

Laurence, who was tall and thin, came from East London and could speak English very well, considering it was his second language. 'Van,' as he became known, ran with ease as he lugged the weight of the machine gun, his number-two, Gall, in hot pursuit carrying the weighted-down patrol bags filled with belts of 7.62mm rounds.

Gall, known as 'Angoose' came from Colenso in Natal, English was his native tongue. Angoose was an extremely difficult character to deal with, always getting in the last word and doing things his way and different from the rest of us. It seemed that he enjoyed living in his own quiet world at a distance from everyone else, but any talk of the RPG – rocket propelled grenade launcher – brought a skewed smile to his fair face and his eyes lit up with glee. This weapon drove him slightly crazy, for he chose to lug it everywhere and proved to be a good shot with it.

This fighting machine, known as the Ratel, was named after the honey badger, which is fast and stealthy in attack. The Ratel lived up to its name, with 16 tons of mine-protected steel sitting on three axles, motored by a huge diesel engine, the glass bullet-proof at three inches thick.

3. De Brug: preparing for battle

The ten of us in 23A were proud to be finally sitting in a Ratel after six months of gruelling training. Now we could really sing the 1-SAI song with every morsel of meaning: 'We are the 1-SAI Ratel soldiers!'

In our new platoon, I got talking to Brian, who I remembered standing next to me six long months earlier at the Natal Command base in Durban. I hardly recognized him with his very short blonde hair, but could not mistake the ever mischievous wide smile and sparkle in his eye. I reminded him of the Alsatian police dogs that had gone berserk over his chicken, and we both laughed, remembering it as if it were yesterday.

'I had it packed full of zol – marijuana,' Brian calmly said, with a smile from ear to ear. I looked at him, slightly stunned, and smiled back.

This guy is all balls or no brains, I thought as I weighed the repercussions had he been caught. Now I understood the dog's uncontrollable behaviour.

Close friendships were formed that would help build our strength through dangerous and uncertain times, even though the word 'fear' never entered our vocabulary. We learned how to choose our close friends and tolerate those we did not trust, in spite of wanting to trust everyone, we just couldn't. There was an ever-growing number in our platoon who had a weakness for the green gold and a select few would beg, borrow, and steal both money and kit to satisfy their cravings.

Most of us tried it – some a lot more than others. I invented my own silent term for this green weed marijuana, I called it 'The Great Escape,' for it allowed us to put our minds on the other side of the five metre barbed-wire fence and enjoy freedom from the prison-like structure that we lived behind day and night.

In a dust-covered convoy Bravo Company, now a fully mechanized unit, left for De Brug in our Ratels. After half an hour's drive of follow the leader, we stopped and disembarked standing in the middle of nowhere. Little hills and wide open bushveld greeted our eyes, and we squinted into the miles of openness that lay before us.

Work began and we started erecting tents, each platoon splitting in half and filling the two tents that had to be positioned in a dead-straight line, lest we have to take them down and start again. Once our sleeping quarters were up, we began work on the mess hall, which was another olive green tent that was the roof to the fold-out aluminum tables and benches that would be our seating.

A cammo net was thrown over the tent to add coolness to the dry heat that sapped continually at our energy. At the back of our tents we dug three holes two metres deep and placed a plastic toilet frame over them. These bush toilets, known as go-carts, became our daily visiting place, where we would have 'races' as we shooed away swarms of flies in the hundreds. Adjacent to the go-carts, were the piss lilies, which were two funnel-shaped plastic urinals that also stank to high heaven.

It was quite amazing how we had managed to carve a niche out of the remote bush and make it a home with absolutely no luxury or spoils from our previous lives.

It was June, and winter was gnawing at our heels. The bitter cold, amplified by the lack of city heat, began to eat at our surroundings and plunge us into an icy misery. Our sleeping bags lay open in rows upon the green groundsheet with our *grootsaks*, or backpacks, standing against the tent wall at the head of our sleeping bags. Boots were polished and rifles cleaned under flickering candle light, our hands chilled to the bone as they worked over the ice-cold working parts of the rifle.

To add extra warmth I stuffed my thick and heavy great coat into my sleeping bag and wriggled my way under it, fully clothed. We tried all we could to bear the cold, as we lay stiff upon a thin blanket separating us from the frigid ground, temperatures dropping as low as minus 11°C. While we breathed, we exhaled clouds of cold air and shivered ourselves to sleep.

In the morning we woke to the usual whistle and the stale cold air trapped in our tent. We pulled our aching bodies into the freezing air, laced up our boots, and exited through the tent flap into the darkness of morning. The cold air hit us like a tidal wave. We thrust our hands into the pockets of our thin bush jackets and kept our heads down, heading for water in the Ratels big water-holding tanks. We carried our rifles wherever we went, with the butt folded in and the rifle belt slung over one shoulder, the weapon hung across our backs so as to not restrict our movement while we washed. Bravely we threw water over our faces, brushed our teeth, and shaved, the razors pulling and slicing as they jerked across our frozen faces.

To have gloves would have been an answer to our prayers, but they went unanswered, as gloves were not standard dress in the South African military. Most of us chose not to layer up with clothing – which we had learned the hard way, having been forced to shed clothing by 10:00 under the heat of the rising sun. In a matter of hours we experienced a shift in temperature from freezing to a desert heat wave.

With shaving out of the way, clean, chattering teeth, a freezing face, and red ears, we darted back for the daily morning inspection, which was held by platoon in front of the mess tent by our loot – lieutenant – and corporal. On the

3. De Brug: preparing for battle

calling of our surnames, we answered with our army numbers. Afterwards we presented our rifles for inspection.

'*Vir inspeksie, hou geweer*!' – For inspection, hold your rifle! – our corporal shouted.

Flicking the safety catches off onto automatic or rapid fire, we pulled back the cocking handle, allowing the rank to look down the barrel. They held their thumb in the opening of the chamber and searched for Ratels, which were dust particles – or rocks, in their skewed vocabulary.

It was impossible to prevent particles of dust from entering the barrel in terrain where the wind blew clouds of dust every day just as sea salt blows off an ocean, they knew it and we knew it. Nevertheless, we all tried in vain to beat the odds with a last minute suck on the barrel, we inhaled the dust into our lungs in order to present a shining barrel. Sometimes it worked and saved us from an *opfok*, but most of the time it just made us cough for nothing.

During one of our inspections, a troop of ours had a live round in the chamber, which scared the living hell out of Corporal Burger. He arrogantly cast his eye down the length of the barrel, not understanding why he could not see his thumbnail at the end of the barrel. When he realized why, he freaked.

'*Jou foken dom troep*!' – You fuckin' dumb troop! – he screamed, beside himself with rage, realizing that if the working parts were released and the trigger was pulled he would have had a bullet through his head.

Whether this was accidental or planned I have no idea, but no doubt there were those in our platoon who were quite capable of making an accident happen. Being the bastard he was, we wished something of this magnitude upon him as payback for all the harsh verbal and physical treatment he continued to inflict upon us.

With the cold gripping our hands, we struggled to hold our ice-cold rifles as we looked forward onto the green board bolted to two yellow poles, which stood in front of the mess tent with an inscription in yellow letters that read: '*B Komp Rhino's Rest*.' A very tall, leafless tree stood as the backdrop, adding further bleakness to the dust and cold that had become a part of life. In any other life, a place with a name like *Rhino's Rest* would be understood as a holiday area in which to rest and relax. Instead, ours became one of anger, with uncomfortable sleep and frustration rising and dipping with the temperature with an inbred, venomous hatred to the shithole called De Brug, where we lived with minimal comfort and even less rest.

Slurping down watery scrambled eggs followed by an extra-sweet, lukewarm coffee, we were told to wait by the Ratels. The drivers fired the Ratels into noisy life, the diesel engines belching out one smoke cloud after the next as they shook the morning awake. Like a magnet, we were drawn to the engines at the rear of the vehicle, and we sought every ounce of warmth that they emitted. Our eyes burned and our breathing became strained as we inhaled mouthfuls of diesel, our hands spread-eagled over the warm metal. When the sun began to show itself, we followed its path and stood in huddled groups, bent on absorbing each ray, hoping to thaw our freezing bodies.

'You can have my daughter but not my sun,' someone blurted out as a fellow troop blocked his warmth.

On the command to board our vehicles, we dispersed from the sunshine and climbed into the fridge. The metal of the chassis helped lower the temperature, giving us the same sensation as if we had just walked into a refrigerator and closed the door behind us.

'Shit I am freezing my balls off!' a fellow troop piped up as we sat on the cold, hard, rubber seating and did not dare to move.

With puffs of steam blowing from our mouths, we nodded in agreement, hoping the vehicles would begin moving so we could gain extra heat from the engine block. In the usual convoy we departed from Rhino's Rest and headed for more open bushveld, beginning with vehicle formations in platoon structure, as if we were entering into battle. Alpha took the left flank, Bravo the right, and Charlie the middle, followed by the HQ Ratel, which remained in the rear.

Bennie, our driver, was gunning the Ratel at 60 to 70 kilometres per hour. We looked through the small portholes and watched the long grass flash by. Still frozen cold, we sat glued to the seats, our metal helmets strapped uncomfortably under our chins and our hands tucked deep into our pockets.

Gall, ingeniously, had run a wire from the Ratel battery to his tape deck, which sat on his side of the vehicle. Very dusty and dirty, it emitted a sound that helped drown out the drone of the diesel engine. 'Big in Japan,' by Alphaville, blared in distorted fashion through the speakers, and we sat back with hatches closed and tried to enjoy the ride and music, leaving Bennie, Toth, and Fox to follow orders through the headsets. Fox and Wayne had just traded places, Wayne opting to lie low in the tail gunner's section in the rear in an effort to sleep off sickness. Fox took his position in the gunner's turret, enjoying a chance to stand tall in the front of the armoured car.

With the words 'Big in Japan' blearing from the small speakers, all of a sudden we flew up half a metre from our seated positions and slammed our helmets, in unison, into the closed metal hatches. Our rifles flew out from our

3. De Brug: preparing for battle

hands and struck the ceiling, and Browning cases crashed onto the steel grids over the floor, causing further panic with the sudden explosion of noise.

Our ears ringing, we dropped like rag dolls, shell-shocked at the sudden lurch of the armoured car, which seemed to bounce as it rose and fell only to rise again and make us feel like we were riding a bucking bronco. The top of our shoulders ached, for the round rim of the helmet had pressed deep into them while our bodies flew up with our shoulders hunched into our necks on impact. All eyes shot forward into the driver's seat and we wondered what the hell had just happened.

When Bennie stopped the vehicle, we all spilled out, slightly disoriented, and looked back past Wayne, who was dangling by his legs out of the back of the Ratel, his head and arms buried in the long grass. Soon our eyes began to regain their focus and we looked with stunned expressions into the depth of this massive hole. Then we heard shouts of help for Fox, who had smashed his face against the metal in the turret. His face was pale and expressionless, and his eyes wide with shock. Blood streamed from his forehead and nose and dripped onto his brown dusty shirt, then into a pool on the outer rim of the turret.

Sax, our platoon medic – known in army slang as the 'tampax tiffie' – was on the scene within minutes to attend to Fox, whose nose was growing by the second through the bloody mess of his face. Stunned and bewildered, Fox was taken away for further medical attention. Wayne, on the other hand, had cheated death from the flying Ratel, with only a few minor grazes to show for it.

Standing close as a group, we surveyed the hole and could see, without a word being spoken, how close we had come to serious injury, and even death, had Bennie lost control of this 16 ton beast. The hole was at least four metres deep and ten metres wide – deep enough to completely bury the vehicle. This enormous opening in the ground was well camouflaged by the tall grass, now flattened down by the nose of the Ratel, which had dug in at the base of the hole. Two deep-set tyre tracks parted the grass as the Ratel ascended out of the depths, and according to 23B we became airborne, all six wheels a metre off the ground for a fleeting, precious few seconds.

Bennie had performed a miracle in reading the situation well in his fight to steady the vehicle while trying to keep the wheel in a straight line. He had proved his driving skill, for which we all gave him thanks and hoped for no repeat performances. Our hated *staaldaks* had saved our heads from splitting like watermelons and snapping necks like twigs on contact with the metal hatches. Thank God the hatches were tightly closed, for if they were not we would have shot halfway out of them, catching our shoulders on the sides and more than likely breaking a shoulder blade or two. 23A had escaped from what at first seemed an unavoidable and serious injury, and as a result we bonded even closer together, for we were a section with yet another story to laugh about.

Bennie drove at reduced speeds for the remainder of the day, all of us still a little shaken up. We sat back and listened to 'Alphaville,' the sound echoing through the vehicle. Soon we began to laugh about our narrow escape, Fox bearing the brunt of our jokes.

'With a big nose like that, he now looks like a real fox,' someone said.

We all laughed, wondering how our friend was making out in the medical tent. Relieved to be back at Rhino's Rest, we were welcomed by a mummified Fox, who had a white bandage wrapped around his face, with an opening for two blackened eyes and a red swollen mouth. With gratitude for his well-being and our own, we shied away from his gaze, and silenced by the drone of the engine we killed ourselves with roars of laughter at the sight of *Howuuuu mannetjie*, the Fox, before he was whisked off to 3-Military Hospital in Tempe for stitches and four days of recovery.

Back in our tent we lined up with our dixies and waited on the meal, which, as always, was, for the most part, equally as disgusting as the last. The simple meal being the highlight of the evening, and as always all too quickly consumed, we headed over to the Ratels and began washing our greasy dixies in cold water with no soap. Sand came to the rescue here, and scoured off any unwanted oil and grease before we rinsed the dixies under the cold water to restore them to their original chrome colour. Our *pikstels*, which comprised of a spoon and a fork that slid into a knife, were washed in the same fashion – in the red sand of De Brug.

As the last light began to slip away, we cleaned our boots and rifles. Sleep was the only alternative to the darkness and cold descending upon us. Under the flicker of a couple of candles, which cast shadows across the V-shaped roof of the tent, we curled up for another freezing night upon the ground, our body heat and warm breath trapped within the flaps as a saving grace against the dropping temperatures.

In the morning, after our rifle inspection we were ordered to fan out into a long line to do a chicken parade across our company lines. This was organized as a cleaning up of rubbish, from *stompies*, or cigarette butts, to plastic and paper, which had blown across the open terrain. The non-smokers like myself became extremely frustrated at picking up the *stompies*, for the smokers had total disregard for where they tossed their finished cigarettes. One early morning I had had enough and vented my anger to my fellow troops.

3. De Brug: preparing for battle

'This is bullshit!' I said too loudly, all within earshot of Corporal Burger.

With a face as mad as hell, he signalled me out and screamed: '*Kom hier jou sleg ding!*' – Come here you useless thing! '*Sien jy daardie paal? Gaan haal hom en fokoff! Vat hom en fokveg, jou hoender hoer!*' – Do you see that pole? Get it and fuck off. Pick it up and fuck away, you whore chicken! he roared with his mouth wide open and his eyes emitting daggers of hatred.

I ran towards the wooden pole that he had directed me to, and proceeded to pick it up. Grabbing hold of it, I thought to myself: What an idiot I have been. Why did I verbalize my frustration? Now I was going to pay for my stupidity with an *opfok* of note. Struggling, I lifted the thick two metre pole onto my shoulder and began to run with it in front of my platoon while they continued with the chicken parade. This heavy pole dug humiliation and anger further into my pained body, and I dragged my feet across the hard, uneven tufts of grass, waiting for the whistle to signal my return. I carried on for at least half an hour, not daring to change my grip for fear of dropping the log and having further punishment meted out.

At the end of the *opfok*, with a very red and bruised shoulder, I had learned not to complain and never again questioned why non-smokers should pick up *stompies*. Our platoon hated this bastard with all the venom we could muster. He was as cold and unfeeling as a snake, having always an unflinching expression drawn across his pale, ugly face. He had reminded us, day in and day out, that we were 'lower than kaffir shit'. There were no words to explain our hatred for this man, other than death upon him as a way to spare us of our living misery under his command.

During another *opfok* flipping Ratel tyres, with at least three troops to a tyre, Laurence turned and faced Corporal Burger and told him outright that he was not going to do it anymore. This was the first time that I had ever seen a troop refuse to follow through on an order, and I knew it would hold serious consequences for Laurence.

Instantly he was marched away and placed in DB – Detention Barracks, where he literally had the shit beaten from him, for he was forced to run from dusk to dawn, with full kit, for three days. He did not stop running on the spot or across parade grounds until the sun went down, and only then could he collapse into a deep sleep.

After six weeks in De Brug, we returned to 1-SAI for a pass to the civilized world and an escape from Corporal Burger and the rest of the *rondfok*, or fuck-arounds, that had us in a daily spin.

After two days at home we walked back through the cold gates of 1-SAI feeling as though we had never left it. When the lights went off at 21:00, two section leaders had not returned from pass, though everyone else had been accounted for. In the morning Toth and Stoop had still not returned and were classified AWOL. Two of our three sections were leaderless, forcing Paul and Grant as 2 ICs – second in command – to take over the reins and give us direction. To our complete satisfaction, after a few days had passed and Toth and Stoop had still not returned, two Durban boys – Paul and Grant – became our section leaders. That night we got our hands on some Castle and Lion beer and drank heavily to our new English leadership. Paul would lead Alpha section, and Grant Bravo.

The following day, Staff Sergeant Nel led our company onto the parade ground, with Platoon 3 well hung over. We marched with arms swinging like pendulums to shoulder height. Once halted, we stood in the blistering heat of the African sun and waited for the next command. After 45 minutes, with legs locked dead still and weighted to the red stony earth, my eyes caught sight of Grant in the front row as he began to rock slightly from side to side.

I knew it was a matter of time before he fell, but he fought on until his legs buckled, and then he fell headlong onto the hard ground. Firmly rooted to the spot, we looked him over, not moving our heads from the empty space, unable to do anything for him as he lay in a faint at our hot feet. On seeing Grant, Paul began to follow suit, and he too seesawed back and forth in a fight against the sun and his extreme hangover.

Somehow he managed to keep his balance under the evil eye of RSM Stone, who dragged on with his message to the unit. Five minutes after Grant had passed out on the parade ground, RSM Stone ordered him to be carried off. Very disoriented, with a medic on either side of him, Grant was escorted from the parade.

Back at the bungalow, we laughed with Grant at how most of us had suffered the same anguish against the sun and our own throbbing hangovers. We knew that if the parade had carried on any longer, we too would have folded and fallen.

Ten days after being reported AWOL, Toth and Stoop returned to base stripped of their one lines. After so much painstaking hardship over the past three months of section leader training, during which time they had strived to earn the stripe, they had blatantly thrown it all away for a trip into Botswana.

They both accepted their loss of rank with no bitter feeling towards their new leaders. They had got off lightly by only losing their rank, and they knew it. They had somehow dodged the detention barracks and yellow *staaldaks* with one *opfok* after the next, and most importantly they had avoided any extra days added onto their two years.

Back at De Brug we dropped our kit into our tents, which had filled up with dust in our short absence. Nothing had changed in this wilderness besides the

3. De Brug: preparing for battle

ground being raked by strong winds and layers of dust upon everything from tent to table. *Rhino's Rest* welcomed us back with more discomfort, as we began to prepare ourselves for the mock attacks.

With our magazines fully loaded and pocketed in the front of our chest webbing, along with a 50 round magazine clipped to our rifles, the riflemen were ready. The gunners, with the aid of the tail gunners, had lugged 20mm rounds in long belts and fed them into the metal boxes within the narrow confines of the turret. The 12.7mm Browning was loaded and ready to go, and so was the machine gun group, their leader Gall eager to put his RPG-7 to good use.

Sitting in the Ratel, bombed up and ready to roll, we waited for the order – which came to us in the sign of the engine kicking to life. We began to roll forward across the plains in a platoon convoy, with Alpha leading Bravo and Charlie with our HQ radioing the orders from the rear. After a slow and leisurely drive, our Ratel veered suddenly to the right, the three vehicles following suit and driving in a line spaced 20 to 30 metres apart. Without warning, Wayne tore into the silence and pounded at the targets, which were at least 300 metres away, filling the Ratel with smoke from the burned gunpowder and empty shells that missed the ejection flap, bouncing instead around the inside of the armoured car.

Meanwhile, Laurence and Toth sucked on their clay pipe, mixing the sweet smell of marijuana with the smell of burned gunpowder. All of us sat trapped in the hot box, enjoying the sweet aroma of the dagga. The unmistakable smell seemed to calm our nerves and dull our senses as we prepared ourselves for an attack that seemed real beyond all proportion. The battle noises, smells, and intense expressions made it even more real, and the adrenaline in each of us rose like a crescendo.

Looking past the swivelling gunners' turret and through a portion of Bennie's three-layer-bulletproof windows, I saw dust and smoke rising in the distance. The gunners, sweating under the heat of the cannon and their green, fireproof, asbestos overalls, kept their barrels tightly levelled on the trenches that zigzagged their way across the earth looking as if a huge mole had tunnelled through the red ground and discarded the excess sand along the edges of the endless burrow.

The Ratel sirens blared over the recoil and thud of each expelled 20mm round and the chatter of the 12.7mm Browning. Sitting perched on the edge of our seats, our minds and bodies were rushing on an adrenaline charge second to none. The turret swivelled, Paul threw a yellow smoke grenade to act as a smokescreen and then wriggled his way down the turret into the heart of the car, still linked with radio contact from his brown-scarred headset. With the Ratel still in motion, the hydraulic doors shot open, and then there was a shout.

'*Stop. Stap uit, nou!*' – Stop. Get out now!

It was Paul, screaming at the top of his lungs.

'Go, go, go!' he yelled again, above the tumultuous noise, as we spilled out of the opening one by one, leaving Paul to follow behind.

The same was happening on the other side of the car, with Gall leading the machine gun group. We burst onto the battlefield through a haze of the yellow smoke, which blew over us in the wind under the cover of Wayne, Solly, and Van Rensburg's cannon bombardment. In position on the ground, JP and I, rifle grenades protruding from the end of our barrels, immediately lined up on the trenches through the dissipating yellow curtain. Sparing our shoulders from painful recoil, the butts of our rifles rested on the ground, and arcing them at 45° we released our grenades onto the tunnels 75 metres away. To see our grenades drop and mushroom over the trenches in a cloud of dust and grey smoke, with only a second's delay, the explosions resounding in our ears, was an unbelievable and very welcome feeling.

The noise, the smell, the taste, and the sight as we tore through the knee-high grass in fire-and-movement, maintaining a line with our Ratel's nose, had to be experienced to be comprehended. The sheer volume of noise was beyond anything I had ever heard, and deafened us to any orders that were being shouted across the battlefield.

Evenly spaced ten to 15 metres apart, we rushed towards the waiting minefield, barricaded with sharp rolls of barbed wire, our rifles ravaging the earth with sharp bursts of automatic fire. With the Ratels on the edge of the minefield, giving us support fire and another smoke screen, we began leopard-crawling under the barbed wire, planting red flags as we went to demarcate the mines as a warning to those crawling behind. The first rifleman to reach the roll of barbed wire threw himself onto it, forming a human bridge offering passage to the remaining riflemen who would run with a light step over his back.

Once everyone was through the minefield, the troop over the wire was pulled up free of it – which in most cases was myself, with a few cuts and scrapes. Cautiously, we all leopard-crawled towards the main opening in the trench system, which had been built to replicate what SWAPO was living in inside their training bases in southern Angola – endless snaking tunnels close to two metres deep.

Under cover fire from the riflemen I crawled up to the break in point and dug my right hand into my webbing and pulled out a high explosive – HE – grenade.

3. De Brug: preparing for battle

Grasping it firmly in my right hand, rifle fire digging up dirt all around me, I pulled the pin out with my left hand, still holding the safety lever down. Once I released my grip, I had four and a half seconds to get rid of this killing oval ball, or it would get rid of me.

The feeling that ebbed through me was suicidal' if I froze with it, I would end up taking my own life. It was a mind blowing experience, literally holding the key to life or death. I knew only too well that soldiers had died or been maimed throwing one of these deadly devices. Lying on my stomach, I counted to two and bowled it into the opening, and shouted, '*Granaat*!'- Grenade!

A loud but muffled explosion shook the earth, and a blanket of dust became my protector as I jumped into the opening, firing two shots and screaming, '*Loopgraaf skoon!*' – Tunnel clean!

I threw myself against the wall of sand, allowing my fellow troops to pass me by as I gave them cover fire. Our rifles were geared for trench warfare, with folding butts, which made the weapon about 20 centimetres smaller and easier to handle in the narrow confines. We leapfrogged past each other left and right through these walk-in graves, throwing a grenade upon each right-angled turn to clean them out.

Fourie had a great learning experience over a practice grenade with a live detonator still capable of blowing off a hand. He pulled the pin, threw the grenade, and followed it into the trench in a panic. When it blew at his feet, he emerged very dusty, as pale as a ghost, and totally bewildered. He could thank his lucky stars that it was only a practice grenade. If it were a highly explosive one, he would have been blown to bits.

There was a time I had to leave the trenches and leopard-crawl to a bunker ten metres out. While I was in the process of reaching for the grenade, I realized how close the cover fire was coming to me. The bullets were literally digging into the sand and lifting chunks of earth onto me, an inch from my legs, which was way too close for comfort. I realized that Toth, who was quite stoned out of his mind, was firing these bullets.

Keeping my cool, I tossed the grenade, just wanting to get out of his line of fire, and as quick as lightning I scampered back to the safety of the tunnel wall. Feeling quite invincible and too trusting of Toth's aim, I let it lie, never approaching him about his reckless act of fire that could so easily have gone awry.

With the trenches cleared, we clambered out of them and stormed over the open ground in fire-and-movement, the 20mm adding to the firepower. After a 30 metre dash at the imaginary enemy, a now very light chest webbing having shot five magazines, we seemed to float over the hard ground littered with relics from former practice battles.

When Paul gave the order to stop firing, we made our burning-hot weapons safe and walked towards our Ratel on the other side of the trenches. Red faced with sweat and dried-on dust, and stinking of burned gunpowder, we assembled by the waiting car with broad smiles and gritty teeth.

Still shaking from all the shudder of shooting, as if we had used a jackhammer on solid concrete for the past 45 minutes, we recounted the action to our fellow troops. Wayne told me how close he had come to firing a 20mm round into Laurence's back. Bennie was flying forward at the wheel and Wayne was letting rip, his cannon elevated above our heads. Without any warning, the Ratel dropped into a dip, lowering the level of the cannon, the sights then centred on Laurence's unsuspecting back.

'Shit,' Wayne said later, with a wry smile. 'I just went cold and froze, ripping my finger from the trigger. I could feel the colour drain from me as I shat myself.'

In a split second the cannon was free of its target and Wayne resumed the support fire, putting into the back of his mind what could have been a gruesome accidental death.

To have been a part of this exercise was the biggest adrenaline rush I had ever been exposed to, wherein the mind leads the body through fear and pain and the eyes never lose focus on the task ahead. Our senses were so highly-strung that we seemed to glide across the surface, unable to feel the exertion on our bodies. It was the most amazing feeling that I had ever felt, being only one step away from the real thing. Tired, our hands still shaking, we climbed into our Ratels, and in a long line of dust and diesel our weary souls were chauffeured back to *Rhino's Rest*, the adrenaline charge quickly wearing off.

Grabbing a towel, soap, and shampoo, most of us walked the 300 metres to the makeshift shower, an overhead tin drum supplying a big canvas funnel with ice-cold water. Standing under the freezing water as the invisible cold wind bit at our nakedness – the temperature was barely above zero – we felt like we had been cast into the wastelands of Siberia. We froze our balls off, though our option was to be cold and clean or *siff* and uncomfortable, reeking of gunpowder and buckets of dried sweat.

Stepping out of the shower and drying off, we were forced into the sand, now muddy with water, and we hurriedly dried and clothed ourselves, trying not to muddy our pants, dancing cold as an ice block within them. Eventually, with clean and dry feet firmly set into our scarred leather boots, we walked back to our tent feeling brand new and glad that we had braved the freezing temperatures.

After a quick meal we joined the rest of our platoon around a fire behind our tent, darkness and a clear, starry sky bringing the cold winter night upon us. Keeping warm by holding our open hands over the flames, we talked until the cold chased us into the warmer tent for an early night, with a smoky aroma now hanging under the canvas.

Our demarcated piece of ground, pegged out by our sleeping bags, was a hospitable sight, we sat upon them and removed our boots. Our hardened feet felt trapped within our boots, for they were hardly ever exposed to the fresh, open air and they sweated daily in dirty, stale socks enclosed within the leather. Thus came the unwelcome gift to every soldier – athlete's foot. Some suffered it more than others, and many a day, a thick slime known to us as toe jam built up between my toes.

'Who wants some toe jam?' someone would shout across the tent, making it sound almost like something one would spread over bread.

Our feet were constantly doused in white army-issue foot powder, which did wonders in drying our fungus-ridden feet and relieving us of the itchiness that nearly had us rubbing our toes off.

Lying within our sleeping bags with a few candles offering valuable light, Brian and a few others grouped together as they 'crushed a blow'. Taking our turn as the pipe circled its way around the group, we inhaled and blew out thick clouds of smoke. It renewed a sense of hope upon our circumstances, somehow forcing us to laugh about a situation not worthy of the amusement. This sharing of the 'peace pipe' strengthened our unbreakable bond, and there was never any time to harbour hate or animosity.

Thirty of the 37 troops in Platoon 3 smoked weed. Some did so occasionally, and others became hooked on it. All of us became very tolerant to our fellow troopies bad habit. Nothing could sever the trust in, or our feeling of safety amongst, our tight fighting unit.

One by one we closed our eyes, lying stretched out toe-to-toe, on the mattress of ground, and our dreams removed us far beyond the tent flaps. Meanwhile others continued smoking and talking into the night. The last one to bed had to extinguish the candle, which we all knew could ignite the tent into a funeral pyre and pile of black ash in all of 30 seconds. At the entrance to each tent were two red fire buckets of sand, in case there was need to extinguish the flames in the early few seconds. During our many nights of cramped sleep upon an uneven surface, a snore would always reverberate around the tent, which would be silenced by a flying boot followed by a shocked snort, and then silence until the next snore.

In the afternoon while training on our vehicle movements, we would halt for a lunch break by parking our troop carriers beneath a tree. The hull, with the aid of the tree, was covered with the camouflaged netting, breaking the shape of the vehicle from overhead aircraft surveillance and also offering us valuable shade in which to prepare our tinned lunch of potatoes, beetroot, and army-ration corned beef. The food was normally thrown into a pot and warmed over a gas stove, which was no more than a cylinder with a flat metal top, on which the pot rested. It did not take long before the food was ready, which we spooned into the ten waiting dixies and then sat down as a group and tried to gain satisfaction from the simple meal. The compressed beef was so salty and greasy, with the distinctive and disgustingly strong smell of recently slaughtered meat – which had been minced into a twist-open can in an embalming of fat.

After our taste buds had recovered from the extreme saltiness, and our stomachs from the grease, with the meal gladly behind us, water was heated for our coffee. One advantage to this bush meal was that, for once, we could actually eat at our own pace without having food rammed down our throats with screaming threats. Without the echoing screams, we continued to swallow our meals in a constant hurry, having been completely indoctrinated into military meal protocol. Two spoons of Ricoffey were spilled into each kidney-shaped fire bucket, along with a mountain of sugar to drown out the salt sitting in our thirsty mouths. Steaming hot water was poured from the blackened cooking pot into each fire bucket, lined up in a row in the sand. Ultra Mel long life milk was added to our metal cups to complete what could be called our 'pudding'. This had to be one of the most satisfying moments, as we sat on the ground with our lips glued to the metal of our canteens. The peace and the quiet were enjoyed over the steam, which wafted upwards while we rested in a mode of recharge before the greasy cleanup.

Back at Rhino's Rest we stood frozen next to a fire, all our eyes on the crackling wood, watching the orange tongues of flame curling around the blackened logs. Suddenly the peace was broken when Laurence emerged out of the shadows holding a plastic lined cardboard box, filled with 20 litres of milk.

'Get your fire buckets!' he shouted with urgency. In a second the fire was deserted, and then a few seconds later it was surrounded with clanging metal canteens, held unwaveringly below the lone plastic udder as pure, perfectly chilled milk was leaked into each of our buckets. With white moustaches we gulped back cupful after cupful of this creamy, delicious delicacy, knowing quite well that it had been stolen from the kitchen quarters.

While we were enjoying our milk and laughing out loud at being one up on the military, Laurence brought out a box of mince, just as big as the milk box. Before it could be opened, words of warning reached the fire.

'They are coming, get rid of it,' a voice uttered in the darkness.

'Where the hell are we going to hide it?' someone shot back.

'In the go-carts.'

The remaining milk and the full box of mince were thrown down the two metre deep toilet holes and disappeared from view below the putrid stench of faeces. Within minutes the rank was on the scene, asking questions about the theft and telling us that someone had used bolt cutters on the lock of the refrigerated truck that held all the kitchen supplies.

We listened and played dumb – we had seen and heard nothing. It was great' we had actually got away with the taste of real milk, thanks to Laurence and his Robin Hood antics in taking from the well-off and sharing with the less fortunate, in this case his own fellow troops. On their departure, we filed back into our tent warm with joy and smiles of gratitude for the smallest and simplest of things, which had disrupted the monotony of how we were forced to lead our lives.

After a few joints, the laughter flowed around the tent until sleep brought our shelter to a welcome silence.

In the morning we trod over sheets of frozen water, which cracked like panes of glass beneath our weathered army boots as we walked over to the standing Ratels and washed our faces and shaved away the previous day's dirt and growth.

After the daily inspection and chicken parade, we tidied up our lines and waited for our 10:00 meal. Brunch was carried down to our area in big, rectangular, stainless steel boxes with clip-on lids, supposedly to keep the food hot. The cooks, all dressed in white, followed the procession of food, armed with ladles and ready for *opskep*, or serving.

We always looked down upon those in the kitchen for choosing the easy route, for they escaped the daily torment and training that came with being Ratel soldiers. Many Jehovah's Witnesses, who had refused to take up arms, found themselves stirring big pots of steaming food instead. There were also those who chose the kitchen to camouflage their homosexuality, which suited us since we felt safer having them out of our showers and tents. The third group of troops who entered the kitchen were the physically lazy and medically unfit. At the end of the day someone had to cook the food, so better them than us.

Once the metal food boxes were placed on a fold-out table, Staff Wiese stepped outside the tent and gave his own taste test. His face tightened into a ball of wrinkles as he spat the food onto the ground.

'*Gaan haal jou maaitjies!*' Go and get your friends!, he roared out in disgust. Now he had our undivided attention, as we watched a bunch of white uniforms disappear through the tall, dry grass. It did not take long for about a dozen cooks to appear before our gloating eyes.

'*Wat is hierdie kak?*' What is this shit? Staff Wiese bellowed, thrusting an angry finger towards the boxes.

They stood still, locked in their formation, with no sound coming from their frightened mouths, and we waited, itching for their inevitable *opfok*. In the blink of an eye, the dusty red earth was covered in a sea of white uniforms, they crawled and grovelled at our feet while our faces towered over them, glowing with delight. After experiencing just one hour of sweating misery, maybe now they could understand the hardship in our daily lives, during which food was the only break in our intense routine. Our platoon enjoyed the show, laughing out loud at how easy they had had army life up to now.

Food, as disgusting and tasteless as it mostly was, was religiously served, on time, with portions big enough to fill the void. The high rank stood firmly by the belief that a successful army cannot fight on an empty stomach. With this conviction in the mind and soul of each officer and corporal, we were never deprived of a meal, no matter what!

Shortly after the cooks' *opfok*, a rumour circulated around our camp regarding some ingredients that the angry kitchen staff had added to the food. Our platoon heard that they had urinated, defecated, and spat chunks of phlegm into the huge stainless steel cooking pots, stirring the concoction into a vile-tasting dish to be served as a meal.

Many months later, these hard-to-believe rumours were confirmed as the truth, recounted by a fellow cook who bore witness to it. Hearing the truth did not shock us one bit, but it did explain why the food tasted so awful and extra-salty.

Our Ratel training continued with countless day attacks and night attacks under an umbrella of light, shot up into the black sky in a whoosh from a brown canister called an 'illumination flare.' The night was immediately transformed into daylight, the tracers arcing themselves through the light and disappearing into the blackness.

It offered all those around a spectacular display comparable to a fireworks show, with all the deafening noise and smells that accompanied the exercise. By now we were so well trained that we could perform the attack from memory

3. De Brug: preparing for battle

under a slice of light from the moon – in order to spearhead the attack without casualty to our own.

It was scary and thrilling all at the same time as we shot tracers past each other in our fire-and-movement towards our goal – the trenches. The gunners pummelled the ground ahead with an onslaught of 20mm fire and the Padmors firing mortar bombs behind us. It was so well orchestrated, with each of us performing our tasks flawlessly, after all, we had practised for months, and our confidence showed and swelled within us.

There was only one slight problem with the night attacks and that involved sidestepping any old and unexploded mortar bombs and grenades which lay abandoned upon the ground, waiting only for a kick to activate them. It had been drilled into us never to pick up or kick a bomb or any device that lay hidden in the sand, but rather to report it. Nevertheless there was always someone who would act against the rule, resulting in death or severe injury.

In this case it was Lieutenant Potgieter, from the mortar group, who lost his right hand as he stooped down and picked up an unexploded grenade. As an officer, who was supposed to lead by example, he should have known better, and kept his hand and his head.

Right from the beginning we had been told that we belonged to the government, with one percent of the National Service intake budgeted for write-off to training accidents causing death or grievous bodily harm. This seemed a very high percentage and had us feeling uneasy about the extremely low value that had been placed upon our very young lives. If we suntanned and burned our bodies, preventing us from carrying our kit, we were charged with 'damage to state property' or, better known to us in the more descriptive words of Afrikaans, *beskadiging van staatse eiendom*.

Els, while standing guard with our platoon at a remote building housing army supplies, had fallen asleep in the midday sun with an empty half jack of brandy at his side. When he awoke from his comatose state, his body was as red as a lobster – a similar colour to that of the rank who threatened to *'klaar him on'* – in other words, document him for property damage – if he was unable to carry his kit. With no other option, he painfully managed to fasten the webbing on his back and avoid punishment.

The rest of us conformed to the typical 'army tan' of bronzed faces, necks, and arms, the rest of our bodies a stark contrast of lily white – something quite comical and equally as ugly, for we glowed in the dark like a bunch of glowworms.

The government owned us from the day we signed the papers, and we had no choice in the matter. By paying us a very minimal wage, feeding, and housing us, maybe they felt justified in owning our lives, in forcing us to live by a foreign set of rules and dance to their control like puppets on a string. It was up to us to mentally strike off each and every day as it drew to a weary close and brought us one small step closer to the end of what we referred to as a two-year 'jail term.'

The rank always enjoyed a good show at our expense. This time it came in the form of a canister filled with tear gas. While we were standing in a group and minding our own business, we heard a loud hissing sound. Turning quickly, our eyes locked onto a canister that was emitting an amplified snake-like sound, and then without warning our eyes began to burn as if wet soap had been smeared into our open sockets. We did not know what to make of it, and we dispersed like a crowd running from the riot police.

Stumbling blindly, we ran in a panic, the pepper spray dealing deep doses of excruciating pain into our vision. Some ran for water and doused their faces, which only added fuel to the fire. They immediately began warning those who stood in wait of water relief that it only made the stinging worse. Out in the open, our eyes watering, we looked through our blurry vision and saw our rank, with smiles of content, hiding behind the protection of their black, alien-like gas masks while we squirmed before their eyes.

After a few agonizing minutes, the burning subsided and our reddened, watery eyes began to feel slightly better. Now we knew and understood the words 'tear gas,' having cried the silent and inescapable tears of pain in that drawn-out moment of pandemonium.

In the afternoon, Staff Nel paid a surprise visit to our tents with an unplanned inspection.

'*Hierdie plek lyk soos die binnekant van n foken hoer se handsak*!' This place looks like the inside of a whore's handbag! he screamed at us in anger and disgust.

When he left, we waited for what we knew was to come – an *opfok*.

'Get your full kit and rifle and *tree-aan*!' came the corporal's order.

With our full kit, webbing, helmet, and rifle we formed up and waited for Staff Nel's explanation before the *opfok* began.

'*Julle tente lyk soos 'n hoer nes*!' Your tents look like a whore's nest he said, his black-as-coal moustache rising into his nostrils and a devilish look drawn across his long, frowning, rat-like face.

'When you were babies you crawled, so crawl,' he shouted, forcing us to throw ourselves at the sand and begin our first baby movements. We went into a leopard crawl, using our rifles to pull ourselves forward over the hardened and uneven ground. As we crawled past his legs, I noticed him towering over us and then I saw a sudden movement. Staff Nel lifted his right leg slightly and then hoofed the nearest troop in the side. I crawled past the troop who grovelled on, wincing in pain.

'You would not have been able to get a job in civvie street, so that is why you made the army your career, you cowardly bastard,' I muttered to myself as the sand and dust stuck to our sweaty and strained faces as we crawled like turtles towards water.

To our relief, he told us that we had grown and had learned how to walk, and so we walked, recovering strength and breath for the run that had to follow.

Our next step was learning to run – which we had gathered.

'*Fokweg, jou dom bliksems!*' Fuck away, you dumb bastards!, he shouted over his menacing finger, pointing into the faraway distance.

We were to return only upon hearing the whistle. Tired and angry, we set off, getting further and further into the bushveld, distancing ourselves from his arrogant, PF – Permanent-Force – temperament.

Those who had chosen to dress against the cold were now paying the price, the soaring heat and extra weight now becoming a burden to them. Luckily I had chosen to freeze in the early morning, wearing only a jersey under my overall, which was bad enough since the sweat still ran off us and the thirst caused our tongues to stick uncomfortably to our palates.

When the sound of the whistle echoed upon our alert ears, it was with thanks that we did an about-turn and ran as one big group to the place where we had started the *opfok*. After an hour of sweat and internal tears of fatigue, we retired to the whore's nest and collapsed in a heap upon our sleeping bags, before the order to clean up was issued.

Corporal Burger left us with these words: '*Maak skoon en saamwerk*' Clean up and work together.

The word '*saamwerk*' was used in most army sentences, as they strove to get us working together in a tightly-knit unit of young soldiers.

Together we set about cleaning the tent with a broom that swept clouds of dust into the air, while others tightened the fastenings on the sides of the tent, pulling it back into a taut rectangle. The grass – which is to say, the sand – was raked neatly in straight lines, and the furrows encompassing the tent-fastening chains were rebuilt into one long tidy mound surrounding our shelter.

The fire buckets were topped up and the *stompies* were removed from obvious view. When the eagle eyes of the rank came to inspect the whore's nest, it had been transformed into a neat, uniform, and very clean – in spite of the never-ending grains of hated sand – safe haven.

While lining up for dinner, we got the horrific news that Alpha Company had just killed one of its own. As the story began to unfold, the tragedy of it set in on us. We knew only too well that the end could come knocking at any time for any one of us. It was an accident, but it was a death – a death that would change a family forever.

During fire-and-movement, in the middle of a live practice attack, the riflemen shot too far left outside their range – known as the 'arc of fire' – resulting in a logistics driver being shot straight through the head. He died instantly.

Eating dinner under the dim light, with thoughts swirling subconsciously through our minds, gave us a perspective on the vulnerability of our lives. We handled live ammo every day, in real-life mock attacks, and there was always a high probability of something going horribly wrong. We lived with hope and trust in the men on each side of us, but first and foremost we lived with a deep sense of being young and invincible.

In the morning we bombed up for an attack, with Commandant Roetz sitting on board our Ratel to critique our live platoon attack on the trenches well within our visibility.

Eagerly we all waited for Paul to give us the go-ahead to cock our weapons.

'Load your weapons!' he screamed over the idle of the huge Ratel engines.

I cocked my rifle and, for some unknown reason, my finger stayed on the trigger and I began squeezing down on it. I immediately went cold with weakened legs, for I knew I was within a millimetre of firing a burst. I had lost my concentration, and could quite easily have seriously wounded or even killed anyone to the right of our Ratel.

It was my secret, and remained my secret, and nightmarish thoughts immediately followed. Had I squeezed off a burst, it would have destroyed our chances of boasting our mechanized skill to our commander, and I would have let my platoon down. Thank goodness it did not happen that way.

The day ended well. We successfully took the line of trenches, and our platoon was rated the best at mechanized and trench warfare over the complete 1-South African Infantry Battalion. Platoon 3 had something that most platoons seemed to lack, and that was spirit. Thirty-seven very different people put their differences aside to help gel a fighting calibre within us and be worthy of performing an attack with accuracy, grace, and ease.

After hearing this, we always walked with an extra step of confidence and a feeling of safety and superiority. If we were called upon to cross into Angola as Ratel soldiers, we could not ask for a finer fighting platoon. We bolstered our own chances of survival.

3. De Brug: preparing for battle

With our *ou manne* – troops in their second year – having taken part in an operation dubbed *Askari*, and having witnessed death, we could only wait and wonder if we too would be following suit.

From the dawn of the eighties, there had been an operation into Angola every year, from *Operation Protea, Daisy, Vasbyt 5* to *Operation Askari* in 1984. The Ratel armoured cars had been at the forefront of each of these battles. Our big question was: Where would 1985 take us?

With our training at De Brug now behind us, we knew we had made Lieutenant Bennett proud of his platoon, in spite of the carefree approach we took to army life.

Another training accident met our ears with a shot being fired inside the Ratel. It ricocheted from one metal wall to the next, like a ball bearing bouncing around a pinball machine, until it finally stopped in the flesh of a frightened troop's arm. It was a close call, but at least he lived. Alpha Company had yet again tarnished its reputation.

Near the end of our time in the bush, nature wanted one last jab at cracking our souls. The heavens opened up as thunder rocked the dry plains, and lightning added sharp cracks, illuminating the torrents of rain against the black of night as they lashed an unwavering onslaught upon our tents. The wind ripped at the tent sails like a sailboat fighting to stay upright in the ocean. The tent chains were pulled taut as our shelter angrily flapped and fanned under the power of the elements.

Water began to flow into the tent, forcing those on one side to seek higher ground on my side, as the level rose by the minute. Still in our sleeping bags, we lay in puddles of muddy water for a few drawn-out hours, hoping and praying that the watery nightmare would just go away. Instead it carried on, rising until it forced us to abandon ship, chasing us out into the open and into a quagmire of aimless running. Our saturated gear became twice as heavy, and our rifle cumbersome, under the stinging lashes of rain.

In disoriented and demoralized groups, we scurried like soaked rats towards some sort of refuge. Some ran to the mess tent and others to the Ratel, as we slipped and fell towards a new asylum. I chose the Ratel as my safe haven for two reasons: it would be a guaranteed refuge from above as well as below – against the threat of rising water. Shivering with the uncomfortable chill, a few of us sat inside the vehicle and waited for the warmth that light would bring. Without a wink of sleep and aching with cold, we stepped into the morning light and surveyed the scene, the clay-like mud sticking with each step, like an extra sole on our wet boots.

Clothes and kit lay strewn across the tent roofs and sides, in a vain attempt to dry them, and troops milled about taking weary inventory of their soaked belongings. Packs lay left behind in the mud from the ensuing chaos of the night before, looking as if a hurricane had just blown through. Away from the tent, a fire smouldered and a few troops tried in earnest to dry clothes and sleeping bags over the smoking logs, only to eventually give in to the screen of smoke and the probability of fire from the waterlogged timber.

Slowly we picked up the pieces and swept the water from the tent. The heat of the afternoon sun came as our saviour, for it began to burn the wetness from our clothes, kit, and most importantly sleeping bags. By the time we went to sleep, it was almost as if the previous day had been erased from our minds. Having being deprived of a night's sleep, we slept very deeply and were thankful for a dry sleeping bag set upon the canvas sheet.

The hard ground felt good, and we shut the day away shortly after darkness fell.

Twelve weeks of intense bush training – from route marches, to surviving on water and tins of beetroot, to attack after attack upon the trenches in temperatures that fluctuated from freezing to sweltering and back – had finally come to an end. The *opfoks* and *rondfoks*, which had our lives in misery on more occasions than we can remember, were being left behind on this wasted piece of earth. The soil of De Brug had sapped the blood of our own, with sweat and hidden tears, while we toiled daily against a thin line of insanity.

Demolishing Rhino's Rest gave us all great pleasure and a sense of accomplishment, for we had survived a very tough time far away from the limited luxuries – a thin foam mattress and a warm shower – that an army base offers.

In a long, jubilant convoy we departed from the dusty plains of De Brug in the direction of 1-SAI, all of us thinking of hot showers and a bed above the ground. Through the dust we pulled zap signs as our goodbye salute to this hellish nightmare of an experience.

With our backs to the streaming dust, we looked ahead, with only 15 months of service left. What lay ahead for us was anyone's guess.

4
A State of Emergency: in Tembisa Township

Driving through the gates of 1-SAI with nine months of service behind us, we entered into our well-guarded base with newfound confidence swelling within us. The Ratels were parked proudly at the back of our company lines, with their V-shaped noses facing our brick bungalows.

It was a strange feeling entering the bungalow and throwing our kit onto a bed, opening trunks and metal lockers – army furniture that we had not seen or used in many long months.

Troops lost no time in flocking into the showers. The first were privileged to get an eagerly-awaited hot shower, while the last had to settle for a cold one. But the simple pleasure of washing De Brug's grime from our bodies, without having to step through mud or freeze our balls off under the open, cutting wind, was heaven in itself. Dressing our spotless bodies in fresh clothes only crowned the feeling, as we became the cleanest we had been in 12 long, dirty weeks.

'Good and clean and fresh!' Els sang, emerging pink and scalded from the showers, mimicking the advertisement for a particular brand of laundry detergent.

'You guys smell like mine kaffirs!' Els blurted out, in his typical racist tone, to those who had not yet washed.

He was quite right, only when we came out smelling like roses were we aware of the stale, pungent odour of weeks of dried sweat, smoke, and dirt on the bodies of our fellow unclean troops. To take a dump on a porcelain toilet was heaven, and to lie on a soft bed and gaze up at a secure roof and a dust-free, polished floor seemed like a miracle – almost as if we were back at our homes in the real world.

In the morning we lined up six deep in company formation in front of our bungalows and waited for Corporal Smith to issue his order. Without warning, he ran straight at us, his eyes locked unwaveringly on a troop. Our ranks parted like the Red Sea, allowing him passage as he bolted through, and to our shock, punched one of his troops in the chest, knocking the perplexed soldier back three rows.

What had provoked his sudden outrage was a mystery to us. We could only assume that he was talking while orders were being given – a huge sign of disrespect in the eyes of any rank. Had the unlucky troop been a part of our platoon, I felt we would have stood unified in his defence and sought some sort of justice for his mistreatment. Our justice would come in the way of laughing off an *opfok* – that is, taking our punishment in a very lacklustre and uncaring light. Laughing off an *opfok* always seemed to *koer their moer* – drive them crazy.

Still taken aback at Corporal Smith's actions, we were marched under his orders to the mess hall, outside which we bowed our heads and gave thanks for the food that we were about to receive. Grace was said in many variations, the funniest being 'Rub-a-dub-dub, thanks for the grub' – which we only said away from the religious ears of most of the Afrikaans rank.

Entering the mess hall felt like crossing a rugby field, with row upon row of wooden tables and benches and each company assigned a certain seating area. To me it always seemed like a prison. One by one we trailed past the food as it was slopped on to our pans, and then we filled up the seating, filing onto the bench one after the other, our rank being the guards, watching every move from what we ate to what we tried to throw away.

On our normal Wednesday church gathering, news shot through our groups regarding three Parabats – from 1-Parachute Battalion – who had just died on the wastelands of De Brug. Their deaths had come about during a night practice attack that had gone dreadfully wrong, and added more blood to the rigorous, real-life training exercises. Being mechanized infantry soldiers, we had an inbred hatred towards the Parabats, who we called 'flying meatballs,' or *vleis bome* – meat bombs – and unfortunately their deaths brought us only smiles and smirks, and so we continued with our battalion rivalry.

It had taken us nine months to realize how our rank had been building us up daily by breaking us down into worthless trash stripped of dignity and then building us up again. This pendulum motion continued each day as we began to gain more and more confidence, honing our skills into well-trained and extremely safety-conscious young soldiers. In so doing, it helped minimize the inevitable accidental deaths that had to come with the law of averages in handling highly explosive ammunition during our many dangerous training manoeuvres.

Back inside the base, we heard a rumour that we were going to Lohatlha for training to perfect our battalion attacks across the barren, sandy flat and uninhabited plains. Before the truth of this rumour materialized, we were granted a four-day pass. We did not waste any time in dressing in our most-faded browns, our cravats, patties, yellow, gold and green belts and berets neatly angled to the right with our new three feathers insignia. We stood proud and looked sharp, and we felt every bit of it. With our carry bags at our feet, we waited for the search from our rank.

4. A State of Emergency: in Tembisa Township

To my disbelief, Brian had smuggled two live practice grenades from De Brug and hidden them in his bag. He had told us with a straight face that he intended to throw them into a black location, hopefully gaining satisfaction from a few injuries. Brian stood as calm as the weather and waited for the search, which in the end did not come about, leaving him able to do whatever he liked with his deadly devices. Little did I know at the time that he had three stolen rifles, disassembled and totally stripped down, which were also in his bag, and had managed to walk out of the camp with them.

After a short but extremely worthwhile pass into our old civilian lives, we arrived back to the rumour that had become the truth. To our anger, our company had been assigned to go to The Army Battle School at Lohatlha. For us, this meant De Brug all over again – cold, rain, hard ground, cold showers if we were lucky and brave enough, and plenty of dirt, dust, diesel, and discomfort. This was a very low point for us, but we had no choice and began packing our kit for the long trip.

In the morning, we stood by our Ratels ready for inspection, and then on the order we boarded. One after the other, in call-sign order, we drove out of the gates of 1-SAI in the direction of the Cape Province. Standing through the open hatches with our fibreglass helmets on, we looked back on our camp as we drove down the Tempe road, wondering what hardship Lohatlha would bring us.

After hours of driving, our company convoy stretching for miles, we eventually came to a stop under darkness, on the outskirts of a town very famous for its diamonds. We lay resting on our Ratels, overlooking the city lights of Kimberley, which had sprung to life around the Big Hole, which had been created by the diamond rush more than a hundred years earlier. This hole was the largest hand-dug excavation in the world – 215 metres deep, with a surface area of 17 hectares. Over 2700 kilograms of sparkling diamonds were mined from this site, solidifying South Africa's status as a very important asset to the British crown.

While we waited, Toth was met by his family in his hometown, somehow they had heard about our movements. Standing next to our Ratel, he conversed with them in Afrikaans while we snacked on our very first ration pack. It gave us the same excitement as if we were young kids opening our favourite treats. The small cardboard box with a number on the covering of plastic contained many white packets of powdered drinks, milkshakes, porridges, coffee, tea, and sugar, a rubbery, nougat chocolate bar, three small tins of meat and vegetables, a tube of cheese and condensed milk, a packet of biscuits, a roll of Super-C energy tablets, a fruit roll, a packet of matches, and a strip of fire lighters. This was one day's supply of food, which could become useless in the absence of the most important ingredient – water.

With great enthusiasm, we swapped and bartered each other for tastier food more to our liking. The milkshakes were the prize and the dog biscuits the losing end of any deal.

After a 15 minute piss break, shouts passed down the line of vehicles, from one to the next: 'Get ready to move out!'

Taking to our vehicles, we followed the lead, leaving the lights of Kimberley to disappear behind us. In the darkness we sat within the hull, trying to close our eyes over the hum of the diesel engine as Bennie kept his place within the convoy, his headlights firmly fixed on the Ratel in front.

Our convoy entered into the northern Cape and continued in a southward direction, passing through a place called Kuruman, until we finally stopped in the middle of nowhere. The ground was mostly flat, with a very rich red soil broken by a few rocky hills and overshadowed by the same dry, burning heat as De Brug.

'Where the hell are we?' someone asked, hoping not to hear 'Lohatlha' as the answer.

'This is the Army Battle School of Lohatlha,' Paul casually commented as he turned and faced us from his position in the turret.

Turning back to the landscape, we strained our eyes as we stared into the distance hoping to catch sight of a building, tar road, railway track, or even an animal to somehow plant a marker upon this vast expanse of nothing. To us, we had felt we had reached the arse end of the world, which was 100 times worse than De Brug's lonely wasteland. Looking into the distance, we thanked our lucky stars that we were not destined to spend two years in this abyss, staring daily across the plain vegetation into a new day, with no difference to the one just past.

Inside the fenced-off compound, we lined up our Ratels and waited in the blazing sun for our next move. It was late afternoon when we were issued with our next ration pack, accompanied with instructions to head out as a platoon into the desert land and prepare ourselves for the night's sleep.

Stopping under the shade of a thorn tree, we began our hunt for sticks and thick, dry branches to make a fire to warm our tinned food. With the three small tins, emptied into our dixie, we placed it over the flames and stirred it with a stick as it bubbled with heat. When one dixie was withdrawn from the flames, another took the vacant place, only to be replaced with cold water to heat at the end of the meal in order to make the cleaning that little bit easier.

4. A State of Emergency: in Tembisa Township

Bundled in our bush jackets to combat the drop in temperature, we enjoyed our piping-hot coffee, which held the heat well in the metal canteens now blackened from the flames. Circling around the fire, with the smoke stinging our eyes, we stared into the heart of the flames, sipping on our coffee and gripping the canteen with our bush hats wrapped around the burning hot, L-shaped handle. The first sip was always taken with great care, for the metal was extremely hot and we wanted to prevent our dry and cracked lips from sizzling on the curved, metal lip of the fire bucket, which had caught us so many times before and would inevitably catch us again.

'Fuck it! someone screamed in anger.

We smiled to ourselves, quite aware that the troop had misread how hot the rim was and sizzled his dry lips. After the coffee was consumed, we prepared a place upon the ground to sleep, kicking away sticks and stones and then laying out our nylon ground sheets and sleeping bags. Under the starlight, we lay in small groups, listening to the crackle of the fire as it slowly began to burn out in the same way that sleep gradually shut us down.

In the morning we woke to radio orders to meet at the ammunition dump and begin bombing up for the afternoon attack. The riflemen loaded their magazines with 5.56mm rounds from plastic carry pouches, the bullets neatly packed 30 to a box. The gunners had an ordeal as they lugged heavy belts of 20mm rounds onto the top of the Ratel and began feeding the long chain of 21 centimetre-long bullets into the rectangular metal boxes that fed to the cannon. While Wayne and Fox sweated, we sat and casually filled our 35 round magazines with 30 rounds each to reduce the chance of a jamming leaving tension in the magazine spring.

Glancing over to our HQ section as they sat lazily spread out on the nose of the Ratel, gave us the impression that they were on a Sunday picnic. With a small radio playing from the turret, Tony, Macky, and Jason sang 'Careless Whisper' – in tune and with the same gut-wrenching emotion as George Michael himself. I am sure he would have been extremely proud of these three *Haa Kaa Piele* – HQ pricks – as they enjoyed their singsong in front of the rest of the platoon, who were so caught up in this hive of activity that it became background music while we prepared for the battalion attack.

Fully bombed up, our Ratels weighed 16 tons as we ploughed through the scrub and across the red earth in battle formation, armed to the teeth and ready and waiting for the doors to fly open. Half an hour into our vehicle manoeuvres, a radio signal came through to halt and begin unloading all our hard work.

'Typical fuckin' army, no one knows what the fuck's going on, load up then unload, dig a hole and then fill it in, stand here, now move over there' what a fuck-around!' I mumbled, frustrated at the continuous lack of organization. It was army fact that on most occasions the left hand did not know what the right hand was up to, thus pushing us in to a very angry and pissed-off mentality.

Taking out the first round with our fingers, we used it to strike out each round from all six magazines, emptying the contents into our open bush hats. This was easy in comparison to the shouting and cursing as the gunners viciously hurled belts of 20mm rounds from the turret onto the ground.

'Don't you think they could have let us rather shoot it out?' Nickol exploded as another belt bit the dust.

In the late afternoon, we exited the lonely and forgotten place of Lohatlha and made our way towards the Transvaal in convoy. After a few hours of driving, the darkness pushed us down into the hull, forcing us to sit and rest and glance through the open portholes every now and then, in complete boredom and discomfort.

The Ratel began to slow and Bennie pulled to the side, boxing up to the vehicle in front. Paul told us to get out and stretch, which we gladly did, and used the time for a long-awaited piss break. Under captain's orders, we looked for sticks and made the most spectacular bonfire – it illuminated a long line of stealthy fighting vehicles, each nose nestled neatly into the exhaust of the one in front.

In my mind, I wondered why we had been stopped minutes away from a major practice attack and led so quickly in the direction of the Transvaal.

What the hell was this about? I wondered as we were drawn like moths to the heat of a lamp. The captain issued a casual order to prepare for sleep in or next to the Ratel, but as usual he gave us no information as to our sudden departure from Lohatlha. After our fill of smoke and fire, we drifted to our vehicles, threw our sleeping bags over a patch of ground, and zipped ourselves in for the night. Peering out of our bags, we watched the fire flicker as it crackled and popped over the rustle of troops tossing and turning in their bags, trying to find a more comfortable position against the unavoidable rocks that dug into our backs.

When morning dawned we slowly rose, still in uniform, sore, having half slept with cold and discomfort, as if we had been woken from the dead. With another rat pack in our dirty hands, we boarded our bus – as we sometimes called it – through the puffs of diesel, and stretched our legs in the back as the convoy started to move out.

In the late afternoon we arrived at the gates of 1 Construction Unit in Springs in the Transvaal, and drove in a long line onto their parade ground. By the time we had finished parking our vehicles, the red earth of the parade ground, which was bigger than a full-length rugby field, was totally covered with Buffels, Ratels, and Samils. I would say close to 100 uniform brown army vehicles had formed neat lines down the length of the ground, waiting with wonder and anticipation at what this sudden mass of armoury was all about.

We disembarked and began setting up the chopper tents, which slept a half section with room to spare, laying claim to a section of space by marking it with a pack and unrolled sleeping bag.

Our food from the ration packs was warmed over the stove, which was a small tin with a fuel tablet placed in the middle of it, with holes punctured all around, allowing the air to flow freely through. The heat from these tablets had our food bubbling in minutes, and we stirred the concoction with a stick, trying to prevent a thick layer from burning onto the bottom of our metal canteens.

While we slaved over our individual meals, our rank told us that they were going into town, which meant booze for us. Money was handed to them with a list of what we wanted and how much Rand we needed to hand over. After a few hours they returned with vast quantities of alcohol, from beer to hard-core spirits. Following the list, the bottles of brandy, whisky, Southern Comfort, vodka, old brown sherry also known as Obees, and beer were handed out along with the change, and we began to ready ourselves for a very drunken night.

With a 750ml bottle in the hands of most of us, we began to drink to the night and make up for months of lost drinking time. I had ordered a bottle of Klipdrift brandy, known to us as Klippies, or in Afrikaans as *Horlosie brandewyn* – referring to the clock face that appeared on the label of each bottle. With my metal fire bucket in one hand, and the bottle in the other, I began to pour a lethal measure. This was followed by a packet of cola crystals from the ration pack, topped with some water from the green, army-issue water bottle, ending with a quick stir.

With my lips to the metal, I began to drink this poor imitation of brandy and coke, and I winced with each swig of the vile combination. It seemed to get easier on the taste buds as the night wore on. Fellow troops had warned each other about brandy drunk in excess, which was known as 'the devil's friend' or 'satan's drink' – *duiwel's dop* – because of the actions and anger that fell upon those who abused it.

Laughter and loud talking flowed from the shadows of the circle as we sipped heavily on our drinks, eager to finish the bottle we had started and enjoying the freedom of getting drunk. After a few strong fire buckets of the devil's drink, I saw Engelbrecht walk in and join the circle next to us. This 23 year-old Durbanite quickly began to make a nuisance within the group as he literally begged everyone for some dagga. In the eyes of all of us, he was a complete and utter 'waste of white skin,' and had not changed since being in my Delta Company platoon during basic training. The only good thing was that he was no longer in our platoon but remained in our company as the captain's Ratel driver.

After a few hours, the devil from the drink came out in me. I walked into the group, half staggering and slurring, and punched the unsuspecting Engelbrecht twice in the face, chasing him away like a stray dog with his tail between his legs. Cheers and laughter rose from the group, with slaps of congratulations across my back, coupled with the words, 'Well done, Ram.'

Feeling a strange sense of pride for helping out my fellow troopies, I knew there was no doubt that my drunken anger and actions had been caused by the now-empty bottle that lay discarded at my feet.

In the morning, with blurred vision and suffering from the stench of booze and a pounding head, I knew firsthand how brandy could change someone from a rational thinker to an uncontrollably angry and aggressive person.

With most of us looking extremely pale and under the weather, we began to dismantle our chopper tents and ready our vehicles to move out. All gunners were ordered to remove their heavy, two-metre-long gun barrels from the Ratel turrets, which were then carried to a waiting Samil and placed in neat rows beneath the canopy. Forming up into another convoy, we drove out of the gates of 1 Construction Unit in the direction of Johannesburg. With our Ratels stretched across the tarmac for as far as the eye could see, we remained one behind the next with the help of the Military Police. They controlled all traffic lights and inroads to our rumbling path, allowing us passage ahead of the civilian motorists. In tight convoy we sped past stationary cars, their engines turned off and family members sitting in awe upon the bonnet, waving us on with smiles and cheers. One Ratel after the other thundered by.

Sitting on top of the Ratel we felt the *nugget gevoel* – pride – and wallowed in the civilians' appreciation of our unconditional duty to South Africa. We waved back, almost in a thank you. A chill of goosebumps shot down my arms as I waved to people on the hill, at the edge of their beautiful properties, and on the roadside as they frantically and joyously acknowledged us. Sitting with smiles drawn across our faces, we basked in the glory of being king of the road for the very first time, as confident and well-trained soldiers. The eyes of the parents, and especially the children, grew to huge marbles, they had to wonder in astonishment at what this convoy, which stretched

4. A State of Emergency: in Tembisa Township

for kilometres and had brought the outskirts of Johannesburg to a standstill, was all about.

The Military Police stood in the middle of the roadway, tough and menacing, as their motorcycles waited on the side for a quick getaway onto the next intersection – in order to repeat the same process.

What a feeling, I thought as we were presented with open passage – in the same way a marathon runner would experience it, with adrenaline heightened, like ours, by stationary cars and bewildered and enthusiastic onlookers.

It was not long before we drove into an area that seemed so foreign in comparison to our white world. Arriving in Tembisa was, for us, like entering an impoverished, third world country far from our doorstep. It seemed as though we had crossed the border into a country elsewhere in Africa. For the vast majority of us, this was the very first time that our eyes had seen the misery of a major black settlement, called – in the South African language of segregation – a location, or a township.

The drab, dusty, and dilapidated surroundings were a stark contrast to nearby, affluent Pretoria. In Pretoria, the picture-perfect homes revelled in the luxury of swimming pools and immaculate gardens, manicured to perfection. Tall trees offered welcome shade over green carpets of well-watered grass, neatly squared-off within the boundaries of high, ugly brick walls.

The contrast was like chalk and cheese. The rows of dun-coloured houses, on each side of the dirt road, were almost a replica of those adjacent, except that the doors were painted a different colour. Each little house had a corrugated tin roof, but hardly any were blessed with the essentials of running water and electricity. Water was fetched by bucket, at the end of every few streets, from a wide opening in a pipe that stood three quarters of a metre off the ground. The water gushed from the pipe, and the spillage formed into muddy pools of stagnant water, which the people lined up in, waiting their turn to fill their well-used and dirty plastic containers. Thin, scrawny dogs made their way like hyenas to scavenge a drink from the growing puddle before they were shooed away. One by one the women left with a full bucket balanced upon their heads, walking up the dirt road with total ease, leaving their arms to hang freely by their sides. With this daily task ingrained into their lives, they performed it with the grace and confidence of a practised circus act.

Trees had been chopped down for wood, and there were very few left to be seen and used for shade, and what little grass there was had been worn into a crisscross of dry and dusty footpaths. There were no street lamps to light the uneven and potholed road that broke the line of small houses. Inside, light flickered through the half-curtained windows – the burning candles and paraffin lamps granting the hard-earned luxury of light. A blanket of smog hovered over the poverty-stricken area, from the thousands of wood fires over which their simple meals could be heated.

The air also held the toxic smell of burned rubber, which served as a reminder of the savagery of black-on-black crime, with death at the hands of the burning necklace – which had become a common practice throughout these miserable locations. The 'necklace' was a rubber car tyre that was doused in petrol, pulled over the unlucky victim's head and down their torso – thus locking their arms next to their sides, like a straitjacket. While the person stood in helpless terror, it was set on fire. The victim would shout out bloodcurdling screams as their skin melted under a black haze of burning rubber, leaving behind a smouldering fire and the charred remains of a person in the wrong place at the wrong time. Although we had never witnessed a live execution of this nature, it was shown graphically on television and splashed across the newspapers.

A very sick joke circulated around our camp with regards to the necklace, which always drew a deep, racist laugh: How many Africans can be necklaced using one tyre? The answer: 365 in a Goodyear.

Unfortunately, we were caught up in our own spiral of fear and resentment, and there was never a moment to ponder how different our lives could have been if we had been born black and segregated from society by the cruel wall of apartheid. Maybe only then could we have understood the life of a second-class citizen stripped of human rights.

Our convoy took us into the heart of Tembisa, where we witnessed recently destroyed buildings, including a cinema that had been burned and reduced to a pile of rubble and the empty shops, half-standing, cleaned out by looters. This was a glimpse into their world, where only the toughest survived and where poverty ruled their lives. Most of them did not know a life any different.

With the violence, chaos, and lawlessness that spread like wildfire across many locations in the country, President P.W. Botha declared a state of emergency. The locations were now under martial law, with a curfew imposed upon the community forbidding any movement outside after dark.

Unbeknown to us at the time, in July 1984 Indian and coloured voters had been introduced into parliament for the first time under the amendment of the Republic of South Africa Constitution Act, albeit with apartheid still firmly entrenched in the constitution. Blacks had been excluded altogether and were left to express their political rights through the 'homeland' to which they were ethnically linked. When the newly elected Indian and coloured members sat

4. A State of Emergency: in Tembisa Township

down for the first time, a smouldering African fuse began to burn with anger and bitterness.

Their being cast aside in the decision-making process caused an explosion of violence to rock South Africa, such as had not been seen since the Soweto riots of 1976. Workers and students staged the biggest mass stay-away across the country that South Africa had ever seen. Three hundred schools closed because 800 000 students and workers chose to disrupt the economy and create strife by not attending school and work. Many of the townships became ungovernable when rioting and looting spread and more victims were claimed by the horrific necklace.

The police force was immediately deployed into these volatile areas with their caged riot vehicles, hoping to restore peace through their presence. But with their force spread so thin, especially across the Vaal Triangle, where the majority of the unrest stemmed from, the government had no choice but to dispatch the army. In October 1984, 7000 troops in Buffels, Ratels, and Samils poured in to the Vaal Triangle, as a show of force through sheer numbers and military might, to instill fear throughout the ghetto-like setting. One thousand troops were Ratel soldiers from 1-SAI.

In the political spectrum, since South Africa was in a state of emergency, the grip of economic sanctions tightened even more. On TV, the graphic and ghostly images of savagery and violence flickered daily, and the unrest continued under the army presence as random attacks were carried out on those Africans alleged to be 'informers' to the white rulers.

The tide was turning. South Africa was facing a critical time and the violence began to spread uncontrollably. Many of the experienced black leaders of the township communities had been detained by the police, upon suspicion of supporting the banned African National Congress – ANC. This now left a gap in the power vacuum and a path wide open for a reign of terror, which was exploited by gangs and thugs as areas were plunged into mayhem, murder, and chaos.

People began to wonder if the war had finally moved inside South Africa's borders. The media, which was controlled by the government, silently depicted the Africans as a people so caught up in violence, with so many tribal beliefs and ethnic backgrounds, that disaster was inevitable. To the white population, the violence only confirmed their belief that the Africans would never be able to run a country without bloodshed and chaos.

Armed with rubber bullets in one magazine and five live rounds in another, we stood outside our hatches and looked through the dust cloud as we headed towards an open, long-grassed field slightly away from the poor dwellings but still within the black community.

Below the shade of a few trees and thorn bushes, we started setting up our chopper tents in a long line with our Ratels shielding us from the front. It felt awkward and out of place for us, as white soldiers, to be setting up a makeshift camp upon the very soil granted to the African people as part of the apartheid Land Act. Our Ratels stood menacingly in our camp, and the sheer presence of these powerful monsters warded off any danger to such an extent that we never stood a single guard beat. Opposite our vehicles, two big holes were dug, and on top of them two tall, blue, portable toilets were placed, offering privacy seldom experienced during our daily calling.

In the morning we departed from camp as a platoon and drove down the long dusty roads, passing men and women walking for miles to their faraway destinations, leaving them to cough on the thick, powdery dust that the massive tyres churned into the air. Back inside the impoverished neighbourhoods, we drove wide-eyed past groups of black men, half expecting them to throw bricks and rocks at us. But they just stood and stared right through us with daggers of hatred. The majority of South Africans lived their life without even bothering to consider the possibility of equality, for they were born to this way of thinking and living and knew no better. Those who did glared at our white skin, anger etched in their faces, painting us all with the same white-racist brush.

From one house to the next, we moved past evidence of a hardened, extremely simple life. The wrinkled lines on their faces told a story of suffering against the cold and the basic necessities of life, made worse by the chaos that had recently rocked their lives. At the sound of our approaching vehicles, many families threw open their red, yellow, blue, and green doors and spilled out onto their well-worn grass. There followed the yaps of underfed, dirty, scarred, and thin mongrels – called *braks* – which went absolutely berserk at the sight and smell of us, the white men. They charged forward towards our Ratel, offering protection to their owners. Dirty, naked kids with big eyes, standing next to their mothers, brothers, and sisters, stared up at us as we towered over them. When we waved a greeting, we were met with smiles and a barrage of returning waves and shouts, which continued throughout the neighbourhood and gave us, somehow, the feeling that we were their liberators, saving them from the hated police and their sometimes hard-line actions.

The majority knew that they needed us in their community for protection. They knew that, for as long as we remained, law and order would bring them peace. Outside some houses, old men and women sat smoking on wooden boxes

4. A State of Emergency: in Tembisa Township

and metal oil drums, and watched us pass them by. In the background a distinct African beat played from a small rectangular radio, which was connected to a car battery with a wire coat hanger used as a makeshift aerial. Washing was hung on wires, waiting for the sun to dry it before the dust did, barefoot little children scurried playfully under it, following us over the rock-hard earth with dirty faces and curious looks.

The vehicle patrols were carried out from morning until shortly after the darkness had settled over the sleepy and quiet, dimly-lit township. Somehow, troops in our platoon got wind of the whereabouts of a *shebeen*. So in the darkness we converged upon this illegal establishment and bought a couple of plastic crates filled with 12 quart bottles of Castle beer.

There were many ironies in the black-and-white policies. Blacks were forbidden to buy alcohol from a 'whites-only' bottle store, only from their own – into which we could go as often as we chose. A couple of such ironies reached our ears through music and television. Bob Marley's reggae created no racial barriers, and yet it had a massive following among young white people, in spite of the fact that reggae musicians were mostly black. 'The Cosby Show,' depicted a well-to-do black American family, unlike any we had ever seen, and it also became a huge hit in the homes of the white South Africans. Many blacks being underprivileged, could not afford the luxury of a television set and instead listened to the outside world through their small and well-looked-after radios.

Back at camp, we unloaded the two crates of beer from the tail gunner's door and began distributing two to each person who had paid for his share of the cheap alcohol. Immediately, the metal bottle caps were knocked off, and chinking a giant, 750ml bottle in each of our hands, we began to drink our worries away. Sitting around a circular, rock-contained fire area, we set about making dinner with our ration packs, in between sips of warm beer. The remaining bottles sat in wet socks and hung from our tents, chilling in the night breeze. While we busied ourselves over our meals, a few of us toyed with the idea of naming our Ratel. It created some excitement amongst our Alpha section, and we produced a clever title within minutes. Having been on the road for a few weeks now, sustained strictly on a diet of ration packs, we came up with the name 'Road Rat.' While we drank to our newly-christened vehicle, Wayne immediately got to work, and with some chalk he lettered out 'Road Rat' with horizontal stripes in red, yellow, and green.

The night passed peacefully, the alcohol adding a new dimension to our usual evening of boredom until sleep finished off another day.

In the morning, we hit the dusty roads for another patrol, and showed our presence and our military strength. At the sight of our vehicles, the young, inquisitive kids converged on us like bees to honey. When a big group had formed around our vehicles, we began to throw our unwanted dry rations towards the outstretched arms belonging to hungry bodies. When the food rained upon them, they scrambled for it, and when they emerged victorious from the swelling crowd, the sheer joy in their button-brown eyes and ivory-white smiles said it all. Standing on the Ratel and towering three metres above the African children, watching them scavenge for scraps, gave us a perverse feeling as if we were royalty throwing food to the peasants.

No matter how it looked, to the young children we were their heroes of the day, and hidden in each one of us was a rich and rewarding feeling at having brought joy in such a simple way to these less fortunate youngsters.

Living on ration packs was starting to take its toll on us, for the bland taste and monotony drove our taste buds crazy. The small boxes of food served their daily purpose, but we all hankered for fresh food – anything that we did not have to mix with water. During one patrol a chicken strutted past our vehicle, and in an instant – without a word being said, but only eye contact made – we determined that dinner had just crossed our path. Leaping out of the vehicle, we cornered the frightened bird and placed it inside the Ratel for the remainder of the day's patrol. We kept a close check on our 'fresh' dinner.

Upon arriving at camp, half of our section collected wood and prepared a fire while a couple of farmers cut the chicken's head off with a small knife. With the warm, bloody bird in our hands, we began the tedious task of plucking its white feathers from the deep pockets of skin and then passing it onto the next troop, all of us earned our share of the pot. One of the Ratel floor grids was placed on the fire to burn off the thick, green, toxic paint, it was used as the grill upon which to braai – barbecue – our chicken. When the bird was free of its feathers, it suddenly had become half its size – making the ten portions a lot smaller than we had first imagined. Nevertheless the filleted pieces were placed neatly upon the blackened grid, and with the ten of us circled around the fire we picked our piece of chicken and guarded it with our lives. To smell the burning meat was a mouthwatering feast in itself, we stared at it before turning it with our dirty fingers, in hopes of expediting the cooking process.

When it was braai'd to perfection we nibbled on our tiny pieces of succulent and juicy chicken, enjoying the moment, for it satisfied our cravings. Unfortunately it was just not enough, but it was worth every bit of hard work for a much-needed change. With satisfied bellies we turned in for the night, stinking

4. A State of Emergency: in Tembisa Township

of smoke, and clambered into the tent with a candle in the middle, guiding us to our brown sleeping bags.

To be awoken at first light by the annoying roosters was a daily occurrence, but at least now there was one less to bug us.

Leaving camp for the day, we followed each other in our usual way before splitting up to cover different areas of the location. Our section came across the shell of an abandoned car that was sitting in the middle of a field. To the delight of a few African children, Toth climbed into the windowless car taking hold of the steering wheel, followed by Laurence, who filled the passenger seat. Bennie connected the thick-wire tow cable to the Ratel and the car shell, and then slowly took up the slack, pulling the car on its undercarriage over the green grass, while Toth acted as though he were steering it with a broken steering arm. It was so stupid, and yet we laughed ourselves silly, joined by the crowd of young onlookers. It certainly made their day too.

In the afternoon we were challenged to a game of soccer with the locals. We parked our Ratels in a line, aiming their noses unintentionally, and yet in an intimidating way, over the field of play. Barefoot against boot, we walked onto the uneven turf, where dirty white goalposts marked the areas of the penalty box. The field had been stripped of all grass, leaving only a smooth, rock-hard surface. Excited spectators filled the sidelines as we began chasing the young, skilled, and very nimble Africans in our quest for the ball. Our fellow troopies lazed on top of the Ratels, enjoying the spectacle with shouts of encouragement and much laughter – for the Africans ran rings around our uncoordinated and slow movements. Sweating in our long brown pants and heavy boots, fearful of kicking our opponents on the shins, we managed to wrestle the ball away and score a couple of goals, though not enough to win the match. To the local Africans, this was a day in heaven and the story could be shared in the poverty of their homes, of how they had beaten the 'white army' at their own game.

On our way through the blocks of right-angled roads, a couple of locals stopped us and invited us into their home. Very unsure, we looked at each other and decided to accept the offer. Under darkness, we parked our Ratel outside the very simple home and left our rifles behind in the enclosed vehicle. A 750ml bottle of Castle beer was thrust into each of our hands – a welcome from the group of ten Africans inside.

'Thank you for bringing us peace,' the woman of the house said as she raised her bottle in cheers. Quite shocked at their gratitude, we also raised our bottles and went around the small, one-room dwelling, clinking them with the men and women. When our bottles were finished, another was set into our hands, and as we talked, our eyes scanned the room, which looked very similar to the servants' quarters in the back yards of most of our white homes. A metal-framed bed stood in the corner along one unpainted wall, with four paint tins under each leg, giving it a needed 20 centimetres of extra height – for many African people believed in the superstition of the little green man, called the *Tokolosh*. They believed that he would come for them at night while they slept, and for their safety they raised their beds so that he would not be able to reach them. Some even went as far as greasing the legs of the bed with Vaseline, so that he would slip down in his bid to get them in the night.

A couple of paraffin lamps illuminated the room of smiling faces, and a small radio played from a cloth-covered wooden box, which was used as a table. The concrete floor was covered for the most part with a carpet and a curtain hung as a partition at the far end of the room. It was kept clean, with an extremely basic setting, the radio being the only luxury.

Someone turned up the volume as Cyndi Lauper's hit single 'Girls Just Want to Have Fun' blared through the speaker, turning the room in to a dance floor. It seemed strange to be listening to a song that had originated in New York, oceans away, only to be appreciated in one of the poorest areas of South Africa. Here we were, in the African's world, so underprivileged and distant from our own, in a room filled with people who were able to somehow share the joy of music in peace and harmony.

They had told us stories of police brutality, and the force they had used to calm the riots. There was certainly a lot of intense dislike displayed towards the South African Police – SAP – and the Africans were only too happy to have us watching over them, instead of the 'hard-core and iron-fisted' white police.

When the time came to leave, we pulled out our wallets to pay for the beer, but were met with smiles and a firm 'No!' The African lady of the house pulled back the curtain that was serving as the partition and showed us a wall of plastic crates filled with beer up to the ceiling. We were standing in a *shebeen*, which did not bother us at all considering how well they had treated us. We knew only too well that their skin colour labelled them as unskilled labour and earned them very low pay. The *shebeen* was how they eked out a living.

Quite drunk, we left the home with appreciation for their kindness and boarded the Road Rat, thankful to find our rifles and our vehicle as we had left them a few hours earlier. With Bennie drunk at the wheel, we navigated our way back through the pitch darkness, returning safely to our base camp.

Sunday for us was a normal day of patrol, but for the community it was the day that their best clothes were worn as they walked or were driven to church.

4. A State of Emergency: in Tembisa Township

Their shoes were polished to a shine, their clothes were clean and starched. To the outsider, it looked as though they were visiting this poverty-stricken area, not actually living within its filth. Families waved at us as we slowly drove by, sitting on top of the vehicle with our legs dangling through the hatches.

In the afternoon we found a crude-looking butcher shop, which would immediately be condemned by the naked eye, but with our yearning for a juicy steak, no flies or lack of refrigeration could turn us away. We climbed back into our Ratel, each one of us clutching a chunk of meat wrapped in newspaper and looking forward to our afternoon feast.

The following day we were ordered to set up roadblocks on the main, tarred road entering into Tembisa. One Ratel parked on one side of the road and another on the opposite, 25 metres away. Orange cones were set up in the road to slow the traffic, and two riflemen from each section were placed on a small hill, hidden from sight. If a car refused to stop and drove directly through our roadblock, the riflemen were under orders to bring the car to a standstill.

Randomly we selected cars, and ordered the occupants out of their vehicles before searching the inside. The driver was ordered to open the boot, and unzip all suitcases. He was told to watch our every move as we carefully unpacked each case in our search for weapons and banned literature. When we finished the search, leaving the cases opened and rummaged through, the driver and his passengers usually became irritated at all the inconvenience of repacking.

Taxis were brought to a stop as we ordered everyone out of the vehicle, which contained around 25 people crammed into a 14-seater E-20 van. How they managed to cram themselves in, in the first place, was a mystery to us, and after the search was completed they squeezed themselves back in and continued at their normal kamikaze speed, angry that their time was thus wasted. When the newspapers reported a taxi crash, which occurred almost daily, one could guess the death toll to be around 20 and be very close to the actual figure.

One driver who was pulled over was so drunk that he could barely stand, let alone drive. His eyes looked like roadmaps and his breath gave off a foul smell of alcohol. The contents of his car was pulled apart and put back together, revealing nothing incriminating, and so we let him by to finish his drunken journey. With our white man's thinking, he was entering his location, and if he accidentally killed someone it would be one of his own.

With no arrests after a full day of searching and repacking, we entered back into the sprawl of the township, with orders to break up any crowd we found, which was considered a group of more than four people. We did this to prevent a large number of people from plotting against us and destabilizing the peace.

On a couple of occasions, we walked into a crowd with our rifles ready and broke up the gathering. Some of the looks we got from the young African men could not hide the anger lined across their black faces, their eyes filled with hatred that could shoot us down in an instant. Kicking at the dust, they dispersed into the hive of activity – of people passing by, coupled with cars dodging civilians and dogs running between the young and old as they scavenged for scraps of food.

Back at base, the roads had turned into a river of mud from the afternoon rain and the countless Ratel wheels that had churned the once-dusty way into a slippery trap. Bennie navigated his course as we entered the campground, and with a little too much speed he lost control, hitting an old car wreck. But more importantly, he missed the two portable shit houses by inches, which certainly would have created a foul mess within our camp.

Our platoon had also taken part in a few house searches, and with our rifles at the ready we knocked on the wooden door. A few soldiers waited at the back of the house, in case the occupants tried to climb out of a window and make a run for it. A lookout remained on the Ratel, while a group of us entered into the small, single-room living area. While the African men and women, with worried faces, took a step back, we began a quick search for any books, papers, and literature with links to the banned African National Congress. Again we came up empty-handed, and exited back onto the Ratel, leaving those inside wondering and angry at our invasion of their living space.

Our company had experienced very little hostility from the local people. Two apples were thrown at us, and another platoon had a few rocks thrown at them. We had got off lightly compared with some of the vehicles in the early days of the riots, which were hit with petrol bombs – more commonly known as Molotov cocktails. When a Molotov cocktail hit its target, it exploded in a spreading ball of fire, engulfing everything within.

We had heard stories of Africans being forced by fellow Africans who victimized them with their ruthless acts of savagery, to eat whatever they held in their shopping bags. In one instance, an African woman was forced to eat a raw chicken and wash it down with a bottle of cooking oil.

After a month of living in the black township, we began to break up camp, and in a military convoy we started our exodus from the poor and hidden life of the underprivileged African people.

As an added kindness to our mission, we had left a mark on the people, for we had donated large portions of our ration packs to the begging throngs, who at times followed our vehicles for a kilometre or so in the hope of receiving

4. A State of Emergency: in Tembisa Township

a sweet or a packet of army-ration biscuits. On an occasion or two, someone accidentally threw a fuel tablet towards the long line of young followers, which was ripped open by eager fingers and thrust into their unsuspecting mouths, only to be just as quickly spat out when their tongue tasted the toxic chemical. On seeing this, we could not help but laugh at the stunned expression, which abated with a handful of sweets thrown their way.

Another laugh came at the expense of all those malt porridges that were carefully mixed in plastic liners. We threw them towards the hungry, fixated eyes, and watched them torn open in a frenzy. Unfortunately the porridge, as might be expected, exploded over their heads and dirty faces, leaving most of them to get only a small taste of what our breakfast consisted of.

In spite of their messy faces, they looked up at us and broke into smiles with a chorus of childish laughter. In their eyes, we just knew, we were some sort of heroes, having taken them from kicking a worn-out soccer ball and guiding an old rubber tyre with a stick to standing next to a Ratel. Groups of young kids were hoisted on top of our vehicle, and with us watching over their safety, we drove them around the block. What a rewarding feeling it was to see these kids waving to their friends and parents, who got the shock of their lives to see them aboard our vehicle, sitting with nervous smiles and feeling extremely important.

With these events ingrained in our minds, we knew the army had helped restore peace in some of the worst-affected areas, and even more importantly, our section and our platoon had left their mark in the lives of some of the less fortunate. In the eyes of the military, we had done our job by showing a powerful force in huge military numbers, further strengthened by the might and intimidating look of the honey badger.

When the long dusty road turned into a smooth, tarred, and level surface, we turned our backs on Tembisa, pulling the black curtain closed behind us as we crossed back into civilization.

By the end of October, 685 Africans had been killed around the country, and 500 had lost their lives due to police action. 20 000 had been injured, and 14 000 had been arrested for public violence. These figures were evidence of the waves of unrest that had swept the country into a scary spiral of ungovernable chaos.

Travelling on good roads and passing new models of motorcars below the backdrop of the towering, concrete pillars of the modern commercial buildings that graced Johannesburg, was a breath of fresh air, and we took in the gratifying sight of our new surroundings. The cleanliness on the roadsides, the smiling, clean white faces that waited and waved their hands excitedly as we drove by, were some of the vivid and stark contrasts, forgotten for the month we had lived in Tembisa's bleak surroundings.

After a long, hot, and stuffy journey, we arrived back at the gates of 1-SAI, with the normal wonder in our minds as someone shouted, 'Soweto Now?' – the name of a major black township close to Tembisa, which if broken down into four syllables reads, 'So weto (where to) now?'

1984-Tembisa. Tembisa township on the East Rand in a state of emergency. 23A parked beneath a giant toilet roll. Looted and burned buildings in the background.

Top 20 Hit Singles of 1984

1. RED RED WINE - UB40
2. CLAP CLAP SOUND - Klaxons
3. I WANT TO BREAK FREE - Queen
4. ISLANDS IN THE STREAM - Kenny Rogers & Dolly Parton
5. SELF CONTROL - Laura Branigan
6. ALL NIGHT LONG - Lionel Richie
7. KARMA CHAMELEON - Culture Club
8. TO ALL THE GIRLS I LOVED BEFORE - Julio Iglesias & Willie Nelson
9. MANUEL GOODBYE - Audrey Landers
10. HAPPY STATION - Fun Fun
11. TONIGHT I CELEBRATE MY LOVE - Peabo Bryson & Roberta Flack
12. FOOTLOOSE - Kenny Loggins
13. JUMP - Van Halen
14. SAY, SAY, SAY - Paul McCartney & Michael Jackson
15. MAJOR TOM - Peter Schilling
16. SUNSHINE REGGAE - Laid Back
17. DOLCE VITA - Ryan Paris
18. BREAK MY STRIDE - Matthew Wilder
19. WRAP YOUR ARMS AROUND ME - Agnetha Faltskog (from Abba)
20. BIG IN JAPAN - Alphaville

1984. The songs and sounds that took us back to our hometowns and faraway from our life in browns.

5

Bloemfontein: last days with 1-SAI

Arriving back in 1-SAI was a very depressing feeling, being suddenly stripped of the township freedom and now caged behind fences and gigantic guard towers, which were still positioned down the length of the straight-wired boundary but with more of an overbearing feel this time around.

Bravo Company's Ratels drove to the back of our company lines and parked in a long line, their distinguishing V-shaped noses pointed towards our bungalows. Our platoon was given a new bungalow right at the back of our lines, a stone's throw away from the small, grey-stoned parade ground on which our Ratels were parked.

We grabbed a bed, with the HQ section and Alpha section sharing half the bungalow and Bravo and Charlie on the other side of the wall, which stopped a metre short of reaching the ceiling. Our kit was unpacked into our green metal cupboards and trunks, which we religiously locked, not leaving the temptation open for a fellow troop to gain a piece of kit that he had lost.

Lazing on our beds with our boots on top of the traditional brown blanket, with the two stripes down the middle, we reflected on the time gone by. In a couple of months we would be *ou manne*, and we could not wait for the hard-earned privilege of looking two years older, with our moustaches and faded, well-worn browns. That NAAFI – no-ambition-and-fuckall-interest – army feeling was rapidly gnawing at our spirits as we lazed around, waiting for something to happen.

In the morning, Staff Nel instructed us to get ready for '*staal parade*' steel parade, which would be inspected by Colonel van Zyl and involved removing from each Ratel every conceivable piece of equipment that was not bolted down. Each section took to their Ratel and began work unpacking the vehicle and laying out the gear on an open canvas groundsheet. The gunners and tail gunners handled their 20mm babies, along with their Brownings' and because of all the outside dust, they decided to clean their guns inside our old bungalow, which had remained empty. These lethal weapons were placed over the mattresses, using the beds as a table, making it easier to strip them down, and clean them from dust, grease, and old gunpowder.

While the eight-gunner crew remained indoors, the rest of the platoon swept, dusted, and washed the interior of the vehicle, making it spotless before we began repacking the foot grids and individual pieces of rubber seating. The outside of the Ratel was washed by bucket and cloth, while we stood on top of the vehicle and threw bucket after bucket of cold water over it. The streams of water took away the dirt and dust, leaving the car a clean, glistening matt-brown.

A group of us went down to the front bungalow to see how our gunner friends were making out. The cannons were stripped and spread over at least ten beds, with grease streaked across each mattress and white-striped '*pissvel*' mattress cover, which did not faze any one of us until Colonel van Zyl walked in with RSM Stone at his side.

The first person to see them screamed, '*Staanop*' Stand up!, which we all immediately did. Walking down the corridor, looking at each bed, we could feel the anger written across their faces at our disregard for state-owned property.

'*Wat gaan aan hierso?*' What's going on here?, the RSM bellowed, pointing an ugly finger at the caked-on grease, which all of a sudden seemed to be everywhere. When they left, we just knew that something bigger was to come.

An hour later, Staff Sergeant Nel had our platoon formed up, and in Afrikaans he began cutting us down with his belittling words of degradation.

'*Julle is n klomp foken doos diewe!*' he shouted with uncontrollable rage. '*Nou sal julle kak!*' You are all a bunch of stupid vagina thieves! Now you are going to shit!

His face was a pale white, highlighted by his dark black moustache as his mouth opened and spat hatred towards our three-deep platoon formation – standing, waiting, and dead still at attention.

Pointing at the guardroom 400 metres away, he barked, '*Fokweg, jou donderse varkseuns!*' Fuck away, you thundering, stupid sons of pigs!

As one we turned and laughed aloud and slowly ran towards the guardroom, joking together as we enjoyed the bond and the spirit that had transpired within our close-knit platoon.

'*Julle is besig om my foken moer te koer!*' You are starting to get on my fuckin' nerves, he screamed in torment, giving the impression that he had lost control over us.

'*Op die grond!*' On the ground!, came the next order as we began leopard-crawling over the hard, dusty ground feeling the sharp, tiny stones cut into our exposed elbows. Covered in dust and sweat as thirst dried our throats, we continued with that unwavering strength of iron, never allowing him to get the better of us.

'*Ek sal jou gat so hard skop so dat jou neus sal bloei!*' I will kick your arse so hard that your nose will bleed!, he shrieked, towering over us like a raving lunatic.

5. Bloemfontein: last days with 1-SAI

After an hour of grovelling in the dirt, he told us to 'fuck off,' and so we did.

Walking past him in groups, covered in dust from head to boot, we laughed with high spirits, having reached that true army feeling of 'no ambition and fuckall interest.' Now whatever they threw at us would not break the safety net that we had enmeshed amongst ourselves into our rock-solid and unbreakable platoon.

In the morning, after our rushed breakfast, we continued on with our *staal parade* that was to be inspected by Colonel van Zyl, Captain de Jaeger and RSM Stone. While we worked, cleaning all the removable equipment from the Ratel to a sparkling shine before displaying it on a thick, dirty, brown canvas sheet, we noticed a man driving a tractor who looked every bit like Staff Nel.

Suddenly a rumour circled through our platoon that Staff Nel had been removed from his post, and slowly – with the uncommon sight of him on the tractor – it made more sense. Again we saw him, solemn-faced and looking like a broken man, the humiliation shadowing his expression as he clutched the wheel of the old red tractor and ploughed the small grey stones into an even surface over the parade ground. Standing next to our Ratels, we watched him drive by followed by a cloud of grey dust, as he kept his head forward, sparing himself more humiliation from our victorious faces, the rumour now confirmed to be the truth.

Very few of the high-up rank held our respect and so seeing Staff Nel stripped of his post gave us no regrets or ill-feelings. Platoon 3 had achieved something very few companies could boast of – we had now degraded someone who had degraded us for so long, by the sheer will of sticking together as a steadfast unit.

'He was a complete bastard!' someone crooned with disgust. 'Remember all those *opfoks* at De Brug!'

'Fuck him!' another added in agreement. 'One less PF to worry about.'

Pass was coming up, and the excitement of a short visit home was tugging pleasurably at us, having not seen our loved ones, or experienced a break in the strict military discipline, in two and a half months. There were only a couple of weeks to go before we hit the road on our journeys home, and we were counting the days to this special occasion that came so seldom – something that we lived for, which no amount of money could buy.

RSM Stone took over Staff Nel's role, and with a stern face he barked the orders at us, looking every bit like a ferocious Rottweiler. While we were standing at attention, Brian sauntered up a few minutes late and tried to take his place unnoticed into the platoon formation.

'*Waardie fok gaan jy?*' Where the fuck are you going?, he snarled in Afrikaans, his stone cold face frowning in anger.

Brian looked at him for a couple of long drawn-out seconds before offering his reason.

'I am joining my platoon!' he replied casually, with a hint of what's-the-big-deal in his clever English tone.

RSM Stone marched up to Brian, and right in front of us he grabbed him in a headlock and tried to force him onto the ground. Brian being short, stocky, and very strong, managed to wriggle free, he stood his ground in a way that few had ever witnessed.

'Get your fuckin' hands off me!' he screamed out, his face reddened from the grip and shaking with anger. He held his clenched fists rigidly at his sides, as if holding them back from striking the RSM.

'*Kry hierdie kak van my parade grond af!*' Get this shit off my parade ground!, the RSM retaliated, unable to do a single thing to Brian as long as we were witnesses and our glaring eyes were angrily staring him down.

Watching Brian disappear towards our bungalow left an uncomfortable feeling in my gut as to what RSM Stone might do to us for the humiliation he had just suffered.

Time passed at the normal army pace while we talked of pass and the freedom of choice that was not part of the army language. Our platoon was instructed to get ready for an inspection, which was going to be led by Colonel van Zyl and RSM Stone.

As usual, we worked hard and made it shine, from the high gloss finish of the floor tiles to the dust sitting on top of the dividing bungalow wall. Standing stiff at attention, we in no way wanted to jeopardize our scheduled pass, so we were confident that our bungalow would be acceptable to their tough and sometimes unkind scrutiny. Slowly they walked between the straight row of beds, looking us up and down, trying to find fault. RSM Stone climbed upon a bed and ran a finger on top of the dividing wall and then looked at it. He turned his index to us and showed us a slightly dirty finger, which he translated back to our corporal and lieutenant as failure to pass the inspection. Lieutenant Bennett told us that there was a possibility our pass might be cancelled due to our failure to present a clean bungalow.

We looked at him in disbelief, not believing that they would try and break us in such a callous way, and if they did, it certainly would not be because of the inspection. When the day of our pass dawned, we formed into a squad at the front of our lines, each with a bag placed next to our feet. Excitement turned to apprehension at the thought of pass being snatched away from us, and the possibility preyed heavily on our minds while we patiently waited.

5. Bloemfontein: last days with 1-SAI

Maybe this is how they would punish us for showing disrespect to Staff Nel by laughing off his commands until he no longer had control over us and had to be removed from his post. Talking amongst ourselves, we remembered the total disregard the gunners showed as they cleaned their cannons over the mattresses, leaving their mark in grease. There was also Brian, who had played a part in angering the RSM, who would definitely want to see us suffer in the cruelest of ways.

RSM Stone walked up to us with his metre long divider stick tucked neatly under his left armpit, and addressed us with his typical stern and slightly drawn look.

'Your pass has been cancelled!' he said in relatively well-pronounced English, without a sign of remorse on his pale, stern face.

Silently we stood and stared, hoping that what we had heard was some sort of sick joke. Our hearts stopped for a second and we could feel our mouths fall open as the realization set in. Inside each of us, we screamed out in agony: 'You fuckin' bastard!'

Slowly we walked past him like a bunch of beaten dogs – our arms lamely carried our bags, which now felt so much heavier as we made our way back to the bungalow in the most dispirited way I had ever seen.

Sitting dejectedly in the bungalow, we looked out of the windows onto the parade ground and watched the rest of our company being loaded into the waiting Samils and driven away, leaving us to think that we could have been them. When the last Samil departed in a cloud of dust, so did any last-ditch thoughts of our pass.

These three or four-day passes were what kept us alive. It was like dangling a carrot in front of a donkey for miles and miles, and then yanking it away without any remorse or explanation. It was mental torture at its highest, and we were livid, but as usual we had no choice but to accept it as something that could never be reversed.

A few of us partook in the smoking of a joint to somehow help cloud the feeling that we were castaways in a prison block. The camp seemed unusually quiet without the rest of our company, as we were left to swear blue murder at RSM Stone as the culprit and bastard responsible for our misery.

The days dragged on, and eventually our company returned energized from their four-day pass, with our punishment now served. We put it behind us and followed our next orders.

Paul called our section together and we crammed like sardines into his sleeping cubicle, wondering what he wanted to tell us that needed such urgency and privacy in such a confined space.

'Alpha Company is looking for another section to bring a platoon to full complement' he said with keen interest. 'Rumour has it that Alpha will be the company going to 61-Mech – the Mechanized Battalion base on the border. 'Shit, we can go to the border and go into Angola, maybe to Ongiva and Cuvelai – like our *ou manne* in *Ops Askari*' he concluded with the passion of a keen Ratel soldier looking for action.

I looked at Wayne, and then turned and faced Paul.

'Those guys cannot even shoot straight,' I said. 'They have already accidentally killed and maimed their own. Shit, what chance do we have with them if we are pulled into Angola for an operation?'

I did not want to risk my life with a new bunch of soldiers, not knowing their breaking points. Heads nodded in agreement, as we knew we could be placing ourselves at risk without the valuable support of Grant's Bravo section and Kleinhans' Charlie, and our HQ section.

'We would be going up with all those *vark* Permanent Force leaders!' someone else added.

'*Ja*, I don't think it is a good idea to break away from the strength of our platoon,' JP said in English with his Afrikaans tongue, and heads continued to nod.

Paul, being the good leader he was, respected our wishes and totally aborted the idea, leaving us firmly within the safety of Platoon 3 and Bravo Company.

I left the room wondering why Paul would even have considered such an offer, but it made more sense when I learned that he had a few close friends who had seen action in Angola, and he wanted us to live that out first-hand.

It was our Platoon's turn to stand guard within the base, something we all hated but had to take our turn at and walk our two-hour beat, seeing it out in groups of two. With my luck, I usually got the 01:00 to 03:00 or 03:00 to 05:00 guard duty, which was the absolute pits because you were constantly awoken throughout the night as shifts ended and new ones began. Two rounds were handed to each troop as they left the guardroom and began their lonely, pitch-black walks along the length of fence and past the ugly and overwhelming guard towers.

During the night, someone accidentally forgot to unload his rifle and ended up firing a shot directly above the entrance to the guardroom, leaving a mark in the brickwork, and scaring everyone awake from a dead sleep.

Just before my beat, Alan began to bug me. Half asleep and frustrated, I warned him to stop, but he still continued to provoke me.

'Stop!' I said in an annoyed tone.

'What are you going to do about it?' he said, glaring at me.

5. Bloemfontein: last days with 1-SAI

Before I realized what I was doing, I punched him twice in the face and then pushed him onto a bed, where I wrestled him briefly to the floor. In seconds it was over, he looked stunned and quiet, and now I was pumped, with fury painted white on my face. Turning, I left the guardroom and began my beat. I tried to slow my quickened breathing as I stepped into the cool, dark, early-morning air with a fellow troop.

On our shift, we looked for *Stompie* – Stumpie – the soldier's ghost who had lost both his legs through a land mine explosion. The story was always told and seemed so real, and yet no one I knew had ever sighted *Stompie*.

Many times we heard sounds of rustling leaves and trees, which always scared the shit out of us but could have been just the wind or our imagination playing tricks. Someone from our platoon, on the other hand, was adamant that they heard the step of army boots – from his supposedly lost legs. Everyone, at the beginning of his shift, would always ask his fellow guards, whom he was relieving, 'Did you guys see *Stompie*?'

Unfortunately, the same answer always came back: 'No, he must be sleeping.'

During one of our guard duties, a rifle was found to be missing from the rifle rack, right under the nose of the corporal on duty for the night. It turned out to be Green, from Platoon 2, who had lost his rifle – which looked really bad when they discovered that his 20mm cannon was also missing after arriving back from Tembisa.

Captain de Jaeger spoke to the whole company, explaining the severity of this issue – something we already knew, which did not need any explanation. Not only was the rifle worth around R2 000, but also it could fall into the wrong hands, with the blame of gross negligence falling upon the troop.

'This rifle has to be found,' he said calmly but with a firm voice. 'I don't care where it is, I want it found!'

Our company was ordered to scour the inside of the camp, looking under every bush and in every hole, in the obvious and not-so-obvious places. The search went on for a week, with Captain de Jaeger not letting up and standing firm that the search would continue until the rifle was recovered.

He promised a four-day pass to the troop who recovered the rifle, and so the fruitless search continued. Unbeknown to the rest of our platoon, Brian had told Sandor that the rifle was hidden in a concrete drainpipe under the roadway leading to the entrance of the base – a stone's throw away from the main gate on the outside of the camp.

Sandor left the camp and returned with the lost rifle, easing the growing tension amongst us, and especially Green, who must have been seeing ten green

Rand notes before his eyes in repayment for his lost property, which belonged to the state.

Captain de Jaeger delivered on his word and granted Sandor a four-day pass back to Kimberley, leaving Brian empty-handed, having come as close as anyone could possibly get, except for Brian, to stealing a rifle. He had so badly wanted to take another rifle home with him, on his next pass, and he told us how he had planned to just walk in to a black township and instill fear. On hearing this I could only assume that he had either sold his previous three stolen rifles or was stock piling them for the day a civil war would break out, a day he spoke about and believed would one day come. Lucky for everyone, he abandoned his well-thought-out plan, getting Sandor a pass and covering his tracks so well that he escaped any investigation and no one was the wiser.

Soon after this episode we were told that we would be getting new leaders to see us through the remainder of our last year, which meant that our new rank would be of the same intake, having also been drafted into the army in January 1984.

Our new lieutenant walked into the bungalow and Grant, being the first to see him, quickly stood up and shouted, '*Staanop!*' Lying on our beds, we slowly looked up, and without a care in the world on seeing our new, clean-cut lieutie, we turned away, angry at the disruption, and continued our conversations and our lazing.

Suddenly a new voice shouted the same order: '*Staan op vir jou nuwe luitenant!*' Stand up for your new lieutenant!, and in walked our new corporal. Again we looked through them, with a silent message that they would have to earn our respect, since we had all been in the military the same length of time, only rank separating us. Their new yellow stars and black stripes did nothing to scare us, but we forced ourselves to stay seated and show disrespect rather than jump up with the ingrained fear we had for so long been conditioned to show.

The NAAFI feeling had been steadily creeping upon us, and we longed for our second year to begin with that vital new army term, *ou manne*, attached to our intake, replacing our current one, *rower*, or new recruit. Our intake needed to serve out the remaining two months of the year, and only then could we christen the milestone with the growing of a moustache. For the moment, however, we would have to wait for this change.

They walked through the bungalow and waited outside, delegating our three section leaders the dirty work of immediately getting us rounded up. They kicked at the dirt in an agitated wait for our appearance. Eventually we stood in front of them like a bedraggled bunch of half-wits and listened half-heartedly to their introduction of themselves in Afrikaans.

5. Bloemfontein: last days with 1-SAI

Our new lieutenant stood stiff and straight, his thin, red, oval face and deep-set brown eyes sizing us up. Our new corporal stood to the side, his six-foot height matching some of our own, and his new stripes as perfectly ironed and black as the day they came off the press. These two leaders told us that we would soon be leaving for Middelburg, to our sister unit at 4-South African Infantry Battalion, and they were here to lead us safely to the end. After their little speech, we were dismissed and trailed back inside, opinions forming in our heads regarding our brand-new rank. We immediately decided on nicknames, and chose 'Bambie' for the red-faced Lieutenant Bam and 'Doep' for Corporal. Du Plessis. Occasionally we referred to him as 'Two plus three.'

In November, Captain Delport and Staff Smit flew down from Middelburg to meet with us, as they were going to become our new company leaders in a month's time. They briefed us on what to expect at 4-SAI and told us that we would be staying at the Doornkop training area for two weeks, until the *ou manne klaared out*.

Our time at Bloem was drawing to a close, and we were yearning for a change from lying around and doing nothing – typical to the army lingo of *ballas bak* or *le laag en skiet vir die mag*.

The army had created a new language for us, with key Afrikaans words used in place of the English meaning and the remaining part of the sentence quite often completed in English – a language that quite easily could have been called *Afrikaanglish* or *Englikaans*. Afrikaans always remained the preferred choice of language, with the majority of the soldiers speaking Afrikaans as their first language. Many of us *souties* could not help but roar with laughter at the vulgarity of the Afrikaans military words that they churned out with such ease in their description of a situation.

One evening as we milled around in the bungalow, Laurence crept into a small, vacant room, where a section leader would normally sleep, and began smoking a pipe packed with dagga. All of a sudden, shouts rang through the bungalow as our new rank walked in for a surprise visit. The shouts reached Laurence before they spotted him, and like a hare stunned in a beam of light, he came to his senses and in fright jumped right through a closed window and made his escape in an explosion of shattering glass. A group of us rushed in to find glass scattered everywhere and that sweet smell still hovering in the room. Laurence was very lucky to get away unscathed, his only setback being a rudely-interrupted high.

In early December, our time had come to leave 1-SAI for the greener pastures of 4-SAI. In platoons we were loaded into Samils and driven to the Bloemfontein station, wearing our most-faded browns and our 1-SAI emblem, the three feathers, for the last time.

Every year there is always a company that shines above the rest, and we had been reminded many times that on the battlefield our company, Bravo had risen to the occasion – which allowed us to walk tall and confident, with a skill that really counted. As difficult as our platoon was, we always knew we could deliver what was required, as we had done again and again through the innumerable live attacks over the dusty and flat plains of De Brug.

With wide smiles and nervous wonder we disembarked from the Samils and were ordered to line up along the platform with our backs to the reddish-brown carriages. In a long straight line of over 200 soldiers, we stood to attention and waited for our colonel to wish us well. One by one he shook each soldier's hand as he made his way down the length of the line. Eventually arriving at my spot, Colonel van Zyl shook my hand with a solid handshake, holding the grip for an extra second, as he looked deep into my eyes.

'*Gaan skiet daai Kaffers*!' Go and shoot those Kaffirs!, he said coldly and firmly, uncaring of his choice of words.

I felt an electric shock pass through my body as my heart swelled with pride, with that perverted thrill to kill. Our one-year of training in mechanised warfare had been served, compared to the infantry foot soldier whose training only lasted six months. With this completed, we felt as ready as ever to be granted passage to 4-SAI with almost guaranteed deployment into the operational area and with a licence to kill if the opportunity presented itself.

Charged with adrenaline, we boarded the train and took our compartments. This train ride was far removed from my first train journey, a few weeks short of a whole year ago. The train jolted its chain reaction down the line of carriages as the engine pulled us out of the Tempe station, and we crowded and pressed against the small windows, catching one last glimpse of the place that had changed our thoughts and our lives forever. The excitement was immeasurable, with shouts and laughter, as the feeling of being one giant step closer to the end overtook us in the moment. It did not take long for thick clouds of dagga smoke to make their way down the corridors of the train. We revelled in the prospect of becoming *ou manne*, which was only a couple of weeks away.

Our company was now operation-ready. The only question was, were we going into Angola? It was a question we could only speculate on, for the moment we would have to wait and see.

6
Middelburg – with 4-SAI

After we had had a good sleep, the train rolled into the station at Middelburg in the mid-morning. Hurriedly we were loaded in the normal fashion into the waiting Samils and whisked out of civilian life and into the bush training area of Doornkop.

Looking out from under the canvas canopy, we saw our new training area, which seemed far more picturesque than the dismal plains of De Brug. The red flowering of the aloes and the short and stocky rare cycads, with their dark green head dress, broke the dry, knee-high, grassed, undulating landscape, offering a fresh array of colour through the steady stream of dust.

The Samils came to a halt on the dirt road, with an expanse of bush all around us. Somehow this was not what we had in mind, and nightmares of De Brug began to jog our memories. Each platoon was given an olive-green tent, which was erected a few metres from the roadway. This would soon prove to be a disastrous decision when the dust rose from the dirt track and settled into everything inside our tent.

This was to be our home until our *ou manne klaared out*, keeping us separate from them for our own good. It spared us the name-calling of *rower*, and the jealousy that would be in us to trade places, with another full year of service left. It also prevented the theft of our kit, which would definitely be stolen by those who had lost vital pieces of equipment that they would be forced to pay for before they were given their final *klaaring-out* papers.

Our lieutenant handed out our new insignia, which was the double-bladed sword, representing the versatility of mobile warfare, with two bolts of lightning on either side symbolizing the principle of Blitzkrieg. Meticulously, we removed our old insignias of 1-SAI's three feathers from our green berets and began replacing it with our new unit insignia, representing 4-SAI. Our flashers, worn on the left shoulder of our epaulette, changed from the three feathers to the rare cycad, found so abundantly at Doornkop. The Bravo Company flasher would remain the same and would continue to be saluted proudly on our right shoulders.

Our company, along with Charlie Company, had made the transformation into 4-SAI soldiers, still with that sister bond to 1-SAI of also being a very proud mechanized unit with Ratels.

After a day in Doornkop, Staff Smit arrived in a fit of shouting and screaming, as our welcome on his behalf.

'*Tree-aan!*' Form up!, he bellowed, with his voice echoing across the bushveld. '*Moenie hanna hanna, whatie whatie. Tree-aan!*' Don't dawdle, form up!, he screamed like a tormented man losing his mind.

Once we were formed up, he ordered us, through another rally of screams, to get our rifles and full kit. Rushing back into the tent, knocking each other in pandemonium as we went, we grabbed our rifles and helmets and emptied our webbings of any extra weight before we strapped them to our backs, and then formed up, waiting for the all-too-dreaded *opfok* that was coming our way.

As a company we began running as a *bos bussie*, or bush bus, with our feet in step as our boots hit the dusty red earth with one thud and then another, as we began sweating under the midday heat that was climbing into the mid 30s Celsius. The medics followed closely behind us in the comfort of their Unimog ambulance, stopping every now and then to attend to a few troops in physical pain and mental distress, while the rest of us were forced to run on the spot with our rifles above our heads until they rejoined our ranks.

Once our squad was complete, we catapulted forward, with sweat burning into our eyes and dripping down our faces. We unconsciously licked at it, stinging our mouths with the salty taste. Our new rank, which ran alongside Staff Smit, stopped us at one point and forced us to drink water from our one-litre green water bottles to ward off the heat exhaustion that was gnawing at our dried-up throats and beaten bodies.

In a bedraggled unit of demoralized men, we ran and ran under the belittling torment of Staff Smit, in the master-servant relationship of rank to troop.

'*Julle is laer dan Kaffer kak!*' You are all lower than black shit!, he screamed with his brown piercing eyes, staring in wicked hatred.

When we could not bear the agony any more and we were close to dropping like flies, Staff Smit brought us to a dramatic halt next to a small river. To see this calm river, with our raging fury and fatigue burning within us, doubling over trying to catch our breath, allowed our frustration to subside. Then Staff Smit did the unbelievable and gave us permission to swim. In seconds we were downing our kit, stripped naked with our hideous army tans before we cavalry-charged the glassy water. Swimming and splashing like young kids, we cooled ourselves off under the beautiful feel of the refreshing water, which washed away the fatigue and frustration of an hour's run and turned us each into a new person.

After the thoroughly enjoyable swim, we retrieved our clothes and tried our best to dry ourselves before forming back into a squad under full kit. The run

6. Middelburg – with 4-SAI

back seemed psychologically easier, as we knew the distance and terrain we had to cover and it helped our bodies to feel rejuvenated. The only problem we had was the stinging burning pain of our thighs rubbing spotted red circles into each other from the friction against our wet brown pants.

In the bush bus formation, we ran through sharp needles of pain that felt more like ants biting at us. As we ascended the last rise, it was a rewarding feeling to see a line of tents in the middle of nowhere, giving us that much-needed second wind to carry us home. After being dismissed we walked bent over and fell in heaps inside our tent' red-faced and huffing and puffing, we lay down until we could muster the energy to move again.

The very next day we saw our medics getting their *opfok* as they were given Ratel tyres to flip. They sweated and battled as each flip worked their arms and began to blister their hands. We could only look on for a few seconds before we turned away, sharing their physical torture and knowing exactly what was going through their minds as their bodies were stretched to the limit.

'Thank God it's them and not us,' someone piped up. The sound of angry orders echoed from the outside into the coolness of our tent, and feeling guilty we lazed comfortably on the ground.

In open Samils, we were driven into 4-SAI to visit our new base that would be our home in a week's time. On the right of the gates, before we entered, we passed a big black statue of two soldiers united in their struggle. Behind them the bold gold lettering highlighted over the white stone background read: '*Ons Sal Hulle Onthou*', We Shall Remember Them. I wondered if those who had lost their lives were truly remembered. We could only hope that they died for a good reason. Making our way through the open gates, we took a left turn and followed the neatly tarred road that wound its way up a small hill on the far side of the base. At the top we saw the brick bungalows where we would be staying, with a crowd of *ou manne* lining the fronts as if waiting for our appearance. On seeing us, the *ou manne* began hurling abuse at us with such phrases as '*Jou foken rower, min dae!*' You fuckin' new recruit, only a few days left!, and 'Take them to the *gwarry gat* for an *opfok!*'

Looking out and over them, we remained calm, knowing quite well that they had earned the right, by doing their time, to say what they pleased. Our time would be next' we would just have to wait for it to arrive.

'Lucky bastards,' one of our platoon commented as our vehicles turned around, leaving the *ou manne* to enjoy their last days of army life and wallow in the precious thought of becoming civilians again after two very long years of service.

The Samils returned us to the dust and dirt of Doornkop, where we filed into our tents, wanting the *ou manne to klaar out* so that we could claim the base and inherit the long-awaited label of being called *ou manne* ourselves.

Halfway through December, we entered into 4-SAI as *ou manne*, proud at finally reaching this mark and no rank being able to do a thing about it. Just as importantly, we now had a base we could call home – a new bungalow, a bed, a toilet to sit on and a hot shower – all of which felt more like a hotel than what we had been used to over the past year. Alpha and our HQ section shared half the bungalow, and Bravo and Charlie the other half. At the far end of the bungalow, our section leaders shared a room with their respective lance corporals, with a door to shut out any unwanted raucousness.

Staff Smit began drilling us right away, teaching us the silent count that the *ou manne* used when stomping their right foot on coming to attention or standing at ease. It replaced the count of *een, twee-drie, een,* one, two-three, one, with boom shakalaaka boom and finally, painstakingly ended with boom shakalaaka boom mouthed without a sound except for 200 boots smashing in perfect time to the ground with one cracking thud.

'*Julle is n klomp foken rowers!*' he shouted when our feet hit the ground at varying times of delay.

'Heyyy!' came our response, as we now deemed this an insult to our newly acquired status.

'*Julle is vet deur die kak*' You are stupid, he retaliated, with a slightly crooked smile, as if realizing that we were now a company of fully trained soldiers, ready for whatever lay ahead.

After being sworn at for a couple of weeks as we practised this technique for hours on end, and hearing our feet stamping into the ground like a stampede of wildebeest, we eventually came together as one boot. Our legs lifted together, with the sole of our boot drawn up to the height of our left knee, and then on the silent count we stamped our right foot down with vicious force, allowing the heel to make contact with the ground first.

One night, as we relaxed polishing our boots, JP pulled out some photos that he had acquired from his cousin, who had also passed through 1-SAI and served in Angola in 1981 as part of *Operation Protea*. The picture showed in graphic detail a few SWAPO guerrillas slumped over the spare tyre and rolled-up cammo net on top of the Ratel. The blood of the dead guerrillas had run down the side of the brown vehicle, streaking the side of it a thick red. It gave off a ghostly image in display of its war trophies. Looking at the scene with a twinge of fear in my gut, I had to wonder how life would be for us if we were to be called into an operation.

6. Middelburg – with 4-SAI

At Doornkop we practised a couple of platoon attacks as we attacked stationary targets over the red scrubby soiled plains and the gunners bombarded car wrecks one kilometre away. It was a great feeling to be firing off ammunition in abundance as the adrenaline gripped at us under the deafening noise and burning smell of gunpowder. It was an 'alive' feeling to have all our senses so acutely active while we engaged our targets through our separate roles and made our section and our platoon something to be reckoned with.

After the attack we rested near an African cemetery, where even in death they were prohibited from being buried next to a white person – the unbreakable laws of apartheid ruling far beyond the grave.

It was an old cemetery, with some of the headstones and crosses having been shot at and chunks of concrete missing, leaving illegibile the name of the person buried there. Lining many of the graves were old glass bottles, with a few coins dropped in to them as an offering to the dead souls. It had been abandoned many years ago in the way that it had fallen into disrepair – headstones leaning over and some lying flat on the blackened ground, the grass overtaking the resting place and purposely burned as a firebreak. Looking at a few dates, which I could read, inscribed on the weathered stones, I found markings dating back to 1935.

To celebrate this find we posed for a picture while Sandor lay outstretched below the old and expensive marble grey headstone over someone's burial space, and Wayne sat on top of the thick slab, Gall and Fox on one side and me on the other. It felt eerie to be lazing around in a deserted graveyard, which had sprung to life with absolutely no signs of habitation around it. After our inquisitive play with the resting souls, we left the site and wandered back over the dirty black ground to our Ratels, which we had left in the shade below some huge gum trees for our return trip to 4-SAI.

Brian had managed to smuggle some live 20mm rounds and a couple of boxes of ammunition from the Ratel, and brought it in to the bungalow – which was absolutely forbidden – safety always being ther top priority in the South African Defence Force. Through boredom, he created a show that captured our attention and was performed within the bungalow under darkness. With all the time in the world, and with no fear in the world, he prised off the heads of the live rounds and poured the gunpowder onto his *trommel*, making neatly-coiled lines covering the entire smooth, green surface. Totally absorbed in his work of art, he heaped up the grey, coarse powder, using a piece of cardboard to clean up any spillage, which he meticulously pushed back into the lines. When it was all complete, he sat back and rolled a quick joint while our whole platoon crowded his bed in eager anticipation for the fireworks to begin. Troops sat on the wall and stood on beds and cupboards, all to get a good front-seat view of Brian's highly illegal demonstration.

'Lights out,' he said coolly, striking a match.

'Turn the lights out,' someone else ordered, turning to the person closest to the switch.

When the lights flickered out, Brian lowered his hand onto the line of gunpowder, which caught fire instantaneously, racing away a burning red as it snaked its way following the grey path and eating the powder with the speed of a fuse.

When it was finished, we added a cheer through some deep coughs – for the sulphur burned at our lungs and filled our bungalow with a haze of smoke. Brian's trunk was now burned with thin lines through the green paint. It left a rewarding mark on us, for the great spectacle added some excitement to our otherwise dull and very controlled lives. Once the windows had been opened and the fresh air replaced the burned gunpowder, no one would be the wiser for our few minutes of wonder.

Christmas arrived and was spent at 4-SAI along with at least a dozen *ou manne* who were serving out their extra days. Some of them had just come down from the border, still wearing their *balkies*, and insignia, from 61-Mechanized Battalion – with the black sword standing out over a yellow background and three red lightning bolts cutting across the blade.

They sat quietly at a separate table, and staring over at them, I wondered what they had seen on the border and in Angola. These extra days that they were serving only reiterated the fact that for each day stolen on AWOL, another was added to square up the time. My gaze shifted from their tanned and older faces to the unbelievable lunch that was decked upon rows and rows of tables, with their perfectly starched, pearly-white tablecloths, under the high roof of the massive mess hall.

Each table had a few bottles of wine in the middle of the feast, labelled with the 4-SAI emblems on each, and sparkling-clean, white ceramic plates marked each place setting. Paper hats in all different colours waited for us to snatch them up and adorn our heads, which we immediately did as we got into the Christmas spirit. Food was served in big stainless steel trays, which we helped ourselves to, covering the whites of our plates with thick slices of turkey, ham, peas, and carrots, drowned under rich, salty gravy.

With our hats on and a glass of wine in our hands, we toasted everyone at our table, briefly casting a thought to our families at home before we dug in with laughter and cheer at the most spectacular meal the South African army had ever prepared for us. I had never seen any of us enjoy a meal so much, being allowed to eat it at our own leisure, off a white plate instead of the hated, stainless steel pig pan. These plates, as nice as they were, would take some getting used to, since each meal in 4-SAI was now to be eaten off a civilized ceramic plate instead of the lowly stainless steel.

We thoroughly enjoyed our Christmas dinner judging by the excited chatter that filled the old hangar as we savoured the great-tasting food, quite sure that we would never have such a meal again. We drank the wine as if it were water, and tried to gain a few extra bottles of the merry liquid from one of the cooks who were waiting on the tables. He managed to get his hands on a couple of bottles, which we gladly took and rationed amongst the empty, outstretched glasses.

After the great meal, we walked, very light-headed, from the old hangar across the open and potholed red earth, back to our bungalow 30 metres away. A few of us set about making tea, heating the water in our fire buckets with the metal-coiled, plug-in element known to us as the 'pig's cock.' Wayne was the master of making tea, and with it he brought an element of surprise, shock, and evil laughter. Once he had finished stirring his tea, he sought his foe, a steaming teaspoon hidden in his hand. Once he found his victim, he held the spoon for a second on the inside of the unlucky person's arm. As if bitten, the person would recoil at the shock of the unexpected burn.

'Fuck off, Nickol' was the angry response as Wayne chuckled, offering a fair challenge to his victim to get him back – which, with Wayne's nimble movements, rarely happened. Once or twice he caught me, but Fox, Grant, and Solly were the continual candidates for the teaspoon treatment, poor Solly getting nabbed every time.

Over New Year we were granted a five-day pass. We hoped for a better year than the one gone by, for we were now officially in our last year.

'One down and one to go,' we reminded ourselves, now seeing a sliver of light at the end of the darkened tunnel.

Soon after our pass, we got the eagerly-awaited news that Bravo Company was going up to the border, which meant the operational area in northern South-West Africa, on the border of Angola. This is what we had trained for, but it still sent a wave of apprehension through me, the unknown looming and horror stories recurring in my mind of unlucky soldiers from recent years past. With mixed emotions, we looked back on a year's training in fine-tuned drills that we could perform with our eyes closed. These drills had brought out in us a close-knit unit of well-rounded soldiers.

A trip to the operational area would be another test, the ultimate experience for a National Serviceman being to serve out border duty, during which there was always a risk of being killed, for blood was shed almost daily, whether from us, or SWAPO, or the local population caught in the middle of the bush war.

Alpha Company had already been chosen ahead of us, as the Mechanized Unit at 61-Mech, and had bypassed entering into 4-SAI, instead being deployed to the border directly from 1-SAI.

Our rank told us that we were going up as foot soldiers instead of a mechanized unit, which really infuriated us because we knew all too well that we were the superior company – we had shown our worth on the battlefield at De Brug. It was a bitter pill to swallow, to know that after all our hard training and mental drain we were going up to the border as a company of glorified foot soldiers, who unlike Alpha had not taken a single casualty throughout our training with live ammunition.

Back in the bungalow, we spoke amongst ourselves with that low-key, lack-of-emotion tone, most of us happy to be going to the border. We knew it would offer a better army life compared to the *paraat* – highly disciplined orders issued within a base – along with danger pay, which came as an increase to what was otherwise a pittance.

To celebrate our call-up to the border, a pipe was prepared in the toilet area, and a few of us chose to participate in the intake of the green weed so common on the inside and used so abundantly in our attempt to escape our entrapment. A large group of us gathered in the safety of an open toilet stall, with some circled outside the door, as we huddled together waiting on our turn to smoke the hot clay pipe. As it was passed to the left side under a billow of sweet thick smoke, the recipient sucked until the coal glowed a fiery red, and then quickly passed it onto the next eager person. Once the last troop had circled his thumb and forefinger around the thin neck and inhaled his rush, the group dispersed as quickly as it had formed, passing the pipe back to the owner and leaving a mist of smoke wafting through the shower area.

Those who had not indulged in the smoking could clearly see those who had, bearing the glazed, blank look and the unmistakable red eyes. We trailed past fellow soldiers sitting on their beds, stumbling on tired legs, trying to make our way to the comfort of our own beds.

The temporary relief from our caged lives had been carried out, yet again rewarding us with a deep sleep into another world, a lot freer than the one we had been living in.

6. Middelburg – with 4-SAI

In the morning we were issued *Dankie Tannie* packages from the Southern Cross Fund, with the zip-up folder case consisting of a writing pad, envelopes, a pen, a pocketknife, and a letter from the president's wife, Mrs. Botha, wishing us well on our border duty, as well as a laminated card inscribed with The Soldier's Code of Honour. The soldier stood proud and smiling, decked out in his browns, with the orange, white and blue denoting our flag flying powerfully in the background. It seemed like propaganda, this lone soldier – the SADF trying to make us feel patriotic and proud, whereas most of us did not give a damn about the army and the life that had been chosen for us by the Nationalist government.

The Soldier's Code of Honour read as follows:

For my god, my people, my country,
My fellow man, and myself,
I shall endeavour at all times to
Acknowledge the integrity of higher authority,
Do my duty conscientiously,
Place my integrity above all doubt,
Be recognised and honoured as a soldier,
Be ready to serve unconditionally,
May we then continue to exist as a nation and to keep our heritages!
'Our efficieny leads to enemy deficiency.'

On the back of the card, the calendar year of 1985 was printed, and with a marker I gladly crossed out the days served for the month of January.

Before I fell asleep on the night of 10 January, the night before we were to fly out to the border, my mind again focused on real-life stories of servicemen who had died or suffered agonising injuries. The most vivid story was that of Alan, a matric pupil for whom I had skivvied during my initiation at Treverton College boarding school. Here was a guy that a bunch of us wished dead for making us the brunt of all his bullying, kicking, hitting, and tormenting when I was a 15-year-old Standard Seven at Harland House. One year later, our wish was delivered in the most ghastly fashion. While Alan was trying carefully to defuse a land mine on the border it exploded, blowing off his hands and blinding him for life before he even reached the age of 20.

Looking up at the shadows plastered over the white ceiling, I could only hope that we as a platoon would be returning home as we left it, sparing us the tragedies of the bush war. With a silent prayer, I closed my eyes, still with that hollow feeling in the pit of my belly, the unknown pulling at cords, while I lay stiff as if standing at attention.

In the morning we woke early, packed the last of our kit into our sausage-like *balsaks*, and waited the long wait for the order to board the Samils and begin a new experience. Physically we were ready as we could ever be, our intense training so ingrained in us, combined with the hardened mental approach that went hand-in-hand.

Standing in front of our bungalow, those who smoked puffed nervously and excitedly on cigarettes, as we kicked at the dust in wait. I watched Kleynhans, the section leader of Charlie, as he took long drags on his Chesterfield cigarette, exhaling smoke through sentences in his native Afrikaans. Here was a guy, the son of a priest, of a very strict upbringing, who when he first entered into our platoon did not smoke, swear, or use racist slander, and then, in a matter of a couple of weeks, had been transformed into a totally different person who freely used and abused all of the above.

When the order to board the Samils was given, we boarded one by one with our rifles, having already loaded our kitbags on another Samil, filling up the long, cold line of metal seating from the front to the back, each platoon in its own Samil 50. Sitting frozen on the metal with our rifles standing upright between our knees, our eyes wandered around the canvas shell encompassing us as we waited for the diesel engines to jump-start us and begin the new journey.

Diesel poured out of the exhausts as one vehicle after the other revved their engines into a roar of life' and then, in a five-vehicle convoy our driver slammed the troop carrier into first and we lurched forward. Passing through the gates of 4-SAI, I looked back with my eyes unavoidably left to focus on the monument to the fallen soldiers, which now more than ever seemed to magnify that ultimate sacrifice of death.

Nervous and excited, thankful to finally be moving ahead, we sat and talked as the driver followed the lead in the direction of Pretoria, to the Air Force base at Waterkloof, for our long awaited flight into the unknown.

7
Our unknown history
South-West African- Angolan border

Under the Treaty of Versailles in 1919, Germany was required to renounce all its colonial claims to South-West Africa – SWA. In 1921, the League of Nations granted South Africa a mandate to administer SWA as part of the Union.

After World War-II the mandate was renewed by the United Nations, but South Africa was more interested in scrapping the mandate and annexing SWA as a full province under the Union of South Africa. Throughout the 1950s, despite mounting pressure from the UN South Africa refused to relinquish its grip on SWA.

In 1959, Samuel Nujoma undertook the leadership of a party called the Owamboland People's Organization. By 1960 he had gathered more supporters and created a party called the South-West African People's Organization, known as SWAPO, its headquarters based in Dar es Salaam, Tanzania.

In 1966, SWAPO took the issue of South African occupation to the International Court of Justice. The court ruled in favour of South Africa, in spite of the fact that the United Nations had voted to terminate South Africa's mandate.

Thus on 26 August 1966, SWAPO launched a campaign of guerrilla warfare in Owamboland, in northern SWA. This war of terrorism and sabotage continued to disrupt the South-West African economy and played havoc with people's lives until the end of the 1980s. SWAPO's leader, Sam Nujoma, remained firmly in exile, under the safety of Julius Nyerere's sympathetic Tanzania.

In the early 1970s, things were coming to a head in Angola, as 500 years of Portuguese rule was coming to an end. In 1975, Angola gained its independence from Portugal and slowly started to sink into a civil war, which would become Africa's longest civil war, taking innumerable lives with it as the country plunged into bloodshed and chaos.

The Soviet Union saw this as an opportunity to spread Marxist ideals through the ruling MPLA – the Popular Movement for the Liberation of Angola – under the leadership of Jose Eduardo Dos Santos since the death of Agostinho Neto in 1979.

Fidel Castro shipped in arms and weaponry, along with 20 000 to 30 000 troops, to help bolster the MPLA. Soviet premier Leonid Brezhnev supplied key military advisors, along with T-54, T-55, and T-62 tanks, MiG-23 fighter planes, thousands of AK-47 assault rifles, and countless landmines – all for the MPLA cause.

All this was taking place at the height of the Cold War, with Communism taking a firm foothold in southern Africa and forcing the United States to enter the conflict on the side of Jonas Savimbi's UNITA – National Union for the Total Independence of Angola – by giving monetary support in order to prevent the spread of the Marxism.

South Africa, under the leadership of B.J. Vorster and P.W. Botha, also fearing a Communist takeover, supported UNITA through the military presence of the SADF (South African Defence Force) – by far the strongest and most disciplined army in Africa. The SADF became UNITA's backbone initiating many external attacks on the SWAPO bases dug deep into Angola. South Africa allowed UNITA to take the credit for many South African-led victories in Angola, helping to minimize world political pressure and yet aiding UNITA in gaining further support through southern Angola.

Because the ANC – African National Congress – was banned in South Africa, it too had many military training bases inside Angola. There were estimated to be 10 000 men and women in these bases, fighting in the ANC's military wing known as *Umkhonto we Sizwe*, who played a defensive role against UNITA even though most of them did not understand why they were involved in the Angolan war.

It seemed as though all of southern and eastern Africa was paying for the liberation of South Africa, and freely offered refuge to exiled political leaders, as well as training areas for tens of thousands of freedom fighters. Many parts of black Africa had become united in a quest for an independent SWA and an eventual break in the 350 years of white minority rule in apartheid-driven South Africa.

The South African military presence in Angola lasted from 1975 to 1989, with thousands of South African soldiers serving along the SWA/Angolan border and also inside Angola, taking part in routine patrols and operations. South Africa had a firm grip on SWA – with strategically placed army bases dotted across the country, mainly in Owamboland in northern SWA and good airfields and road links to get supplies to the frontline.

In February 1984, Angola and South Africa negotiated the Lusaka Accord, whereby South Africa offered to withdraw from Angola and drop support for UNITA in exchange for the closure of SWAPO training bases in Angola. By doing this, it only allowed SWAPO to regroup and escalate the terrorist influx into Owamboland, to such a degree that the first seven weeks of 1985 produced the highest insurgent death toll since the border war had begun.

By 1985, the war was costing the South African government around US $250 million a year, which along with tough worldwide sanctions began to put a stranglehold on the suffering economy.

7. Our unknown history: South-West African - Angolan border

At the end of 1988, under Resolution 435, the stage was set for the withdrawal of all South African troops and weaponry from Angola and SWA, the same applying to the Cubans from Angola.

In 1989, under the presence of the United Nations, Sam Nujoma returned from 30 years in exile, and in 1990 SWA/Namibia had its first free elections as it prepared for independence from South African occupation.

On 21 March 1990, the orange, white, and blue of the South African flag was lowered for the last time and the blue, red, and green, with the yellow sunburst, was hoisted proudly in its place.

The founder of SWAPO, Sam Nujoma, was elected as president of the country known today as Namibia.

1985-Angola. Angolan money traded for rat pack food. Antonio Oscar Carmona, the 11th President of Portugal, dated 24 November 1972.

1985-Angola. The Angolan Kwanza which replaced the Portuguese Escudos, with Agostinho Neto.

8
Adjusting to a new setting

Our feet cooked inside our highly glossed army boots as we stood on the paved runway at the Waterkloof Air Force base, waiting in the sweltering heat for our flight to an uncertain future in an African land very foreign to us.

It was 11 January 1985, and we were about to be deployed into the operational area. Milling about, we were apprehensive and excited all at once, wanting to fulfil the ultimate challenge as a soldier – that of serving on the border in repayment for one unforgettable year of torturous training.

Stories of gruesome deaths and severe maiming again plagued my thoughts, with our turn now at hand to defend a border in a land we knew very little, if anything, about.

A C-130 Hercules aircraft landed on the runway and came taxiing towards us, stopping not far from our position. Slowly the cargo hold at the back of the short but stocky plane opened and a casket covered with the South African flag was carefully and respectfully carried off. Our eyes remained transfixed on the wooden coffin, pangs of fear shuddering through us with that cruel reality at what could befall us on the border.

'I am not going to die for this government,' I said, turning casually to Wayne.

'No way!' he quickly answered.

'We have to look after each other so we can come back home,' we vowed to one another, with no clue in the world what to expect on our landing in SWA.

Bravo Company began to board two C-130 flossies, our platoon being the one to board the plane from which the dead soldier had been carried off. In two long lines we nervously boarded through the cargo hold, like cattle shuffling to the slaughter, walking between the hammock-like seating to the very front of the plane. Once at the front, we dropped ourselves left and right into the red netting, holding our rifles rigidly between our legs and pointing the barrel skyward. Snapping the belts together, we strapped ourselves in as we waited fearfully for the takeoff, which could not come quick enough to begin our border duty so we could finish it.

I, along with everyone else, sat trapped in the plane in four long lines, which bobbed back and forth with each shift in posture. I felt like I was in the film *Where Eagles Dare* as we sat in silence and faced each other with our eyes darting around the cargo hold, scanning the line of faces noting fear glazed in some eyes, and fidgeting with our rifles breaking the cold silence.

1984-Natal Command. This is where I entered to begin my National Service, with call up papers for Bloemfontein, 1-SAI. Picture taken in 2005.

1984-1-SAI. 1-South African Infantry Battalion, Tempe, Bloemfontein. Mechanized Infantry Unit.

1984-1-SAI. Standing outside Bravo Company bungalows. L-R. Grant, Hennie, Alan, author and Darin in front. Note washing chained to washing line.

1984-1-SAI. Bokkop insignia of the infantry soldier worn after basics and three feathers of 1-SAI worn after completing mechanized training. 4-SAI and 1-RNT unit insignia on the bottom left and right.

1984-1-SAI. Sew on name attached to our browns after first pass. 1-SAI flasher after the completion of mechanized training.

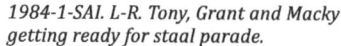

1984-1-SAI. L-R. Tony, Grant and Macky getting ready for staal parade.

1984-1-SAI. Ratels lined up on the parade ground facing Bravo lines.

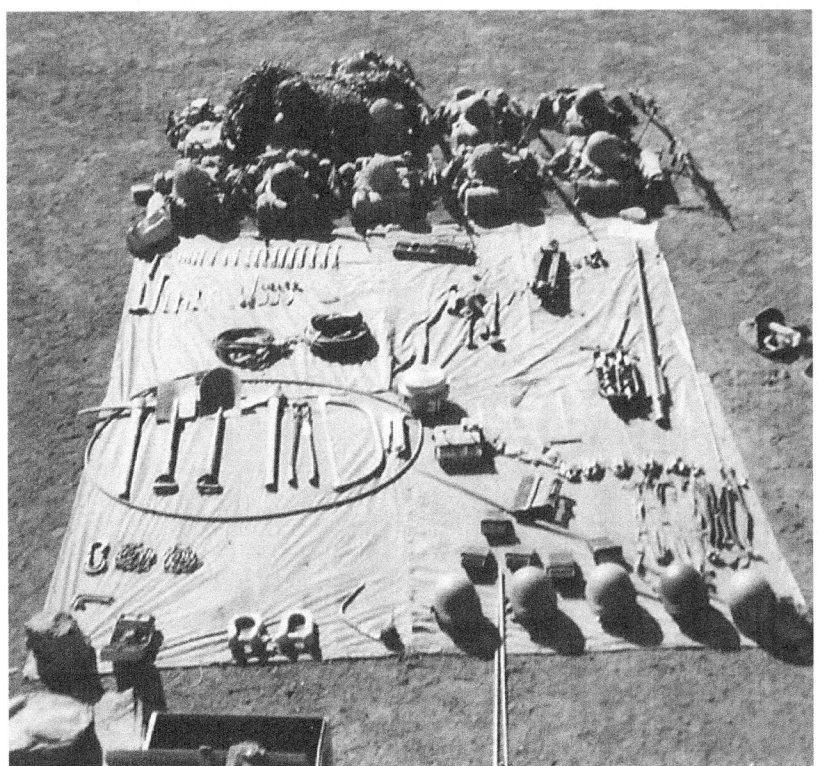

1984-1-SAI. Staal parade. The complete Ratel tote unpacked and displayed for inspection. A gunners nightmare.

1984-De Brug. Ratel 23A. L-R. Wayne, author, Fox, Paul, Bennie and JP.

1984-De Brug. Ratel 23, The HQ Piele. L-R. Sax, Rob, Tony, Stoop, Norman and Macky at the back.

1984-De Brug Rhino Rest camp. Our mess hall in the bush and our parade ground where we assembled for roll call and inspection.

1984-De Brug. Picking up the pieces after a severe storm and a sleepless night.

1984-De Brug. Setting up chopper tents and standing by a fire to keep warm.

1984-De Brug. Platoon 3 troopies walking through the tents with rifles in hand.

1984-De Brug. L- R. Alan, Gall, Grant and Rob sitting in a trench they had dug.

1984-De Brug. Lt Bennett waiting to lead Platoon 3 into a live attack.

1984-De Brug. L-R. Alan, Rob, Gall, author, Brian and Paul finishing our meal from our dixie's and fire buckets.

1984-De Brug. Grant leading 23B with Stoop looking on.

1984-De Brug. Grant leading 23B into a live attack.

1984-De Brug. Grant and author standing very cold on the small parade ground with our army style brush cuts.

1984-De Brug. Lt Bennett with Platoon 3, Bravo Company, after a successful mechanized attack.

1984-1-SAI. Returning to 1-SAI after months of training in De Brug . Ratels lined up on parade ground facing Bravo lines with Oscar Coy in the background.

1984-De Brug. L-R. Grant and Paul. Two Durban boys who would become our Section Leaders of Bravo and Alpha sections.

1984-1-SAI. Author retuning to base as a merchanized soldier with the three feathers of 1-SAI.

1984-1-Construction unit Springs. Massed up on the parade ground en route to riot torn Tembisa township.

1984-Ride Safe dayglo sash worn on the road to keep us safe on our journey home for pass.

1984-Tembisa. Children waiting for rat pack handouts.

1984-Tembisa. Ratel towing a car off a soccer field with Toth and Bennie in the front.

1984-Army Battle School Lohatlha. Wayne on 23A.

1984-Tembisa. 23B throwing rat pack food to throngs of hungry children.

1984-Tembisa. On patrol through the township.

1984-4-SAI. In December, 4-South African Infantry Battalion becomes our new unit with new insignia.

1984-Tembisa. Wayne on Ratel Rat, the name we gave our Ratel in the township.

1984-4-SAI. Our new flasher.

1984-Doornkop. On arriving in Middelburg Bravo Coy was stationed in tents in Doornkop while the ou manne klaared out of 4-SAI.

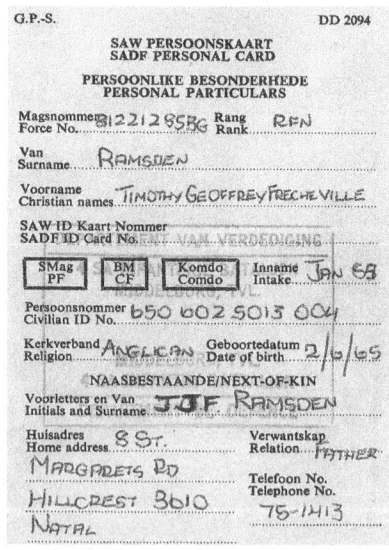

1984-personal card. This was issued at 4-SAI on our arrival to Doornkop.

1984-Doornkop. Relaxing in an old graveyard dating back to the 1930s, that we stumbled across during our fire and movement training. L-R. Gall, Fox, Toth, author and Wayne on the headstone.

1984-Doornkop en route to 4-SAI. L-R. Ratel 23A. Gall, Laurence, Toth, JP, Bennie and the author with Grant leading 23B in the background.

1984-Doornkop. Training with our newly aquired Ratels in Doornkop.

1984-4-SAI. Bottle of wine given to us at Christmas signed by Platoon 3.

1984-Doornkop. Paul and Wayne in their turrets.

1984-Doornkop. The author after some fire and movement.

1984-4-SAI. L-R. Alan, Deon and Fox with a min dae sign. We were finally ou manne.

1984-4-SAI Memorial at the main gates. Ons Sal Hulle Onthou- We Will Remember Them.

1984-4-SAI. Our new bungalows with real grass and not the stones we had to rake in 1-SAI.

1985-Owamboland. Grant, Tony and Macky pissing over the border into Angola.

1985-4-SAI. This card was in our Dankie Tanie parcels from the Southern Cross.

1985- Owamboland. Laurence and the author leaning against a giant anthill.

1985-Owamboland. Dug in on the Yati in ambush positions. L-R. Laurence, Toth, Bennie, Gall and Arthur.

1985-Ovamboland. L-R. Toth, Bennie, Laurence and the author on patrol.

1985-Owamboland. Jason and Macky on the Yati.

1985-Owamboland. Phamphlets dropped by the SAAF over Owamboland offering rewards for information on SWAPO or weapons.

1985-Owamboland. Phamphlets offering rewards for weapons recovered from SWAPO.

8. Adjusting to a new setting

Looking at some of the 18-year-old faces, I had to wonder if the same outcome as the dead soldier exiting our plane would come about with any of us.

The wait for take-off felt like an eternity, and when it came it brought with it a sigh of relief' we began inching forward towards the runway. Sitting stiff and unmoving, I readied myself for my fear of flight as the flossie built up speed for the takeoff. It rumbled down the runway and just kept on going, and suddenly I was gripped with terror, thinking that this huge bird would not have the speed to lift us into the air. As if in slow motion, it groaned and creaked, gradually gaining altitude, seeming to climb forever at a 45° angle.

When it levelled out, it rose and fell as it hit every air pocket, lifting and dropping our stomachs and paranoid minds at the same time while I sat stuck to the netting, envisioning our plane spiralling down to earth in a fireball crash. I wiped my sweaty palms on my browns as I took hold of my R4 rifle again, and watched condensation droplets drip like slow rain from the ceiling onto us, adding some Chinese torture to the flight experience.

After close on three hours of flying – due to South African planes having long been forbidden to fly over Botswana, thus adding time to each troop's journey to the border – we finally landed in silence, which further amplified the treacherous creaking.

Disoriented, we stepped out into the pitch darkness and into the uncomfortable dry heat, grouping together like lost sheep while we waited for an order. Forming a long human chain, we began unpacking the flossie, passing *balsak* after *balsak* down the dark line before they ended up in a Samil troop carrier.

Once we had unloaded the plane, we were herded through shouting orders to board a Samil 100 called a 'cattle truck.' It could not have been named any more appropriately to the way we were feeling. In less than half an hour we were departing from the Grootfontein Air Force base, with our kitbags following on a separate truck as we made our way through the blackness to the Grootfontein army base. We entered a small brick bungalow and laid claim to a bed, our sleeping bags covering the dirty foam mattresses. Tired from a long, draining day of hidden apprehension, we turned the light out early and slept well.

The torching-dry heat woke us early and drew our inquisitive stares out of the cream-painted doorway. We walked into the open and instantly became blinded by the intense glare that reflected off the beach-white sand that was spread over parts of the base and would certainly have been deemed beautiful had it been spread over a beach. Making our way to the shower area, we washed our faces with cold water, which had now heated due to the high temperature, into uncomfortable warmth that tasted salty as we sipped at it from the rusty taps.

Reboarding the cattle trucks, we headed northwards to Oshivelo, 200 kilometres away. Braving the 40°C heat, we sat packed like sardines on the ribbed metal flooring, unable to stretch our cramping legs, thirsting for a drink of water, and unable to take a leak.

After endless pain of sitting still in the heat, we eventually stopped 24 kilometres northwest of Tsumeb, at Lake Otjikoto – a Herero name for 'deep hole.' This lake is the only one of two natural lakes in Namibia, and measures 100 metres by 150 metres, with a depth of 55 metres. The bottom of this lake is a treasure trove of old army relics dumped into it by the retreating Germans in 1915, in their attempt to prevent any weaponry from falling into the hands of the advancing South African army. A few ammunition wagons and a cannon, along with other military hardware, have since been salvaged at great expense and effort and are now on display at the Mining Museum in Tsumeb.

It was a strange feeling to look into the hole dressed in uniform and holding our rifles while tourists dressed in bright and casual clothes snapped away with their cameras, oblivious of our predicament as they focused into the depth of the limestone sinkhole.

With a quick break behind us, and a fresh set of legs, we crammed back into the trucks and continued north along the paved, single-lane roadway. Under our shirts we wore our dog tags around our necks, concealed from the reflective rays of the sun. These two paper-thin pieces of stainless steel, measuring an inch in length, had been handed to us as standard army issue for each and every troop serving on the border. Inscribed into the metal were our ten-digit army numbers, which had become our name, our initials and surname, the words S.A.Corps, and our blood group. If we got shot or were badly injured, these tags were what the medics would search for. If we lost our dog tags and needed blood, the medics would look under our pocket flaps on the left side of our uniform, or on our web belts in the front and centre, where they would also find our blood groups in black marker.

Arriving in Oshivelo sore, stiff, and quite sunburned, we passed through a border post manned by fellow South African troops, who waved us through across a two-metre-wide cattle grid made from railway tracks. Passing over the grid, we had now entered into the Red Zone, or Red Line, or, as we preferred to call it, the 'Danger Zone,' since it was from here on up that we would be receiving danger pay.

The Red Line demarcated the Animal Disease Control checkpoint, separating the commercial cattle ranches of the south from the communal subsistence

8. Adjusting to a new setting

farming lands in the north. This control fence barred the north-south movement of animals as a strict precaution against foot-and-mouth disease as well as rinderpest. Animals bred north of the Red Line could never be sold to the south or exported to overseas markets.

Sector 10, pronounced one zero, based in Oshakati, was the main headquarters for Owamboland and controlled the fighting through radio signals and troop deployments. It was from here that some of the wacky orders were dispatched that made our blood boil.

Later on in the day we were joined by the rest of Bravo Company, who were on the second flossie that had encountered engine trouble shortly after takeoff and had to turn back and land at Waterkloof. They made it on their second attempt, re-uniting us into a complete company again, with myself truly grateful that I was not aboard the engine-plagued plane.

In platoons we began retraining on fire-and-movement, with some training on claymore mines administered by the rank of another unit. These were very lethal mines and were set up on stands as opposed to being buried. The brown plastic face of the mine is packed with precut shards of metal and ball bearings, with an explosive layer behind it to drive the shrapnel horizontally into the target. An electrical wire ran from the mine to the firing device for detonation.

With a few days of training behind us – a mandatory routine for every new company entering the border – we once again were given the order to board the cattle trucks for the trip north to Ondangwa. Before we climbed aboard, Captain Delport informed us that a Buffel – which was a mine-protected infantry vehicle built on a Unimog chassis – had just struck a landmine. The Buffel was manned by a section of 8-SAI troops who, because of its mine protection, managed to walk away with shock rather than injury.

Heading away from the Red Line, we noticed a vast change almost immediately in the landscape the further north we went. The vast, open cattle farms with big old farmsteads at the centre of their lands were left behind, along with the rocky, scrubby bushveld, and replaced with a very rural third world setting. Circular kraals dotted the flat, open terrain with ugly, massive baobab trees and makalani palms, which added life to the otherwise bleak landscape. Local Owambo Africans wandered alongside a narrow road, in the hope of collecting a ride from motorists flying by where speed limits played no significant part in the laws of the road.

Squatting and sitting encased within the four low metal sides of the open cattle truck, we thundered forward with our eyes squinting through the glare as we stared across the open expanse of dry land that whizzed by. The wind whipped at our faces and our clothing as we sat motionless under the burning and unrelenting sun. The Samil 100 charged up the smooth, paved road in a northwesterly direction towards Ondangwa, passing countless donkeys and goats as they ran the gauntlet of death, crossing the busy and only paved road connecting the north with the south, leaving behind many stinking carcasses cooking and rotting in the heat as trophies to roadkill.

Some local Owambos milled around and sat next to their handwoven basketry, which they sold from the roadside stalls that Owamboland was very well known for. Some rounded baskets, with perfectly round lids were a metre in diameter, with simple designs usually incorporating a brown geometric pattern neatly woven with great skill and expertise into the pale yellow reed.

Others sold chunks of meat butchered from cows with pangas – machetes, which hung from wire hooks over a makeshift wooden frame, pooling blood in the dust. The blood attracted swarms of flies, which hovered around the meat under the shade of a tree that gave off the impression that they were there to help prevent the sun from totally drying it out.

Abandoned cars wrecked and beyond repair, littered the roadside, standing as crosses to the stretched out metal graveyard, victims to animal kill, pedestrian and night driving. Statistics marked the country with one of the worst road deaths per capita. Flashing past these wrecks, donkeys slowly pulled a cut-off metal bin that had been scavenged from a small truck. Under the harsh crack of a whip, it edged forward with its heavy load, a young Owambo driver proudly steering them forward as the original wheels and axle, bouncing and cushioning with the suspension, rode over the dry, cracked, and eroded earth.

With road deaths far from our thoughts, our vehicle flew by along the road, blaring its horn at the docile donkeys deep in a trance, frozen and oblivious in the middle of the road. At times we crawled to a stop before the donkey would move out of our path, allowing us to continue tearing up the road that was a black, hazy line for as far as the eye could see.

This land was so vastly different from the land of our birth and its picturesque, rolling hills, its plentiful rivers and fertile farming lands, and its added abundance of colour and natural beauty awash from interior to ocean. Instead we were presented with a flat, rugged landscape deeply and desperately shrouded in drought, scattered with sandy plains and dried pans and makalani palm trees standing tall over the castle like structures of the solidified, rock-hard ant heaps.

Cuca shops had sprung up along the busy road, some of them made from hardened-brown mud bricks. Painted advertising decorated the outside walls.

These Cuca shops were named after the Angolan brewed beer, which had been sold from these stores until the brewery in Angola ceased brewing. This left the shops with only the name.

The lettering of Coke and Pepsi, with their respective trademarks, offered a bright splash of colour to the otherwise dull surroundings and spoke a million words. We looked on, confined to our vehicles, drooling with thirst.

The air was filled with wood smoke from cooking fires that rose in grey wisps towards the huge, open, blue sky, while the locals sat and talked, their scrawny, wild-looking dogs scurrying in and around them at will.

The sun burned at our open scalps like hot needles through our hair, parted by the wind, and we watched the second hand tick slowly by, each second drawing us closer to the border line. I wondered about an attack, and how easy it would be for the terrorists to launch a RPG7 rocket in our direction, killing a large number of us.

Well, maybe this stretch of road is safe, but who knows? I tried to reassure myself as I sat still, pondering the idea.

These journeys were mainly undertaken in daylight, it being far too dangerous to travel the open road in the pitch dark.

'Miles and miles of fuckall!' someone shouted over the rumble of the diesel engine.

'What the fuck are we doing here anyway?' another troop echoed.

'What a shit hole,' a third added, and heads nodded in agreement.

The rugged beauty had immediately become scorned as an ugly wasteland, our predicament being to see only through the blinkers of our army eyes. Our brown uniforms were ideal camouflage for our new environment – in body, but certainly not in mind.

Aching and stiff, our bodies in a state of *rigor mortis*, we finally arrived in the small town of Ondangwa. Crowds of Owambo people and traffic, and the further movement of army vehicles – mainly the camouflaged Casspirs, with black policemen sitting leisurely on top of the four-wheel-drive trucks – were our welcome to this town of great strategic importance to the SADF.

The cattle truck wound its way down a narrow street and then took a sharp right as a boom operated from a sandbagged guard hut shot up into the air, allowing us access into the Ondangwa base.

When this bastard of a ride was over, we grabbed at the sides of the truck and levered ourselves up painfully slowly, our bones locked and bent in agony, like old men using their arms to rise from a chair. When the ache had been stretched from us, we now focused on our thirst and began to search for the liquid. A group of us found the main ablution block and rushed to the nearest sink, twisting the tap as quickly as we could, cupping our hands as we sucked up the dusty, warm, and very salty water with complete gratitude. Now, with moistened mouths, having quenched our thirst, we thrust our green water bottles under the tap and filled them up for later use when the emergency arose.

Staff Smit was enraged on hearing that we had drunk water from our fellow National Servicemen's base without being granted permission. He formed our platoon together, with all of our water bottles filled to the brim, and then he began screaming at us, drawing stares from the base's soldiers.

'*Moenie vir my loer nie, ek is nie in hoer nie!*' Don't look at me like that, I'm not a whore! 'I haven't got the time and you haven't got the money', he added with sarcasm.

'*Drink jou foken water!*' Drink your fuckin' water, he barked at us.

While we drank, we realized that this was just another excuse to beat the shit out of us in an attempt to break us.

'*Voorste posisie af!*' Go into the first (push up) position!, he screamed like a man delirious from the heat.

Together we dropped to the ground, taking the position of a push-up, staring into the powdery white dust, and waiting for the next insane order.

'*Op die maag af! Staan op! Drink! Op die rug af! Staan op! Drink!*' On your stomach! Stand up! Drink! On your back! Stand up! Drink!

And so the commands went on, our faces burning with rage and embarrassment as he degraded us in the face of the base's soldiers, forcing them to witness our *opfok* on their terrain. Sweat ran from our faces as we threw our bodies at the white concrete earth and glared through the sun at its zenith, our clothes covered in the white, flour-like powder.

After a while we all stopped and looked at Staff Smit with hatred painted in greyish white streaks across our faces, listening to his forceful threats to get us to drink as he screamed at us like a cruel slave master.

'*Ek sal jou bliksem, jou sleg moer!*' I will hit you, you bastard!, he bawled at us.

Holding eye contact, we stood there dead still as one, blaring a fuck you response back at him as we all opened our water bottles at the same time and tilted them upside down, pouring the liquid at our feet while still holding eye contact. This all too precious ingredient splashed our boots as it hit the white, powdery ground before being swallowed almost immediately into the thirsting earth.

8. Adjusting to a new setting

Our look of don't fuck with us' we have live ammo gave him the message, and it triggered a mean look in him as he came to realize that some soldiers played by different rules. In the past and present, troops had reached that breaking point and had cracked, using their loaded weapons as a threat on the dictatorship of rank' and he knew he was walking a fine line with a few individuals from Platoon 3.

What a feeling it was to have stood like David and faced Goliath head-on without wavering, gelling us even closer together into that tight-knit fighting unit. We knew that his days of getting to us were almost over. Covered in the white powder from head to boot, walking with an air of confidence, we laughed victoriously within our groups and drifted off.

After a wash we milled around aimlessly under the noise of Alouette helicopters flying to and from the Ondangwa Air Force base, either returning from a mission or about to embark on one. A huge white water tower, used now more importantly as a lookout post, rose high above us with soldiers perched on the very top with rifles and binoculars. A tent offered valuable shade, which could be seen from within the base's heaped-up, sandbagged walls.

It felt strange trying to get our bearings and our thoughts together within this garrison, with the continual and real possibility of enemy fire that could be launched in and around us with no warning. This base, along with Oshakati and Ombalantu, acted as major supply centres to the smaller and more vulnerable bases positioned further north. The supplies consisted mainly of ammunition, diesel, and gas cylinders to feed the portable canteen stoves and food in the way of wet and dry rations.

The wet rations consisted of the main necessities for the kitchen, with some of the important commodities being coffee, sugar, long-life milk, condensed milk, eggs, bacon, meat, bread, potatoes, cooking oil, butter, and most importantly a good supply of Castle and Lion beer that was bought and consumed by the six-pack. The bland, dry rations that would be coming our way came in the form of the boxed ration packs, which would be nothing to write home about.

In the middle of the base, outside the canteen that sold those luxurious items – such as chocolates, sweets, chips, and ice-cold beer – we sat in a terraced-off area clutching our beers and our rifle, while we waited for the cloak of darkness to cover us. When it was dark enough, a movie flicked onto a white screen before us as we sat like parked cars at a drive-in, thoroughly enjoying a setting that seemed so out of place, in an area where anything could happen at any time.

Through our laughs of enjoyment, we were continually brought back to reality as we constantly cast our eyes and our hands towards our rifles, never allowing them out of arm's reach. The smell of salt lingered in the air, and we sipped on our beers, guarding the remainder of our six-pack from falling into drunken, thieving hands as we shared the camaraderie under the starry night, surrounded by built-up, sandbagged bunkers.

When our beer had been consumed and the movie had ended, we trailed off, half staggering into the darkness. Finding our packs, we rummaged for our groundsheets, which we laid over the dusty earth, and placed our sleeping bags over them.

Lying drunkenly on our backs, we looked up into the heavens before passing out on our solid mattresses, waiting for tomorrow to dawn and our deployment to the SWA/Angolan border line.

1985-Owamboland. Crammed into the infamous Samil 100 trucks and heading north to the South African Airforce Base at Ondangwa.

9

A long patrol and a dugout on the Yati

The heat of the early morning sun forced us groggily up, and we set about rolling our sleeping bags and packing our gear, being for a change one step in front of our rushed orders. Sitting on our *grootsaks*, a group of us brewed our coffee over a fuel tablet, relishing each sweet sip of this beverage that played such a vital part for each soldier, for he used this as his kickstart to a new day, offsetting any hangovers from the night before.

With the coffee half consumed, we were directed towards the waiting Buffels. We were each issued a few rat packs and tons of ammo, ranging from mortar bombs for the Padmor to hand grenades, rifle grenades, grenades for the *Snotneus*, smoke grenades, flares, Claymore mines, six loaded magazines, and belts of 7.62mm rounds for the LMG – a light but still very heavy machine gun. Our platoon was now loaded to the tits and ready for whatever war was out there.

Weighted down with our packs strapped to our backs, we clambered up and into the Buffel, with one section to a vehicle. Buckled down into our rubber seats, we left the base in four vehicles, our platoon heading in the dusty direction of the Yati. The Yati was a depopulated, no-go area, cleared of bush that was the frontier between Angola and South-West Africa, with a sand road running down the middle. It is also known as the Cut-line or *Kaplyn* in Afrikaans.

To our disgust and anger, the drivers of the vehicles followed their orders and told us to disembark after only a short ten-minute drive, abandoning us under the shade of a few trees.

'What the fuck!' we said as we looked at one another, following the trail of dust and watching the tail end of the Buffels disappearing into the flat terrain. Standing and stumbling in disarray under the cumbersome weight we had strapped to our backs, we looked like overweight babies trying to hold their balance with their first steps.

Under the orders of Lieutenant Bam and Corporal Doep, we set off into the distance with all eternity lying sprawled before our sand-blasted eyes, dusty and booted feet, and demoralized spirits. With our rifles cocked and ready to fire, we were now a part of *Operation Salamander*, patrolling within Owamboland northwards towards an area where most of the incursions were taking place.

Owamboland had the densest population in SWA, totalling close to 650 000, and most of the local Owambo Africans were loyal to SWAPO because they saw

SWAPO as their liberators from South African colonial rule. Through years and years of the bush war dragging by, it got increasingly harder to change what beliefs lay in the locals' minds, and many of these rural Africans saw SWAPO as the banned party that would lead their country to prosperity through independence.

Bullets had killed thousands of these so-called 'freedom fighters' known as SWAPO, or more commonly to us as terrs, but it was not enough to rid the problem of SWAPO's influence spreading amongst the indigenous people as South Africa fought to keep control of the last colony in Africa.

In 1981, a SADF general admitted in an interview: 'We can actually destroy our military enemy. But this is not to say we will destroy SWAPO. SWAPO is in the minds of the people. Bullets kill bodies, not minds.'

Walking in an arrow formation, we carefully stepped across the terrain, looking nervously behind each bush and up and beyond each thin tree. Our eyes hunted for the enemy while our fingers remained on the trigger and our barrels remained pointed in the direction we looked. It was a scary feeling, and we tried to accustom ourselves to the threat of danger within an unwelcoming land that had already started to punish us.

Our legs grew weak as they struggled forward through the soft, beach-like sand, and our backs ached under the enormous weight stuffed into our packs. The sun scorched our arms and faces, and the army bush hat served to protect our scalp from those penetrating hot rays. The tighter we strapped our packs to our backs, the easier the load seemed to be on our bodies. Yet we still wrestled like docile pack mules with our heads down, placing one foot in front of the other and following the course over the open terrain, as flat as a table top.

With a few gruelling kilometres behind us, and thirst gnawing at our dry mouths, we were ordered to stop for a break. While we lowered ourselves slowly to the ground, our packs catapulted us back into a disorganized heap - we fumbled with the zippers to get at our water bottles. Propped against our packs, we gulped at the water, which was now a hot and disgusting temperature, and it trickled warmly down our weary faces and onto our sweat-soaked shirts.

When we regained our strength from the rest and water, our thoughts shifted to the burden of weight we were carrying.

'I wish I had not packed all this shit!' a troop remarked with remorse.

'I know how we can lighten our loads,' another said.

'How?' All our heads turned, waiting for the answer to our cursed baggage.

'Bury it.'

After a few seconds, we all began to dig shallow holes and immediately started to discard our unwanted weight. Extra uniforms, loaded magazines, grenades, mortar bombs, rifle grenades, smoke grenades, flares, water bottles, and some ration pack food filled the holes as we threw earth over our belongings and continued with our much-lighter loads, never bothering to even cast a glance back. The sun continued to burn down, and our backpack straps cut lines into our already red and raw shoulders, and our mouths thirsted with each struggle to step over the godforsaken land.

It was not long after our rest that we encountered our first kraal, which consisted of a cluster of huts encircled by a wooden enclosure.

Passing by in a long, tired line, we saw a middle-aged Owambo woman pounding corn in the hollow of a cut-off tree stump. She looked up at us with a message of hatred plastered over her face as she continued to pound, each stroke growing in intensity. Once we had passed by, we looked back and saw her hanging red, washed clothes over the stockade.

We had been told that these were some of the methods used to signal SWAPO that danger was lurking in the area. The fast-pounding sound would travel a fair distance over the flat land, acting as a warning, and the red cloth a danger symbol to any terrs within visibility of the kraal. Whether this was true or not, it certainly spooked the hell out of those of us who read into these telltale signs.

We disappeared into the distance, crossing through wide-open grassland, and in the middle of this vast, green area, a few hundred metres away from us, we made out the shell of an old house. Curious, we beelined for it and saw the discoloured white walls of an old farmhouse, abandoned many years ago through the strife of the bush war. The roof and supporting beams, along with the doors and window frames, had long since vanished, leaving the shell as the only reminder of the strong German colonial past. The closer we got, the clearer we saw the bullet-riddled walls, which had chunks of concrete the size of saucers dug out of them through heavy-calibre fire. The inside was no different, for we were met with the same pockmarked walls as we looked from one open square of window, through the next, and into the adjoining room – with the same result. The freedom fighters had left their mark a long time ago on this old house as they moved through the area, confirming their presence with the word 'SWAPO' scratched with stone deep into the mortar of the solid brick walls. Small trees, bushes, and grass had grown through the old concrete floors and cracked brickwork, as nature reclaimed the land with some of the small trees having grown to the height of the rooftop.

With an eerie feeling, I wondered what had become of those early white settlers who had tried to carve out a livelihood from this brutal terrain in a new life of uncertainty, from which they had been forced to flee for safer ground.

After a few more kilometres we stopped, for hunger eroded our empty stomachs. Throwing down our sweat-sodden packs, we began collecting sticks and dead branches to make a fire for our evening meal. Out came our fire buckets from the water bottle pouches, as well as our *'pikstels'* utensils. We readied ourselves for the big decision – what to eat. With my knife I punctured a tin of corned beef and began cutting off the lid, followed up with a tin of meatballs – *meatballas* – and mixed vegetables, which I poured sloppily into the dusty fire bucket. Sharing our fire with close friends, we cooked our food over the crackling heat and stirred our individual concoctions.

Dodging the curling flames, our hands shooed away the burned ash from our bubbling food, and we engaged in small talk – always keeping any fears well hidden. When it was heated to our satisfaction, we plucked our bush hats from our heads and used them as oven mitts to retrieve our fire buckets from the red-hot coals. The embers and ash, which had fallen into our meals as we hastily yanked our burning-hot metal canteens from the fire, got casually stirred in, adding a slightly burned taste to our bland recipe.

Sitting on the ground wherever we chose, we spooned our tinned food from our metal cups, enjoying our simple bush meal. We observed the hive of activity of fellow troops crowded around fires and shrouded by the plumes of smoke rising amongst them. In less than a couple of minutes, we had consumed our food, and all that remained was to clean our fire buckets and utensils in the sand.

We added a ration of water to the dirt to help with scouring them clean in readiness for a nightcap of coffee. Again we placed our fire buckets upon the coals, and once the water had come to the boil, we added coffee, sugar, and condensed milk to the ash-blackened water. This was without any doubt the highlight of the day – to sit and contentedly sip our coffee and watch the sun slip gracefully away behind the tall makalani palm trees. The powder-blue sky quickly began to change colour, and the wisps of white cloud became reddish orange, spreading across the skyline like wildfire setting the heavens into a burning haze, as if it had radiated from the scorched savannah. Pinks and purples arced the horizon, darkening into streaks of blackened smoke that hung suspended like a painting with the beauty of oiled colours brushed over canvas.

This was African beauty in its glory, rewarding us with a sense of tranquility and a time to set our spirits free. To be able to trap this moment in the dying minutes of light made us feel such an integral part of untamed Africa, with that unspoken pride for having been born in this glorious continent.

Before the last light slipped away, we packed our gear and moved out, making our way to a new section of bush, which would become our sleeping position for

9. A long patrol and a dugout on the Yati

the long night. To prevent the enemy from knowing our exact position, we never made fires under darkness and never slept where we ate, for fear of a night attack. A fire at night would certainly be a suicidal mistake, offering a target for the terrs to set their sights on and blow us out of our sleeping bags with bombs from their mortar pipes.

With our rifles linked to our arms like an invisible chain, we walked into the disappearing light, which gave us valuable camouflage. In pitch darkness we held hands and stared our fears down, tiptoeing in silence, led by a fellow soldier's hand. In pairs, we were deployed in a complete circle, protecting ourselves from an attack from any angle, and leaving Corporal Doep and Lieutenant Bam the comfort of being in the centre.

Silently and carefully, we laid out our sleeping bags and placed our packs at our heads, giving ourselves a slight bit of cover if the need arose. Our rifles were set on automatic fire and rested on their tripods next to our sleeping positions and never out of arm's reach.

Before we slept, we tied hands together with a string, fastening the right hand of one troop to the left hand of the soldier a few metres away. This procedure had a dual purpose. If we heard or saw something in the middle of the night, we would tug on the string – a quick and silent way to wake a fellow troop. We also used this as a way to pass on guard duty without us having to get up and disrupt the silence, which could result in a shot being fired accidentally through the disorientation of sleep.

When the string was jerked later, I jolted out of my light sleep into a reality of wonder and fear, mixed together. I was now guarding everyone's lives with an overwhelming responsibility, and a lonely feeling crept upon me. The night threw an array of sound across the open, cool bushveld, leaving me to interpret every noise, from the shrill of Christmas beetles and crickets to the belch of a frog and the bark of a dog.

When the shrilling sound stopped, my heart skipped a beat along with it, and I strained my eyes into the darkness and through the bush in front of me. I heard yaps in the dark distance and made out shapes that looked human within the shadows of the overgrowth.

Reaching for my rifle, never losing sight of the shapes, I pointed my barrel at the shadows and held my breath while I strained to hear the sound of breaking twigs. Instead, I was met with the sound of my heart pounding like a drum. Stalked with paranoia, I sat with itchy and sweaty fingers, which never left the curved trigger area while I continued, rigid and tense, to stare into the dense bush, waiting for any movement so I could shoot.

After a wait that felt like time had stood still, the music of the bushveld came back to life, and at the same time I realized that the shapes belonged to the bush' and with this verification a sense of calm flowed through my clenched fingers and stiff torso. I sighed with relief and smiled to myself at how completely paranoid I had become – having been only seconds away from tearing up the bush with automatic fire. After an hour of guard watch, that flew by, I tugged on the string and gladly passed the responsibility to the next in line.

Thankful as I was to be alive after my waking hours of paranoid fright, it did not seem too bad to have the sun baking us in our bags and the flies buzzing around our sunburned faces and crawling up our nostrils and into the corners of our mouths. This was our first taste of the bush alarm clock, which would welcome us in the same way each and every morning, forcing us to rise and deal with the pests on our feet rather than be tortured awake.

After a coffee and a quick snack, we packed up and headed nervously towards the Yati. Just before we reached it, Rob emerged from a dry but dense section of bush with hands cupped together, holding a massive brown toad the size and shape of a soccer ball. To me it looked as though someone had taken a pump to a normal-sized frog and blasted it with a strong jet of air. We had never seen anything like this before and we crowded around Rob, staring at it while it sat calmly in his hands, its wide eyes blinking at us. Finally it urinated in his hands, forcing Rob to let it go as this giant creature sprung awkwardly away into a new resting place in the coolness and safety of a hole.

On reaching the Yati, we passed some infantry troops who were dug in on the South-West African side. We continued past them, heading parallel to the Yati in an easterly direction for a few more tiring kilometres.

Eventually Lieutenant Bam brought our platoon to a halt and began deploying us in half-sections, with Alpha being the first to be positioned along the border line. Paul, Fourie, JP, Fox, Wayne, and I were left behind as the rest of the platoon continued forward to their ambush positions.

Lowering the weight from our sore backs, we surveyed the area of bush that had been designated to us. Slowly and nervously we walked up to the Yati and looked up and down the long, flat, and very straight roadway that separated trained guerrillas intent on infiltrating into the Owamboland region that our company had been assigned to. Walking across this road with our rifles at the ready, half expecting to see SWAPO hiding in the bushes on the Angolan side, we forced ourselves over and into a new country, marking our spot in Angola by urinating in wide arcs across the sandy soil.

This road, which served as the border line, had not been used as a passage in many a long year because of the threat of landmines, placed maliciously by the terrorists to disrupt and create panic throughout the ranks of the South-West African Territorial Forces, the South African Defence Force, and the local Owambo population.

After our little jaunt, proud to have placed a boot print on Angolan soil, we returned to our packs and began selecting a cut of bush in which to make our homes for the next while. Wayne and I teamed up and chose an area 12 metres from the road, below a small green bush, maximizing all the shade and camouflage from the otherwise open and scattered clumps that dotted our side of the border.

With a shared fold-out shovel and our metal drinking cups, we began scooping out sand and piling it up on the sides around our two man sleeping position, to a depth of nearly half a metre. After a couple of hours, we had four shallow graves dug in a line, with enough depth to give us cover if we came under fire. Wayne used his bivi, or his groundsheet, as a roof, stringing it to bush on all four corners to aid us against the 45°C heat and the possibility of rain' while I used mine to cover the ground in our dugout.

Together we threw green branches of bush over our brown roof, adding camouflage and further shade to our ambush position. A dried-out branch was dragged up to our head area and placed next to our packs to serve as extra cover from the front of our position.

When our homes were complete, we began placing the Claymore mines on their stands, a few metres in front of us, with the electrical wire carefully hidden by sand and leaves trailing back to Paul's dugout, where the firing device was positioned.

Our work done, we scrambled into the shade and started our war of waiting, for the time began to stand still. Our sanity was strung to the limits, the heat sapping at our energy and the flies teasing and torturing us as we swatted at them in vain, staring at a blue sky and a clump of green bushes, totally alone, feeling as though we were stranded on an island devoid of water. Bored to death, we looked forward to our meals as a break from the monotony of waiting upon no excitement or activity of any sort.

At around 19:30 darkness came, bringing with it the joy of coolness. But on the flip side, on many of those moonless nights when we couldn't see a hand in front of our taut faces, it dealt us many a frightening night. There were nights when every noise played cruel tricks, working our young minds into a raging fit as we fought to place in context what were nothing more than the sounds of nature, as we lay positioned in the heart of the area used by incoming guerrillas.

During the day we paid a visit to some of our half-sections dug in further east of us and fighting off the same insane elements as we were. Passing the remainder of our section, we stopped and spoke to them for a while before moving on to Grant and his section. Grant recounted a story from the night before regarding Loots, which could so easily have turned dreadfully ugly. In the middle of the night, Loots had got up and, unknowingly, had walked in his sleep across the Yati and into Angola, in the direct firing line of his own forces.

When he awoke in the pitch-blackness, he realized what he had done – which forced him to remain trapped where he was for fear of being shot as an insurgent if he crossed back. Without a rifle, and hardly sleeping a wink, on top of being a vulnerable target from both sides, he waited until first light before he could make a safe return.

Back at our ambush site, with darkness upon us, Fourie had unwittingly wandered out of his position, into the bush behind us, to relieve himself. I heard movement, in the form of breaking twigs and the rustle of leaves. I started to freak, and my heart and mind raced out of control.

Could this be a terr? I questioned to myself as I flicked the safety catch onto automatic fire, as the sound came rushing closer.

'Who's there?' I said firmly, but no answer was returned.

I knew I was taking a chance by speaking out, for if it was SWAPO I had provided him with a target at which to shoot.

In the next second, *Vark* Fourie, whom we often referred to as 'Stupid Fourie' because of his unthinking actions – broke through the bush right in front of me, almost walking into my rifle, which I held at waist level ready to spray the bush with bursts of fire.

'You fuckin' arsehole!' I shouted in relief, shaking at what I could so easily have done.

Fourie looked at me pale-faced, suddenly comprehending what his fate could have been.

'Why the fuck didn't you answer?' I blurted out before walking away trembling without waiting for his reply which was no longer needed.

In this new land, we were living on the edge, ready to blow anything away, gripped by the invisible claws of fear. Countless soldiers had died in similar situations, and Fourie was just plain lucky that I had waited instead of shooting and asking questions later.

On the fifth night of our ambush, Paul – for some unknown reason – ordered us to stand guard in front of our dugouts and just behind our minefield, instead of seeing out the watch from within our shallow holes.

All five of us looked at him in disbelief, blatantly telling him, 'No way.'

We went on to explain our fear of placing ourselves in the firing line of our own troops. Paul, being the reasonable leader he was, agreed with us and abandoned the idea, leaving the guard to continue the same way as before.

That night we were startled awake. All hell had broken loose, and the chatter of automatic fire tore into the dark silence. Disoriented for a second, we realized that we were under attack' a continual shower of lead cracked like whips and hissed about our ears and just above our heads' we heard the shots thudding into small trees all around us.

Under frightful confusion, we opened fire in unison from our lying positions, our bodies tightly pressed to the ground. We figured we were under attack from the Angolan side.

Red tracers bounced into the dark bush, lighting up the night sky, offering a spectacular show that, had we been in a different situation, we might have enjoyed.

'It's coming from behind us,' Fox screamed over the noise to Wayne and myself. Fox and Wayne immediately turned around and returned fire, and Paul and I continued shooting into Angola, fearing that they were wrong. We watched our red flashes disappear deep into the Angolan bush. Fox, in a squatting position, clipped a 50 round magazine to his rifle and screamed, 'Look!'

Tracer after tracer flashed red from the barrel, the bullets expelled into the distance, the *doppies*, or shells, flying from our rifles into the air and bouncing around us with tinny sounds.

A multitude of bullets kept coming at us, the cracks getting lower and lower with every passing second. In less than two minutes, which felt more like 20, and a couple of magazines lighter, it was all over and silence once again reclaimed the bushveld. Rushing on adrenaline, our hands shaking from the jumping of automatic fire and our noses burning from the scent of burned gunpowder, we caught our breath and began asking each other down the line if everyone was OK.

Relieved to hear that there were no casualties Wayne and I aid down, our adrenaline slowly wearing off into an uncomfortable and stunned silence' we lay with our backs to the ground, absolutely shit scared and waited for the long night to drag by. We lay like two dead bodies, stiff and rigid, the hairs of our arms pushed up by goosebumps, and stared wide-eyed at the groundsheet a metre above our heads. Our breathing was rushed and our hearts continued with an accelerated beating from within our tightly bound chests, and we tried to somehow relax ourselves. In what seemed like an out-of-body experience,

I replayed the scene in my mind while I diverted my gaze from the overhead groundsheet towards my feet and beyond, into the outside world of untouched land, through the shadows of branches, and towards the stars that twinkled brightly around us. Suddenly the true impact of this event sank in. How close we had come to being snatched away into the plastic, zip-up body bags, only we would truly know.

What would have happened had we obeyed the order and stood guard by the minefield? I asked myself, knowing the answer already.

With no one to turn to, we withdrew into ourselves, trapped within the walls of our minds, and played the scene over and over until sleep came – in short intervals.

Unwittingly, we had just proven to ourselves that we could face danger head-on without falling to pieces. Our intense training had taken over, and adrenaline had overridden fear. No one had frozen in fright, and that proved to us the most valuable lesson any soldier can learn: We will not let each other down, but will stand firm together!

When the morning light finally cast the darkness away we ventured forward, eager to survey the scene, hunting for bullet marks amongst the thin trees. It did not take long before we found the markings that told the same story, except this time we could see them in the light as they scarred trees above and past our sleeping area, well below our standing height. Branches had been ripped off, and bushes and trees were oozing sap through the chunks that had been shot out of them, only a metre to a metre and a half from the sandy ground. Looking at the oozing sap reiterated for me the miracle that we had not witnessed our own blood being shed.

Lieutenant Bam arrived at our ambush site and began surveying the area with us. While he was looking at some of the trees, he informed us that a guerrilla had slipped through our platoon's ambush positions in the night, crossing back into Angola.

In the afternoon, we walked to the ambush site, housing the rest of our section who were positioned south-east of us. They told us that they had heard movement in the night and had opened fire with their R4 rifles and the LMG, but that they fired blindly into the dark. They never realized that their shooting had swayed too far left, exiting their arc of fire and placing our lives at high risk. Whether they really heard the enemy or not, we will never know, but what we did know was how close this friendly-fire fight had come to scarring our lives forever had one of us been shot.

Back at our position, a radio signal crackled over the set, with a welcome break to the daylight silence.

9. A long patrol and a dugout on the Yati

'Yati, Yati – gunship. Yati, Yati – gunship!'

This was a warning from a helicopter that was in our area – us being the Yati, and the helicopter being the gunship. Within seconds of radio contact, a camouflaged Alouette MK III helicopter, of French design, broke the silence with its heavy rotors and loomed into sight. Together we rose to our feet, to show our presence and not be mistaken for SWAPO, which might have made us targets for another friendly-fire incident. The gunship flew at tree-top height right over our position, giving us a quick two seconds to see the gunner tightly strapped in behind his 20mm cannon, which protruded from the side opening.

Looking down on us, he raised his hand in greeting as the two-man crew disappeared over the Yati into Angola. It was an amazing feeling to be acknowledged, especially from the skies, for we had sunk into our filth and isolation and were cut off from the outside world – boredom and nightly fears were in control of our dismal lives.

These fighting birds in the air added security to our vulnerable position. Gunships are generally only called in when the enemy's chevron-patterned boot print is only half an hour old, and they fly only during daylight hours as it was too dangerous to fly at night.

A couple of minutes passed before we heard the 20mm cannon at work, a few deep thuds echoing back to our ears and bringing a smile to our dirty faces at the kill that had just taken place.

A few minutes later we heard the gunship returning to our side of the border. We wondered if this was the terr who had got through our platoon ambush into the relative safety of Angola. Our few minutes of excitement over, we returned to the shade of our bivis with thirst gnawing at our throats.

With the unbearable heat topping 45°C, our six-litre water ration was rapidly disappearing, leaving us no option but to scout for a waterhole. Wayne, Fox, and I left our area with our rifles and began walking south, each with a couple of empty green water bottles. After walking a few kilometres, half expecting to see a SWAPO on the way, we eventually found a waterhole and joyously walked into the cool pit, which had been dug down to a depth of three to four metres. A circle of crystal-clear water filled the pit and it was beautifully cool and refreshing to our dry mouths and dirty hands, arms, and faces. To escape the heat in the depth of this pit surrounded by a low wooden stockade was pure heaven on earth for us. Clean, cool, and content, we filled our water bottles to the brim and returned happy to our waiting troops, with one less worry on our minds.

In the latter part of the afternoon, Staff Smit and Sergeant Piet Muis came bundu bashing in a Kwevoel parallel to the Yati because of the possibility of striking a land mine along that unused stretch of roadway. In a swirl of dust they drove right into our minefield, smashing some of our Claymore mines in half under the weight of the huge mine-protected troop carrier, which came to a halt right in front of our dugouts.

Bastards! I thought as I looked up to Piet Muis with absolutely no respect. His long, thin, pointed face looked just like a mouse' his ears were the size of the open Kwevoel doors. He was a PF who had chosen an extended career in the military, and he enjoyed putting people down and creating misery for us. With choices in life limited for a person of his stature it seemed unlikely to us that he would be able to eke out a living in civilian life. From the vehicle they threw down a few boxes of dry and boring rat packs, then drove off into the bush, leaving us to swallow the Kwevoel's dust and endure more waiting and wondering.

Early the next morning, Paul received a radio signal from our lieutenant to pack up and meet the rest of our platoon at a position further east of us along the Yati.

Racked with excitement, we tore down our homes with that urgent need for a change in scenery and a reunion with our platoon mates. We then departed, ready for our next step into the wide-open wilderness of northern South-West Africa.

1985-Owamboland. Wayne and the authors camouflaged dugout on the Yati. It saved our lives in a friendly fire skirmish.

10
And the rains came

What a great feeling it was to see familiar faces we had not seen in over a week as we reunited from split-sections back into the strength of a complete platoon.

Burdened with our gear which felt twice as heavy because we had not had to pick it up for so long, we set off in single file behind the long strides of Lieutenant Bam. Earlier in the day, we were averaging three kilometres in 45 minutes which considering our hefty packs, the heat, the soft sand, and the unevenly ploughed stretches of land was good. Fatigue and thirst were sure credits to our *vasbyt* of stamina and endurance. Through last light, and into the shield of darkness, we continued forward, angry and disgruntled by our lieutie's slave-driving commands.

'How much further?' someone asked of the dark night.

'*Moenie moffie raak*,' our loot answered back hastily. '*Nog n kilometer*' Don't act like a queer. Just another kilometre).

Brian angrily shouted through the darkness, 'Fuck this! I am not walking any further!'

He stopped and dropped his kit and rifle. This stopped our lieutie in his tracks and forced him to retrace his steps to the troop who had cracked and reached that breaking point that could come and go so easily.

'*Kom nou Brian, moenie moffie raak*' Come on Brian, don't act like a weakling, said Lieutenant Bam in a pleading way, frustrated at his vain attempt to get Brian moving again.

Brian refused point-blank to pick up his kit, giving those around him no choice but to grab his gear and share the load amongst themselves. Only then did Brian join the tired line of weary troops as we cut our way through the darkened surroundings. The thought of sleeping on any patch of ground passed through all our minds.

After 12 kilometres of hell, we arrived at our Company Headquarters in the middle of the bush, physically exhausted, thirsty, and hungering for a tin of food. It did not take us long to realize that our lieutie had pushed us to the limit for his selfish, personal gain – racing our platoon against Platoons 1 and 2 in his quest to reach the Company HQ first.

He achieved his goal with a smile and a few congratulatory remarks from Captain Delport, and also with subdued anger from us for not caring one bit who came in first or last in this game of platoon rivalry in which the victorious lieutenant had hoped to gain some respect from his superior.

Lieutenant Bam led us into our TB, or sleeping positions, for the night. One by one we filed past him in a hushed and depressed silence, still boiling with rage at the unnecessary pace of the patrol. Standing like cattle, waiting for his tap on our shoulders so we could proceed past him and take position in the circle of *rondom verdediging,* or defence on all sides, seemed to take forever, for we were desperate to strip ourselves of the 30 punishing kilograms of gear.

'*Kom verby, kom verby!*' Come past, come past!, Lieutenant Bam said as he hurried us by.

Wayne, who was behind me in the line, imitated the lieutie's command.

'*Kom verby, kom verby!*' he said sarcastically in his English accent.

I was standing next to Lieutenant Bam, waiting to be tapped on the shoulder to take up my position, when he cracked. He thought it was me who had imitated his order. Losing his temper, he pushed me backwards, his face staring me down in rage.

I stumbled back a couple of steps and lost my footing, buckling under the weight of my gear, which pulled me to the ground. I landed on my back in a patch of mud and rested on my pack for a couple of stunned seconds. Then I began struggling like a tortoise stranded on its shell, fighting to get back on my feet.

Lieutenant Bam stood over me with his close-set eyes and stern, thin, boyish face, staring menacingly at me. I was livid and my face contorted with anger as I looked up, locking eyes with him as he stood towering powerfully over me.

In those helpless seconds I cast a thought back to boarding school, when I had been pushed to the ground in a fight. I had two choices – either to remain seated and allow the heat to subside, or stand up like a man and take whatever came my way.

My mind was racing, and I said to myself: No one pushes me down' I don't care who the hell you are!

'Fuck this!' I swore, and found enough strength to get out of the mud.

'If he pushes me down again, I'll shoot him!' I said, under my breath, while I struggled to hold my balance in the slippery mud.

'You fuckin' *poes*!' I swore at him. I wrestled my rifle sling free from around my neck and shoulders, and using it to force myself up, I faced him in an almost berserk state.

His right index finger was still wagging annoyingly at me, only centimetres from my face. With my free right hand I grabbed his finger and crushed it back

10. And the rains came

into his palm, while my left hand clutched my loaded rifle with 30 rounds in the magazine.

'You fuckin' dumb arsehole!' I bellowed readying to swing my rifle at him.

My uncontrolled fury had taken me close to flicking off the safety catch and putting a bullet in his head. He had pushed me over the limit into a state of border-line insanity, in which my actions strayed well beyond my mental control or care for any later repercussions.

Corporal Doep heard the commotion and naturally went straight to the side of the lieutenant, threatening me with challenging an officer – which, as we all knew, held serious consequences.

His words sank in and my anger began to slowly abate – he could quite well have saved both our souls from serious harm. I turned from his face and without another word took up my position for the night, along with the rest of the weary platoon.

Still shaking with adrenaline, anger, and resentment, I kept to myself and unrolled my sleeping bag onto my groundsheet. I placed my boots next to the head of the nylon bag along with my R4 and climbed in fully clothed. The stench of my uniform was now at least ten days old, and ripening.

I zipped myself into the safety of the bag and lay on my back, looking up at the sky for help. I searched for the stars, but unfortunately found none. Instead I saw adark, purplish-clouds hanging low over us, and from nowhere a deafening sound of thunder shook the dry plains. A voice inside of me pleaded with the heavens: No, not now, not tonight! I felt the first soft drops of rain upon my upturned face, which began to quicken with the tormenting growl of the thunderstorm until it was beating down with the intensity of a showerhead.

There was no escape from our position or our predicament as we threw groundsheets over our packs and curled up in foetal positions in the hope of gaining warmth. The water quickly settled on the ground and began to saturate our sleeping bags, and us in them. Tired, cold, and very frustrated, we battled against the torture of the stinging raindrops against our faces and bodies. It became impossible to sleep, and instead I closed my eyes hoping to shut out the discomfort, and ducked my head further under the cover of my groundsheet to avoid the torrent of rain. There was nowhere to run for cover and warmth – the driest place was underneath the Captain's Buffel, which was already occupied by our rank. All we could do was lie still, whimper under the mercy of the above, listen to the frustration of those around us, and wait for ten hours to drag slowly by until the new day dawned.

We began to rise from the mud looking like drowned rats, slowly moving about and feeling as stiff as cardboard as the breeze hit our frozen bodies. Only too glad that it was daylight we stretched away our aches and pains and surveyed the chaos that we were sharing. A few troops tried in vain to dry themselves and their sleeping bags over a smouldering fire while others, yearning for a steaming fire bucket of coffee, began making use of their fuel tablets.

Thankfully the rain had stopped, leaving behind soft muddy ground, slightly cleaner clothes and bodies, and boots half-filled with rainwater, which were turned upside down and placed onto our already cold and wet feet. After coffee, we packed up and threw our saturated packs onto our sore backs, and we began to move out in one long and very depressed line.

Our next orders were to walk to a rendezvous point and wait for Buffels that had been dispatched from Ondangwa for our retrieval. After a long wait, they arrived and we quickly loaded ourselves in by sections. We were extremely thankful for the ride, for had we walked with our wet packs it would have pushed us beyond the limits. It did not take long for the sun to come out and burn the wetness from our kit and our sleeping bags, which hung like washing from a line over the steel-sided plates of the vehicle flapping dry in the cool breeze.

After the bumpy and dusty drive, we arrived at the Ondangwa base and waited on the next order, which was to disembark from the vehicles. Not long after that, the next order came to get back on the Buffels. After five times of climbing on and off these mine-protected vehicles, our tempers soaring through the *rondfok*, we were finally ordered to board a waiting Kwevoel. Packed again like sardines, we headed towards Ombalantu, all our kit still quite wet and now very dusty – back to the territory base close to where we had just been lifted.

We never understood our orders and never tried to, for they never seemed to be of sound judgment and never made any sense to us. Time and time again we had been told never to question an order, for our rank reminded us that we were not being paid to think but rather to do. Our job was to follow through on the orders, no matter how absurd the command seemed to be – and with niggling frustration and buckets of anger, we generally put on a brave face and went with the flow – which was always so much easier than going against it.

After another agonizing long drive through a damp drizzle, we arrived at a very wet and muddy base called Ombalantu, marked by a giant baobab tree at least a thousand years old. Our Kwevoel entered the base and parked alongside one of the fortified walls close to the entrance. Sitting in the rain, we watched vehicles pouring into the base, churning the ground into a quagmire while we sat and wondered about the next move.

Cold and angry, I stared through the rain and saw a thin black dog, which had strayed into the base, giving chase to one of the passing Samils. It ran alongside the front tyre and tried to gnaw at the giant turning rubber, but unfortunately it got too close and fell under the massive rolling weight. After one quick yelp, it was flattened into a bloody pulp and buried beneath the thick mud, the driver totally oblivious to what had just happened.

Nothing stopped as the stream of vehicles and soldiers moved in against the discomfort of the rain' we gazed onto the rectangular, ash-brick kitchen and toilet block, wishing for cover under the corrugated tin roof. Meanwhile we sat in our usual wait, never knowing what to expect next.

Eventually we disembarked from the Kwevoel into the mud, but instead of being given a tent we were told to set up our bivis under the stars, next to one of the base's huge sandbagged walls. Picking the driest patch of earth that we could find, we began setting up for another long and sleepless night. There were no stars to take our minds off the torment, and the drizzle turned to rain, throwing us into panic. Anger was welling up in all of us because of the torture of not having slept in two days, and it drew us closer to that dangerous breaking point, our bodies weak and sick with fatigue.

'Fuck!' someone screamed out, drawing out the 'u' in reaction to the lashing rain.

'Fuck this place! What the fuck are we doing here?' another troop added.

We felt trapped, like wild, raging animals, unable to escape.

Eventually, when we could no longer stand the sharp stabbing of the rain and the pool of mud, we took our rifles and began searching for cover. Most of us ended up congregating in the toilet area, within the ash-block walls and behind the black meshed windows – thankfully under the cover of the tin roof. A group of us sat next to the toilet pits, which were just a couple of holes in the ground with a plastic cover. The smell that rose from the stinking pit was deplorable, and it gave off a sulphurous stench that attracted a swarm of flies to crawl constantly across our faces – and we knew only too well where they had come from.

The smell and the flies were certainly better than the rain, and the hard concrete floor was certainly better than the mud. Sitting numb with cold and soaked to the bone, we waited for morning, when we hoped to see the burning sun. But once we were warm and dry, we would curse the wretched ball of fire for bringing us thirst and sapping us of energy for the next patrol.

This was the life we were living. Our bodies were constantly tested by both extremes of weather. Most of us sat in silence, though others cursed the darkness and the shambles we were in. Again we were driven into the path of border-line insanity.

I internalized my pain and mental chaos, for I knew that voicing them would not free me from the grip of hardship. I needed to save my energy for the next day so that I could reform, and get myself through, and take a step closer to the end. Our lives had become a survival against the elements and the invisible enemy, which bit by bit were driving us insane through the silent mental and physical demands.

First light broke through the thin black meshing, bringing with it a sigh of relief – because now, at least, we could see our distress and deal with it, as opposed to walking blind and shivering in the darkness. The rain had halted, giving us a chance to dry out our water-filled sleeping bags and clothes. In small groups we converged on a smouldering fire giving off more smoke than heat, and stood like statues, holding our bags over the grey, rising cloud. Because we did not realize how much heat there was below the smoking logs, a few of the nylon sleeping bags began to melt and were immediately yanked from the smoking circle – followed by some choice words.

Before we had time to sort ourselves out, we were given the order to move out. Our kit, still very wet, was packed up and thrown onto the Buffel, followed by our rifles, which were now showing signs of rust and neglect. Next, our tired bodies followed. Riding into the distance, we again relied on the sun to dry our kit and rejuvenate our souls from the deep-set aches and pains of the dampness.

Our patrol was short-lived, for the vehicles could not churn through the mass of water on the ground. In some places, these *oshanas* were ankle deep to a metre deep and spanned for miles' they could quite easily be mistaken by an outsider for a dam or lake. The *oshanas* would spring to life through a web of ephemeral, vegetated watercourses, which are filled during a four-month period of heavy rainfall beginning in January. Once the watercourses are filled during this period, known to the locals as *efundja*, the runoff flows onto the sandy soil and spreads into shallow lakes called *oshanas*. But we referred to them as *shonas* – a word we despised for all the blisters we had to endure to cross them.

But in spite of being cruel to our feet, the *shonas* were kind when we thirsted, for the heat constantly overwhelmed us. Since water was so scarce, the locals never complained, for they knew the struggles that lay ahead when the heat burned down for the remaining eight months of the year and barely a raindrop fell.

After a few swear words, we all climbed off the vehicles with our kit and rifles and immediately sank into the mud and water. Leaving the bogged-down vehicle and its driver to navigate their own way out of the *shona*, along with

10. And the rains came

the rest of the drivers and their Buffels, we began walking out of this mess, heading in the direction of Beacon 10, which was on the Yati. These solid, two-metre-high, four-sided concrete slabs known as Beacons were positioned ten kilometres apart along the length of the Yati, starting in the west and continuing far into the east, along the old cut-line separating Angola from SWA. These beacons were few and far between, having been either shot out or destroyed through the many years of the bush war' or the overgrown bush had hidden them from our searching eyes. These weathered slabs of dulled concrete, with a number imprinted into them, acted as our reference points. The rest of our navigation was handled by compass, which directed us time and time again to the Yati. Once on the cutline, the beacons brought us much cheer upon reaching far-flung destinations on many a patrol. But on the flip side, it also brought much anger and frustration to the surface, for we knew what distances we had to cover to reach the next point east or west of it.

Shortly before we reached the Yati, we stopped for a much-needed rest under a few trees. Tired and exhausted as usual, we threw down our gear and then grabbed at our water bottles, downing the warm contents before resting against our packs. There was a big anthill close by, and Macky and a couple of others – who for some reason still had energy within themselves – began chopping at this built-up heap of rock-solid sand with sticks and a shovel. When it was time to continue with the patrol, we began walking over hard chunks of earth, which had been chiselled off this huge mound that stood over five metres in height. In front of this anthill was a smaller heap of built-up earth at least three metres high, into which they had sculptured a face. What they had done was remarkable – carving a face out of the anthill and bringing it to life with a resemblance to the Polynesian rock statues on Easter Island. The man's huge head was elongated, with a straight, long, and thin nose, deep-set eyes, and a wise frown across his brow, a curved mouth, and a little undergrowth over his head. Unfortunately, at the time we were so tired we barely cast a second glance at this amazing piece of artwork, which would certainly scare the living crap out of any terr that walked through the thick bush and unexpectedly came face-to-face with it.

Just south of Beacon 10, we set up our TB for the night, choosing a thicket of green bush for extra cover. With time helping us to adjust, having been constantly on guard – especially through the nights – it seemed to somehow get easier as we drew closer to each other with a silence that in a soldier speaks volumes.

The next morning, after a quick meal and a hot, sweet coffee, we set off for Beacon 12 – a patrol of 20 kilometres away. Our mental strength and resolve was tested again as we willed ourselves through *oshana* after *oshana*, dragging our boots, which – filled with water – were now twice as heavy. Our pants, too, were wet up to our thighs, and our packs shifted awkwardly as we took our course through the muddy brown water.

One could not help but notice the colour that these rains had brought to the vast, dry plains, replacing the dull, creamy brown with a lush green. With each step, we could see new shoots of grass pushing through irrigated cracks in the wet earth. Nature had begun to blossom with a fresh, new, vibrant life. The sudden change helped lift our spirits from the usual dusty dry African plains – one serious drawback being the mosquitoes, which multiplied in the thousands in the stagnant waters and ate us alive.

Daily we doused ourselves in Tabard and vast quantities of mosquito liquid that smelled worse than kerosene. That became our protective armour against the onslaught of the ferocious and annoying pests. It did not matter how we smelled, or the taste of this liquid on our hands when we ate, so long as we could keep them at bay and prevent the pink swelling from the bites and the severe itchiness that followed each attack.

The flies were just as bad, or even worse, for they also bit and flew about our faces, sucking on our sweat like a hive of bees around honey.

'*Fokweg*!' Fuck off!, we screamed in anger as we shot our arms out, sending a few flies on their way for a brief moment – until they returned for a repeat of our frustration. With anger growing in us, just to shout out seemed to ease our sense of helplessness and balance our minds for the time being.

Reaching Beacon 12 came as a relief, finally bringing an end to our 20 kilometre patrol. When we took our wet boots off, along with our saturated socks, we looked at our deathly white feet, which were extremely wrinkled and very blistered. What pleasure it was to have our feet naked and breathing as the cool breeze blew a massage across our worn soles, taking with it the aches and pains and recharging us for the next patrol. Thoroughly enjoying our rest, we made our cooking fires and ate before setting off into our ambush positions, under last light, for a guarded but deep sleep.

In the morning, after a quick coffee, we set off for Beacon 13, ten *clicks* away to the east. After a few kilometres of walking with the sun burning down on us, we decided to strip off and cool down within one of the *shonas*. We waded into the metre deep muddy water and sank our bodies below the warm surface, and stretched and relaxed without a care in the world – tall grass, lilies, and a backdrop of mopane trees around us.

While we sat in a group, we watched Grant, Wayne and a couple of others picking large green lilies from the water. They placed the long stem of each lily down the length of their R4 rifle barrels, leaving the green leaf protruding from the end. The four of them then proceeded with fire-and-movement as they ran – splashing, dashing, and diving into the water in a complete mockery of our strict bush-training drills.

Rocking with laughter, we doubled over, our sides hurting from watching their antics. If any terrs had been sitting in the bush watching this circus act, they too would have burst into laughter and left the area thinking: These South Africans are a bunch of clowns!

En route to our next destination we saw two goats wandering aimlessly, and impulsively, yearning for fresh meat, we made a decision. A group of us gave chase after them and managed to force them over the gravel road and onto the free-for-all Angolan soil. Once on the Angolan side, we believed that whatever crossed our path in the way of food was ours for the taking.

Bennie and Sandor lay in wait for the goats and then pounced on them. Their knives drawn, they slit their throats before they even had time to bleat. Their legs were tied together, and a strong stick was slid through – and with one troop on each end, we shouldered our dinner and walked off. The carcasses swayed from side to side and dripped blood onto our boots as we walked like cavemen towards a bearing set out by Corporal Doep. I walked, holding the stick at the back of the tandem, looking down at its neck as it flapped open and closed like a fish's gill. The two of us struggled with the dead weight, coupled with our own gear.

Eventually we arrived at our sleeping place for the night and set down the two large animals. At once we all began rounding up firewood, placing the smaller pieces in a pyramid above some dry leaves and grass. Once lit, it smoked away, identifying our position with ease – not that we really cared, hunger now dictating the order of the day.

Crowding around the fire with the two dead goats at our feet and the flies feeding off their blood, we eagerly waited for the coals to simmer down so that we could begin our bush braai. With a small penknife in each of our hands, we began hacking out chunks of bloody meat from the warm animal and threaded our savagely cut out pieces onto green sticks which we placed over the fire, balancing them on a mound of sand built up around the base of the fire pit. While the meat sizzled over the heat of the coals, we looked at the animals with huge hollows chopped out from their upper bodies, and yet most of the animal was still covered in its brown fur, somehow disguising our kill.

Making eye contact with the slit, evil-looking eyes sent a chill down my body, and a feeling that I was about to eat the devil's animal. It forced me to turn away or lose my appetite, and of course, without hesitation, I chose to turn away. After a fair while of turning our green sticks, the meat blackened on the outside and cooked as much as our hunger would allow. Without a moment to waste, we tore into the strips of meat with our dirty and greasy fingers.

Sitting around the fire and talking, the juice ran down the sides of our mouths in our devilish lust for animal flesh. It came as a wonderful change from the dry ration packs. The juicy but tough goat tasted wild, and was still bloody in parts, but our jaws chewed and pulled at it like carnivores, having been deprived of this luxury for weeks.

While we rested under some shade with our bellies bursting, I saw another group of goats wandering around aimlessly and unattended, far from their owner's kraal. Watching them, I wondered how the owner would react when he found out about the devastating loss we had inflicted upon his investment. Every evening at dusk, all goats automatically made their way back to their kraal, as if some sort of built-in remote controlled them. This time, unfortunately, two would go unaccounted for – for those two sat in our bloated but contented stomachs.

Bush life had now become a part of us, and we did what we could to make life easier with what came our way. Three weeks had passed since we left South Africa, which now felt more like an eternity ago. Secretly within ourselves, each one of us had transformed from scared young boys into a breed of toughened survival fighters, ready for whatever the bush threw at us. We had learned an attitude of I couldn't care less.

Our faces had become bearded and hardened, only breaking for a quick but nervous smile. Our once neatly ironed browns had not been changed since we landed, and they had become torn and blackened with dirt. Some of them, modified for the brutal climate, were worn with cutoff sleeves. Our boots were now scuffed and covered in dirt and dust, and our rifles – once so well looked after – were now showing signs of rust.

Our platoon had begun to look like a mismatch of rebel troops, far from the neat, clean, and crisp-looking soldiers that we were only weeks ago, when we had boarded the planes with the fear of the unknown riding with us.

With time wearing on, we began to worry less and less about the threat of death, and our actions became ruthlessly careless. Fires occasionally sprang to life within our nightly sleeping circle, in addition, cigarettes were lit up inside the bivis, amplifying the glow like a lighthouse casting a beam across an ocean. Less frequently did we stand guard over our fellow platoon mates with any consistency, for the first guard watch was normally placed upon the troop who fell asleep the quickest, and thus he never transferred the duty to the next of us.

10. And the rains came

Our minds had become nonchalant. We figured, if it was our time to be attacked, so be it. That did lift a certain amount of tension from us. Yet in spite of this approach, it is human nature to fear the unknown and the unseen, and the terrorist movement in the area was obvious. Thoughts of this nature played through our minds and on too many occasions that underlying fear was upon us, no matter how we tried to disguise it.

It was 30 January, and Wayne had just turned 19 in the middle of the bush. Naturally there were no beers or cheers for his celebration, but instead just a few handshakes and a similar day of boredom and patrol to the one gone by. It was just another day in the open bush as we walked west, parallel to the Yati, towards Beacon 11 – staying off the road for fear of stepping on a land mine. After another gruelling 20 kilometres, we arrived at the same place we had been a few long days ago.

With hunger again wrestling at our guts, we allowed Paul to do the unthinkable. Looking up at an extremely tall and straight tree, we saw a Martial Eagle sitting proudly at the very top, gazing over its territory oblivious to Paul's rifle, whose sights were lined up on the big bird.

'Should I shoot it?' Paul asked.

'Go for it,' we answered, expecting that he was either bluffing or would miss the target altogether.

Paul took aim and fired. The crack snapped at the silence, and another followed in quick succession. The red tracers shot up into the tree, striking this glorious bird in the wing and forcing it to fall, flapping in panic down the middle of the tree, hitting each branch. The eagle landed close to our feet, frozen with shock. Armed with sticks, we began clubbing it to death, which somehow added to its suffering even though we were trying to put it out of its misery.

I will never forget that feeling of weakness in my legs as I looked down upon this huge majestic bird, which was so much bigger as it lay sprawled on the ground than it was only a few moments ago. Still we rained our blows – repeatedly in mercy – upon it. It seemed such a waste of nature to have this bird of prey dead at our feet, its life taken by our callous hands and unthinking, selfish thoughts.

Some of us began collecting wood for a fire while others started filleting steaks from the bird whose flesh looked the same as a chicken's. When the fire was ready and all the meat was cut and the time came to braai, we could not bring ourselves to eat. All of us had silently given Paul the go-ahead to kill the eagle, but now we were sickened to our stomachs and had lost our appetite to eat it.

Deep inside, I knew that this dark day would live with me forever, because of the selfish part I had played in the wasted death of a magnificent bird. I took a good look at the head, with its big eyes and beautifully curved black beak, before I cut it off, along with two of its claws, and placed them in a plastic bag. I tied the bag and used an elastic band to further seal it before placing it in a pouch inside my *grootsak*, zipping the pocket firmly closed.

Walking away from the scene, I still could not believe what we had done, or that I had been a part of something so totally contrary to my love for nature. I think I wanted the head to somehow balance the wrong, and I kept it in my *grootsak*, rotting with maggots for two weeks inside the zip-up pouch. Eventually I felt ready to bury it, and placed it in a hole far away from where the rest of its body had been left to rot.

My thinking and actions had become irrational. We drove ourselves forward in different ways to combat our wild, crazed life at nature's fingertips, and bush survival was beginning to drive us slightly insane.

Ever since that event, there is not a single bird that enters my vision, flying the open skies or sitting in a treetop, that does not shock me back to that sad and so-selfish day.

That night, we took up our sleeping positions in a straight line with Bravo section, placed 50 metres from us, followed by Charlie, also 50 metres apart. Our ears blocked out the odd bark of a dog in the distance and the nightly sounds of bushbaby cries, which seemed all around us as our eyes shut out another day.

On hearing movement, we jolted from our shallow sleep, springing to full alert and grabbing at our rifles. Instantly we hammered off rounds into the dark bush, spraying sweeping, automatic fire into the position where we heard the disturbance. Tracers gave a brief illumination as lines of red disappeared into the night, offering a rare glimpse of a tree or a bush.

With no return fire, we quickly stopped and strained our ears against the silence and our racing hearts. All of a sudden, Bravo rocked the silence' they had added their firepower along with Charlie's. To us it sounded as though our invisible target had moved westwards by 100 to 150 metres across our platoon's fire, and then vanished into thin air as silence once again reclaimed the night.

Whenever we heard a sound, we gave no thought as to where our bullets could end up. We knew quite well that we could have shelled a kraal full of locals. Had we done this, we would have been none the wiser, unless it was reported back to us the following day.

That morning, when we woke as the sun broke through the trees, we had a very strange feeling, for a totally new area had presented itself and we were unaware of our surroundings, having taken our sleeping position under darkness. Crawling out of our sleeping bags, we looked up to see a forest of thick, straight, and very tall trees stretching 20 to 30 metres above us. The ground was hilly and so out of character to the normal flatness of SWA, with a beautiful coolness about it as the green trees shielded us from the daily fireball.

Barely awake, we looked around believing that we had awoken in a different land – a place that seemed more soothing and comforting in comparison to the scrubby and never-ending, dusty, and waterlogged plains that we had become so used to. These small banks now explained why we had rolled from our initial sleeping positions with some of us waking up in the dip of the bank a few metres from our rifles. To see our rifles further than arm's reach was a shock in itself, to have woken without our rifles at our sides, in the darkness, was like playing a game of Russian roulette.

Grabbing our rifles, we scouted the hard, uneven area over two-metre-high hills, only to drop down a few metres over a meandering course of hills and hollows, all in a vain attempt to find any telltale signs of enemy presence. All we came up with were a few footprints, now days old, in crisscross patterns across the cool dusty earth, below the old steadfast trees.

The scenery change was short-lived. We emerged out of the forest and back onto the plain where a two-metre-high anthill reminded us that we were most definitely still wandering over the soils of SWA.

One good thing that came from our sleeping spot was the fact that we were all at least one magazine lighter for the onward patrol, where every ounce of weight counted, especially when we were the ones lugging it on our backs.

After another ten kilometres, we arrived back at Beacon 10, the point we had started from exactly one week ago. Nothing had changed on the scenic front and water still covered huge parts of land, and the long green grass was now waving to us in the breeze. Our faces and lips continued to burn under the haze of the sun, our bush hats offering some relief to our scalps. Flies still buzzed about our faces, pestering us as they crawled in and out of any opening, into our eyes, ears, noses, and mouths. How this action angered us was a torture that words cannot come close to describing. These lightning-quick pests bugged the hell out of us from one step to the next, never leaving us alone for one minute.

After staying one-and-a-half days in one place, we got the order from Lieutenant Bam to prepare to move out. Having dried our boots in the sun, we now pulled them onto our feet, which had now shrunk a size. The leather had become rock-hard. Our feet ached, and we began treading lightly around our gear as we began packing up. With a swing of our packs onto our backs, locking the plastic clips together and pulling the straps tightly down our chests and one across our stomachs, we were now prepared for the next patrol.

Greg sat comfortably, like a king in his bivi, under the shade of a huge makalani palm tree and blatantly told Grant that he was not going to move. Grant, his section leader, had no choice but to inform Lieutenant Bam of his troop's insubordination.

Lieutenant Bam emerged through the open bush and cracked' he began cursing Greg, calling him every word under the sun as he too tried to get him up and moving. The rest of us were not too happy as we watched, wasting time, standing still loaded like docile donkeys with our overweight packs buckling our backs. Eventually, after more threats, Greg finally succumbed to the inevitable, rose up, and broke down his shaded camp and joined the rest of Platoon 3, which had waited nearly half an hour for him to join the line.

Platoon 3 moved out and joined up with Platoons 1 and 2, and we began our walk from the Yati in the late afternoon, under a dark sky in a southwesterly direction towards Ombalantu. With the ground completely waterlogged, we had no choice but to walk out of this mess, for it was impossible for the vehicles to reach us and lift us out of our position.

It was just as well that we had no idea what we were in for. Had we known, a few of us, irrationally, might have inflicted injuries to spare us from the ordeal.

Our patrol began with at least 100 of us spread out in a long line, walking in the same direction under a refreshing, cool drizzle. It did not take long for the drizzle to turn to showers, blinding our vision as it belted down, lashing at our faces as the water ran from our heads and down our angry faces.

The lieutenants and corporals constantly egged us on, and we averaged four kilometres an hour, stumbling onward, cursing through more water than land. One minute we were trudging through knee-deep water, and the next we were dropping to our waists as we walked into concealed holes. Our clothes were soaked to the skin and had been for hours, adding weight and discomfort to our already unbearable patrol with absolutely no end in sight.

Soon the darkness was on us, adding more gloom as it blanketed our clenched expressions of physical discomfort, our heads swirling in madness. Our thighs had been rubbed raw, along with the cracks of our buttocks from the constant friction of wet cloth against tender skin, which added further insult to injury. The heavy army boots felt like lead weights pulling down at our blistered and raw feet with each weary step. Blindly we followed each other through the sounds of splashing and cursing, we literally felt our way forward.

Most of us walked on in a numbed silence, internalizing our pain, while others shouted into the night to relieve themselves of their anger.

'Fuck this shit!' someone yelled out.

10. And the rains came

'Keep quiet! *Hou jou bek!*' Hold your mouth!, the rank howled back.

Inside our minds, we were stumbling through the threshold of insanity, cursing at our misfortune, driven on with this forced march. Splashing with each step, I walked past Van Dyk, a big Afrikaner from Platoon 1 who was openly crying through his pain and exhaustion in this helpless situation that we were all in. He had shed his brown pants and his kit and stumbled on in his white underwear to prevent further chafe between his thighs. His LMG was slung over his neck and shoulders, and he bowed over it as if in prayer, whimpering and sniffling with each heavy step. He had reached his breaking point, but he had no choice but to continue on, with the three platoons, on this devilish march.

Our intense training at 1-South African Infantry Battalion had stood us in good stead, with an unbelievably strong mind-set and an extremely high threshold of pain. Our minds began to tune out the pain and dull the anguish through *vasbyt*, as we faced up to the bleak situation with perseverance, stamina and endurance, which led us forward.

Our sense of time and distance had long abandoned us' we had hit this invisible brick wall, and only our legs could keep stride with a fellow troop, hardly visible through the darkness.

When thirst overcame us, we either drank from the ground or wrung out our sodden bush hats into our dry mouths. There were times when we held our trembling hands cupped to our mouths, slurping at the water in hungry gulps as it pissed down upon us.

With the hours drawing painfully by, I secretly wished for an attack so we could just stop and take our chances with death, which had to be better than the torture we were struggling through.

Thunder rolled about us, followed a few seconds later by the sharp, cutting cracks of lightning, which shot across the blackened sky, striking at faraway, imaginary targets.

As we walked, jumbled lines of a Laura Branigan song I had heard so many times through basic training, and in and out of my first year, shot through my mind with so much meaning.

I could hear her catchy voice echoing through the darkness with only the slosh of boots and heavy breathing to distort the sound, as if she was pulling me through the night. Even though, in her words, we barely had the will to keep up the fight, it certainly took all my self-control to hold myself back from 'cracking' and screaming out to the heavens for an end to the torment.

I began thinking about this border war, and wondered how anyone in his right mind would sign-up for extended service or choose a career as a soldier to experience these miserable conditions. On this border I couldn't help but think, by the law of averages increasing over time, how soldiers would see contact and be dealt severe injury or even death.

Shaking my head as if to bring myself back to reality, the words of the song seemed to sum up my mental breakdown – very little control left in me as I literally willed myself on from a reserve I had hidden deep within, a reserve that I had no idea lay in my character and that was also very evident in the rest of Platoon 3. I had to believe that this night would end, otherwise I would have ended up like Van Dyk, crying in delirium, having hit the wall, with no will to try and fight, moving hopelessly forward to an end that had to come.

After walking and swaying on stumbling feet for eight hours without stopping, covering a distance of 25 to 30 kilometres, we saw bright lights bursting from the rainy darkness ahead of us.

'Could this be the end, or are these lights a figment of our imagination?' we asked ourselves with hope.

Getting closer to the light, the flat, waterlogged terrain became visible, which made it slightly easier to navigate our steps. It really did not matter any more, as we had fallen in fatigue and the unevenness of the surface so many times' once more would not matter. But it was the light that was drawing us to it, like a moth to a candle, as we walked on with a second wind in its path. It was not long before we noticed the built-up sand walls of a base camp. Which one we had no idea, as it illuminated from the shadows growing in size with each energized step.

With our bodies doubled over our rifles, we dragged ourselves through the entrance in a semi-conscious state, totally blinded by the light as it bore burning holes into our sockets and made us feel like we had entered through the gates of heaven.

It did not take long for us to realize that we had finally reached our destination, and when we did we dropped to the ground where we stood. Our bodies shut down, and we sat with the million-mile stare frozen into our pale faces as the torrents of rain continued to lash at us. Totally oblivious to the rain and the mud, we huddled against the storm in depressed groups while we waited on the order that would again move us.

This had been the most challenging and demanding march that we had ever been exposed to in our army lives, and words will never come close to capturing the full extent of how the event was played out. To totally comprehend this episode, from walking through the overcast day into the hellish night, our lives had to be lived for those eight hours, within our boots and souls, with a saturated

30 kilograms of gear strapped to our backs and our minds raging with anger and hatred at this land, the army, and the turmoil we were trapped in.

'Coffee, coffee!' an excited shout echoed from somewhere in the base.

The next minute we saw an urn of hot coffee sitting on a fold-out table under the shelter of an overhang, and a dry troop from the Ombalantu base standing next to it. Feverishly we dug into our packs in search of our fire buckets, and with them clutched in our hands we joined the long line.

With our hands outstretched and shaking like leaves in the wind, the troop flicked the handle, allowing the warm coffee to spill into our smoke-blackened and dented metal canteens. We all eagerly awaited the warmth that the coffee would bring to our freezing bodies. Sipping at it in silence, we cupped the metal warming our hands as we shook, frozen to the bone, each sip doing little to console our desperate condition. But nevertheless, it did help.

Within minutes, a crisp and very dry-looking Staff Smit emerged before us and bellowed into our faces: '*Klim op die Samils!*' Climb on the Samils!.

We looked at him with hatred, and everyone was thinking the same thing: You fuckin' bastard, do you have any idea where the fuck we have been while you have been sitting dry on a bed in the base?

Unable to move, he screamed at us again: '*Fok weg nou, op die Samils!*' Fuck away now, on the Samils!, with not a hint of sympathy or compassion for our helplessness.

Feeling like animals herded from one nightmare to the next, we climbed onto the open Samil and sat, quietly dreading the next nightmare soon to begin. Waiting on the open trucks, the rain continued to torment us and our minds began to wonder why we had been marched with such urgency from Beacon 10 to Ombalantu.

Now, with further urgency, we waited to be driven out without time for a quick rest. Suddenly a few of us began to worry about being pulled out for an operation into Angola. This thought began to fuel panic within us, for we knew only too well that as Ratel soldiers we would be used first in an attack on a SWAPO base. Immediately we began to doubt how invincible we were, and we closed our eyes on our world, these fears still running rampant through our minds, and the line of insanity tugging again at our mental being.

When the Samils started, our eyes shot open and our hearts seemed to miss a beat as the two-vehicle convoy left the base at close to 02:00. Huddled together, the wind ripped at our wet clothing and through our chilled bones as we sat like statues, glued to the metal floor and surrounded in silence and blackness – all of which heightened our unknown fear. Our energy had long deserted us, and our spirits were at an all-time low, leaving us with no will to even crack. So we let time and pain take its course, believing that life could not get any worse.

Internally we cursed this country, with all of our inflicted suffering, aware that the earliest escape was serious injury or death. With our rifles tightly gripped in our frozen hands, we sat unsleeping and stiff as the wind cut through us, while we waited for daylight to wash away our hardship and take with it our burning red and raw rashes, between our legs and the cracks of our buttocks.

On reaching the tar road, the Samils raced full-tilt in a direction that we were none the wiser, but we no longer cared.

We were at the end of our tether, and I could not care less anymore if I lived or died. Either way, I just wanted this nightmare to end!

1985-Owamboland. Patrolling the Yati and laden like mules, crossing an Oshana in the height of the rainy season.

11

Etosha National Park
Ambushing the enemy

After three hours of wallowing in our deepest nightmare, we drove into the Oshivelo base camp as the sun was breaking over the peaceful bushveld. Our Samils were met by the Ratels of Alpha Company from our battalion, which were now based at 61-Mechanized Battalion.

This was the base where we of Platoon 3 believed our company should have been stationed, considering our proven superior combat skills over Alpha Coy. Now, with their unexpected meeting, we most definitely began to suspect that something major was on the cards.

After a brief chat with some of Alpha's troops, we were ordered into the tent area of the camp, and our platoon designated two tents to dump our gear and grab a section of ground on which to sleep. At once we set about reorganizing our kit, fear of the next order driving us out and into another distant nightmare. Our wet sleeping bags and clothes were hung over the tent sides and we welcomed each ray of burning heat upon our strewn-out kit, which looked as though a bomb had just exploded within our new dwelling.

With a little free time on our hands, we took the opportunity to wash our clothes under cold water for the first time in three-and-a-half weeks. Equipped with a hard scrubbing brush and a block of Sunlight soap, we made our way to the toilet area, where we found a few stainless steel sinks into which to throw our half-wet clothes, still wet from the night before.

In spite of the downpour, our shirts were still lined with salt stains from all the sweating, and our collars were as black as the ace of spades, and were hard and solid. Our upright collars would have made Elvis very proud, except for the fact that they stood stiff around the backs of our necks – not from starch but from filth and grime. Our brown uniform, which was certainly browner before the wash, came out a lot cleaner and had a friendlier smell to it. Our hands instantly became spotless and wrinkled pink – a feeling we had not been used to but enjoyed nonetheless.

On our first night in Oshivelo we were given the green light to buy beer, and it was such an exciting time to somehow feel normal again, even if only for the duration of the six-pack of ice-cold Castle or Lion. With our beers clutched in one hand and our rifles in the other, we made our way to a screen and parked ourselves in rows, waiting for the light to fade so that the movie could begin.

For us, something so simple became so thrilling as we sipped on our beers and got caught up in the moment, leaving behind the patrols, ambushes, and nightly sleeps in tight circles.

The following day, with a clean and slightly more faded uniform, we left the base in Buffels for another stint in the bush. The Buffels branched off the tarred road and took us into one of Africa's finest game reserves. We entered at the Namutoni Gate into the Etosha National Park. Short of reaching the old white German fort, we branched off to the right on a dirt road, driving for half an hour along the length of border fence while looking through the dust over the vast, open, flat plains. In the distance we saw a giraffe, towering over the green canopy of the thorn trees, which were scattered across the dry and dusty terrain. This was such a typical African scene – one of calm, peace and beauty. Unfortunately, for us this moment was lost and could not be appreciated, as we journeyed on under rigid orders.

Dust poured out from behind the vehicles as we followed the thick, heavy, and sandy road, only accessible by a four-wheel drive. The Buffels took us in a north-easterly direction, into an area of wooded savanna in contrast to the western side of the park, which was stripped of shade, leaving a dry, rocky surface covered with thorn scrub and offering little cover to the herds of animals that wandered across the plain.

Our Buffel came to a stop within a clump of trees on our left and the three-metre-high electric fence on our right. In sections, we began digging shallow holes under the shade and cover of the overhanging trees, with our positions facing onto the sandy road and fence. Shortly after we had dug ourselves in, Captain Delport came over the radio, informing us that ten terrorists had been spotted in the area where we were now positioned. After a few minutes, we heard the unmistakable sound of the Alouette gunships as they flew over our position in the hunt for these ten, but ended up returning to base empty-handed, leaving them to hopefully run into our ambush position.

Fully aware that terrs were in the area, we took up our guard duty in a tree overlooking the fence five metres in front of our dugouts. When I was awakened for my one-hour stand, I climbed up the tree with my rifle slung over my back and a set of night-sights in my one free hand. I climbed at least three metres up and found a good position in which to lean back against the trunk of the tree, with my feet standing on a thick branch. Once in a comfortable position, with my rifle slung with its belt around one shoulder hanging in front of me, I put the night-sights to my eyes and began scanning through the thick bush on the other side of the fence – through a hazy, slimy green, illuminating the night into day.

After close on ten lonely minutes in the tree, with each sound threatening me, I heard a rustle that sounded very close. Instantly I felt my heart smacking against the walls of my chest as my legs went weak with fear and my eyes stayed transfixed on the area of bush before me. I held my breath under a cold sweat, waiting for that sound to come at me again, but all I could hear was my heart, pounding with the intensity of a sledgehammer.

'Where are these fuckers?' I mouthed through dry, unwavering lips.

I felt sweat sticky on my hands and gripped my rifle tighter.

I continued scanning the bush with the night-sights, and the harder I looked into the vision of green, the more I saw a tangle of darkened, shadowy shapes, closely resembling faces. Paranoia gripped me. Desperately trying to untangle the shapes, I pushed my back into the tree, and with my legs positioned on two firm branches, I readied myself to fire. I flicked the safety to automatic and, with my finger glued to the trigger, I was ready to fire at a split second's notice. All of a sudden I heard the same rustling, and I again fought against the darkness. I tried to determine its origin, despite my disorientation and the otherwise silent blackness. Again I waited, but this time I was ready for the figure or figures to emerge from the bush at any second. And yet they stayed hidden.

I knew I was a vulnerable target, and if I shot I would give away my position – making myself a sitting duck, with no cover to hide behind. I too would have been in the direct fire of the rest of my section, which could easily shoot upwards from disorientation through sleep and the ensuing chaos.

After listening intently for a few agonizing minutes, paralysed with fear, I realized to my shock that the rustling was coming from behind, and then it hit me' I made sense of the sound. It was one of the troops rolling and turning in his sleeping bag. What a sense of relief it brought me, and I sighed through heavy breathing, strength quickly returning to my tense body.

I had been fighting waves of paranoia for at least 20 minutes, and to say that I was shit scared would be putting it very mildly. That was one of the quickest and scariest hours that I had experienced, drawing my watch to a close. Thankful, I climbed down the tree and gladly passed the sword to the next in line.

I crawled into my shallow dugout, welcoming the safety it offered compared to the openness of being perched in the tree. Fully clothed, I climbed into my sleeping bag and zipped myself closed. Lying still on my back, my head resting on a small brown towel, I gazed at the beautiful clear sky through the overhang of branches.

My attention was directed at the stars as they twinkled above me, sparkling like diamonds through the clarity of a pollution-free skyline. I followed the path of a falling star as it dropped from its suspended position and fizzled out to nothing, and then my roaming eyes caught sight of a satellite.

I found the Southern Cross, marked by the stars, and close to it the arrow pointing northwards. This picture above us was an unforgettable sight, with no city lights to dim the beauty and no aeroplanes or traffic to disrupt the calm. We were at peace with nature, which I used as my escape from the tension that came with this on-and-off hell that had become our way of living.

Wayne and Alan, who were with Charlie section just east of us, had a similar experience to mine. They had left their section's ambush position in search of water but had somehow lost their bearings on their return. With their heightened anxiety as darkness began to set in, they kept on moving forward until they heard a rustling in front of them, which brought them to an abrupt halt. They froze in fear and flicked their safety catches onto automatic, holding their breath for the next rustle. When it came they were ready to fire, but they still could not quite place the direction of the sound.

'If we hear it again, let's just shoot!' Wayne whispered to Alan.

Stiff and tense, they waited for what could be anything from a lion to a terr. Then, like a puzzle piece falling into place, they spotted a landmark through the darkened shadows and instantly realized that they were standing only a stone's throw from Charlie's ambush position. The section was asleep in their sleeping bags, which had again caused all the rustling.

Again friendly fire could easily have brought death to some of Charlie section and destroyed that young and invincible shroud that we wore more often than not.

On the fifth night of our ambush, we were startled awake by gunfire to the right of my sleeping position. Bennie, Laurence, and Sandor, positioned behind a huge fallen trunk of a tree, had heard movement and opened fire with R4s and the LMG, ripping at the calm silence with a constant barrage of automatic fire. I grabbed my rifle and was ready to shoot, but waited to see if I could see any flashes of fire coming towards us, but I saw none.

After about 20 seconds the firing stopped, and through the chilled and churned-up silence we heard the moaning of a cow on the other side of the fence. Suddenly it was evident what had just happened. The movement through the bushes were cows, which had been cut down through the hail of fire.

The painful moaning carried on through the night and into the early hours of the morning, which was made worse by the shrill laughter of a hyena that smelled fresh blood. The moaning ate and gnawed at us, and it grew louder when the hyena began to rip out chunks of the cow, which was still barely alive.

The night was long, and we could not sleep, and lay paralyzed and wide awake, listening to the distress of the animal, unable to move from our positions and end its misery with one more bullet, helpless in wait for first light.

When morning came, we headed to the fence as a group, and with the aid of a stick pried open the electrified strands of thick wire. We climbed through, careful not to touch our rifles against the metal. Once through, we began our search, which did not take long to produce an astonishing sight. Emerging through a thick cluster of bushes, we found three dead cows.

Twenty metres further on, we found another dead cow its rump completely eaten away by the iron strong jaws of a scavenging hyena. The poor beast had been carrying a calf, which would have been born in a week or two. I remember thinking: What a waste of valuable meat in such a poor country. The local who owned these four cows must have suffered a huge setback cattle were a measure of wealth in this land.

Watching the flies crawling over the bloody flesh and shooing them from our faces, we walked off and left the cow for the scavengers. At the three untouched cows, we drew our Okapi and Swiss Army knives and became scavengers ourselves. We hacked out thick chunks of bloody steaks the size of our arms. We gave absolutely no thought to the possibility that the cattle might have been carrying a sickness that could have drastically affect our health. Why would we even bother to worry? After all, nothing could touch us' at 18 and 19 years old, we were invincible.

With our hands bloodied and our mouths watering, we carried away as much meat as we could back to our dugout positions, leaving behind three mutilated carcasses far worse than what the hyena could have done. We collected wood and prepared the biggest braai that the Etosha had ever seen.

While we sat around our fires, we wondered if the owner would report his loss of cattle, like the local a couple of weeks ago who had lost two of his goats to two of our knives. Those two goats had to be paid for by Corporal Gregan, who in turn we had to pay back.

But in the end it was all worth it to have that great taste of meat again. Time would tell if we had to pay for this meat, but this time we would definitely get our money's worth.

Looking at our piles of meat, we literally had enough meat to feed an army, and we braaied and braaied for days.

Some of the meat we passed on to our fellow platoon mates further down from us, and the rest we braaied over the hot coals before placing it in the plastic wrapping that covered our ration packs. With the package tightly sealed, we buried it in a shallow hole within our sleeping area, under the coolness of the soft sand – marking the burial spot with a stick, to be dug up for a later meal. This became our refrigerator and our safe haven against prowling animals attracted by the scent of meat.

What a treat it was to chew on fresh meat again, but unfortunately our stomachs did not take kindly to the overload of this rich overload and as a result we suffered chronic bouts of gippo guts. This soon passed, and we resumed our feast, constantly digging into the earth to retrieve nice cool steaks and we hardly touching our dry rat packs – except for that all-too-important coffee fix.

To an outsider looking on our group, we must have looked like a bunch of cannibals. Ripping hungrily at the dried meat with dirty faces and blackened hands covered in dirt, and with grime stuck deep under our fingernails, we sat totally oblivious to the world around us, our sole focus being the meat clutched in our hands.

With bloated bellies and a few luxurious days of bush feasting behind us, we were lifted by Samils and taken back to the Oshivelo base. Once back in the base, Brian – who had laid ambushed with Bravo section a few hundred metres from our position – swore that he had seen a black face in the bush through his night-sights, but before he could fire, the face had disappeared into the shadows.

Was it real or was it his paranoid imagination? We would never know, but one thing was for sure – the terrs were definitely in the area.

Inside the tent we unwound, enjoying the safety in sheer numbers within the base. After a shower, we relaxed, feeling like new people, having washed the past from our dirty bodies and then topping it off with a few too many cold beers. This always restored us to normality, and we laughed through our drunken slurs, sharing stories from our past ambush positions.

Daily I entered information into my pocket diary, logging events and experiences that we were exposed to – something I had kept up secretly from the very first day I entered the operational area. This was a highly illegal practice, and I always did so away from the watchful eyes of the rank' for no one from the outside world was allowed to know what was going on up there – including the South African public.

Had it been found, this little brown book would definitely have been destroyed and I surely would have faced repercussions. To my knowledge, I was the only one logging information of our experiences. To make matters worse, I had a smuggled camera, which fitted perfectly into my chest webbing along with my five magazines. The thin, black camera took up the sixth pouch in the middle, which at a quick glance could easily be taken for a magazine. The two rolls of film I carried would definitely have been destroyed had the camera been found. This was not a place where cameras were welcome, and journalists and camera crews were forbidden to record any footage in SWA or southern Angola, unless by rare invitation of the South African Defence Force.

All letters written within the operational area were read and censored with a thick black marker, erasing names of places, events, and dates before being stamped '*GESENSOR*' censored in purple ink, and initialled along with a number logging the letter. After this letters were mailed on the Hercules flights between Ondangwa and Grootfontein and Pretoria's Waterkloof Air Force Base.

What happened up here in northern South-West Africa and Angola was for us of the SADF and other military units to know, with no formal backing, which could be used as proof against the SADF and in turn the South African government. Secrecy was definitely the byword in the South African Defence Force.

After a drunken night we were back in the Etosha aboard Buffels, with all of us suffering hangovers, along with the latest news from Captain Delport in our thoughts. Seven Ground Force PLAN had been spotted and were on the run inside the park. Almost immediately we were dropped in an area and set up an ambush in eager anticipation. We wondered with hope if we would get our first kill. With time drawing out along with our patience as the heat and hangovers tortured us, word came over the radio that the Parabats from 1 Parachute Battalion, our neighbours in Tempe, Bloemfontein, had shot and killed two, and that Koevoet had claimed the other five. One of the five was a senior colonel, whose head was worth R20 000.

Koevoet was a police counter-insurgency unit, which operated from the South African-designed Casspirs, which for their part were mine-protected infantry fighting vehicles ideal for the harsh terrain. Most of these vehicles had twin MAGs mounted in a roof turret and a second for the gunner, who stood next to the driver. These fighting units comprised mainly ex-terrorists who had been captured while fighting for SWAPO. After many long interrogations, and in many cases torture, they had turned and chosen to fight alongside the South Africans.

Most of the vehicles had white leaders, some of whom signed up after completing their National Service. Rumour had it that some of these white guys had dropped out from National Service, having spent time in military jails with their hard-line approach to authority and couldn't-give-a-fuck attitude to the regimental order of strict discipline. How true this was, we had no idea, but one thing was for sure: When we saw them aboard their Casspirs, we looked at them with respect and at a safe distance, believing that what they had seen had altered their minds.

Some of the Koevoet policemen were ex-Rhodesians who had experienced a decade of bush war within their own country. With their war over as Rhodesia lost its name to the newly independent Zimbabwe, they entered into a new one with the same bush principles and bloodshed and led some of the Casspirs into battle. It was mentalities such as these that made Koevoet one of the most successful operational units, with a very high kill ratio.

Rumour also had it that they were stoned most of the time and drank spirits heavily. Again, whether this was true, we had no idea, and it certainly was no business of ours if they did. I would think it normal to find some way out, and to dull the after-effect of killing.

The English word for Koevoet is 'crowbar,' and I can only imagine that they got their name from leveraging information from the tough local Owambo population loyal to SWAPO, which in turn led to numerous SWAPO deaths.

When we heard that Koevoet and the Parabats had made the kills, it really angered us, for in all honesty we believed that today would be the day that we killed a SWAPO guerrilla. Unfortunately that hunger was short-lived. Some of us were lucky, and others very unlucky, that the terrs had chosen a route slightly away from our ambush site.

At 11:00, Samils lifted us out after only one peaceful night in the quiet bush amongst animal sounds – something an avid camper would have given anything to experience, with the exception of bodily tension. Over the sandy roads, we bounced up and off the metal lines of seating on the ride back to the Oshivelo camp, gulping down mouthfuls of dust as the brown cloud settled under the canopy and covered us from head to toe. Once in the camp, we lined up for our pay, which amounted to R30.

It went straight to beer and cigarettes, with absolutely nothing else to spend it on. Fortunately for us, beer cost barely R1, so we were able to purchase a fair amount with our measly pay cheque. The more we drank, the more it drowned the tension and brought us back to a feeling almost normal – close to that of a summer campout, with jokes and stupid antics shared around the fire and within the canvas walls of the candle-lit tents.

With the arrival of another morning, however, reality dawned upon us through a thick cloud inside our heavy heads. We were ordered to board the Buffels for another patrol. Strapped in and ready to go, we left the base at 09:00, with one ration pack to last for three days. In other words, we would go hungry for two of the days. The only comforting thought was that we were in a vehicle instead of on our feet, and that meant a lot.

Somehow we managed to stretch our rations over the three days, more thankful to be moving in a vehicle than burning our energy with foot power. So long as there was always one hot coffee to begin the day and one to end it, that was all we really needed from these survival kits, which we loathed with such passion.

Back in base, Captain Delport summoned us to the small, open parade ground area and informed us that from 1 February to 13 February, a total of 43 terrorists had been killed, with a loss of 20 of our own. Unfortunately, many of our own had lost their lives through negligence, friendly fire, and – to a lesser extent – malaria.

Another piece of information our Captain gave us involved an ambush that comprised around 40 terrorists, whom a coloured unit drove into. They had suffered severe casualties, but to what extent we were not informed.

In another incident, one of the local Owambo civilians picked up a Russian SKS grenade that had been hidden for later retrieval. Unfortunately it exploded, killing one and badly injuring four others. It was almost as though this information was purposely fed to us as a reminder that our own people were getting killed in SWA' and in a subtle way I think our captain was trying to tell us to keep our guard up.

On the next patrol, two Bushman trackers joined our platoon from 201 Battalion, and one of them rode with us in our Buffel. These two Bushmen looked so out of place clad in South African browns, with the smallest size hanging off their slender frames and big boots protruding from their feet – looking every bit too heavy for them to lift off the ground. Their G3 rifles looked cumbersome in their grasp, in comparison to the grace with which they carried a bow and arrow.

They are a very small people, with an average height of between 4'10" and 5'2". Their features are adapted to the extremely harsh desert climate. Bushmen are hairless, except for their heads – which with their tightly coiled black peppercorn hair leaves patches of scalp exposed, allowing them to stay cool.

Their flat yellow faces hung loosely, the folds of skin forming a very wrinkled and wise old look. Two slit eyes gaze out from beneath a weathered face that is protected from the glare by the fat of their laden eyelids. With a wide grin, their smiling faces stretched apart, showing off a beautiful set of ivory-white teeth. The wind ripped at us while we stood straight, gazing at the dusty road and hunting for spoor – that is, footprints from our enemy's boots.

The San were amazing trackers and could read spoor with the Buffels travelling at 30 kilometres an hour. Our eyes darted from the road and back to the Bushman, who scanned the ground with deep concentration.

Suddenly he signalled a sighting and Bennie immediately stopped the vehicle. We all clambered out, following the Bushman's lead as he stooped into a squatting position and examined the prints. The boot print was old, with many telltale signs to prove its age. Insects had crossed the print, leaves had fallen into it, and the wind had blown sand, distorting the indentation. Reading out the information, our Bushman tracker told us that our enemy had passed through a couple of days ago.

While we took a break from our driving and rested next to the Buffel, our Bushman tracker started to dig into the earth. He squatted and dug, his hands pulling out a brownish root from the dry soil. He held it above his head, and with his mouth wide open he slowly milked tiny droplets of clear juice from it.

We watched and listened in awe as they broke into an excited chatter in a language of short pops and clicks, made by the tongue as it moved to various parts of the mouth. Smiling with fascination, and having no idea what they were saying, we enjoyed the sounds, which flowed like music to our ears. We were excited to have been exposed to a culture so far removed from our own.

Once back on patrol, Paul relayed a message that had just been transmitted over the radio. Another eight terrorists had been spotted in the Etosha Park, with Koevoet in hot pursuit. It was not long before we heard from the radio that Koevoet had made contact and killed all eight, dashing our hopes for some action.

After a dusty and uneventful day, we returned to the Oshivelo base, still with lots of energy – having not been forced to use our feet, which was a huge blessing.

Lazing in our tents, we were suddenly startled by an earth-shattering bang. A group of us rushed from our tent into the neighbouring one with that feeling of hoping for the best but expecting the worst, converging on the place the explosion had come from. Barging into the tent, we were met with a stunned, ghostly silence, and then we saw Oosthuizen's face, covered in blood and frozen with shell shock. Norman, standing next to Oosie, was also bleeding from his injuries and was equally as pale. Automatically I assumed that a shot had been fired accidentally, but that was not the case.

Oosthuizen had been playing with the Claymore mine detonator, and for some unknown reason he had made contact with the electrical wires on the battery. This immediately fired off the detonator, propelling sharp shards of metal across the tent and into his knee and face. Norman, who was sitting next to him, also absorbed some of the flying shrapnel.

Our medic, Thackery – whom we called 'Sax' – quickly attended to him, applying pressure to his facial wounds before he was carried away to the medical tent, where he had the shrapnel carefully removed from his face and knee. With sobering thoughts, we looked down upon the droplets of blood circled on the dirty canvas floor. None of us could quite believe, not only had he survived the blast, but also that he still had two eyes in his head.

In the medical tent he lay resting for the next couple of days, awaiting his fate. When we saw him again, his face was scabbing, with pink cutlines across his cheeks and around his eye sockets.

For the damage he had caused to 'state property,' and for endangering the lives around him, he was confined to barracks and handed over to the RPs. In the hands of the tough and unforgiving Regimental Police, Oosie was given three days of intense CB drills, which lasted from sunrise until sunset.

Returning from one of our Buffel patrols, we caught sight of his red metal helmet, which he had been forced to wear as a statement for all to see that he was serving out punishment for his stupidity and disregard for his fellow troops' lives. He ran and sweated with his full kit, at the mercy of the RPs' and I bet after the first day, with all the physical abuse and the scorching heat, he must have wished he were dead.

On the next patrol, Brian for some reason had wound up in our Buffel, and while we were stationary he fidgeted in his webbing and pulled out a mortar bomb. Casually he stood up and held the bomb to his chest, and to the utter disbelief of all the watchful eyes around him, he released the bomb from his grasp. It landed on its head, bouncing off the metal floor with a hollow thud before rolling to a stop against the base of the metal side plate.

'Are you fuckin' mad?' we all screamed out, racked with fear.

'These things can go off at any fuckin' time!' another troop yelled out.

To our shock, Brian again raised the bomb' and before he could drop it, we bailed over the side to the safety of the ground below.

'Go ahead and kill yourself, but don't wipe us out,' someone shouted.

With a glint in his eye and a malicious roll of laughter, he dropped it twice more. We watched, believing that he was about to blow himself sky-high. Brian was crazy and had no fear of death' he cherished the gamble as a huge joke. Fortunately for him, and to our astonishment, the bomb did not explode – leaving him to laugh aloud at our wound-up paranoia.

The heat and the boredom were starting to take their toll on us, and actions like these drew us dangerously close to losing our lives on account of sheer stupidity and gross negligence.

Is this the *bossies* or *bosbefok* – the madness – we had heard about when soldiers began to go crazy on the border? I wondered, having no idea and nothing to compare it with. But it was madness – something that would certainly have never been tolerated in the eagle eyes of any rank higher than a section leader.

After a short stay at base, our Buffel took us back to the Etosha Park for another patrol. An urgent message shot statically through the radio, blatantly stating that three terrorists had been spotted in our area.

With the keen scent of our trackers we picked up their tracks, which were only minutes old and raced towards the sound of gunships flying very low over the open bush – not much further ahead from us. On approaching the site, we were surprised to find almost 30 vehicles, which had formed three sides of a wall, with the two gunships hovering over the middle.

On our arrival, we were ordered to close off the only open side, forming a squared-off barricade of 150 metres made up of Casspirs, Buffels, and a couple of Samils. Our bodies were racing on adrenaline under the cutting drone of the rotors, and we thrust our 11 rifles over the side of the Buffel, pointing them into the long, dry grass. Our eyes remained transfixed into the square enclosure and our fingers frozen to the triggers, eager for the terrs to present their heads so that we could blow them out of the thick grass and riddle them with holes.

Staring unmoving down the length of our brown barrels, we watched the Alouette gunships swoop like overgrown birds, rising up and dropping down with their tails in the air and their blades to the ground. The pilots manoeuvred them within two metres from the ground, using the rotors like giant combs as they parted the grass in their bid to flush out the terrorists.

The pilots' concentration was written on their brows, and we looked in through the rounded glass bubble and watched them grapple with the joysticks as they fought to control their whirlybirds. In their peripheral vision, the pilots could see us soldiers with that evil glint of killer instinct, ready to pounce on the slightest movement and fire volleys below them in a split second. Both gunners were strapped behind the 20mm cannons, and they looked eagerly for their prey in the area their pilot had presented to them.

After a drawn-out hour of wait and searching, with surges of adrenaline charging through us, we were ordered to abandon our positions.

Shocked at the order, we began to depart from this dusty piece of open bush. A radio message reported that the terrorists had managed to break free from our barricade and win their freedom to live another day. This came as a decisive blow for all of us, for we were quite certain that three kills were going to be carried out.

To all of us, it proved what masters of the bush these terrorists were' having been born into it, they knew how to read it and live off it better than we would ever know.

11. Etosha National Park: Ambushing the enemy

That night we spent under the stars in the Etosha Park, still grappling with the fact that three terrorists had slipped right through our hands. The following morning, however, brought great news to our ears, via the signal from the A54 radio. A reaction unit operating under the call sign of Romeo Mike – the fighting arm of 101-Battalion – had picked up the spoor and chased the three down. They made contact, killing one and seriously wounding another, who later died. The third was later captured.

This was a great radio message, and it brought a broad smile to our faces, even though we had missed the opportunity ourselves. But at least another unit had the chance for the last laugh at their cunning expense.

News reached us regarding a local who stepped on a land mine that had been planted on a road in our area. He was severely maimed, and we were given the task of sweeping the roads for more mines. By planting these deadly mines, SWAPO had achieved their goal of creating disruption and sabotage and instilling terror into the local population.

Standing inside the mine-protected Buffel, behind the small driver's cab, we screened the sandy road ahead as we drove, hunting for any telltale signs of soil disturbance. After hours of riding into the glare, and with faces covered with dust, we returned to base with no news to report.

After a cold shower, a few warm beers, and a short but safe sleep, we were back into the bush for further road-sweeping, and then a patrol along the outskirts of the Etosha Park. After the patrol, we were given a site to set up an ambush and remain in position for the next four days.

In the front of our encampment, we set up trip flares, which consisted of a line of gut connected to the round ring-like pins in the flare itself. The gut was then pulled tight, about eight centimetres from the ground, between the two flares, which pointed skywards.

If SWAPO walked into our position through the line of gut, the tension would automatically pull the pins out and fire the flares into the sky, illuminating night into day.

The purpose of this night-time ambush was surprise. Surprise would give us the edge and allow us to hit our target before it hit us.

Wayne and I teamed up for the night, and as always closed our eyes with some hint of wonder at what the night would bring. We slept as well as a soldier could possibly sleep in an area where there seemed to be a constant threat of enemy presence, and yet we still had not seen a single terr.

In the morning we spotted a herd of eight to ten elephants that nonchalantly ploughed through the vegetation like a convoy of giant steamrollers, flattening a path and leaving behind waste in the form of round, tightly-packed, grassy, steaming balls. These graceful monarchs had very small tusks, which in the Etosha Park was quite normal, due to a chemical deficiency in the soil that inhibits the growth of ivory. From a poacher's perspective, such a circumstance certainly protected them. Captivated by their prehistoric looks, we watched these beasts trail each other in a long line. They swung their long grey trunks and grabbed at what they wished, before they were lost from our vision amongst the thick bush and mopane forest.

Unbeknown to us at the time, this elephant herd walked right into Bravo section's ambush site. Darkness gave an additional fear to the touchy situation. They came extremely close to trampling through the trip flares, but with shouts – and some loud banging of dixies on rifles – Grant and his section managed to divert these beasts and change the circumstances, which could so easily have turned ugly. Had the flares detonated, with blinding flashes and high-pitched swooshes of sound as darkness turned to light within a second, they would have panicked and could have trampled the section in their haste to escape what they would have considered an attack.

The next day, we heard a gunship through the silent, dry heat of the afternoon. The noise of it bounced off the flat, open plain. With that reassuring sound coming from the lethal flying machines, it felt good to know that we were not alone in this bush war. Seemingly out of nowhere, the camouflaged Alouette came into view and shot right over our heads, only a few metres from the ground, in its race to catch the Koevoet Casspirs. Koevoet was in hot pursuit, tracking a terrs fresh spoor, which had been tagged as a Dispatch Commander. That would be a very important kill or capture. We never learned of his fate, but judging by the thud of the 20mm cannon, we could only imagine.

On our return to Oshivelo, we were told to get packed up and be ready to move out. At midday we boarded the infamous cattle trucks, preparing our minds for the long and cramped journey that lay ahead, with our departure northwards on route to Ondangwa.

My thoughts pulled me back to that march on Ombalantu a short time earlier, and I had to wonder if our return to the area would be equally as demanding and demoralizing.

12

Patrols between beacons on the Yati

The guards manning the entrance to the Ondangwa base waved our vehicles into the well-guarded camp, in welcome for our second visit. For some reason, this time around we seemed to have a better picture of the layout and its close proximity to the local, thriving market on the outskirts of this small but important town.

Suddenly we noticed the high barricaded walls of white sand, with neat cut-ins walled with sand bags, acting as lookout and guard posts. Barbed wire adorned the length of these walls, adding further protection and stealth to this very important base, which acted – along with Oshakati – as a vital supply link to bases further north, situated along and very close to the Angolan border.

There was a hive of activity, with lots of vehicle and troop movement to and from this base. It seemed a big base to us, with straight rows of tents and neatly parked columns of Buffels, Kwevoels, and Samils lining the dusty white sand. In the centre of the camp there were high communication towers that linked northern Owamboland with the headquarters at Sector 10, along with the rest of the military bases dotted across the top part of the country.

Those lucky enough to have these camps as permanent bases for their duration of service in the operational area were spoiled with the luxuries of a life close to civvie street. There were real beds with soft foam mattresses, under the coolness of dry tents, a canteen with a never-ending supply of ice-cold beer – a dart board, television and video – good wet rations cooked over a stove in the base's kitchen – and most importantly, safety in numbers behind the towering walls. Unfortunately our berets were green and we were from 4-SAI, which meant that struggle and strife in the open bush was what had been cut out for us by the military in control of the placement of the various units in Owamboland.

With the base occupied by another unit, and with every tent taken, we were designated a dusty patch of ground on which to spread our groundsheets and sleeping bags. Lying on the stony earth and wriggling around for a more comfortable position, we looked at the dark sky and waited for the droplets of rain that would surely fall. It was no use worrying about the rain, as we needed the sleep. And so we closed our eyes, with rain hanging over our heads like an alarm clock set to go off at any minute.

The pitter-patter of light rain upon the tents around us and on our sleeping bags woke us up from a short but deep sleep. The slight warning gave us enough time to scramble into the toilet area, escaping the worst of the downpour as we sat the rest of the night out, the rain beating at the tin roof and the wind blowing some of the wetness onto us through the mesh window openings. No smell or discomfort under a shelter could compare with that cold, saturated feeling that had come our way all too often. We sat down, our only wish to remain dry. Sleep did not matter' that luxury would come later.

The month of February had been with us for two weeks, and with it came the height of the rainy season – with an average of 108 millimetres of rainfall, along with a hive of terrorist movement from southern Angola into northern SWA. These heavy rains played in favour of the terrorist influx, the pooling water concealing any trace of enemy tracks.

By mid February, small groups totalling 700 insurgents were said to be active in the operational area. Security forces were engaged in some of the fiercest fighting. By 15 February, a total of 130 insurgents had been killed, which was the largest death toll for PLAN – the People's Liberation Army of Namibia, which was SWAPO's military wing – for the first seven weeks of any year since the war had begun. There was a down side to these statistics. Five security forces were killed when their vehicle hit a land mine, which came as one of the single highest fatalities for some time.

In the Ondangwa base, while we waited patiently next to the vehicles for our orders, we saw a SWAPO terrorist being led in through the main entrance. His dark Owambo face had a white bandage, normally used for a wound dressing, bound around his eyes blindfolding his view of the strong South African presence, which looked upon him with hatred. His dirty, unbuttoned shirt hung loosely over his thin frame and medium height, and he shuffled his booted feet nervously in front of us, led on by two soldiers – one pulling at his arm for direction, and the other with his rifle levelled at the guerrilla's upper body. As suddenly as he had appeared, he disappeared for his interrogation, unaware what pain lay ahead for him.

News reached us pertaining to one of the African units, which were stationed in the area involving the death of one of their troops, who was shot by a fellow soldier. His death was blamed on excessive alcohol and jealousy over a local Owambo woman. Unfortunately, stories of this kind filtered out from less-disciplined units with some frequency, and hard spirits were one of the main factors that swayed minds to actions in some cases beyond their control.

Any downtime in the operational area went hand-in-hand with beers and hard spirits, and soldiers turned to drink through boredom. Those who had seen fighting turned to it as a stress-reliever and medicine, and for them it became a tool to keep any of those silent and tormenting demons at bay.

12. Patrols between beacons on the Yati

At 10:00 we departed from the Ondangwa Air Force base, having enjoyed some rare luxuries in the way of chocolates and small bags of chips – a taste that we savoured not knowing if it would take another seven weeks to sample such civilian food again.

After another blistering afternoon, we arrived at the Okalongo base courtesy of the cursed cattle trucks. We waited in the truck in a state of disarray from the first order, and then there was a long wait until the next, but when it came we met it with relief. Our platoon had been assigned a tent and a certain degree of respite from the rain. We had barely thrown our gear down when Corporal Doep shouted at us to form up, and so we joined the rest of our company in the centre of the base, with Captain Delport standing next to a map. With a stick in his hand, he pointed to the map of SWA and southern Angola and then moved the thin piece of wood up to our area. There, he told us, intelligence gathered from the field estimated that anywhere between 30 and 40 terrorists were operating in our area.

He told us that SWAPO was becoming sneakier, hiding their AKs and uniforms in holes below the ground, and then mixing with locals in the daytime, only to return under darkness and move off as guerrilla fighters in their quest for freedom for the people of South-West Africa.

Under last light, we all made our way to the bunkers within the fortified walls of this base and began familiarizing ourselves with the landscape relative to our arc of fire – a duty known to us only in Afrikaans as *klaarstaan*. Looking over the sandbagged walls, we watched the bushes and trees grow dark, making mental notes of certain shapes that could be mistaken for people. We did this so that when we took up our guard duties through the night, we would be familiar with the surroundings.

In the morning we left the base for another patrol, and after walking for only a few hundred metres we came across an old brown Bedford army truck, shot up and out of action, left to rot on its disintegrating rubber tyres as a reminder to the struggles of the 1970s.

On 27 February, we patrolled over the Yati and into the Cunene Province of Angola for the very first time. It now seemed so long since the first time that we had all decked, or covered, each other as we stole across the old road to place our boot print upon the Angolan soil – an achievement seeming to rival that of Neil Armstrong's landing on the moon. Then, with two prints firmly in the soil, we christened it by urinating in wide arcs, as a symbol of hatred of this land and our loathing at being here.

Platoon 3 had now walked into the Angola that we had sung songs about during those dark and distant days running in a squad in 1-SAI.

We gonna march into Angola, we gonna kill them Sam Nujoma! immediately came rushing into my mind as we walked across the beautiful, flat, tropical green savannah that stretched for miles – a sight that would have made any farmer envious.

Is this Africa? I asked myself, for the terrain seemed so vastly different from what we had seen up until now. To me, it looked as though a cutout of a green English pasture had been transplanted into this wild, open part of Africa. There were no low, neatly piled English stone-wall boundaries, but instead there was this unbroken green grass belt that carpeted the saturated ground with only a few clumps of bush, and trees in the far distance to break the expanse before us.

Spread out and sweating, we walked past round, dried-up balls of grass, which we kicked at as if we were striking a soccer ball. After the kick, we realized it was elephant droppings – or more like bombs – evidence of an elephant herd that had passed through some time ago. I would say that this was the first time any of us had witnessed such a find, with the moulded footprints baked into the soil and the grass balls proving to us that there were still roaming herds of wild animals passing freely across the savannah, without the restrictions of a boundary. This was truly wild Africa, where the animals followed their own course, hopefully being able to steer clear of the evil poachers who would go to great lengths for an old ivory tusk.

Walking further north of the Yati, still thinking of the elephants, I got the fright of my life. The bushes rustled, sending me into a panic. A second later, we saw a frightened impala spring from its hiding place and race across the open plain, leaping with agility as it floated away to the safety of the distance. Once my heart regained its beat, the buck now filling my thoughts, I wondered how long it would be before this animal became a meal for a few hungry UNITA or South African soldiers.

A few tiring kilometres of patrols behind our aching backs, we stopped for a rest under the shade of some bushes and big trees. Cushioning ourselves against our sweaty packs and enjoying the breeze blowing at our wet backs, I saw movement from the side of Crompton's *grootsak*. I had to look again to make quite sure that I was seeing what my eyes were telling me. A black-and-white striped snake, at least 60 centimetres in length, slithered out of his pack and casually descended the side of it before disappearing in its sideways movements into the thick green grass. It left us wondering how long it had hitched a ride within the comfort of Horse's pack – I mean, Crompton's – and also whether it was venomous or not. Luckily, we did not have to find out.

Our friend Horse was a tall, dark, 17-year-old from Ramsgate in Natal, who always had some guessing his race' his dark complexion and curly-black, wiry hair would throw us off. In our racial thinking, we classified him as a mixture of black and white, falling into the racial status of coloured – not that it bothered us in any way. He was a part of our platoon, and that was all that mattered. I am sure that, if he had pursued his racial classification with his military call-up, he probably would have got an exemption. His dark, long face made his green eyes stand out even more, and his tall, thin body seemed to lengthen his already long arms, which would hang down to his knees. For this bodily misfortune he was granted the name 'Horse,' and after each walk through the *oshona* we would laugh with fun at how he dragged his arms through the water, and on reaching dry land we would check his knuckles for roasties – skin that had been rubbed off.

'Horse, are your hands Okay?' we asked in our witty and sarcastic tones.

'Fuck off,' he replied in good humour, with a laugh, in total acceptance of his name and what went with it.

After an enjoyable rest behind us, we set off through the waterlogged earth, which was a breeding ground for frogs. It was as though a plague of these amphibians had hit earth, making it harder for us to step a few paces. Eventually we said, 'Fuck this,' and walked through them, squelching the frogs into the soft earth as we went. Wherever we looked, these small green frogs were teeming in their hundreds – and possibly thousands – sitting, leaping, and eating each other, an extraordinary sight. As always, nothing in the world could deter us from quenching our thirst, and after clearing a pool of the muddy water we dipped our water bottles in and watched them bubble under the murky water until they were full. If a frog did happen to get in the bottle, we just tipped it out and began filling it again, and then we closed our eyes and drank to our heart's content. Before moving on, we filled our bottles again, never wanting to be left stranded in this heat with no liquid, even if it was muddy and flavoured by a thousand frogs.

Further into Angola, we came across a rusty, yellow, metal enclosure below an old tree in the middle of nowhere. Getting up close, we realized it was an old grave overrun by weeds. A faded inscription on a metal cross gave the name of an old Portuguese colonist who had died there in the early 1900s. It left me with a strange feeling – this lonely grave of some significance, positioned in an area without a single trace of the old civilization that had once been there.

Leaving the grave behind, we continued on until a radio signal interrupted our pace. An Afrikaans voice stated that a contact had just taken place at Beacon 15 and we were to immediately head in that direction, because a group of five to seven terrorists carrying AK-47s and RPG-7 rocket launchers were heading in our direction.

Stepping up the pace with newfound energy and a goal in mind, we readied our rifles and darted our eyes across the landscape, in and out of bushes. We hunted for tracks with the skill of two Owambo soldiers, who were patrolling with us under new names we had given them – for we did not know how to pronounce their Owambo names. Moving as fast as we could with *'Talk'* Interpreter and *'Skilpad'* Tortoise, we eventually came across the enemy spoor who had crossed our area within the last ten to 15 minutes.

Crowding around the find adrenaline racing, we examined the prints close up, with verification from our two trackers that these were fresh spoor – no disturbance to the tracks in the way of leaves, insect crossings, or sand. They were perfect in every way, and the more we looked into the sandy earth, the more we could read. We could see they were on the run' the heel of their boots hardly touched the ground, for the sand had flicked out from the indentation with each running step.

While we were looking at the prints, Toth, Bennie, and a couple of others dropped their kit' and with their rifles hanging off one hand, they gave chase, following the tracks like dogs on a foxhunt.

In the distance we heard a drone of a Casspir coming from behind us, and approaching fast. Immediately we started kicking at the terrorist prints and dragging branches over them, in the hope of granting our platoon the kills – since we had found the spoor first.

With a thunderous breaking of branches, the camouflaged vehicle burst through the bushright next to us, with two black Koevoet policemen running in front of the vehicle, holding their AKs with the long, 50 round, banana-shaped magazines clipped to them. The two runners had their eyes fixed on the bushes ahead of them, one hand clutching at their rifles and the other pulling at the air to drive them forward. Sweat poured from them, running down their stoned-looking faces as they rode on waves of adrenaline.

'Money, money, money!' one shouted through clenched white teeth, without the slightest movement of his head to cast a look in our direction. They were running like two hounds, with the scent of their bounty hanging in the air. The wide-open whites of their eyes were menacing and without fear as they stared through the mopane scrub, leaving behind their prints and tyre tracks as the only proof of their whirlwind entrance and exit before our startled eyes. They were paid per kill, and yet ironically they might have ended up killing their former comrades if they had changed sides from SWAPO.

The white commander of the Casspir stood in the turret behind the Browning 12.7mm machine gun, and with a scowl he openly swore at Lieutenant Bam for

12. Patrols between beacons on the Yati

allowing us to cover the tracks. His rounded, scruffy face was covered with a ginger beard, his cold eyes shadowed under a mean frown, with a look of don't fuck with me, I can kill in a flash.

His dusty hair was short and red, and he wore a cutoff cammo shirt exposing his shoulders and arms, which were as big as thighs. He was a big, mean Afrikaner who – we all knew by his persona and vibe – had killed before. Sitting like a king in his turret, he looked down upon us, snarled in sarcasm, and was then swallowed into the thick bush as the Casspir rumbled away.

The drone gradually got fainter leaving us with dwindling hope of our platoon being able to boast of a few kills. Shortly after the Casspir had left our position, Toth, Bennie, and the others returned, very disappointed at how close they had come to a contact, only to have it snatched away by a section of mobilised Koevoet policemen. They recounted to us how they were gaining on the terrs until Koevoet drew next to them and, with a sly smile on their faces, left them choking on dust with their spirits demoralized.

After our evening meal and a hot canteen of coffee, we began setting up camp for the night at the site of joy and despair where we had found and lost the spoor. Sleep came to us within the circle of all-round protection, a slightly higher scare to it with our first sleep in Angola upon the imprinted earth of a band of ruthless and well-armed terrorists.

Through a light sleep of wonder at what had become of this group of terrorists, I lay still, taking in the silence that seemed even quieter than across the border. Thankful for the safety of our numbers under this darkness, with only a slice of moon adding a dim light to our surroundings, our eyes automatically flicked open at the slightest sound.

Looking over at my loaded rifle, I drew comfort from this cold piece of metal at my side.

In the morning we packed up and followed Koevoet's tracks 13 kilometres into Angola, walking north of the Yati. Unfortunately, after a long walk, we found nothing, losing the tracks to a *oshona*, and with this outcome we were ordered to rest and prepare our meals.

Under the sinister and watchful eyes of huge black crows, perched in the trees and glaring down at us, we began to prepare a warm meal from the ingredients of our ration packs. They constantly watched over us, squawking and calling to each other as they waited with all the time in the world for us to turn our backs on our food' and we knew if we carelessly did, our meal would become theirs.

One of these vulture-like birds swooped down when I made the costly mistake of walking over to my pack to fill my fire bucket with water, and in those fleeting few seconds it stole my red sausage-like tube of cheese. On returning to its elevated position within the tree, it screeched with glee, and they all joined in, in what felt like bird laughter directed at us.

'Piss off,' I screamed in anger, having lost the most enjoyable part of my meal. Picking up a stick, I threw it towards them, sending them into temporary flight. Unfortunately they were like mosquitoes – pests that we could not shake off – and after a very short break, they would inevitably return to try our patience.

'Watch my food,' we would say to each other if we had to step away for any reason. Grant walked away from his food without having it watched, and paid the price for it. One of these big black bastards flew down from a tree and scooped up some of his ration pack. Grant cracked, cursing these pests that were adding frustration to our already frustrated lives.

'I am going to fuckin' kill you!' he swore as he grabbed his rifle. Taking careful aim, he squeezed off a shot and blew the bird out of the tree, spraying bird and black feathers everywhere and scattering the rest of the crows in the process. After a good laugh, we enjoyed our simple meals in the silence of nature, without this unbearable and annoying bird cry that never stopped.

In the early morning, under the cooler temperature of first light, we began walking south out of Angola, looking for that all-too-important border crossing. Close to the Yati, we came across photocopied leaflets written in Owambo, lying like litter blowing in the breeze on the ground. Picking one up, we studied it, and gathered by the pictures, each having a monetary denomination attached to it – that it was offering a reward for weapons or information on any terrorist infiltration. The reward was in South African Rand, and was quite substantial for any local person living off the dry land. These papers were dropped from planes and left for the wind to disperse across the open land. Many locals would give in to the temptation and trade off an arms cache, or knowledge of SWAPO's whereabouts, for a good payday in the strong value of the Rand.

Walking for 15 kilometres, we still could not find the border, with many long stretches of it no longer a road but replaced by overgrown bush. Pissed off, we realized we had walked right over it and now had to retrace our steps two kilometres north.

'Fuck. Who the hell is leading us?' I swore, with welling anger at having to walk another two kilometres for someone's stupid mistake.

'They don't know their arse from their face!' we muttered after each added, unnecessary step, discontented with our nagging thirst and burning sweat.

After half an hour of dragging ourselves through that continual ebb of frustration, we eventually found the roadway and joined up with Corporal

12. Patrols between beacons on the Yati

Gordon's Platoon 1 for the night. Crossing back into South-West Africa, we somehow felt safer to be on this side of the border, even though it did not make any difference – with the enemy still out there somewhere.

Sweating in the morning heat, we woke to the usual whine of *'mossies'* mosquitoes, and mopane flies, which crawled up our noses and into the corners of our mouths and onto our tongues. Spitting and slapping at our faces, this was our call to rise and face the new day. The sun soon began to heat the land like a slow oven, and we knew too well that it would not be too long before it was baking us in mid-stride.

Lieutenant Bam led a group of ten of us along the Yati, and Grant led another group of ten in the opposite direction. Our group came across a kraal, with a bunch of locals sitting around their brew of *'mahango'* millet beer. This concoction sat fermenting in dirty plastic buckets inside a huge, round, woven basket at least a metre in width and height, which sat on a six-legged wooden stand. The beer was made from the marula fruit, which was allowed to ferment with the help of the acid from old batteries and discarded leather boots. It cost us ten cents for a plastic jug that at one time was a cream colour but over years of use had become extremely dirty and brown. A yellow calabash was lowered into the thick, soupy, brownish-green liquid, and a jugful was scooped out and poured into the only plastic holder. One by one we drank this lethal brew, wincing with each sip until we closed our eyes and downed it before passing it to the next paying customer.

After one jug and the heat of the midday sun, I lay on the ground and immediately passed out next to a worn path leading to and from the kraal. I awoke feeling the urge to vomit, which I could not control, and ended up spewing the vile concoction all over myself. Wasting my precious water, I cleaned my face and shirt and then found the rest of my fellow troops, who were all merrily drunk.

Thirsty and dazed, we patrolled on, totally whacked out of our senses, and ended up completing a 15 kilometre patrol with no further excitement. When our cloudy heads seemed to see the light, it dawned on us what could have come of us had we walked into an ambush. We seldom reflected on the severity of past occurrences, but as drunk as we were – for the first and only time while on patrol – we knew all too well that had we walked into a contact we would most probably have been shot where we stood.

One of our daily sights on our endless patrols was that of the termite heaps, or in our language the 'anthills.' These monstrous mounds were a work of art and some stood at least three to seven metres in height, standing on a base which could measure between five and seven metres in circumference. They looked like large cones, with a wide base tapering to a point at the top, and were as solid as brick houses. These anthills had been made completely by worker termites, from the regurgitated mixture of sand and saliva that acted as cement, making each mound extremely difficult to break open. Inside the ant heap there are a maze of passages and chambers acting as highways for the movement of these blind insects. The sun and the rain also played a vital part in helping to keep the outer casing of this castle rock-solid.

While killing valuable resting time on patrol, we watched Brian and Wayne climb a tree. This was no ordinary tree, for it had an anthill right in the middle of it that looked more like an octopus, with all its green, branch-like tentacles protruding from the solid sand of this massive mound. It was by far the widest and tallest and oddest-looking sight that we had seen and stood higher than the seven metre tree itself, offering Wayne and Brian a hazy view of the flat and monotonous land that surrounded our lives daily.

While we sat and rested between patrols and meal times, we often fidgeted in the soft sand like young kids playing in a sand pit. Our eyes would always be hunting for an odd beetle or a strange insect to study and pass the boredom of the waiting game. On one occasion, we came across columns of soldier ants at least an inch in length, looking stealthy with their huge jaws as they passed us by in straight rows, as if they were on their way to launch an attack. They looked like a model version of a military exercise, with the termites on their way to battle in the formation of a three-pronged attack.

Out of sheer boredom and the inquisitiveness of children, a few of us decided to sabotage their battle plan by launching an attack on them with a fuel tablet, which we placed in their path. The intense heat given off from this round white tablet did not deter the advancing column in any way. Instead it maddened them, as line after line of these army ants, as we called them, sacrificed themselves in a bid to extinguish the flame and save their fellow soldiers.

It was absolutely mind-boggling to watch, as one wave after the next fizzled and popped upon the heat only to be replaced by the next advancing wave, without so much as a falter in the attack. Hundreds of these ants perished and lay charred over the battleground until we finally sprinkled sand over the heat, putting an end to the attack, which would not have stopped otherwise.

Another pastime was placing two scorpions in a bush hat or dixie and taking minimal bets on them as they stung each other to a slow death. It was cruel, but no crueller than to wait in the unrelenting sun upon this land that we had not been given any choice to serve in.

12. Patrols between beacons on the Yati

Boredom played the devil in us, with nature at our fingertips sometimes paying the price for strayed actions, which somehow kept our spirits alive as we wandered from point A to point B with little or no interest in life. Walking back to base camp after being lost to the bush for the duration of the patrol, which normally lasted between seven to ten days, we gave off an air of people not to be messed with.

Our suntanned and unshaved faces were sweaty and streaked with days of dirt, and our hair stood or lay as it wished upon our itchy scalps. Our bodies smelled of wood smoke from all the cooking fires and dried salty sweat, mixed with dust and dirt. Our hands were burned from reaching into the fires with fingers cut by bush whacking and the menacing thorn bushes, and the dirt was uncomfortable as we scratched at our filth. Our slimy feet oozed with 'toe jam,' which had built up between our toes from sweat and the confinement of our feet in hot leather boots and a ten-day-old pair of khaki socks. Even our own noses winced at the smell that we gave off, especially from our rotting feet. Our breath stank through our furry teeth, made worse by each spoonful of curried and pickled fish from the rat packs. The collars of our shirts were black and stiff from dirt and sweat, and the backs and underarms of our shirts were marked with salty white rings, ingrained like targets into the brown of our ragged-looking uniform.

In this way we had blended into the local population with the same offensive, pungent odour that they carried. But at least we knew a day would come when we could wash it off – if only to regain it on the next patrol. Soon life would repeat itself and we would forget when our last wash was, falling into that putrid way of life again until the next visit to running water.

Tired but excited, we approached the guarded entrance piled high with the protection of sand bags, and entered into the Okalongo base. My feet slid in my socks, with athlete's foot being my problem and the skin moist and cracked in between my toes. I carried my supply of standard, army-issue foot powder religiously in my pack, though it did little to rid me of this uncomfortable and slow, niggling, itchy torture.

Our platoon was granted a day's stay in the base, which gave us enough time to wash our clothes for only the second time in nine weeks, and most importantly cleanse our bodies with a bar of soap underneath a slow-running cold shower.

Our meals while in base were wet rations cooked over a portable stove from the kitchen, which were always met with excitement for a taste so different from the vile dryness of the ration packs. Breakfast consisted of eggs, bacon, toast, and hot coffee, and lunch of meat, potatoes, and gravy, eaten in the luxury of a tent, our dixies set upon fold-out tables while we sat strangely upon a row of benches in an almost normal environment.

Our spare time was used to sort out our kit, clean our rifles, and ready ourselves for the next patrol. This was a time when we could get access to our thick canvas *balsaks*, which seemed to pose more problems than they were worth. This sausage-like bag, which stored all our excess gear, stood more than a metre high and half a metre wide when packed full. The only problem with these bags was something quite simple, which always turned into a nightmare of frustration. Whatever we wanted always seemed, without fail, to be at the bottom, and as a result we had to unpack the whole bag to get at the last item.

I remember watching the expression on a troop's face as he dug into his bag, only to realize that a tube of condensed milk had burst over all his clean clothes and much-needed gear. His face changed to shock and then to anger as he lashed out at his *balsak* with his foot.

'Fuuuuck!' he swore, having more work on his hands and no choice but to clean it, for it would not be long before he had an infestation of ants in his sticky clothes. Turning away, a group of us laughed, grateful that it was his bag and not ours.

These bags were always clipped closed with a padlock to prevent any fellow troops from helping themselves to our army supplies. It seemed so ironical that we trusted our lives to the fellow soldiers within our platoon's camaraderie, and yet our few but necessary army belongings were not safe in the wandering hands of some of our clan. Amongst ourselves, we knew who could be trusted and who could not, and that became a measure of true friendship and respect for one another, along with the person's property.

With a clean uniform and feeling like new people, we loaded up our new ration packs and left the base in two lines under the rising morning sun.

Stopping just out of the base, we raised our weapons with the barrels pointing upwards and cocked them within our two rows. Without any warning, a burst of automatic fire shot an inch or two above Greg's head, arcing to the right, bullets and shells spraying just over the line of heads. Stunned and in a shocked silence, we looked over to the culprit for a few long seconds before turning with that invincible armour and walking off to begin the patrol.

Deon had cocked his rifle with his index finger on the trigger, and while he held his left hand on the piston grip he pulled it back, sliding a round into the chamber' and with this action, he in turn applied more pressure on the trigger mechanism. The result was such that an inch or two lower would have had us covered in the blood and brains of our own. How close four or five troops came to death that day was quite unbelievable.

Our lives had become conditioned to a whatever-happened-happened approach, and we were hardly fazed by such a close call. We shrugged our shoulders and treated it more like a training exercise.

The route for patrol was in the direction of Beacon 16, a torturous 30 kilometres away. Our packs were now always loaded with only the bare necessities, and even though water was our main lifeline, only one bottle was carried to minimize weight, which forced us to replenish from the land. There was many a time that we stooped down and filled our bottles from the stagnant, brownish-green waters of the *shonas* and swallowed the liquid with gratitude.

After half a day's walk, I became so exhausted from the thirst that rasped my dry throat – so much so that when I saw a *shona* I shuffled my tired legs with extra haste and beelined for the water's edge, into which I threw myself. My head landed right next to a heap of floating donkey droppings the size of golf balls. Casually I pushed them aside with one hand, and with the other I cupped the muddy water to my mouth and drank until my belly hurt. My eyes darted over to where a group of donkeys frolicked in the water, their front legs tied together to prevent them from venturing too far from their owners. I did not even bother to think of the urine that must have been excreted into the pool of cloudy water from which I had just drank. This was part of the existence, moving through from one tired day into the next, one experience following the last – a life far removed from the taken-for-granted amenities of a civilized world.

It gave us an insight into the life of the PB's – or *plaaslike bevolking*, the local population – who lived a life of subsistence, working their patches of dry, hardened earth by hand and hoe, yielding fields of *mahango* crops that helped feed the hungry families and livestock. The goats were plentiful and wandered free, and they destroyed what little they could nibble on and yet looked a lot healthier than the thin, underfed cows. Chickens produced eggs – along with that annoying sound of roosters crowing so early in the morning. Their dogs were mangy and very thin looking, scarred from many a dogfight, and in spite of their loveless treatment they always remained loyal to their masters, acting out the duty of watchdogs.

This rural lifestyle of agriculture was so typical of Owamboland that was disconnected by rail, and the further inland we went the less reliable road links there were. Most of the sandy roads could only be traversed by the power of the four-wheel-drive army vehicles. The locals were forced to walk for miles for their provisions, but they seemed to manage with ease, compared with our struggle with the land and our gear.

The young, dirty-looking kids clad in torn, filthy clothing free of footwear, their faces crawling with flies, watched over the cattle while the women, young and old, tended to the needs of the kraal. The young women walked, balancing water buckets on their heads and returning to the older ones, who sat around a smoking fire as a meal was being prepared in the hard clay cooking pots.

The men – when they were home, which was seldom – sat together under the shade of a big tree drinking *mahango* beer in deep, meaningful conversation. Most of the young Owambo men were involved in the bush war, either fighting with us as translators, or as soldiers within the ranks of African units. Many, on the other hand, became freedom fighters – either by choice or by the force of indoctrination, having being abducted from their families at a young age and moulded into fighters for the Communist cause.

Our feet trampled over endless *mahango* fields, with the grain crop recently planted in straight rows evenly apart, looking every bit like soldiers standing in company formation. In our uncaring strides, we kicked at the heaped ground, in total disregard for the backbreaking manual work it had taken to cultivate this staple, which stood out like a sore thumb surrounded by the dry bush and baked earth, pitting green against dusty brown. This is what would feed the undernourished mouths of which there were so many.

Our attitude became one of fuck them, this was their problem, and we have our own. We dragged our feet and lashed out at the towering mahango stalks in our wrestle with sanity, through waves of heat and anger. When we had long passed into the distance, we left a line of boot prints and broken crops, along with the repressed fury of those who had slaved over the land.

To us, most of the locals were loyal to SWAPO, and so they also became a hated enemy who offered hidden and silent support while we struggled with our call of duty and displayed our show of military force. Our strength was visible across many painstaking miles through the heart of the insurgency influx, and we knew it would not be long before our position circulated through the area by bush telegraph, again forewarning SWAPO into an early hiding.

Halting for a rest, Norman decided to discard some of his heavy ammo. He dug a shallow hole and placed a couple of magazines and a white phosphorus grenade inside it, and with a thin layer of sand he covered the deadly contents. Turning our backs on the resting place, we picked up our kit and trudged away, continuing our patrol and thinking nothing of it.

Unbeknown to us three young local children found the arms cache, and being inquisitive, they tugged on the pin of the phosphorus grenade. The pin came out of this lethal grenade, which exploded in a shower of sticky white blobs of phosphorus, sticking to their skins, literally burning holes into their flesh.

Scared and stunned, they walked back to the Okalango base still clutching handfuls of Norman's ammo. The medics along with Wayne, who for some reason had remained behind at base, quickly attended to the three children by throwing them into the swimming pool. They each grabbed a child, and as fast as they could, they proceeded to scrape the burning blobs from their scarred flesh with the use of surgical blades. With smoke filtering out of their black hair, they winced and wriggled under the extreme pain as the burns gnawed deeper into their flesh, while Wayne and the medics did what they could to ease their sufferings.

The children remained quiet, choked with fear, their wide eyes searching in vain for a halt to this burning that had their skin blistering and bubbling and resembling a scene from a horror movie. To ease the agony of the burns, they were all administered a syringe filled with a large dose of morphine.

The water helped to prevent them from burning further, since phosphorus does not burn under water' it needs oxygen to work its torture. One by one, they were pulled from the water so Wayne and the medics could see the blobs and scrape them off, but as a result, the burning began all over again. In the darkness the phosphorus glowed green, making it easier for the doctors to find the burning spots. They continued to draw the blades over their flesh, which was peeling off in their hands.

After hours of exhausting work, the children were bandaged. The child, who pulled the pin, having taken the brunt of the explosion, was bandaged from head to toe. His father came to the base to see his child, and with a look of shock he saw his son bundled up, looking more like an Egyptian mummy – which only added to his worry. The three children were loaded into a vehicle, along with the one parent and a couple of the medics, and left the base in the direction of a hospital in Ondangwa. It did not take long for word to filter back to the base that the child who had pulled the pin had died.

Norman would only learn the trauma and torture of his careless act when we returned to base, at the end of our week-long patrol. A young innocent child had been snatched away in an action that could have been prevented. Norman could not take the sole blame for something that we had all played such a selfish part in, in our self-absorbed struggle from one patrol to the hated next. We could all relate to the careless and needless way in which this young child had died, in spite of our lives being taken over by total disregard for the value of anyone's life but our own. We had all buried ammo at some stage to lighten our loads, and in my case I had left behind a rifle grenade somewhere in this land of misery.

Shit how I hate this land and the wrongs that go along with our duty, I said to myself. But there was no escape from the turmoil except to keep plodding on and going with the flow.

Norman was called in front of Captain Delport and Lieutenant Bam. His punishment was a week's hard labour within the confines of the base, which would involve repairing the sandbagged bunkers and adding sand to the walls in those areas that had become eroded through runoff.

It was a small price to pay for his negligence, and yet somehow, in a mixed-up way, we blamed the higher echelons for putting us in this mess. Right from the beginning we had been loaded to the tits with too much ammunition, forcing us to discard it to save our breaking backs.

Leaving Norman behind to ponder his actions, we left the base wondering what, if anything, had come of the ammo that we had discarded in the weeks past and whether it would turn up to maim or kill the most vulnerable again.

Walking through the roughed-up *mahango* fields, we trailed each other's boot prints, thus stamping our authority into the dusty soil. Fox walked ahead of me with short strings hanging from his bush hat, which swung like pendulums with each step. This was an ingenious discovery of his, to keep the mopane flies and the regular black biting flies at bay as he walked in luxury – in contrast to us, with our sweaty faces that attracted this vermin like a swarm of flies to crap.

Bridger, who was following in the line, not only barked like a real dog almost continuously, but also walked with his hands out as though he was clutching at a pair of handlebars, riding a motorbike as he revved at an imaginary throttle. Changing into a lower gear, he accelerated, throwing his body forward with the action, and sped past a fellow troop, gaining a place in the straggling line. Shaking our heads with a smile, we wondered, as we often did, if he had lost his marbles. He quickly steered himself in after pulling on the front brakes with the squealing sound of rubber on tar.

Just ahead of Bridger was Gall, cradling his beloved RPG-7 with a rocket tucked into a side pouch in his brown webbing. He never once complained about the extra weight that he wanted to carry in addition to his rifle and pack. Why he chose the added burden was a total mystery to us, for we knew if we walked into a contact he would never have the time to fire this weapon. The struggle, as we laboured under our weight, was marked with the salty white rings dried into our shirts and pants through the buckets of sweat that ran like rain from our serious-looking red faces.

On passing each kraal we were met with the bark of scrawny and underfed dogs, who went crazy at the scent and sight of foreign, white people. They barked madly and bared their teeth at us as they guarded their owner's kraal, but became timid as we approached with our rifles at the ready, forcing them to back off as our sheer numbers bore down on them.

Once out of sight of the kraals, and earshot of the barking dogs, we dropped our packs down on the earth and stole a much-needed and deserved rest. The first thing we reached for were our water bottles, which we could not thrust into our open mouths quick enough. We swallowed the liquid, now warmed to the outside temperature – a heat that would have been comfortable to take a shower under. It was water, nevertheless, and served its purpose, moistening our bone-dry mouths. Enjoying the rest, we leaned against our packs as content as we could ever be, and dead to the world we scanned the open landscape, shutting out our nomadic wanderings for the time being.

Matches flicked, sparking across the flint, lighting cigarettes to combat boredom, addiction, and stress while others peeled wrappers from the rubbery and chewy chocolate, mint, or rum and raisin bars. Some picked up round husks the size of tennis balls, littered below the shade of the makalani palm trees. Those who had energy smashed open the hard outer casings to get at the seed, which was covered in brown, stringy matting. With our knives or a sharp blade, we began to clean the seed and then proceeded to carve a design into it until we reached the white of the seed. After much practice, we became quite good at displaying our unknown artistic talent on these small, teardrop-shaped pieces of vegetable ivory. With all the time in the world on our hands, we carved some unique-looking pieces with the bulk of the design in brown, and the rest of the seed left a creamy white. Wayne and Macky excelled at this skill and were forever fixing our carvings and adding helpful hints to our technique, which ended up producing such works of art as 'Camel,' taken from the cigarette pack' 'Hang Ten,'with the trademark bare footprints' and 'SWA 85' and 'Angola 85,' marking our duty within these two African countries.

Looking around, I saw each soldier preoccupied in a task that, whatever it was, certainly took him to a faraway place, with thoughts more rewarding than those that would begin again as soon as the patrol resumed. Some wrote letters on creased paper, with dirty fingers clutching at the pen, while others reread letters pulled from their packs now dog-eared, worn, and dirty. It was the ink with the connecting thoughts that always brought a smile to a soldier's face, no matter what the situation, and giving us that vital link to the outside world that reassured us that someone out there was thinking of us. Cigarette smoke hung over our huddled groups for a few seconds before the thick grey cloud was dispersed by a slight breeze into the hot air. No matter how we used our time, our rifles always remained within arm's reach as a reminder that we were not on a holiday.

Macky was an amazing drawer, and knowing this, I wanted him to put his mark on my well-used diary, which I was writing up each day. In a matter of ten minutes, with the use of a blue ink pen, he drew the most remarkable picture of life on the border, which could not have been depicted more accurately by a professional artist. It was a simple picture drawn across the brown cover, which served as an excellent bleak background so true to the setting, with a man sitting next to his bivi strung from beneath a makalani palm tree, offering valuable shade. The soldier sat next to his pack, staring into the distance, surrounded by the round husks that had fallen from the tree. On the right of the palm tree, a rock-solid anthill stood to a height of at least two metres – a statue that marked the plains of northern Owamboland in abundance. Turning my diary over, he drew a few sets of boot prints in stride across the background, thus depicting our endless route marches.

Before we moved out, Lieutenant Bam and Grant conferred with each other to plan our route from a map of northern Owamboland, which they spread over the dry dusty soil, with small sticks preventing the corners from blowing closed in the slight, beautiful breeze. With the aid of a compass, they determined our direction and plotted a course over the block we had been designated to patrol.

When that dreaded order was delivered to move out, it was always met with resistance, for our bodies had grown accustomed to the rest and did not want to give it up for the sake of a patrol. After the usual round of cursing, we rose like robots and continued walking like pack mules, our rifle belts slung over our necks and resting in the cradle of one shoulder – which also gave us easy access to our triggers if the need arose.

In the background, Els' voice could be heard' the words flowed from his tongue with the crudeness and filth of a sewer. Suddenly our faces cracked into smiles as he broke the silence' his straight-faced way with every swear word in the Afrikaans language gave us a new lease on life, and we stepped from one boot print into the next.

'*O Katrine is 'n naai masjien, u hum, u hum, O Katrine is 'n naai masjien, u hum, u hum*,' he sang, and we joined in with the chorus – making light each step, with laughter and rejuvenation and the unbreakable spirit of camaraderie. We had covered a fair distance before we lapsed into that silence of hidden thoughts, plagued by heat and thirst. It was not long before he again roused us from the pit of silence, shouting '*Jou ma se mangwap skiet pap*' and '*Waar is jou groot slang, chic 'n lang, chic 'n lang?*' and once again the laughter returned to our wincing, sweating faces, amused by his vile and perverted Afrikaans humour.

When all was quiet Els spoke out, in good English, a deep-rooted statement to the Owambo people. 'The black Southern African, will have to realize that life on earth is very hard!'

He said this with such sincerity and sarcasm, and yet it was so true to their harsh life, caught in the middle of this bush war. His words rubbed off onto all of us, and became a hit on our patrols. Everyone took his turn at delivering this piece of made-up political propaganda.

But with all due respect, it was very hard for the locals to play both sides in this war where they suffered all too frequently. Coming up to a kraal, we went in and did a routine search, peering into the darkness of the smoke-filled huts in our search for anything suspicious. The headman of the village spoke with our lieutenant, Talk, and Skilpad, and they asked him about SWAPO activity. He replied in Owambo, telling them that terrorists had been in the area yesterday but that he was not sure in which direction they had headed.

The information was of little use to us, and we headed off into the late afternoon heat to find a place to settle down and cook our meals over the crackling fires. After we had eaten our fill and washed the warm, boring meal away with a hot fire bucket of coffee, we watched the burning ball of the sun sink below the wide horizon. What a feeling it was to have the cool air blowing over us while we enjoyed what little we could savour from the end of the day, all charged with that inner joy of crossing off another day and watching the beauty of the lingering sunset. Those amazing fiery reds, mixed with oranges and purples, were splendid to witness as we sat around our small fires with our Owambo friends and our rifles next to us.

In our normal fashion, under last light we moved out and made our way towards a bushy area, where we would sleep. Suddenly we were signalled to stop, and through the sudden silence we heard movement approaching our position. Our hearts beating, we flicked off our safety catches and waited. The sound seemed to come faster out of the darkness towards us. Waiting for the signal, we stepped out into the roadway, our rifles ready to spray fire on the approaching sound. Suddenly a bicycle appeared with a very shocked local man upon it. Skidding to a halt, and lucky to be alive, he was bombarded with questions from our two Owambo translators as to why he was out of his kraal, breaking the dusk-to-dawn curfew. Confident that he was not a terr, we granted him permission to leave. Very apologetic for his lateness, which could so easily have cost him his life, he pedalled into the darkness, which swallowed him up immediately, leaving us to ponder on the thought of his death had we opened fire.

Riding on the adrenaline clock, we found a patch of bush, and closing off in a circle we lay down for the night. It seemed so ironic that we could share our place of sleep, eat alongside our translators, and cook around the same fire with people of another race. I don't know if anyone questioned this in his mind, but we knew the racial rules in our country. No black person could eat at the same restaurant as a white person, stay at a 'Whites Only' hotel, or ride on a 'Whites Only' bus – and the list went on, yet in the bush they were considered equal for their part in helping the white South African soldiers win the war on terrorism. As a white person deprived of schooling with anyone from another race, I found it educational to learn more about Talk and Skilpad, both of whom had been drawn into the war for money – to give their families a better chance of survival – even though Talk was only a 15 year-old kid himself, carrying a G3 rifle and capable of using it. They both belonged to 101 Battalion, which numbered around 2000 men in the mid 1980s, including about 200 South African and South-West African whites. This unit supplied guides, interpreters, and trackers to those in the field, which became a vital link in gaining information on SWAPO movements.

After a good sleep, we got news from Company Headquarters involving a D10 cannon, which had been dragged by a bunch of terrorists into SWA to be used against South African occupied bases. On the same radio message, we learned that the Reaction Force of 101 Battalion had lost a Casspir in a fierce firefight, from the fighting arm of Romeo Mike, resulting in one captured terrorist from the contact. In a separate incident, two Buffels had rolled over, pointing towards driver error rather than conflict – with no mention of South African casualties.

We always listened to these bits of news carefully, even though it felt as though the incidents were taking place well out of our area. In fact, some of the action was only a short patrol away – usually just east or west of us along the Yati. It reminded us of our vulnerable position, even though we still walked with an air of invincibility. We also learned that the headman who had divulged information to us on recent terrorist activity had been killed by SWAPO. The news did not come as a surprise' a few headmen had been killed over the past weeks, solely for talking to us.

From Beacon 13 we lugged ourselves and our weighted packs another 30 kays, past some of the old cement beacons with SWA marked into the cement on one side, and Angola on the other, now lying in ruin from bullets and decades of neglect. Following our lieutenant, with his boyish and worried look, we eventually arrived at Beacon 16. In front of us we saw a small army base right on the Angolan border, which stood alone in an open area totally devoid of all civilization. The area around the base had long since been abandoned due to its dangerous position.

'This patrol better have been for a damn good reason!' I said as we unloaded our gear and dropped it to the ground. I looked upon the sand walls of this camp, wondering what it meant for us. After all, we had only walked a gruelling 30 kays to get here.

1985-Angola. Owambo knife. A prized souvenir from Angola.

1985-Owamboland. The cover of my diary, depicting a typical army scene of a bivi next to a makalani palm, along with an anthill. Drawn by Macky.

13

Our very own base camp

It was late in the afternoon on 9 March, as we lay in sprawled heaps only a stone's throw away from the Beacon 16 base camp. Sitting propped up against our packs, we felt the drizzle teasing our tired faces as we waited, eagerly anticipating what lay on the other side of those white-heaped walls.

The longer we waited, the harder it rained' and the more we fidgeted, with time standing still, the angrier we got. The rain dotted and danced at our booted feet, making life even more uncomfortable and leading us to an acceptance of yet another wet and sleepless night – short of a miracle sparing us from this ordeal.

After a few hours of abandoned wait, we got the order we had hoped for but somehow never expected to be issued.

'Stand up and move into the camp,' came the order from Corporal Doep, who led our soaked and very happy platoon onto the thick, sandy road that led into the camp. Walking past a guard bunker at the entrance to the base and past the three and a half metre sand walls, we were now inside the base camp known as Beacon 16.

It was a small camp with a few olive-green tents pegged to the earth and a couple of huge old trees offering colour, and more importantly shade, to the two big black bladders containing water and diesel – both vital ingredients to our survival. A couple of Buffels, a Samil, and a Kwevoel were parked in a row outside one of the tents, which seemed to take up quite a bit of space for the small size of this camp that could only hold one rifle company at any one time.

Waiting outside a small tent, sheltered by a tree from the unwanted water dripping from the heavens, we continued scanning the base with that ever-present wonder at what lay in store for us. A 30 man tent was brought to us and we were instructed by Staff Smit on where to position it. With each man delegated a task, we erected it in record time, the rain doing little to dampen our spirits as it played its devilish pitter-patter on the taut and dusty canvas.

After two months of nomadic patrols from one area of bush to the next, we now walked into a tent within a camp that we could actually call our own – a feeling that seemed so out of place. This was now our place to leave any extra kit and what few valuables we had, and a dry place from the dreaded rain.

Grateful for the sheltered ground, we lay in two long lines with our feet pointing to the middle, below the high ceiling of the tent, which was held

13. Our very own base camp

upright by two tall metal poles. Closing my eyes that night, I smiled with a sense of belonging, having felt like an orphan for the past eight weeks, shifted from one orphanage to the next until a home eventually came up.

The morning brought great excitement to us, and we looked forward to scouting around our new home, which seemed to be positioned like a fortress, an expanse of open bush surrounding us. Leaving the tent with our rifles, we ventured out in bare feet but did not get very far. The early morning sun had already scorched the soft brown beach sand, which scalded our feet with each stride, as though we had stepped into a pot of boiling hot water becoming trapped for a few lingering seconds. Returning to the tent as quickly as we had left it, we pulled on our boots and resumed our inquisitive tour of the camp, which looked to be about 40 to 50 square metres.

Looking over the wall facing north, we were amazed to see another camp about 400 metres away, just across the Yati, well-camouflaged beneath a thick forest of mopane trees on the Angolan side. It did not take long for us to realize that this was a UNITA camp, which was fighting alongside us in a bid to win power over the ruling MPLA forces inside Angola.

Speaking with a few of our Company '*HK piele*' HQ pricks, we soon learned a few things about this base, which they had learned from Captain Delport. The base had been built by bulldozers in the mid to late 1970s and served as a South-West African Police base, which later swung over to a Koevoet base with the formation of Koevoet in 1979. With their heavily-gunned, armoured Casspirs, Koevoet patrolled along and over the Angolan border, reacting without delay to information they received concerning the movement of insurgents. They acquired a fearsome reputation from both sides of the border, having scored the highest kills of any security-force unit up till the end of the war.

Another piece of information was one that we did not want to hear. This base, situated right along the border line, had been mortar bombed three times in its short history – suddenly it made sense why there were no brick buildings in the camp. Looking into this old Portuguese colony called Angola, I wondered if we would be spared such an attack, and turning from the hardened wall of sand I mouthed that secret and silent motto of mine: Whatever will be, will be. There was certainly no use in adding further worry to our situation.

We passed a small tent with its sides built up by thick railway sleepers – adding protection if the need arose – which was positioned conveniently beneath a big old marula tree, thus offering that ever-important shield against the penetrating sun. It turned out to be the base's kitchen, containing a Garry – which is a stove with hotplates on a small trailer with a tow hitch. There was plenty of fresh air blowing through the tent as a result of the tent flaps being permanently clipped down.

Our group could not help noticing the stocked pantry, ranging from tins of condensed milk and a variety of meaty tins to loaves of bread, dozens of eggs, and bags of potatoes. Someday we will taste some of this food again, we all thought as we smiled at the appeal of these staples – staples for those in a base, but not those in the bush. Just past the kitchen we stepped through the rotting marula fruit that had dropped from the massive tree, which marked its shade with a fermenting mess landing upon the rubber diesel and water bladders.

On the south side of the base, we found the magazine dump, which had sandbagged steps leading down into the coolness of the ground, at least three metres deep. Sandbags lined the walls and covered the tin roof. In the event of an attack, these sandbags would cushion the explosion and hopefully prevent the whole magazine dump, with all the extra ammunition, from blowing sky-high and taking us with it to kingdom come.

In each corner of the base there were lookout bunkers cut into the walls – which were lined with sandbags – with a crude piece of corrugated tin overhead. These bunkers were lined with more sandbags on the roof, which acted as further protection against the unforgiving sun and rain, and most importantly against any mortar bombs. There was another bunker at the entrance, and two more in the middle of the longest walls, offering further lookout onto the open terrain. They were about two metres deep, and were built higher upon the walls by potato sacks filled with sand, which had long since baked to the hardness of concrete. These potato sacks were a good buffer against flying shrapnel and bullets, if any were to come our way from Angola.

It did not take long for us to notice where our rank slept and on what they slept. Their tents had been carefully dug out from the ground, so as they walked into their shelters they stepped down into the coolness and the safety of being below ground level. On the level of the metre and a half deep hollow, they were met with the luxury of metal-framed beds with soft foam mattresses, and with the good fortune of real light, which was powered through the genie – generator. It was a life way above the likes of us common troops – something we could only dream about.

The toilet area was a brown wooden outhouse, which was placed over a pit in the ground teeming with the largest and fattest flies I had ever seen. We had to fight them off, along with the potent smell of lime powder, which was randomly poured down the shaft. Next to this delightful setting was the shower area, which consisted of a big, brown, funnel-shaped canvas bag, known to us as the 'African condom,' which was suspended from a tree branch by a rope and pulley.

On the rare occasions when we could wash below this prehistoric device, which nevertheless worked, we stood below it and turned the black nozzle cap, allowing water to spray upon us with the same intensity as a civilized bathroom shower. The only disadvantage was that we only had about two minutes to wash before the water ran out, and then it had to be lowered again and refilled by the next troop in line who had a bucket. This 'condom' had caught many a troop standing fully-soaped, thus causing soap to run from his head into his eyes, and in turn causing a yell for help – an urgent need for more water. Having a clean body gave us a feeling that money could not buy, for it lifted us to a paradise well beyond the dusty plains, and the fear of there never being an end in sight to our misery.

After two nights in camp we were issued three ration packs, which we immediately began to break open and discard and trade what we had no liking for, hoping to gain a good deal from a friend who was also trying to weed out his food. Before we left for the bush, I went to the tent kitchen and asked someone I knew if he could spare a few potatoes and a tin of condensed milk – which he did, away from the sharp eyes of any rank. It seemed like nothing – a few potatoes and a tin of sweet condensed milk – but it was more the breaking up of this monotonous bland ration that we had lived off daily, for breakfast, lunch, and dinner, for the past eight weeks.

Corporal Doep led us out of the base on a bearing that only he and his compass knew, and we again patrolled the land, which had no attachment or value to us and which we viewed more and more as a heartache and an *opfok* than anything else.

After a few silent kilometres we came across a Cuca shop, which was situated in the middle of nowhere. It was a small square shack held together by wire and a few nails and screws pierced through the rusty corrugated tin walls, and to us it looked more like a house in one of the poor black locations, known as a 'tin shanty.' The door was firmly padlocked, and it gave the impression that its owner had long since abandoned it. Wayne and I decided to take a look inside, and managed to open a corner wide enough to slip through. Once inside, we felt the intense heat cooking us like an oven. We struggled with our vision in the darkness, waiting for it to adjust. There was an old table, and stacks of crates containing empty beer bottles with the South African Brewery mark on each, and one-litre bottles of Coke and Pepsi – all dusty and undisturbed, except for the many spider webs woven and plaited across the crates and the corners of the heated, metal walls.

Sweating buckets, we scanned the room, once more hoping to find something full. In the far corner our eyes caught sight of two quart bottles of Castle, brewed 3000 kilometres south of us, in our homeland. Each of us grabbed one of these hot bottles and made quickly for the chink of light and escaped from the claustrophobic heat into the cooler outside with our treasure. Full of old dust and dirt, and covered in broken web, we pulled the bottle tops off and tasted the Castle beer, which as hot and ugly as it was helped dull our senses. Passing the bottles around, we all enjoyed a few swigs, sharing the moment like a close family struggling through each day.

Happy with a slight buzz, we trailed into the distance behind Corporal Doep, who led us into a kraal for a random check. Walking into the kraals, we were always on high alert, with our safety catches flicked off and our fingers curled like snakes around the triggers. We knew what a great ambush position this was, and we had to remain ready for any surprise that could transpire.

We followed through the maze of this fenced stockade, passing a cooking area with a fire still smouldering and pens of livestock, before emerging into an open, smoke-filled living area. Fanning out with our rifles in front of us, we pointed them into the dark huts, waiting to hear Owambo voices, but found them oddly deserted.

With no one around, we suddenly felt the urge to lay claim to a few of this Owambo family's possessions – as souvenirs to remember the daily thoughts we harboured towards the people of this land. Wayne and I both took a neatly carved wooden chalice, with a thin stem joining the perfectly rounded base, looking exactly like a wooden wine glass with a beautiful design cut into it. Three other troops grabbed pangas – thick-bladed knives, half a metre long, and we departed from this rural dwelling. I felt weird leaving the kraal knowing that what I had hidden in my webbing was not rightfully mine, but in a selfish way I took it as repayment for all my internal anguish, which festered in me like a plague and could explode from the depths of my soul like a pressure cooker, without any warning.

Once we were on patrol again, what had happened at the last kraal remained at the back of our minds – until a local man came running up to us, appearing out of nowhere. With the help of our translators, his Owambo was deciphered back to us in broken English. To our amazement, it turned out that he was from the same kraal we had just come from, now at least two kilometres away. He was a religious man, and the two cups that Wayne and myself had taken were needed for one of his religious rituals.

How the hell he knew that we had them is beyond me, I said to myself as we waited for the outcome.

Corporal Doep asked if anyone had seen these cups, expecting the answer to be a flat 'No!'

Instead he got the shock of his life when Wayne and I dug into our webbings.

'Do you mean these?'

We held the two wooden cups aloft, turning our entire fellow troops' heads onto our admittance of guilt. The local man nodded with a frown across his wise old face, showing a glint of yellowy brown teeth as he sighed lightly, with absolutely no emotion, before stepping forward to reclaim his property. With us taking the lead, the remaining three knives suddenly appeared before the local man, with apologies in English following.

For some unknown reason, this local tribesman decided not to report our actions to a higher authority – which would certainly have landed our half-section in some hot water.

Watching the old man cross back over the roughly ploughed patch of land, and over the scrubby terrain with his belongings, we smiled cynically, unable to understand his feelings of anger towards us South Africans.

'There's a guy who has just changed sides,' someone said, realizing that what we had done had suddenly damaged the trust he might have once had in us, as soldiers who had such a strong presence in and across northern Owamboland.

In all likelihood he changed sides to avenge our negligent action, and turned to SWAPO as an informer to regain face.

Leaving the past behind, we walked on, wincing at the dried, sweaty smell of our bodies. The odour blended into the environment, there being no point in using soap or deodorant. In this land of bush, there was certainly no one to impress – not to mention the scent we would give off, making it easier for a terrorist's keen sense of smell to detect us. The only time we laughed it off was when we could not take the feel of our furry rough teeth anymore and smeared toothpaste on a finger or a brush, if we had one, and scrubbed them clean – transforming us once again into new people.

Going to the toilet in the heart of the bush was an experience in itself. We took up our daily squatting positions behind the privacy of a tree or bush, our rifles sitting on their tripods next to us. Before the few white squares of paperwork were complete, huge dung beetles bigger than the old one rand coin flew at us from out of thin air and dive-bombed us beneath our bare backsides, landing in the middle of our excrement. These round, inch-and-a-half, black, prehistoric beetles, coated with the protective armour of a rhino and with two curved-looking tusks, immediately began to roll our waste away from beneath us, even before we had placed the white flag crowning our land mine. Standing upright, with front legs above their heads on top of their newfound prizes, and with strength more than double their size, they wheeled the sandy balls into view. From our squatting positions we watched the beetles hard at work, using their small spiky legs as steering columns while they spun in the sand, fighting each roll of the ball. If it were not for the cloud of flies that our discharge had attracted, I could have sat and watched these insects for hours with admiration for their sheer determination. To witness nature at work right before my eyes, as the beetle played out its part in the environmental cycle, was a masterpiece of splendour that no city life could offer.

`On a few occasions we could not help but notice the colour of our excrement, which was as black as coal and sent panic through us. The shock of being unable to fathom such a colour exiting from our bowels forced us to share this news with our friends, who were just as glad to learn that they were not alone in this strange phenomenon.

Our alarm subsiding, we tried to find out why – which did not take long, as we recalled our eating and drinking habits. Having continually drunk from the ground, our systems had become very high in iron from the muddy waters, causing the sudden change in colour.

In three days we had covered a distance of close to 50 kilometres, taking in the all-too-familiar flat and colourless terrain. Our eyes hungered for a change in scenery and bright colours away from the continual browns and greens. Our ears wanted to hear noise, whether it be a civilian car racing in traffic or a train flying over the joints in a railway track. We wanted to hear anything but the buzz of the flies and the creepy breeze that silently passed through a bush or a *mahango* field. Instead we saw the dented and rusty skeletons of old car wrecks, stripped of all parts from wiring to wheel, to be used in this simple life of re-using anything and everything for a temporary fix.

The axle, along with the wheels, were transformed into a donkey cart' a metal bin had been removed from one of the many wrecks and bolted atop the axle, which now made an ideal wagon for the transport of water and firewood, with suspension to go with it. Young African kids no more than five years of age would sit in the bin and steer these docile donkeys with a stick and a thin leather string tied to the end, meting out a crack for speed or change in direction, showing off their art in driving one of these contraptions set by the pace of these slow beasts. Unfortunately, this was the sound that we heard that replaced the breeze, and not since passing through Ondangwa had we seen a civilian car, which felt years away in a life now very foreign to us.

While resting, Corporal Doep relayed a message to us that Lieutenant Bam and his half-section of Platoon 3 had captured three suspected terrorists. It later turned out, after some intense questioning, that two were not terrorists, and they were allowed to walk away from the pointing R4s. The remaining young African man was taken away to one of the main bases for further questioning, but what came of him we were never informed.

Another message of importance that echoed from the green handset of the A54 radio was that a contact that had taken place very close to our area, involving 8-SAI.

A Puma helicopter had urgently been called in to 'casevac' – evacuate casualties – the three injured and airlift them back to the Ondangwa Air Force Base. One terrorist had been injured in the contact, and the following day had been tracked down by 8-SAI and found a few kilometres away, propped up against a tree and badly bleeding from his injuries.

Next to his bloodied body were two AK-47s, six rifle grenades, and three landmines. 8-SAI troops with fresh memories of injuries to their own did not take kindly to his pleas for mercy. What became of him, we never knew.

It was funny the feeling we got from these radio messages, which somehow shrank the open bush and thus brought life and death a lot closer to us. Walking on daily with this nothing-can-touch-us mentality gave us that much-needed awareness that contacts were taking place within our vicinity.

These terrorists had been trained in Angola, Tanzania, and Zambia, and also as far afield as Cuba, East Germany, Russia, and Czechoslovakia. Inside their camps and military bases, they had been trained in the Communist way of thinking, its ideals brainwashed into them. On their return, they lived with the belief that Angola and SWA would become the Communist utopia of Southern Africa, led by the terrorist's favourite weapon – the hard-line symbol of Communism – the AK-47. With Marxism on the march southwards, they also believed that their repressed 'brothers in chains,' under the apartheid regime of South Africa, would also soon be free.

The banned African National Congress within South Africa also had military training bases within Angola, training the military wing of the ANC, which was known as *'Umkhonto we Sizwe'* Spear of the Nation. The purpose of their training was to infiltrate South Africa and perform acts of sabotage by planting bombs and creating chaos in the hope of weakening the white government's grip on the country and freeing the black majority from 350 years of white minority rule.

Through another radio report to Corporal Doep, we learned that Lieutenant Bam and the other half of Platoon 3 had come across a local whose wife had been killed by SWAPO. In the process of killing her, the terrorists had left behind two Russian hand grenades. These two grenades were taken by Lieutenant

Bam and handed in at our base at Beacon 16, and in turn for his good deed the local was given R100 for each grenade. This, of course, would have been a lot of money for such a poor man, but it did little to replace the void of losing his wife.

After the long patrol, we entered into our base under the shade of the tree marking the entrance, and wearily fought our way through the thick dune-like sand towards our tent. Once inside the tent, we welcomed the coolness and collapsed on the groundsheet marked by our waiting kitbags, which looked as though they had been standing guard over our sleeping space while we had been away on our bush patrols. Thinking that we could lay back and relax in the comfort of our tent was short lived, for Staff Smit had other plans to fill the rest of our day. Our instructions were to clean out all the loose sand in the bunkers and use it to refill new sandbags, which were to be placed on top of the existing ones to add height and further strength to the walls.

At the end of a hard afternoon's work, having already patrolled back to the base in the morning, we were rewarded with a two-hour guard beat for our efforts. It pissed us off to watch our Company HQ personnel lazing around with no worries in the world while we slaved over their fortress, where they permanently lived, adding strength, neatness, and a guard beat to break up our one and only deep sleep in the all-around safety of a built-up base.

'Fuck this,' someone muttered. 'We are better off in the bush away from this law and order.'

We had to agree with him, but as always we had to sit tight, bite our tongues, and just wait our time out.

While the sun started to drop in the early evening, we all departed to the newly-renovated bunkers with our rifles and familiarized ourselves with the outside surroundings, taking mental note of bushes and the odd tree in our arcs of fire. It was a peaceful time for all of us to sit undisturbed and reflect, and with all the time in the world we watched the light change into shadows of darkness. It was not long before we sat engulfed in the evening blackness, which in this way-out place in northern Owamboland was darker than ever, there not being a chink of light to be seen anywhere other than from a few twinkling stars.

This was always an important practice in a new surrounding, to prevent us from overreacting in fear and mistaking a small bush for a terrorist. It was a common fact, and one we all knew too well, at how a bush moving in the breeze or a tree branch could play tricks with our paranoid minds, its shadows and movement played out below a slice of the moon.

I took up my lonely watch at 02:00 for two whole hours, taking up position at the corner bunker closest to our tent. I sat in the bunker behind the sandbags, with barbed wire running down the length of the solid mound, walling us in. It was scary to be alone, looking out into the black night at those darkened shapes that we had seen not too long ago, as trees and bushes hung over the base through the ghostly silence.

A little while later it started to rain, turning the hard earth to mud while I sat in my barricade under the tin roof with its sandbagged covering, watching the rain cut into the earth and tear at the tents in the base. Time, being always on our hands, played towards the thinking game – and we used it to pass the time during our long, unwanted guard period.

A thought passed through my mind concerning television footage of soldiers in World War-I. I wondered what kind of hell they went through as they stormed trenches and bunkers in a boot's-depth of mud and over the cutting circles of barbed wire. For me, sitting under a roof with only a little rain blowing onto me, and a shallow level of mud – which in comparison seemed like paradise – only helped lift my silent spirits. I gazed down onto the face of my digital watch, hoping for an unlikely speed-up of time, but it only seemed to stand still and add to my loneliness.

All seven bunkers were filled with a soldier in each, to guard our fellow troops' sleeping lives. We all knew that attacks had been launched on this base. Whether there had been death or serious injury we had never been informed, but with bombs landing within the walls we could only assume that there had been some casualties.

In the morning, before we left the base, we were informed that 11 terrorists had been killed in the previous week, and between January and mid-March a total of 188 terrorists had been wiped out.

Leaving the base with our clean bodies, our webbings packed with five ration packs and a sensible load of ammunition, we loaded our rifles and began the patrol, which lasted five kilometres on the first day. On reaching a kraal we stopped and entered for a random search, which only produced a group of young, scared children who raced off, shrieking, to the protection of their elders, who sat hard at work around the baked clay pots nestled into the smoky coals of their cooking fires.

With looks of invasion into their space directed at us, followed with some Owambo only understood by our trackers, we moved out in search of a spot to cook our dinners – away from any locals' watching eyes.

It was late in the afternoon when we dropped our packs and began preparing a few small fires. I decided it was a good time to cook my potatoes, which I still had from the base kitchen. With my knife I began to peel these items of luxury with my dirty hands, cutting them in long slices into my dixie. They came out a lot darker than a potato normally would, thanks to the juices, which cleaned my hands in the process. Somehow I had managed to lay claim to some cooking oil, which I dripped onto the potatoes before placing them over the hot coals.

Rushing against my hunger pains and the smell of oil cooking over the fire, I stirred the chips around, which stuck to the bottom of my aluminum, rectangular plate cum pot. Ash, as always, found its way into our dinners, adding a smoke-filled aroma to our food. When I could not wait any longer I ate my fried potato which tasted raw and burned. The heat scalded my tongue. In the end it was worth the effort, since it added a change to the menu – which counted for so much to our conditioned taste buds.

The tin of condensed milk was another exciting experience in the world of sweetness. It was placed unopened in a fire bucket full of water on top of hot coals. When it came to the boil I topped up the water level to avoid exposing the tin. I left it to boil for a couple of hours until finally the bloated tin was lifted from the fire and cooled off in a canteen of cold water. When cool I used the tin opener on my knife to cut off the lid which exposed thick brown caramel. Licking my lips in anticipation I would spoon out a mouthful of this warm and delightful luxury. It seemed like a sin to eat this in an environment where we survived only on the necessities.

It was normal to share windfalls sparingly with a selected few adding excitement to our existence where the simple things meant so much. Minutes after it was ready, a handful of troops appeared with spoons and dug into the tin in turn satisfying their sugar cravings and smiling ingratitude.

It had been worth all the effort of watching over the fire to produce such a smooth dessert, It was a cooking technique I had learned from Wayne some time before. The sugar made us very thirsty, but it bolstered our spirits with new energy as we washed the thirst away with warm water from our water bottles.

On the last day of our patrol we walked the last three kilometres to base and immediately collected R15 of pay that was due. We blew it on spoiling ourselves with chocolates, chips, soft drinks, and later in the evening six-packs of beer. Letters that had been flown up from South Africa were distributed which revived our only contacts with the outside world. We had been deprived of radio, television, telephones, and newspapers for such a length of time that it felt like years.

We followed the base routine for the single day we remained behind its sand buttresses. It flashed by as we cleaned our bodies and our kit, getting ready

13. Our very own base camp

for the next patrol. Leaving the base was always a good feeling with the bush in charge instead of our bosses Staff Smit and Sergeant Piet Muis. We left them behind to push around the HQ troops permanently stationed in the base.

We walked into the furnace of dry heat glad to be free from the base orders but at the same time dreading the long foot patrol ahead and the kilometres we would be putting behind us. A few days later a radio signal came through to our half section reporting stolen pangas and the rape of local women at a kraal within our patrol area. To our disgust and disbelief we found we were the prime suspects. Lieutenant Bam had to advise Captain Delport of our coordinates so that he could rendezvous with us to question us to find the culprit, or culprits, in our ranks.

He soon arrived in the comfort and safety of a Buffel driven by Donald. Donald had matriculated from Weston, a farming school in Mooi River – the same area as Treverton the boarding school that I had attended. Weston and Treverton had been archrivals for many years. Unfortunately for Treverton, the 'pig farmers,' as we called them, invariably beat us at rugby and cricket – which always added salt to our wounds.

I will never forget an event in my final year at Treverton College, when close to 35 of us, including the head boy and prefects, grabbed the biggest sticks we could find and headed as a huge group for the river, where supposedly two of our school's pupils had been beaten up by a Weston student.

We arrived to find at least 100 Weston pupils lined up on one side of the shallow river, facing us menacingly, also with stick-like clubs. They suddenly stormed through the river like charging Zulu warriors, swarming towards us with sticks, golf clubs, and axes wielded high in the air accompanied by spine-tingling yells and shouts. To their shock, we stood frozen to the ground and raised our weapons – more in fright than in anger. Seeing this their charge seemed to peta out and slowed to a crawl. This left the battle to be fought by fists, one of ours against one of theirs. As it turned out, blood was shed on both sides, in an even fight. Our agreement to fight one-on-one had averted a fullscale bloodbath and what would probably have become a barbaric scene for students who were supposed to be civilized.

In my mind's I saw Donald storming forward against our small contingent of Matrics. When I first saw him in Bravo Coy many months before I reminded him of that day. It was a day that lived vividly in both our memories. Seeing Donald again this time in the driving seat of the Buffel silently played the event back to me again with a chilled feeling of what might have been.

Our half-section came to attention on the order of Lieutenant Bam, who saluted the captain as he disembarked from the Buffel. Once on the ground, he walked down the line of scruffy soldiers gathered in the middle of a thicket of bush. With a stern and solemn face he began asking questions with Lieutenant Bam respectfully returning answers.

Before the arrival of Captain Delport we had already begun to speculate who the rapist could be. But we just could not get our mind around the idea of a white soldier raping a local African woman. Some, of course, might have been diseased but it was mainly the lack of personal cleanliness that accompanied their simple lifestyle. Unfortunately, it was not the first time, nor would it be the last, that a young white soldier had committed such a criminal act.

After five minutes of questioning, Captain Delport realized that we could not be the guilty ones and left.

Shortly afterwards a radio message confirmed that a section of 101-Battalion were the culprits. This included a white driver from our Company HQ who had been based at Beacon 16 before being detached as a driver to 101-Battalion for a short stint.

He was arrested and placed under Military Police guard before being driven to Ondangwa and then flown out of SWA, to face a military court hearing in Pretoria. What became of him we never heard for he never returned to our unit. We guessed that he was serving out the remainder of his two years, and probably more, within the confines of a military jail.

The guilty one was still from our Company ranks, though, and it was hard to believe that one of our trusted own, from Bravo Coy, could have stooped so low.

Watching the dust dwindle into the distance, we set about finding a sleeping place for the night. To our amazement we were awoken at sunrise by a few local Owambos who had wandered into our sleeping circle undetected and had coughed us awake. They were seeking medical attention and believed we were miracle workers who had easy cures for their illnesses.

Suddenly people more appeared. It was as if they had stepped from the shadows of the thin mopane trees and the scarce bushes. It was an odd feeling to have our 'concealed' place of sleep so rudely invaded by a group of poor and forgotten people who looked more like the walking wounded.

Thackery, our platoon medic, began to work on a line of Owambo patient many of whom's faces were contorted with pain.

There was a young Owambo girl who was so bloated that she looked pregnant, but her pain was caused by her having been unable to urinate for weeks. Sax worked his miracle with a small piece of hosepipe, which he thrust up inside her in full view of those lined up waiting for their turn with the healer. After a few minutes of excruciating pain, her urine began to flow like a dam with

13. Our very own base camp

its sluice gates fully open. The relief visibly showed on her young face as she stood weakly in the muddy pool of of her own discharge.

Those in the line who had witnessed this miracle began fidgeting and coughing in the hope of an immediate cure to whatever they were suffering from. One at a time they were attended to by Sax, with the help of Wayne and a couple of other willing troops. The coughs got louder and the pain seemed worse. Their eyes had sadness in them, and the whites of most of their eyes were a dull, yellowy brown – possibly due to malaria. Their clothes looked as though they had been washed and used countless times hung on them and seemed to be holding together by threads alone. Most were shoeless, the soles of their feet now cracked and leathered from the terrain.

Maybe many were genuinely sick, but it seemed to us as that some were having us on, desperate for the white man's medicine – which, in their eyes, could cure them of the most deadly diseases.

Bandages and band-aids were handed out for minor cuts, along with malarial tablets and the odd injection for pain relief. Sitting in the shade of some trees, we watched an old man step up to Thackery and Wayne with a deadly cough.

'Watch this,' Wayne said as he handed the old man a malaria tablet and silently acted out what he wanted him to do.

Wayne opened his mouth, popped in an imaginary tablet, and began to chew. The old man followed his act and chewed on the vile-tasting pill until he had broken it down into a paste, then swallowed it with disgust. There was no telling us how bad these tablets tasted, for we had been through the routine time and time again and had never tried to chew them, for it caused a revolting bitterness in one's mouths which would stay with you for the rest of the day.

Looking on, we had to laugh at Wayne's comedic approach. The old man looked at Wayne with a big smile after he had swallowed the white paste which exposed his brown- stained teeth. Miraculously, his sudden cough disappeared – cured by the malaria tablet.

Sitting in the shade of a marula tree we watched the line of waiting grow as more people arrived from miles away. It seems they had heard we were there by bush telegraph, the only form of communication in this most rural part of Africa.

An old woman sat down next to our group probably to escape the mid-morning heat that had already begun to burn us. Why she had chosen to sit next to us white soldiers we had no idea. She was certainly not scared of us and began talking to us in Owambo, but we had no idea what she was trying to say.

She was old, at least in her 80s, and her face was a map of rural African life, weathered by tough conditions of survival and a meagre subsistence existence.

The leathery skin of her face broke into a broad smile that exposed a mouth of missing teeth.

From the cloth covering her head, she pulled out an old and dirty folded document typed in Afrikaans, along with a black-and-white photograph. The document looked every bit as old as she was. It was stamped in faded ink, with the words Windhoek, SWA clearly visible, along with her birth date which was shortly after the turn of the century. She drew patterns in the sand with her index finger and tried to explain in Owambo what she was trying to say. We looked at the document again and found a name.

'Monica,' Wayne and I said simultaneously.

This brought a smile to her old face. Her eyes made contact with ours and she tried to tell us about her tale of hardship in a life.

With a small stick she began pointing to the lines she had drawn in the sand, as if counting them.

'How many?' we asked, getting a reply in Owambo that made no sense to us.

'Howamany?' Wayne asked again trying to imitate an African accent.

But Monica looked straight through him without a glimmer of understanding.

We Christened her Monica Howamany and we gave her the square 'dog biscuits' from our rat packs which we considered were only fit for dogs. But Monica surprised us for she really enjoyed them and contentedly nibbled small pieces as she sat unmoving, surrounded by a group of bored white soldiers.

Wayne and I decided to teach her a little English. With the aid of a stick, we scratched lettering into the sandy soil and pronounced it as we completed the writing of each word. It did not take us long to move on to some choice swear words, 'shit,' 'fuck,' and 'arsehole' being a few of them. After each word, the audience laughed, along with her, as she pronounced each word in her Owambo accent. I kept egging her on with new words which helped to produce much-needed laughs.

After ten minutes of swearing and without warning she pointed her index finger in my direction.

'Fuckin' arsehole,' she shouted out in perfect English.

There was a spontaneous roar of laughter from the guys that was so loud that Sax spun around to see what he had missed. The group including myself laughed so much that tears ran down our faces.

Monica threw back her head and joined in the laughter, enjoying every moment of it at my expense.

Sax continued with his psychological battle to ease 'sickness'. The people departed as cured after swallowing a tablet or having had bandage wrapped around a sore leg or arm, a few plasters stuck over cuts, and a couple of injections into their thin arms. They left Thackery and the platoon medical bag a lot lighter for the rest of the patrol.

When the last of the locals had been taken care of, we readied ourselves to move out. Monica also stood with the alacrity of a person half her age. She raised her arm in farewell and set off for her kraal which was some kilometres away.

Wayne's eyes had been irritating him – so much so that he joined in for the medical handout and got his hands on some eye drops, which he promptly squeezed into each of his red eyes. It was not long after the drops were in his sockets that he realized that something was wrong with his eyes. He had the feeling as if they were set wide open in a fixed stare. Rushing back to Thackery, Wayne grabbed hold of the small plastic bottle and looked carefully at it to make sure that it was in fact eye drops. The faded label clearly read 'Eye Drops,' but it was now a solution of eye drops that had expired years ago' and who knows, maybe the heat had helped turn it into a glue of sorts. Wayne walked around for a few hours looking more like a bushbaby with similarly big, saucer-like eyes, firmly open and unable to force a blink. It was impossible not to crack a smile at his comical appearance, amazingly unseen by his wide-eyed vision.

With our rifles in our hands and our packs strapped to our backs, we set off into the heat with the sun at its peak. I had to wonder what would become of Monica Howamany, with her age and waning strength against her, in a rural part of Africa where life was short due to disease, hunger, and civil war.

The other half of our platoon reported that they had found a yellow smoke grenade in a waterhole. This precious necessity of life was covered in a yellow film of powder, destroying it for human consumption. It had to have been one of our own soldiers, who must have thirsted for this cool liquid' and on drinking his fill' he ruined the gift for all who would follow. He most probably was thinking that he was getting back at the terrorists, with whom we 'shared' these deep pits – for both sides relied on the land for survival. Whether the guilty troop realized the depth of his selfish act or not, no one knew, but one thing was for sure: Water was worth more to us than its weight in gold in the land of never-ending heat, and he had made our platoon suffer for it.

On our patrol, we met a local man who had found a Russian SKS grenade over a year ago, and in Afrikaans he recounted his story to our interested ears. It seemed weird that we were able to understand an Owambo man for the first time after all these weeks, speaking our second language in this foreign land.

In his drunken state, he had picked up a deadly grenade, and not knowing its nature he threw it against a tree with force. On hitting the tree, it exploded, blinding him in one eye, blowing his left hand clean off, and covering him with scars of shrapnel. Looking at his crippled body, we understood that he was just another innocent statistic in this daily bush war.

Lieutenant Bam asked him in Afrikaans if had seen or heard of any SWAPO movements within the area. He replied firmly: '*Nee!*' No! We looked at him as if he were a liar and left him standing with his crippled frame as we continued onward, distinctly believing that he had been in contact with SWAPO and knew of their whereabouts. Maybe in fear for his life, he would not divulge this valuable information to us.

Soon after this, Wayne's eyes began to loosen up, as the scare of permanently being stuck this way began to subside. He started to blink again after hours of torture from his wide-eyed vision.

We emerged out of a cluster of bushes to the sight and safety of our fortress at Beacon 16, which stood out like sore thumb in the middle of nowhere – besides the open bush and the UNITA base camp just over the border line in Angola.

It signalled the end of another patrol, which of course was a good thing. We followed each other to our tent, where we dropped our kit like lead weights and leaned our rifles against the canvas sides before lowering ourselves in exhausted, sweaty heaps upon the canvas groundsheet, which was our floor.

Staff Smit summoned us to the middle of the camp for '*pos parade*' post parade, where we saw a number of parcels covered neatly in brown paper and tied firmly around all sides with white string. First of all, he began calling out surnames for the letters, which we always greeted with a huge smile upon hearing our own name.

Looking at the parcels, we sat in the sand like kids below a Christmas tree, secretly wishing for our names to be called so that we could open a present. Wayne and I were both called forward to receive our gifts, and then we returned to our places in the sand feeling 'as happy as two pigs in Palestine' – a saying we had learned from Els, who always said it in Afrikaans.

Immediately we began opening our wrapped boxes, first of all cutting the string, and then ripping at the paper like two excited young children.

'Is this fuckin' licorice?' Wayne blurted out, as mad as a snake, while he waved a pair of black shorts in the air.

'It tastes like black shorts,' he said after trying to bite into them. Laughter erupted all around him as our troops enjoyed his sarcastic humour.

'More bloody Super-C's and another fuckin' brown army vest!' he shouted in disbelief.

13. Our very own base camp

'What the hell is my mother thinking?' Wayne begged in despair, as if looking for an answer from his mother, with a sudden change in mood and mixed feelings of anger at having been robbed of his short-lived excitement.

We had all been living on Super-C glucose tablets daily, for weeks on end, and the last thing in the world that he needed was more of them.

The rest of Wayne's parcel was made up of non-edibles' polish, a letter-writing pad and envelopes. It was impossible to hide his disappointment, and he did well to conceal the depth of his feelings about being robbed of something he had longed for, for such a long period of time.

My parcel, on the other hand, was a gift from heaven, with the likes of a small box of neatly-packed squares of homemade fudge, homemade fruitcake, and Madeira cake, tins of sausages, Melrose cheese wedges, packets of 'Smash' powdered potatoes, and sticks of dried meat known as Biltong.

Wayne's state of mind began to improve as we opened the fudge and shared a few pieces, along with a couple of wedges of fruitcake. The beautiful taste sent us out of this world, and we reconnected with the pleasures of home a million miles away.

After a good dinner of wet rations, we were instructed by Staff Smit to form up in a platoon. The darkness had begun to encroach upon us. While we waited in a three-deep formation, a tiny grey bushbaby with enormous eyes and large round ears in comparison to the size of its small head, sprang from one shoulder to the next, using its thick bushy tail as a guide. This little creature began to burrow inside our shirts, and then popped its head back out between the buttonholes, its eyes focused on the troop in front. While it sat on my shoulder, I opened my mouth to see what the little guy would do. Cautiously, he placed his paws onto my tongue, and he gingerly felt his way forward before sticking his head inside my mouth for a couple of seconds. I never for one-second thought of any diseases that could be transmitted this way, or the possiblity of swallowing a tick or flea.

These little bushbabies only came out at night, and lived off insects and gum from the sweet thorn trees. The Lesser bushbaby, named after its plaintive wailing call, brought smiles and an inquisitive joy into our world, where very little raised our spirits.

Staff Smit began speaking to us as the little grey creature sprang from shoulder to shoulder in rapid, agile leaps. He told us that an arms cache consisting of two mortar pipes and 24 bombs had been found hidden in some thick bush, well within target range of our camp. This news should have shocked us, but it did not, since we knew the history of this base and how it had been revved in the past.

At 21:00 we left our base, a little disgruntled after being ordered out on a scouting patrol with the hope of surprising the terrorists as they returned to their arms cache. We walked for an hour, straining our eyes and ears for any sounds out of the ordinary. But all we heard were the plaintive cries of the bushbabies as they defended their territory and communicated through the stillness of a cool night. Shortly after 22:00, we lay our sleeping bags upon the dewy ground and settled down for the night, our rifles very close at hand.

It was dark, cool, and eerie, especially with the knowledge of an arms cache found so close to our sleeping position. It was another night of waiting as our eyes looked up, losing our vision and our thoughts in the dark depths above. A chink of moon shone a slim white light through the black sky, and hung as if suspended by an imaginary cord above our deathly-quiet sleeping circle. It offered us that valuable visibility in what was otherwise a mineshaft of blackness, adding further scare to an already scary environment.

After sleeping on and off throughout the night, we woke shortly before 06:00 and returned to base with nothing to report. Hungry, we made our way to the kitchen for a breakfast of greasy eggs and bacon, a 'doorstep' thick slice of bread, and a hot canteen of coffee. It tasted good and was worth the aggravation of being a slave to the upkeep of the base.

Shortly after completing the meal we washed the grease from our dixies and waited for the next order.

Staff Smit did not waste any time in putting us to work, for he decided the magazine housing the ammo needed attention. With two of us to a heavy metal ammo case, we began lugging the rectangular boxes from the cool deep pit, where they sat below the wall. With all the cases laid out in the sand away from the bunker, we began work fixing the walls by filling sand bags with the loose sand that had sprinkled like salt through the cracks and onto the floor of the ammunition dump. When the work was complete, we began carrying the cases back in and piling them, one on top of the next, until they were all in the safety of this confine.

It now felt crazy, how we had yearned for a base for so long and when we finally got one we could not stop bitching at all the hard work and *rondfok* that went along with one of these safety havens. We still felt deprived of not having a TV and a video to watch a movie, like the rest of the bases scattered across SWA. Again, Platoon 3 and Bravo Coy had missed out on a luxury that so many troops were enjoying as a clean, rewarding break to the rough-and-tough bush life, which did wonders to break the monotony.

What we did have was a base for a day after our six to seven day patrols, and ourselves to communicate with over six-packs of cold beer – to help conceal our feelings.

Without any forewarning, we were again turned from the base and deployed for a scouting patrol, with five loaded magazines in our chest webbing and one clipped to our loaded rifles.

Into the darkness we went, in a long line, following closely behind the troop ahead, wondering silently what the night might bring.

1985-Angolan Border. Beacon 16 base camp right on the border overlooking a UNITA base. Kitchen tent on the right and tents half below ground to protect mainly the rank.

14

Actions of stupidity
And more rain

An hour into the patrol, the radio broke the night silence with information on a police base that had just come under attack by mortar fire. No casualties had been reported through the shelling, but the terrs were apparently on the run. This base was within our area, and so our platoon was ordered to begin setting up an ambush – which we did, along a worn sandy path close to where we had found some boot prints.

It was 01:00 when we lay down in a long line, listening for any sounds out of the ordinary. A little way up the path, a local dog broke the silence with repetitive barking, giving away our ambush position.

Els and Solly, being the closest to the kraal, walked up with their rifles and converged on the dwelling. Upon their sudden entry, the barking escalated. The dogs became wilder with the strange scent of the two white men, and they howled into the black night like werewolves under a silvery slice of moon. Thoughts of, shut those fuckin' dogs up, reverberated through our minds, with a fear that our ambush would itself be ambushed, and that the terrs were running close to where we lay in our scared wait.

'Shut your dogs up before I shoot them!' Els said in Afrikaans, raising his voice as it travelled down to us. When they continued to bark, he kicked at the dogs with his thick and heavy army boots – which instantly restored calm, though not before a final yelp was emitted.

'*Jou dom kaffer*!' – You dumb kaffir! – he uttered in nervous frustration, and then followed his verbal abuse with a sharp slap across the local's face that we again heard from our position. With the silence returning to the cool night, he trailed down the path and took up his position as though nothing had happened.

Lieutenant Bam tried in vain to contact Kleinhans over the radio to find out if his section was in place. 'Two Three Charlie, Two Three Charlie, *kom* in.' But no response was returned to the frustrated Lieutenant.

'*Waar die fok is Kleinhans?*' he blurted out, quite shocked that he had not responded.

Suddenly Kleinhans' voice whispered scared over the radio, in Afrikaans. 'I can't move,' he said. 'There is a snake crawling over me.' There followed a hushed radio silence.

14. Actions of stupidity and more rain

The snake had rendered him frozen with shock, and he lay face down in the sand, unable to move as waves of shutdown paranoia shot through him. On realizing there was a problem, fellow troops came to his rescue, and managed with sticks to flick the long, slithering reptile from his radio strapped to his back.

All of a sudden we heard dogs barking in the distance, and then after a minute had passed a few more dogs broke into a chorus of barks, which were now a lot closer to us. Our hearts and minds began to race with whatever was disturbing the dogs, for it certainly felt like it was bearing down towards our position. Looking through the sights of our rifles, we visualized the terrorists running scared through the open bush, passing kraals as they went, disrupting the sleeping night as they tore through the black curtain of darkness.

Unmoving, we waited with our rifle butts tucked into our shoulders in the lying position, with our elbows steadying our life line as we pointed our barrels forward, our sweaty fingers ready and willing to squeeze bursts of fire. Our nerves drawn tight, we seemed to hold our breaths as we waited for the approaching alarm, set off by the local dogs, to draw steadily closer.

When all was silent, Lieutenant Bam shot an illumination flare into the darkness. It whizzed and whistled skywards before culminating with a popping sound, and a bright light was cast all around us. It was the weirdest feeling, to be in a place that we had walked into, under a shield of darkness, having absolutely no idea or bearing to what was around us, feeling like we had been dropped in from the sky. Now we could see trees and bushes and the local kraal extremely close to our ambush site, painting a picture of what lay around our position. Our eyes darted over the openness, trying to pick up something out of the ordinary, but nothing stood out. Within seconds the light fizzled out, and our eyes began to adjust back to the darkness.

Unfortunately the wait produced nothing, and silence returned to the night. After an hour we closed our eyes and used the rifles on their tripods as pillows. Slumping over them with our bush hats used as padding, we stole a few uncomfortable winks before setting off at first light towards our base camp.

The cool early morning seemed to have abandoned all life' the bushveld slept in silence except for the brash movement of heavy boots stamping a path through the dry land, snapping a few brittle twigs, and crackling the grass and leaves as we went. Our line moved quickly towards the orange awakening of a new day, with hunger gnawing at our empty bellies.

So near and yet so far, we had entered back into Beacon 16 with nothing to report.

Our reward came in the way of another greasy breakfast, which we gladly scoffed down with a canteen of hot, sweet coffee from the stainless steel urn. Ultra long-life milk was always used to dilute the strength of the Ricoffey, which had become the choice coffee in the South African army. So long as it was hot coffee, it really did not matter, for in our position we were the beggars who could not be choosers' and naturally we took what we got.

Before we left the base we were notified that six troops from 8-SAI had contracted yellow jaundice, but there was no word on the severity of their condition. Again we wondered if this information was fed to us to shock us out of the boredom and carelessness that we existed in, so that we could pay more attention to our own health. The high threat of malaria was treated with very little to no respect, and most of us threw our white Daraclor malaria tablets to the wind, taking our chances with the mosquitoes and our rank for disobeying orders. We also had the tsetse fly to worry about, which carried the dreaded sleeping sickness that had already left its mark on a number of soldiers from different units. The further eastwards we patrolled, the greater became the risk of encountering this sickness. We had no way of telling which were tsetse flies and which were not. In our usual frame of mind, the threat was shrugged off in the same way as the enemy threat was. There was absolutely nothing we could do about it.

Our ration packs were collected, numbering the length of our patrol. In this case it was six, which meant another six nights in the bush. To Staff Smit and Captain Delport, it did not matter that we had already done five days plus another two in the field, meaning that it should have been time to unwind and relax our minds and aching bodies in the base. Further rations signalled that we would have done 13 nights in a row when we finished our next patrols in the bush – which was not the end of the world, as we did not care one way or another. It was more about our platoon always seeming to draw the shorter end of the stick, though in the end it only drew us into a tighter-knit unit.

'I will give you two tins of curried flesh – fish – for one tin of Owambo *piele* – small sausages,' I shouted across the tent, hoping to draw an exchange as we ripped apart our ration packs. Shouts went back and forth as this dried food traded hands and we gained what we liked and discarded what we did not. I traded hard to get ahold of the red tubes of cheese, which had to be one of my least-hated items in this bland survival pack. I also managed to palm off my rubbery chocolates for strawberry or vanilla milkshakes, which were a treat especially with cold water. Dog biscuits, super-C tablets, and the apricot fruit roll generally got tossed into the rubbish bin at the entrance to our tent. Before

14. Actions of stupidity and more rain

I left the tent, I added some valuable contents of my parcel to my webbing, stuffing in some ostrich biltong, fruitcake, and some tins of sausages. One thing was for sure: I would be eating like a king on this patrol.

The rest of my parcel was locked inside my kitbag for consumption on my return. Food from the outside world became priceless, with each soldier hungering with a watery mouth for a taste of such rare commodities. The temptation to steal was so great that some so-called friends would rob your stash to taste anything but the powdered rations that were beginning to drive our taste buds and us mad.

Leaving the base with another six 'rats' having completed the usual trades, and feeling lighter and content with our wheeling and dealing, we set out on our way. Corporal Doep led us out into our familiar terrain on a six-kilometre patrol, which we were never very enthusiastic about. It was common knowledge how he followed orders according to the book, *paraat* for whatever lay ahead. But on most occasions he was overprepared, adding unnecessary stress that we certainly did not need, since we were already living the life of a nonchalant soldier who really did not care one way or the other what lay ahead.

Carrying our daily anger towards anything and everything brown in colour, and linked to army life along with this foreign soil that we were sweating upon, we selfishly looked only at ourselves. We never paid an ounce of thought at what it was like to be in the position of our section leaders, corporals, and lieutenants as they listened daily to our whining and complaining. But instead, they all remained positive and continued to lead us in the roles they had chosen.

Our section leaders bore the brunt of most of our frustrations, and we looked at them on the same level – except that they now carried two stripes, having received the second shortly after arriving on the border. Paul, Grant, and Kleinhans had the never-ending task of keeping us motivated and moving with alertness as we continued knifing through the bush with our couldn't-care-less attitude towards life or death – a feeling that continually gnawed at our angry minds, rising and falling like waves in an ocean.

The slightly extra danger pay was a pittance in comparison to the added stress and aggravation that our platoon rank had to endure at our expense. They guided us through countless grid positions blocked out on maps, steering us clear of friendly fire with the aid of a compass and reference points that were few and far between. Daily our positions were radioed in to Company HQ, who in turn shed light on enemy activity in the area before we headed off again in our pack-mule fashion.

When the six-kilometre patrol came to an end we found ourselves in familiar terrain, quickly confirmed by the unearthed wrappings of our ration packs that had been dug up by scavenging dogs and locals.

We took our sleep in the exact position in which we had slept a couple of weeks earlier, within the same laager formation, in our nightly, all-around protective position. Something like this could have proved suicidal to us, for the terrorists were known to booby trap areas frequented by South African soldiers with mines and trip grenades. If they had been tracking our movements using the local Owambo intelligence network, they could have beaten us to our area. Higher rank had instructed us never to sleep in the same area twice, for reasons of this nature, but naturally we did not care and took our chances. I usually paired up with John in our sleeping positions. He was the second in command of Bravo section, and carried one stripe with his duty. Pixie, as John was known, was another Durbanite, with a short, thin frame, who wore glasses and had a happy-go-lucky nature. His short legs would take two steps to my one. He was a year older than most of us, and had a year's extra black stubble covering his long, thin, olive-tanned face, along with his trademark dirty white piece of cloth, which he wrapped around his head and used as his makeshift sweatband. Another bonus about John was that he smoked, which I chose to ward off the mosquitoes' it repelled them instantly with the same effect as a burning coil – something that was not included in our survival kit.

'John, light up another cigarette!' I said as we lay under the bivi, whenever I heard a buzz that unnerved me. Within minutes, our sleeping area would have a cloud of smoke blowing through it.

Corporal Doep ordered us to stand guard, and again we chose Bridger to kick off the first watch, for we knew that he would not last his hour before he succumbed to sleep and gave the rest of us a guard reprieve, thus forcing us into a game of Russian Roulette.

Upon waking the next morning, we felt stiff but happy that all had gone well during the night, and we had stolen a pretty good sleep without the disruption of a guard beat. Scratching our dirty skin and feeling hung over from a sweaty sleep, we pulled on our boots and set about making a fire for our coffee. Once the fire was crackling with heat, we filled our metal buckets with water up to the curved rim and waited for it to boil. Our dirty hands ached and had all kinds of burns and scrapes from going in and out of the fires to retrieve our valuable boiled water. Once our buckets were out of the fire, we would quickly add the coffee sleeve and sugar sachets, followed by the white tube of condensed milk. After the hard work of preparing our coffee, it gave us the biggest pleasure to just sit back in the dirt,

14. Actions of stupidity and more rain

resting on our packs, and sipping at this delight while everything remained so still around us. Nothing could touch us in this moment, with the rise and fall of the sun the only visible changes to this otherwise unchanging environment.

At least one person a day would burn his lips on the burning hot metal of the curved lip from the fire bucket, upon which the silence would be broken with a shriek, followed by cursing. After a laugh from the onlookers, the victim resumed his coffee sipping, but this time he paid a lot more attention to how he placed his lips upon that deadly curve.

Another aggravation in the bush was the dreaded tube of condensed milk, which on occasion would burst in our webbings, leaving a white, sticky mess over everything, with no way to clean it up short of wasting valuable water or coming across a waterhole. Naturally, if it was not cleaned before reaching base – which was normally days away – the ants would be attracted to it like bees to honey, adding further frustration to the uncomfortable situation.

The fires quite often became a place of fright and laughter when a troop would walk past and toss a live round into the orange flames, quite unnoticed by those huddled around the cooking area. After a few minutes, a loud crack would shatter the quiet and in one movement as if joined at the head the circle whirled round in fright.

'Are you fuckin' mad?' someone would shout.

This would be met with laughter from those who had been let in on the secret, but it was a careless act and a very stupid one, for the head of the bullet could have struck someone.

'Don't shit yourself, it was only the live shell.'

Maybe it was just a live shell, and maybe it wasn't' we had no way of knowing other than by hearsay, or until someone got hurt. I had often seen a bullet, head and all, thrown into a fire, forcing me to vacate my position until it exploded. But here we were, adding fright to our already tense situation, almost working against each other as boredom began to eat away at us. It produced a nervous laugh from those around the fire, and our hearts began to pump again and we continued with our tasks – as if it were just a firecracker that had been thrown and not a round that could kill.

That invincible shield had once again played a vital role in our thoughts and feelings, which could be turned on and off with the ease of a switch.

The daily radio contact from our Company HQ passed on information regarding SWAPO, who had converged on some schools and had kidnapped Owambo school children as young as 15 years old. They had been led away at gunpoint from their schools and families to training bases deep into Angola, where military training and indoctrination awaited them. Eventually they would return as 'freedom fighters,' their minds converted to Communist ideals and brandishing the symbol of Communism – the terrorists' favourite weapon, the AK-47. Many families never saw their children again after they got embroiled in the bush war that cost so many of them their lives.

Our new orders pointed us in the direction of Ongenga, a small village eight kilometres from the Angolan border. After patrolling for a couple of hours, we came across an old school in a state of disrepair, with a hint of German architecture. It was odd to see a brick building for the first time in ages, even if it had been left with no budget for upkeep – it stood against the dry heat and wind, its white and yellow paint flaking and fading with each passing day. Most of the dirty and dusty panes of glass were missing or broken within the cracked wooden frames. The concrete-pillared corridors gave off a colonial feel and looked out upon an open, dusty courtyard with a well in the middle, surrounded by a circular stonewall, neatly puzzled together, guarding the deep pit of water. An old black, plastic bucket hung from a frayed rope between the wooden poles, which acted as the anchor preventing the bucket from being lost to the dark depth of the hole.

In the classrooms, old, solid, wooden, beams supported an even older tin roof, and the bare walls hungered for paint surrounding a very well used chalk blackboard. The wooden desks and benches sat in rows, their uniformed students paying attention to the lesson as they stared, unmovingly, straight ahead.

Once we had been seen, a stunned silence fell upon the room as they sat and glared at our half-platoon, with our rifles looped over the front of us and our scruffy appearance in torn uniforms, sleeveless and dirty shirts, and unshaven faces that added a mean look to our intimidating stance. While we milled around the courtyard, Corporal Doep spoke to the head of the school, seeking information on SWAPO's movements and whether his school and his students had come under any terrorist threat. The old Owambo principal refused to divulge any information on the enemy. This we knew he was doing to safeguard himself and his flock of children from the lurking terrorists, who always got wind of what was said to us.

It was an uncomfortable feeling leaving the school with our guts telling us that he knew something but chose to keep it hidden for reasons of his own. Turning on our heels, we headed for an old round concrete tank that acted as a water reservoir for the locals in the small village. On reaching the tank, we cast our kit down and shed our clothes, climbing up the old rusty ladder that took

14. Actions of stupidity and more rain

us three metres off the ground to a circular mass of water filled to the brim. One after the other we dropped into the coolness, with laughs of joy as the odour and sweat was cleaned from our bodies, but unfortunately into the drinking water of the village. For our sanity, this cool refreshing swim was a gift from heaven' it rejuvenated our spirits from the heat that burned so harshly upon us.

Once we had had enough, we clambered down and began drying off in the sun, sitting on our browns as the sun absorbed the water drops over our tanned bodies.

'Look what I found!' Solly exclaimed as he held up a FAPLA bush hat.

'Shit, they were here!' someone uttered, in reference to the terrorists being in the area very recently. We took it in turns to hold the hat that had been worn by one of SWAPO – its fold-out earflaps and neck covering intended to ward off the burning sun, aggravating flies, and mosquitoes.

'Don't tell anyone that I found it!' Solly said nervously – for fear of having it confiscated.

Casting our eyes back at where he had found it below a cluster of thorn bushes, we could now make out a few boot prints which were now a couple of days old. The terrs were now long gone, but now at least we had a garment to prove they were definitely here.

These ugly thorn bushes were called *'hak en steek'* hold and stab because their thorns would grab ahold of you, catching on your clothing and packs. Upon moving to free ourselves, they would prick us and rake bloody lines across our arms and faces. The ominous white, needle-long thorns often stopped us in our tracks, and we had to carefully pick ourselves free from their grasp. Once they had got us, we fell victim to what the Afrikaans called *'wag 'n bietjie'* wait a bit – which is what we did until we had gently sidestepped our release from this bastard of a tree.

The secret of Solly's hat stayed with us, Corporal Doep being none the wiser. To pass the time before the next move, we dealt worn, dog-eared cards and played hands of poker. Greg moved away from the group and got hold of a tube of toothpaste, which he squeezed into his brown T-shirt. Before we knew what he was up to, he began to laugh and walk towards Solly, by far the smallest guy in our platoon. Greg grabbed hold of Solly and began wrestling him to the ground, and Solly tried to fight back through his laughter' he now realized what Greg was about to do. Suddenly the card game came to an abrupt end. Solly – or 'Solamonkey,' as he was known, for his monkey looks and small frame – had a head of coal-black hair and a dark complexion, which were due to his Portuguese ancestry. His parents had left Portugal for a new home in the then old Portuguese colony of Mozambique and when Portugal granted the African land its independence, they fled for a safer life to South Africa.

Greg forced the shirt covered in toothpaste past Solly's struggling arms, and then dropped it over his exposed groin area before rubbing it in for a quick couple of seconds. The laughter was unbearable, and we watched our good friend squirm as the heat began to sting him' and all he could do was laugh, his face drawn in pain.

It was situations like these, when laughter flowed unceasingly, that lifted us out of our otherwise unexcitable predicament and presented us with something to believe was worth living for.

After an enjoyable rest with time to feed ourselves, we moved out in search of our nightly sleeping area, as the light began to dim on another long day.

During our many patrols in the darkness, we always had to pay careful attention so as not to walk into the two or three strands of wire that were nailed to wooden poles to demarcate local boundary lines. In pitch darkness, while we walked in a line, the person leading would come to a stop upon feeling the taut strands of wire, and then he would climb through with the aid of the troop behind him holding the wires open – each one helping the next until we were all through. This was performed countless times, and the action was now second nature to all of us.

While I was leading the line, I abruptly stopped creating an accordion effect as I lifted my leg and swung my body through an imaginary fence wire. The next in line began edging forward, reaching out like a blind man, feeling his way forward, waiting to catch the wire. At least a minute passed by before I heard 'Fuck off, Ram.' They realized they had been had. Another laugh had been shared from the trick that Wayne had performed flawlessly in the past, cracking many a tired smile upon a dry mouth.

We found an open area with soft mushy ground, and being tired, we decided to take our chances with the site of an empty *oshana*. Looking up at the star-studded African night, I said, 'There is no way it is going to rain tonight.'

'I think we should still spin the bivi,' John said, with little trust in the clear, still night sky. The decision made, we strung our bivi between a tree and a stick, holding our two joined groundsheets to a V and anchoring it to the soft mud with a string and a few metal pegs.

Our home for the night was now ready for the rain, but no one else had decided to rig up a bivi, believing that rain could not come from such a covering of stars.

It was not long after we lay down upon our bags and stretched out our sore muscles, that we heard the demon sound of thunder rolling over us, followed

14. Actions of stupidity and more rain

by a crack of lightning and the whiff of wet soil with a damp, dusty, salty odour. These signs only confirmed that the rains were on their way yet again.

'Fuck this,' someone swore, knowing quite well what awaited us. And then it came.

The drops began to play slow, unwelcome music on our taut bivi, and with them followed the desperate cries of frustration.

Then the rain began to beat at the bivi with no warning, and the thunder and lightning played havoc in a scene that we dreaded more than anyone will ever know. Flashes of light eerily lit up the inside of the bivi, and the thunder splintered the night with crashes and rolls, while the landscape absorbed the rain. Everyone but us was now paying the price for not erecting his coverings, and I could say a 'dry' thanks to John for his decision to take the time to build a home. Lying stiff and tense and unmoving in our sleeping bags, we listened with dread to the rain as it showered down and luckily ran off our shield. We felt privileged to be dry. The cruel sounds of the night echoed through the sheets of rain, and our fellow friends braved the storm with nowhere to hide.

The gushing torrents of water and wind had our bivi fighting against its pegs, and John and I believed that we would shortly be joining the rest of the troops under a waterfall of water. When the water started to run inside, we quickly pulled our fire buckets from our packs and began scooping out trenches all around the inside, building up a wall to prevent the inflow.

After we had finished this task, we lay back, satisfied that it would hold. A few troops came to our home, seeking shelter. Knowing only too well what they must be feeling, we allowed them in without hesitation. Sitting up to make more space, Rob, Alan, and Bolt entered into our bone-dry abode.

'Ship ahoy, ship ahoy,' Grant shouted into the rainy night, wading through the water that had swelled from nothing into a small lake and trapped angry bodies that had no opportunity to escape. Corporal Doep kept on shouting for silence, but there was no way that anyone could keep quiet in this deplorable and miserable situation, no matter how close the enemy might be.

After a dry but sleepless night, we stepped into the morning, and into the waterlogged earth, under the blessed sunshine. We stared into the *oshana*, where we saw a muddy mess of soaked packs and disillusioned troops, stumbling around as they gathered their wits and their belongings. John and I could not help but share a smile at our good fortune, for we saw ourselves standing in our fellow friends' boots, understanding their dispirited feelings, having had too many soaking-wet experiences of our own.

A group of us converged on higher ground and began preparing coffee over our tin stoves, with a fuel tablet burning hot within it, bringing our water quickly to the boil. Sipping on the sweet medicine, which always seemed to wash away our helplessness and sleepless nights, allowed us to regroup our thoughts. Our strength began to flow again.

After our coffee, we packed up and loaded our heavy packs onto our backs and headed back to the reservoir for a swim. Our packs were stripped apart, and everything was hung over bushes and on grassy patches – to allow the heat to dry them. We climbed into the tank, and into the mass of cool water, allowing it to wash away the night gone by. Swimming and lazing about, enjoying the paradise that we had discovered, we gazed into the open wilderness, watching donkeys stand dead still and goats mill about, chewing the grass down to the roots. Refreshed, we dried off and began repacking our kit for another patrol.

During the patrol I met a local man within his stockade of the kraal, who had a traditional Owambo knife tied with a white string around his waist. Approaching him, I offered food and a R5 note in exchange for his knife and a couple of worthless Angolan Kwanza bills. He took off his knife and took a good, long look at it, withdrawing the steel blade by the hand-carved wooden handle from the perfectly fitted wooden sheath, which had been burned out by the heat of the blade to gain a beautifully snug fit. It was a wonder that such a magnificent item could have been handcrafted without the help of modern machinery. This was his hunting knife, and I could see that he really did not want to part with it, as his mind swayed back and forth, looking at the pros and cons of having a little money and a fair handful of ration-pack food as compensation for the loss of a knife that, with time, he could remake. After a long time in thought, he nodded his old head, and with his cracked working hands he handed over his knife and an old, crumpled, dirty-green Angolan 100 Kwanza note, Agostinho Neto's face and begging hands gracing the worn bill, in exchange for the South African hard currency, dry sachets of food, and packs of dog biscuits. With little emotion showing in his dark eyes, with the whites long ago turned to brown from sickness, he watched us drift through the greenery that the rains had brought, waiting patiently as the distance swallowed us from his vision.

Our patrol came to a stop and a voice mumbled over the radio, requesting that we make contact with our Company HQ. In Afrikaans, a voice informed us that a base 36 kilometres away, in an area we had been in not too long ago, three-and-a-half beacons away, had just been mortared and machine-gunned.

Oh well, poor bastards, was the common thought to our invincible young minds' we showed no emotion or feeling for this dangerous life.

14. Actions of stupidity and more rain

When the information had been relayed through our only connection from bush to base, we continued in our uncomfortable boredom, and another day was logged and lost to a worthless page in my brown pocket diary.

Leading each other into our laager, we again went into our guard of nightly protection, unravelling our now-dry sleeping bags and settling in for sleep. It was not long after we had taken our positions and lay still, waiting for sleep to overtake us, that we heard rustling through the nearby bushes. Instantly wide awake, we grabbed our rifles and stared into the night, waiting as the adrenaline surged through us like a drug and transformed us into a wired and fully-conscious state.

From the middle of our TB circle of protection, Corporal Doep shot off an illumination flare that whistled up into the night sky before cracking into a bright light. It burned brightly, transforming the cover of night to day as it hung suspended from a miniature parachute before slowly floating down to earth and giving us that valuable, bright daylight to see what lurked out there. Automatic fire rocked the night' we opened fire all around us with a chatter that churned the still night into a chaotic upheaval. Tracers darted through the blackness like a fireworks display all around us' we emptied a magazine each with great speed, spraying the bush as if we were using a hose to water a grassy lawn.

When the illumination flare burned out and the shadows of darkness once again crept back, the firing seemed to fade away, bringing with it the strong smell of burned gunpowder, which hovered in the air, burning at our nostrils. Still on guard, we strained our ears for any movement while we lay, stiff with tension, our hands shaking from the vibration of the automatic fire, waiting again for the safety and reassurance of first light.

We drifted in and out of sleep until the welcome sight of morning had us blinking awake. We began scouting around our sleeping positions for spoor. But, unfortunately, we could not find anything to prove enemy movement and justify the trigger-happy overreaction that our nerves, being so highly strung, had dictated to us. No excuse was needed for our display of firepower, for we would rather be safe than sorry and live by the rule of, shoot first and ask questions later.

Off we went again, embarking on a six-kilometre patrol, with Stoop at the helm navigating our course with the compass. The only problem was that he forgot to take a bearing before we set off, which caused us to veer off course, with no landmarks or signs to use as reference points. Corporal Doep shouted and swore in Afrikaans at Stoop and his stupidity, joined by the rest of us as we too cursed his carelessness in adding unnecessary steps to our patrol. After some backtracking, and more unforgiving anger, we eventually regained our bearings and continued onwards, disgruntled, to the end point of the extended six kilometres.

Under first light we surfaced, having survived another heavy downpour – our bivis being our saving grace against the torment that these rains continued to mete out to us in such a cruel and unrelenting way.

Moving like the nomads we were, we set off on a very short two-kilometre patrol before stopping to eat our midday meal amongst the shade of some green bushes, with an *oshana* of water right next to us, which had helped turn the earth into a quagmire of clay. Our soles pulled up thick wads of earth with each step, doubling the weight of our already-heavy boots while we moved, with uncomfortable footing, amongst each other's cooking areas.

Loots, for some unknown reason, thought he would be funny. He looked for a reaction by tossing a two-star grenade close to where we sat, sending fright and anger through us at his stupidity. He startled the hell out of us, and was sworn at by those close to where the explosion of hissing light had erupted. Corporal Doep was immediately on the scene, and continued the onslaught, wagging his finger and cursing all the more in the Afrikaans language, native to both of them.

It was becoming more evident that the uncomfortable bush boredom was beginning to play games with our fellow friends, their sense of reckless carelessness governing their actions.

Continuing with our meals, which were the highlight of the day – giving us something constructive to do, even if the taste was not what we had anticipated.

Now on a full stomach, we decided to look for flexible green sticks in order to engage in 'claylighting,' which involved placing a piece of clay at the end of a stick and, as if it were a fishing rod, pulling it back and casting it off at each other with a flick.

While we played like young teens far removed from a border war, enjoying ourselves in the moment with our toys, we noticed Brian minding his own business, sitting in his own world, cooking over his stove. He always put a lot of effort into his meal. Chunks of clay flicked everywhere, slapping against naked skin, and crashed through bushes, followed by shouts and healthy laughter.

A lump of clay landed very close to Brian and his dixie of food, which was balanced precariously over the tin stove, holding the blue flame of the fuel tablet.

'Move away,' he patiently warned everyone, then turned and continued to stir his bubbling food.

It was not even two seconds later that another 'claylight' careered through the air towards him, landing inches from his meal.

14. Actions of stupidity and more rain

'If another one lands near me, I will shoot!' Brian threatened, his stern face pale with anger.

Loots flicked a shot in Brian's direction – it stopped an inch from his food and narrowly missed him as he taste-tested his meal. Brian, who was a person of his word, took a running step to his rifle and, shouldering the butt, levelled it at Loots and fired a single shot. The shot cracked the silence and blasted into the earth less than half a metre to the left of an extremely stunned Loots. Standing next to Brian, I watched with disbelief as I saw a chunk of earth torn from the ground and flicked up, coming to rest at his frozen feet.

'I am going to fuckin' kill you, you dumb *soutie!*' Loots screamed across the open expanse, anger flowing from his Afrikaans tongue. His face was drained of colour, his sense of shock evident, as he delivered these words with believable meaning.

Brian remained calm, still pointing his rifle at Loots over the 20 metre gap of land, as they faced each other in gripping silence. Loots broke the stare, grabbed his rifle, flicked off the safety catch, and pointed it menacingly at Brian. He was immediately joined by three Afrikaner friends, who also flicked off their safety catches and levelled their R4s at Brian – who with his confidence had somehow made his small but stocky frame look larger than life.

With no need for a warning, we scattered for cover, leaving Brian to face certain execution by four deadly rifles, pointed at his upper body as though by a firing squad. Standing well out of line, we feared the outcome – believing that we were seconds away from witnessing the blood of our platoon shed upon the clay, at the hands of our fellow soldiers.

The standoff lasted a few agonizingly long minutes while Corporal Doep pleaded for the five of them to lower their rifles. Eventually, after a lot of repetitive, nerve-wracking persuasion, Loots and his group dropped their rifles to their sides. Brian was the last to lower his. With immense calm, he placed his rifle on the ground and continued to stir his meal as if nothing had ever interrupted him.

This life was starting to wear us down – its torturous patrols, the overpowering elements of nature, the large doses of anxiety and fear, the loss of self respect and dignity, all together with our intense hatred of this life and this land. The descriptive Afrikaans word we had given to this mixed-up mentality was *bossies*. We often used it with each other, snapping in and out of this phase as the days dealt their seemingly insurmountable frustrations cruelly upon us.

At some point in this lonely hell we all encountered our breaking point, at varying intervals and levels. Some things were wilder and more bizarre, and others were more trivial, but nevertheless we all reached it with the same dangerous levels of uncontrollable anger – made worse by the fact that we had live ammo at our fingertips.

With our 'no-care attitude,' life had certainly become more ludicrous as well as dangerous within our ranks – we lived each day with thoughts of the future freeing us from this life of border-line insanity.

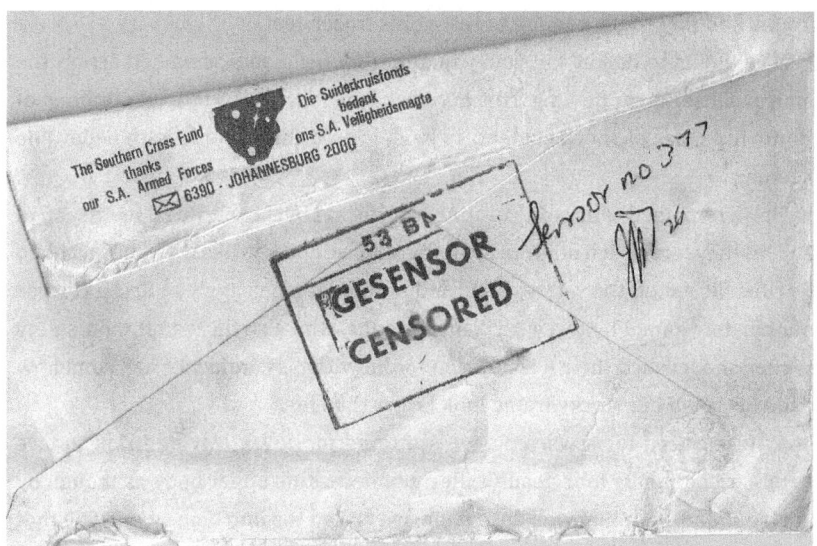

1985-Border. All letters from the operational area were read and censored, before being stamped in red ink, Gesensor-Censored along with an initial, and then flown to Pretoria.

1985-Border. Our hard earned danger pay spent on beer, as we yearned for pass and Civvie Street.

1985-Oshivelo. L- R. Sandor, Bennie, Stoop and Rampie, knocking back a few beers.

1985-Dolfyn Base Omuthiya. Lt Bam shaking hands with RSM WO Eddie Heyman.

1985-Owamboland. Lt Bam with a captured AK-47. SWAPO's favourite weapon.

1985-Owamboland. John and the author with Stoop climbing a makalani palm.

1985-Owamboland. Brian scooping water from the oshana with his fire bucket under a beautiful South-West African sunset.

1985-Owamboland. Never far from the sights of our R4 rifles.

1985-Owamboland. Patrolling the Yati. Cpl Gregan getting some shut eye with his rifle close at hand.

1985-Owamboland. A mine protected Buffel troop carrier bogged down in the height of the rainy season.

1985-Owamboland. Patrolling towards the Yati. L-R. Gall, Alan and Deon looking down at a despondent Grant.

1985-Owamboland. Cpl Gregan.

1985-Etosha Game Reserve. L- R. Fourie, the author and Fox cooking steaks over the coals after some cows paid the price having crossed our nightly ambush position.

1985-Owamboland. Cpl Gregan cleaning his rifle on patrol.

1985-Owamboland. crossing an oshana into the sunset.

1985-Owamboland. Relaxing on the Yati after another long patrol. L-R. Greg, Fox, Macky, Cromps, the author, Solly and John.

1985-Owamboland. Patrolling in half sections along with two Owambo trackers.

1985-Oshivelo. Alouette gunships outside the base.

1985-Owamboland. Cooling off in an oshana. L-R. Paul, Toth, JP, the author, Cromps, Fox and Laurence.

1985-Angola. A kraal cruelly wiped out by SWAPO and its inhabitants massacred.

1985-Owamboland. Lt Bam filling up water bottles from an oshana.

1985-Angola. Burying the dead in two mass graves.

1985-Owamboland. Kleilaat in an oshana with Cpl Gregan taking the brunt.

1985-Angola. Looking on with shock and revulsion. L-R. The author, Fox, Wayne and Grant, while a UNITA soldier gets ready to dig a grave.

1985-Owamboland. Patrolling across one oshana after the next.

1985-Owamboland. A kraal setting.

1985-Owamboland. A faced carved into the side of an anthill by some members of Platoon 3.

1985-Angola. A Portuguese grave in the middle of nowhere.

1985-Owamboland. Cpl Gregan 'winning the hearts and minds' by feeding a hungry young girl with a child on her back.

1985-Owamboland. On patrol. L-R: Solly, Macky, Wayne, Greg, the author, Fox and John in the background.

1985-Angola. Patrolling through some thick bush.

1985-Owamboland, Beacon 16 Base. Playing soccer with UNITA right on the border of Angola.

1985-Beacon 16 Base on the South West African-Angolan border.

1985-Ondangwa. Boarding a SAFAIR C130 for return to the 'States'-South Africa.

1985-4-SAI. Standing in Bravo lines. L-R. Front. Rob, Fox and Alan. Back. Macky, Tony, Wayne and the author.

1985-4-SAI. Getting drunk outside the bungalow. L-R. Greg, Cromps, Fox, Solly, Macky, Wayne, Rob and the author.

1985-Kruger Park, Kostini Base. Lt Bam in the ops room.

1985-Swaziland border, Intelligence House. Wayne solemnly pointing to the bullet hole that could have been my head.

1985-Swaziland border. The Intelligence House where Wayne and myself stayed along with other black berets.

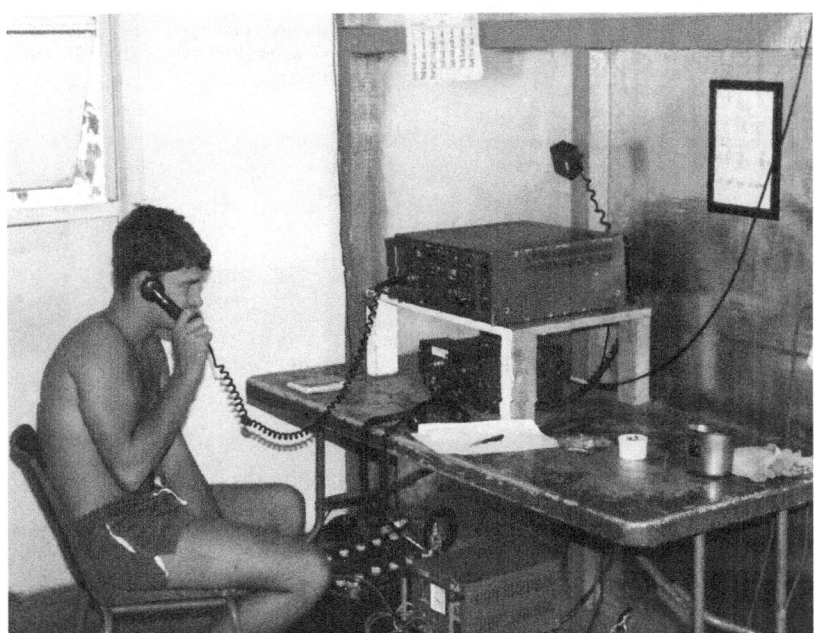

1985-Kruger Park, Kostini Base. Bennie on duty manning the radio.

1985-Kruger Park, Kostini Base. L-R. Fox and Cromps in the front and Bennie and Els standing in the doorway of our bungalow.

1985-Kruger Park, Kostini Base. Alouette about to land on the helipad with Minister of Defence, Magnus Malan on board.

1985-Kruger Park, Kostini Base. Our rank and three very good leaders. L-R. Lt Bam, Cpl Gregan and Cpl Doep.

1985-Kruger Park, Kostini Base. L-R. Wayne, the author, Bennie and Fox. Stunned at hearing the news that our three missing section mates had been captured by FRELIMO in Mozambique.

1985-Kruger Park, Kostini Base. Captured refugees fleeing the civil war in Mozambique.

1985-Kruger Park. Our home for a night in these abandoned huts.

1985-Kruger Park, Kostini Base. Relaxing in base after 10 days in the bush.

1985-Kruger Park. Patrolling across a river with little thought paid to hippos and crocodiles.

1985-Kruger Park. Standing in a Samil 20. L-R. JP, Stoop, Els, Fox, Bennie, the author and Wayne.

Platoon 3

1985-Kruger Park. Bravo section arising from their chopper tent. L-R. Brian, Cromps, Greg and Solly.

1985-Kruger Park. A Samil 20 bringing supplies to the sections in the bush. L-R. Fourie, Fox and Wayne with Louw driving.

1985-Kruger Park. A braai in the park. L-R. Wayne, Solly and Fox.

1985-4-SAI. 23 Alpha's final day of National service and at full compliment. L-R. Front row. Els, Bennie, Paul, Laurence, the author and Wayne. Back row. Gall, Toth, Fox, Fourie and JP.

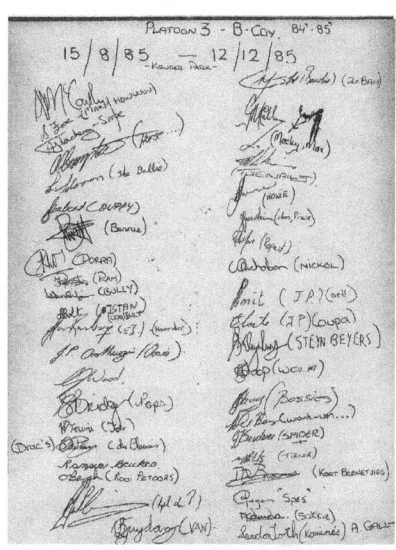

1985-4-SAI. Platoon 3 signatures. Note the last three are Paul, Laurence and Toth after their release from Machava Prison in Mozambique.

1985-4-SAI. Laurence, Toth and Paul with Lt Bam after their release.

1985-4-SAI. Staff Smit forming up Bravo Company for the very last time as we prepare to klaar out.

1985-4-SAI-23 Bravo. L-R. Front row. Bridger, Brian, Solly and John. Back row. Grant, Deon, Loots, Greg, Gouws and Cromps.

1985-Middelburg. Most of Platoon 3 meeting up for a swig of champagne to celebrate our 'freedom.' Lt Bam in the front with his platoon.

1985-4-SAI. On the other side of the 4-SAI gates and offically klaared out.

15

An unforgettable scene

Once back at base, Lieutenant Bam informed us that a whole section of South African soldiers had been killed where they slept in laager position. When I heard this, it certainly made the hairs stand up on my neck with worry. I knew quite well that on too many occasions we had let our guard down during the night.

This had to be a ploy to get us to stand guard, I wondered, along with a few other troops who also believed he was trying to scare us with the fear of losing our lives, and more importantly his own.

On the first night back into the bush, we slept as though we were on a camping holiday at a wild bush resort – sleeping the deep sleep of babies. His ploy had certainly not worked, and he was as furious as a bee smoked from its hive.

'I told you to stand guard!' Lieutenant Bam shouted out in Afrikaans, his red face wrinkled in frowns as he looked at us, waiting for an answer. Shrugging our shoulders and raising our hands with blank expressions, we stared back at him as if to say, we don't care any more about this invisible enemy.

Lieutenant Bam went on to tell us that spoor had been spotted at Beacon 17, which only brought a response of 'Fuck this' – for we knew only too well that this was ten kilometres from where we were only the other day.

When orders of this nature were transmitted to us, it gave us this fantasy of two well-dressed generals sitting comfortably in leather chairs, below an overhead fan in a boardroom, facing each other at opposite ends of a chessboard. Clean and content with life, they reached out and took hold of the crystal glasses and swirled the whisky, the clinking of ice cubes being their only distraction as they contemplated their moves. The pawns of both colours were moved at free will across the squares, which were like grid blocks imprinted into the map of northern Owamboland. The troops had became the pawns, of little worth as we were patrolled from one Beacon to the next, from east to west and north to south, shuffled across the board, the moves becoming more ludicrous with each passing swig of neat whisky.

While we sat resting next to the Yati, Company HQ made contact with Lieutenant Bam and passed on information regarding four kraals that had been burned to the ground in Angola.

'I am looking for volunteers,' Lieutenant Bam blurted out, which turned the talkative noise to a sudden silence. No one was willing to offer an extra foot patrol or unnecessary kilometres to our tired legs.

'I'll go,' Grant piped up. Fox was the next to raise his hand. Soon after the ice was broken, Wayne, Macky, and myself followed by Gouws volunteered – giving the English an edge on the Afrikaners, who were outnumbered for a change five to two.

With our rifles, seven of us – with chest webbings, some filled with magazines and others empty, and a water bottle each – parted company from our half-section that was to rendezvous at this point until our return.

Disappearing over into Angola on 29 March, we began walking northwards through open grassland, which seemed to get greener the more distance we put between the Yati and our platoon buddies. Our alertness was at a higher tempo than normal as we walked the land these terrorists trained in before being dispatched on missions of sabotage and destruction over the border into SWA/Namibia.

After 16 kilometres of nonstop walking, we arrived at the first kraal to see the dwelling, now a charred pile of ash. Clay cooking pots were the only possession to survive the flames. In the middle of the kraal were four neat mounds of earth, which sat with some kind of peace amongst the black, depressing circle of ash that encompassed the well-worn earth, which had recently been the floor to a simple but humble home. There were no crosses or rocks to place on the mounds marking the site where the four murdered locals lay – in what must have been a straightforward burial, but without the dignity of a service, ending their lives in much the same way they had been led.

Wasting no more time, we set off again in search of the second kraal, and it was not long before we came across a local Ovimbundu man. With a stroke of luck, he could understand a little English, and knew exactly the location of the next kraal. It seemed so strange that there was not a soul in this open bush, but as fate would have it we were presented with a guide local to Angola.

We followed his lead at a lightning-fast pace, with Lieutenant Bam following closely behind, the rest of us making up a line that snaked its way through the thickening bush and tall green grass, in a direction that only the guide and possibly Lieutenant Bam knew.

Without a sign or a warning, we stepped through the long grass and found ourselves standing in the remains of the second kraal, which had been deliberately burned to the ground in the same way as the first. In the middle of the black ashes were five mounds of fresh earth, covering another dark event that had so recently occurred.

The local man left us standing in a group to survey the scene while he wandered to the perimeter of where the kraal once stood, coming to a stop at the edge of the ashes where it met the beautiful, tall green grass. With his back to the curved

15. An unforgettable scene

humps in the ground, he bowed his head as the grass waved in the breeze, giving him his peace to break down and grieve, with silent tears streaming down his dark, leathered face.

Not wanting to hold us up, he cut short his grieving and turned around to face us. Only when we saw his old face did we realize that he had been crying – which was more evident after a quick sniffle and the wiping of his red eyes on his dirty shirt cuffs.

Looking back once more upon the out-of-place mounds, his malaria-riddled, bloodshot red eyes mixed with a yellow tinge, he looked into our steadfast eyes with such sadness and yet so much courage.

'This was my family,' the old Ovimbundu man said in broken English, through a hardened face that seemed to have seen it all. On hearing this, we went silent and cold. We each mumbled a poor 'sorry,' then, turning amongst ourselves, said, 'Poor bastard' – the word bastard uttered in a meaningful tone of respect.

In spite of our hatred of this land and some of its people, there was still a heart of compassion in us. There was no denying that we felt his loss.

'Shit,' I said casually. 'Here is a man who has just lost everything – his wife, children, home, and all his meagre possessions. Now he has got fuckall to live for.' I was unable to truly fathom the enormous weight of such a devastating loss.

Now it was our turn to look back at the heaps of sand covering such untimely deaths, and with this we were only too grateful that he had been spared the ghastly sight that would have made a lasting impression on him.

Following the old man, we trailed off in search of the third kraal, and headed into what I believe was true Africa – not a dust road in sight, not a building, a car, or even an aircraft flying through the powder-blue, crispy clear sky. There was no pollution to dampen the beauty of massive trees, standing like giants over the lush green plains, with only the bird sounds and the swish of grass in the breeze breaking the high pitch of silence. The odd ant heap stood like a stone statue curving upward, and the sun shone harshly as we stepped across the plains, feeling like we were the only ones alive in this part of the world. When the first ox wagons rumbled and rolled across Southern Africa, this is what they must have seen and – I am sure – what they would have felt, with the gap of a few hundred years in history not dulling the open beauty and unbelievable quiet that engulfed these plains.

Carrying a rifle and having passed two kraals of buried dead, it was still a magical continent, with adventure mingled with the vast beauty – not that we had chosen to be here for either. On the long walk to the third kraal, we paid little attention to the fact that we had not seen a single dog, donkey, goat, cow, or village besides the two kraals that had just been burned to the ground. This was proof of the clearing of a buffer zone in the early 1980s, wiping the area clean of all people and livestock that could aid SWAPO in their efforts to blend in with the local people, feed off them, and ferry ammunition and supplies by donkey in their quest to liberate SWA/Namibia.

After a few kilometres, our local tribesman met up with another Ovimbundu man, who was also on his way to the third kraal, and so we continued forward with them in the lead.

While we crossed a section of open grassland, with the green grass standing tall up to our chests and at times tickling our faces, we were suddenly alerted by the contrasting sight of four African soldiers at least 200 metres from us.

'Get down!' Lieutenant Bam ordered, his thinking being the same as ours.

Have we just spotted four terrs? We wondered, while we crept forward with our safety catches off and our fingers at the trigger mechanism. Now we could see their AK-47s and their clothing, and it was not until one of the locals recognized an arm raised aloft, with a finger stabbing into the air, followed by the lifting of their hats from their heads – which was supposedly the confirmation pledging their loyalty to UNITA, that we were able to relax. They were not SWAPO and that was all that mattered. These soldiers were fighting for their leader, Jonas Savimbi, who controlled most of southern Angola and had been embroiled in two decades of a costly civil war with the MPLA, aided by the South African Defence Force and South African-led operations into Angola.

Walking up to them with renewed confidence, we greeted each other while our two locals conversed with them in their own language, before we again set off, following them with complete trust as they walked us deeper into Angola.

They wore no uniforms and looked more like a rag-tag bunch of rebels, with their AKs being the only symbol of any military connection. The feet of some of them were clad in black scruffy boots, while the others had well-used ordinary shoes that had travelled many dusty miles. They carried no packs or extra ammo, using the land to guide them forward in the way of food and water' in much the same way we had begun this patrol.

It was not long after meeting the UNITA soldiers that we were led into a *mahango* field with the green millet crop reaching into the air to a height of three metres, engulfing us in a sea of green. These fields of millet were always planted around a kraal in northern Owamboland – as it was part of their staple diet, the crop also being used for brewing alcohol.

Turning around in this field, I cast a look over my shoulder to see my footprints being filled with another troop's. The crop opened like the Red Sea and we passed through it, dwarfed by the height. Without casting a thought to the kraal that should have been nearby, we emerged from the field as if we had opened a green curtain illuminating a scene through the now-open window of the crop – which took us all of a few seconds to work out.

'Are they drunk and passed out?' I wondered as I looked onto a heap of bodies lying unmoving in the middle of the kraal. I took another step closer, and a stench as vile as one could ever imagine hit me like a gigantic wave, knocking me back a step, as I struggled to hold my feet on this shifting landscape. Slowly we edged forward, the smell gaining in potency, until we were standing above the bodies, with the smell of death assaulting us, and lingering over the charred remains of the third kraal.

The flies were like vultures as they sat and buzzed in frenzied swarms around the bodies. Forcing ourselves forward, we were aware that these locals had been killed and left to cook and stew in the sweltering heat, and then through blurry vision our eyes focused on the most unforgivable sight, which remains etched in my memory.

None of us had any idea what we had just walked into, and there was nothing that could have prepared us for what we saw.

An eerie calm hung over the scene, as we looked nervously at the dead, counting to twelve the number of Ovimbundu who had been so barbarically slaughtered. It was unbelievably hard to comprehend that it was for real, and if it was not for the awful smell we could have mistaken this scene for a stage on a film set.

In this killing field, the battered bodies had already begun to turn an ugly, yellowish blue, lying open to the ruthless elements for at least two to three days. We could literally taste the smell of death, we sucked it into our throats with each breath while it hung over the carnage like a putrid cloud. The hard brown earth had been stained crimson red next to the limp bodies that outlined their positions in death while the dry soil soaked it up like waters from a rainstorm.

My legs felt weak, and they tingled as I began walking slowly through the pile of bodies that lay within a six-metre area. As I walked, I could not help but think that at any moment one of them would come alive and grab at my ankle, clinging on for protection. Five bodies lay huddled together in a heap, another six lay in front of the five, and one lay alone to the side. They were all shoeless, their leathery, cracked feet exposed, along with their torn and tattered and bloody clothing.

With a taste of poison in our dry mouths, we had just witnessed first hand the brutal and cruel savagery that plagued the beautiful African continent.

Forcing myself forward, I made eye contact, looking into their glazed-over eyes, my hand shielding my mouth and nose from the odour of rotting and decaying flesh. I stood over a young but unrecognizable young girl. Her head had been stripped of all flesh, exposing a skeleton mask as a face, leaving her grinning skull to stare back at me with a spine-tingling scare before I had to turn away. Standing with my scuffed and dirty boots inches from her skull, and clutching my loaded rifle, I feverishly stole a second glance as I fought to control the queasiness in my stomach. My shocked but inquisitive vision again settled onto her white skull and two wide-open eyes, and I returned the stare with equal amounts of fear. The jaw was tightly closed, forever held tight with the last scream, showing off her long, gleaming white teeth still embedded in her partially removed gums, smiling back at us in an evil way.

'Great teeth for a Colgate commercial!' someone piped up sarcastically, as if trying to make light of the gruesome reality that encompassed us.

The skull looked as though a chemical had been poured over her head, eating away at all the skin, leaving a pearly-white skull free of all flesh and black hair. I am not sure how the skin was so perfectly removed from the skull, except that maybe it was burned and then torn off by wild, hungry animals.

I had to keep looking away, feeling spooked by the eye contact that seemed to hold me magnetized to the victim. Goosebumps grew over my arms and travelled down my rigid body at the speed of light.

Stealing glance after glance, I stared at the right side of her creamy skull and saw trauma at the temple. Her skull had a hole smashed into it the size of a baseball, and I saw flies buzzing in and out, becoming lost within the dark space of the opening.

My tired and watery eyes, burning with the unwelcome acidity of the stench, shifted to the neck, where a white-beaded necklace hung in matching colour to her skull, with the joy it once held now long gone. A thin blue and white, cotton-chequered shirt had been pulled up, exposing her yellow belly with a round mass that looked like a snake coiled upon it. I stared at this coil through another wave of nausea, and then it hit me that she had been bayoneted or stabbed with a sharp bladed knife. After a few stunned seconds, I realized that this brown coil was in fact her entrails, which had spilled out of her into a neat mound infested with flies under the burning African heat. Her red and white skirt lay above her knees, exposing her long, thin legs crossed elegantly in a relaxed fashion – in a contrasting situation to the upper half of her disfigured form.

I hurried a last glance at this girl, thinking that I had now seen everything, and then I noticed her arm was missing at the elbow, the stump covered by the blood stained blue and white of the shirt cloth.

15. An unforgettable scene

With another awkward shudder, I tore my eyes from this mutilation with a sickening dread in the pit of my stomach, feeling guilty for staring at the brutality she had been dealt.

Turning to the next body, my legs felt heavy and my stomach felt knotted and tight, I tried desperately to hold my breath to avoid vomiting from the sight and, worst of all, the dreadful smell.

While we walked through the unforgettable scene, we could not help noticing Gouws on his own, 25 metres away, throwing up every few minutes as he tried to find relief in the fresh air, distancing himself from the flies and savagery. Here was an Afrikaner who had seen death as a fireman in his civilian job, and yet he could not find the stomach to deal with the murderous death scene, which was further amplified by the rotting flesh. It surprised us to see him acting as a spectator while us English city boys stepped over the bodies, gagging silently on the smell as we took in the surroundings with internalized shock.

Next to the faceless girl, another woman lay with a splintered bone broken like a twig as it protruded out of her flesh at the arm. The bone of her arm had been gnawed on by hungry, scavenging dogs and had been stripped clean of all flesh. It pointed upward, with the rest of her arm lying in the sand, shredded at the elbow joint.

The carnage continued, with each small step imprinting another lasting image into our minds, which had been so well trained at suppressing feeling and emotion. An old, crippled woman had a hole chopped into her head the size of two fists, a heavy axe-like knife called a panga having butchered her to her gruesome death. The hole was so big and brutal we could look right inside her skull, where we were convinced we saw her brain. Flies flew in and out, feasting in the pool of blood, and then flew onto us, crawling into our mouths and noses as we shooed them away with twice as much venom, considering that they had sat on these rotting and bloodied corpses. Pieces of her skull, flesh, and brains hung from the hole like a cracked, open coconut, held together only by the matting of her hair. Forcing myself closer, I realized how wrong I was. It had not been a clean chop to the skull, but rather a shot from a rifle held very close to the back of her head, that had blown out the fist-sized hole at her temple. When the bullet exited her skull it had exploded in splinters of bone, which had peeled back the scalp, exposing the devil's work with blood, brain, skin, and skull expelled around her in the dirt like some sort of twisted collage.

The old woman had died while she kneeled over another woman – possibly her daughter, in a last-ditch attempt of motherly protection. She sat like an angel, her arms resting over them in one last act of motherhood, her head slightly bowed as if deep in thought.

Another woman had been panga'd in the mouth, cutting her face clean in two, and another had her throat slit wide open, and yet we still had not seen the worst.

The saddest, which at the time could not be felt, had to be the two children who were both less than four years old and were culled in the same barbaric way as an elephant herd, where not a single animal from the herd is spared. The two children had been shot while tears had dried in lines down their small baby faces. One had his white shirt stained in dried blood from shots to his small back, and a two-inch hole in his neck where a bullet must have exited. He rested upon his mother, they had huddled together before the end came. The other child had been shot, dying a couple of metres from the closest person in his kraal, and looked more like he was trying to flee the turmoil.

Another of the women died from a bullet to her head, which had blown a hole in the back of her skull. The lone old man was shot cleanly, and thus had escaped the slaughter that the rest of his family was dealt.

We could see that they had been severely beaten, as they stood together in the open, before the panga began to swing under the fiery light of the burning kraal. The silence must have been splintered with blood-curdling screams through the spilling of blood. When the butchering began, they must have wished for the *coup de grace* from the AK-47s as they sprayed bullets into them, the empty shells lying scattered on the earth.

Looking at this blood bath, we were not capable of showing any feeling or emotions, for our intense training had turned us into hardened, uncaring soldiers. To deal with this massacre, we joked and laughed, and did not allow the full horror of it all to sink in.

Turning to Wayne while choking back the smell and dodging the flies that sat like vultures on a kill before settling on us, I said – referring to the faceless victim – 'They could have fuckin' pulled her out of the hut before they torched it.' Wayne laughed at these remarks, which seemed to be a diversion from the horror of this sight.

'Thank God they are black,' someone uttered uncaringly. 'If they were white people, I would have flipped.' These words had been shot out under the barriers of apartheid, without a glimmer of thought paid to the innocence of women and children caught up in a massacre over a war not of their choosing.

'Just another 12 less to worry about!' another racist comment rang out, but he was cut short by the smell that made it hard to talk and hold our breath.

15. An unforgettable scene

Such comments represented the way we had been born into South Africa – segregated by race, with the white way of thinking that went along with it. Life was black or white, lucky or unlucky, trouble-free or hardship' and it depended on what side of the coloured fence you were born, and we in South Africa were lucky to be born on the white side.

The hardship of the army for a white male was just a small price to pay to sidestep the word misery, which had been carved into so many black Southern African faces and remained hidden by ivory-white smiles.

A UNITA soldier emerged from the *mahango* field with a shovel, which seemed so out of place in an area that was nothing more than trees, bush, and open savannah for as far as the eye could see. To us it looked as though he had just returned from the hardware store, which was at least a three-day walk away, with this important tool to be used for the burial.

He began to dig, breaking up the silence as the lone shovel struck the earth – the only noise chopping at the constant buzz of flies. The shovel did not stop its daunting task as it was passed from one UNITA soldier to the next, and then onto us to carve out a hole deep enough to hold six bodies. When the first hole reached two metres, we began on the next. But the deeper we dug, the worse the inescapable smell became.

During the digging, Captain Delport made radio contact with Lieutenant Bam and told him to get us the hell out of Angola. Through army intelligence, he went on to say that our group was situated in an area supposedly crawling with around 30 terrorists – most probably the ones who had committed these atrocities.

Suddenly we sensed panic in Grant's voice. He had just been conversing with Lieutenant Bam, but together they had not let on as to what was said over the radio.

'Come on. We have to dig faster so we can move out!' Grant said, in an audible tone of panic.

'Take it easy, Grant,' we said in relaxed voices, giving the impression that we were enjoying a holiday in the sun and treating Grant's panic as a humourous joke. He pleaded with us again to speed up.

Here we were, 20 to 30 kilometres into Angola, only one or two of us with full chest webbings holding six magazines, and the remainder with only the magazine clipped to the rifle. If an attack came our way, our minimal firepower would be a concern, and the hunger, thirst, and fatigue that plagued us seven and four UNITA, against an enemy of 30. With this in mind, we had to hope for a clear passage back to the Yati, to the rendezvous with the remainder of our troops.

When we stood above the bodies the smell was revolting, but when our noses were on the same level as the rotting corpses the stench was abominable, rushing us out of the hole within a couple of minutes. We held back waves of nausea as the odour took a suffocating hold over our senses.

Macky took my camera, and as we walked through the area we heard the blunt click in the background' the film froze a frame as proof of this barbaric carnage, before the evidence was placed below the ground and covered up for good. No shot from this illegal camera could capture the truly graphic, ghostly, and grisly images that assaulted our vision, or what it was like to see it as it was, and smell it, with nothing to dampen the vulgarity.

The seven of us, like it or not, had witnessed the aftermath of a war crime' and closing our eyes, we could almost hear the screams and feel the tension still hanging in the dirty air.

Talking amongst each other as we sat, waiting our turn with the shovel, we tried with time on our hands to piece the event together as it would have unfolded. We believed the terrorists had run their gauntlet of death through the night, waking and forcing their victims into the middle of the kraal as they set it alight, and then, under the bright and burning torch of dry wood and straw, they began their killing spree.

United in fear, we could see how they latched onto each other while they stared death in the face, before they agonizingly succumbed to their violent wounds, one by one. We could almost hear their screams frozen into their facial expressions, which seemed as though the volume had been turned off, cutting short the spine-tingling wails that must have splintered the night silence while the world slept and the explosion of horror erupted.

Taking in the horror of this scene, there was no doubt that a clean slaying by a bullet was easier to bear than the gruesome butchery that we witnessed. Each step we took required willpower to fight the sight and smell with each passing and dragging minute.

There was a group of five bodies linked like a chain, their ages depicting a succession of generations lost in a single night. A grandmother lay with her arms spread-eagled in protection of her daughter and grandchild. The mother lay next to her child, and he leaned upon her looking as though he was nestling into a sleeping position. The fifth of the group, possibly the grandmother's sister, lay a couple of feet away.

Sitting to the side, on a piece of wood that was once part of the stockade, I found a couple of AK-47 shells in the sand. I picked them up and cupped them in my hand. While they jingled in my palm, I realized that I was holding the very

15. An unforgettable scene

force that had expelled two bullets into the flesh of these innocent Ovimbundu people caught up in a war, with no place to escape to.

Next to me, propped against the seating of wood, was an AK-47 belonging to one of the UNITA soldiers.

'Look at this,' I exclaimed to Grant and Wayne.

We looked at the condition of his rifle. It was not only dirty and rusty, but the barrel was plugged with sand. If he had had to fire a shot, most probably he would have killed himself instead of his target.

On the ground close to where the AK-47s stood, a few of the belongings were collected from the bodies and placed in a pile. There were a few necklaces, and a black plastic pouch holding a very worn typed document and a dog-eared 50 Kwanza bank note.

'I am going to take that as a souvenir of being in Angola!' I told Wayne, and pilfered the note from the worn plastic sheath, to add later to my collection of different denominations of this worthless currency.

Looking at the black soldiers roaming the devastated area, we saw a ruffian, ragtag kind of army clad in a mismatch of civilian clothes. One wore a tartan scarf and sunglasses with a brown beret, and another had a leather hat similar to one worn 'down under', in Australia. His blue pants were rolled casually upto his knees. The captain wore a dirty black set of boots, minus the laces, and the only thing that they had in common was the AK-47 and the fight for UNITA rule in Angola.

Soon after the digging came to an end, to make matters worse we lost radio contact, and Lieutenant Bam and Grant were sent into a second wave of panic. Now we were totally on our own, and if something happened and we needed reinforcements, we had no way of relaying our position.

'The radio's dead,' Grant told us anxiously. At the time this meant nothing to us, even though his panic definitely gave us cause for worry. It was a lonely feeling for Grant and Lieutenant Bam, knowing what they knew and not wanting to tell us, and not being able to leave this area until the bodies were buried.

A wall of orange, fertile sand now lined the two dark pits, surrounding the openings in the ground, into which the corpses could now be lowered. While we waited for the burial to begin, the four UNITA soldiers disappeared into the millet fields and emerged five minutes later with a pile of cut green stalks, two metres in length. They began platting at least four strands together, making two firm ropes out of the green leaves. The two green strands were slid underneath the sides of each victim, and with a man at each end, the slack was taken up and the body was then lifted from the ground and carried like a stretcher to the gaping hole. There it was gently and respectfully lowered. Each body was carefully placed onto the next, until six bodies filled one hole, allowing the soil to seal the smell within the pit.

The group of four that were entwined had to be pried apart by long wooden poles from the stockade. It forced the old woman to roll like a felled tree trunk, spilling a pool of thick syrupy blood from the opening in her head. Flies converged on the spot, and another dreadful whiff of death blew into our lungs and deep into our nasal passages. We swallowed the stench of death and fought the vomit that was waiting to be expelled from our dry mouths. The young children were levered from their mother's encompassing grip, forcing her to keel over from her kneeling, *rigor mortis* position into a lying posture. She had certainly done what she could, spreading her arms as a protective shield to cushion her children against the brunt of fire.

Callous or cruel, we had to laugh at the sight of this old woman as she rolled like a drunken bum before falling on her face into the dry earth. Maybe this was our way of shielding feeling and emotion in such a desperate situation, where we drew strength from our brothers in ways that made little sense.

After the bodies were separated, the matted ropes were pushed underneath them and carried to the waiting open hole. While the third body was being lowered into the ground, the UNITA captain lost his footing in the loose sand and fell, with the body, headlong into the grave, landing upon three stiff corpses at the bottom of the hole.

A group of us saw this and could not believe how lightning-fast he moved. He clawed and pulled at the loose earth, emerging with his dark face a shade lighter, as if he had been blown out of the hole by a highly explosive grenade.

This had to be the highlight of the day. We pissed ourselves laughing, with our backs to him and our stomachs knotted in painful amusement, seeing the lighter side in death.

Sitting to the side, we watched the last of the mutilated bodies disappear into the earth. It was the child, and for some reason they were both layered on top of the mass graves. All the bodies had been placed into the holes in some definite order. The middle of the kraal was now naked without the corpses, but still clouded with fresh and dried blood, leaving the flies to chase the scent in the reddened ground and settle on our faces in their distracted search.

The shovel was once again passed between us as the last hole was covered, leaving two heaped mounds at the gravesite. The sun still beat down as relentlessly as the afternoon African sun could. The graves had been purposely dug at an angle, so that when the wind blew it would blow at the head of the mound, along the length of it as opposed to the width, thus minimizing the amount of loose soil that would be eroded.

With the tedious job complete – where black had killed black, and black and white had dug the graves in the middle of nowhere – we had lain to rest these souls that had been wiped so easily from the face of their warring land.

This was Africa, where these kinds of atrocities could be committed before fearing eyes and blindfolded from justice, where there seemed no respect for the gift of life, which could be snuffed out at the click of a finger.

Easy come easy go, as the southern African came into the world and left it, seldom reaching old age.

Els could not have been more right with his harsh but truthful saying: 'The black southern African will have to realize that life on earth is very hard!'

The UNITA soldiers told us that one child had managed to escape the massacre with only a bullet wound to his leg. He apparently had made it to the safety of our base camp at Beacon 16, where he had received medical attention. The terrorists had stolen their cattle, using the herd to conceal their tracks as they made good their escape. In payment for all our help, they offered a couple of cows to us, which we declined, but accepted the offer of two chickens, which the soldiers seemed to pluck from the air. These chickens had belonged to the murdered locals and had now become ours for the next meal.

The sickening smell had now vanished, replaced with the fresh-smelling earth from the mounds concealing the dead. A calm silence once again settled over the area.

Amongst the charred remains of where the huts once stood were dozens of clay cooking pots and water calabashes carpeted in the black circles of ash. Some of the pots were cracked and broken, and we left them to stand like headstones in an abandoned graveyard of broken souls. For the last time, we stepped across the creamy brown earth that had been stained with their blood, and we left behind the shell of the humble abode that was now only a grim reminder of the savagery of war.

There was no landmark to ever find these graves again, and with no parting last respects to their shortened lives, we began to get ready to move out. Saying our farewells, we parted ways with the UNITA soldiers as they disappeared northwards, deeper into their territory, and we began walking southwards in the direction of the Yati.

Hurriedly, under persistent orders from Lieutenant Bam and Grant, we began to move for the first time in many long hours. Those hours felt more like days in one place, and we picked up the pace, putting distance between us and the shroud of gloom. Grant and Gouws carried the chickens, their legs bound firmly together to make them easier to carry and less likely to escape. Grant even went so far as to name his chicken 'UNITA,' after the soldiers who had given it to us.

While we walked, we gritted our teeth and harnessed our strength against empty stomachs and the mental drain of images of contorted faces. Our heightened anxiety seemed to subside with each step towards SWA/Namibia, and we shelved what we felt and masked our fear inside hidden, internal tunnels, and buried it as we had buried the corpses. We were well-trained soldiers and it was our silent, unwritten code of honour never to admit or show fear. And so the unforgettable scene remained buried at an unknown place in southern Angola.

The seven of us crossed *oshana* after *oshana*, dragging the chickens through the mass of rainwater, sometimes with their heads below the water level. Urgently we worked our legs knee-deep through the 200 to 300 metre expanse of dirty brown water as we made our way out of the Cunene Province of Angola.

Under Lieutenant Bam and Grant's leadership, we navigated through the body of water like a lonely ship over an ever-darkening ocean. The weather began to turn on us. The skies started to grow dark – the threat of rain loomed, along with the darkness that was quickly closing in on the daylight. It did not take long before the skies opened and the shafts of unrelenting rain began to prod, stab, and sting us. The drops bounced off our heads and weakening bodies, soaking and abusing our spirits to the very core.

The African downpour masked our concealed rage, and we pushed on, blindfolded in a destitute mess, the scene of slaughter now at the furthest point in our minds. Cold and wet, we longed for the rendezvous point with our friends who would bring an end to this nightmare, and for food, and rest. Our legs ached with the kilometres we had already walked on blistered feet' they slid in the wet boots while we stumbled forward, following Lieutenant Bam as he steered us towards what passed for our home.

I remember seeing a small, curved, concrete milestone, which must have been positioned on the cutline. At that particular point it was no more than an overgrown road reclaimed by bush and grass. It was a great feeling to be on the Yati, for it meant that our remaining section was westwards, on the left-hand side of this border line, at a position that we could not miss.

Walking next to Grant, I saw UNITA sitting contently on top of his radio, which was strapped to his back. As always, we offered words of encouragement to one another. We walked numb and cold into the darkness, with no idea if we were close or still far from the end point.

15. An unforgettable scene

Eventually, at 20:30, the murderous 40 to 50 kilometre patrol came to an end, and we stumbled into our waiting half-section that had begun to worry for our safety, for darkness had set in.

I hope they don't shoot us, I thought as we emerged tired and weak from the darkness, bursting through the overgrowth like the walking wounded, into an unbelievable greeting from our fellow brothers.

'Hey Ram, howzit going?' John said, and thrust a dixie of warm food at me.

'I am fucked. What a patrol. Thanks for the chow!' I tried to gain my bearings and make sense in my disoriented state of mind. Meanwhile I spooned a few warm mouthfuls into my belly.

Our bodies had been willed on by sheer determination from shortly after first light until the cloak of darkness had overtaken us. The seven of us had been moving for around thirteen and a half hours at an incredibly fast pace, barely stopping to catch our breath. The only rest came at the expense of the dead, as we sat in wait for our turn to dig. And, worst of all, we had not eaten during the whole patrol, having survived the day on pure rushes of adrenaline.

'Did you guys find Brian?' one of the troops asked.

'No. What do you mean?'

'Shortly after the seven of you left, he began following you,' John said. 'About 30 minutes later, he followed your boot prints.'

We looked on in disbelief, hardly believing that he would be so foolish.

'If he is not with us, where the fuck is he?' we all wondered aloud, in shock.

It did not take long before Lieutenant Bam got the news that Brian was missing. It sent a wave of panic and anger through him at how stupid Brian could have been to take such a chance alone, in this land where one man could be a sitting duck with the enemy.

There was nothing we could do until morning arrived, and so the questions turned to our long day of events.

'Did you find the kraals?'

'Did you see any bodies?'

'What did it look like?'

And so the questions went on' our eager friends wanted to know all about our experience. With details and gore, we spilled it out, answering questions until we had to stop, for our wet clothes and sleep had got the better of us. Retreating to the warmth of our sleeping bags, spread upon patches of uneven ground, we settled down for the night. Within minutes I had fallen into one of the deepest army sleeps that I had ever had.

In the morning I woke stiff and sore, very grateful that our voluntary patrol was over. I wondered where Brian was, and if he was all right. A few hours into the morning, a radio signal came in from Platoon 1 informing us that Brian had walked into their position. Together with Corporal Gordon's Bravo section, they located the fourth kraal and witnessed a very similar scene. They had come across five bodies, lying open to the heat, amidst the ruins of their burned kraal, before laying them to rest in one mass grave. One of the locals from this kraal had been led away at gunpoint by SWAPO, and he was taken deeper into Angola.

Brian had no way of getting back to our position and was ordered to remain with Platoon 1, with no sleeping bag, kit, or food. They were good enough to share their ration packs with him for a couple of days, until it was their turn to return to base.

We, on the other hand, had to lug Brian's pack along with us as we headed towards Beacon 16, around five kilometres away. While we walked, that unmistakable smell of rotting death trailed us. It had become firmly embedded into the cotton of our filthy uniforms, and gave us no escape from that ghastly scene.

Another radio message broke the airwaves from Sector 10 in regards to our sister company, Alpha Coy, based at 61-Mech. While they were on patrol, one of their platoons had strayed out of their area block, and in the darkness had made contact, killing two and wounding several. Their rejoicing over their kills was short-lived, for the dead and wounded were identified as an African unit fighting on our side. Once again, friendly fire had unnecessarily caused the loss of valuable lives.

In a totally separate incident, one of Alpha Company's troops was accidentally crushed as he walked between two Ratels within the 61-Mech base. In a weird and selfish way, news of this nature only confirmed what we already knew. The *'varkseuns'* stupid ones had been given the Ratels, even though we had been far superior in our battle drills during our first year of intense training. We could only laugh at their stupidity and ignorance in losing soldiers while we, as glorified foot soldiers, were proud to have not lost a man, or committed the worst deed of all – death by friendly fire.

While we sat, allowing the news flash to sink in, I could not help but watch Grant, who had become quite attached to his bird in a funny sort of way. While we rested, he called out for this chicken.

'UNITA, UNITA!' he said. 'Where's UNITA? Has anybody seen UNITA?'

'I just killed it!' Oosthuizen exclaimed, stopping Grant in the middle of a stride, as if he had just pulled off a round.

Grant whirled around. There was nothing he could say or do' UNITA was dead, along with the other' they lay with their heads cut off in a pool of blood, and a sharp knife lay next to them. All of us pitched in and began to pluck the feathers from these scrawny birds, and then with our knives we cut thin fillets of meat for a small braai.

Not even the smell of rotting corpses on our clothes, or the fact that these chickens came from the kraal of the dead, could deter us from this bush feast. Eating a juicy piece of meat braaied over a fire, the aroma of burned meat released into the air, was heaven for us, and we passed up on the ration packs for a small but tasty meal.

Packing up after the enjoyable meal, we headed out on the last few kilometres to Beacon 16. Those who had seen the massacre were yearning for a cleansing wash. When the camp came into view, we left behind the unforgettable trail that had so viciously claimed 26 innocent lives in a single night of murderous rampage.

The day had started off like any other, but it had ended far beyond our teenage imaginations, with the look and smell forever imprinted into our minds. There was no denying that this unforgettable scene would sleep inside us forever.

Entering the base, all we could think about was a shower to rid us from the putrid smell that had walked, eaten, and slept with us over the last five days.

For now, the scene was left behind in Angola.

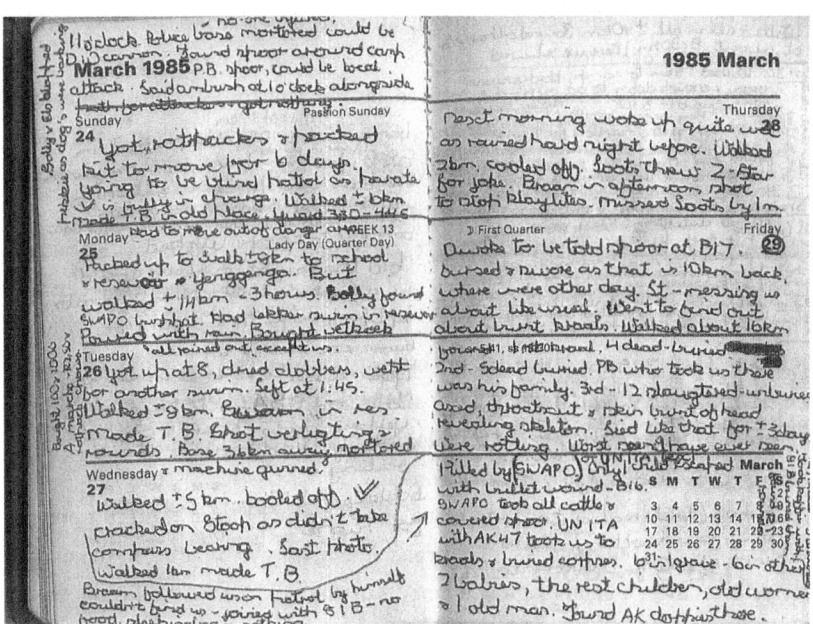

1985-Angola. A page from my diary entered on 29 March 1985 recording the massacre. Entries were logged daily.

16

April fools

In the tent we dropped our webbings and rifles, stripping off the filth of our uniforms, and then raced like madmen to the single shower strung up in the tree. After a patient wait, we took our turn under the luxurious warm water, scrubbing ourselves clean with a bar of sweet-smelling soap while we soaked up the pure feeling of cleanliness.

Returning to our tent like soldiers who had been through a transformation, we could not help but smell our old clothes, which seemed to wreak twice as much with death as before we stripped them off. The stench was left to hang like a bad omen above our sleeping places.

'Is that you?' we joked, hardly recognizing each other with clean-shaven faces and combed hair – a sight that we were not too familiar with and had never seen in the bush.

Lazing in the tent, we traded events with the other half-section. We could relate to common stories of the bush life that was so much a part of us. We heard a story of how Bennie had caught a highly poisonous puff adder that could bite like a dog and kill within an hour. Being the farmer he was, he skinned and filleted the reptile, then cooked it over an open fire, sharing the chicken-like taste with his close friends.

That night, for some odd, unknown reason, our rank threw us an unbelievable braai, with huge steaks twice the size of our hands. Together we placed these chunks of meat upon an open grill, above a deep fire pit of glowing red coals that burned and cooked our individual pieces to juicy perfection.

The meal was topped off with six-packs of ice-cold Castle, which was a rarity in these soaring temperatures. We had been used to chilling beer and cans of Sprite and Coke in a wet sock, hung from a tent flap or a tree branch until the night breeze had chilled it to our satisfaction. This was our bush fridge – a technique that worked brilliantly and brought a smile to our faces. As we walked our ungodly patrols, we also doused our water bottle pouches in water, a chilling method that also worked wonders.

It was great to get drunk and place ourselves away from this entrapment, in which we crossed the days off subconsciously, always thinking of the end of our service. After a good laugh and much slurring talk, we retired for the night, passing out on our sleeping bags.

In the morning, we lined up in front of Staff Smit, who held a sheep shearer in his hand. One by one we stepped up to the box and had our hair completely shaved off, leaving us with a number one army cut, only two millimetres of bristles covering our scalps. Instantly our heads became cooler' our new hairstyle was easier to maintain and keep our scalps free of fleas, lice, and other nesting insects.

Good news was on the horizon, we were getting a pay increase – back pay since January, for the time we had already served on the border line in our war on terrorism. Our danger pay was being raised, which was great news for us considering we were paid a pittance so out of proportion to the conditions and life-threatening situations circling our daily lives. We were always amazed at how little our 19 and 20 year-old lives were worth and how easily they could be replaced. At the end of the day we had to remind ourselves that we were just a number, not paid to think but to follow through on orders.

After lunch, we were informed on news that was coming out of the operational area. A lieutenant from the Ombalantu base, where we had done that murderous night walk two months ago, had just been killed. We were left to presume that he died in a contact.

Another soldier in Oshivelo had contracted malaria and died. This news seemed to kick-start our malaria pill routine. Once again we began to fear for our safety, signing and sealing our fate before swallowing those God-awful pills that only made us feel nauseous. Tired of feeling sick, most of us decided to stop taking them once and for all. We took our chances with the disease – which certainly made us feel a lot healthier.

Things were happening in our zone of the bush war, and our Captain began to elaborate on the details. A land mine planted on one of the many sandy roads had just detonated, striking a Buffel but luckily causing minimal injuries. An AK-47 and a Russian pistol had been found hidden in our sector, to be retrieved later, and there was information regarding a ground force unit of terrorists that were moving through our area.

On top of this, we were told that there was a high probability that our base would be attacked in the night. We found this hard to believe, but any piece of information retrieved from the field had to be treated as a real threat.

During the night, our turns were taken in the bunkers' we nervously waited for the attack that never came.

Another scrap of information, told to us the following day, had little relevance to us but nevertheless played a big role in the distribution of arms to the terrorists. A ship had just docked in at the Luanda harbour with containers full of AK-47s, ammunition, and landmines – a gift from the Communist satellite states to SWAPO and its drive for independence.

If everyone knew this, I asked myself, why was nothing done to stop this flow of arms that would eventually find their way to where we were stationed and claim lives. It was politics' knowing was one thing, and acting to stop it was another. So we continued cleaning our kit and rifles, casting the information aside, for it held no value to us at all.

While we milled about within the walls of the base, we found ourselves in a group that was standing in boredom on the outside of a 16 man tent, enjoying the shade of an old tall tree that spanned its leaved branches like the spokes of an umbrella.

Out of nowhere, Staff Smit walked up to us, anger welling in him as he stood and swore at us with a face full of revulsion. Our group looked back at him as if to say, 'What's your problem? Leave us alone!'

He must have read our thoughts, for he exploded in a fit of rage, picking on the closest and smallest troop amongst our seven or eight man group. Raising his arm above his head like an abusive father to a son, he cracked, and swung his open hand down like a forehand tennis shot, dealing Solly a flat hand across the side of his face, knocking him clean off his feet. The sound gave a smack to the silence, and we stood as paralyzed onlookers, shocked with disbelief. We watched helplessly as Solly landed flat on his back, the wind knocked clean out of his sails. He lay at our feet before we began to move, out of our trance-like state, towards our fallen good friend.

Then, as he came to, we looked up coldly at this bastard of a man, showing our distaste at his action and looking at him with all the bitter hatred that we could muster on our clenched, angry faces. As the situation heated up, Piet Muis arrived on the scene, shouting and swearing at us, in defence of his Permanent Force brother, who were by now only hiding behind their three stripes – or, in Staff Smit's case, three stripes and a castle.

'What a waste of white skin,' we mumbled to each other after being dismissed by the cursing of '*Fok weg*,' uttered by the two ignorant Permanent Force leaders. Before we followed their orders and left, we stared them down for an extra second, our faces speaking out to them with all the loathing that we could muster from within. As we carried Solly away like a wounded troop, with a friend on each side of him, he hung on to our shoulders in a daze. We trailed away to our tent, our tempers reaching a crescendo.

'Fuckin' Dutchmen!' someone swore, in reference to the Afrikaners who seemed to hold most of the rank in the army.

'If only we could put a bullet into them by accident!' someone said, and the reality of this statement was instantly checked by another, as if to strike the notion immediately from our minds. 'We would never get away with it,' he said. 'It's not worth it.'

How we hated these PF's, who in our eyes could not fit into a normal civilian role in life and so had turned to the army as a career. They thrived on the daily power trip that rank gave them, knowing full well that we were helpless to fight back. Their selfish control forced us to live by their rules, with no escape until our two years of service was up.

'Solly, you have to *klaar* that prick on,' we told him.

He was sitting still, slightly disoriented, in the safety of our tent. *Klaaring aan* was the Afrikaans term for bringing someone before a military court, which could only be done within South Africa. It was much easier said than done.

What Staff Smit did, for absolutely no reason, was reason enough to bring him in front of a military hearing. The only drawback for Solly was that following through on it would bring upon him a life of living hell, which Staff Smit would see was meted out to him for the remainder of his service.

Weighing the pros and cons, Solly decided to handle the situation as though nothing had ever happened – which we could not blame him for, since he was the one who would have been victimized until the end.

While we stretched back in the tent, having allowed our anger to subside, a small radio distorted a song from its speakers. It was Cyndi Lauper's song 'Time After Time' – which had an emotional edge to it, and her words reverberated through the tent with much meaning. Time after time' patrol after patrol' ration pack after ration pack' *oshana* after *oshana*' and day after endless day – we just existed in this monotony of a life that was being lived 'time after time.'

We were waiting for our time to come so that we could leave this land. We saw no value in being here, laying our lives on the line. For this reason, we harboured untold bitterness for University students. It seemed so unfair to us that they could live carefree lives of freedom, in contrast to our lives of filth and fear in dirty dugouts, seclusion and boredom tugging at our shirtsleeves while we sweated in raging temperatures, placing our lives on the line for South Africa. Whereas they drank and partied and enjoyed the pinnacle of their teenage years, with no worries in the world, while we struggled endlessly to guard their drunken lives, which we loathed and could never come to terms with.

News reached our tent that Brian had returned, having been led back to the base by Platoon 1. For his total disregard of his life and his fellow troops, when he followed us alone in the hunt for the burned kraals, he was banished to the bunker at the entrance of the base, to serve out a sentence of solitude as his punishment. His quarantine forbade us to make contact with him, but when the rank was not looking we did, and passed over some food, with idle chat to help pass some of his uncomfortably slow time.

Meanwhile, Laurence and Bennie got into a heated fight in our tent. Our platoon was at a loss who to side with. Being in such a tightly-knit platoon, it was extremely hard for us to watch such dissension within our ranks, so we stood to the side and waited for the anger to abate and colour to return to their viciously pale-looking faces. We pinned the blame on outside factors that were debilitating our characters into some kind of animal instinct controlled by the puppet strings of tension and frustration.

Soon after the fight, Laurence got hold of a bullet from his R4 magazine clip and shone it into a gleaming and glinting brass prize. Placing it in his pocket, he crept into Staff Smit's tent, which sat below ground with the protection of umpteen sandbags. Under the generator light he found his bed and carefully placed the shining bullet on the blanket at the head of his mattress. He hurriedly left, leaving Staff Smit to understand that one of his troops wanted him dead.

Somehow word filtered back to the Staff that Laurence was the culprit, and so he was taken from our tent by HQ troops, their loaded R4 rifles ready to be used. He was placed in a nearby tent, where he was guarded the whole night. To their shock, Laurence slept like a baby – not even waking to add fright to the HQ *piele*, who were convinced that Laurence was going to put a bullet into Staff Smit as he slept. I cannot believe Staff Smit slept so well that night. It was as if Laurence had said to him: Don't fuck with Platoon 3! For we all knew, only too well, that we would stand together to lift and carry each other that extra mile for the spirit of our enmeshed platoon.

That night, after a few more cold beers, we settled down in a candlelit tent, with shadows bouncing off the sides and ceiling as we wriggled our bodies into our sleeping bags on the groundsheet. It was 31 March, we closed our eyes, crossing off another day from our imaginary calendars.

In the early hours of 1 April, all hell seemed to break loose. Explosions rocked the silence with piercing cracks and whistles that smacked like fireworks above our tent, in the fragile night.

'Fuck! We are under attack!' a voice screamed through the tent. In synchronized reaction, we were up and mobile within a split second' we ran barefoot and stripped to the waist, and sprinted to the nearest bunker, our weapons clenched within our hands.

Shouts of panic created more confusion' troops dashed, disoriented, through the darkness, seeking the protection of sandbags within the deep bunkers. Our

16. April fools

camp was buzzing like a disturbed ant heap' men tumbled from tents, shocked rudely awake, rushing about in confusion for safety.

Waiting in large numbers within our sandbagged hideout, fear gripping us, we watched the flashes explode with sharp, cracking bangs, turning the darkness into a lingering, bright light.

Our sleepy eyes burned as we scanned for a target from the bunkers. Our fingers curled reassuringly around the triggers, we waited for a sign to fire. But from our bunkers, we could see no evidence of an attack. So we presumed the mortar bombs were coming from the other side of the base and were falling short of our walls.

The gunpowder stung our noses as the night breeze carried it across the base' our blood rushed with the pace of thuds and flashes, and we remained on full battle alert.

After what felt like was an eternity, Staff Smit screamed over the lull in fire and told us to assemble outside the base kitchen. Wondering why he would pull us from our positions so quickly, we trooped through the darkness with little understanding of his urgent order.

After our platoon had formed, he stood before us like a man drunk on power. 'April fools!' he shouted into the night – a cry that he followed with a deep, cynical laugh that left us stunned.

Is this guy for real? What is this bullshit? I wondered. I could not believe what I had just heard. I turned to look at a few faces, for confirmation that I was not the only one who was shocked. By the returning stares, I realized I was not alone.

Silently I thanked my lucky stars, and then cast a look to his smiling, arrogant face.

'You arsehole,' I mumbled through clenched teeth. I heard the nervous laughter of those who still did not fully comprehend what had just happened. Yet what we had felt – the tension gripping us with fear – was as real as the real thing could possibly be.

Slowly we walked away, back to the tent, with the tension easing through jumpy, excited chatter. Relief began to replace fear. Inside the tent, lighters and matches flicked at the darkness, and cigarettes were hastily lit while the non-smokers stared at the ceiling. We did what we could to calm our nerves, which had been strung as taut as piano wires. With the knowledge that our base had been mortared three times in the past, we had to assume that this was the fourth – plunging our minds into a mess of uncertainty.

The April Fools Day of 1985 will always be remembered as the day Staff Smit acted out of total disregard for our declining mental state, and a day that symbolized our continual search for a reprieve from this shit hole of a land.

Life seemed to be going haywire. We all felt like we were losing our marbles. I cast my thoughts back over the last two weeks and saw the strains that seemed to be pulling at the seams of our 'unbreakable' platoon. First there was Brian, who nearly shot and killed Loots' and then Brian again, who followed us on his own and got lost in the kraals of death – then Staff Smit, who hit Solly for no apparent reason – Laurence's fight and his shining the bullet as a threat – and now this April Fools joke by Staff Smit, the leader of the base in the absence of the captain.

What the hell is happening to us? I wondered, worrying that this place, and our situation, was creeping up on us to such a degree that, if we were not careful, something dire might accidentally befall us. Sleep eventually came to us, sleeping within arm's reach of each other – the only platoon in the base to fall for this sick joke.

When morning dawned, the previous night had become history. We moved on as though nothing had ever happened. Word reached us from a headman of a village at Beacon 14, who reported to HQ that a group of between five and ten terrorists had been spotted moving through the area.

Having been refitted from head to heel, and feeling clean and refreshed, we were issued ten ration packs, which caused the tent to fall into a ruckus. We traded goods with the air of a stock market.

'Anyone for snake and onions and a tin of piss?' – snake meaning 'steak,' and piss 'peas' in our wry pronunciation.

'I'll give you Owambo *piele*, and a tin of shrapnel' Vienna sausages and mixed vegetables.

'Deal.'

'And who wants my pickled and curried flesh – fish?' I shouted, hoping to rid this meal of fish breath. Thus we disposed of our dislikes and replaced them with our not-so-dislikes. With a pile of tins, from mince and noodles to musical beans, we began to load our webbings for the ten-day-long patrol with the ration pack diet that was supposed to be balanced and healthy.

Unfortunately, we begged to differ, and only ate it to fill our growling stomachs. We certainly did not enjoy it, for it rotted our guts with foul wind and constipation. But it was food – more than most of the locals were used to – and it did provide the energy for our lengthy patrols.

Grateful to be out of the base, we left with our packs bulging in weight and set off on a 15 kilometre patrol, the sight and smell of death now far in the back of our minds.

In our normal way, we made our fires under the backdrop of an ever-changing sunset, which always made us so proud to be born African. As always, it was a calming moment – the African sun lowered itself with a pleasant coolness. At last we could leave behind the troubles and struggles and agony of reality and absorb the moving picture of tranquil beauty.

While we hurriedly ate a warm meal with our fingers, burned a dirty brown and black – we watched the scene as if in a drive-in. The fiery orange glowed through the tall makalani palm trees before radiating into beautiful shades of red. The beauty was a pleasure to absorb, and yet at the same time seemed so out of place in a land where death came and went with each setting of the sun.

Each sunset was like each day. Every day offered something different, whether it be frustration, excitement, or an adrenaline rush, in the same way that no two sunsets were the same, and yet each was as rewarding to our souls as the last. Sitting still, we watched as the colours swirled and filtered across the blues, reaching high into the clouds as the shades of colour changed with each minute that ticked by.

Each night we took part in this ritual, until the mesmerizing colours of fire slowly and peacefully became diluted and we waited for our nightly curtain of darkness. Unfortunately, we could not appreciate the full splendour of the sunset with the ever-present rifle at our sides. In our subconscious, it detracted from the beauty, which shone upon the same open plains that we shared with our SWAPO enemy.

With night upon us, and our circular position set in place, we settled down into a protective sleep. I woke early in the morning, and felt as sick as a dying dog – my bones cold and weak, and my body burning in and out of fever.

'Oh, shit,' I groaned to myself. 'Is this what malaria feels like?' I began to get ready ahead of time, knowing that I would hold up the rest of the platoon with my painfully slow movements. At 07:15 we left our sleeping area and made our way to a position called Hotel 5, four kilometres away, where we were to receive further orders.

I dragged myself like an old man across the uneven ground, feeling each jarring step of agonizing pain. I fought the weight of my pack, which now felt double the weight. Shivering spells racked my body like an arctic chill. My feet seemed to sink into the sandy earth, and the weight of my gear pulled me down, forcing my legs to work twice as hard to keep my body upright and moving. No one could help me' I was on my own, and I mustered all I had to just keep up with the patrol. My teeth clenched in chattering song. This was the sickest day in my army life, but I forced myself to march on, denying the request of my fellow friends to report my condition to the corporal so that he could arrange for a *casevac*. Only I knew how sick I was – and by God I really needed to be flown back to base – but my stubbornness refused the easy route. I trailed the patrol with a few friends, who stopped every now and then to wait for me, and offered to carry my gear. But I would not have it. I darted in and out of bushes, with diarrhoea further weakening my predicament. I fought off the cold sweats, and burned up at the same time. But I hauled my body onwards. Eventually, pale faced and extremely weak, I arrived at Hotel 5 utterly exhausted, as we began the wait for our captain and his orders.

The orders were definitely not what we had expected, and were met with loud cheers of jubilation. In less than a week, we were flying back to the states – border lingo for South Africa. This was great news, and sent all the troops into a buzz of loud talk – along with smiles, which said a million words. Through my pain, I managed to force a weak smile, disappointed that I could not savour this moment with the same joy that the rest of the platoon had. Nevertheless, our days in this country were numbered, and that was worth a nice cheesy (smile), whether sick or not.

As if a miracle had overcome our tired legs, we walked with a second wind to Block 7, ten kilometres away, where we made a TB for the night. Having walked 14 kilometres over the day feeling like death warmed up with each step, I did not even bother to make a meal' instead, I began to prepare for sleep. I laid my sleeping bag on a dry patch of earth, and with all the clothes I could wear I wrapped myself up like a mummy and started to sweat the fever out.

The morning brought a new feeling. I felt a lot stronger, and ready to handle the new day. On our walk to Block 8, we saw a small herd of sheep for the first time, and licked our lips at the vision of fresh mutton, unfortunately, this luxury never came our way. Once in Block 8, we took part in *Operation Musket*, and were given two talks by Owambo's who acted as translators and patrolled with us. They were the same two who had patrolled with us over a month ago – Talk and Skilpad, who carried G3s (ex-Portuguese Army rifles used so widely in Angola in the 1970s). Standing upright like disciplined soldiers, they looked professional in their clean and smart, camouflaged uniforms. Talk was a mere boy, not older than 15 and Skilpad was in his late 20s. Again we took our two new soldiers into our ranks, without a single question about their race.

Skilpad had adapted his name from the English translation for the Afrikaans word '*skilpad*,' tortoise, because of the way he removed his brand-new, soft-cream leather boots before he entered an *oshana*. With bare feet, he walked through each body of water, carrying his precious boots until he reached dry land, where he would lace them up again, only to repeat the sequence on reaching the next *oshana* a few hundred metres from the last. For the time it took to catch up, he

16. April fools

received the name Tortoise – which sounded more meaningful in Afrikaans, and so the name Skilpad was given to him.

These two Owambo trackers earned huge amounts of respect from us for placing their young lives, and their family's lives, at risk of SWAPO attacks by siding with the South Africans – all for a pay cheque of a few hundred South African rands.

Half our platoon went on a short patrol, and the remainder stayed behind, under the shade of a few old and huge trees. While we waited, a few inquisitive goats came grazing towards our place of boredom. Out came the dog biscuits' we flicked them at these beasts like frisbees, trying to entice them closer with each throw. When we had them practically eating from our hands, we reached out and grabbed their curved horns, and held on to them while they bucked, wrestled, and turned their heads in a bid to escape. Their devilish eyes showed the fear that they were about to die at the hands of these odd-scented white men. But instead, after we had had our fun catching this cunning animal, we let it go before trying to lure another. It passed the time, and was certainly less strenuous than a patrol.

While thus engaged, we heard some heavy bursts of fire and automatically thought it was from our half-section on patrol. Scanning our surroundings, we saw no activity – leaving us to wait and wonder who had been involved in it. Sound often travelled far over the flat, unoccupied terrain, disorienting us to the origin. Our half-section returned, having also heard the shots, but they had not discovered where they had come from.

While we were on patrol again, the rains came down – as if to have one last laugh while it bucketed down. The dry earth quickly turned to puddles of mud, and we patrolled on, before stopping at our navigational point.

Again surrounded by bush, and weakened by the hardship, we settled down for an uncomfortable and sleepless night of helplessness and desperation. Our only wish was for there to be an end to this extended nightmare.

Not long after we had settled in for sleep, the rain stopped. But the water damage was already done, and we waited for morning and the heat of the sun to dry us out.

The sun never let us down, and we were dry before long. Holding a warm fire bucket of coffee in our hands, we got information over the radio regarding five terrorists who had been spotted at Oshikuku, which was south of us.

Loaded with our gear, we set off on a 15 kilometre patrol across the terrain, which had formerly had our boot prints cemented into it from all the long patrols through northern Owamboland. Our talks led us to a Cuca shop, and began questioning the owner on SWAPO's movements. As usual, very little information was shared – they wanted to protect themselves from the hostile retaliation of SWAPO soldiers, who would be back once we left.

Sitting on a log outside the square, corrugated iron shop, we were handed a few bottles of warm Castle beer, along with a jug or two of the potent and revolting *mahango* beer. I chose the warm Castle – my memory of vomiting from the local African beer was still as clear as the blurred day I passed out. Sipping on the beer in the afternoon heat, with the temperature soaring to 45°C, took its toll, for our slurred reactions were proof of the heat. We watched the local people mill about us, buying the simplest of foodstuffs from the small shop – in the way of matches, paraffin, sugar, and the odd loaf of stale bread. They looked at us impassively, showing no signs of joy or displeasure that we were in their village, consuming their beer outside the only shop for many miles.

Content with a few hours of relaxed drinking, our rifles propped against a log within a fingertip's grasp, we decided it was time to move on – but not before we purchased a couple more bottles of Castle for the road.

With the bottles tucked carefully into our pouches, we ambled away into the heat, which seemed to cook us where we stood. It was not long after our first steps that we fumbled for our water bottles with that dry thirst at the back of our throats. Drinking to our content, with our heads tossed back, we gulped at the warm water, allowing it to spill over our faces, cooling us slightly as we stood in the furnace of the afternoon African sun. When my bottle was empty, I looked into it and saw black gunge that had stuck to the sides in a slimy kind of black mould. Inserting my index finger, I turned it in the hole and tried to clean it, though my finger was not much cleaner. When I pulled it out, it was dark black and slid, with a thick, muddy feel, against my thumb as I rubbed them together to get a feel of the texture. This was the water that we had been drinking from the ground, which sustained us in a survival that could have caused my sickness a few days ago. What parasites and bacteria were living in these pools of stagnant water was anyone's guess – answers we would rather not know, for quenching our thirst came first and safety a distant second.

The black inside of my water bottle did not faze me, but I did try to clean it with my dirty shirt cuff, which I screwed into the opening and turned as though I were tightening a screw with my hand. The inside came out a lot cleaner, and the shirt a lot dirtier.

A little further on we found spoor. They turned out to be the footprints of Koevoet, who had recently been in the area and were most probably responsible for the heavy firing a day earlier.

16. April fools

Finding a comfortable and shady area, we stopped for a long rest and used it as our time to prepare dinner. While we collected wood and made our fires, we opened another bottle of beer, giving off that air that we were on a camping trip in Southern Africa with no threat to our well being at all. With dixies burning hot in the fire, the aluminium blackened, bringing our concoctions to a bubbling boil, we dropped our empty glass bottles into the red-hot fire and watched the froth fizzle until it disappeared. Using sticks, we scooped and flicked the coals towards the bottles until they were covered in a kiln of heat' we began to bake them in our hope of melting them. Our food suddenly did not matter, we focused on our glass skills, watching the brown bottles change shape as the intense heat worked its magic like a glass blower at work. In between mouthfuls of our food, we watched the bottles begin to flatten, and then with the glass soft, we tried our hand at sculpting. We prodded the glass, making a hollow in the middle, hoping for a unique ashtray when the heat died down. Leaving the glass in the dying coals overnight, we fell into our sleeping positions hoping that the glass would keep its form without cracking when the heat died down.

The alcohol, in combination with the fact that we had less than a week in this end of the world, produced a fine and deep sleep for us. Before we packed up, we checked the fire and found our work cracked in half – which only meant that we would have to try again. We had attempted this many times, but only once did I actually see a completely flat bottle emerge from the dusty coals of a fire without a crack in it.

After hot coffee, the march back to Beacon 16 began' it was our final patrol over a distance of 24 kilometres. On our way, we passed a group of four Koevoet troops carrying R1 rifles, the short, stubby magazines holding the 7.62mm rounds. These four black soldiers were, in all probability, ex-terrorists who had been caught as SWAPO fighters, interrogated, and turned to fight against their old comrades in arms. Why they were patrolling with R1 rifles was a mystery to us, since they were heavier and bulkier to handle. But in Koevoet's case, each soldier had his own preference, whereas we had R4s and there was no deviating from that. After raising our hands in greeting, they disappeared in one direction, and we in another, over the flat land where bush was the only buffer from the wide-open spaces.

It was 16:30 when we reached our base, with untold relief spread over our tired faces at the reality that our border *opfok* had come to an end.

Beers flowed with uplifted spirits, and we chinked our beer tins in cheers to the end of our time in this forgotten place of misery. But as always, when we were on a roll someone had to step in and demoralize the high wave we were riding.

At 22:00, Staff Smit and his Prince Charles equivalent, Sergeant Piet Muis, decided it was time to give us an *opfok*. We laughed it off, partially drunk and partially not giving a hoot in hell for these men, who were bored and just wanted to see some suffering on our behalf.

Screaming at us like rabid dogs, they shouted: '*Fok weg om die tente!*' – Fuck away around the tents! – and so we ran into the darkness, the laughter and shouts within our platoon directed back at them, and with insubordination in our tone. Stumbling and tripping on tent chains and tent pegs, we rounded the tents and returned to more demeaning accusations and slander, which were heaped upon us with such free will. Again we were sent around the tents, with another burst of drunken laughter, producing one of the most amazing feelings within us. Here we were, once again proving that we could stand as one and face whatever was thrown at us and take it as a platoon – a platoon that was as strong as its weakest soldier. Platoon 3 certainly had an air of anti-discipline inbred within us. We hated the unnecessary *rondfok*, and yet we had shown the skill with which we could launch a full-scale mechanized attack. To us, that was what really mattered.

After ten minutes, the rank abandoned their hopes of getting the better of us and chased us away, cursing at us to *fok weg*, and so we returned to our waiting beers in the tent.

In the tent I spoke with Corporal Gregan in regards to my two rolls of camera film, for I was quite aware that we would be searched before leaving SWA/Namibia. The reel of film was about eight centimetres in length, and so we decided to make it smaller by breaking the plastic canister in half, keeping the smaller reel holding the film and disposing of the rest.

Thinking where to hide these two films, I decided on two places – giving me a better chance of getting at least one through. I placed the first roll of film into my rifle by the trigger mechanism, and for the second I cut the seam of the material inside my beret, making a small hole into which I could insert the reel. There I placed it behind the double-bladed sword and laurel wreath of 4-SAI.

I decided to place my diary in a side pocket in my brown pants, and I passed my camera to Wayne, who placed it in his chest webbing, which at a glance looked like a magazine. I did not want the Military Police to find a camera on me and force a further search, for my gear would be ripped apart until they found the film and possibly the diary as well.

Packed and ready to move out, we closed our eyes one last time in Beacon 16 eagerly anticipating the morning, so that we could begin the journey southwards for a long-awaited and exciting step closer to the states.

17

Going home at last

The warm morning air was filled with a buzz of excitement. We rolled our sleeping bags up and trooped out of our tent, our kitbags shouldered and our rifles in hand.

At the entrance to the base, a Kwevoel waited for the order that would have our balsaks loaded into the metal-walled sides of this mine-protected carrier. Once our kit was taken care of, we boarded four Buffels in our appropriate sections, carrying our rifles and our chest webbings. With six vehicles lined up in convoy, the diesel engines broke into a chorus of revving. The noise further elevated our soaring spirits, and we sat engulfed in smoke. The Kwevoel, driven by Sergeant Piet Muis, took the lead' its thick tyres dug into the soft sand, blowing clouds of dust while we moved forward and out of the entrance for the last time.

Standing in the Buffels, we cheered with jubilation equal to that of being granted a pass home. With that army feeling of 'seeing was believing,' we now knew that our departure was being carried out true to our rank's word.

A few hundred metres from our camp, we had a good view of UNITA's base, hidden behind a stockade of wooden poles, looking far less barricaded and not nearly as neat as our camp. Looking back on Beacon 16, we saw a few heads watching our dust trail – belonging to the Company HQ, which had remained behind to watch the base until Platoons 1 and 2 arrived from their patrols. With faces laughing uncontrollably like a bunch of madmen, shaking and waving our hands, we screamed whatever came to mind through the clouds of dust. Our emotion and glee was directed at this base, and our staff sergeant within it. We had not an inkling of regret to shed from our Buffel along with the three behind us.

It was not long before Beacon 16 was swallowed into the storm of dust disappearing from the horizon for all eternity. Turning around, we slapped each other across the back' our excitement set in with smiles such as I had never seen. We truly were on our way. The Buffel jumped and shook over the deep and bumpy roads, and we were unable to strap ourselves into the rubber seating, or to contain our excitement in a sitting position. The end of this place had to be seen from as high as we could elevate ourselves, and by standing we were able to view the landscape over which we had toiled – at a height of four metres above the ground. The anticipation of a homecoming charged us beyond control, and we gave no thought to the fact that mines had been laid upon dirt roads of this nature. That is why it was mandatory to stay seated and strapped firmly into our rubber bucket seating, our rifles between our knees, the butt on the metal flooring, and the barrel pointing 45° away from us. Following this safety plan would prevent us from being catapulted high into the air, our rifles striking us before we could sustain injuries or smack down to earth with the force of the blast.

Being invincible, and riding a non-fearing wave of adrenaline, we rolled on standing and swaying in the ride that felt so much like a roof ride, and nothing anyone could do to strip this moment from our lives.

Eventually the dirt road met the main tarred link that had driven countless army vehicles to and from the frontline of northern Owamboland. Entering the major town of Ondangwa, we were met with strange sounds and noises not seen or felt in many long months. The marketplace was a-buzz with activity' the locals bought and sold, and then traded the basic necessities, with a lot of loud noise. Young children were strapped to their mother's backs by a blanket tightly wrapped about their frame, which acted as a seat while the young child's legs dangled freely at the hips.

Civilian cars the worse for wear hooted and backfired as they navigated the narrow tar roads in between buildings with familiar names. The two most prominent were the blue and white lettering of the Standard Bank and the First National Bank, in black over a green and yellow background. The Banks seemed to be quite well looked-after compared with some of the other low-level buildings, which needed paint and maintenance. Rusty holes in the tin roofs attracted the heat while providing a cool shelter from within. Black electrical cables ran from one building to the next in a haphazard pattern of woven artwork, linking each to a power source within a low-lying mess of cables. The cables were strung from wooden poles and sunk at a point that seemed easiest and most convenient. It was a picture of a poor Africa where scrawny dogs, in between the fast-paced hustle and bustle of organized chaos, wandered in search of discarded scraps. The Owambos came and went, bartering in the currency of the South African Rand – which was by far the strongest money in Africa. It was an overwhelming feeling to see such throngs of people again, having gone many a day on our endless patrols without laying eyes on a single African face.

Casspirs, with Koevoet policemen sitting on the roof of their vehicles, drove past us with their AK weapons lying across their legs, looking every bit a group of kings as they looked upon the Africans in the crowd, who took a step back, allowing the Casspirs to speed by.

'Did you see that dead terr strapped to the mudguard?' someone shouted above the noise. By the time I had turned, the only thing I saw was the dusty, camouflaged back of the Casspir heading in the direction of Oshakati. It was common knowledge that Koevoet kills were strapped to the mudguards, with space inside the fighting vehicle at a minimum. I am sure it was also used as a warning for any future SWAPO

17. Going home at last

guerrillas to think twice before they joined the fight for freedom – for now they had seen a comrade bleeding and dust-covered, looking more like a sack of potatoes than a human.

Facing forward again, and slightly upset at not seeing a dead terrorist, my eyes focused upon the town, its walls a dirty brown and its flaking and fading paint adding a change in colour that gratified our sight. Whites and reds seemed so alive compared to the muddy browns and olive greens, as did bricks and mortar to mud and sand.

Our vehicles continued over the flat, well-paved road, passing the local Owambos, who were so used to the South African vehicles that rumbled the roads of this town daily. Our vehicles, along with countless others belonging to National Service troops, were a display of the control that the SADF had in northern SWA/Namibia. Some looked up, but most were unfazed by our presence.

Our small convoy drove into the Ondangwa Air Force base with a feeling of security blended with happiness. We drove behind the high wire fences topped with razor sharp barbed wire. There was lots of activity in this base, C-130 Hercules transport planes took off and landed, ferrying troops and supplies with drones of noise as the Alouette gunships hovered around them like seagulls scavenging for scraps. They were in the air, acting as roving guards to the massive and unprotected target of the Hercules' it would have been a devastating blow to the SADF if one of these planes were knocked from the sky.

Platoon 3 was dropped outside a tent, which was our designated home for one night. Unloading our kit from the Kwevoel, we carried our belongings into the cool open shelter, with only a groundsheet on which to sleep. Booking our places of sleep, we dropped our gear where we pleased.

Our final cash payment of danger pay was paid out, which was R86, and at the time it seemed like a lot of money to have in our hands in one lump sum. A few of us scouted around the base until we found a canteen, where we bought an average of six beers each, and then returned to our tent. It felt like a hotel in this neatly tarred and concrete base, with huge watchtowers watching for enemy presence. It was a pleasure to be here, compared with our months of aimless bush wandering and living like dirty animals.

In excited, drunken conversation, we wondered why our platoon had been chosen to leave the border first. Casting our minds back to the last two weeks, we had to believe that all the craziness within the platoon – the threatening bullet, Brian's walk alone after our patrol, Solly, and worst of all our couldn't-give-a-fuck attitude to this life and our invincible characters – had forced our rank to get us out before unnecessary harm came to one of us.

After another great sleep upon the concrete floor, we got up early and carried our kit to the runway. As a safety precaution, all our ammunition was handed in and our rifles were checked to make sure that no bullets had been left sitting in the chamber.

To the side of the runway we stood in three long lines' and with our kitbags in front of us, we were ordered to take off our boots and begin unpacking every last item onto one of our groundsheets. The Military Police – or, as we referred to them, 'Meat Pies' – stood in front of our platoon, looking menacing as they waited to rip into our kit.

Laurence, Bennie, and Toth stood at the front of our platoon, and so they were the unlucky ones to get checked first. They had Owambo knives, a bow and arrow, and bushman spears and arrows that they had bartered and bought from the locals on one of our many patrols.

'Where is the paper clearance for these items?' they growled, demanding to see a piece of paper proving that they had been sprayed for bugs and infestation before they would allow their entry into South Africa.

Unfortunately for them, they did not have the paperwork, and therefore were told to leave the items behind. By leaving them behind, they knew that the 'Meat Pies' would snatch them for themselves, and so together they decided that, if they could not take them, no one would. Picking up their souvenirs, which they had selected in remembrance of a place hardly worth remembering, they walked up to a rusted oil drum that was now a rubbish bin, and with anger in their eyes they began to smash their curios into splinters of broken sticks and bent metal before discarding them into the barrel. Empty-handed and shaking, they returned to their positions.

This episode seemed to divert the kit check, and we all stood still, waiting for our turn. My film and diary remained well hidden, and my legs and stomach waited with pangs of nervous anticipation.

The kit check was over, and the Military Police left us to pack our gear into our balsaks and wait for our flight – which could be an hour to five hours away. 'Hurry up and wait,' one of the most famous army expressions – rather too early than too late – was another hated test of military discipline. It left us to wait at the edge of the runway with no shield or cover from the boiling sun, performing the old soldier's trick of sleeping anywhere and in any condition.

Like hobos strewn along a deserted street, we slept propped against our packs, our bush hats pulled over our faces, protecting our skin from the penetrating sun. We hoped that sleep would bring the flight to us sooner.

At 15:15 we walked onto the runway, after a whole day's wait in the exhausting heat. Wearing our cleanest and most faded brown uniform, with our bush hats traded for our green berets' we walked towards the plane looking every bit like a platoon of well-rounded soldiers. There before our eyes was our plane, with her cargo hold open like the mouth of a huge whale, waiting to swallow a mountain of kit into her belly.

The plane was a C-130 Hercules aircraft, which was operated by SAFAIR. It carried a thick, orange stripe with narrower blue and white lines on either side. We walked in a line behind the plane, into the hold and placed our gear in a heap, stuffing the opening that quickly grew to a huge ant heap of layered balsaks, firmly anchored by the cover of green-spider-web like strapping fastened to the floor.

With only our rifles in our hands, we began entering the plane from a side door behind the cockpit, and under the small overhead lights we followed the line to the back of the plane. Still in a line, we dropped ourselves into the red, hammock-like strapping that was to be our seating for the trip. Waiting and staring at the enclosed, windowless hull, we fidgeted with our rifles and swayed like people on a rocker, feeling every movement from the troops on either side.

When the engines sparked to a drone of life, turning the four propellers, it sent a wave of euphoria through us. Our priceless smiles were worth a thousand words.

'Here we go back to the states!' an excited troop shouted over the deafening noise, while we sat motionless, strapped into our moving seats.

It felt like a decade since we had been in this same position. Now our tanned faces looked older and wiser than our years, and survival instincts were now deeply inbred in us.

Sitting quietly, I used the time to reflect on a chapter of our lives that we had entered, not knowing what awaited us, and yet we had emerged as a closer group of individuals through our daily struggles.

Over the last three months we had left our boot prints from Beacons 10 to 17, a 70 kilometre distance walking along the border road, and both north and south of the border line on our daily patrols. Excluding the month of vehicle patrols with our Buffels, we had walked a staggering 500 kilometres in 60 days, strapped with 30 kilos of gear and moving pretty much daily from one expanse of bush to the next.

In the three months, we had only been in a base within the fortress of sandbagged walls 18 times, and most of those times were just for refilling our food and ammo before being sent into the field again. Our platoon had spent a total of ten nights within a base, rewarding us with the safest and deepest sleep for the duration of our border trip. The ground had been our mattress and our friends had been our entertainment – unlike most National Servicemen, who were gifted with beds and a communal TV and video for pleasure. Beers and other luxury foods came every so often to us, and not daily from the canteens in most of the bases. Our patrols remained ingrained into each one of us, and we moved like pieces in a chess game, steered across the mapped-out board of northern Owamboland, stopping before moving on like nomadic wanderers, at the whim of those with military power.

Our first patrol had been so different from the last. With our rifles at the ready, we looked behind each bush and up into every tree with taut nerves, alert eyes, and bodies stiff with tension, in hunt for the enemy. Many patrols later, we lowered our guard and questioned our place in this land that we began to view as 'the arse end of the world.' Our thoughts began to mesh, and became written into our faces and our body language, while our frustration level ebbed: What the hell are we doing in this country, anyway?

I thought back to the abundance of kraals that we had walked into, invading the locals' space and meeting them with equal amounts of fear as we searched through the dark huts for SWAPO. These terrorists used the kraals as refuelling stops for food and water' they infiltrated into the local population before continuing on their missions of sabotage and killing. These patrols had certainly built us into a closer unit of young men with a high threshold of pain, but nevertheless it was a job we hated. We battled the flies and the hardship – hardship that will never be forgotten.

Those long hours of darkness, dismally lying in mud and water, having endured the worst rains in 150 years' the boredom of waiting for something to happen in our many ambush positions' and the inescapable, burning heat that meddled with our minds, having driven us to our breaking points, also could never be forgotten.

The agonizing patrols through day and night, sleeping at times on high alert and paranoid with fear, in and out of ambush positions in shallow dugouts and living like dirty, forgotten animals, with the threat of death by friend or foe overshadowing our daily lives, all this was over for now at least, and so too were the plaguing thirst and the dry food cooked over open fires, our iron will our saving grace. One word that came out of our harsh training was *vasbyt*, which in English means, 'to just keep going no matter what physical or mental strain stood before us.' By living up to this word, we had dragged ourselves through a mind-building experience that would help us in later life. Very little in the way of hardship could be worse than what we had lived through.

It was 15:40 on 7 April when the big bird began moving forward under the drone and vibration, slowly picking up speed into a bull-like charge, thundering down the runway while we held our breaths. If I could have scripted a song for this take-off, 'Major Tom – Coming Home' – a song that all of us knew so well from our first year, would have been my choice:

The count goes on:
Four, three, two, one.
Earth below us, drifting, falling,
Floating weightless,
Coming home.

Each of us secretly willed the flossie up into the sky. Its creaking and groaning grew with each nerve-wracking second' our palms were sweaty and our legs weak. It shook and rattled as the pilot made a thundering effort to get it off the ground' and then, miraculously, it rose. Now we were 'coming home.'

Hell I don't want to die now' after all we have been through! I said to myself, irrationally, as the plane rose and fell on hitting every air pocket. My brow and palms began to sweat further. How I hated flying! I thought about home in South Africa, realizing that this was the first time I had left the country. How I had missed that magical land of such untapped beauty. I could not help but look back on the friendships I had made cooking around the fires and in the safety of the base fortresses, the anger, the fear, the tension, the aggravation, the drunken laughs, the suppressed feelings and the control that this land had over our actions and inactions.

Eventually, after a very long and drawn-out flight – these thoughts of the past having kept my mind active over the three hours, though my body sat as rigid as it had during some of those pitch-dark nights in the open bush – the plane touched down, making a couple of bounces before the pilot steadied it. Suddenly I felt pure relief, and the flossie erupted in cheers and clapping: 'We are back in the states!' Little more needed to be said to mark our long-awaited homecoming.

Filing down the passage in between the now vacant row of hammock netting, we shuffled towards the front of the plane. I could not wait to get the hell out of this claustrophobic aircraft and stretch my cramped and weak legs. After some time, I was at the front of the plane, standing at the only door, and then finally I stepped onto the tarmac at the Waterkloof Air Base in Pretoria.

To have our feet standing firmly on our own soil was an event of mighty proportions. Many of us stooped to kiss the tar, while others took in the surroundings with pride. Up until now I had not had such a feeling of strength and survival, as I had upon returning to the safety of our motherland. Three months had felt like three years – long days of boredom moving into long nights of little sleep' the salt cellar of time poured its sand at a snail's pace.

Instantly we noticed the temperature was cooler' there was no dust in the air, and the military airport looked extremely modern and well kept in comparison with what we had seen on the border.

Forming a human chain, we unloaded the plane one kitbag after the next until the cargo hold was empty and a pile of gear sat on the tarmac. Once we had found our balsaks, we lined up at a guard post and passed our kit through an X-ray machine. Again I worried about the two rolls of film and the illegally written diary pertaining to events and places in the operational area. The Military Police seemed more concerned with studying the X-ray on our kit than our persons, and so we marched through the customs check without a hitch, into the 'free world' of South Africa.

We waited, wondering what our next move would be. We assumed that it would be back to 4-SAI, and then off to our hometowns for a ten-day border pass. I could not help but remember the casket that was taken off our plane before we flew out. The only difference now was that we had lived our fears firsthand' they lurked and pounced, and then subsided, only to pounce again if only for a minute – but in that minute it certainly left its mark.

Climbing into a Samil 50, our platoon sat with our rifles while another Samil transported our gear. Rumours circulated that we were not going to 4-SAI and then home, but instead we were off to guard an ammunition dump.

'What's this crap?' someone muttered. 'They have to let us go home.' We sat hoping that the rumour was not true.

Driving away into the darkness, we left the base and got on the civilian roads. After a couple of hours drive, we reached a very tightly guarded main gate and another base, still in Pretoria.

Our lieutenant was met by another officer, who directed us to an open bungalow. We filed in and sank ourselves onto the soft foam mattresses, which covered the metal-framed beds. Now it was for sure that our pass home had been delayed – which did not sit very well with us, having 'psyched' ourselves up for home every day for the last three months.

Still, we slept very deeply, not moving or waking once in the night' the comfort was like that of a hotel. The showers with hot and cold taps, and the flushing, porcelain toilets, were two commodities we had long since forgotten.

In the morning Lieutenant Bam relayed to us some news from the border, which he had received through the communication network from this base. After we had been dropped off at the Ondangwa Airforce Base, the convoy of

Buffels and the lone Kwevoel returned to Beacon 16. On that same road of dirt and sand, the leading vehicle – being the Kwevoel – struck a land mine. The force of the blast blew Piet Muis out of his seat and out of the door, into the sand. The front of the vehicle was beaten up, but he survived the blast – which, to be quite honest, we did not care about. In our minds he was a 'permanent-force arsehole and a waste of white skin' who treated us with no respect, and his close call with death was met with callous laughter. Someone added further mockery, making a joke about his elephant-sized ears – which must have flapped like crazy as he flew from the vehicle. It gave us another laugh about the coward who backed Staff Smit when Solly was knocked off his feet.

Then we remembered how we had stood for miles while travelling on this same road, defying our orders to strap in while we celebrated our departure. Suddenly it struck us what our predicament could have been had we detonated the mine. We wondered if it had been planted after we had passed over the area, or if our vehicles somehow miraculously missed running over it. It is a question to which we will never know the answer to, but either way we were lucky!

At the next bit of news, our ears strained to get all the details. Platoon 1 had walked into a group of three terrorists as they knelt in an *oshana*, drinking the water in the same way we used to. By the element of surprise, they managed to catch one alive, but lost the others as they sprinted away. The captured terrorist was supposedly a detachment commander who had received training in East Germany – known as the DDR, and carried kit manufactured in East Germany and Czechoslovakia – both Communist satellite states loyal to the spread of Marxism through Southern Africa. With his AK-47 firmly in the hands of Platoon 1, he spoke freely with his enemy while he waited to be picked up and taken away for his interrogation at Oshakati. The two terrorists on the run were not as lucky, discarding their Soviet kit to lighten their load in the hope of getting clear of the gunships that had been radioed in and chased them like eagles after their prey. It did not take long before they were cut down in full stride by the deadly thud of the 20mm cannon, with Platoon 1 hearing the muffled thuds that they hoped was the end of the two escaping SWAPO.

When Platoons 1 and 2 returned to South African soil, uniting Bravo into a company once again, we could boast of returning from the operational area without suffering a single casualty. It was an incredible feat, considering that most units had lost soldiers to enemy contact, friendly fire, vehicle or weaponry accidents, diseases such as malaria and meningitis, and even suicide. Not only did we have a clean sheet, but also our company could now take credit for one SWAPO soldier captured, and indirectly for the deaths of two more.

Having suffered many close calls, it was as though a hand of protection stretched over us like a shield, driving away danger. We had been spared killing or being killed, but there was always the thought of how close we had come to mistakenly taking one of our own lives.

The year of 1985 produced the following statistics in the operational area within SWA/Namibia:

CONTACTS	252
INSURGENTS KILLED	590
CIVILIANS KILLED	56
CIVILIANS ABDUCTED	179
MINES DETONATED	170
DISCOVERED VEHICLE MINES	147
DISCOVERED PERSONNEL MINES	284
CAPTURED RIFLES	514
CAPTURED RIFLE GRENADES	1006
CAPTURED HAND GRENADES	512
CAPTURED MORTAR BOMBS	1966

This information was acquired from *The Frontline Special Report*, published in March 1989, and from *South Africa's Border War*, by Willem Steenkamp.

Also in 1985, according to Eugene Griesel, 88 security forces died – in contacts, accidents, and disease. With thousands of troops in the operational area, this figure has to be attributed to the extremely high standard of training and discipline within the military units of South Africa and South-West Africa. The rank's goal, first and foremost, was to return us safely to our worrying mothers.

For now it was over, and we could feel safer within the borders of our own beloved land – far from the border-line insanity that had festered deep within us for so long. Our life of hardship, which words do not come close to describing, had been lived the only way our teenage souls knew – and that was through the unbreakable bond of camaraderie.

Standing in the bright morning light, still adjusting to life outside of the bush, we scoured our new base, wondering what we had been placed here for.

However, we were home – and to all of us, that was all that really mattered, for we could finally close the most demanding chapter in our young, teenage, army lives.

18

Guarding an ammo dump
An overdue pass

A gloriously crisp morning greeted us, from an unbroken spell of fine South African weather, in an array of colours. The perfectly manicured grass, like that of a bowling green, was as green as an English meadow – the plants, in a built-up, weedless rockery, were out of this world, flowering in reds and yellows, with a couple of flatcrown trees adding the finishing touch to a simple paradise below the backdrop of a sea-blue sky' the odd, wispy white clouds were moving freely with the breeze.

What a powerful contrast this was with the scenery during the past 16 months of our National Service. Within a day we had come from the wild, rugged African bush to the neatly carved-out beauty of a well-maintained garden of colour – a sight that seemed out of place to what we had become accustomed.

We had arrived in the darkness, winding up a tarred road to the plateau on top of this hill, quite oblivious to where we were. Now standing outside the clean brick bungalow, we looked upon the city below us, with buildings dotted in blocks amongst the intersections of paved roads. This was Pretoria, and we were now sitting on top of one of the biggest ammunition dumps in South Africa, with a network of tunnels excavated into the hillside, filled with a stockpile of ammunition and explosives.

Word had it that there had been a threat to blow it up, and so we had been placed here to add to the guard roster – which was surprising, since our platoon was known to have had a bad record when it came to standing guard' we had demonstrated that on so many occasions on the border.

Through the day and through the night, we walked to these concrete guard towers positioned in the corners of the base. We climbed the stairs, spiralling 15 metres up from the ground, our rifles and a radio linking us to the same frequency as the other towers. Sitting and standing in these cold, damp, cylinder-like structures for two hours, we gazed around at our surroundings. The time passed through radio contact with our friends and brief naps upon the damp, urine-smelling, concrete floor.

Walking to the towers at night was quite an experience. Everything was dark, quiet, and eerie, and we had only a torch to illuminate the farthest, desolate corners of the base. We heard – and felt – every sound. I climbed into the tower with a sense of safety, and only returned when I sat in the circular area, having sent a few bats flying from the ceiling with the bright beam from the torch. Looking down upon the lights of Pretoria was quite a sight, having not seen a city of twinkling lights in over three months. To me it looked like the night sky on the border in South-West Africa, except not as beautiful and tranquil.

It was always a relief to pass guard duty to the next unlucky man and obtain a warm bed, as opposed to the cold concrete floor. At 06:00 we often heard screams and shouts from the city below us. We believed that they came from Pretoria's main prison, where death row inmates waited for their 06:00 execution by the hangman's noose. Whether our speculation was correct I do not know, but these shouts and screams certainly carried with them an uncomfortable fear. Silence almost always returned shortly after the clocks struck 06:00, the gallows doing justice or injustice to the irreversible crime and fate of the perpetrator.

A week into our guard duties, Lieutenant Bam ushered all of us out of the bungalow and onto the green carpet of grass. While we stood as a platoon, he questioned us on the theft of Bridger's wallet, which had his cash from yesterday's payday in it. While our lieutie threw the questions at us, Corporal Doep, unbeknown to us, climbed a tree and watched our movements and expressions in his quest to catch the culprit or culprits from within our ranks.

This episode left a bad taste in our mouths and wiped away the notion that we were as one with each other, with bonds as strong as steel. It just went to prove that, even amongst our own there were thieves, and we could not fully trust the person who slept on either side of us. There was a slight exception to this rule – the bunch of Durbanites that were bound so close, knew we could wholeheartedly trust one another.

The money was never recovered, and the dirty deed hung over our platoon like a disease, forming a rift between us. Our silent suspicion indirectly pointed towards a few of the really hard-core dagga smokers. A few of us English were sure as all hell that Bridger's measly army pittance had gone towards the next stash of marijuana.

After two weeks of guard duty at this very vulnerable and explosive target, we packed up and left for 4-SAI, which could only mean one thing – our overdue pass.

A Samil drove us through the gates of 4-SAI. We were floating on adrenaline and excitement at the thought of a visit home, to places we had not seen in over four months. The vehicle dropped us outside our bungalow, which looked exactly as we had left it months ago. Trailing through it with our kit, we dropped our gear on our mattresses, and after a shit, shower, and shampoo, we packed our kit away and packed a bag for home.

After a good night's sleep in our beds, we woke and dressed in our most faded browns, our spit-polished boots gleamed brown and Toney-red. We wore

18. Guarding an ammo dump: An overdue pass

our flashes on our epaulettes, along with our cravats, staple belts, white boot cuffs, and our green berets tilted sharply to the right. We looked sharp, every bit like a professional unit, with a highly-disciplined soldier's edge, even though we were an army of conscripted teenagers, we were older and wiser than our years, and were as professional as any professional army around.

A Samil loaded us up and took us out of the gates and dropped us on the road at the demarcated 'Ride Safe' pick up points. There was a silhouette of a soldier on the sign, marking this as a safe point to hitchhike from. These silhouettes had been placed at strategic points along main roads, in an effort to reduce the amount of troops who were killed as they stood in the middle of nowhere waiting for a lift. Most troops teamed up with a friend to wait for the ride that would take us closer to home. Standing with our 'Day-Glo' sashes, we stood as free soldiers, with ten days of border pass ahead of us.

After at least ten different rides, with a story to tell on each, we had travelled close to 1000 kilometres along quiet secondary roads and main roads, with the long journey taking us well into the night. We remained wary of each driver, even though nine out of ten were whites who either had a son in the army or had just finished a stint of service themselves. Our guard remained up, generally one of us slept while the other spoke to the driver. It was common knowledge to us, the high death rate of soldiers killed in road accidents' and Wayne and I, who hitched together on most occasions, made sure that we would not become one of those negative statistics.

When our ride finally reached a small town called Hillcrest, we shook hands before I stepped out onto the Old Main Road. I walked the last 200 metres to my parents' home, and Wayne continued towards his hometown in Pinetown, another 10 to 15 minutes away.

It was a great feeling to walk through the big three-acre garden and see the tall flatcrown trees, azalea bushes, and the massive jacaranda tree, which in full bloom spread a canopy of purple flowers. It was pitch-dark when I walked through the garden towards the old farmhouse, whose typically wide-pillared veranda glowed with lights to await my return. Tired and excited, I climbed the stone steps and lifted the brass fox knocker and hammered two sharp strikes to the thick-oak stable door flanked by two Victorian carriage lamps. While I waited to surprise my parents, I looked upon this beautiful, open-grassed garden, with trees as old as the turn-of-the-century home, standing in the shadows, and the moon and stars adding a sparkle to the stillness, and the solitude reminding me of the border. The dew had descended' cooling the night after a blistering hot day while a thin blanket of mist blew across the open lawns. Because of the high altitude, the night was comfortable, free of humidity and itchy, sticky heat.

When the stable door was opened in its two halves, I was welcomed home with hugs and handshakes, smiles and the instant offer of food and a cold beer. What a feeling it was to be back home and catching up on news in person, in a familiar and safe place – even if it was for only ten days.

The excitement began to slowly wear off, and sleep edged its way in, and like a new person I dragged myself off to bed with a full stomach, a happy heart, and a slightly cloudy head from the few quick beers. Sleep came easily on my familiar bed, and I sank into a deep, unmoving rest, knowing that I did not have to rise at 06:00. As deeply as I slept, I still jolted awake at sudden, out-of-place noises, which on more than one occasion had me fumbling for my rifle. One night I heard branches brushing and scraping against the window with the wind. I woke up, wide-eyed with paranoia, and in my effort to grab my imaginary rifle I knocked the lampshade off the light above my bed. I tried to place my surroundings, and it took some long drawn out seconds before I managed to regain my bearings. With a wry smile, I dropped back onto the mattress, my heart still pounding. I wondered what the hell was going on with me.

It was amazing how ingrained our reactions had become to the slightest sound. We overreacted to each unplaced noise. I can clearly remember my mother tiptoeing over the oregon pine floorboards, through the billiard room, towards my room at the end of the house, with a morning cup of tea. As silent as her footsteps were, at the odd, muffled creak of a floorboard my eyes shot wide open and my body remained dead still and as stiff as a plank, waiting for her to enter my room. Only then did I realize where I was, and only then could I relax.

'Oh you are awake. I thought you would still be sleeping!' my Mum said, not aware of the wave of paranoia that was inside me.

What the hell? I questioned myself – having no idea of the meaning or context of the word trauma. I am safe here. Why the anxiety and tension?

Wayne and I saw a lot of each other over the course of the pass, drinking at all hours and making up for lost laughs in the civilized world out of uniform.

One drunken night we were met by one of Wayne's friends, Paul, in the parking lot outside the Imperial Hotel in Pinetown, with his newly-acquired motorbike. I took it for a ride first and careered straight towards a concrete wall. I had only a split second to brake before hitting it head on, with no protection for my head other than the 12 beers that we had recently consumed. I managed, though, to spin it around – which felt spectacular in my drunken daze – and

I drove it full-throttle back to where Wayne and Paul stood. I drew up next to them, looking as though I was in full control of my actions, and stopped. I forgot to put my foot out to balance the bike, and as a result it toppled onto me' we crashed together on the hard tarmac. I was so intoxicated that I could not even feel the embarrassment, let alone any pain. Paul hurriedly picked up his bike and left us standing in the desolate car park in the early hours of morning. Climbing into my mother's Opel Kadett, we headed towards Wayne's mother's apartment for sleep.

On the way through Pinetown we saw a lone figure walking through an open, misty field, following a well-worn path on his way to work at around 03:00. This open area, with long grass, was close to Wayne's mother's apartment, and was used as a cut-through into the city of Pinetown.

Drunk and angry for the way our lives had been dictated to, under strict discipline in an army that we did not want to be a part of, with hatred like we had never felt welling up and consuming our dulled drunken minds, we watched this African man making his way innocently through the open field. In our drunken state we got out of the car and made our way towards him.

'You fuckin' bastard,' we swore at him. 'You are the reason we have been on the border shitting ourselves and why we have to do the fuckin' army!'

He looked at us, stunned and scared, and then we committed the most cowardly act there is to commit on an innocent person. We started punching and kicking this Zulu man until our hands and feet were throbbing with pain – we used his body as an outlet for the uncontrolled rage that had been building in us over the last 16 months of hardship.

'Fuck off, you dumb black!' we swore at this crumpled heap of a man. He lay still in the long grass before we turned and made our way towards the car.

It felt like the tables were turned, and we were the rank verbally abusing the troop – for we spat out the racial abuse that had been driven into us daily.

Completely out of it, our breath reeking of booze, we drove around the block to try and calm our out-of-control actions and regain our breathing, which had become loud and heavy.

After the short drive, we returned to see the beaten man rising to his feet. This action of defiance sent us into another berserk state, forcing us to rush at him again and rain more cowardly blows upon him. He was quickly on the ground before a white woman's scream of 'What's going on?' rescued him from further torment.

'He tried to steal my friend's motorbike,' I shouted out into the night trying to appease the worry in the woman's voice. I looked down at the cowering man in an effort to justify our most heinous crime, committed upon an innocent person minding his own business.

Sore, tired, and drunk, we left the beaten man lying like a rag doll in the damp, long grass. The mist began to move in, to somehow cover up this despicable act of cowardice. Arriving at Wayne's mother's apartment, I said to him, 'We have just made another person join the ranks of the ANC.' We shared a sheepish smile as we entered the main door and hurriedly closed it – as if to close our minds upon the dreadful past.

The morning brought with it blurry vision and a throbbing, heavy head – our hands and feet ached terribly. As soon as I felt the pain, I was instantly shocked wide-awake in the awareness of what we had done only a few hours ago.

I will never be able to justify our actions on that dark misty night for as long as we live. It was so out of character for both of us to instigate such a terrible act, even as we struggled to fit back into a society we seemed to have lost touch with. Our actions had been driven by the subtle and incomprehensible words of racism that had been thrown at us daily, causing us to blame the blacks for our predicament in the army. Fuelled on by drink, which only raised our already-high levels of anger and hatred, accumulated during months of hardship and fear on the border line, we became embroiled and mixed up in our own little war of insanity. Distorted thoughts had become knotted in our brainwashed heads, leading us to behaviour with no plausible excuse.

I have always lived by the motto: 'What goes around comes around,' and for my punishment I would have to wait ten years for justice to take its course and the tables to be well and truly reversed.

We enjoyed the rest of the pass with more drink at hotels, clubs, and braai's. The time passed very quickly, and we had to get dressed back into our browns and begin the trip back to camp.

I met Wayne in Pinetown, leaving as late as possible for the 1000 kilometre journey back to Middelburg. It was 14:00 when we stood patiently waiting for the first car or truck to stop, but before we began I pulled out a six-pack of Lion Beer for Wayne and a six-pack of Castle for myself. Now we were ready for the journey, for as long as it was going to take.

'Cheers,' Wayne said with a big broad smile – we cracked the bottles together without a care in the world while standing on the roadside. Three beers later, a car eventually came to a stop, and took us all the way to Newcastle, the hometown of Macky, the artist from our platoon. Spotting a hotel, we walked in and sat in the lounge. There I pulled out a plastic bag with four cheese hotdog rolls, which my mother had made for us as *pad kos*, food for the journey. We immediately began eating with our boots resting on the table, quite oblivious to the stares. We tore into these fresh bread rolls, dropping crumbs onto the clean carpet. Once we were done, an Indian man from the hotel approached us and, suspecting trouble, we placed an order.

'Can we have one Lion and one Castle?' I said.

'I am going to have to ask you both to leave. We do not serve people in uniform.'

Shrugging our shoulders and feeling a lot better for the hot dogs in our stomachs, we trailed out and twisted off two more caps, sipping while we waited, and emptying our full bladders against the closest tree. The darkness began to set in just before another car stopped.

'I am going as far as Volkrust, is that OK?' the tough-looking Afrikaans man said.

'Yes that's fine!' we replied, only too grateful to be moving forward with this great trek of ours once more. After a short drive, we were dropped off in this one-horse town' quite sure the horse was dead. Feeling thirsty, we walked into the one and only bar – or the only one we saw – and ordered two beers from the wooden-topped bar area. Sitting at the bar, we could feel the piercing stares directed at us' our uniforms had grabbed their attention. Being two English boys in an Afrikaans town, we sat talking to each other and wondering how this would turn out. We were well aware of the resentment between the English and Afrikaans, which stemmed back to 1820, when the English settlers arrived. A few of these big, rough-looking men came over to talk to us. They asked which unit we were from, and then told us where they had served. We could see instantly that they welcomed us – they saw our uniform as a sign of 'white duty' to our country. We were the ones playing our part in keeping it safe under white minority rule.

From Volksrust we headed towards Ermelo, a couple of hours away, but not before having another beer as we waited in the darkness with our 'Day-Glo' sashes illuminating our presence on the desolate roadway. The next car ride flew by, but unfortunately went only as far as Amersfoort, the home of Lieutenant Bam. It was a small village – one of these places that, if you blinked while driving past, you would miss entirely. This time we definitely walked into the one and only bar and were again welcomed by some hard-core farmers who refused to let us pay for our beers. After two beers and lots of talking to the people from this small, isolated community, we stumbled out of the bar and into the chill of a very dark and still night.

It was 22:00 and we were already late getting back to base' there was nothing we could do about it now – we would have to deal with what awaited us in the morning. Disoriented, tired, and drunk, we began to hitchhike in the wrong direction – the direction of our homes. After five minutes we realized our crucial mistake, and turned our swaying bodies to face the right way to our base. The cars were few and far between, until a white Valiant passed us after a cold, half-hour wait and pulled over at least 200 metres from us.

I broke into a run towards this stationary car, wanting and needing a lift to get out of the cold, the alcohol slowing my swerving charge.

'Tim, what are you doing?' Wayne shouted after me. 'He did not stop for us.'

'Just watch,' I bellowed, charging towards this vehicle. Upon getting closer, I realized it was a taxi.

Pulling the door open, I looked upon a black man, who was suddenly illuminated by the light of the door. I looked back to Wayne for confirmation whether to ride or not, but he was indecisive.

Hesitant for another long second, I blurted out: 'Thanks a lot. You have no idea how long we have been waiting in the cold for this lift.'

'I was not really stopping for you,' he calmly said 'But I can give you a lift to Ermelo.'

'Excellent!' we echoed. Wayne took the back while I took the front. I smiled wryly at having wangled a lift out of nothing.

We were now in a position that sent a scare through us. We had never had a ride with an African at the wheel, and if he bore hatred to white soldiers who happened to be drunk, all he had to do was drive us into a black area or, worse, pull a gun on us. I hoped my gut feeling would not let us down and we would get to Ermelo as quickly as possible.

Soldiers had been run over accidentally, and on purpose, and stoned by Africans bitterly opposed to white rule. On one occasion, while we waited for a lift under a bridge in Colenso, stones were thrown at us from a speeding car, which narrowly missed us, striking the bridge. We would just have to ride this lift out and see if we arrived safe and sound in Ermelo.

The radio played an African beat, and a typical African jive filled the air, which because we were white was quite foreign to us. The big man, with a round smiling face, slouched behind the wheel, giving off an air of contentment. His headlights bore down on the long, straight, and flat, open road.

'Is this your taxi?' I asked, trying to make conversation and not daring to sleep, even though I wanted to so badly.

'Yes, I have had this business a couple of years,' he answered, without taking his eyes from the road.

'We don't really want to be in the army, but we have no choice in the matter,' I added, trying to excuse our positions.

'Oh? I did not know that!' He looked at us, quite shocked at the statement I had just made.

Rambling on with drunken comments, we spoke about the barriers of apartheid. Wayne and I made a point of showing compassion for the quality of life that his black colour had been forced to live under in South Africa. He did not have much to say, having been born into such a life. He also made the comment that his situation, along with that of over 30 million of his fellow Africans, was something that could not and would not change in his lifetime.

At 01:00 we arrived in Ermelo to find the town completely shut down, without a single soul about, and also out of luck for a beer at the bar. Standing under one of the few street lamps, we opened our last beer each and waited for a lift, which in this desolate place on the map was like waiting to win the lottery. It was cold and aggravating, and we wanted to sleep. We looked down the long road, hoping to see two beams of light to raise our dispirited hopes. When the last beer was finished, we threw our bottles into the long grass and sat on our bags at the edge of the road. We had nothing left to do but watch time tick away. It was after 02:00 when a car appeared on the horizon, and like two survivors trapped on an island waiting for rescue, we jumped up and successfully waved it down. Unfortunately he was not going to Middelburg, but instead was going to a small village called Hendrina. So we got in, getting another step closer and warmer to our base.

After a safer and shorter drive, we arrived at Hendrina and were dropped off at a sign that read 'Middelburg 30 kilometres.' This had to be the end of our journey' everything was in darkness and asleep and there was absolutely zero chance of a lift. Drunk and tired, we stumbled upon the closest house, which was ten metres from the roadway, and banged on the door. Instantly dogs began to bark, which only led to a further outbreak of barking all around us. Lights flickered on, and then we heard movement. We expected to see a huge Afrikaner with a gun. Instead, when the door opened, the frame was filled by a mother and daughter, dressed in white nightgowns, with pale and confused faces of wonder at what this 03:00 awakening was all about.

'We cannot get a lift back to Middelburg!' I said to them, and without a hint of hesitation they said, 'Come in' in their Afrikaans voices. 'Do you want coffee?' the mother added.

'Yes, please,' we said – not believing our good fortune and the trust that these people had in us.

I had never, before this moment, set foot in an Afrikaans house' and while we looked around us, mother and daughter put the coffee on. The white walls had a few pictures hanging in old frames. Black-and-white family photos rested on antique furniture. A carpet covered most of the old wooden floorboards, which had been sanded to a rich glossy finish, but still creaked, with each step. I estimated the house to be close to, if not more than, 100 years old – judging by the inside, the style of the outside, and the old tin roof.

Having put a mug of steaming coffee into our hands, mother and daughter continued to fuss over us like mother hens. Two mattresses were suddenly dragged into the lounge, and we sat on old comfortable armchairs, watching the activity and hardly believing the effort that was being put into our stay. Two pillows were added to the mattress, and then fresh sheets were pulled over the mattresses. They each refused to allow us to help. The mother asked us what time they should wake us, and looking at our watches we said '6:30,' which was only three hours away. Once the beds were made, we thanked them for their kind hospitality, and as the lights went out so did ours.

At 06:30 we rose with pounding heads and dry mouths, which were remedied with hot coffee and a bowl of corn flakes. With sincere thanks to our saviours, we walked with them to the wire gate entrance that we had entered only a few hours before. Turning to the mother and daughter, we shook their hands with more words of thanks that we knew could never be enough, and with a final wave we began walking and thumbing a lift.

Cars were now travelling the road, and it became only a matter of time until one stopped.

Together Wayne and I had completed a pub crawl from Pinetown to Middelburg, spanning a distance of close to 1000 kilometres in 13 hours excluding the sleep time, with a beer or two consumed in each town, along with the six-pack that was polished off in between the bars. The beer count was beyond our wildest guesses, but judging by our hangovers it had to have been double our normal intake.

At 07:00 we walked up to the gates of 4-SAI, dreading what awaited us on the other side, where we were immediately warned by those guarding the entrance that Staff Smit was waiting for us – which is what we had expected – but we did not want to hear it.

We had completed the final leg of our journey, with a hangover to remember. But now it was time to pay for our sins and accept the punishment that would soon come our way.

19

Mischief in the barracks
Life in the Intelligence house

After a hurried walk through the base along the winding tar road we eventually arrived at our bungalow, with some relief to be back. We walked in with a sense of hope that we had not acquired an extra day added on at the completion of our two years. It was great to be reunited with our friends, but before we could catch up on each other's news we were formed up in front of the bungalow, and then as a squad we were ordered off at a run down to the parade ground, at the entrance to the base, to meet a fuming Staff Smit.

Corporal Doep brought us to a halt in front of him and he immediately took control, drilling abuse into us with his blasphemous tongue, calling us each and every name under the sun from *'dom etters'* dumb pusy sores to *'laer dan kaffer kak'* lower than black shit.

'Ek sal jou bors oopsny en in jou longe kak, so dat jou asem kan stink!' I will cut your chest open and shit in your lungs, so that your breath will stink!

Staff Smit continued on with his rampage of degradation.

'Sak vir twintig,' he screamed, his face contorted in rage.

So as a platoon we dropped to the ground and gave him 20 pushups at our own pace. There was no way he could break us now, with less than eight months left in this dictatorship of a world. Standing up without a care in the world, we looked at him in wait for the next order.

'Voorste posisie af!' he bellowed again, and we dropped to the hard stony ground in the 'the first position,' our bodies inches off the ground, held up by our legs and arms, in preparation for push-ups.

Stuck to the stones, we remained like that for at least ten minutes – our arms burning and our brows sweating out beads of alcohol. My head continued to pound, and I felt ill' I wriggled and moved for comfort while the sun added further misery to our situation.

There had been a few troops who had arrived late, making the *opfok* easier to bear – for Wayne and I were not the sole cause of the hardship we were now toiling under.

'Staan op jou klomp suurstof diewe!' Stand up you clump of oxygen thieves!, he ordered.

We slowly raised ourselves painfully from the ground, with our hands roughed and bruised from the stones that had pushed into them.

'*Kry daardie foken civvy kak uit van julle!*' Get that fuckin' civilian shit out of you!, he roared, while he threatened us with a wagging finger.

'Lieutenant Bam, *vat hulle Gwarry Gat toe*' Take them to the Gwarry *Gat*, he barked.

At a run we departed for the human and Ratel obstacle course at an old quarry not too far from our bungalow. Before we reached the Gwarry *Gat*, Lieutenant Bam instructed us to go to our Ratels and lift the tow bars from their fastenings at the side of the vehicles.

With two to a bar, we ran towards the quarry, knowing full well that this punishment had been at the orders of Staff Smit. These four metre long solid bars, capable of towing a 16 ton vehicle, rested on our shoulders like a telephone pole, digging and niggling into our flesh as one pulled and one pushed with each uncoordinated step. The ends of the bar were square, making it harder to find a comfortable position, and it bruised and rubbed, and alternating our shoulders made not the slightest difference to the intense pain that numbed our skin and had our ears ringing while this bastard of a pole banged against the side of our heads. Cursing our way forward with thirst dried within our mouths, we made our way to where Lieutenant Bam was standing, which was at a position on a flat piece of ground overlooking the obstacle course.

At his feet stood a white pail of water, brought up to satisfy our thirst. Slowly we made our way towards this bucket, but before we reached it Stoop cracked and lashed out at it with his boot, spilling the contents into the dry sand, which swallowed it before it could pool.

'What the fuck did you do that for?' came a shout of shock from behind my head. There was no need for a reply, for Stoop had reached that breaking point through pain and frustration, and had lost sight of the big picture. Now we all had to suffer for his stupidity.

By this time I was feeling green and nauseated. The sweat dripped from my pores, saturating my shirt. Placing our bars down, we lowered ourselves to the ground before a whistle pierced the silence from below us, followed immediately by a deep scream.

Staff Smit had arrived and had summoned us from this small hilltop to the obstacle course down below. Leaving the tow bars, we descended down the red earth, only realizing now the ascent we had made with these heavy bars of metal. We made our way towards this hated man in a stampede of dust.

'*Fokweg om die pad!*' Fuck away on the road!, he swore as he sent us running up and over the red mounds of earth, which had been positioned for a Ratel course.

While I ran, I fought back the continual surges of vomit that rose and fell with

19. Mischief in the barracks: Life in the Intelligence house

each labouring step' thus I struggled through my drunken punishment. After completing the first lap of the course, he shouted out: 'The first five back can sit out.'

And so off we went again. Knowing full well that I would not be able to make it in the first five, I kept in the middle of the pack, and two thirds into the course I dropped down in the valley of a mound and let everyone pass me. The first five sat out, and the rest were sent off again – with me still sitting, shielded behind the mound, waiting for my fellow troops to round the circuit once again. When they came stumbling over the small hill and descended onto my hiding place, I took up the chase, and having rested I found myself a couple from the front. Running like a bat out of hell – to steal my selfish life-or-death reprieve from my drunken nausea – I made it in the first five, granting myself the promised rest. Sitting totally out of breath, I watched my fellow troops running while the salty sweat poured from my face and stung my blurred eyes with an aroma of Castle beer wafting about me.

It was not much longer before it was over, and my hangover a thing of the past. With enough energy left in us, we ascended the small hill and retrieved our tow bars before making our own way toward our Ratels in our groups of two. After placing the bars back on the vehicle sides, we were free to go back to the bungalow, where we collapsed in untidy heaps – boots and all – upon our brown-blanketed beds.

We had experienced the Gwarry Gat, and hoped that it would be our first and last visit to that site of suffering.

Our platoon went through days of doing nothing except lazing around and killing time. On most days, after the lunch in the mess hall, having eaten off plates like civilized people, we would sneak into an unoccupied bungalow next to the one that had been gutted by fire from our ou manne, and we would embark on an afternoon siesta. On one occasion, Corporal Doep came to our bungalow to round us up for Staff Smit, who wanted to talk to our platoon. To his shock, we were nowhere to be found, except for about five or six troops who did not know about our hideaway. Corporal Doep took the small squad down to the buildings at the main gate, where Staff Smit patiently waited.

'*Waar die fok is die res van julle?*' Where the fuck are the rest of them?, he roared at Corporal Doep, who looked back at his superior totally lost for words.

'*Staff, hulle het net verdywn*' Staff, they just disappeared, he sheepishly replied.

When we heard this from those few who were present, we roared with laughter, now wishing we could have been there to witness the dumbfounded look on his face and the anger in Staff Smit's.

At night we stood guard, walking between the double fence to and from the concrete guard towers, which stood every few 100 metres to a height of six metres from the ground. Some nights were better than others, depending on what shift you got and what area of the base you were assigned to guard. There were times when I walked through a blanket of mist, totally alone at 02:00, with everything eerily dark and quiet. It gave me the feeling that I was walking onto the set of a horror movie. On many nights the sky was black, with only a chunk of moon protruding, giving me some much-needed light – for I walked through the grass, knee-high, half expecting to see a werewolf or a wild animal.

The nights in the bungalow we used at our own discretion. Some of us shined boots, cleaned rifles, and ironed browns to a knife-edge, while others got high on whatever their hands touched – from tablets to cough medicine, from glue to dagga.

A word of warning had been set up and agreed upon, which we used when rank unexpectedly walked into our bungalow. The word was meant to give those doing illegal activities the time they needed to clean up or clear out. 'Arra' was the word, and it worked like a charm, spreading through the bungalow at the speed of light' the urgent message was responded to without another word having to be said.

A few of us had tried the 'white pipe,' which was a white mandrax tablet crushed to a fine powder and then sprinkled onto the marijuana at the end of the pipe. While someone lit a match, another pulled at the neck of this 'white pipe,' burning the powder and weed into a red-hot coal. After one hit of this lethal intake, we would forget our names and walk like zombies down the row of beds, our faces as pale as ghosts, looking for our beds. Why we tried this was beyond me, for the high sapped our energy and rendered us lifeless, with barely the strength to drag our feet from the toilet block and back to our beds. Boredom had once again played its part in the destruction of our brain cells' we passed the time in any way we saw fit.

Smoking dagga had become a way of life, especially after dinner, as we wasted the night away with blank expressions and out-of-place laughter. There seemed to be more dagga within the walls of Platoon 3 than the rest of the Battalion, Brian being one of the main dealers in 4-SAI. Just about everyone in our platoon had tried this weed. Some got hooked on it, while others got sick – trying it and ending their experience in coughing fits. It was always around, and the sweet smell never left the bungalow, and the stoned glaze remained on most soldiers from one day to the next.

This heads-up warning of 'Arra!' had saved many from the clutches of high rank and extra days with precious seconds in warning' but more importantly, no one succumbed to an overdose of tablets or mandrax from the white pipe, even though many looked as though they were heading that way.

19. Mischief in the barracks: Life in the Intelligence house

Our daily awakening in our bungalow was met with the disgusting smell of cigarette smoke' more troops than not lit up and began puffing on a cigarette as they struggled to wake up, expelling the smoke into the air and stinging our puffy eyes as we began moving around.

To the non-smokers, it was funny to watch the smokers falling asleep with a cigarette burning in one hand until it burned the skin between their fingers, jolting them awake in a shriek of pain and sending us laughing into the toilet block to shave, wash our faces, and brush our teeth.

'Arra!' was shouted through the bungalow as Staff Smit entered for an odd, unplanned inspection of our quarters.

'*Hierdie plek lyk soos 'n hoer se handsak!*' This place looks like a whore's handbag!, he screamed and Lieutenant Bam and Corporal Doep stood behind him while he surveyed the scene.

Referring to our bungalow, which was neat and clean but not up to his high standard of army presentation, he roared out, '*Dis uit soos boknaai op a Sondag middag voor die polisie stasie!*' It is out like fucking buck on a Sunday afternoon in front of the police station!.

Struggling hard not to laugh at such an outrageous remark, we stood still and waited for him to finish. He informed us that the commander of the base would be coming in tomorrow to inspect our bungalow, and with a '*maak dit reg*' make it right he left us to it.

In the morning we were ready for the Commander, who performed a close inspection of the bungalow, looking for fault – as they always did. The day before, Staff Smit had told us his name – instructing us to remember it in case he decided to ask one of us who he was.

Walking slowly down the glossy floor and past the neat rows of beds, in a perfect line, with us standing unflinching to attention in neatly-ironed, faded browns, he drew face to face with Macky, and looking into his eyes he stopped.

'*Wie is ek?*' Who am I?, he asked in Afrikaans.

Macky looked at him for a few seconds, and then replied in English, 'Captain, I really do not know.'

'I am not a fuckin' captain!' he barked, under the insult of having his castle and star mistaken for a lowly captain.

We knew this was a bad sign' his whole demeanor changed. Suddenly – as if by magic – he found some dust on the top of a wall, and in a cruel tone he said, '*Vat hulle volgende pass terug!*' Take their next pass away!, leaving us standing in dumbfounded, fuming rage.

Macky felt terrible, but we reassured him that it was not his fault. We knew quite well that he was looking for an excuse to demoralize us and break us, in a way that no one had been able to until now.

The next pass, due in a week, had vanished under the same thoughts of you selfish bastards. We fell back onto our neatly made beds. I wondered how long we would remain in this base before being given another assignment and taken away from the strict order of army life, behind the secluded barriers of these wire fences.

To pass time, the two best artists – Macky and Wayne – and their two helpers – Alan and Fox – embarked on painting on a huge metal board, which lay on the ground. They pencilled outlines to a name and insignia that would be erected in front of Platoon 3s bungalow. Over a painted green and black background, with Bravo Company in yellow down the sides, they painted a huge elephant with its ears fanned out, its white tusks hanging down, and its trunk elevated in a sign of good luck. It was a work of art, handled with limited resources, and it stood proudly four metres in the air – acting as a clear break between Bravo and Charlie Company lines. The comments they got from their painting did us all proud' there was never a moment in which we were not swollen with gratitude to be a part of Bravo Company, with our platoon leading the way.

The bungalow adjacent to us housed Platoon 2, and one day while they were exploring the ceiling of their bungalow, a guy from Cape Town found a black R4 rifle hidden in the rafters – which must have been up there a few years, since the R4s were no longer black but brown. The person who had concealed it there must have been planning to steal it, and then as the time drew closer he abandoned his plan, selfishly leaving it to the dust and cobwebs. By doing this, the thief had allowed a fellow troop to be blamed for the loss of his rifle – for the real thief would definitely not steal his own and land himself in hot water' that would result in him being forced on orders to explain what had become of his weapon.

Had the Capetonian stolen it and managed to get it out of the base, no one would have been the wiser, but instead he turned it in, and for his good deed he was rewarded with a pass home.

On hearing this, our platoon began climbing into the ceiling, hoping to find a rifle or two ourselves. But this was not to be the case. It dawned on a few of us that this would be a great place to smoke a joint – being the most concealed place that the bungalow had to offer. At least five or six of us entered the cupboard, where we stored our civilian carry bags, extra blankets, and brooms. Using the shelves as stairs, we opened the wooden roof hatch and climbed into the dusty ceiling. There we passed a joint from hand to hand and mouth to mouth, until

19. Mischief in the barracks: Life in the Intelligence house

only the filter was left. With the ceiling filled with smoke and our heads clouded over, we navigated our way down like drunken sailors, stumbling and missing our footing as we crashed in fits of laughter. Those in the bungalow must have wondered what all the ruckus was about.

When pass came and we did not go, our corporals went into town with our money and stocked up on half jacks of brandy, whisky, old brown sherry, and beer. Sitting in the sun on mattresses, we began to drown our sorrows, with no one around to bug us, and we laughed our misfortune off, with the consolation of having our good friends to share this drunken moment with. Els had us in hysterics when he acted out a sermon, taking on the role of priest. With a stern and serious face, he preached to us, throwing in swear words that rolled from his lips like sewerage. I have never heard such funny filth in the descriptive Afrikaans language as what Johannes Jacobus Bernadus Christophilis Els could expel from his mouth. His vocabulary got worse with each swig of brandy.

In the morning we woke with hangovers and dry mouths' the previous night was now a distant blur. Forced to rise by Corporal Doep and Corporal Gregan's wake-up calls, we began to move around at the pace of seniors three times our age. For some reason, Els was not himself, he grumbled and moaned as he made his bed next to where Wayne was sweeping. For some unknown reason, he walked up to Wayne and began swearing at him, and then struck him twice across the face with his flat hand. A group of us stood and watched, hardly believing what we had just seen – a temperament change in a split second, with hidden, subdued anger randomly coming to the fore for no apparent reason. It was seldom unleashed upon our own, and our facial expressions showed our distaste' we did not welcome Els' actions at all. I was standing next to Wayne and felt horribly guilty for not jumping in for my friend, but I knew that if I did, those siding with Els would also have jumped in – which would have led to an out-of-control brawl amongst our very own.

Time dragged, as it always did in the base, with the only solace being a roof over our head, a soft bed, and a daily shower – a luxury that we had not been used to for many a month.

One morning, out of the blue, we were rounded up and told that we were leaving for Nelspruit in the Eastern Transvaal – which brought relief to us, as we needed a change of scenery to speed up the dragging days of boredom.

In Samils, we departed the base for Nelspruit – having no idea as usual why we were to head in such a direction. Under darkness, we arrived at an old hotel with tall-pillared corridors and red, polished concrete floors acting as verandas. There, we were told, we would be sleeping the night.

While we slept, Brian and Stoop decided they needed some of their mind-relaxing medicine. They broke into a car that was parked in front of the hotel, and took off in it for a marijuana hunt to satisfy their craving. On their return, they were caught red-handed as they pulled into the parking space' and to make matters even worse, the car they had borrowed belonged to a general. Lieutenant Bam was fuming when the general notified him that two of his troops had gone AWOL in his car, thus making Lieutenant Bam look as though he had lost control of his platoon. The situation was left to rest for the moment, and was to be handled upon our return to 4-SAI.

The following day we went into the small Afrikaans town, shepherded by our rank and watched by the keen, sharp eyes of shopkeepers who believed that we were on a mission to pocket some of their stores' inventory. Music from certain stores had us moving to the beat, while kind smiles and the aroma of perfume had our senses on alert. We walked in a group, savouring the freedom as if we were on a day parole from prison' enjoying the life we had lost touch with.

On returning to the hotel, Wayne and I were told to board a Buffel, which we did – with no idea of the reasoning behind it. Shortly after strapping in, we left Nelspruit in the direction of Barberton, a small town that had sprung to life with the discovery of a gold reef in 1884.

The driver of the Buffel continued past Barberton, with green road signs flashing before our eyes, proclaiming: Swaziland.

After a long drive, the Buffel veered off the tar road and followed a bumpy and dusty wide path, towards an old-farmhouse with a tin roof and a couple of boarded-up windows. The rest of the openings were covered in screen netting. On getting closer, we noticed that there was not a pane of glass in the window frames, and at the entrance to the farmhouse was a two metre high sand barricade, which immediately put us back onto the SWA border at Beacon 16.

'What the hell are we doing here?' I asked Wayne, speaking aloud rather than looking for an answer. When the driver cut the diesel engine, Wayne asked him what this place was and why we were here.

'This is an intelligence house, and we have had reports that it might be attacked!' he said. While that sank in, we both turned to each other, and without uttering a word we both thought, how are two extra bodies going to bolster the defence of this house?

'How do you know this?' I challenged him.

'We go into the field everyday, talking, helping, and mixing in with the locals, trying to gain valuable information. A reliable source has told us of ANC

19. Mischief in the barracks: Life in the Intelligence house

movements in this area, who have recently crossed over the Swazi border. They are on a mission of sabotage, and we believe something will happen.'

The National Serviceman was also completing his two years, but in a way very different from what we had been subjected to. His beret was black, which gave him the ears in the field of intelligence' whereas ours was, green which gave us many diverse roles – from foot soldier to Ratel soldier and everything that went with it. Under the umbrella of iron will, and wearing our Infantry berets with a pride second to none, we would not have wanted to wear another colour on our heads. The struggles and tribulations of what we had experienced – compared with most of the non-combatant units within the National Service battalions – were like comparing chalk and cheese. What we would have given to have their lives for a few months and enjoy a holiday free from the screaming and cursing of our rank. It was something we could only enjoy for now, for we knew it would not be too long before we were back to reality within the confines of the barracks.

The interior of the house was more civilian than military – posters of beautiful women and fast cars adorned the creamy white walls, and each room had the privacy of a door that locked. Two beds filled the space in each room' a small carpet helped cover the scuffed wooden floorboards, and an enclosed window allowed the light to filter through the tiny-holed screen netting. The communal kitchen – equipped with a fridge, stove, and sink, along with all the necessary cooking utensils – helped to keep all ten National Servicemen assigned to this house fully-fed and in good spirits. There was also a lounge area, with sofas and chairs facing a small television set, allowing us to view the only two channels that were aired from 18:00 to 24:00 by the South African Broadcasting Corporation.

The rifles, ammunition, uniforms, and a tall antenna protruding seven metres into the air from the roof, were all that gave this place away as military rather than a small civilian farmhouse with an overgrown garden of flowering, hardy plants and a patch of tall, withering stalks of corn, already harvested.

'What a *rustig* life,' I uttered to Wayne.

We both compared our new life in browns to something equivalent to life in an army hotel – a place we could have used in our previous border life of survival, from hard uneasy sleeps to dry tasteless food in the stifling heat, with boredom always tugging restlessly at our wits.

A few of the intelligence troops went on pass, leaving us to do as we wished in the comfort of their military home. It did not take us long to meet the housedog cum guard dog, who had just given birth to a litter of puppies that looked like rats with large heads and frolicked before us in playful but clumsy excitement.

Exploring the back of the house, we found a volleyball court with a net pulled taut between a rectangle of white-washed lines, laid upon the flattest piece of land, with an overgrowth of trees and bush circling it. Through some of the thick bush, we came across a half-finished swimming pool made with rocks and concrete, and a stagnant puddle of dirty brown water covered with a swarm of breeding mosquitoes.

It was an amazing place, quite simply carved from the bush in the simplest way, with electricity run from a generator, the water heated over a burner, and the outside toilet taking care of the smell and the paper business.

After a deep sleep in a place feeling more like home, we got up at about 09:00 to find the house deserted. We decided to take a walk along the dirt road to the Wareings Bread plant, where thousands of loaves of bread were baked and sold to the hungry locals at an affordable price. Walking next to the high fences, with barbed wire coiled along the top to keep out any intruders, we arrived at an opening in the fence, which housed an office. A local African man popped his head through the opening, and on seeing our uniform he immediately thrust out two loaves of white, burning hot bread – the top of the loaf blackened to a hard crust – into our grateful hands.

Racing back to the house with hunger and burning hands speeding us up until we broke into a run, and made straight for the fridge and the block of butter. Tearing at the bread while the steam poured from the middle of the loaf, we dropped chunks of butter into the bread, which melted like ice cubes in a kettle of bubbling water. Tearing pieces off, we feasted like kings. I boiled a pot of water for the morning coffee, which helped wash the fistfuls of baked dough down our throats.

With our rifles, we boarded the Buffel and were driven, along with a member from the Intelligence house, into the adjacent African area, looking for information or a threat to our presence. Over hours of bumpy and very dusty driving, we passed hundreds of round, mud-brick, thatched huts. The round grassy overhang of the roofs looked far too big for the houses. The houses themselves looked so sturdy and withstood wind and rain' and yet they were made entirely from grass and mud and were supported by some thick sticks for a roof and entrance. Through the clouds of red dust, we passed cheering throngs of kids, who chased the stream of dust with whistles and screams that soon engulfed them and rendered them invisible in our wake. Life here was also poor, and far more rural than our township experience in Tembisa – and even though we gained no information from the area, we did gain a true picture of the poor Swazi life, which was comparable to the subsistence life of SWA/Namibia and southern Angola.

19. Mischief in the barracks: Life in the Intelligence house

Our freedom was enjoyed like that of a holiday – with an absence of the daily shouts of orders from leaders in a crazed state of being. Relaxing and playing volleyball and hands of cards in between the Buffel patrols, we embraced each day without a single complaint, even though we still had no real understanding of our task – which we now did not need to know.

On a bright morning, with the house quiet, we began moving around with too much time on our hands. There was an R1 rifle lying on a made-up bed, belonging to one of the black beret Intelligence troops who had gone into the field without it. I had never seen an R1 up close, let alone handle it, whereas Wayne had one during his basic training in Pretoria, before being sent to the mechanized infantry unit of 1-SAI.

Wayne became quite intrigued with this weapon' he picked it up, flipping it over in his hands, with the short, stubby magazine clipped to it' our eyes scanned it from barrel to butt. He unclipped the magazine and began stripping the working parts from the 7.62mm weapon. Looking at each part with keen interest, we disengaged it from the next piece, comparing it continually to the working parts of our R4 rifles. It seemed heavier than our rifle, and was not as user-friendly' we laid out the working parts on the blanket of the bed. When we had had enough of our fascination with this new weapon, we began to piece the metal puzzle back together while we sat on the bed. We stood up together, and Wayne stepped back, elevating the barrel slightly to my right, and then, as I moved towards him to cross his path, a shot rang out, blasting into the wall with an almighty bang. Pieces of concrete splintered from the wall and were propelled into my face and hair with only a slight sting, for the shock of the rifle shot overpowered any other feeling.

Everything stopped, our ears were buzzing and a throbbing silence rang through the room. I tried to make out what had just happened' I had no idea where the shot came from until I saw the stunned and pale face of Wayne, the rifle now hanging limply to his side – like that of a defeated soldier.

'Shit, I nearly killed you!' Wayne mumbled in shock.

His frozen face said it all, and only his mouth moved – barely – to throw these words from his numbed lips.

'I am okay,' I calmly told Wayne, trying to reassure him in an effort to break his dumbstruck expression, which was still firmly plastered over his disbelieving face. Wayne had squeezed the trigger, and to our astonishment, a shot was expelled' the bullet had been in the barrel the whole time.

On regaining my bearings, I expected the whole house to be converging into the room at any second. But to our astonishment, no one came in. Both of us shifted our glance to the wall, which had a gaping hole ten centimetres wide and five centimetres deep at the level of my head – which stared back at us as if to illustrate what my head would have looked like had I crossed in front of the barrel. Around the hole, the wall was scarred with shrapnel' it cut and peppered tiny streaks into the cream paint – as another reminder of what could have become of our faces. At the time of the shot, we paid no attention to the possibility of a ricochet, which could so easily have killed one of us – for we were less than a metre from the wall when the shot was fired into it at point-blank range.

While we cleaned the room of concrete chips and dust, we searched for the bullet – looking into the hole in the wall and under beds. But it was nowhere to be found. We welcomed the fact that there was no one else in the house to witness this incident, which if it leaked out would be deemed a military violation, bringing Wayne on orders before heavy-duty rank for action of negligence.

When the room had been swept clean with our hands, we looked back to the wall and wondered how the hell we could hide such a crater – and then together we burst out laughing. The laughter helped calm our nerves, and it carried on as we took a picture of a solemn-faced woman in a vain attempt at a modelling pose and stuck it over the hole to conceal the evidence. The laughter did not stop until we had tears in our eyes' we laughed at the sad-faced woman who had come to our rescue, and then finally – with not a single soul the wiser – we left the room with our legs still weak. Tiny pieces of concrete were stuck in our hair, and I had a slight cut on my cheek from one of these flying chips. We shut the door with grateful thanks that we had emerged in the same way we had entered less than half an hour before.

With ten days of glorious rest and one very close call behind us, we were reunited with our fellow platoon mates, who had also been dispatched to these various remote outposts in the vicinity of the Swaziland border.

After exchanging stories, we set off for Middelburg, in wait for another army command. And I did not believe for one moment that our next set of orders could improve on this kind of life. But as usual, we would have to wait with hope and see.

20

Kostini Base
Kruger National Park

Halfway through the month of August, we were told to get packed up and be ready to leave before first light on board small Samil 20s, one section to a vehicle.

Only too glad to be leaving base, we bundled into the back of these open troop carriers with our rifles and *grootsakke*, dressed in jerseys and bush jackets against the bitterly cold morning chill. In the cab of the vehicle, Paul, our section leader, sat next to Bennie, the driver for Alpha section, in the comfort of a padded seat and the warmth of the heater. Meanwhile we sat upon the metal benches, exposed to the icy winds, which after two to three hours would be replaced with scorching heat.

In a platoon convoy of five vehicles, with Corporal Gregan at the wheel of another Samil loaded with supplies, we drove very enthusiastically out of the gates of 4-SAI, welcoming a new adventure far from the wire fences of the base.

Leaving Middelburg behind us, we headed towards Nelspruit with darkness and cold all around us. As we tried to sleep and stay warm, the vehicle jolted with each gear change – which seemed to rock us asleep for a few minutes before another bump had us bouncing awake and sliding across the metal barred seating, followed with mumbled cursing.

When the sun began to rise like a light switch dial turned on ever so slowly, it illuminated the barren countryside with hushed silence all around us, except for the diesel drone of engines. Stretching away the aches of cold and the stiffness of sitting, we sat uncomfortably and watched the morning come alive before our eyes. Long grass waved along the roadside on rocky scrub' huge mountains loomed in the distance, the seemingly endless road leading us towards these massive mounds.

Following the lead of Corporals Gregan and Doep, with Lieutenant Bam riding behind and Tony driving the HQ section with Alpha, then Bravo and Charlie in the rear, we kept to our order in the convoy. Before reaching Nelspruit, we turned off at a signpost directing us to Lydenburg, which took us northwards towards the Transvaal Drakensberg Mountains.

Without stopping at Lydenburg, we headed towards Sabie on the Long Tom Pass, which had been nicknamed by the British forces during the Anglo Boer War after the Boers' 15 centimetre guns. The guns had been used during a long and thunderous battle on this very pass. The Long Tom Pass snaked its way up and around hills for 57 kilometres, taking us to the top of the Transvaal Drakensberg – a summit of 2 149 metres above sea level.

The scenery on this slow and tedious journey was breathtaking' we rounded the curves in low gear, and they hairpinned back to where we had already been, allowing us to see up close and shout across to our fellow vehicles before they too rounded the curve and began the low, snaking ascent. The uphill gradient took hours to conquer and gave us a panoramic view that any avid traveller would revel in. There was absolutely nothing but mountain after mountain after mountain, with greens and browns and a hazy blue sky, and not a person other than us to be seen, and not a single man-made creation other than the tarmac and its solid white stripe.

With the long, winding roads behind us, we headed through Sabie and following the Sabie River, we were led to a main stretch of roadway that led us, in turn, to another ascent. Travelling northwards along the smooth tar roads, our vehicles dwarfed by the rugged mountain range, we continued in convoy along the path that had been blasted so calculatedly from the rock years ago. Those sitting on one side of the vehicle stared into a brown wall of shale cliff face, while the other side sat rigidly, looking down a sheer drop of 1 700 metres into a furious flowing river deep below. Only a half metre high barrier kept us from plunging over it.

Daring ourselves, with knots in our stomachs, we looked over the edge while clutching the metal Samil seating, viewing a sight whose breathtaking beauty – had we not been in the controlled army uniform of thinking – we may have appreciated as out of the ordinary. In tow with the rest of the vehicles, we wound our way through the pass, entering a few long, narrow, straight tunnels that transported us through a huge mountain toward another one, waiting for us on the other side – wherever we looked, there were only mountains of rock.

Half way up Shangaan's Hill Pass we stopped for a rest break at a tourist viewing point. This much-needed stop allowed us to get a full view of this out-of-this-world sight of mountains and the deepest valley I had ever seen, with the crags painted in many shades of green and orange lichen. Ferns and moss hung over damp rocks, and tiny water droplets ran down the shale, leaving slimy lines on the polished slabs of rock. Shouting obscenities into the cliffs as loud as we could, the rocks echoed back the call three or four times, as clearly as it was emitted. The vulgarity forced a laugh from each of us on its return. Els had taken the initiative, and as always used a particular part of a mother's anatomy to echo into the vast hills. '*Jou ma se moer!*'he shouted, and it was still echoing when some South African tourists stopped at the lookout, and then quickly left as the echo resounded through the pass.

After a short but refreshing rest stop, we continued on, passing through more tunnels and meandering roads until we reached the Olifants River at a place called Mica, where we followed the signs to Phalaborwa in a northeasterly direction.

After close to ten hours of sitting on hard strips of metal, our buttocks now thoroughly numb, we eventually pulled into the army base of 7-SAI at Phalaborwa. Our arrival held the secret to our next set of orders, but what they were we had absolutely no idea. While we waited, stretching away our discomforts, Lieutenant Bam met with the commander of the base and received our orders, which were to enter into the Kruger National Park.

At 17:00 we departed 7-SAI, and entered South Africa's biggest wildlife reserve at the Phalaborwa gate as the light began to fade on us. It was a strange feeling to enter the park for the first time, and be in the home of the lion, leopard, rhino, elephant, and buffalo.

As we all wondered why we had entered this nature reserve, we passed a huge monument of a stern-faced Paul Kruger. His bearded, rounded face and shoulders stood atop a rock structure. It gave me the impression that this 'Old Lion of the Transvaal' was watching over his domain' in the same way he had done so many years before as president of the old South African Republic. On 26 March 1898, President Paul Kruger signed a proclamation establishing a sanctuary for wildlife – being the first of its kind in Africa. It was man's first offer of friendship on a continent where he had been waging a war of extermination with the once-abundant herds of wild animals.

For this unselfish deed to save nature, Paul Kruger was honoured by the changing of name of this wildlife reserve from the Sabie Game Reserve to the Kruger National Park.

The tar road soon led us onto a dirt track with a few herds of animals milling about the roadside' their ears pricked up and their tails swooshed from side to side in nervous wonder at our presence. Instantly we caught the flavour of this exhilarating atmosphere' a barrage of colour, sound, and smell met our alert senses. Zebras and impalas stood frozen with unbroken stares and twitching tails' their black and white stripes and white underbellies blended into the cool, darkening evening. Then, when one of these animals could not stand still any longer, it broke from the group into a snorted gallop, plunging the whole herd into a panic' in a cloud of dust and frantic stamps, they charged and sprang their way to safety, away from the strange sound of our vehicle. We were in awe at having witnessed wildlife an arm's length from our vehicle – a scene that would enlighten most of us to a better understanding of nature in its own habitat.

Departing from the disturbed herd, we continued, doubling back to a smooth, tarred road on which we drove for about half an hour, until we were radioed to stop and ready ourselves for the night's sleep. It was a scary feeling to be in a reserve with ferocious wild animals. We wondered whether, if we did close our eyes in sleep, we would be eaten while doing so. Wearily and nervously we climbed onto the ground, and literally felt around to see whether we should sleep on the scrubby earth or in the back of the vehicle. Suddenly, out of the pitch-black night, a growl echoed across the plains – which instantly forced a decision from us with regards to our safety' except for Gall, who as always had to be different, and chose the ground over the discomfort and safety of the Samil. Sitting in our sleeping bags, we looked out at the night from the back of the Samil, hardly managing to sleep in the small confine of a double row of metal benches and too many bodies spread over the small space.

We were grateful to watch the sunrise when the new day began, though we were still unsure of our role in this animal kingdom. Gall seemed to have got more sleep in his bivi than the rest of us in our crammed confines, two metres above the ground.

After morning coffee, a signal came through on Paul's radio from Lieutenant Bam, informing us to head north. As we drove, animals popped up from everywhere, crossing the dirt road, grazing in the tall grass, or just standing under the shield of a flat-topped African thorn tree.

Here we were in a land teeming with wildlife, watching the morning sun cast a gleam upon this timeless gem of such splendid wonder, displayed for us city-boys to awaken our senses to wide-eyed adventure and intrigue. This was nature's paradise, and as I gazed upon this setting, I felt my love for nature being born, and for the moment I forgot that I was still in the army.

On the drive we crossed a narrow river divided by a shallow concrete bridge, and before we reached the other side we saw half a dozen crocodiles spread over flat rocks, basking in the sun and smiling through their elongated mouths. These huge prehistoric monsters were well over four metres, and they lay unmoving and unblinking, their big bellies pressed against the rock. Their midget-like clawed feet rested next to them, quite out of proportion to their long frames and curved, whip-like tails. It looked as though these body parts did not belong with this animal.

Before noon we drove through a no-entry sign, drilled onto a concrete

20. Kostini Base: Kruger National Park

beacon that read 'Kostini SAP Coin Unit' Counter-Insurgency Unit, which was a base positioned in the middle of the park, away from any tourists' eyes.

We entered the Kostini base reckoning that this could not be for us' for there were camouflaged bungalows with beds, a swimming pool with a volleyball net, and a kitchen with a fridge. These were gifts from above, which Platoon 3 could not have the privilege of enjoying – for we had never had the luck of landing such a score.

Alpha section walked into the nearest bungalow, and by throwing kit onto a bed, we laid claim to a mattress' and then we began to scout the base, still waiting for the catch.

'This base cannot be for us!' we told each other at the same time, remembering the last 20 months of our service, which had been more like disorganized hell than luxury.

Walking around the camp, we could not believe the sight of such beautiful green grass – so perfectly trimmed in comparison to the wild dry scrub only 30 metres from where we stood. In the middle of the camp, there were a few rondavels with neatly thatched roofs, positioned under thick, tall trees, shielding us from the penetrating rays. And there were bushes and tall plants, which helped fill the openness of this cut-out. There was a concrete wall near another thatched overhang, and a circular pool nearby, which was only waist deep and not more than five metres in radius. Many hardy and exotic plants had been planted by those who came before us, along a neatly-lined stone rockery, adding colour to this out-of-place little oasis of paradise, with the barren wild only a stone's throw away. On the other side of the rockery, a helicopter landing pad had been cleared and marked by sandbags in a square – should the need arise for a chopper to casevac someone to the hospital.

Are we really going to stay here? I asked myself with hope. Or is this only going to be an overnight tease? While I thought about this, we were told we could swim – and with five on a side, we played pool volleyball with all the excitement and laughter we could muster as we wallowed in the warm water – which helped to cool off the dry, 40 plus °C temperature.

After the swim, Lieutenant Bam gave us our orders – which were to capture the refugees who were escaping over the border from Mozambique in a bid to flee the raging civil war for a safer life in South Africa. With the war between Communist FRELIMO and the South African supported RENAMO intensifying in the mid 1980s, the locals had been fleeing in their thousands across this divide – they were running from a country in collapse and totally ravaged by the destruction and crippling effect of war. Famine and ill health were driving them towards a better life – ironically, into the apartheid regime of South Africa.

In their escape, these poverty-stricken and frightened Mozambicans had braved AK-47s brandished by brainwashed soldiers, both man and boy. They had sidestepped through minefields, carrying a few belongings – mainly clothes in a nylon bag – and climbed through and over electrical fences along the length of the border. Once inside the park, they still had wild animals – in the form of lion and leopard – to contend with, along with the brown uniform and aggression of the South African soldier. Some had tried the 'escape' three times, failing each time, to be returned to the other side of the wire only for a repeat performance – for they lived in the hope that, with the next attempt, they would reach their freedom. Groups of these people, we had been told, were not so lucky as to get a second, or even a third, attempt at the crossing. Some of these ill-fated refugees had become statistics, falling victim to prides of hungry lions.

After an exciting day and a good night's sleep, we arose with the hope that we would be venturing into the park. Our wish was granted, and with seven ration packs we were cast from the base into the wilderness. Our eyes peered through the bush until we spotted an animal, and then we pointed, and shared the prize with our friends. Bouncing over the dirt roads, out of view of the public eye, we continued northwards until we reached the Shingwidzi River. Half of our section was deployed on the one bank of the river, while the other was positioned directly opposite us, and yet close enough to shout across the muddy river that separated us. On each side of the river we set up chopper tents only a couple of metres from the border of Mozambique, and what we saw of our neighbouring African country had a very similar terrain to that of the Kruger Park.

We lay in wait for the refugees, expecting them to cross at any moment between the fence and the riverbank, where the fence came to an end. As time drew on, we became bored and restless with the midday sun, beating down with just as much venom as it did on the SWA/Angolan border, as well as curious about this new land on our doorstep. A few of us from our chopper tent walked over the border and looked up at the small hill that overshadowed our position in Mozambique.

'If we climb that, do you think we can see the sea?' I asked Wayne and Fox, who immediately replied, 'Let's climb it and see!' And so we set off into foreign territory with no weapons besides our sharpened, inquisitive outlook. After half an hour of voluntary *opfok* in shorts and boots, we reached the top, hoping to see Maputo, the capital of Mozambique with the Indian Ocean breaking towards it. But unfortunately, all we saw were the mountains of the Lebombo Range, which were a sight in itself but not one that could match an ocean with oil tankers dotted on the horizon and white crests on breaking waves. Careful not to stay too long, we caught our breath and shrugged off our disappointment, then began the descent towards the fresh but muddy water of the Shingwidzi River. Red-faced and sweaty, we arrived at the sandy banks' and walking through a clump of reeds, we took off our boots and swam in a shallow part of the river – still in Mozambican territory. Afraid of a crocodile attack, we kept our eyes on the alert for a sudden disturbance in the reeds upstream' and because of this threat, we did not stay in the water too long. Feeling a lot cooler and relaxed after our bath, we carried our boots the last 30 metres onto our side of the border, to our chopper tent.

Our section's deployment was in the northern part of the park, only 100 kilometres from the border of Zimbabwe. Until its independence in 1980, it was known as Rhodesia, and had also suffered severely through a decade of bush war, with the white minority clinging to power until the politicians paved the way for free elections. Many white Rhodesians saw this as the time to 'run' south, following the trend of the Portuguese in Angola and Mozambique and the British in East Africa – all seeking stability and safety within the borders of a white-controlled South Africa. Rob, from Charlie section, was born a Rhodesian, and he told us stories of land mines and civilian convoys, led by army vehicles along farm roads, towards towns and cities. His family had left the country they adored; taking what possessions they could during the height of the bush war, and started a new life in South Africa.

After a dinner of tinned food cooked over a flickering fire, we had our nightcap – a steaming fire bucket of coffee – to round off another day in the heart of the African bush. When the night was upon us, we got into the chopper tent and zipped the oval archway closed – leaving an opening at the top for fresh air, the mesh netting keeping the unwanted whine of the mossies at bay. During the night we heard a variety of animal sounds, which were amplified in the stillness of night. By far the most chilling was the call of the hyena. This started as a deep sound and ended in a high-pitched shrill, which left us quite uncomfortable – until this undertaker of the grasslands left us to sleep once more.

Each day in this new world of ours helped build more confidence as our admiration and respect for nature grew. We trusted that the animals were just as scared of us as we were of them. When we left camp our rifles always accompanied us, in case we walked into a compromising situation with a threatening animal. Out of boredom, and curious what the sound of rifle fire into the river would be like, we decided to try it. We shot a magazine each into the muddy expanse of the Shingwidzi and watched the bullets kick up spray when they hit the surface. They created a circle of widening rings in the same way a stone does. The sound was unbelievable – the bullets cut into the water with a whiplash, reverberating off the mountains and back to us. The chatter of fire had to have travelled a fair distance, and we were left wondering whether we would be receiving a radio message warning of gunfire within our area. Luckily nothing was reported, and so we decided to do some scouting in the Samil 20. We zipped our tents closed and waited for Paul and his half section to pick us up. Holding our rifles, we climbed aboard the vehicle and bounced over the dirt roads, the metal benches punishing our backsides and whacking at our backs.

Driving through clouds of dust, the soil as dry as a bone, we eventually came to a wide river dammed on the one side. There we saw hippos at play, fighting with their jaws stretched square and open. Others wallowed like submerged rocks, and white tick birds walked over them – they plucked and feasted on these blood-sucking parasites. Now and then they snorted like tug boats and shot jets of water into the air from their round nostrils. On the other side of the bridge, at least six green monsters lay basking in the afternoon heat – lying dead still, without blinking an eye or twitching a muscle – their long jaws locked firmly shut. What odd docile creatures these crocodiles seemed to be upon the rocks, and yet in the water they were as quick as lightning. The sights and the sounds pleased me' this time in the Kruger Park was the absolute best I had experienced thus far in the uniform of a National Serviceman.

The first seven days in the bush went very quickly, and on the seventh day we entered the Kostini Base for our turn for a rest. We cooked our food over a real stove from the base kitchen. Our week in the bushveld had been a great wildlife-viewing experience, but it had proved fruitless because not a single refugee had been spotted. How amazing it was to rest on a foam mattress, without rocks digging sharply into our backs on the unevenness of a slight slope. The one day of base granted to us was not enough, but it did recharge our spirits with a warm shower and a comfortable sleep and a decent meal in our bellies, christened with a few ice-cold beers. Swimming in the pool had to be one of the highlights, especially as we came into the base one section at a time. As a result, fewer troops needed to use the pool, and so we had the luxury all to ourselves. The afternoon was spent with match after match of volleyball, and shouts and laughter amplified throughout the base. We looked and felt more like tourists enjoying a great holiday in an upmarket resort.

There was a big baboon that watched over our camp, and every now and then – when his inquisitiveness became too much – he ventured into our space and went straight for the kitchen. Once in the cooking area, he got into the fridge and made off with a big block of cheese. At first it was amusing, but soon it began to irritate everyone. Day by day we lost provisions – mainly in the way of fruit – until a trap was laid for him within a wired-off enclosure that we used to store the garbage. After hours of waiting, the baboon carefully made his way through the spring-loaded door and into the cage. Once inside, someone grabbed the stick that had been holding the door slightly ajar, and ripped it out, causing the door to slam firmly shut. The baboon viciously threw his body and face against the wire, shrieking and crazed in his effort to free himself. He bared his eyeteeth at us, which were at least five centimetres long – and when he lunged for us, we took a step back, hoping like hell that he did not break out. Lieutenant Bam got the game warden's approval to shoot the baboon, and duly carried out the execution. After this episode, we never lost any more rations to a wild animal – especially not one that was so cunning and similar to us.

In the late afternoon, after an enjoyable day of rest, and completely caught up on washing, we started to pack and get ready for another week in the solitude of the bush. With our rifles, packs, and clean browns, we climbed onto the Samil 20 and left the base with the A54 radio turned on and the nose of the vehicle headed back towards the Shingwidzi River. Staying on the dusty back roads, Bennie gunned the small vehicle, hoping to set up camp before dark. We drove with the sun setting to the left of us – a gift in itself, with the array of rich colour streaming over the horizon and only the groan of our engine breaking the stillness. We arrived at the Shingwidzi River in the same position we had been in a couple of days earlier, and under the headlights of the Samil we set up our tent before the rest of the section departed to their side of the river.

In the morning we went on a vehicle patrol, and were rewarded with the prize of all prizes – we saw the fastest animal on earth, sitting proudly on a small anthill, and her baby cub playing mischievously in front of her.

'Look, it's a cheetah!' a few of us exclaimed at the same time. Word reached Bennie in the cab, and he slowed the vehicle to a crawl and then a stop, 15 metres from the graceful feline. The spotted, long-legged cat turned her small head towards us – two distinct, black tear lines ran from her eyes as she scouted the plains like a sentry. It is quite seldom that one has the good fortune to view this animal up close, and we savoured it for all it was worth. In less than 20 seconds they were gone, vanishing into the bush, leaving us in admiration of a creature that none of us had ever seen but had heard so much about.

Feeling as though we were moving in slow motion, we departed from the sight that had now become a memory – the stamp of Africa firmly pressed into our consciousness. Bouncing over the roads, we passed lots of animals in small herds – zebras, antelopes, and giraffes – but nothing as inspiring as the cheetah and its baby cub. On reaching the river, where we had seen the hippos and crocs over a week ago, we came to a stop on the concrete ramp dividing the dammed-up water from the narrower part of the river on the other side of the bridge. To our disbelief, Gall shed his clothes and decided to take a bath.

'Angoose, *jou dom poes*' Angoose, you dumb *poes*!, we snapped, trying to dissuade him, but to no avail' for he broke the water in a splash, swimming furiously away from us. He swam 30 metres into the muddy water, to the very place we had spotted crocodiles' and then he turned around and swam back.

Stunned, we looked at him, shook our heads, and laughed in disbelief. Standing on the stone wall, he soaped himself' and before he dived in again, a few of us told him bluntly, 'Gall, no matter what happens, we are not going to save you.'

Shrugging his shoulders, he dove, leaving only a soapy trail behind him. If there was a croc out there, that would have been the time for it to strike – for after Gall's first dive it would have thought that an animal was in distress, and would have waited there for the kill.

But to our sheer amazement, Gall swam back to the safety of the low stonewall with a told-you-so attitude written upon his face – having beaten the crocodiles at their game. 'Angoose,' by which name we knew Gall, always did things differently, no matter what it was. I think he did it for the satisfaction of bugging the hell out of us. He always had a sly smile on his pale face, and this – with his ginger head of curly hair – made him stand out amongst us even more. Gall had an answer ready for whatever was said to him or around him. He was just one of those annoying people who knew nothing about everything. He was clever in his own complicated way, but he was a harmless loner at heart – living within himself, jotting down notes in a book that he carried daily inside his pack.

One night we moved camp and set up our chopper tents temporarily next to this same dam-like river, at a place elevated from the waterline. While we set up, Gall – as could have been expected – set up his own sleeping area about 20 metres away. Turning in for the night was another experience in itself, for it was then that the bushveld came alive, offering us a symphony of sound – always a song to my ears. The quietness of the night heightened the sound of the animals, which moved with ease through the cool black night. Then out of nowhere came the deep roar of a male lion, which echoed like thunder next to us. We bolted straight for the safety net of the Samil.

'Where's Gall?' a troop asked. 'Shit, he is on his own down there!' A finger stabbed through the darkness, in the direction of the lone bivi. 'Gall! Gall!' we shouted, and then finally he crawled out of the opening and stood up facing us. 'I can see them just as well from here!' he exclaimed, before turning and wriggling back into his sleeping nest, quite unfazed by all the commotion.

'Gall you fuckin' *dom soutie*!' Els shouted.

Either he had big brass balls of courage, or he was suffering from stupidity. Personally, I think the latter was more likely.

When the quiet returned, we ventured down from the vehicle and back to our tents. In the morning we tried to scout the area for the lion's footprints, but came up empty-handed.

In the afternoon we tried our hand at fishing. I landed myself a useless mudfish – which I then used as bait, hoping to catch one we could all eat. I fished at a spot where only a day earlier crocodiles had been lying on the rocks, only a few metres away. As I stood nervously and stupidly in the reeds, I hoped like hell that one would not emerge right in front of me. Fortunately for the crocs, and unfortunately for a decent fish, it was not to be – but on the other hand, Bennie proved very successful in catching a nice-sized bream.

Back at camp, Bennie went to work' he began to prepare a feast for us, with what little provisions we had. We made a fire and waited for the dry sticks and branches to reduce themselves to hot coals. Next to the fire, we dug a small hole 30 centimetres deep, and using a stick we pushed and prodded the hot coals into the shallow pit. Bennie wrapped the bream inside a wet newspaper and placed it upon the coals, and then carefully placed the sand over the top – burying the fish into an improvised oven. For a few hours, the fish remained forgotten and untouched within the earth – left to slowly cook. When the time was right, Bennie went to the hole and carefully removed the layers of soil until he found the dirty wrapping of the newspaper. He opened the pages, and inside was the bream, cooked to perfection. Crowding around the small feast, we reached out with our dirty hands and took a piece of fish – which broke free of the bone at the slightest touch. The bream was moist and succulent, and had a mouth-watering, smoked flavour to it. But unfortunately, with ten eager mouths to a small fish, it was finished far too quickly. Still it left a taste that bettered any fish that I have ever eaten. We all heaped Bennie with praise for his accomplishment of a splendid meal, made with absolutely no cooking supplies or spices other than pepper.

Happy with life, and quite content with our wild and carefree spirit in this park, we headed back to the Shingwidzi River – to our positions on either side of the river – for more days of wait and wonder under the burning-hot African sky.

21

Leaderless
A dark shadow of doubt

It was 12 September, and it was no different from any other day. The sun shone, there were no loud, barking orders from rank, and for once in our army lives, time was governed as we wished and not used as a tool of discipline – in the way it had been for just three months shy of two years. We rose from sleep when we wished, or when the tent became too hot, exposing our dirty, shirtless bodies to the bright morning light for coffee while sitting on a rock, our gaze set upon the glimmer off the still river on our doorstep.

After a small breakfast of porridge and a rat pack milkshake, Wayne, Fox, and I crossed the border into Mozambique, as we had done a few times before. The three of us walked past the border fence, and along the sandy riverbank that separated South Africa and Mozambique. The high barbed-wire fence came to an abrupt end when it met the Shingwidzi River, which filled the 25 metre void and acted as a border in itself. On the opposite river bank, the boundary fence resumed its snake-like path and wound its way over hills until it became lost to our squinting sight.

Once we had walked 40 to 50 metres into Mozambique, we crossed a shallow part of the river and set our sights on a rocky hill that we had all climbed before. The tedious climb took us a slow half hour to complete' we navigated a path through the rocks and scrubby dry ground, and beneath small trees growing on the hillside, which brushed our backs with some discomfort and irritation.

The very first time we ascended this hill, we tackled it with a painted picture vividly set into our minds. The visual I had was one of a beautiful coastline, with oil tankers motionless on the horizon, ferrying cargo upon the Indian Ocean, and Maputo in the foreground. This visual kept me going, and I believed if I willed my mind on with enough hope, the vision would miraculously present itself.

Upon reaching the summit, we were met with the same disappointment as before, for the picture in our minds had not materialized. Instead we saw the rugged, rolling hills of the Lebombo Mountains. They were a magnificent sight, for they rolled from one hill into the next, filling the wide expanse before us.

For the few Durbanites from our section, nothing could come close to equalling the beauty and ruthlessness of a raging ocean. Huge waves, curling and crashing onto a sandy beach and washing cleanly over the soft sand – and a fresh aroma of salt blown into our open nostrils by a cool sea breeze, was what our young and keen senses ached for, in or out of our bush living.

21. Leaderless: A dark shadow of doubt

Sitting with sweat cooling on our skin, under the shade of a small tree, we continued talking about the ocean. Our eyes looked down into our beautiful land, upon the nearest thing that resembled an ocean – the Shingwidzi River. Our vision followed its meandering course into the hazy, heated distance before becoming lost to the lush greenery that adorned the banks.

Under some trees and bushes we saw our 'homes' – we made out the dome shapes of the two olive green chopper tents, split apart by the shimmering water of the Shingwidzi. Even though they were positioned very close to the break in the border fence, the tents remained well camouflaged by the green surroundings.

There was movement around Paul's tent – a few figures milled around, preferring the heat of the outside to the oven-like setting and stale-smelling air inside. After a few minutes, a fire sprang to life, made for the purpose of heating water for the morning ritual of sweet, steaming hot coffee to kick-start another day in the heart of the bushveld. Looking down upon them, we watched the smoke rise and the wind wafting streaks of grey towards the crystal-clear, sea-blue sky before it thinned to nothing and disappeared into thin air.

With a nice long rest behind us, we gathered our strength for the descent from this hill that had held so much promise for us. Slowly and carefully, we zigzagged our way down until we reached flat land, where we raised our hands in greeting to our fellow troops – Paul, J.P., Bennie, Els, Laurence, and Sandor, who had spotted us on the Mozambican side.

At the shallower part of the river, the three of us shed our clothes and walked into the cool, muddy-brown water, which soon covered us up to our necks. We gave no passing thought to the parasitic worms that could have entered our bladders, as in the case of so many African rivers, known as Bilharzia – or, as we sometimes referred to it, 'Bill Harris.' While we took pleasure in the swim, we kept a sharp, vigilant eye for the crocodiles, which we had seen basking on rocks further upstream a few days back. The dirty-brown water, to us, was like relaxing in a spa. We smiled with the refreshing feel that the cool water had over our bodies' standing or lying back, we laughed, enjoying this paradise of simple pleasure.

'This is the life!' I exclaimed, with a feeling of satisfaction in army life for the first time in nearly two years – revelling in the fact that we had just over three months to serve.

Once we had dried off under the blazing midday sun, we walked the last few metres out of Mozambique to our tent, recharged for the stifling heat that would soon be sapping our energy. Our group began collecting wood for our lunchtime meal. We made a fire to warm tins of corned beef and vienna sausages and a canteen of water each for our tea. While we consumed our meal under the shade of a tree, unbeknown to us, Paul, Laurence, and Sandor crossed the border into Mozambique – in the same way we had done only a few hours before.

Resting in the shade, we amused ourselves by throwing stones in the river, reading, and sleeping off the heat. In the late afternoon, we were surprised to see Els and Bennie with their rifles on our side of the river.

'Have you guys seen Itzie, Paul, and Laurence?' they asked, a worried tone to their voices.

'No. Didn't they go swimming in Mozambique? Why?' Something did not seem right.

'*Ja*, they went into Mozambique shortly after noon, and we have not seen them since!' Els replied, with a very serious expression that seemed out of place to his normal, humourous demeanor, which was such a daily laugh in our platoon.

'They left their rifles as well!' he added.

'Well, there are still a few more hours of daylight left for them to turn up. Let's wait and see what happens' they cannot be far away.'

Our concern was slowly mounting.

Bennie and Els left us and returned to a waiting J.P. with an agreement that whoever spotted them first was to immediately tell the waiting ears on the opposite banks of the river.

When darkness began to descend around us, a horrible feeling entered our guts – having not heard a word of their whereabouts. Suddenly we had to assume that they were lost. But now, with no rifles or sleeping equipment, they would have to rough the night out until morning, and hopefully they would find their way back to us' after all, they only had to follow the river.

A shout reached us from the opposite bank: 'Have you seen them?'

'No!' we replied flatly, through the dimming light.

'If they are not back in the morning,' Bennie said, 'we have to make radio contact with Kostini and notify the lieutie of their disappearance.'

'*Ja*, he has to be told,' we said. We did not want to get our friends into trouble, but now we feared for their safety and well-being.

Silence returned to the river, and our fears swirled through our minds. We watched the darkening night encroaching on us like a fog of blindness' it chased us into the comfort of our tents, where the shadows of candlelight danced through the blackness.

After an uneasy sleep, plagued by the worst thoughts imaginable, we rose early and shouted, across the glassy surface of the Shingwidzi, to our fellow troops.

'Any sign of them?'

'No, they never came back.'

Now it was time to follow our gut and do the right thing. Bennie got hold of Paul's A54 radio and made contact with our home base Kostini.

'Two three, two three, this is two three Alpha. Do you read me?'

'Two three, reading you loud and clear.'

'Two three Alpha, reporting the disappearance of three troops.'

'Two three, what happened?'

'Two three Alpha, they crossed the border to swim.'

'Two three, shit – crocodiles!'

'Two three Alpha, maybe we don't know.'

'Two three, sit tight and wait by your radio.'

'Two three Alpha, affirmative.'

Lieutenant Bam immediately radioed Captain Delport at the Letaba Base, who in turn radioed even higher. By mid-morning the chain of command had set the wheels in motion – two camouflaged Puma helicopters flew over us at tree-height, the sudden sound coming out of nowhere and scaring the living shit out of us. They chased each other down the length of the fence, with pilot and co-pilot scanning the terrain in Mozambique for any telltale signs of the missing three. When these huge choppers reached the most northern point that they thought could have been reached on foot, they abruptly turned and headed south to re-search the area they had already flown over. Under strict military orders from the South African government, they had been instructed not to violate Mozambican air space – for the Mozambican authorities had flatly denied the request to allow the search to cross the border line.

'Do you think they were eaten by crocs?' I asked Wayne, for I now started to believe that something terrible had happened.

'Lions or crocodiles' I don't know. Maybe,' he said. We did not know what to think or believe anymore.

One thing was for sure, for the Pumas to be here, it was serious – but just how serious, no one knew. Our feelings said it all – a soldier knows when something is not right, and this was definitely not right. Feeling alone, the eight of us continued to stand apart, the watercourse separating us, making the divide even greater.

While the helicopters chopped at the air for a deafening few seconds as they whizzed over us, Wayne and I decided, of our own accord, to enter Mozambique. With loaded rifles and a 30 round magazine clip, we crossed the border and made our way along the river under the whirling sound of rotors as they flashed by overhead. Coming to a shallow point in the river, we crossed it in our takkies towards the sand bank, half expecting to find their blood from a crocodile attack.

But instead we saw the unmistakable footprints and boot markings printed into the soft beach sand.

'They were here,' Wayne said. 'But what are all these boot prints?'

'I don't know, but it does not look right!'

'Let's follow the trail and see if we find anything on the way!' I said, raising my voice over the noise of the rotors. Turning to Wayne, I waited for his nod of approval' and on his nod we began moving, flicking our safety catches off and onto rapid fire.

Walking slowly next to the river, we placed our feet in the line of prints and followed the trail down river. Our hearts pounded – we distanced ourselves from the border fence, our eyes constantly scanning the thick overgrowth from right to left and then back to right – we jittered through barriers, bordering on fear and adrenaline.

The undergrowth got thicker and the air became cooler, the branches from the tall trees and thick, overhanging bush shielded us from the warmth of the daylight, as it tried in vain to stab rays through the knotted creepers. The river shrank in size under the ever-darkening cover of foliage, a dead silence hung in the damp air – except for the slow trickle of water and the rotation of blades, now close to two kilometres away.

The path of footprints continued over the moist sand, through the curtained enclosure from the riverbanks, taking us further away from the safety of our border.

'How much further do we dare to go with no guarantee of finding anything?' I said, turning to Wayne. We both realized the grave danger to which we were exposing ourselves. Here were two white South African soldiers on foreign soil with loaded weapons, and we were shit scared of walking into a FRELIMO patrol two long kilometres from the protection of the South African border. Moved by these considerations, we decided to turn back.

It felt very eerie to be alone with Wayne so far from the safety net of our fellow friends with no idea what lay in wait behind the walls of bush – whether it be a uniformed soldier or a wild animal. Our faces, as always, concealed the fear that ran wild within us and festered in our anxious stomachs while the element of the unknown played in its own devilish way.

Our hearts racing and our bodies racked with tension, we hurriedly retraced our steps – our eyes darting in and out of overgrown entrances to this umbrella of bush. Every few paces we turned and stole a glance backwards, half expecting to see something standing in the long, dark corridor. The coolness in the air had covered our arms in goosebumps, and we moved our feet silently through the thick, wet sand in a walking charge towards the openness of daylight and the familiarity of the South African side. Every rustle of a branch had us on alert –

our fingers curled more tightly around the trigger, ready to fire at the slightest movement. Once we reached the safety of our border, we returned to our normal selves, leaving behind the nervous energy that we had carried, and welcomed the sound of another Puma rocketing over us.

The pilots were by now our only hope of finding our three lost friends alive. Wayne and I had done our part, with total disregard to our safety, but even though we had turned up nothing, at least within ourselves we could say that we did what we could for our friends.

Once we had regained our breath, we spotted Lieutenant Bam on the other side of the river, talking with Bennie, Els, and J.P. An hour later he visited our side of the river, looking red-faced and worried about the situation – which was only made worse by the noise of the camouflaged helicopters, churning and charging the airwaves with anxiety.

Quiet, disoriented and preoccupied in deep thought, he told us to remain in our present positions for one more day – which was when we were due to break camp and head back to Kostini anyway. On this order, he turned and departed in his Samil 20, leaving the area a totally different person from what we had come to know. We could not help but notice what the disappearance of Paul, Laurence, and Sandor had done to his demeanour.

In the late afternoon, silence returned to normal' the helicopter search had been called off, leaving us alone to ponder this highly mysterious vanishing act. We questioned ourselves and our fellow troops, trying to make sense out of this extraordinary occurrence that had us questioning our invincibility – which for the first time seemed to have made its point, for our young lives were no longer as invincible as we had once thought!

It was a long night, and many thoughts passed through our minds – and a dumbfounded wonder of what could possibly have happened to them. I could not believe that they would have gone on AWOL with only three short months remaining of the 21 already served. Hopefully time would shed some light on the mystery, which we suspected lay within the tent on the opposite bank.

Did they know more than they let on? We wondered, still trying to find that last piece to the unsolvable puzzle.

When the sun rose, we rose with it, hoping to find our friends returned – but it was not to be. The water already boiled, we sipped hot coffee from our metal canteens and our stare set upon the calm Shingwidzi. After lazing around for much of the morning, we began to dismantle the chopper tent, roll our sleeping bags up, and pack our gear in wait for Bennie, J.P., and Els. They arrived at noon to pick the five of us up, and our belongings, which we tossed up into the back of the Samil 20.

Leaving the Shingwidzi River seemed like a stab of betrayal and abandonment to Paul, Laurence, and Sandor. We drove out of the area, scanning the bush one last time for some vital clue. Our guilt was dreadful, and we turned our backs with a sombre mood hanging over us – and the realization, sitting in our guts, that our shield of invincibility had been dealt a severe blow.

Their rifles and kit sat packed at the sides, with us in the back of the vehicle – which made it feel that much stranger to have their gear, but not their persons.

Leaderless, in a dark shadow of doubt, with the worry of what was next hanging over us, we ambled on, silent with our own thoughts, the excitement beaten from our sails. We passed herds of wildlife we could no longer admire for their beauty. Staring upon the open plains, we either remained quiet – listening as others communicated – or discussed amongst each other the severity of what had befallen Platoon 3s Alpha section.

It was a long, lonely drive back to base. Our dampened spirits were slightly lifted, but offered little to rejoice in when we spotted our little utopia of thatched huts and greenery adorning the cut-out from the rough terrain surrounding it. On driving into the base, down the narrow dusty road, we were met by Lieutenant Bam, who had rushed out to meet us half expecting to see Alpha section back to full complement.

'No sign of them?' he mumbled, expelling a disconcerted sigh, he shrugged his shoulders and kicked at the dirt in disgust, and walked away crestfallen, disappearing between the bungalows.

As a unit we had to allow everyone their own way of dealing with this event, and in our lieutie's case he had shown his torment the most noticeably – his one pip carrying with it the responsibility of leading all of us to safety.

Personally, I did not know what to do. I had no idea how to grieve, and I questioned whether I should grieve with no confirmation of their deaths or whether I should live with hope. I chose the latter, looking at the hopeful side but still believing that we needed a miracle to get them back.

While we ate dinner that night, we could not help but notice Lieutenant Bam openly shedding his tears for his lost 'sons' – he declined to eat his meal, but swigged down can after can of beer. The more he consumed, the deeper he sank into a depression, for the worry stared him straight in the face, forcing out a wave of anger – which he followed with more tears.

Amongst ourselves we drank too, we drowned our sorrows with a six-pack, in the comfort of our bungalow – the kit and rifles of our missing comrades placed upon their waiting beds.

21. Leaderless: A dark shadow of doubt

Passing out on the soft comfort of our mattresses, we blanked out the night, and any thoughts that tried to enter our comatose sleep. With the afternoon to ourselves, we used it to recover, and rest in between 'volleyball swims,' relaxation, and reading in the sun upon the short green mat of grass.

When the late afternoon came, we were ready to leave the base for the bush. Our somewhat smaller section felt quite different without Paul, Laurence, and Sandor to fill the empty spaces.

Driving out of Kostini and down the dusty roads, the familiarity of nature once again absorbed our attention, casting aside those wandering thoughts and helping soothe the questions which we constantly asked, but for which we received no answers.

What exactly had become of them?

Search for three S A soldiers who disappeared

Military Correspondent

THE search for three South African soldiers who disappeared from their base in the Eastern Transvaal five days ago continues.

Yesterday, a ground and air search was launched for the men, who went absent without leave and might be in Mozambique. Their unit had been involved in border control of illegal immigrants from Mozambique.

The three men are Cpl P Kolenda of Ramsgate in Natal, Rfn L R van Zydam of Bedford, and Rfn S L Toth of Kimberley.

A spokesman for the Defence Force in Pretoria said the three men were wearing civilian clothes, were unarmed and it was believed they could have wandered into Mozambique.

The Mozambican authorities had been notified of the ground and air search through the Nkomati Operation Centre at the Ressano Garcia border post near Komatipoort, according to the spokesman.

He would not say whether Mozambican soldiers were assisting in the search.

Late last night there had still been no sign of the men, a Defence Force spokesman said.

Maputo releases three S A soldiers

PRETORIA—Three South African soldiers held by Mozambique authorities since September were back home, the SADF said last night.

The three disappeared from their unit in the Eastern Transvaal along the Mozambique border on September 12.

A Defence spokesman said the men had been in the hands of the Mozambique authorities since September 23.

The three are Cpl P Colenda, Rfn L R van Zydam and Rfn S L Toth.

They would be placed in quarantine at 1 Military Hospital, Voortrekkerhoogte, while undergoing comprehensive medical examinations.
— (Sapa)

Soldiers cleared by inquiry

Mercury Reporter

A MILITARY board of inquiry has found that Cpl Paul Colenda of Ramsgate and two other soldiers could not be held responsible for their detention by the Mozambique authorities earlier this year.

Cpl Colenda, Rfn L R van Zydam and Rfn S L Toth were released by the Mozambique authorities after being held since September.

Defence Headquarters also announced that the trio had completed their national service yesterday and were on their way home.

The board of inquiry said the three members were not absent without leave and could not be held responsible for their detention after they were caught in Mozambique territory while swimming.

1985-Kruger Park. Our three soldiers who disappeared, leaving us to fear they were dead.

22

Cause for celebration

The days went by, crowned with beautiful sunsets and the enchanted sounds of the wild echoing crystal clear over the savannah, under the welcoming coolness of night.

Our camp had been set up under the shade of some trees' our chopper tents a stone's throw away from each other – and this time nowhere near a river. One at a time we stood guard, with the aid of the radio in case an urgent message was transmitted from the Kostini base, through the airwaves, to our waiting signal.

There was no activity and no excitement to help pass the time' no beers or luxuries, but just the annoyance of mosquitoes and flies that pestered us to insanity. One major piece of news that did reach us was that somehow the newspapers had got hold of the fact that three soldiers had disappeared, and under the heading 'Search For AWOL Trio' it suggested that they had run away. This angered us, for we knew our friends well, and one thing was certain: With minimal time left to serve, no soldier in his right mind would jeopardize his discharge. Breaking the rules, whether in prison or the army, only got you time added on' and after all we had all endured as a platoon, we wanted nothing more than to complete our National Service together as the tightly-knit unit of the young men that we were.

When our seven days were up, it was a thrill to head back to Kostini for a hot shower and a cold beer, or six – not to mention the bed. On our arrival into base on 23 September, we had barely set foot into our bungalow when Lieutenant Bam met us, his face flushed with excitement.

'They are alive!' he blurted out. It took us a few seconds to comprehend what he had just said, and in what context. After a short pause, having captured our full and undivided attention, he went on.

'They are in Maputo! They were captured!' he said' his voice trailed off with the realization that they were alive, but far from free to leave.

'Who captured them?' All of us suspected that it was FRELIMO, the Communist-backed, ANC sympathizers who were fighting the South African-aided RENAMO.

'FRELIMO!' Lieutenant Bam said, cutting the silence with a stab of the word.

We looked at each other with shock and joy to hear that they were now accounted for, and best of all, alive, but when I heard that they were being held by FRELIMO, I honestly did not believe we would ever see them again. There

22. Cause for celebration

were only three months left before our klaaring out papers were handed to us, granting us the freedom to walk back into civilian life.

On 23 September, the Mozambican authorities had notified the South African government that they were holding three white South African soldiers captive in Maputo. South Africa in turn notified the SADF, our 4-SAI unit, Captain Delport, and then Lieutenant Bam at Kostini. The news reached our ears via this chain of command.

Then it hit me like a slap across the face. I turned to look for Wayne. 'It could have been us,' I whispered to him, sensing that same shock in his stern looking face. Looking back at me, he nodded, recognizing that fate had been on our side when we crossed into Mozambique.

Had a FRELIMO patrol spotted us that morning and laid in wait for us to cross again? Who knew? But the questions were real and too close for comfort. 'What about our two kilometre walk along the river?' Wayne reminded me. Reliving that walk sent a wave of shock through me, and I thought about our holding loaded weapons across the border – which would have been deemed a threat by any soldier and given them reason to shoot at us. The rest we left to pure speculation.

'Shit we were lucky!' All of us agreed – though we had not lost our focus on our three friends, held as prisoners far away, in unfamiliar territory – within the confines of a third world jail.

With the good and bad news dominating our thoughts, we continued with our day, taking full advantage of a hot shower, a shave, and a dump in a real porcelain toilet – the army ritual of a shit, a shower, and a shampoo.

By mid afternoon we decided it was time to approach Fox, who had volunteered to manage the canteen from a refrigerated Samil. He was in his element, surrounded by cases of Castle and Lion, bars of chocolate and boxes of Simba chips ranging from cheese and onion to smoked beef. He took his job seriously, and tried to manage his stock in accordance with his sales, balancing his money at the end of each day – or at least trying hard to. Our section all had a six-pack in our hands' and with this 'medicine of laughter,' we congregated under the thatched eating area while a radio belted out tunes from the 80s. Sitting on the wooden benches, our beers resting on the thick wooden tabletop, cut from a huge oak tree, we enjoyed the taste of the beer and the uplifting feel it gave us as we listened to the music and spoke amongst each other. Not forgetting our friends, we raised our tins in salute, wishing them a speedy and safe return. We sat, only imagining what kind of ordeal they were suffering in contrast to our casual banter and backdrop of music. Lieutenant Bam joined us with a bottle of brandy, which he drank like water – with the aid of Coke to cut the taste. The capture of three of his troops was already taking its toll on him.

'Food's ready!' came a shout from the kitchen, and with our dixies we ambled towards the smell that wafted from the huge, round, stainless steel pots. Mashed potatoes, gravy with meat, some peas, and a slice of bread with margarine – and so dinner was served, with a scoop from a ladle into our aluminum, rectangular containers. During dinner, we continued to drink, using the food as a cushion for all the beer that followed it down. It was a good bonding time' we enjoyed each other's company, and the music, between noisy scrapes of cutlery over the bottom of the dixies. Quiet only returned when the cutlery was dispensed with and the bread, which had been saved until last, was used as a sponge to wipe our containers clean.

With time wearing on, we noticed that Lieutenant Bam began to reel with the effect of this highly depressive drink – which started to take control of him. Suddenly the silence was shattered' he stood up and shouted into the air while holding his plate of food.

'If they can't eat, I am not going to eat!' he slurred, and in the next moment he launched his plate into the wall – splattering gravy, mashed potatoes, and meat and splintering ceramic across the stone flooring. The food ran down the cream painted wall in slow silence, landing in a heap at the base' and then, through the stunned hush, his tears flowed freely through muffled sobs. The demons in the alcohol, and the numbing news of their capture, had taken their toll on our leader, who in his weak but justified moment of emotion had won our full respect. This single act proved to us how valuable each one of us was, and his steadfast quest to return each and every soul from Platoon 3 alive and well to our parents.

After Lieutenant Bam had been taken back to the comfort of his bed in his rondavel, we continued with our celebration – their lives now accounted for, for the first time in ten long days. There was nothing we could do to bring them back' we had no choice but to wait and let time take its course. We still had to eat and live and keep strong, and pray in our own ways for their safe return.

With the booze running low, we persuaded Fox to reopen the canteen, and with another six beers each we got hammered – toasting each beer to our three soldiers sitting in darkness and desolation in the far off capital of Maputo, a city we knew little to nothing about. After a long night, having consumed far too much alcohol, we retired to bed with the full knowledge that we would be suffering for it the next day. But in the moment, for them and for us, it had been worth it.

As expected, we rose when the sun warmed our bungalow, and nursing severe hangovers, we staggered around the base like brain-dead zombies. By

22. Cause for celebration

the afternoon, having filled our bellies with two square meals, we began to feel more like our old selves and began preparing for another week in the bush, with seven ration packs handed to us.

At the usual time in the late afternoon, we packed the vehicle and paid Fox a last visit to stock up on some beer and chips, for our nights ahead in the isolation of the bushveld.

It still seemed quite strange to depart from the base with barely half a section – minus Paul, Laurence and Sandor as well as Fox, who remained behind to man the canteen. Els had already been with our section, making our tally seven, and with Stoop moving from our Bravo section into Alpha, we now numbered eight.

Leaving base with our coordinates handed down from Lieutenant Bam to Gall and Bennie, we headed towards the Letaba River to lay an ambush on one side of a bridge. Countless weary legs of these war-torn refugees, trying to flee a land so ripe in civil conflict, had regularly traversed this crossing – and now it was up to us to surprise them in their earnest quest to reach peace.

A hundred metres from the bridge, we set up camp and left all our gear behind – only taking our rifles with us to the bridge, where we found a good vantage point to observe the crossing. We took turns standing guard over the tarred concrete bridge – a route well travelled by tourists, who were not meant to know that the army was wandering within the park, helping to control the influx of illegal immigrants. The night played out a performance of animal calls – the most notable being the whooping of the hyena, which sounded uncomfortably close to us. Our beat for the night produced nothing, and so in the early hours of morning we returned empty-handed to our makeshift campsite. Upon reaching our camp, we immediately noticed paw prints, and then smelled the foul odour of rotting meat. We realized that the hyena we had heard on the bridge had walked through our camp. Then I noticed muddy prints in our tent, which for some reason had not been zipped up – thus giving him free access to pilfer as he wished. I looked at my pack and noticed right away, holes in one of my side pouches, which was streaked with rank, wet saliva. Cautiously I unzipped the pouch, half expecting to see a hyena inside – the overpowering, rotting carcass smell seemed to be everywhere. While I slid the zipper open, I wondered why he had gone for this particular pouch, but once it was fully open I realized why. I had packed my tins of meat in this pocket and having punctured these tins with his teeth, he had caught the smell of food – which threw him into frenzy, and he fought with the nylon material to gain access. Looking more closely, I noticed that his teeth had squeezed holes into them with the ease of a can opener – proving the hyena to have the strongest jaw in the animal kingdom.

It had not been too long ago that we had been told of an unfortunate incident that had occurred within the park, involving a National Serviceman from another unit. He had fallen asleep, or had passed out, halfway outside his tent and in the middle of the night, a hyena had ripped a massive chunk from his face. It verified further that these grotesque, deformed, dog-like animals are not just scavengers, but when hungry, they will attack to survive – sometimes hunting in packs to corner an animal for a meal.

After a quick breakfast of porridge and coffee, we headed out by Samil, driving along the dusty road that took us along the banks of the Letaba River. It was here that I viewed the most graceful of all cats, the leopard, with his camouflaged coat of black paw-print markings hiding him perfectly within the shadows of a tree overhang. He had made his way down from his resting spot in the thick branches to the river's edge, where he licked at the water in the same way a cat licks from its bowl. This is one of the hardest animals to spot in the wild, for it barely shows itself for a few seconds before it hides again. It was the first and only time that I had been granted the privilege to view such a fine creature' and like the cheetah, it remained ingrained in my memory as being at peace with nature.

Further down the road, we were treated to another rarely witnessed spectacle. Close to the waters of the Letaba, I watched a fish eagle drop from a treetop in directional flight. It dropped like a stone, and just before it touched the water it stretched its legs down, then dipped them like arrows beneath the surface. In an unbroken flight, it fanned itself forward, and its legs emerged from the water having speared a flapping fish between both sets of claws. What a soothing sight it was to witness the freedom of this bird' it disappeared just as quickly, with its well-deserved catch of the day held firmly beneath its wingspan.

On our return, we noticed a spiralling swarm of vultures hovering overhead, waiting for the right moment to descend upon a fresh kill – to scavenge a few leftover scraps of flesh, left behind by the full-bellied predators.

Back at camp, we were thankful to see that the hyena had not returned, and even if he had, we had made sure that the two sets of zippers were firmly zipped to the top, denying him easy access into the chopper tents. After a small meal, a few of us decided to take a short walk down the river to try and find Charlie section, who were camped a couple of kilometres from us. Taking our rifles with us in case we were attacked by an animal, we headed into the afternoon sun with hardly a care in the world. Walking along the bank of the river, I spotted what looked like a big rock amongst the reeds' but it struck me as being too large, and so – being inquisitive – I ventured closer. I took a few paces back and

22. Cause for celebration

took a running jump from the riverbank onto a small island of land, big enough for only one person to stand on. After nearly jumping too far, I landed neatly onto it, using my arms to steady myself from falling into the water. This placed me only five metres from the big rock and armed with a small stone, I threw it at this big, polished, grey object – which to my horror erupted like a volcano from within the reeds, rising like a hovercraft from the water, and growing in size by the second. Waves washed over my feet for what felt like an eternity before I broke from shock and performed the greatest long jump record in the Kruger National Park – I vaulted from the island back to land. Safe at last, I managed to turn my head and catch sight of a massive hippo, bursting down the river, parting the water as it went, leaving two waves to roll with white crests as they washed over both riverbanks.

When I regained my wits, I realized what had happened. I had selfishly and unknowingly disturbed this gigantic creature from its sheltered place as she was trying to give birth. I was lucky to get away unscathed – considering her anger and shock at being disturbed at such a painful moment. Nevertheless, I had given Wayne something to laugh about, and a story to pass on to Charlie section.

A little further from the hippo incident, we found Charlie section relaxing in a shallow river to cool them from the relentless dry heat. The first thing I noticed was Brian, who held a beer in one hand – giving the impression of a Sunday picnic at the beach, rather than guard beats to catch refugees. It was great to see them again, for it had been weeks since we had last spoken with the base rotation – and thus we'd been prevented from seeing much of one another – only one section returned to Kostini at any one time. When a section was in base, two would be left in the veld to await their turn for a humanizing experience, in the form of a shower and a square meal.

Charlie had come across two massive skulls – one of them a buffalo with two huge curved horns, which they had balanced upon a bigger but oval skull, belonging to a hippo. We took turns picking up the hippo skull, just to see how heavy it was' and it weighed an absolute ton. After a good laugh and a long rest, we said our farewells to our Durban friends and headed up river, hoping not to see our new enemy the hippo, and eager to make it back to camp before the night was upon us.

Back at camp, we surrounded the fire, enjoying the crackle and pop as the dry wood burned fiercely creating a passage of light into the black hole of darkness. Busy with our meals, we opened tins and mixed them into a concoction. Then we stirred it as it bubbled in our dixies and fire buckets. The burning embers rose and fell, settling into our food only to disappear with the next stir.

The nights and the days continued in the same way as the ones before, and the only things that broke the monotony were the animals and the weekly visit to base. When we became frustrated with the boredom and the intensity of the heat, we reminded ourselves what life could be like if we were back in 4-SAI under the strict discipline of marching and running. Here, at least, we could sweat with no interruptions, or uncalled-for shouts from insecure rank, or opfoks like those horrendous walking patrols that were an almost daily occurrence on the South-West African border.

Kostini always helped lift our dirty, downtrodden spirits and normalize our lives within a tiny fraction of civilization. As we returned, Bravo section left – having left a story swirling around the camp about Grant and Tony coming face to face with a lion. They had gone for a walk with their rifles, and upon rounding a bush they walked headlong into a huge lion, its tawny mane puffing up around an already-large muscular frame. They stared into each other's eyes for a couple of seconds, which must have felt like an eternity, before the lion broke the spell, turning and disappearing into the long dry grass. Grant's legs had turned to jelly, and he could barely move his body from the spot. He made no effort to hide his fright, openly joking about how scared he was of being eaten – 'even though there was not too much to eat.' His slender build resembled mine at the time – not much wider than a rake handle. They had been lucky to walk away, for if the lion had been as hungry as Bravo section, we might have been looking for a new section leader and the HQ section a new driver.

Another story Bravo told was of the time Greg had been out in the late afternoon, collecting wood for the evening fire, barefoot and clad only in his underwear – looking more like a Neanderthal man than a soldier. Sauntering through the bush, a pile of sticks slung casually over one shoulder' Greg continued to collect wood close to the tar road that ran north and south through the heart of the reserve. A few German tourists drove by, stopped, and then reversed in disbelief to look at this wild animal. They had spotted a tall dirty, unshaven, man, tanned as bronze as the soil, walking casually – and, in their opinion, aimlessly – in the middle of a park that was home to the most ferocious of all animals. Greg made eye contact with them and raised his hand in a calm greeting, which caused them to immediately speed towards the closest rest stop. There they placed a report with the warden, who was forced to hold back his surprise and laughter at this story of a wild man roaming the Kruger Park.

When Louw finished telling the story, we were in stitches of laughter. We tried to imagine the facial expressions of the tourists, who had no idea we had been living like this for weeks on end.

22. Cause for celebration

Clean for a day, we departed for the dust and filth that accompanied the scorching African heat – for sweat and wood smoke replaced the sweet smell of soap, and once again became the normal rank odours of the bushveld.

On our drive, we spotted a herd of elephant led by a huge bull – weighted down with his old pillars of ivory, walking in a column one behind the other, each trunk curled around a tail, linked in a long, unified line of security. They intrigued us, and we wondered why the herd was performing this charade. Then we noticed that in the middle of the procession were two baby elephants, dwarfed by their elders as they shielded them from the dangers of the bushveld – the steering arm of their snake-like trunks rested protectively upon their little heads' and holding onto their tails, they stamped a beaten path through the dry grass. A little further from us, they crossed the dirt road – as human in their mannerisms as I have ever seen, the adults shepherding the kids across the road like a crossing guard directing small children.

Observing these roaming giants, I thought of Solamonkey, who had actually crept up undetected and managed to lay a careful hand upon one of these majestic animals. He told us that it felt like bristles from a wire brush – short, thick needles of hair protruding from its canvas-grey, wrinkly skin. His daredevil act thankfully had no repercussions – for these animals have a keen sense of smell' and with an inbred fear of poachers turning their hacked-out ivory into blood money, they remain alert to the threatening smell of humans.

A few days later I thought I would show off my bravado when we spotted another herd of elephant feeding in a shallow riverbed surrounded by reeds. Leaving the section sitting comfortably on the dam wall to await my return, I set off with my camera, hoping to get a close-up picture of the fine-looking bull. I walked a few hundred metres from Alpha section, which sat as spectators on the wall, waiting for a show to begin. I jumped from rock to rock and narrowed the distance between the bull and myself, creeping the last few metres through a thicket of rustling, long green reeds. Carefully parting the vegetation so as not to make any noise, I saw him through the window frame of the reeds. Sitting excitedly and yet nervously, I observed this massive creature at only five metres away. He was totally oblivious of my presence. His trunk swayed freely from side to side as he ate and drank, using his large ears to flap and fan away flies, his sad-looking brown eyes stared through me, his poor eyesight unable to detect my presence. I was down wind, so his sense of smell was powerless to capture my scent. But it all changed in a second when I stood up to get a better angle for a photo shot of him.

Suddenly he had a bearing on me – he sensed a threat and let out a deep trumpet sound. His ears pricked up and began to flap like sails in the wind, enlarging his already-huge physique. Then, with increasing fury, he lifted his trunk high in the air and whipped it down, only to raise it again, waving an all-too-clear signal to immediately get the hell out of his territory. He started to trumpet again, and rocked his body back and forth with his ears still flapping and his trunk snaking like a cobra, ready to strike as the final warning for me to move on out. I raised my camera and looked through the lens' and as I clicked the small black button, I turned in haste and fled. My legs were running even before I realized that my brain had told them to do so. I sped through the reeds and jumped from rock to rock like a rock rabbit, without daring to cast a glance back. I had a feeling in my gut that this giant was bearing down on me. I ran and ran, without stopping, until I reached the dam wall red-faced and totally out of breath. It was only then that I looked back to see the elephant moving away from his feeding area. The spectators had enjoyed the show, and doubled over in laughter at the speed of my escape. Unbeknown to me at the time, he had performed a mock charge, running at me for at least ten metres before I sprang to safety using the rocks as stepping-stones.

'Ram, you should have seen your face!' Els shouted from the wall, and followed it with another laugh.

I had provided the day's show of entertainment, having experienced the largest animal in Africa at only a few steps away. I had seen each wrinkle in his hanging folds of leather skin, and the enormous size of his tree-trunk-like legs as they pressed the scrub of ground into round, flat markings. His big old face and round tired eyes had stared me down, and he was quite prepared to steamroll over me as safeguard against my being a poacher and a serious threat. After all, I was in his territory, and therefore I should obey his command' and in his language he had told me to stay well clear.

Once the laughter had subsided and I was breathing normally again, we decided to head back to our bush camp to prepare our dinner over our bush oven. Having enjoyed hot coffee around the crackling warmth, absorbing the peace and quiet, we climbed into our tents under the glow of a candle set in an empty tin in the middle of the floor. Circling the flickering light, we began to play cards to pass a couple of hours of early darkness before sleep would come to put a close to another day.

With the tent opening unzipped to allow the cool breeze to filter in, and the burning smoke from the wick and wax to waft out, we began to play poker with our dog-eared and well-fingered cards. Into our second game, I noticed a shadow expand from the light of the candle onto the tent wall.

'I think I just saw a rat!' I shouted out, interrupting the flow of play and forcing heads to turn in search of something resembling a rat.

22. Cause for celebration

'It's not a rat, it's a fuckin' massive spider!' Wayne exclaimed, sending panic through the tent. Next to the candle was a huge, red roman spider as big as an outstretched hand and as hairy as our arms. Its long, black, hairy legs began to move its huge oval torso up to the warmth and light of the candle, totally unaffected by our presence. While we proceeded to corner it in one of our boots, we noticed another one of these spiders heading towards the candle and then, when things could not get any stranger, we spotted three more crawling over our sleeping bags.

'Lights out!' someone shouted, and out went the candle, leaving us to crawl and feel around for these terrifying-looking spiders, which we trapped with dixies and boots before tossing them back into their world, far from ours. Somewhat satisfied that we had nabbed all the culprits that had disrupted and brought our card game to an early end, we climbed into our sleeping bags hoping for no surprises. Having learned our lesson – to keep our tents zipped up throughout the day and night – we tried to sleep, which eventually came with no further unwanted, scary intrusions.

In the morning, having survived the spider threat, we now had a water shortage to deal with. The ration of water that we had brought from Kostini had been used up the previous night, and our coffee nightcap left us urgently awaiting replenishment from base. By mid afternoon, under the tormenting sun, we still had not received our promised supply, which began to drive us into a crazed state of distress.

Further radio signals were transmitted – the response being, 'We are on our way' – and so the wait continued for our lifeline, which we had more often than not, taken for granted. Our position this time around was far from a river. We had been warned countless times not to drink the water from the rivers, and yet we had swam on many occasions oblivious to any diseases that lurked within them. Lying in the shade to prevent the sun from sucking our energy completely dry, we tried to sleep off the uncomfortable thirst, licking at our lips, anger welling up in us with the feeling that we had been forgotten about. When I could not take it anymore, I decided to open a tin of peas and drink the juice – which seemed a good idea at the time. I pried my leathery tongue from my palate, but as the minutes ticked on my thirst returned with a vengeance, aggravated further by the salty content.

In the late afternoon we heard a drone, but could not see a telltale trace of a vehicle approaching, for we were positioned behind a rocky hill. A few minutes later, the drone seemed to grow in tempo, and then in wonder we stared at a brown Samil 20 – which appeared before our eyes with Louw at the wheel.

Before the jerry cans of water touched the earth we had the lid unscrewed, and poured the water at will into our fire buckets – not worrying one bit about all the spillage that turned the dry sand into a miniature river as we stampeded it into mud – drinking to our hearts' content like wild scavengers around a water hole.

We had been without water for 15 hours in this sweltering temperature – a test of anyone's sanity and patience, being by far the longest we had ever gone without. It gave us a taste of what it must be like to be shipwrecked on a remote, scorching-hot island, gripped by lonely wait and strangled with thirst, sapped of energy, feeling constantly tired and useless.

Once our smiles returned, we asked the driver why it had taken so long to get to us, and the answer – as stupid as it sounded – was true: He had been given the wrong coordinates on top of having to deliver water to Bravo section. Our anger had long ago dissipated, and there was no point in taking out our frustration upon someone who merely delivered the ration – even though we had wanted so badly to hold someone responsible for this unneeded torture.

It was great to feel strong again, with enough water in us to prepare a meal and a sip on a hot drink while we stared at the hilltop, watching the fiery sun descend behind the rocky outcrop as coolness once again returned to the plains under fading light.

The morning gave us something to cheer about, for it was our turn to head into base, and like bingeing alcoholics, all we could think about was a few good ice-cold beers from Fox's well-stocked canteen truck.

Once in base, we satisfied our craving by lining up outside the canteen, greeting our friend Fox and then departing to the bungalow with a six-pack in hand. Opening a can each, we toasted each other, along with a reminder for our three section members sitting in jails.

'To Paul, Laurence, and Itzie!' Els chanted, and we smacked our tins of beer against each other, unified in celebratory hope for their return. Time was racing on, and their capture was now nearly six weeks ago – though the span felt longer than it actually was. For the seven of us remaining, we moved from one day into the next, and the passing time had made us stronger – but still there was a lingering doubt that we could not quite place – for if we allowed ourselves to think about it, we would feel guilty. The feeling was that we would never see our three section mates again. In a cruel but realistic way, we believed it would be years before they returned to their homeland.

If by chance they were granted their freedom one day, we would have long gone our separate ways after our klaaring out. But in celebration of their memory, good laughs shared, and a true bond that had been forged throughout our platoon, we drank once again to their confined souls – and wondered at their predicament.

Top 20 Hit Singles of 1985

1. LOVERBOY - Billy Ocean
2. ONE NIGHT IN BANGKOK (from Chess) - Murray Head
3. CARELESS WHISPER - George Michael
4. RING OF ICE - Jennifer Rush
5. WOODPECKERS FROM SPACE - Café Society
6. POWER OF LOVE - Jennifer Rush
7. YOU'RE MY HEART YOU'RE MY SOUL - Modern Talking
8. WE ARE THE WORLD - USA For Africa
9. THE LOST OPERA - Kimera
10. I KNOW HIM SO WELL (from Chess) - Elaine Page & Barbara Dickson
11. SOUNDS LIKE A MELODY - Alphaville
12. I WANT TO KNOW WHAT LOVE IS - Foreigner
13. AGADOO - Black Lace
14. WHAT'S LOVE GOT TO DO WITH IT - Tina Turner
15. WILD BOYS - Duran Duran
16. SHOUT - Tears For Fears
17. NIGHTSHIFT - Commodores
18. LOVER COME BACK TO ME - Dead Or Alive
19. LIKE A VIRGIN - Madonna
20. NEVER ENDING STORY - Limahl

1985. The songs that eased our minds through some tough situations in our second year.

23

Refugees
40 days left to serve

The days were now speeding by quicker than they had ever done, and we rapidly approached that army milestone of only 40 days left to serve.

Juddering over the hard, uneven surface of roadway, spewing clouds of fine dusty-brown powder into the air, we sat without a care in the world, waiting to take the stage for our final bow before we turned our backs and waved farewell to a life in uniform. While we pondered, we watched a dust cloud billowing on the horizon.

'Look over there!' we nudged at each other, setting our eyes on this area that seemed so out of place in such fine weather, with not a cloud to clutter the calming blue sky.

'Its coming closer!' a voice added. Bennie cut the engine drone, which was instantaneously replaced with a rumble that carried on like rolling thunder.

'Look, it's animals – thousands of them.' These last words were lost in the deafening stampede, as wildebeest bore down upon us, galloping past our vehicle in full flight – in numbers unimaginable.

The ground shook as they passed us by, locked head-to-tail in the herd like a runaway train turning the blue sky to a dirty brown' and they charged blindly through the dust. It took a full five minutes for the thousands to rush past us as we sat like a vehicle caught at a railway crossing, waiting for the seemingly never-ending train to pull its last carriages through.

Covered in dust from head to toe, and with ringing ears from the roll of thunder, we watched the last few animals amble past as they followed the dust of their herd on their migration trail northward towards greener pastures.

When the dust curtain settled, exposing a steam-rolled plain of churned earth, we stared out at it, hardly believing what we had seen only a few metres from our vantage point. Coughing and spluttering, I rubbed my eyes from the penetrating dust particles and marvelled at this wonder that had come and gone so suddenly.

What we had been so lucky to witness, we knew that few visitors to this park would have the good fortune to gloat over – something so powerful, which had been given to us for no charge.

All agreeing upon a wash, we made our way to a big concrete tank that was only accessible by using the Samil as a ladder, to reach the circular mass of rainwater that fed a waterhole nearby. Cooling off, and most importantly ridding ourselves of the dust that instantly turned the water brown – we enjoyed the moment with gratitude and continued to talk about the wildebeest stampede.

With clean and refreshed bodies, dressed in dusty clothes, we passed more animals on our way back to our encampment. We paid little notice by now to the strong presence of warthog, which broke cover as the engine echoed its 4X4 diesel drone across the dry scrub, chasing them in circles, they strutted like royalty, their erect, aerial-like tails cutting through the dry grass. Their long, bearded faces, with two small, curved ivory tusks curling from their upper jaw, gave them the look of much leaner but nevertheless hairy, ugly pigs – which were quite comical to watch as they ran stiff-legged in search of a hole in which to hide from the threat of our passing vehicle.

Still laughing at these unattractive beasts, our concentration turned to a lone ostrich that ran through the grass and onto the road – running in front of our vehicle as if leading it. Standing up, we crowded the cab and laughed hysterically at this big bird galloping flat-footed down the middle of the road while we unintentionally bore down upon it. It did not waver or yield, but continued to hog the dusty road, running upright on its straight legs, its feathers fluttering in the wind and giving the impression that, if it ran a little faster, it might take off. Its long, thin neck stood rigid, like a broomstick with a small head perched on the end. This caused another laugh when someone commented that the ostrich looked more like a giant feather duster than a bird.

Watching it strut into the bush, we continued unhindered along the dusty road, back to our temporary camp under the carefully chosen canopy of shade. To pass the time, we often resorted to the game of Peggy-Peggy, which we played with a sharp knife and two players. The object was to spin the knife through the air and peg it into the ground. Once pegged, your opponent was forced to meet the entry of the blade in the soil with his foot. Each throw opened up the stance, until one body was awkwardly standing in a splitting position, his legs opened in a full V, trying to meet the knife point. If it could not be met, he was declared 'dead' – allowing his opponent to walk away victorious. Wayne continued on his winning roll as he had done on the border, throwing with great accuracy and pegging it into the hard soil when it counted most. There seldom was a challenger who could derail his winning throws. There had been many close calls – knives bouncing off trees and boots, cutting clothes, and drawing small amounts of blood with no serious injuries.

When we became bored with this dangerous game, we decided to do a little target practice on our worst-tasting tins. Lining them up in a row, propped up on mounds of sand, we walked back a few metres and squeezed a round into each of these disgusting tins, blasting them high into the air and peppering the surrounding bush with the 'shrapnel' of mixed vegetables, potato salad, and pickled fish. The bullets entered the tins cleanly, blowing the contents through jagged, gaping holes of peeled-back metal – a graphic illustration of the damage that an R4 could inflict upon a head full of brains.

Wiping off food that had splattered upon us, we marvelled at our shooting and the excitement of tins launching into the air. The bullets resounded around us in the hills, cracking like whips in the silence. The thrill was short-lived, for we still had to ration our food to last a week, and we dared not shoot ourselves in the foot and be left high and dry, having literally blown our food away.

Saving our tins, a few of us went for a walk with our rifles and came across some pheasant and guinea fowl. Wayne took a shot at a pheasant sitting in a tree, and I took aim at a flock of guinea fowl about 100 metres away. Feeling hungry, I fired – thinking I must hit one of the dozen or so that stood on the dust road – but I missed. I took another shot and missed again – which only helped disperse them – and then in frustration, I let off a burst of automatic fire – to really send them on their way.

Walking along the wire border fence with Mozambique, we searched for one of these birds, but came up empty-handed. It was just as well that my shooting was inaccurate, for at certain times of the year these birds are full of worms. And knowing our luck, we would have cooked and eaten one full of them.

With only the mountains to hear our shots, we trailed back to camp, having disobeyed the strict instructions handed down to us by our rank – not to fire upon any wildlife unless we were placed in a life-threatening position. To my knowledge, no animals were shot, but an impala was run over under the blinding lights of a Samil 50 as it travelled between Kostini and Letaba. It was joyously devoured by all of us, even though it was as tough as leather and as wild as a recently killed animal could be. In spite of its smell and taste, it was a great change from our dry rations, which by now were normal routine for our bush survival.

The following day, in the early part of the afternoon, we broke down the tents and headed along the border fence, passing the biggest baobab tree that I had ever seen – just over the fence on the Mozambique side. Had we tried to surround the circumference, with all eight of us linking arms around the base, we would not have made it. Standing extremely old and ugly in disfigurement, in its unique way it looked as though it had grown the wrong way up – its branches totally leafless, looking more like roots growing haphazardly at very peculiar angles.

23. Refugees: 40 days left to serve

Passing by the base, we stopped and paid a visit to the canteen for some beer and spirits before making our way to the bush again. On our drive, we came to a section of the park that seemed off the beaten track' the dirt road came to an end and turned into a rocky trail that led between two huge hills. In low gear, we began a slow descent on this road of loose stones, which moved like marbles under the thick tread of our tyres. After half an hour of slow, tedious driving – having being rocked and belted against the metal with every lurch and bump – we finally reached the bottom, and to our amazement found two abandoned rondavels. They seemed so out of place, with nothing but dry terrain all around them. The mud walls were cracking, showing the skeletal structure – mud bricks built between and over thick sticks as support structures around the perfectly circular walls. These walls had set like cement and supported a roof of dry grass, tied together to make up the covering, a circle of concrete centred at the top of the dome holding the thatch in place. The thatch had long since dried and weathered with time and neglect. The floors were sandy and cracked and, yet smooth in some places, having once been layered with cow or animal dung – which was always a great way to keep the floor free from dust and sand and make the surface hard, cool, and easy to sweep.

Looking at these huts, we decided it was as good a place as any to see the night through without the hassle of setting up the chopper tents. Stepping up to the huts, we passed the rusted remains of a corrugated iron door, which had long ago come adrift from its hinges and lay in a discarded heap amongst the tall, dry grass. The grass waved in the breeze, as if in waiting for that moment when it would one day retake the crumbling little houses that had once been home to African wardens.

Cautiously we entered through the low, narrow doorway and into the circular interior of utter blackness. We allowed a few seconds to adjust to the bleak and musty aroma of the windowless room – we half expected a bat or wild animal to fly at us as we surveyed the inside of this old relic.

Happy to find no threat inside, we returned to the vehicle for our bottles of brandy and Black Label beer, and sitting pressed against the curved wall, we christened the huts with fire buckets of brandy and dumpie bottles of beer. A candle was suspended from the ceiling in a tin, and we sat below it dodging drops of hot wax, which dripped through the flickering shadows. The more we drank, the more we laughed' Els led the way, his humour as vile as a sewer fermenting in the desert heat. A great actor with an unwavering, straight-faced expression, he made us laugh until our sides felt like exploding, from his English cum Afrikaans interpretation of a priest, to the sarcasm and mockery of the army rank that had dealt us hardship and misery never to be forgotten. The amusement, encouraged by the swigging of brandy and beer, was much needed, once again we used the alcohol to wipe clean a tough two years. In our usual way, the fire buckets clanged together, along with the bottles of beer, and we saluted our friends on the other side of the fence.

Each one of us had his own ideas on their fate, and was resigned to the fact that we had seen the last of them – unless they were released and by chance we ran into them many long years into the future.

When the drink had run dry and the candle had burned down into a pool of wax, with a little wick of light left, we stumbled outside and grabbed our sleeping bags and what little gear we needed before splitting up into the two huts and passing out for the remainder of the night.

The burning morning heat had us groggily rolling around in our sleeping bags, sweating and thirsty. Somehow, in the middle of the night I had rolled around and found myself half in the hut and half out, my legs out of the bag and spread in the dusty sand. I felt a severe itch between my toes, and with my puffy eyes I cast a glance down at them. Still not seeing anything, but feeling a biting itch, I spread my toes apart' and there, between the soft skin, were two huge ticks the size of a fingernail, sucking at will on my alcoholic blood.

Not overly shocked, I pulled with force at this small, ripe, blueberry tick that had embedded itself into my skin. It instantly came loose, and popped within my grasp, leaving a thick, sticky, bloody paste between my thumb and index finger. The other I plucked off in the same way, and was able to discard this one into the sand without it popping. I examined the rest of my body and found a few more of these insects crawling over me. I managed to brush them off before they bored into me. With everyone awake, we made our exit from these tick-infested huts, taking a close look from head to toe and paying particular attention to any soft spots of skin – especially under our arms and on our private parts. Most of us had been bitten, making it an easy decision to move deeper into the bush, away from our newfound homes.

These old huts must have been used as a shady resting place for animals, who in their time of itchiness would have brushed against the walls, dropping their unwanted batch of ticks into the earth and leaving them to wait for another host to latch onto.

Glad to move from this area, though still with some irritation between my toes, we headed up the rocky, unsafe road, those of us in the back opting to walk up the steep incline – in case the vehicle veered too much to the right and rolled. Ambling well behind the vehicle, we watched its tyres flicking stones in all directions as it spun its way at a crawl up the steep path, finally coming to a halt when it reached level ground. Once we were all back in the Samil, we moved away from the border fence, making our way along the seldom-travelled dirt roads for about half an hour, until we came across a beautifully green area of trees with an overhang of branches – the perfect umbrella to shield us from the penetrating afternoon heat. When our tents were assembled in our new resting place – which was a haven of coolness from the usual blazing heat – Els pulled out a small package of newspaper from his pocket and began preparing a joint.

When it was ready, we passed the thin, torpedo-like cigarette from one dirty hand to the next, puffing casually on it as the normal channel to clear away the long-unwanted hours of boredom. We mellowed, taking in complete peace and quiet as we lay upon the moist carpet of green grass, the pleasant coolness touching our skin. There we gazed past the network of branches and into the powdery blue sky. There seemed to be no worries in this castaway existence, and we covered our eyes with our bush hats, shielding us from the glare above.

Suddenly a man shouted: 'Get your rifles! Hurry! Get your rifles!'

What is this? I wondered, believing it to be a dream – until I saw a short and very red, round-faced man with a long ginger beard, dressed in a khaki shirt and shorts, leaning over me in a stooping kind of way, his hat looking more like two big rounded ears. I panicked as he came into my view, for I had mistaken him for a huge hyena. He was ugly and quite scary, and sent me jumping back a pace or two, I searched for a stick with which to defend myself.

'Get your rifles and follow me!' he repeated, in an effort to get us coordinated and moving. Standing dead still, I stared at him – realizing now that he was not, in fact, a hyena. But I still wondered who he was, for he had appeared with a suddenness that seemed as though he had parachuted into our camp.

'Hurry up, get moving! There are refugees out there!' he shouted, and then things started to make sense, he was a game warden, with a certain amount of authority. Totally disoriented, we ran around in circles in an attempt to locate our rifles – which we eventually did, though in a much longer time frame than the warden expected from trained soldiers. Following the red-faced warden in a long line, stoned 'out of our trees,' and with our rifles in our hands, we set off through the long grass. We walked like a herd of elephants into whatever was in our path. The warden turned and faced us.

'Get down and be quiet!' he scowled. 'They are just over there.' He pointed across the dry plain, but all we could see through the afternoon haze were thorn trees and grass.

'Stay here and wait for them' I will chase them your way,' the warden said, then dashed off into the bush in a quest to herd them our way for easy capture.

After an hour, he returned to tell us that they had got away. Surprisingly, he still thanked us for our help. We accepted his thanks, knowing full well that we could not have been much help – having felt more like bumbling idiots, thanks to Els and his laughing medicine that had made us comatose and paranoid.

When the game warden disappeared we broke into hysterical laughter – still not believing his whirlwind entry and exit, or that we looked more like idiots than soldiers.

Laughing about the incident, we succumbed to sleep, thinking about the excitement of the next morning's return to the paradise of base. Shortly after arriving, we got the news that Lieutenant Bam caught 12 refugees, who turned out to be the same group we were trying to corner. They had been impounded in the storage room, awaiting their inevitable and dreaded return to the border fence. It seemed so ironic that three of ours were imprisoned in Mozambique and groups of Mozambicans were imprisoned in South Africa, but unfortunately, 12 civilians had no bargaining power compared with that of the three white South African soldiers.

While they sat locked in the shed, we enjoyed the afternoon, playing our normal volleyball games in the pool and drinking a beer or two while watching the sun going down. After obliterating our senses well into the night, we returned to our beds in various stages of drunken stupor.

With a breakfast of fatty eggs and bacon, and plenty of hot coffee, we felt ready to tackle another day. Our orders were to drop off the refugees at the fence bordering our two countries, and then continue with our normal one-week stint in the bush.

The refugees – who consisted of men and women young and old, along with their children – climbed aboard the Samil 20, entering from the back with the flap lowered for easier entry. They took up the two rows of metal seating, leaving us no space but to stand over them with our rifles in our grasp. We dared not leave our rifles on top of our gear at the feet of these frantic people, who could quite easily be tempted to use one of our loaded weapons upon us in a single second of uncontrolled desperation.

Their faces were weatherbeaten with hardship, having lived through a war that killed and maimed at will. Some of them had never known peace. They sat still and unmoving, staring over a mountain of red and blue nylon bags, stuffed with all their worldly belongings' not even a bounce from a bump could lift their subdued expressions. They had paid large sums of money to experienced

23. Refugees: 40 days left to serve

guides, to ferry them through the park to a safer life – free from starvation and malnutrition and the chatter of bullets. This group of people had withstood ten years of fighting, watching their land turn from one of beauty, with rich fertile soil, into one with little hope of growing a meagre crop to feed a small family.

Without needing to plead, their hollow hungry eyes said it all, they continued to sit in silence, with only a few worrisome coughs barking at the stillness within the confines at the back of the Samil. Each set of dark brown eyes held a sinister story. Most of them had seen a lifetime of misery and war, and had lost loved ones needlessly. Their loss was worn in etched lines across their faces, which had aged them far beyond their years.

In just short of an hour, we drew up next to the border fence in ghostly silence. Bennie cut the engine and brought the vehicle to a grinding halt. The coughs became louder and the eyes seemed to plead for mercy, and their faces looked at the wire and the hardship beyond. They sat unmoving, as if stuck by fear to the rigid metal seating.

'Come, you have to get off!' we said to them in a caring way, pointing over to Mozambique.

But still they did not move, as though they were waiting for a miracle to spare them the toil that was about to begin for them.

'Fuck off!' Els screamed at them, his round puffy face filled with revulsion at the 12 refugees, now overstaying their welcome.

Yet still they sat, and stared with dazed confusion, as the frail old woman coughed into her thin blue dress – as if trying to buy some sympathy.

Orders were orders, and they had to be obeyed without a single sign of weakness, we were here to expel them from our soil and back to theirs. Before we could tell them to move for the third time, two shots rang out in quick succession – their sharp, cracking echoes bouncing off the mountains and returning with another two whipping cracks. Their eyes changed from confusion to terror in a split second, sending the Samil into a panic.

The 12 refugees scattered like seeds in a storm, along with all their belongings, to the fence – which some scaled, while others wriggled underneath, throwing the big bags over the wire. Some of the bags got caught in the barbs at the top and had to be knocked free by long branches. In a matter of seconds, they were within their rightful border' and as they became lost from view in the thick bushy scrub, they became lost from our minds too.

By following our orders, we had in all probability sent these people to a certain death in one of the poorest, most war-torn lands on earth – where one stood more chance of seeing an AK-47 than a cultivated field. These people were a living misery, who had become hopeless walking souls with only an existence of hardship to show for their years, and our orders only added further plight to their sufferings. Unfortunately, in South Africa we had enough of our own hungry and poverty-stricken Africans to feed and worry about – Mozambique would have to attend to their own.

Leaving the scene with a strange feeling brewing within us – from still seeing those pleading eyes and silent, uncomplaining mannerisms – we increased our distance from the fence, in an effort to help clear our conscience. An order was an order, and it was not for us to discuss or question it – it was to be followed through on, no matter what the cost.

Unfortunately, I felt in my gut that the cost was definite death. If the raging civil war did not get them, exhaustion and thirst from the hundreds of kilometres of walking that lay ahead of them would' or, if not that, starvation – having little or no crops to harvest – would be their death.

Having reclaimed our seats, we scanned the vast plains and looked down upon a world of mountains, each decked in scrub and rock, they peaked and fell, rolling away into the haze upon the horizon.

After a long drive, and with our backsides numb from all the jarring and jolting, we arrived at our reference point below a big mountain. Slabs of rock were littered over the ground, and there was hardly a tree in sight for that so-needed shade to keep us sane. Once we had chosen two areas to sleep upon, we began the daunting task of rock clearing, and – with many hands making lighter work – we had our two chopper tents erected before we knew it. To our dismay, after all this effort we realized that the tents were on a slight incline, which would hamper our sleep' but by now, with the light beginning to fade, it was too late to do anything.

After a terrible sleep, with all four of us having rolled to the bottom of the tent, we stumbled uphill and out of the tent, tripping on a rock or two as we plunged into the fiery heat that waited to welcome us. While we boiled our water for coffee, the radio crackled to life from the Kostini base, informing us that Brian from Bravo section had gone unaccounted for.

'What the hell – not another one!' someone muttered. Our minds raced, wondering what Brian was up to with less than 50 days to serve.

'Maybe he went AWOL to get dope,' Els piped up. That was quite feasible, and well within Brian's daredevil character.

His disappearance automatically reminded us of the fate of Paul, Laurence, and Sandor, and left us again to wonder how they were surviving as they slowly rotted away in body and mind, within a third world jail, starved of human rights.

23. Refugees: 40 days left to serve

In the afternoon we got a very unexpected and surprising visit from Staff Smit and Captain Delport, which was our first contact with them since we had left 4-SAI. Expecting shouts of verbal abuse, we gave them the respect due their rank – standing immediately to attention, shirtless, scruffy, unshaven, and unable to salute the Captain's three stars for lack of any headdress.

Walking through our camp area, which in Staff Smit's evaluation looked like a *hoer nes* whore's nest – kit strewn across the rocks, and fire buckets and dixies around our neatly built circle of stones, used as our fireplace. He picked up Fox's rifle and looked down the barrel, and upon seeing the thick layers of dirt and rust build-up, he passed it back and with a wry smile said: 'If you have to shoot someone with this, you will kill them with blood poisoning instead of the bullet!'

The response had been so different from what we had expected – having been hammered for the slightest fault, both verbally and physically, for nearly two years, with an aggressive bark that sent shudders through us. His tone for the first time was more humane, which seemed so out of character for him. When they left, we laughed amongst ourselves. Maybe they finally realized that our time as National Servicemen was drawing to a speedy end, and so they could permit themselves to give us the necessary leeway to serve out our sentence in the most normal way a soldier could.

Taking turns, we climbed the mountain – which we used as a lookout post, observing the escarpment for any illegal immigrants trying to sneak across the rugged and challenging terrain. Sitting through one hour of peace atop a big boulder, with a pair of binoculars and the A54 radio, we passed the time sun tanning and watching huge blue lizards scurrying like rats across the rock surfaces before disappearing into a crevice. These prehistoric creatures were at least 30 centimetres in length and would keep us company, for they too enjoyed basking on the rocks and soaking up the midday sun.

On one of my many returns from the summit, I heard a commotion filtering up to me from our camp below. There was a mix of angry shouts and pleas' two of our troops had succumbed to the torturous bouts of insanity due to the escalating temperatures and the boredom of trekking across the border line. We all fought to keep control of our varying degrees of burning frustration. It did not help that we lived with the same faces and behaviours day in and day out, for weeks and months on end, fighting the same annoyances and looking for an outlet to somehow divert the ever-rising crescendo that was building up within us.

'Come on, Nickol, don't do that.' Gall said.

'Fuck off, you stupid prick!' Wayne shot back, following his rebuke with a bombardment of rocks and stones at Gall and his lone bivi – his sleeping quarters were always 15 to 20 metres away from ours.

'That hurt! Come on, stop!' Gall shrieked in pain, but Wayne pelted another rock at him, making a cutting blow to Gall's arm.

'Angoose, jou poes!' Wayne shouted before turning to leave a bewildered and hurt Gall to lick his wounds within his bivi. It was always amazing how the mood could swing from laughter to aggression at the slightest, most trivial thing, and develop into a near-bloody brawl. In this case, judging by Wayne's pale-faced rage, Gall was lucky to be getting a stoning instead of lead from an R4 rifle.

It all ended well, as it usually did, within the confines of our platoon: Gall was banished into his usual seclusion, a stone's throw from our sleeping quarters.

The night saw us rolling around with an odd, rock-jabbing discomfort in our backs, and the morning found us bunched up at the bottom of the tent like a concertina, having slithered down the slope, in our nylon sleeping bags, into a tangled heap.

After a few trying days in this uncomfortable site, we were rewarded with the lush and relaxing surroundings of Kostini.

Some of the HQ drivers welcomed us with great news about Brian, who had been missing now for five days. Brian had achieved the unthinkable, he had walked from Bravo section's temporary bush camp, through the pitch darkness and across paths of wild, roaming animals, to the Phalaborwa Gate that our convoy of Samils had entered so long ago. Once on the tar road, he had hitchhiked like a normal troop on a pass, making his way towards Durban and his hometown of Malvern. After a day and a half of stepping in and out of cars, he arrived home and immediately began acting out his mission. He stuffed his empty backpack with dagga, which he purchased in a nearby African township and thumbed his way back towards Phalaborwa and his fellow troops of Platoon 3.

Brian left thinking that he would return undetected. After all, who would know that he was gone – other than his section and Grant? And he felt they would do their best to keep it a secret. But unfortunately, totally out of the blue, Staff Smit and Captain Delport did their rounds, and knowing Brian well for all his daredevil actions, they asked where he was. Grant had no alternative but to tell them he had no idea, and had not seen him since the morning. This had bought Brian some time, which until now had gone unreported.

Knowing full well that something was up, Captain Delport radioed Lieutenant Bam and informed him of the disappearance. Now three heads were filled with anger, and wanted immediate answers' but no one but Brian could give them.

23. Refugees: 40 days left to serve

On his return, he was surprised to learn that his disappearance had been noticed' but in with his uncaring nature, he shrugged his shoulders, quite prepared for whatever punishment would come his way. Grant immediately radioed Lieutenant Bam, informing him of Brian's return – upon which the whole section was ordered back to base. Brian was brought before Lieutenant Bam on Orders for his days on AWOL, but the issue was laid aside without any immediate retribution – leaving the matter to fester and be resolved at 4-SAI. No evidence was found with regard to Brian's backpack of dope, for he had cleverly hidden it in a hole before entering Kostini, and only his section of Bravo troops were aware of it.

Once again, Brian had cleverly sidestepped the strict army rules and discipline, and he celebrated with the breaking of a pipe. Smiling like a cheshire cat, he blew clouds of thick smoke into the air with sarcastic satisfaction – as if in defiance of the army and his awaited hearing.

On the eve of our 40 days, we were granted permission to enter Phalaborwa to purchase a few supplies for ourselves. Loaded into the Samil 50 as a complete platoon for the first time in months, we ventured into town – a place so foreign to our conditioned senses. Seeing cars, traffic lights, shops, and people in civilian clothes' hearing the honk of horns' and smelling restaurant smoke from the grills sent us all into a frenzy. We took in our surroundings like excited kids on a school outing. One thing we all had in common was our search for a bottle store to buy some much-needed alcohol for a celebration we had been dreaming of ever since the day we entered the army. Finding the most important store in the town, we began to empty its shelves. Most of us departed with a bottle of spirits and a mix in our grasp. Then we ventured into the butcher shop and had a huge steak cut to perfection for the braai that would be the centre of our festivities.

Smiling, with our important necessities in hand, we climbed onto the Samil and headed back to Kostini, watching the bushveld from the back of the vehicle – the only area that was not enclosed by the brown canvas sail. While the dry grass and flat-topped thorn trees flashed by, we chatted excitedly to each other, thinking of the drunken night that awaited us.

The Samil had us back in base in the late afternoon – enough time to get the braai prepared, charcoal and wood filling the bottom of the half-metal drum. Once the drum was ready, it was lit to allow enough time for the burning hot coals to cool off – so as not to burn our monstrous and juicy steaks.

We wasted no time in twisting off the caps from the whisky, brandy, vodka, and Southern Comfort bottles' and with our fire buckets in hand we mixed generous helpings of spirits to see us on our merry way. A radio had been set up close to the braai area, and a cassette tape played memorable 80s songs – sending our minds racing back over the tumultuous 22 and-a-half months we had served. We drank to the loud music, and to our absent friends behind bars, and we drank to the sobering thoughts of our freedom – with the real countdown just beginning. When Bruce Springsteen's *'Glory Days'* played, we met it with a chorus of 'Forty Days' – stirring us into a crazed and berserk drunken state. We screamed out 'forty days' with such heartfelt emotion, and goosebumps lining our arms' we met the milestone in typical army fashion.

When the song finished, we clanged the metal of our fire buckets together, careful not to waste any alcohol, but knocking them together hard enough to unify us in remembrance of our daily struggles.

'Min dae!' Few days! someone shouted over the noise of the music, and we smiled, knowing that the end was finally in sight.

Lieutenant Bam, on the other hand, remained subdued' his mind was still punishing him for the loss of three of his flock – and still not a word on their condition, let alone their return.

Our 'forty days' celebration continued well after we had consumed our thick slabs of meat, which acted as a good buffer to our stomachs – for we were suffering under the heavy abuse of the strong spirits, beer, and wine.

Grant had consumed a bottle of wine, glugging it back like a bottle of water – which was something to see, he being a person who never drank and was not able to handle the alcohol in his blood stream. We all watched Grant with keen interest as he tried his best to hold his stance while the wine took the effect of slurring speech and uncontrollable, swaying movements. Not long after the bottle was finished, he began vomiting his guts out, huddled over a bunch of bushes' oblivious to the careless laughs directed his way. He stood in that pathetic position – which we all at one time had been in – wishing for an end to the burning torture.

Someone had entered the toilet area, and in his drunken stupor had become disoriented, defecating in the middle of the cement floor. We were unable to blame the baboon that had been sneaking into the camp for this foul deed, since it had been shot and killed months ago. After some investigating, Kleinhans was named the culprit' he admitted to his wrongdoing, and blamed alcohol for it. He was the son of a priest, and in the process of becoming one – he was as clean as a whistle when he entered the army – but after being in Platoon 3, his life took an about-turn. He was smoking like a chimney, drinking like a fish, swearing like a trooper, dabbling with the odd joint' and now he was crapping on the floor – not a fitting image for a future priest.

23. Refugees: 40 days left to serve

The morning after was not a pleasant experience – we struggled with heavy heads, marking our official 40 days left to serve. Walking through the area of the previous night's celebration was like entering a war zone' cans and bottles littered the grass, stark reminders of why we were hanging our throbbing heads.

It was a day worth remembering, christened in the only way that a soldier knows – and that was to drink until you dropped, which we did – the heavy price to be paid later.

Our platoon remained in base for two more days before we were granted a pass, which had to be taken from 4-SAI. Loaded into a Samil 50, we headed excitedly back to Middelburg for our very last pass – which had an indescribable feel to it. Pairing up with Wayne, we took to the road with urgency, yearning to free ourselves from the soldier's uniform bond and begin our integration into society. This was our trial run to the real end, which was looming just over the horizon – just over a month left. What a feeling it was!

Once back into society and clad in civilian clothes – any colour but brown – we followed through on our prearranged plan of meeting up with a few of the Durbanites from our platoon. Wayne and I took the trip into Durban and met up with Alan, Rob, Darren - Istanbolt, and John at the 'Med' – a nightclub at the corner of Brickhill Road. Together we had a great time, and continued on with our 40 day party, though this time in civilian clothes and with civilian minds. Drink flowed and laughter rolled into the early hours of the next morning, when we staggered out of the club and onto the street. On the opposite side of the road, we spotted John sitting in his mother's white Toyota Corolla. The four of us bolted across the busy street, dodging cars, making it to the small island that separated the two lanes of traffic. Like a tightrope walker, we balanced our swaying bodies upon this concrete partition while waiting for a gap in the traffic, and then we launched ourselves towards John and his 'transport.' Converging upon the car, we climbed like monkeys – sitting on the roof and the bonnet and banging on the windows – the high level of alcohol in us driving us crazily onwards.

A police van rounded the corner and headed straight towards us, coming to an abrupt stop next to John's Toyota. Two white policemen, dressed in greyish blue uniforms of the SAP, got out and marched towards the four of us – their menacing hats adding further authority to the already intimidating uniforms.

'You are all under arrest for being drunk and disorderly and disturbing the peace!' they stated in broken English, followed by an order to get into the back of the van.

'We are in the army! It's our 40 days!' I answered, hoping to buy some sympathy from our military counterparts.

Unable to deter their thinking, however, we climbed into the back of the van and sat like wild animals, caged behind the mesh of the thickly woven metal. Expecting to be let out, we were suddenly startled when the metal door slammed shut and then locked upon the dank holding area.

'They are just going to drive us around the block to scare us, and then they will let us out. Watch,' I said, in the calmest and most positive voice that I could.

They careered around as if taking us on a roofie ride, sliding us around and smashing us into the sides of the cage as we fought to steady ourselves with each sudden turn. Wide-eyed and somewhat sober, I began to worry, though without divulging my thoughts to the others. I prayed that we stayed on all four wheels, and that the claustrophobia that was filling the air within this tight box would not get any worse – for I feared being trapped upside down without an escape route.

'We are going to jail, and we are going to get extra days for this!' Alan said.

Not knowing what to believe, but trying to remain positive, I replied: 'They will let us go. Just wait and see.'

The police van pulled into the C.R. Swart Police Station and stopped short of the main entrance. One of the policemen opened the door and waited for us to get out before escorting us to the main charge desk.

Relieved to be out, we now began to worry about the next step, for they herded us towards this high desk, and the crowd of ruthless and stern-faced policemen that leaned and stood around it.

Each one of us was forced to give his name and address, telephone number, identity document number, and – most surprising of all – his fingerprints. Things began to feel weird and blown-out-of-proportion, and it looked as though a charge was being laid against us. The fear of a court case now entered our hazy heads. That would naturally lead to extra days – something we had avoided painstakingly for two years' and we did not intend to get a single day added onto our already-long service.

The policemen – all much older than ourselves – looked powerfully down over us, as if repulsed by our drunken looks and actions. Facing the charge desk, I mumbled something – which was taken completely out of context. The African man who was standing behind the high, flat-topped desk suddenly looked at me with fierce hatred set into his wide-open eyes.

'You black swine!' the African policeman shouted out at me.

'What do you mean? I am not a black swine!' I replied calmly – that all-too-common racist thinking suggesting, to me, that he was the black swine.

In the wink of an eye, he vaulted like a gymnast, swinging his body in one motion over the desk like a true Zulu warrior. His right hand raised, he swiped it through the air, striking me with a resounding clap – the flat of his open hand made contact with the side of my face. I did everything in my power to remain upright and unmoving, though the force hit me with a burning sting and caused my eyes to water and my face to redden with both anger and pain. I remained standing like a statue, without the slightest flinch – so as not to grant him any satisfaction of knocking me off my balance. Keeping my composure, I looked at him with scorn in my eyes for his wrongdoing and my inability to defend myself against such corrupt authority.

'Ram, just leave it,' Alan and Rob said. 'It's not worth it.' They saw no point in standing up for something we would surely lose. The Afrikaans policemen, who had witnessed the assault, just stood by and told me not to retaliate – conveniently conforming to the government-controlled uniform of the police force. Ironically I had been hit by a black man – who was an equal within the police, though in the outside world of South Africa we had been groomed to think we were better than him – the laws of segregation dictating that to us.

How ironic it was to have been slapped by a man who was not an equal, who was not permitted to ride on a whites-only bus, use a whites-only toilet, eat at a whites-only restaurant, who was forbidden to live in a whites-only area. And yet he could wear the same uniform as his counterparts and get away with slapping a white face.

It is confusing to remember living under those dark days of apartheid, when segregation was just a part of life and the colour barrier unfairly favoured or scorned at will, depending solely on one's pigmentation.

With a slap in the face – literally – under the apartheid laws, the four of us were led away to the holding cells. Alan and I were ushered into the first cell, and before we could even turn around, the door had slammed shut on us.

'How long do you think we will be locked up for?' Alan asked, as he fidgeted nervously – waiting in anticipation of a hopeful answer.

'It doesn't look good. I hope like hell they let us out in time to get back to camp!' I answered, with concern in my voice.

We had come so far, and I could not imagine having time added on for such a petty crime. It would certainly be a cruel blow to bear, being handed extra days – with us sitting on less than 40 days to serve.

Tired and drunk, we lay on the rough, thin, black mats' and looking through the bars, we waited to pass out, casting our unsolvable worries aside. Suddenly I sat up with a jolt and blurted out: 'Did Wayne see us being taken away?'

'No, he was inside the club.'

'Shit, I gave him a lift.'

How will he get back? I asked myself – anger rising inside me because of this hopeless and unnecessary situation.

Helpless to do anything, I closed my eyes and wished for the morning – which came quicker than I had expected.

At 06:00, a policeman rattled the bars and told us to leave the cells – which we hastily did, carrying our throbbing hangovers along with relief that we would not be given extra days.

Hungry, tired, and very grateful to be out, we walked through the early-morning crispness and fresh, salty air towards the beach, and along the Durban beachfront towards my mother's silver Opel. Wayne was nowhere to be found, and I began to wonder how he had made it home. We forced a laugh over the previous night's predicament before parting ways and echoing to each other: 'See you back in camp.'

I soon found out that Wayne was fine, he had called his mother for a lift back home after the cold had forced him into a stranger's car for warmth. The warmth was short-lived, however, for a few seconds later the man – who was a homosexual – tried to flip Wayne's seat back. That drove him out of the car in a flash – the evening cold now quite bearable in comparison to what the stay inside the car could have meant.

The story raised a laugh while we joined up for our very last team effort, hitchhiking back to Middelburg, the end of our two years a calendar page away.

For the first time in our army lives, we were actually glad to get back to camp, reunite with our friends, and relive our stories from the short pass. We sat, confidently united with eagerness to get back to the Kruger Park to finish our long journey. The time was nearing the end – an end that would allow us to start living our lives freely and as we pleased, far from this controlling and bullying army world.

We could certainly see the light at the end of the tunnel, and it felt brilliant.

24

Farewell to the Kruger

In the early morning we climbed onto the Samil 50, taking the two rows of metal benches eagerly, wanting to get away from the brick and mortar of 4-SAI and back into the paradise of the animal kingdom.

Wearily, we arrived at Kostini in the late hours of the night, after a gruelling and extremely uncomfortable day's ride. Breaking up into our respective sections, we made our way to our prefab, camouflaged bungalows, where we retired to the comfort of a pillowless bed for a deep sleep.

Fully rejuvenated after the long trip, we made ourselves ready for more days in the African bush – another experience to whet our appetite for more adventure in a part of Africa that was true to its depiction. This was army life at its best, we were the lucky souls who were living in nature's habitat, roaming free as the animals, as we crossed the plains between the murky dust and unpolluted skyline.

During our many drives, wearing the dirt roads thinner, we would pass a huge, open water tank where we had stopped on a few occasions to cool ourselves. This round concrete tank acted as a rain catcher and a holding tank, to channel water to a nearby drinking hole where we swam. It was also frequented by passing elephant herds, who would casually dip their trunks and shower away the dust and heat from their leathery grey skins.

Bennie manoeuvred the Samil to the rounded side of the tank and then, using the metal railings there to hold the canvas sail that enclosed the back, we hoisted ourselves into the cold water. This instantly shocked us out of our heat daze and injected refreshing life right back into us. We passed the time enjoying this spot – the equivalent of a health spa in the outside world – when an Alouette helicopter appeared out of thin air and began circling over us within a 50 metre radius.

'Now we are in deep shit!' a troop remarked.

Some tried to hide under the water, and others climbed on the Samil and then to the ground, in a bid to distance themselves from an area out of bounds for us.

The helicopter continued to circle, but its focus was not on us, but on a clump of trees about 40 metres from the water tank. We stood on the ground and watched with keen interest trying to find out the reason for its circular flight pattern. It banked time and again looping widely around us. After the fifth circle, lifting the dust and churning the silence into a chopping buzz, it continued overhead, disappearing into the scrubby distance and leaving us to stare after it, grounded in awe by this sudden, inexplicable event.

Still shaking our heads, we continued sorting our kit next to the vehicle, while others swam or sat, drying off under the scorching sun. In the cooler part of the afternoon, we watched with keen interest as a small herd of bosbok timidly made their way towards the water hole. Aware of our being there, but with thirst driving them on, they lined up along the thin concrete channel of water, leaving one to stand guard while the others bowed their heads to slurp at the warm liquid. It was always a unique and interesting sight, watching animals at a waterhole, ears and senses finely tuned as they placed themselves in this most vulnerable position.

With the Alouette still plaguing our thoughts, we returned to base, and it was there we heard the story. Unbeknown to us, General. Magnus Malan, the South African Defence Minister, was aboard that helicopter. The reason had been to view a pride of 17 lions, hidden from our sight by the long grass and shady trees – so close to our position that it wasn't funny. On hearing this we smiled, thanking our lucky stars that they were not hungry enough to eat a few skinny National Servicemen, for we could quite easily have become their next meal.

We soon forgot what might have happened to us. More important was that we had bypassed trouble. We looked more like a bunch of wild bush warriors than soldiers. Tanned a healthy golden brown and clad only in shorts, our rifles and kit strewn around the Samil, they could see from above our enjoyment for the simple things that we utilized in our bush life – things that brought instant pleasure to our worn and tested spirits.

After passing over us and away from our swimming pool, they had landed at Kostini, where the general met Captain Delport and Lieutenant Bam. It was assumed he was there in an effort to get Paul, Laurence, and Sandor back to South African soil as soon as the slow political process between the countries would allow.

These questions Lieutenant Bam met with a depressing tone.

'They are still in jail. That's all we know,' he said, a frown appearing on his red-sunburned brow, which his beret had been covering until recently.

Another refugee had just been caught – this time a middle-aged woman carrying a small baby in typical African fashion, bound by a blanket and nestling tightly into her back. It was another act of courage and determination to flee her war-ravaged land, defying death in an attempt to reach peace. Not only was she carrying her child, but she also carried a big, overloaded bag on her head with all her belongings. It was a sight that could not be forgotten' the little child raised her hand to us in greeting, totally oblivious to her mother's trauma at having to be returned to the border post at Komatipoort – having come so far for absolutely nothing.

Each day in base was celebrated with an abundance of drink and loud music. The countdown of days was now in the thirties and we gladly supported the canteen and its manager – who could not be happier than with a six-pack under one arm and a bag of chips in the other. The 'Man,' who went by numerous nicknames – such as 'The Leman' or 'The Woo-man' – always ran his canteen with an open beer within reach, always making sure he had enough ice-cold stock on hand to quench our thirsts. Fox took little care of his personal appearance and always wore his hair in a peak. A comb or a brush hardly ever made it through his hair. He enjoyed the shade and sported an army tan with his dark arms, legs, and face, contrasting to his lily-white upper body that chose shade in the repressive heat.

We enjoyed the camaraderie over a few beers in the cool of the evening. Our drinking was interrupted when someone told us that a vehicle had 'accidentally' run over an impala. This gave us an excuse to have a braai. While the Afrikaners amongst us cut up the animal, the rest of us started the fire. We braaied chunks of meat and then began to eat – which was more like chewing than eating. It tasted wild and rubbery with that uncured smell of not having hung for long enough to let the blood drain. Nevertheless, it filled our hunger gap, and we washed more Castles' down, ridding the wild, salty taste with the bitter taste of beer.

In the morning we took a long drive by Samil to Phalaborwa to visit a bottle store to get a bottle of hard tac, then to the butchers to get thick steaks. Thinking of the free life that we would soon be living, we climbed back into the Samil. Back in Kostini, we packed our gear and headed for the bush along with Solly who had agreed to join us – adding a much-needed laugh to our section. Alpha was divided into two half-sections, with Fox, Wayne, Solly, and me making up one and Bennie, Stoop, Els, and JP the other. Once our sleeping place had been selected and the tent pitched, we immediately began collecting wood to braai our thick slabs of meat. We carefully arranged the dry sticks to allow enough space for the fire to breathe before sparking into life.

There was no rush so we sipped brandy and vodka and swallowed mouthfuls of beer. The fire warmed our bodies, and our eyes became transfixed by the dancing flames as they licked around the dry logs. The peace was pure bliss, with only the crackle and pop of the fire breaking the evening quiet, shooting red sparks into the pitch-blackness. The shadows played across our faces as we talked and laughed while at one with nature, enjoying the friendships that had been rock-solidly forged over the past many months.

'At least we don't have to worry about the threat of mortar bombs!' Solly chirped up, referring to our many border patrols when fires were forbidden after nightfall.

We heard the whoop of a hyena and imagined the big, round-headed creature with its head drooping down to the ground, swaying with its ungainly gait as it dragged its hindquarters through the bush in our direction.

'It must have caught a whiff of our steaks!' someone said as another whoop echoed through the pitch of night, followed by a spooky laugh.

These animals carried the most deplorable odour, being known to roll in the rotting remains of a carcass to mask the smell of their own filthy stench. The sound, which met our alert ears, annoyed us and conjured up a certain fear – we could not trust these cunning animals one bit. The call was taken as a sign to begin the braai, and each of us slapped a massive steak onto the makeshift grill above the red hot coals. They sizzled as we kept a watchful eye on our meat. Juices dripped into the fire sending puffs of smoke into the starry night.

We said 'cheers' to each other and to a life that could only be dreamed of. The radio/cassette player stopped playing and was immediately attended to. Fox wound the dial and picked up a song so fitting for that night, called '*Tarzan Boy*' – which had us all singing. Here the four of us were living wild in the bush, the only difference was that we Tarzans had consumed alcohol like water, as if there was no tomorrow. When silence again reigned in between songs we realized that the hyena had left – most probably chased away by our poor and out-of-tune singing.

When they were ready we lifted our steaks from the grill with a fork and dropped them into our dixies. With our hands acting as the cutlery, we ripped into the juicy meat with our teeth – tearing off chunks, relishing the taste with a smile of satisfaction, washing it down with yet more spirits and beer.

Such times shared around this fire, and countless others long gone, always provided an opportunity to sit back and ponder. How many faces of men with different values and ideals, had stared into those flames, knowing little about life except that we were in uniform with rifles never far from our hands.

The four of us laughed about the past as we drank to our *min dae*, clanging bottle against fire bucket, longing for our long-awaited civvie street rebirth to begin.

When we had eaten to capacity, the drink had dried up and the fire had burned out, we stumbled into the tent – if we made it that far – and passed out.

24. Farewell to the Kruger

The next day the heat was on us again, sweating us out of the tents with bloodshot eyes and dazed looks, into a frenzy of flies that buzzed in pestering circles around us.

A mumbled 'fuck off' was heard as we waged war against them, swatting in vain and shooing the buggers from our itching faces. We looked as if we had been dragged through a bush backwards, our hair all dishevelled and our clothing dirty and creased.

'Coffee?' someone shouted.

'*Ja*, of course!'

We heated the water in our mess tins which were still unwashed from the night before and were tainted with traces of brandy and Coke. We disguised this by adding sachets of coffee, packets of sugar, and generous helpings of condensed milk squeezed from its white plastic tubes. Savouring each sip in an effort to clear our heads, we readied ourselves for another boiling day in the rugged bush.

In the latter part of the morning, we were collected by Bennie and his half-section for a routine patrol in the vehicle. We had not gone very far before we spotted a pack of ten wild Cape hunting dogs, trotting together upon their long skinny legs, a force to be reckoned with. Their big, thick, pointed ears and their blotched, black, brown, white, yellow, dirty-looking coats made them unmistakable. They remain one of the rarest animals in Africa, having been hunted almost to extermination prompted by man's fear of them. They continued to hog the dirt road as we trailed on behind them.

A little farther on they gave up the road which allowed us to continue the patrol. We caught sight of vultures swarming and circling in the sky so we made our way towards them. To our delight, we came across a lioness and a young cub that had just finished feeding on a zebra kill. Having seen them we could boast that we had seen every species of animal in the park in our four months there, except for the mighty rhino.

Here we were, only weeks away from re-entering the civilian world, and most us still had little or no idea as to what we were going to do with our lives. We were living up to one of our favourite songs from the mid 80s, the Talking Heads' wacky *Road to Nowhere*. Like the song we drifted in the moment along the well-travelled road to nowhere, complacent, taking one day at a time until our army days ran out. Only then would we think about our futures.

Dusty and dirty and bedraggled we returned to base after completing our last bush patrol in the Kruger Park. On entering Kostini our full platoon was reunified with all sections having been ordered back to base.

Calling us together, Lieutenant Bam told us that the next day we would be leaving the base – the base that had become our 'home' for the longest period of our service. A Citizen force unit – we referred to them as 'Campers' – had arrived to replace us and would sign for our vehicle and assume control of Kostini.

This called for a last party to celebrate a life that would never be lived the same again. It had been a life under the stars in a pollution-free environment with wild animal sounds echoing throughout the night, the glory of viewing the game in their terrain, and a beautiful sunset to end each spectacular but dusty day.

Lining up outside the canteen truck, most of us bought a dozen beers each. Keeping them hidden and cold, we began to drink to a time that had enriched to our souls and made long lasting friendships that had blossomed from enduring struggle and perseverance together.

Milling about in the open grassy area between the bungalows and the toilet quarters, just about every troop was drinking beers. Music and drunken laughter filtered throughout the camp with the sound of empty aluminum beer cans being crunched indicating that more cans were being opened. Drunkenness had become a way of life with us young soldiers who used liquor as medication to release tension. Senseless drunken talk made sense to us as we struggled to cover our well-hidden tensions.

A loud bang ripped through the darkness, disrupting the disorderly but peaceful scene.

'What the fuck was that?'

We all looked at each other, suddenly sober and wide-eyed in frozen shock. I looked to where the sound had come from and saw Brian holding his rifle with the butt into his shoulder and still squinting down the sights with an expression of disbelief on his face. He had shot at troops in the grassy area. I rushed to where I imagined the shot fired had been aimed, expecting to find a soldier dead or severely wounded. The odds of the round having missed someone when they were all milling around on the grass seemed like a million to one.

Everyone seemed in a state of shock, standing still and unmoving for a couple of seconds before urgency prevailed and shouts replaced the shattered calm.

'Was anyone hit?' I shouted as a few of us hunted through the darkness, eventually making our way into Charlie section's bungalow.

I saw Fourie sitting on his bed, with his back to the door and his face turned, looking a million miles past me. His face was a pale shade of white, drained from the shock of the rifle shot that had glued him in deathly fear to his metal-framed bed.

'Are you OK?' we asked, looking for blood.

Amazingly, we found none. Someone pointed at the metal frame of the bed where we saw the bullet had struck and roughed-up the metal. Other than the sheer shock of the crack as the bullet whistled at him, Fourie – although terribly shaken – was uninjured.

We soon learned that the bullet had been shot between Corporal Gregan's legs as he crossed the open grass in front of the toilet block. It continued its flight and smashed into the toilet's asbestos wall, shattering a drain pipe as a Camper sat on the throne attending to his own business, His buttocks were lacerated when the ceramic exploded underneath him. The bullet then exited the toilet wall and entered Charlie section's asbestos bungalow, where it struck the metal frame of Fourie's bed. If it had been a couple of centimetres higher, it would have blown a hole in his back, paralysing him. If it had been a couple of centimetres lower it would have taken out a chunk of his upper leg.

By the time I reached Brian he was surrounded with every demanding answers for his stupid action that unbelievably, had not killed anyone.

'I didn't know it was loaded!' Brian explained, having already told everyone that he had forgotten to expel the round from the chamber after unclipping the magazine. He had forgotten to perform the most standard drill, which we had performed day in and night out for practically two years – to ensure that our weapons were safe at all times, especially inside a base.

I remembered a saying taught to us during our basic training in 1-SAI, in regard to our deadly rifles: 'Always treat me as though I were loaded. Never point me at any living creature you do not wish to kill.'

Unfortunately, Brian had deviated from the basic rules of weaponry – not only creating chaos, but also nearly taking three lives in the process. Had someone died, it would have been a cruel tragedy to mark the end of our service. Lucky for us, that did not happen and so it was not worth worrying about. Still it was hard not to replay it within our minds.

We were becoming *'slapgat'* lax in our actions – which seemed to be working against us as drink and drugs led to unnecessary havoc. Brian, like all of us, was drunk and smoked out of his mind, but still there was no condoning his squeezing a trigger at moving targets – especially at his fellow soldiers.

The drunken party seemed to die shortly after the shot was fired, and we retired into our separate bungalows for our last night's sleep in the game reserve.

In the morning we rose early and dressed in our most faded set of browns, with boots highly glossed and berets folded and tucked neatly through our left epaulettes. Packing the last of our belongings and rolling up our sleeping bags, we carried our gear outside – along with Paul, Laurence and Sandor's – and then re-entered to give the bungalow a clean sweep.

One by one we got aboard the Samils, and in our small convoy we stared into the dust as the last of Kostini was swallowed from sight. There was a mixture of sadness, which was soon overshadowed by the exciting prospect of walking free. Making our way through the park, we headed for the Phalaborwa gate, travelling this time on the beautifully smooth tar roads instead of the potholed dirt roads, which had shaken us around like a ration pack milkshake more times than we cared to remember.

Here we were, paying our last respects as we viewed the last of the game from the place we had called 'home' – the place where we had lost three of our troops in the last chapter of our service. It felt selfish to think of the game and the park when we were leaving three of our comrades behind. Having heard no word of them forced us to imagine the worst, and we were left to wonder whether they were alive at all.

Since their capture along the Shingwidzi River all those months ago, we had never returned – having never chosen to and never been ordered to. All we could do was live with the hope that someday they would be released into South Africa and into the care of their devastated families.

There was a sombre mood in the vehicle as we passed through the Phalaborwa gate, each one of us was lost in his own thoughts. We held onto the fond memories of adventure, as well as the threats of insanity – having travelled another border line through the tormenting strains of the bushveld.

Our emotions were running on an all-time high, and we could now count the remaining days on both hands. We sat back and smiled contentedly, letting the Samil take its course to the boundary fences of 4-SAI.

Our time had now reached that stage when we could actually feel it dwindling away like sand in an hourglass – the words 'home sweet home' calling the tune of our soon-to-be-realized dream.

1988-Pretoria. Convoy en route to the border with drivers and gunners.

1988-Owamboland. Dakota flying in with high-ranking Generals and Brigadiers for a briefing with our rank. Orders were to head towards Ruacana.

1988-Owamboland. Grant and Paul holding a dead two metre spitting cobra.

1988-'Blue Route.' The author covered in white fine dust from the dry salt pan.

1988. Waiting on the order to move out.

1988-'Blue Route.' Driving across the salt pan en route to Ruacana.

1988-South of Ruacana. Macky using his staalduck to shave.

1988-'Blue Route.' Samil 50 and water bowser both stuck in the mud on exiting the never ending salt pan.

1988. Taking a well needed rest with Ratels nose to tail in long lines before heading out again in convoy towards Ruacana.

1988-South of Ruacana. Olifant 105mm tank on our flank.

1988-Oshigambo. Entering the base with Van our gunner on the right.

1988-South of Ruacana. Inside Ratel 11 Charlie. Fossie on the radio, the author, Macky and Nic.

1988-Oshigambo Base. Picture taken from the water tower on the inside of the base.

1988-Oshigambo Base. Picture taken from the water tower on the opposite side of the base.

1988-South of Ruacana. Brian inside 11C.

1988. Patroling the South-West African/ Angolan border in our Ratels.

1988-South of Ruacana. 11C waiting to go into Angola. L-R. Front row. Brian, Sarge, Fossie, Piet and Van. L-R. Back row. Riaan, Nic, the author, Darin, Macky and John.

1988-South of Ruacana. Ratels and Olifant tanks going into mock attack. This is how it would have looked for the real thing.

1988-South of Ruacana. Lined up and waiting for orders.

Platoon 3

1988-Oshigambo Base. Loading up ammo with the expectation of an Operation into Angola firmly in mind.

1988. A foot patrol on the border. Riaan armed with his mag leading the way.

1988. A typical Owambo kraal. Doing a random search for tell tale presence of SWAPO.

1988. Ratel patrols along the border. Brian and Riaan resting on his mag.

1988. Riaan, Macky, John, the author and Brian.

1988-Oshigambo Base. On the South-West African beach. L-R. Wayne, Brian, John and the author. Old Platoon 3 mates.

1988-South of Ruacana. South African forces ready and waiting to rumble into Angola.

1988-Oshigambo Base. On the outside walls of Oshigambo. Ratels hidden by camouflaged netting in between rows of trenches, where we slept.

1988-Oshigambo Base. L-R. The author, Wayne and Grant.

1988. On patrol. Another meal in the bush. John peeling the potatoes, Riaan pointing to the dish and Darin, Nic and the author looking on.

1988. On patrol with our cut off browns to combat the heat. L-R. Piet, Brian, Macky, Darin, Van, Grant, the author, Wayne and Riaan.

1988. The author riding patrol on the Ratel.

1988. Riaan on his way to take a leak, totally naked except for his socks and his weapon that never left our sides.

1988. An old mud walled church with nothing around it for miles.

1988. On patrol and checking a kraal for signs of SWAPO. L-R. An interpreter, Brian and the author.

1988. On patrol and resting under the shade of some makalani palms.

1988. Ratel 11 Charlie with its name Madonna etched onto the hull. L-R: Piet, Van, the author, John, Brian, Besem Bek, Riaan, Macky, Darin and Wayne.

1988. Patrolling the border and passing a joint around to combat the extreme boredom.

1988. On patrol with Grant acting as Satan, with Cpl Bean and an Owambo interpreter looking on.

1988. Riaan with Grant acting as Satan with a pitch fork and poncho and Cpl Bean in the background.

1988. Riding on top of 11 Charlie. L-R. John, Darin, Riaan, Brian, the author and Nic.

1988. Looking for signs of SWAPO around a Cuca shop.

1988-Okatope. Clean after a night stop en route to 'Grooties'. L-R. John, the author, Macky and Brian. Unaware that we were the vanguard of the historic SA troop withdrawal from SWA.

2003-Ombalantu Base. The famous hollowed out baobab tree in the base.

1988. On patrol and looking dirty and worse for wear. L-R. Brian, Wayne, Macky and Riaan.

1988. Ratel 11 Alpha watching over some Owambo women as they collect water from a well.

1988-Oshigambo. Leaving Oshigambo Base in convoy bound for 'Grooties,'Grootfontein.

1988-Windhoek. All smiles as troops board a SAFAIR C130 for the flight home. L-R. The author, Brain, Macky, Darin and John.

2003-Ombalantu Base. An army stove abandoned when the SADF withdrew.

2003-Ombalantu Base. An eerie silence hung over the base that once sheltered thousands of conscripts over the duration of the border war.

2003-Ombalantu Base. Taken 15 years after the border wars end with a bevelvoeder's bunker now an Owambo home.

2003-Ruacana. Angolan border post still in ruin from the border war. This is where we would have crossed in 1988.

2005-Maputo, Mozambique. Laurence, the author and Wayne catching up on 20 years since our Platoon 3 days of 1984 and 1985.

2005-Maputo, Mozambique. Samora Machel, the leader of FRELIMO with Laurence and myself flanking the mural. FRELIMO had captured Laurence in 1985, and had him imprisoned in Machava.

25

Farewell to National Service

After many miles sleeping in the sitting position, holding onto our rifles as we nodded our heads with every turn and jolt that the endless tarmac threw at us, we finally rolled through the two big black gates of 4-SAI.

'*Min dae, jou foken rover!*' Few days, you fuckin' new recruit!, Els screamed at the top of his lungs from within the Samil, at the new recruit who was still in his first year of service while he nervously swung the metal gate open for us.

We met it with a loud roar of laughter, we rode the wave with seniority of service now firmly taking precedence over sympathy for the new, lowly recruit.

The Samil wound its way along the smooth, paved road, passing under an umbrella of flamboyant trees lining the roadway, until we reached the rows of red brick bungalows, where the vehicles came to a stop. We made our way into the front bungalow, which had been designated to Platoon 3 a few weeks short of a year ago. Reclaiming our beds with a mountain of gear placed upon the white covering of the mattress, we sat down and rested against our belongings, waiting to regain energy before we began the tedious task of unpacking.

After everything was packed into our metal cupboards and metal trunks, we locked them up – not giving our fellow troops the temptation of thieving an item that had previously been lost. In a matter of days we would begin signing back our army gear, and any items that we could not present we would have to pay for. With this in mind, we watched over our kit with the keen eyes of a hawk.

Those who wanted to partake in the smoking of a clay pipe congregated in the toilet area, as we had done before, blowing thick clouds of marijuana smoke up at the ceiling to mix with the steam. Once a few brain cells had been demolished, we ambled back towards our beds, with no energy left in us to do anything but laugh at the most trivial thing that crossed our sight and minds before closing our eyes on yet another day.

After an easy and deep sleep, we surfaced at the usual time and got ourselves ready for breakfast in the mess hall a short walk from our bungalow. Sitting down in plastic chairs at a long table, we ate like royalty off ceramic plates instead of dixies – using full-sized metal cutlery in place of the stubby pikstel that we had survived with in the open bushveld. The good old fire bucket, which had served us so well as our portable cooking pot and coffee mug, was now replaced with a pearly-white ceramic mug with a handle. The new and uncomfortable grasp took some getting used to.

After a filling meal, we returned to the bungalow with that typical NAAFI feeling, for the days now in single figures. While we killed time talking in small groups and drinking tea saved from our ration packs, we waited for the next order – which came quicker than expected with the startling and hurried entrance of our lieutenant.

'*Luister hier'so!*' Listen up! he ordered, with a hint of well-concealed joy upon his stern face.

'Paul, Laurence and Toth are free!' he gloated.

His face blossomed into a wide smile. It took us a second to register what he had just said, and when we did our platoon erupted into a chorus of cheers, immediately followed by a barrage of questions.

'When will we see them?'

'Will we see them?'

'Are they okay?'

'Where are they?'

And so the questions went on, and our lieutenant looked every bit – in Els' words – 'as happy as a pig in Palestine'' a fitting catchphrase to the elation that he showed as he moved around us with the feeling of a person untouchable in his happiness. He grinned from ear to ear, proud to be bringing Platoon 3 back together with good tidings of an early Christmas present – a present that could not be a more worthwhile gift to all of us, having shared the inner agony of separation for such a long time.

When the noise began to abate and the bungalow returned to normality, he began to answer some of the questions.

'All three of them are in the Voortrekkerhoogte Military Hospital in Pretoria undergoing tests and examinations. They are all weak, and when they are strong enough they will be going home to see their families before returning to 4-SAI to klaar out.'

'Grant and I will be flying up to see them,' he added.

'Say howzit from *Peloton Drie*' – Say hello from Platoon Three – Els shouted, which cast a joyous smile across our faces and warmed our hearts with inner jubilation. When the lieutie left the bungalow, we stood unmoving, not quite believing that this was all happening so perfectly coordinated around the completion of our two years. Brian, Stoop, and Els rounded a few of us up for a pipe of celebration' and in the normal way we lost ourselves in the warm rush of the high as we looked forward to seeing our friends again.

The following morning, Lieutenant Bam and Grant left the base for the hospital, flying from Middelburg in a small plane to the Air Force base at

Waterkloof. Upon landing, they were whisked away by a waiting army car to the military hospital, with the excitement running a mile a minute through their pumped-up veins.

Once in the immaculately clean hospital, they were directed by the kind, smiling nurses in white uniforms to the separate rooms where Paul, Laurence, and Sandor had been placed. They came across Paul's room, and Grant – being a fellow Section leader to Paul – stepped into the room first and saw Paul half facing him.

'Sakkie!' Grant uttered, using Paul's favoured nickname, a broad smile lighting his face with gratitude that his friend and fellow leader was alive.

But Paul's response was not what he had anticipated. Paul turned slowly and faced Grant, with a pale, blank expression and not an ounce of excitement. Grant looked hard at Paul for an extra second, feeling like he was staring at a friend with dementia – until he saw the scared eyes welling up with tears of recognition. The tears sat within his red eyes, which stared with deeply hidden fear, and hung there without flowing. They looked at each other, their silence speaking volumes, until Grant took a gigantic step towards him, embracing his friend and wrapping his long arms around Paul's short upper body.

Grant stood like a giant, his thin frame and six-foot height towering over Paul, feeling absolutely helpless to offer aid. His arms felt the skin, and the knobbly ridges of bone that protruded from his thin vest as testament to the cruel month's just past. Paul's zest for life had been extinguished, leaving behind the shell of a man that Grant had come to know so well. Feeling out of place and in the way, Grant knew the mental scars hidden within the walls of his friend's mind ran through him like a deep, turbulent river.

'Laurence and Sandor had a shit time!' Paul spoke, softly uttering the words of a true leader – putting his troops' wellbeing before his own.

'*Ja*, I know. But what about you?' Grant asked, with a sense of worry for his frail friend.

'I'll be okay,' Paul replied flatly, not looking for any sympathy as he let a glimmer of a smile slip from his otherwise expressionless and deathly-pale face.

Lieutenant Bam and Grant made contact with Laurence and Sandor, who also looked very weak and pale as they lay in bed connected to the intravenous drips that fed them a saline solution. Smiles and handshakes locked the moment.

After the quick but emotionally draining reunion, with only a little talking having taken place and a lot of sighing filling the silent gaps, Lieutenant Bam and Grant shook their weak hands one last time and waved farewell to their troops. Stepping out of each of the rooms, which all had a scene of pain and equally-high levels of trauma wedged into them, they exited down the corridor and away from their troops, leaving them to recover in the capable hands of the doctors and nurses.

'Look what those bastards have done to them!'

Lieutenant Bam turned to Grant, his stern face filled with rage and hurt as they walked quickly down the corridor, wishing secretly for retaliation that they knew would not be possible.

Grant and Lieutenant Bam were the only ones to see those faces fighting to regain their senses in the overwhelming change that had transpired in a matter of a couple of days. They left the hospital floating on a high, with more gratification than they could have wished for – having being allowed to see the three captives alive and free.

Their flight back to 4-SAI was filled with happiness. They knew quite well that the whole of Platoon 3 was eagerly awaiting information on their friends.

When Grant entered the bungalow, he was bombarded with questions from all angles, pertaining to his short but intense visit to the military hospital.

'What do they look like?'

'Are they bruised and battered-looking?'

'What actually happened? How did they get caught?'

'How thin are they?'

And so the inquisitive and prying questions were unleashed on Grant who was unable to answer many of them.

'They are skin and bone. They managed to survive on rice alone. They are all weak, but they are doing well.'

Trying to dodge another onslaught, he added: 'They are going home for a few days to see their families, and then they will be coming here. They had a tough time.' And with this solemn statement, he stepped away, leaving us to absorb the information.

We received the news without any shock, having expected it from a starving third world country that did not adhere to the Geneva Conventions.

It was satisfying to hear that they were now shielded by caring hands and being nursed back to full health. We paid little thought if any to the mental trauma of their wounds. Only time could possibly heal them, and that would require far more rehabilitation than their malnourishment.

Our platoon broke into chatter and began dispersing soon after Grant left the curious circle that had formed so magically around him.

The days began to drag by as we prepared and cleaned our kit. The first item to be handed back – which brought great relief – was our R4 rifles. They were thoroughly inspected before our rifle number was checked against our name and army number. With a match in place, we finalized the document with a signature to confirm that it no longer belonged to us. We felt quite naked without them, as if a dead weight had been removed and the invisible shackles finally cut loose, for we had lived with our rifles at arm's reach through pretty much every hour of the past two long years.

Our fibreglass helmets, chest webbing, combat webbing and grootsaks were taken to another store room and signed back in the same way – except with less of an inspection. Each signing back brought us one step closer to reaching the end.

A couple more days went by, and we were really itching to see Paul, Laurence, and Sandor for ourselves. It was not much longer before that day came. Lieutenant Bam went down to the main gates, where he met his three troops with open arms and fought back his emotions. The four of them climbed into the car that had driven them from Jan Smuts airport and ferried them slowly along the smooth road and up the slight hill towards the bungalows. The car stopped outside the big painted elephant that marked the line of bungalows belonging to Bravo Company, and out they stepped onto the red earth, metres from their fellow platoon soldiers. It felt like years for them since they had seen this base, their old bungalow' and now all that remained for them to see were the familiar faces within.

Walking in the shadow of Lieutenant Bam, they followed behind him, Paul leading Sandor and Laurence' and like a proud father showing off his three sons, he stepped to the side, putting them in the spotlight. The bungalow instantly erupted with loud cheers and clapping and we rose to our feet, coming almost to attention as we gave them all the respect that they deserved – and certainly more than we would have given any rank. Troops stood on beds and sat on the dividing wall that separated the bungalow – all to get the first glimpse of something we had long ago written off' for we never expected to see the day that they would return to Platoon 3.

The shouts and cheers continued, and we stood as one and clapped them home with broad smiles spread across our enthusiastic faces. Goosebumps popped onto my arms as we witnessed this miracle – still not believing that it was actually happening. Out of the corner of my eye, I saw Lieutenant Bam standing still with tears of joy welling in his eyes, with admiration for the spirit of his platoon – now complete for the first time in over three months.

For a long few seconds, Paul, Laurence and Sandor stood frozen to the red-tiled floor, for they too had abandoned hope of returning to their platoon. By this time the whole platoon was on our side of the wall, and as Paul, Laurence, and Sandor stepped forward, so the corridor opened like the Red Sea. We pushed back, lining up in a dishevelled crowd along the edge of the beds. One by one they walked behind each other, down the line of eager faces, and we clapped and shook hands while they passed us by, as if in slow motion.

In their eyes we still saw some fear – fear that would be extremely hard for a person outside the army to understand. The whole platoon had walked in and out of fear for two years, but our fears could never come close to what they experienced. Their faces were drawn and as white as sheets, and their bodies tired and much thinner, for they had lost 15 to 20 kilograms in three months.

The half smiles they wore were controlled and guarded' they had the overwhelming feeling of being the centre of attraction' their minds raced with confused excitement and they stepped forward with a subdued reaction. They hoped we would not bombard them with questions, but rather allow them to gradually settle back into the safety of the platoon.

As they made their way towards the end of the bungalow, we realized that the SADF had delivered the best possible gift to us. Our platoon was now complete, in mind and body count, with only a handful of days left to rekindle old memories and share a laugh – if it were at all possible.

When all the commotion had ended, we continued with what we had been doing. For me, I joined most of the Durbanites and made my way into the tiny cubicle at the entrance to the bungalow, where I found Paul in the middle of the crowd.

'Hey, howzit going, Paul? Welcome back.' I shook his hand firmly and stared into his eyes.

'Ram, good to see you,' he replied with a wry smile, and he stood in quiet confusion of his surroundings. Shortly after offering our individual greetings, we sidled out of his room and back into the main bungalow, leaving him in peace with his own thoughts.

When the lights went out that night, I took the time to reflect on my two years. Friendships were my saving grace, having undoubtedly willed us on and through it. While I drifted from the past to the present, I accelerated to the very near future with the question, what now? I imagined without this safety net to fall back on. Smiling, I closed my eyes – more than satisfied to be leaving this dictatorship for the freedom of the outside world.

After an unusually slow breakfast, we lined up in a squad at the orders of Staff Smit, who began fine-tuning our marching drills for our final parade. After hours of turning, coming to attention, and resting within the squad – our right

25. Farewell to National Service

foot stamping authority into the hard ground – we finally succeeded in mastering our drills without someone within the formation shouting out the time of een, twee-drie, een. With 200 feet hitting the soil together, it gave off a loud smack and emitted a feeling of working together – or saam bewerking, as the army liked to refer to it. With the silent sound of 'boom, chic-chic, boom' uttered inside our heads, we turned on the command and stamped our feet as one, from knee height into the red earth, with pride in our accomplishment – looking every bit like the professional soldiers the SADF had moulded us into. Our arms swung to shoulder height and our legs moved forward, right then left, in perfect harmony with the soldier on either side, driving us forward like a steam train with the metal arms turning the wheels in one synchronized movement.

In between rests we heard bits and pieces of stories from the captured three, who had been told by authorities in high places not to divulge any information about their experience. It was inevitable for some of it to come out, with us being their closest friends, and so bits and pieces in jumbled order filtered through to us – Els being the one who constantly niggled them for more details.

We listened intently as we were taken back to the Shingwidzi River, where it all began with a FRELIMO patrol capturing them within shouting distance of our encampment. Laurence mentioned handcuffs, dirty jail cells, huge rats, tough guards, and meals of fish heads and rice. They told us their stories with strained aged faces, the frowns creasing their brows and fresh pain clouding their eyes as they re-lived the torment.

Mention was made of being tied to a tree and ammunition dumps exploding on their jail-cell roof in Maputo, orange flashes lighting up the night and raining debris onto the roof. At the time, no mention was made of the fear that must have rocked them through their ordeal, but in the true fashion of a soldier, we knew it was there, lying under the surface – and telltale signs of it emerged through body actions and facial expressions.

As we looked at all three, it seemed to a few of us that Paul had taken the nightmare a lot harder than Laurence and Sandor. He had become very withdrawn, in contrast to his normally upbeat self. Laurence shocked the platoon, along with his good friend Brian, having given up the green weed that had flowed through our platoon on such a regular and recurring basis, freeing our minds on more occasions than we cared to remember. Toth stepped back into the platoon as if nothing had happened. We were quite aware of his physical strength by the way he had manhandled his heavy LMG machine gun, he always had an extraordinary amount of fitness in reserve, along with a very strong mental side that could weather anything thrown at him, without complaint.

Paul picked up where he left off' and wearing his Section leader stripes, he led us – hiding as best as he could the mental torture he had suffered at the hands of the Communist FRELIMO. With mounting respect for our leader, we followed his orders, helping him in what way we could, aware that his unspoken fears haunted his actions.

The last nights were wasted away with bottles of brandy and other hard-core, clear spirits' now we were willing the days on. With two nights left to serve, I fell under the influence of these dreaded spirits, and with brandy directing my path, I challenged a first-year lieutenant who was walking through our lines. Ignoring his authority of rank, I told him to leave which he refused to do, instead pushing the power trip of a newly promoted officer onto me.

'I am a lieutenant' you can't tell me what to do!'

'I don't give a fuck. Get the hell out of our lines!' It was the brandy doing the talking for me. When he did not move, I pushed him' and by doing that I had struck an officer – which carried dire consequences. Unfortunately, I should have realized that brandy has a way of bringing out violence in people, especially soldiers – as I had seen throughout the two years' but I had not learned the lesson, and with already too much consumed I had not heeded the warning.

It did not take long before the Military Police arrived with a caged van, arresting me and placing me in the back – in exactly the same way as had happened on our 40 days. Riding away alone, I felt doomed – with extra days hanging around my neck like a noose.

The van came to a halt at the main gate, and I was led from the back of the vehicle by the two burly Military Police and into the guardhouse, towards two thickly-barred cells just big enough to hold a bed. I was instructed to leave my boots outside as a precaution against suicide with the bootlaces. Once inside, the iron door closed with a sinister and cruel feel, instantly expelling my freedom and replacing it with a cloud of doom and worry. I lay on the bed and thought about my situation, which could carry extra days or a military court for pushing an officer – all while drunk with only two full days remaining. I would have to wait for morning to see how the event unfolded, hopefully with a clearer head. With my mind still swirling at my stupidity, and my thoughts now beyond my control, I succumbed to the excesses of drink.

'Wake up. Wake up!' the Military Police shouted.

I rolled over and looked at them for a few long seconds, groggily wondering why they were waking me after just putting me inside. The door was open and they were standing by it, willing me out of the tiny cell.

25. Farewell to National Service

'You have to get back to the bungalow. They are having roll call!'

Their words of warning now began to make sense.

I was being let out, and had to run like hell across the base and back to the bungalow before my name was read along with the rest of the platoon. Lacing up my boots in double quick time and thanking them while I did so, I bolted out of the guardhouse, and with alcohol still heavy on my breath' I cut through the middle of the camp towards the bungalow. Through the moonlight and my stumbled running, I managed to glimpse the time on the digital face of my watch. It registered the odd time of 04:50. Rounding the hangar where we had spent last year's Christmas, I saw Platoon 3 with their backs to me and Staff Smit in front of them, reading surname after surname in alphabetical order. Slipping through the shadows, I joined the back of the platoon in time to hear the name 'McCallum' '*Teenwoordig*, Staff' Present, Staff, came the reply.

Nicholson and Oosthuizen were called and then Ramsden. I also replied '*Teenwoordig*, Staff' – trying to hide my heavy breathing.

At the end of the roll call I walked back into the bungalow, feeling vastly relieved at having escaped the dreadful probability of extra days. I felt as though I had redeemed myself, in the nick of time.

When the sun rose on that very last day, we woke early – shaving and washing our faces and getting dressed into the set of browns that was the most *houding*, oldest and most faded. Our flashes were placed on each epaulette, with the cycad depicting the unit of 4-SAI on our left and the black-and-yellow bordered square, split with a horizontal line into green and black of Bravo Coy, proudly worn on our right.

We were ready to salute our company flasher for the superiority we felt it carried within the battalion. Our green cravat was worn around our necks' our green, gold, and black-striped staple belts were worn around our waists, our white patties were worn like ice-cream men around the top of our shiny boots, and with our berets worn on our heads, proudly tilted to the right, we were ready for the *Klaar* Out Parade.

It seemed just like any other day, but it wasn't, the end had finally dawned. Like children around a Christmas tree, having waited for an eternity until they were allowed to open their presents, our eternity had also arrived – with the best present of all soon to come: the gate opening to allow us the freedom to go home.

Our last meal was nothing special, but it was a time to say goodbye to some of the troops in Platoons 1 and 2, and some of Charlie Company and Alpha Company who had returned the day before from their base at 61-Mech.

In the mid morning we formed up in our three companies and marched as a battalion onto the parade ground in front of parents, family, and friends. The feeling it gave was something that I will never forget. Our hearts were swollen with pride as we marched in total synchronization, our legs and arms linked with an invisible cord. Coming to a halt, we turned on the order, and with the 'boom chic-chic boom,' we planted our boot heels into the earth with one loud smack – our chests bulging and our hearts pounding with honour.

At attention, Alpha and Bravo Companies were awarded the octagonal 'Pro Patria' medal of patriotism, for our service in the operational area of South-West Africa and Angola. The ribbon displayed the colours of the South African flag – the orange, white, and blue with the South African coat of arms stamped into the back of the medal.

Receiving the medal meant very little, and yet the moment meant a lot. On looking at it, two words instantly came to mind, afkak and mindfuck, from shitting off from one patrol to the next along with the mental agony of toiling with all the frustrations. If we could have traded it for a reprieve for our two years we would have, but now that it was all over it seemed worth the agony.

At the end of it all, all that really mattered was the achievement of finally reaching the end. The weight of the metal could not come close to the weight of the mental strain that we carried in and out of the two years, following orders that had forced us to dig continually into deep reserves to see us through.

After the parade we carried our balsaks to the office buildings just around the corner from the gate. Staff Smit called us together as a company, and while in formation he spoke to us with pride, having being chosen to lead Bravo Company along with Captain Delport. He thanked us for being so successful as a unit of men faced with numerous challenges' and then, choking with emotion, he wished us well for civilian life – which came unexpectedly from his hardened heart.

He seemed like a different person speaking to us. Here was a man for the first time showing a hint of compassion, a world apart from the evil man who had shouted racist abuse at us, constantly demeaning us into feeling – in his words – 'lower than black shit.'

To my mind, it was too late to feel any warmth for this bastard of a man, who not only had hit Solly clean off his feet but had also, on too many occasions, made our lives a living misery.

He reminded us that we as a company, had achieved almost the impossible over our sister units across the country. 4-SAI's Bravo Company had not lost a single life, unfortunately Alpha and Charlie could not boast the same clean sheet.

We had survived the operational area, many very near accidents, the temptation of suicide or desertion in our weakest moments, the capture of three of our men, road deaths on pass travelling home, wild animals, malaria, meningitis, over-exertion through heat and raging thirst' but together as a company – and more importantly as a platoon – we had survived the ordeal.

Our unit had gelled us into a tiptop quality of soldier and, coupled with our young ages and the fact that this was not our profession of choice, we had served as an integral part in one of the mightiest military machines in the world.

Lined up six deep, Staff Smit brought us to attention and marched us off for the very last time.

'*Aandag!*' Attention '*Regs met ses afmarsjeer!*' Right with six in a line march off! '*Regs om!*' Right turn '*Bravo Kompanie voorwaarts mars!*' Bravo Company, forward march! '*Mag in, bors uit, nek teen die kraag, pinkies teen die nate!*' Stomach in, chest out, neck against the collar, little fingers along the seams!

With these commands we experienced an overwhelming pride at having served and served proudly and literally floated towards the main gate. Just short of the gate, Staff Smit brought us to a halt.

Bidding each other farewell, we remained at attention with mixed emotions. A bittersweet feeling ran through us and we knew that the bonds of friendship, forged through the hardships, were moments away from coming to an abrupt end.

Our lives would soon be scattered across the vast country, back to where we had left an eternity ago. The camaraderie and comfort, which we had so painstakingly built, would soon be disappearing. Had we gone into an operation into Angola in the way we had been trained for – like those in the years ahead of us – there would have been no question that we would have sacrificed ourselves to save a friend. The bond we had was second to none' I could never have wished to serve with a better group of soldiers – some wackier than others, though that only helped our platoon stand out more than the rest.

The gates slowly opened, like an iron door to a cell, and when the order came we marched through and into the real world of family members standing on the side of the road, waiting for us. The moment we had been dreaming of, with the sweet smell of freedom in the air, had finally arrived. When the whole company was outside the gates, we were brought to another halt. The final order was only minutes away – the order to send us back to civilian life.

'*Salueer, Saluut!*' Staff Smit roared.

As one we proudly saluted our company and our unit our green berets angled sharply right side down with the emblem of 4-SAI's double-bladed sword in the middle.

We saluted once, twice, and for a final third time before marching three steps in unison. On the fourth step we dismissed, flinging our berets high into the air like frisbees. For a couple of well remembered seconds the powder-blue sky was speckled with a sea of green.

It was strange to say our goodbyes with such finality we kept our emotions in check before we dispersed to meet our waiting families. We had decided to meet in a parking lot in the centre of Middelburg for a final farewell. My dad picked me up along with John, Rob, and Tony who filled up the back seat.

Dad took us to the rendezvous point where we met about three quarters of the platoon for a last laugh in uniform as Platoon 3. Toth passed a bottle of champagne around and we all took swigs while it lasted. It was a fitting toast to the milestone that marked us becoming civilians again. After that we shook hands in fond farewells and drifted off in opposite directions.

John, Rob, Tony, and I made our way back to the Mercedes, with my father patiently waiting at the wheel' and with the final wave at faces never to be seen again, we began the journey towards Natal and home.

We had done it' we had reached the near-impossible end, having wavered in our expectations of getting through that mental and physical abuse. Iron will had prevailed over weakening thoughts throughout this strict military order, with that mixed feeling of I am glad we did it, but I am glad it is over.

For one whole year, we had slept on the ground, under trees, in dugout holes and tents if we were lucky, staying dirty for weeks on end, eating off and around fires, and surviving the hardship that was thrown at us with barely 50 days granted for pass, with a day on either side spent on the road getting home and back to camp, all in two very long years. We had lived an existence far removed from the normality and comfort of the civilized world, forcing us at times to become more like animals – for we had lived so long like them.

It seemed like decades ago that we had entered the army as young, innocent boys, only to emerge as toughened-up men trained with the skill of mechanized warfare. Being so young, we had been easily moulded and indoctrinated in mind and body to comply with military situations with little or no emotion. The harsh training had taught us to conceal our feelings and our pain, for no one – not even our closest army friends – should see us weak and vulnerable.

Two of the most important formative years had been snatched from us, depriving us of a smooth transition from school to the workforce. For most of us thought that army life had not really changed us' but it definitely had. Our fears were never addressed' we never spoke of them, and so we carried them like a dead weight for years to come. When young boys become soldiers and are trained to kill, and are placed in dugouts surrounded by open bush to lie and wait for the enemy for a week or more, something happens to their nerves, creating an imbalance, and tension overrides boredom with anger and frustration – both playing a vital role in the mixed-up puzzle.

All that we had left to show for our time were memories, both good and bad – which had been engraved deep into our minds. Memories to stand as solid reminders of the forced sacrifice that we had given as the 'call of duty' to the white government of South Africa.

We had done the honourable deed, to serve and take our chances' and now that it was all over, we could sit and cast judgment on our past and our country's political stance on the world stage as it tried to defend its actions. Or, on the other hand, we could walk away enriched with friendships and a unique experience that nothing could ever come close to matching' and that is exactly what I did.

Thank God it was over, for all it was worth.

1985-4-SAI. Minutes from klaaring out. Platoon 3. Macky, Rob,Tony, Jason,Solly, Alan and Wayne. Free at last and with thoughts of what now for life in Civvie Street.

26

Mozambique
A journey through hell

In January 2004 I contacted Laurence having not seen or heard from him since we completed our National Service in 1985, a gap of 19 years.

Through many long distance telephone calls and letters back and forth I finally managed to get his complete story of what took place in Mozambique.

In April 2005 Wayne and I met Laurence at the Durban airport for our prearranged trip to Maputo in Mozambique, to find and see for ourselves the Machava Prison.

To be standing next to Laurence a full two decades later, as we came face to face with the walls that had imprisoned him for so long, was a riveting moment. One could not help but notice the tension drawn across Laurence's face as he began to relive his nightmare. While standing at the entrance, deep in thought Laurence spotted a rat, the same size that had scurried through his cellblock daily' its appearance seemed to confirm that this was indeed Machava.

After desperately trying to persuade the guards to allow us to look inside but to no avail, we drove around the towering walls to another entrance. Wayne and I got out of the vehicle and walked up to the main gate hoping to look through one of the narrow guard lookouts. Suddenly soldiers appeared looking through the slit openings while another three in uniform ran at us from the main gate, shouting and waving their hands with faces taut and menacing.

It not only spooked us but it terrified Laurence who had remained in the vehicle. Wayne and I quickly jumped into the vehicle leaving our African translator Miguel to confer with the soldiers in Portuguese.

'I would rather die than go back in there!' Laurence quietly mouthed as he pointed to the intimidating walls, remembering the hell that lay beyond them, the hell that only he knew.

I have to commend Laurence for making the difficult journey and allowing himself to re-open already healed wounds. I know it could not have been easy and I pay tribute to him for his courage.

I want to thank Laurence for closing Platoon 3s 'unknown chapter' that ended our National Service.

This is what he told me:

The new day had brought with it another barrier of unrelenting heat to stun

26. Mozambique: A journey through hell

the dry plains with the chirp of crickets and the buzz of flies, filling the haze of silence.

Paul, Laurence, and Sandor ambled away from their camp area, deciding it was as good a time as any for a swim to soak away the heat from their burning bodies. They headed drowsily through the thick grass, clad in their black, army-issue P.T. shorts for the shallow part of the river over in Mozambique – to avoid the hippos and crocodiles in the wider part of the river on the South African side.

Forty metres on the other side of the high wire fence acting as the boundary between the two countries, they stopped and swam in the same part of the river that Wayne, Fox, and I had enjoyed so much a couple of hours before them. They swam for close to an hour, savouring the coolness of the water against the sweltering, dry heat of the afternoon, and then sat on a small sandbank in the middle of the river, taking in the peace and stillness that surrounded them on foreign soil.

'There are black soldiers pointing AKs at us!' Sandor suddenly exclaimed in a nervous whisper. Laurence swung his head around and looked over Sandor's shoulder, not knowing what to expect, and was met with a sight he could hardly believe to be real. Amongst the tall grass and reeds on the riverbank, nine African soldiers in camouflaged uniforms stood with menacing looks and AK-47 rifles pointed aggressively in their direction.

The stunned silence was broken with angry shouts in Portuguese directed at the frozen three, who continued to sit, unsure what to do and unable to understand Portuguese. Another rally of screams tore into them as they were summoned to stand up' the soldiers raised their rifles and then quickly locked their sights back onto them, as the signal to stand up.

Raising their hands above their heads, Paul, Laurence, and Sandor stood up as if in slow motion, their weak legs filled with dread. Following the Portuguese orders, they stepped into the muddy water and began wading towards them with their arms reaching skywards and their chests pounding. Once they were on the other side, the soldiers summoned them out of the river with cupped hands and the AK rifles thrust at them, inches from their bodies' shouting at them again in their urgency to get answers.

Standing scared and dripping wet, Paul and his two riflemen tried in vain to reason with their captors, but because of the language barrier, it was to no avail.

Unfortunately, Paul, Laurence, and Sandor were so close to our position that we could have heard a loud shout for help, had they been able to try. But with nine rifles cocked and ready to fire, it was no wonder that they obeyed the soldiers.

The FRELIMO patrol had come from Paul's side of the river, having descended the hill we had just climbed only hours ago' and then, using the thick reeds along the bank as good concealment, they cornered the three with total surprise, giving them only one feasible option, to follow orders or be shot.

The AK-47s, combined with the fearsome looks and tense body language, directed the three South African soldiers to follow four FRELIMO. It was shortly after 13:00 when the soldiers trailed down the river – Sandor, Laurence, and Paul boxed in, snaking away in a line behind the leading four. The remaining five took up the rear, never lifting their AKs from their shirtless backs.

These fit and lean FRELIMO soldiers carried no extra kit, besides a water bottle threaded through their web belts – their saviour against the intense heat and aching thirst. Their camouflaged uniforms added further stealth to their already mean and overpowering characters, and their weapons acted as the law enforcer to this small, ragtag-looking army.

One heavy step after the next led them further and further from the safety of our country into the scary unknown, fear and panic tightening like a noose around their necks.

Where are we being taken? All three asked themselves, still numbed with the fact that they were captured soldiers, and hardly believing that their lives had done an about-turn and the threat of death was now a reality.

In a long line they made their way down the sandy and very shallow river, walking barefoot with Sandor in the front, Laurence in the middle, and Paul at the rear. After walking two kilometres over the soft sand, shadowed from the burning sun by the thick overhanging branches, creepers, and bush, they forked away from the shallow water onto a beaten and well-worn path. The bush got thicker, the ground got harder, the sun got hotter and beat down upon their naked backs, stinging like salt on an open wound. Their tired bodies cut through thick patches of dense bush, and thorn bushes raking them with the devil's thorn, 40 centimetres long, drawing blood instantly. Thin green branches flicked back at them, whipping at their heads and trunks and adding to their drawn-out pain.

Staring forward with their eyes squinting against the sharp rays of light from the sun, their feet stumbled over the burning ground and scrubby, flat terrain. Each step became more painful than the last, and blood trickled from cuts and broken-off thorns that remained firmly embedded in the soles of their feet. Flinching with pain, they agonizingly kept up with the pace set by these FRELIMO soldiers – the South African army word *vasbyt* ingrained in their minds and driving them forward.

26. Mozambique: A journey through hell

The deeper they walked in to Mozambique, the more unsettled they became, for they realized that without a doubt they were in grave danger of being killed and buried in the wide-open bush, never to be seen or heard of again.

One of the FRELIMO soldiers was extremely aggressive and angry, he shouted through clenched, pearly-white teeth, his face creased with wrinkled lines of bitter hatred for his white captives. Stabbing the ground with his free hand, he conferred in Portuguese with his troops, getting angrier by the minute. His hand continued to point at the ground, unrelenting in his fight to win the argument that he voiced so passionately.

Laurence believed that, with all these hand actions pointing towards the earth, they were looking for a place to execute and then bury them, with no one around to act as a deterrent or witness.

But to their astonishment and gratification, they continued on, the sun setting on their burned backs, welcoming the gradual drop in temperature. By now their mouths were bone dry' they wrestled their tongues free from their palates, which felt like they were glued together.

With a torturous, non-stop, five-hour walk in an easterly direction, they eventually walked into a FRELIMO bush camp with olive green tents erected in a neat circle. They were immediately met with the confused stares and fierce looks of 20 to 25 FRELIMO soldiers, all dressed in the same camouflaged uniforms, with green berets and brown leather boots. The extremely weary three followed the most senior soldier, under the silent direction of the AK-47, to a lone tree in the centre of the encampment. The senior soldier was joined by a few others who held pieces of thick rough rope. They turned Paul, Laurence and Sandor around and began tying their hands behind their backs. When their hands had been tied together, they were instructed to sit with their backs to the trunk, circling the tree. Their hands were then further tethered to the hands of the person on either side of them, and then the rope was fastened above their heads and anchored around the thick branches – making escape near impossible.

The soldiers turned and left them tied to the tree like lonely stray dogs. Darkness crept in, leaving them to ponder their predicament. They bowed their heavy heads, with their chins digging into their chests as they rested them on their drawn-up knees, and quietly came to terms with the unfortunate situation they were in. Thirsting for liquid and hungering for food, they sat dead still, their hands numb behind them. Together they gained silent strength through eye contact with their friend on either side.

'How could it be?' they asked themselves. One minute they had been enjoying a carefree and relaxing swim, with the freedom of nature at their fingertips and the next they were confined to a tree at gunpoint.

The ropes gnawed at their wrists, chafing and burning the skin as they wriggled in and out of a new position, in the desire for one of more comfort. Cautiously, they whispered to each other, toying with an idea of escape.

'My ropes are loose,' Sandor whispered. 'I can get my hands out easily.'

'Which way is the border?' Paul said.

'But what about the guards?'

'They would shoot to kill!'

The answer to their questions came with these resounding words: 'How far would we get until they tracked us down and shot us!'

The idea of escape thus squashed, an uneasy and lengthy silence filled the air, until it was broken by a whisper of warning.

'Watch out, here they come!'

Twigs broke under moving boots and long shadows stretched out of the blackness, growing taller with each step. The guards towered over them, and slung their AK weapons casually over their shoulders. The whites of their eyes glowed with hatred – they stared down at the sorry state of the captured three. Looking upward, an uncontrollable fear stalked them, like a hunted animal frozen in fright.

Mumbling to each other, they checked the ropes and then filtered back into the darkness at the perimeter of the bush camp, where they slept. Minutes later they would reappear, stalking up on their prey with scowls of revulsion – to check on their 'trophies.'

Still dressed in thin shorts, they shivered with aching shoulders and heads bowed as if in prayer, the night chill set in and dew descended upon and around their vulnerable bodies. For added warmth, they drew closer and waited out the night. Nodding off for a few minutes at a time, the cool night dragged by until they watched a new morning dawn – hoping that it would bring a miracle.

Now they could see the bush camp more clearly, compared with the dimming light and fatigue from the night before. They realized that they were very close to the operation room or radio control centre, for they saw the high, protruding antenna placed in a nearby tree. Most of the tents remained closed and securely fastened, preventing Paul, Laurence and Sandor from learning what lay hidden behind the four dirty-green walls of canvas.

The three soldiers wondered about their friends in their chopper tents, and what they were making of their sudden vanishing act.

26. Mozambique: A journey through hell

While they sat, looking forlorn and abandoned, tied to the tree like three unwanted dogs, the sound of helicopters echoed through the open bush, pricking their senses into full alert.

'Can you guys hear that?' Paul whispered excitedly. 'They are looking for us.'

These whirling messages of hope reached deep into Mozambique and into the bush camp, sending electrifying energy through the three soldiers. They knew, without a shadow of doubt that these helicopters were flying in search of them. They sat with goosebumps creeping up their arms, helpless to react – the guards overshadowing them at gunpoint.

The FRELIMO soldiers became very nervous with all the noise. One soldier placed his index finger over his thick, rubbery lips and signalled 'Quiet' with a tense frown. The Pumas sounded a lot closer than they actually were, for the terrain played tricks upon their ears, forcing them to ready themselves for an attack from the air. Each FRELIMO soldier clutched his rifle firmly and looked through the bush from their sprawled-out positions, in the direction of the noise, waiting for the expected flyover from the helicopters. After a tense wait behind trees and bushes – with Paul, Laurence, and Sandor still tied to the tree – the soldiers realized that the helicopters were keeping to their flight path within South African airspace. So with untold relief they resumed their activities.

It left the three dejected, with shattered dreams of an immediate rescue – they sank back hopelessly against the tree, their bodies still stiff with tension. Paul, Laurence, and Sandor took turns being led away for a piss break. Stretching their cramped and sore legs, they hobbled away from the tree and urinated onto the dusty soil while the AK-47 never left their backs. After the brief but worthwhile release, they returned to the same dusty spot beneath the tree, allowing the next one to enjoy his stroll on revitalized legs.

Unbeknown to anyone at the time, a handful of Recces, Reconnaissance Operators, had been dispatched by the South African government to help locate Paul, Laurence, and Sandor. They tracked their spoor and located them at the FRELIMO bush camp – seeing them quite clearly tied to the tree. They had the ability to free them, but the command from the South African government had been one to just observe. There was no doubt that politics was playing a role. Although superbly well trained as fighting soldiers, their actual role was infiltration and observation. Being the elite soldiers they were, they relayed the information back to the SADF, and having accomplished their task, they left Mozambique with no one the wiser.

The three white soldiers sat weak, unfed, and thirsting for a drop of water, but nothing came their way. With the never-ending heat of the day finally drawing to an end, the sun eventually began to set on another blistering dry day across Southern Africa. Slowly the fiery ball dropped, and with it a cool silence cloaked them. The helicopters had stopped flying – the danger of poor visibility being the determining factor. Suddenly the silence felt naked, without the whirl of hope chopping through the air – leaving them to bow their heads and wish for an end to this lingering hell.

At around 10:00 they were untied from the tree and forced to stand up, still with their arms firmly bound behind their backs. Awkwardly, they forced themselves up, slowly straightening their stiff bodies with a light-headed and dazed feeling brought on by hunger. The soles of their feet ached with blisters and embedded thorn needles' their upper bodies were streaked with caked-on dirt and lined with scratches of dried blood.

Intimidating shouts in Portuguese from six of the original nine FRELIMO soldiers forced them forward, away from the tree, and behind the leading soldiers – the rear guard pushing them onward. With their heads bowed and their hands still tied together – their fate in the hands of these soldiers – they wrestled with fatigue and dizziness over more flat, thick, and bushy terrain.

Their short 19 and 20 year-old lives began to flash in front of them, along with thoughts and visions of loved ones. They questioned whether they would have their lives spared and be reunited with them.

The helicopters launched their search again, but with each step a stride away from the border, the hope of rescue began to dwindle with the sound of the rotors that eventually faded into thin air. Instead it was replaced with the shuffle of footsteps over the dried earth, and the heavy breathing and odd word of Portuguese.

The sun continued to burn upon their open backs and sweating heads, at a temperature above 40°C – sapping at their waning strength and spirits. Walking hunched over with their heads lowered, and fighting to straighten their sagging shoulders, they hobbled over the dry scrub like three old men. Staring at their dirty, brown, and cut feet, their wrists rubbed red and raw from the rope burns, they said a silent prayer in the hope that God was listening.

After walking for half a day, they came to a walled-off area with a sign in faded black lettering that read 'Masenjerry.' Barbed wire lined the top of the walls and high-wire fences, behind which they were escorted. This camp was a permanent FRELIMO base, squared off by a high-wire fence encompassing many olive green tents and at least 60 soldiers' along with six green Russian troop carriers similar in design to the South African Saracen, which were parked together close to the tents.

In a repeat performance, upon their entry into this second FRELIMO camp, they were again greeted with shouts of excitement and sneers and snarls of hatred from the crowd of young African soldiers. Fearfully, Paul, Laurence, and Sandor stood their ground under the verbal assault launched at them in the language of their colonists.

'These bastards also wear green berets, but they are our enemies!' Laurence said – a comment on the similarity between the South African Infantry green beret and theirs. He had to cut short his idle conversation, however, for he noticed a bunch of soldiers walking hastily towards them with their AK-47s.

The group of soldiers led them away from the prying eyes to an open-sided tent, where they were left under the guard of a lone soldier. Wearily they sat, still with their arms tightly fastened behind their backs as they looked out upon the base. They followed the soldiers' steps as they hurried between tent and vehicle. The faded, dirty, and slightly torn flag of Mozambique fluttered in the breeze from a tall wooden pole, marking the entrance to the FRELIMO base. They sat and stared at the Communist symbol imposed over the faded horizontal stripes of green, black, and yellow. The red triangle along the length of the flagpole housed the Communist star and over it, an AK-47 with the bayonet attached and a worker's farming tool formed an X, which stood over an open book. The five-pointed star shone prominently through.

The idea of escape again nagged at their minds, but led them to the same answers. They knew if they attempted to escape and failed, that they would most certainly be executed. The body language of the FRELIMO soldiers reiterated that truth. The daylight would make it impossible for an escape through the guards and roaming soldiers' and on the other hand, darkness would provide them with cover but would make it near impossible to find the border. They needed to walk towards the setting sun in the west, which after a couple of days of hard walking would see them safely on the South African side.

This virtually impossible escape plan was shelved' the decision was made easier by the look in their eyes, which spoke volumes in itself. All they could do was sit and wonder about their fate, wrought up into a mental and physical state of fear and desperation.

Three days dragged by, each day similar to the last. They survived on small scraps of dried bread – amounting to a single slice – washed down with a few sips of water. The night brought more uncertainty, and their only solace came from the splendour of the peaceful, twinkling, and starry sky above – seemingly out of place and far removed from their silent turmoil.

On the fourth day they heard a vehicle approach the camp, and not knowing what to wish for they kept their eyes on the entrance to the camp. Through the entrance, a green Russian troop carrier entered in a cloud of dust. It had six wheels and was similar to the vehicles already parked in the camp – resembling the Saracen used at 5-SAI in Ladysmith.

Paul, Laurence, and Sandor were immediately dragged to their feet and pushed towards the waiting vehicle. They cautiously climbed in, through the open doors at the back, and seated themselves beside a couple of armed African guards. They drove out of the camp in silence, gazing out of the open portholes, watching open bush and trees flash by while they bounced around over the uneven dirt roads.

After a few hours of uncomfortable driving, the vehicle stopped on the side of the road. One of the guards exited from the back holding a jerry can, from which he proceeded to pour diesel into the fuel tank.

Eventually, five hours later, the vehicle drove into another permanent camp, this time with rows of brick bungalows – ten in all. This primitive camp was also enclosed with a wire fence and was filled with lots of soldiers. The camp was well maintained and had three tall, cold, concrete watchtowers with spotlights – which at night pulled circles of light through the darkness, guarding the quiet camp against attack.

Paul, Laurence, and Sandor were met by a tall, clean-cut FRELIMO lieutenant, who to their relief spoke quite good English. So far he was the only person they had come across who could speak with them. The lieutenant lost no time questioning them about what had happened' and then, to their astonishment and gratitude, the ropes were untied, freeing their hands for the first time in days. It felt abnormal – a naked and strange feeling – to have their hands hanging in front of them. They studied and rubbed their hands, now a painful red with raw patches around the wrist areas, and enjoyed the feel of the blood pumping back into them.

From being treated like animals, they were now treated very well, and food and clothes were passed their way. Laurence inherited a pair of brown corduroy trousers, a cream shirt, and a brand new pair of crisp white takkies. Paul and Sandor also received clothes and footwear to cover their near-naked and battered bodies.

The African lieutenant stood smartly, with his medium build, dressed in camouflage, two black stars decorated the epaulettes of his uniform. With a friendly and trusting face, he looked over his newly dressed captives, making eye contact with them, and then, in broken but clear English, he spoke.

'Everything will be alright' you three will soon be going home,' he said with complete sincerity. Looking up at him with the reverence of a god, they smiled for the first time in what felt like months' sighing with relief, that the nightmare was soon to be over, thinking it could not be long now. Home was all they could think about, and with smiles that spoke volumes they felt rejuvenated.

The following day the three of them climbed into a waiting vehicle, entering into two wire cages, which were then closed and locked behind them – leaving them to sit like three dirty, wild animals. When the engine revved to life, so did their spirits – this being the journey to their freedom. A week had dragged by, feeling more like six months. Somehow their resolve held them together' it drew them through this lonely hell, uniting them further into a band of brothers.

Home, South Africa, family and friends, showers, food, and drink occupied their minds as the vehicle drove through potholes and bounced them around. Wrestling against the driver's poor road navigation, they clung with all their strength to the mesh openings. The tarmac had long ago disintegrated through neglect and civil war' this was third world Africa, where the decaying roads were one of the first signs of the declining economy.

In the late afternoon they drove into the Maputo Base Camp, where they spotted another Mozambican flag demarcating another important place. They were now inside the main headquarters of FRELIMO, where the high rank sat and significant decisions were made.

The back of the vehicle was hurriedly opened, and Paul, Laurence, and Sandor spilled out upon the dry dusty earth, before being ushered with haste to an empty room. The room was dark, but as their eyes got used to the dim light, they could make out the cream colour of the brick walls and the dirty square tiles covering the cool floor. The old, heavy, wooden door was immediately slammed shut and locked, leaving soldiers posted on guard outside the doorway.

In the room, there were three very old grey blankets, with almost more holes than blanket, and a few dirty, smelly old mattresses. Taking one blanket each, they spread it over the cool tiles and lay upon them. In the night they all began to scratch at their skin, with a sudden bout of itchiness. Out of the blankets a swarm of fleas had emerged, latching onto their gift of new, unsuspecting flesh. They scratched and itched the night away, eventually discarding the blankets into the far corner of the dark room and accepting the hard floor rather than be eaten alive.

Hidden from the light, they huddled together, propped against the walls, wondering what had become of the word 'home' – uttered only a day ago by the friendly-faced FRELIMO lieutenant. Those surges of excitement now seemed so far away! Desperation turned to anger, and quickly ended in a relapse of helplessness as their broken souls fought against the mental torture.

While they sat like shadows of their former selves, slouched in darkness, a sudden explosion rocked the room, instilling further fear into them. Through the barred glass windows they saw red and orange flashes of light exploding like fireworks into the night sky. A thunderous bang shook the roof, followed by a hailstorm of bullets and shrapnel that rained like a storm upon the old tin roof – which amplified the sound tenfold and sent a wave of panic through all three.

'Grab the mattresses!' Paul yelled above the noise. With one mattress to a person, they rushed for the window and leaned them against the threatening area – to shield the glass from flying into the room and lacerating them like shrapnel while they cowered for protection in the furthest corner.

'Do you think the roof can hold up?' Paul asked when another barrage of rock and shrapnel showered down with a deafening thump.

'They are coming to rescue us!' someone shouted over the roar – reference being made to the SADF – but unfortunately it turned out to be RENAMO, blowing up a FRELIMO ammunition site. The smell of gunpowder soon infiltrated into the room and burned deep into their lungs. It hung in the room long after silence had returned to the dark, lonely isolation' coughs chased away the silence while the three bodies rocked in fright.

Laurence cast a glimpse at his friends, and within their sad eyes – now sunken into their gaunt faces – he saw the same hidden fear he was feeling, the same tired and sluggish look from lack of food and nutrition. They had all lost weight, and their clothes hung limply from their frames.

One at a time they were led away from the darkness into the burning light, and taken to a solitary room next door for interrogation.

It was 23 September – 11 days since their capture – and word had finally reached South Africa that they were in the hands of the Mozambican authorities.

Paul, Laurence and Sandor faced up to their interrogations, totally unaware that the SADF had been notified of their capture, and to top it off, they had been declared AWOL. Unfortunately, they had no way of knowing how dumbfounded their parents were at the accusation, with barely three months of service left. To their parents – and to us their fellow soldiers – it was ridiculous that they would do something so stupid and risk having extra days added onto their two years, which they had nearly completed.

One at a time they were taken through the open cement courtyard, outside their locked room, towards the rows of brick, bungalow-style buildings, their arms cuffed in front of them and their legs shackled and a chain giving them

26. Mozambique: A journey through hell

the awkward leeway of a foot in between shuffled steps. The guards directed the single soldier to the main building, where they passed below a big painting of Samora Machel clad proudly in his battle fatigues and displaying his power as the first black leader after the Portuguese had abdicated their colonial rule.

Once in the main building, Laurence was led into a small, brick, cubicle-like room. An old, scarred, wooden table and a chair were positioned by the single barred window. Two FRELIMO soldiers, with holstered 9mm pistols, green berets, and sharp looks of hatred welcomed the handcuffed Laurence into their presence with expressions of disgust. In the interrogation room, Laurence looked at the lone picture of the Communist leader staring down at him from the off-white walls – again clad in uniform, frozen stiff within the square of glass.

Two soldiers conducted the interrogation and shot endless questions at him – probing for information about military bases within South Africa.

'What's your name?'

'Why are you in Mozambique?'

'Did you come here to fight?'

Laurence answered these questions without a problem, and then the questions turned to the military role within South Africa – to which he hardly uttered a word of answer.

'How many troops are in your camps?'

'Guard duties – how are they carried out?'

'What vehicles are in your bases, and how many to each base?'

'How are your bases laid out?'

'How much ammunition do you have in your camps?'

'What kind of food do you eat in the bases?'

And so the questions continued.

Laurence bravely held his ground and refused to give any information, for fear of an attack against one of the many bases dotted around South Africa.

'If you don't talk, we will shoot you,' one of the soldiers said.

Then the other soldier slammed his fist upon the tabletop' the crack shook the table and echoed around the small room, startling Laurence. The two soldiers, whom Laurence believed to be officers, were convinced that the three South African soldiers were aiding their RENAMO enemy as resistance fighters' and they were not letting up on their interrogation until they got the information they were looking for.

The interrogations took place daily – sometimes lasting an hour, and other times an agonizing 12. Twelve hours of verbal abuse while standing handcuffed against a firing line of repetitive questioning, delivered through shouts of anger and aggression in broken English, sapped Laurence's resolve and yet he remained silent. The soldiers circled around him like flies to bloody meat, shaking fingers in his face and snarling like dogs through bared, white teeth, trying desperately to draw information from their captive.

Without breaking Laurence, he was led away in his handcuffs, back to the room where his two friends waited eagerly for his return. They told each other about the questions they were asked, and decided to begin talking – answering with lies, and therefore not divulging any critical information. They planned their lies for the following day's interrogation while sitting in the middle of the floor' they knew it would bring satisfaction to their armed interrogators.

Food came twice a day, consisting of small pieces of bread and a helping of rice covered with tiny dried fish heads. When the mealtime arrived, their handcuffs were removed' and with their dirty hands, they devoured their food, leaving an empty, dented, and very dirty metal plate.

The daily interrogations carried on into the second week, until on the 12th day Laurence was summoned by the guards and taken to the main building, where he received the gut-wrenching news that Paul and Sandor had been led away for execution. A wave of nausea hit him with the force of a tidal wave. His legs weakened and his breath became short – he looked mortified as he stared through the guards – now feeling totally abandoned and alone.

What is happening? Is this for real? He asked himself. Not knowing what to believe anymore, Laurence knew that his time must be short' and then it came. A soldier from the interrogation room walked up to him and, with uncaring intimidation and evil looks, stared him square in the face.

'Your turn will be before sundown,' he said, without a sign of remorse.

Laurence stood glued to the ground, understanding now that his life was in the hands of these ruthless and rough-looking soldiers, who would not hesitate to put a bullet through his head.

The end is near. That was the lonely feeling that occupied Laurence's mind. Absolutely shit-scared and now totally alone, without words of encouragement from his two friends, he leant against the wall in darkened silence, such as he had never experienced before. He waited and waited, and time stood still – his nerves were strung to their breaking point and his body was stiff with tension. He kept on guessing it must be time – the sun must be setting by now – the key would be turning in the lock any second and they would be there to take him away. Sitting without a wink of sleep, he again thought about his army friends, guarding the borders within the Kruger National Park, his family, who would be worried sick for him and his two friends. The break with this link was the cruellest, stripping him of a vital support system and leaving him with the loneliest of voids in the pit of his empty stomach.

On the 14th day – two days after Paul and Sandor had been taken away – the soldiers came for Laurence. The sitting and waiting had been torture, but now it somehow seemed all right. He weakly got to his feet and steadied himself on trembling legs. He was quickly blindfolded with a crude piece of cloth and was ushered like a death row inmate from the lonely room towards the warm light that filled the doorway. Stepping out into the bright and alive world on the other side of the archway, he could only expect the end to be near, and with pangs of fear, he was led towards a green land rover, his hands still cuffed behind his back. He was helped up by one of the soldiers, who grabbed his arm and pushed him into the vehicle. He sat in the back, next to a tall thin African who went by the name of Mashona. Mashona's one hand was cuffed to Laurence's – making it harder for an escape. Another soldier positioned himself next to Laurence, nullifying any thought of escape. Two soldiers filled the front and rattled him with their very loud talking, which came across more like shouting. And so they waited in the boiling sun for the order to move out. Mashona could not speak any English, nor Laurence any Portuguese – which left them to wonder at what the other had been accused of doing. The three soldiers all had AK-47s, and the soldier in the rear had his positioned across his upper thigh – the barrel pointing into Laurence's stomach as a further threat.

Laurence sat still and stiff, wallowing in paranoid thought, with no vision to break the dark spell of hopelessness that overcame him. The engine turned over, and with it his heart missed a beat. Without warning, the vehicle lurched forward with a crunch of the gears towards the main gate, which was immediately opened by the guards' and with the opening, the fear of death rushed upon him.

Am I being driven to my death? Laurence wondered.

The land rover transported them over a very neglected and potholed tar road, and then into the heart of Maputo. Passing through the city, everyone but Laurence saw once-beautiful Portuguese architecture standing as a reminder of the country's proud colonial past. The buildings were disintegrating through years of civil war and neglect. The pale stucco shades, which adorned the brick structures, were flaking under the sun, exposing big cracks through the brickwork. Empty wooden window frames with broken panes of glass stood beneath roofless structures' the round roof tiles had long ago been looted. They passed by a hotel, no longer servicing weary travellers with board but now offering free grazing to scrawny cows, which chewed on the tall grass in the overgrown lobby.

The open vehicle travelled down the wide streets. Huge, flamboyant trees grew along the roadside, granting throngs of people an umbrella of shade from the scalding sun. These majestic trees spread their branches above the potholed roads, adding colour to a depressing scene' and the majestic palm trees towered over the lower, drab buildings giving the ocean city a beautiful, tropical feel.

In the gracious squares with their perfectly-cobbled walkways, people sat and moved and went about their business – unaware of the splendour and excitement they would have experienced in the early 70s, when the capital was called Lourenco Marques after a Portuguese trader who visited in 1544. One could almost visualize the grandness of this sea capital at its peak, before civil war had ripped its guts out and left behind the tarnished remnants of a jewel that once sparkled so brightly upon the eastern shores of Southern Africa.

Poor African civilians moved about – some with babies cradled on their backs, bound tightly by a thin blanket, others dodging traffic and hooting to get to the other side of the crammed road. Some carried baskets of fruit and live chickens towards the market place, hoping to make enough money to cook a meal for the day. Poverty was clearly penciled into their tough faces as they embarked on another challenging day in one of the poorest countries in Africa.

The five of them were rocked from side to side as the speeding driver swung the wheel left and right to navigate the minefield of holes dotted in the roadway. The cool breeze blew his dirty, black hair away from his forehead – with the hope that a few fleas would be blown from his itchy scalp in the process. Laurence's arm felt like it might get ripped off at the wrist as the vehicle lurched in and out of the deep craters. The land rover reduced speed as it approached a grey metal gateway surrounded by a ten-metre high solid brick wall. Laurence was still oblivious to his surroundings.

The sun was setting and darkness was rapidly drawing in, the coolness upon Laurence's skin told him that the sun had set – which meant that he was at the place of his execution. The engine was cut off with a splutter and a stall, and another lurch forward brought an end to the hectic half-hour's drive, which had thrown him around with more force than a roller coaster.

Sitting still, Laurence said a prayer and waited for the soldier's arm to lead him away to his death. He took hold of Laurence, forcing him to stand with what little strength he had.

'Let it be quick – I want it over!' Laurence mouthed to himself as his feet touched the earth.

Laurence had no idea where he was. The soldier led him like a blind man over the uneven, loose-stoned surface, where the tar had long since peeled from the

26. Mozambique: A journey through hell

roadway, and towards a high, grey double gate. A soldier took hold of Mashona's arm and released his hand from Laurence's cuff, only to fill it with Laurence's free hand, cuffing them firmly behind his back. Laurence and Mashona were led to the gates and then were ordered to step through a small side door cut into the left side of the main gate. They had now walked into a holding area, bordered by another wall of solid grey gates – walling them in.

They had stepped into the Central Jail of Maputo, also known as the notorious 'Machava Maximum Security Prison.' The locals knew that once you entered this prison you never came out. It was said that six months inside this hellhole would be enough to kill you. Little did Laurence know that his execution had begun when the gate closed coldly and heavily behind him.

Hurried talking took place in Portuguese between the soldiers and the guards, ending with the soldiers departing back to the land rover having fulfilled their orders.

With his hands securely fastened, Laurence walked with Mashona, under guarded escort, to the guard office under the dim light of the entrance. The metal gate was opened and the two of them stood for the first time on the gravel that was home to Machava. Laurence was left with the feeling of what now? With fear tugging at his demoralized soul yet again.

When his blindfold was removed, he blinked under the dim light that filtered from a light socket hanging from a rusted wall bracket. They were welcomed within the gates by 12 to 15 African prisoners, young and old. Together they stared through them in the hope of seeing freedom on the other side of the metal gate before it was slammed shut, closing out their short-lived dreams of being on the other side.

The prison looked old, and not at all well maintained. Gravel had long ago replaced grass, a few trees stood isolated within the middle of the compound, overlooking the walls with ten long, rectangular cellblocks, covering off the bleak surroundings within the high, evil boundary. Sinister metal lamp poles curled over the solid, thick-bricked wall – on either side of freedom and imprisonment – and the hooks were silhouetted against the light outside. Very few worked, the bulbs had burned out or exploded years ago and were another reminder of the neglect that had spread through this country, from beautiful hotels and government buildings right down to prisons.

Glad not to have the blindfold bound around his head anymore – although the darkness was nearly as dark – Laurence was led by a couple of guards through the uncomfortable dark screen, towards a cellblock. The main gate acted as the entrance to the cellblock, and it creeked and groaned open like an old dungeon door. Laurence was led into the block and down the long, blackened corridor. Immediately the overwhelmingly damp and musty odour hit him smack in the face. His nostrils sucked the dampness into his lungs and his eyes began to water, he shivered through the coolness of the air.

He walked deeper into the cellblock until the guards directed him to stop next to an empty cell. Standing uncomfortably still, he waited while one of the guards produced a long key, which rattled with an echo until it found the slot and turned, opening the thick-barred metal door. Laurence was shoved into the room, and before he could turn around the door slammed closed upon his life – leaving him with the same helpless and lonely feeling.

This will be my end! How will the South African government know where I am?

Out of nowhere a bat flew into his face, whirling him around with the fright of his life. Still standing with his hands behind his back, he slowly stepped back, seeking comfort in the corner of his cell. Standing completely still in darkness as black as coal, he remained frozen in fear until his legs became lame. With his back pushed hard against the wall, his body slid – as if in slow motion – down the brick wall, until he crumpled in a heap along with his broken spirits. In a half-sitting position, he remained painfully awake, wide-eyed and motionless, he stared out into the nothingness until he saw the darkness grow ever so slightly lighter with the dawn of a new morning.

Aching and disillusioned, Laurence sat stone-faced, staring far beyond the barred cell door' still with his handcuffs biting into his raw wrists. His body felt cold and numb from sitting upon the hard concrete surface. Incoming daggers of light illuminated a square cell, four metres by four metres' a barred window sat three metres above the floor, linking one cell to the next. The three cell walls were painted a rusty red, and deep scars scraped into the surface, covering the walls in Portuguese graffiti, the only words of any meaning were 'RENAMO,' which had been very carefully etched into the paint in large lettering.

RENAMO had been formed in 1977 by the Rhodesian Central Intelligence Organisation and was strongly supported by South Africa until 1984, when the Nkomati Accord ended the cross-border ties. Pik Botha, the South African Minister of Foreign Affairs, signed the agreement relinquishing support to RENAMO and its credibility as an anti-Communist movement. It was signed with the provision that Samora Machel stop supporting the armed wing of the African National Congress and allowing them to run training camps within his country only to leapfrog over the border into South Africa.

26. Mozambique: A journey through hell

RENAMO and FRELIMO had been warring for over a decade, with Communist FRELIMO clinging to power with Samora Machel as president, instilling his Marxist ideals upon his struggling country.

FRELIMO had been formed in 1962 in Dar es Salaam, Tanzania, and a couple of years later it launched an armed struggle in northern Mozambique. FRELIMO had been formed mainly by the presence of the Makonde tribe from the north, but many of its leaders had joined the party from other parts of the country. Samora Machel had risen to power in 1969, taking over after the assassination of Eduardo Mondlane, and he subsequently began mounting further attacks.

By 1975, chaos ensued across the country, resulting in white Portuguese settlers fleeing in their thousands to the safety of South Africa. Families took what they could pack into their cars and small trucks and drove south in quest of a new and peaceful life. These settlers left a legacy on the country, in successful businesses and prosperous farms and years of hard work in Lourenco Marques – all of which had made it such a thriving and important seaport.

On 25 June 1975, Mozambique gained independence – and without any elections, Portugal recognized FRELIMO as the new government.

Samora Machel and FRELIMO's ideals had successfully destroyed the social and economic fabric of the entire nation, plunging it into a disastrous civil war. Law and order had long ago vanished, along with human rights and fair treatment of political prisoners. There were no courts operating in Maputo – which Laurence soon learned from one of the guards.

People had been put in to jails by soldiers loyal to the FRELIMO government, and then were forgotten about, left to rot like animals behind bars for crimes hardly worth mentioning.

With a level look fixed on the barred cells, Laurence stared across the corridor and made out the shapes of fellow humans, who were also trapped behind the thick iron bars. Their freedom had been torn from them, along with their human dignity' their spirits were left to waste away with their bodies.

Laurence's blank stare was broken by the groaning and squeaking from the rusty hinges holding the door to the main gate of his cell block' it swung open with some persuasion. A dirty, old, rusty, brown wheelbarrow was being pushed on its single wheel, and it made a groaning stop at each cell. The wheelbarrow stopped outside Laurence's cell, bearing a very dirty and dented metal plate of rice, which had been scooped out from the heap. It was placed upon an even dirtier floor, with years of filth caked over it, and slowly pushed, by means of a boot, into Laurence's confines. The guard unlocked the door and released his cuffs, allowing him the chance to eat – after the cell door had been slammed sharply shut.

'Eating food out of this wheelbarrow is like giving food to pigs!' Laurence mumbled to himself when the wheelbarrow had groaned away – its load looking as though the sticky rice held it together.

He looked at his food with revulsion' but with hunger dictating, he sank his dirty hand into his plate and squeezed a helping of sticky rice between his fingers. Using his thumb to mould the staple into a small ball against his four fingers, he placed it into his dry mouth and began chewing uncomfortably on it. It tasted sour and stuck to his dry palate' he did not know if this would be his only meal of the day. He licked his fingers like a cat would its paws, cleaning them of the last grains' he looked down upon the well-used and empty plate, wondering how many imprisoned mouths had fed from it.

In the morning, Laurence was allowed ten minutes outside his cell to wash and use the toilet. Followed by guards, he walked down the corridor, passing rows of cells where Africans gripped the iron bars – some staring with faces of anger and hatred at the passing white man.

Laurence counted 17 cells in his block, all the same size, and equally as dark and dank as the next' the only difference was the unlucky human jailed within its solitary confinement.

Shuffling ahead of the guards, Laurence was directed to the toilet area, which consisted of a round, dirty hole cut neatly into the concrete floor. The smell that rose up from the old, caked-on excrement would turn the toughest of stomachs. A crude, rusty pipe protruded from the green and black, mould-covered wall adjacent to the hole, which marked the spot where the prisoners washed.

When the hole was used, Laurence was never alone. He squatted over it in full view of the guards and fellow prisoners lined four to five deep, waiting their degrading turn. The humiliation and loss of dignity weighed heavily on Laurence as he performed this daily ritual in front of his audience. His urine was extremely light through lack of nutrients, and he suffered severe constipation from the only meal of rice that he was eating. While he squatted over the stinking circle, rats the size of meercats scurried in and out of the hole at will, right beneath him. The rats were black and grey, and measured around 45 centimetres in length, and lived below the cellblock in the old sewer system. Their beady eyes, showing no fear of the movement around them, looked at the rows of feet and then scampered across the wet concrete floor, dragging their long, pencil-thick tails behind them as they disappeared below the next prisoner's bared buttocks in a splash of water.

Stripping naked in front of the guards and fellow prisoners, Laurence stepped beneath the cut-off pipe, and with cold, yellowy water he proceeded to wash off the previous day's sweat and grime' without the aid of a bar of soap.

After the brief reprieve from his cell, walking back along the corridor, Laurence could see out of his cellblock through a small window. He saw the big grey metal gates, guarded by sloppy-looking soldiers who walked up and down holding their AK-47s below the fluttering flag of Mozambique. A faded, painted sign in Portuguese hung on the wall next to the main entrance, standing as a lost but vivid reminder of the colonists who had constructed this prison in 1963 to preserve law and order. It had been built on 22 hectares of land, a massive, Portuguese-style wall encompassing the area in which 850 prisoners could be held. In 1967 it was divided into two prisons – one on 12 hectares and the other on the remaining ten hectares, notably referred to as 'Big Machava' and 'Small Machava.' Laurence was in the 'Big Machava' area, under maximum security.

Guard towers were positioned along the walls, cutting into the thick brick, and curving out from it on either side before protruding upwards three metres above the wall. The towers offered the guards a valuable lookout over the prison's derelict surroundings, through the narrow open slits and a horizontal line of glass at standing height, now broken with shards filling the open holes. A forgotten feel hung like a cloud over the many imprisoned lives that should not have been there in the first place – projecting a cold, uncaring, and very tense atmosphere.

Feeling slightly better after the wash, he was marched back into his open cell within the ten-minute toilet time frame. His metal cuffs were tightened around his red wrists and legs' and once secured, his cell door was slammed shut for the rest of the day, leaving him alone in maddening thought.

The days dragged by, each slower than the last. Sitting in the corner, Laurence's eyes moved around the dark cell, fishing for something to help pass the time. Above his head, in the centre of the white, flaking, concrete ceiling, wires dangled from an old rusty light socket – which had clearly not dispersed light in many dark years. Laurence, sitting in his sweat from the sauna-like temperature, gazed in delirium at the indecipherable writing inscribed on the walls' passing time through the restraint of boredom.

Directly across the corridor from Laurence, a father and his son shared a cell. Together they would stare at him across the tunnel of dark space, with open, silent looks of hatred for him and his white skin – their hatred inherited through years of repression under their white colonists.

'Keep to yourself!' Laurence screamed at them.

Each day fuelled more anger within Laurence, welling up like a volcano ready to erupt – but unable to, and with no constructive way of releasing his raging fury. He had become a caged animal, pacing within his squared cell, his anger now overruling his fear. Laurence waged his anger towards the jail, the hardened guards, the third world order in Mozambique, the desperate feeling of abandonment by the SADF and in turn the South African government, and worst of all the unknown fate of his two loyal friends.

How will I ever get out of this hellhole? He asked himself. No one knows where I am. He was looking for the impossible answer. Silently, he said, 'This is where I will most probably die a lonely death, and be buried in an unmarked grave. I want to die!'

With his handcuffs off, some unknown slip-up from the guards, Laurence launched himself upward, like the wild animal he was, towards the hanging strands of wire. Not caring whether the wires carried current or not, he grabbed hold of the straggly mess, and with a tight fistful of wire he dropped back down to the concrete floor. Somehow shocked to be alive – having expected the wires to be live – he half-heartedly smiled to himself, realizing that the end to his living nightmare had not come. Looking down for quite some time at the two long strands of copper wire insulated in a plastic coating, he wondered what he could do with them.

With plenty of time on his side, he decided to make a necklace, and so he began plaiting the black and white wires together. Weaving the wires with skill, he lettered the necklace with a name – a name that he prayed to daily, asking for strength to see him through his ordeal. In beautiful even letters, the name "JESUS" could be easily seen, the band looked so well made that it could pass for merchandise sold from a shop.

Laurence was forbidden to have anything in his cell other than his ruthless cuffs, which left him no option but to hide his work of art in the pocket of his baggy pants. Holding his new necklace proudly, he stroked the lettering and prayed for his freedom.

Sleep could only be had in a sitting posture, or in a curled up foetal position. There was no cushioning to buffer against the cold, cracked, and yet smooth concrete floor – nor was there a blanket to bundle up against the chill, or a pillow to prop up a weary head. Closing his eyes, even if it was for a few minutes, helped remove his mind from the bars of his prison.

The cellblock was full of crazy and aggressive Africans, who emitted lots of intimidating noises – some having lost their minds in their banishment within concrete and darkness. Some laughed insanely into the encompassing blackness, while others shouted at the walls or banged at the bars – adding further fear to Laurence's deepening nightmare.

'If these walls could talk, they would scream out the suffering from each

26. Mozambique: A journey through hell

foul, dark, locked-up box" and so varying sounds were emitted daily from the zoo-like cages of these trapped animals, and the noise resounded in a dull echo through the cellblock.

Sitting and scratching at itchy, flaking skin, Laurence sat in the heat of his cell, drawing comfort from the cool floor. The shouts and screams travelled their usual paths through the damp stench, while he looked across at his fellow prisoners with revulsion. He mumbled to himself, through the taste of sour rice in his dry mouth, his thoughts were confused – madness seemed to be closing in upon his life of seclusion.

After just over a month of living in the same cell, starved of walks and precious sunlight, the guards opened his cell and led him up the corridor towards the main gate. Laurence weakly dragged his weary legs past keenly-interested African faces, clutching the metal bars as they watched him move slowly past them – the highlight of their day.

When the leading guard pushed the solid main gate, it groaned open and a flood of sunlight poured into the darkness. Laurence winced in pain and his eyes burned as if red-hot pokers had been speared into his unsuspecting sockets. Unable to shield his sensitive eyes from the burning glare – for his hands were still cuffed – he shut them tight and turned his body awkwardly against the sun. He squinted, blinking away the throbbing pain while the guards tugged him forward, latching onto one of his arms. In spite of his body being weak, it tingled with renewed hope, the rays of sunlight warmed his soul and the cool breeze seemed to blow away the damp and dirty smell of the cellblock. He caught sight of a high metal water tower on four metal legs, holding a rectangular tin tank to catch the rainwater, and standing well above the high, thick, brick walls. Besides the grassless ground, it was the only landmark that he saw in his blinded life behind the fortress walls.

They stopped at the cellblock next to his old one, opened the main gate with a similar groan, and marched him back into the corridor of darkness.

The invisible and overpoweringly putrid odour of dampness hit him in the face, forcing him to hesitate with his next step before following more deeply into the new block of cells. Slowly his sore eyes began to adjust to the dark, illuminating a different set of African faces, barred behind identical cells. The guards brought Laurence to a sudden stop halfway down the corridor and opened the vacant cell with a jingle of keys. Once inside, the door was slammed shut, leaving Laurence with his face devoid of all expression and his tortured mind ready to shut down. Leaning against the wall, he slid himself brokenly down onto the red and cracked concrete floor. In a heap, he lowered his head towards his knees and screamed with blood-curdling ferocity, which sounded more like a wounded animal and echoed through the jail, bouncing off the brick walls only to return with a haunting echo. Out came the release of weeks of built-up anger, aggression, and frustration – which seemed to help for the moment, before he lapsed back into boredom.

After a few days in his new cell, he heard a voice at the barred window. Excitedly he broke into conversation with this English-speaking person hidden from view. The stranger had a white, South African accent, he began to ask questions concerning Laurence's well-being.

Laurence soon learned that this man had been sentenced to a life of imprisonment for the role he had played in blowing up a major oil pipeline in Mozambique. Many long years had passed while he languished in the Machava Prison, and he had been long ago forgotten by society. This old prisoner had been granted the freedom to walk in between the cellblocks and converse with fellow inmates. Each day he passed Laurence's cell, striking up a conversation with the deteriorating soldier and gladly offering valuable words of encouragement.

Leaning with his back against Laurence's cell and looking away from his barred window – so as not to create suspicion – the old man spoke to Laurence with his distinguishing South African accent. He sounded clever, with a casual approach, and came across very friendly, with a hardened, rough edge to his voice – and yet his words were kind and seemed to flow from the heart.

'Keep your hopes high – you will be released one day,' he said with sincerity. Laurence, on the other hand, struggled to believe these words. And yet the calming sentence had been offered freely by the friendly, faceless voice of a lost and broken soul.

Sometimes this 50 year-old man, who looked more like 65, would throw pieces of stale Portuguese bread through the cell window, followed by a few loose Palmar cigarettes bound together with an elastic band. They were as stale as the dried bread, but gladly appreciated all the same. On one occasion a tube of toothpaste came flying in, like a gift from heaven, along with a box of Pala Pala matches. Laurence had last tasted toothpaste in South Africa, and was now quite used to the furry feel in his mouth and the pieces of rice wedged between his yellow teeth. Using the toothpaste for the first time in weeks, with his finger as a brush, burned his mouth – but it gave him a clean and refreshed feeling. Sitting as content as a person could, while he puffed on a stale cigarette, he thought about his old friend who cared for him. It brought a lump to his throat – that there was someone out there who took an interest in his well-being, for the first

26. Mozambique: A journey through hell

time in two months. Blowing thick clouds of smoke into the air, Laurence could only wonder if his sentence would also be life. Shuddering at the notion, he diverted his train of thought – not being able to handle the idea of living out his days behind these walls. When he had drawn the last drag from his cigarette, he flicked the butt through his cell window and into the outside world, discarding the evidence from the guard's sight.

When there were no cigarettes or scraps of dry, salty, and chewy Portuguese bread to be tossed into Laurence's cell, the older man still came around to check up on him and pass time with idle chat. This man was a gift from God, placed here to keep Laurence going when all he wanted to do was just curl up and die. Laurence had contemplated escape more times than he could remember. This was the Alcatraz of Africa, where if he managed to somehow escape from his cell and scale the thick high walls, he was still a glowing white face in a sea of black with no sense of direction in this foreign land with a foreign language.

On one occasion the man gave Laurence some really encouraging news.

'The Minister of Foreign Affairs from South Africa, Pik Botha, has met with Samora Machel to negotiate your release,' he said with confidence – in a tone that Laurence had never heard since his confinement. Laurence remained silent, allowing what he had just heard to sink in.

'How do you know?' Laurence said – trying hard not to sound overjoyed, for fear of being let down again.

'I heard it from one of the guards.' Then, in a voice filled with hardened hatred of FRELIMO and the guards loyal to the ruling government, having been a rebel himself in his allegiance with RENAMO, the old man added: 'I hate these fuckers! They are all the same!'

This was great news – if it could be believed – and it gave hope to Laurence's desolate soul.

One day, very unexpectedly, Laurence received one of the most useful gifts he could ever ask for.

'Are you still cuffed?' the old man asked, shouting upward towards the cell window, three metres from the ground.

'*Ja*, I am,' Laurence said, wondering why he would bother to ask.

A few seconds passed, and then a small metal object bounced across the cell floor, landing close to Laurence's feet. After a closer look, he realized it was a key and immediately he went to work with his cuffed hands, scrambling to pick it up.

The key was a small piece of smooth, crude-looking wire, stronger and thicker than a hairpin and gunmetal grey in colour. Picking up this well-used piece of wire, Laurence played with it through his fingers and tried to get a good grip on it. He was sure that it had been crafted by the old man and used by him to also grant his limbs a little freedom.

'You have lots of time to practise unlocking your cuffs!'

Laurence thanked him for the precious gift – second only to freedom – and caught a glimpse of the Good Samaritan as he wound his way between the cellblocks in the fresh air. He was tall and thin, dressed in baggy clothes and long pants, with a wrinkled and very weather-beaten face – aging him beyond his years. His face had a Portuguese look to it, with a rough, grey stubble of beard and long, dirty, greying black, curly hair that had not seen a comb or a brush in many years, hanging greasily down to his stooped shoulders. From the short distance, Laurence saw this man smile through a mouth of missing teeth and a grey, untidy moustache, until he became lost behind another concrete cellblock.

Here was a South African man who had chosen to live in Mozambique, and because of his acts of sabotage, he had been stripped of his freedom and sentenced to serve out the remainder of his life behind the high walls of the Machava Maximum Security Prison. His family knew of his whereabouts, but because of his life sentence they were forbidden to visit him. The only outside contact that reached into his isolation came in the form of parcels. These small boxes, packed with tinned food and cigarettes, helped break the terrible monotony of prison life and added a little excitement at the same time.

On one of his many visits to the outside window of Laurence's cell, he told a story of an African civilian who was also serving time in the prison. FRELIMO soldiers entered into a prominent RENAMO stronghold in a rural area of Mozambique, and to win the local population's support they began distributing handfuls of rice to the hungry community. An angry man, loyal to the South African-backed RENAMO party, stepped forward out of the thin and undernourished crowd with his dented enamel mug to accept his handout of the rice. When his cup was filled, he threw the rice at the feet of the ruthless soldiers with a fierce look of hatred and revulsion. For this act of disrespect to the ruling FRELIMO government and its soldiers, he was handed a five-year jail sentence, with no court ruling or records to document his entry into Machava.

After listening intently to this story, Laurence began to use his time to practise unlocking his barbaric cuffs, which for the most part had been locked tightly to his wrists and ankles. After many hours of trial and error, coupled with frustration and swearing, Laurence finally mastered the art of opening his cuffs and re-cuffing himself within a 15 second time frame. The freedom it gave him to have his hands dangling loosely around his body and his feet apart transformed him in to a new person, it rejuvenated his spirit and lifted his soul well beyond the bars, granting his limbs the liberty they rightfully deserved.

This key became Laurence's treasure, he concealed it carefully in the inner pocket of his pants, along with the odd cigarette and box of matches. It also became the tool to scratch days served into the red wall – which left a white scar below the paint.

'Another day for fuckall!' Laurence mouthed as he marked another stripe of six – the seventh crossing through it on a diagonal to record a completed week. He had transferred his 35 five days in confinement from his first cell, along with the 14 days in the bush camps and headquarters of FRELIMO. These lines, cut like grafitti into the prison walls, displayed a lengthy picture of confined torture.

How many more lines will I have to scar into this new wall before I will be free? Laurence asked himself, through silent tears.

He generally released his cuffs at night, for fear of a fellow inmate reporting his actions to a guard' but if he had to unlock the cuffs in daylight, he made sure it was away from the untrusting, watchful eyes of those in his cellblock. He was the only prisoner to be cuffed, eating with the humiliation of a wild monkey – his hands locked together as he scooped rice with trembling fingers into his dry mouth.

At night he tried to do some stretches and pushups when his strength allowed, and occasionally he pulled himself up by holding on to two of the four bars from the outside window. When his hands could not hold the metal bars any longer he sank to his knees and, with tears in his eyes, he prayed to God. His prayer begged for freedom, promising his life to the Lord if this miracle were ever granted.

When the main gate groaned its usual rusty warning, it gave Laurence the precious time he needed to relock the cuffs to his wrists. Once the prying eyes of the guards had checked the cells and Laurence's cuffs, they left, closing out the warm rays of sunshine that had stolen their way through the slightly ajar main gate at the far end of the corridor. The door grinding shut was the signal Laurence listened for and when it did, he whipped his cuffs off like a professional' and with a wry smile he enjoyed his newfound freedom.

The night blanketed the already-dark cells in further darkness, like a mineshaft with an abandoned tunnel, and the prisoners settled down for the night. With the cellblock in dead silence, Laurence could hear the sound of rats scurrying across the cement floor. He sat and watched these huge rodents fighting over pieces of rice that had spilled from the wheelbarrow during mealtime. Scratching and splashing echoed from the toilet area' more and more of these monstrous rats surfaced from the sewer and entered the cellblock on a scavenge – sending a feverish chill through each wide-awake prisoner.

These cunning creatures darted in and out of the cells, creating pandemonium as they went. Obscenities were shouted after them, followed by a slow kick – an effort to scare them off. With his eyes half closed in narrow slits, Laurence kept his focus on these dirty pests as best as he could while they cut their way through the cells – another fitting scene for a movie thriller. Their white teeth were as long as a cat's, and they were not at all scared to challenge the prisoners for a grain of rice. Only when they got too close for comfort would a plate be banged against the bars or the floor, to send them on their way. And only when the scratching disappeared, with a splash of water in the toilet area, did Laurence's tension dissipate. Plucking up the courage, he lowered himself onto the cold floor, and with hesitation he closed his eyes, blinked them back open, and then shut them again.

On many occasions, singing flowed from the blackness of the cells, making Laurence feel as if he were in a different place at a different time. The beautiful voices, singing in a totally foreign African tongue, with a sound that could be mistaken for happiness, brought comfort and soothing to his spirit while reassuring him that he was not alone. The melody traversed the bare corridor and echoed from the walls and through the cells, reaching the welcoming ears of the 17 prisoners incarcerated in Laurence's cellblock.

There were nights when the unmistakable rattle of automatic gunfire reached their alert ears. The sound had been carried the distance by the stillness of the night, and became just another normal nightly noise.

Daily the guards came and went with their usual arrogance and open display of hatred. There was one guard who was different from the rest, and showed Laurence compassion. It seemed so out-of-place to see a guard act with sympathy in this ruthless setting, where guards did their job with complete disregard for human rights. The guard with kindness in his heart gave his name to Laurence – 'John,' or 'Joao' in Portuguese, and in doing so, he offered his trust and friendship.

'Where am I?' Laurence asked. His tired eyes focused on the guard – not knowing what the answer would mean anyway.

'You are in Machava.'

Indeed Laurence did not know what that meant, but the word 'Machava' sounded vulgar and guttural – every bit of a death trap.

Joao entered Laurence's cell and came over to him with a ring full of keys, he immediately unlocked his cuffs, and then left the cell without a word. Joao had no idea that Laurence had been able to undo the cuffs for the past few days, and Laurence certainly was not about to let him in on that secret. Laurence appreciated the humane gesture, but still he could not trust a single soul – let alone a FRELIMO guard. On the completion of his shift, Joao returned and locked Laurence's cuffs back onto his waiting wrists.

Laurence cast his mind back to his last cellblock and now believed that it was Joao who had managed to have him transferred from the shouts of madness, anger, and hatred, into a more peaceful cellblock. He remembered asking Joao to get the prisoner opposite his last cell moved – for he had purposely bumped into him in the corridor, having a blatant hatred of Laurence's white skin.

'He is a threat to my life,' Laurence had told Joao' and now here he was in a more stable environment, thanks to the actions of the one and only sympathetic FRELIMO guard.

He seemed so different from his colleagues for he treated prisoners with respect and dignity – which Laurence was not at all used to. Joao carried himself through the prison with such a distinct and calming difference instead of angrily barking orders of intimidation like the other guards. While he was on duty, it was a pleasant change – giving Laurence a chance to lower his guard and relax as best he could.

On one of the days, Laurence made his way down the corridor under his usual armed escort towards the toilet area for his allotted ten minutes. One of the guards, walking up the corridor, came right up to Laurence and stopped, then, without any warning, he spat a thick chunk of phlegm that landed menacingly upon his shirt. Anger welled up in Laurence, 'you black bastard' he cursed in silence, but before he could react, he was pushed on by another guard, out of harm's way, towards the toilet area.

The cold wash of water running over his itchy skin did nothing to hide the damp smell that covered the cellblock and lingered in his dirty, smelly clothes, reaching deep into his nostrils. The sticky humidity was unbearable' the sweat poured off him like a marathon runner chasing the finish line. His wash-down quickly forgotten, he sat back in his cell drenched in a pool of sweat, looking ahead into oblivion, with a stare frozen in his gaunt and pale face.

Cockroaches the size of big beetles darted across the floor, and then suddenly disappeared with fright into another part of the cellblock. Large flies and mosquitoes circled the cells, adding more anger and resentment to his helpless situation – especially when they chose to settle on his sweaty face.

'*Fok weg!*' he screamed while trying to swat one of these bastard pests.

When the days turned to nights, and back again to days, Laurence began to feel the effects of isolation taking its toll – starved of all the vital ingredients of a healthy life.

Through lack of exercise, nutrition, and vitamin D, Laurence began to grow tired and weak, and suffered severe headaches from malnutrition. His already-thin frame had lost so much weight' he survived on rice alone, and some days went without because the guards forgot to feed him, or chose not to. When he dozed off in spells of delirium, he would jolt awake at the slightest noise – only to realize that he was still living inside his worst nightmare. Unable to do anything to help his hunger pains, or the dizziness, he rested his head upon his hand – which he used as a pillow against the cold concrete – and then shut his eyes again. He continually itched at his black beard and his head – from the lice and fleas that had nestled within his long, matted, and straggly hair and bit and pestered him at will. When Laurence chose to stand, he rose slowly, as if he were an old man. He reached out with blurred vision to the metal bars, to steady himself as he straightened his arched body into an upright position. The fluctuating temperatures and damp, sauna-like conditions had been cruel on Laurence's bones – giving him the feeling that arthritis had set in. His pants hung from his thin waist, held partially up by a thin, dirty string that circled crudely below his belly button. He stood and stared through the row of bars with a death wish – for death had to be better than this life beyond hell.

When the door unexpectedly groaned open, Laurence quickly snapped out of his trance and tightened his cuffs, as if he were performing a well-perfected trick. From his cell window, which he could barely see out of, a flood of sunshine shone in, circling the floor with comforting warmth and chasing away the shadows. Laurence sat in the glow, basking in the soothing feel of the rays as they needled their way into his pale, white skin. It was not long before the rays arced away, leaving Laurence deprived of his few minutes of pleasure and allowing the shadows to creep back and reclaim their space.

Laurence prayed and prayed, but his prayers went unanswered. Again he asked himself: Does anyone know where I am? Does anyone care, or have I just been forgotten about? These thoughts were a cry for help, and they circulated continually around his disoriented mind.

How am I ever going to get out of this stinking shit hole, or will I ever? Laurence tortured himself with the unanswerable question – he allowed himself to slide down the dirty red wall, holding his face tightly within his clenched, grubby hands as if he were trying to squeeze an answer from his muddled head. He began to feel that he was losing his mind, trapped within the claustrophobic walls of the cell, and he tried to find some encouragement to fight against his depression. He was careful not to allow his thinking to skip too far into the distant future, for that would only expose him to more torment at the agony of being abandoned by the land that he had carried a loaded rifle for. Subdued in desperation, with his head bowed and shielded from view, fleeting tears rolled down his bearded face until the words of the old man resounded loudly back to him: 'Keep your hopes up high.' And with that mental boost, Laurence felt the strength return to his frail body.

On Joao's next guard shift, he walked up to Laurence's cell and greeted him with a broad smile.

'You must be prepared to go home.'

Laurence looked back at him, not understanding or believing what Joao had just said.

'I don't know when, but it will be sometime soon.'

Can this be true? Laurence wondered' hope flooded his withered soul.

He waited patiently as the days turned to weeks, but there was no follow up on the hopeful news' it was like waiting at an abandoned train station. There was always that faint glimmer of hope that maybe one day a train might come past – in the same way that maybe one day he would be led down the tracks of the corridor and taken away from this station, which had been abandoned for so long.

Again Joao told Laurence that he would be going home. Laurence looked at him with disbelief, resigned to the fact that only a miracle could free him from Machava. Another week dragged by, with no change. Freedom seemed like a mirage – he could see it and sense it, but as he drew closer to it, it was gone. It was another cruel blow to him, adding heartache and disillusionment to his nearly 13 weeks in captivity.

The third time that Joao visited Laurence, the words he offered were the same as the previous time.

'Prepare to go home!' He said, with a similar tone as the last time. It was hard for Laurence to believe him now – the words had lost their meaning. And yet deep down he wanted to believe – and had to for the sake of his sanity. Laurence knew that Joao was only passing on information that he had heard. With just as much hope, Joao wanted to see Laurence free from his suffering.

In the morning the guards came to Laurence's cell and told him yet again to prepare for home.

What do I need to prepare? He would be ready in a flash – there were only his old dirty clothes and rotten-smelling takkies.

Two hours passed, and then Laurence heard the unfamiliar sound of a vehicle coming to a stop in front of his cellblock. His heart began to race, bits and pieces of what Joao had been trying to tell him now made a clearer picture in his dazed mind. He looked at his cell wall, he had now cut 90 lines into the red paint – 41 of them representing days in his present cell, over 2000 hours of hell with no end in sight. No words can come close to describing it, unless you have lived it.

The door opened abruptly, and a bunch of guards walked briskly down the corridor and stopped at Laurence's cell. For a split second they looked him over, before one turned the key and swung the door open. They summoned Laurence to follow, which he did, shuffling down the length of the block like a man four times his age, the guards trailing him at his slow pace. He came to a halt at the closed door of the main gate, not sure what to do until a guard shoved his way past and pushed the heavy door open. The sun immediately lashed at him, drilling into his eyes and blinding him. So he walked with his eyes tightly closed and they burned through a black cloud of pain.

Where am I going? Can this be what Joao has been telling me all along? Is this really happening? Laurence wondered, with his mind racing out of control.

Suddenly the warmth and fresh air had blown the stench of the cellblock from his nostrils. Could this be freedom he was smelling?

A guard reached for his hands and released him from his chains. Thoughts were racing through his mind with the speed of a roller coaster: Am I actually going to be freed? Can this be true or is this just another mirage?

Focusing on the white three-ton truck with a big metal canopy enclosing the back of the vehicle, Laurence moved towards it' upon closer examination, it looked more like a United Nations vehicle of Russian origin. It now felt like years since Laurence had last seen a vehicle, let alone ridden in one.

Slowly he ambled to the back of the battered and scratched vehicle, and towards the open doors. Climbing up and peering in, he saw two white men in separate cages. They looked demoralized, and cowered deeper in their cages, their scruffy, black and ginger, bearded faces half hidden by long, matted, dirty hair. Their sunken eyes, underlined by black bags of sleepless nights, stared from their red cages in the direction of the white man standing in front of them – equally as dirty and thin as they. Laurence's pale face stared harder, and with a blank expression, into these two square cells' and then in a split second all three sets of eyes lit up in unison with a sparkle of recognition, and their mouths fell open with priceless, heartfelt smiles.

Laurence could not believe his own eyes. He blinked to make sure that they were not playing a foul trick on him. His heart pounded like a drum. He laughed anxiously, for before his blurry vision sat Paul and Sandor.

For a few stunned seconds, there were just three broad, silent, overjoyed smiles. The deathly silence spoke volumes. They could see the suffering in the subdued body language, their smiles only temporarily overshadowed the horrific past. Some of their fear was released through the bond that these brothers in arms had forged – a unity that would always be even stronger than any that had been formed with the rest of Platoon 3.

Laurence was shoved into the third cell in the back of the truck – the fourth remaining unoccupied. Once in his cage, the red door was slammed shut on him, as a zookeeper would lock up a fierce animal. The back door was closed too, leaving the three again in darkness' but at least this time there was happiness within the blackness.

'I thought you guys were dead!' Laurence blurted. 'Shit, it is good to see you guys again!'

'Great to see you, Laurence. Fuck, we never expected to see you again!'

'Where are we going?' Paul asked, his eyes close to tears.

'I think we are going home!' Laurence said. For the first time he believed those words.

'Home, home,' one of the others said – as though he was trying to fathom the true meaning of that.

The dirty white vehicle exited through the big, grey, metal gates and around the circular, cracked, concrete base below the flagpole, it made its way up the potholed road towards the tarmac. Machava was now behind them, but would forever be with them. Oblivious to everything but themselves, they did not feel the jolt and took no notice of Maputo that filtered through the rusty cracks of the jail box in jumbled segments of differing shapes and faded colours. The three of them sat shell-shocked, still not able to believe that they were together again after two months of being apart. The noises they heard seemed strange to them.

Africans walked freely along the pavement, while trucks, busses and cars hustled along the roadway, hooting and jockeying for position and spilling out clouds of diesel fumes. Over a few deep coughs brought on by the dust, they continued to gaze blankly, managing to catch a flash of colour among the neglect of the city buildings. Everything seemed to rush by with the speed of a video played on fast forward. The driver and the soldier, who guarded them with his AK-47, conversed with each other in Portuguese, and Paul, Laurence, and Sandor watched the built-up city turn to open bush and Maputo disappear through the cracks.

The darkened journey took them from Machava to the FRELIMO headquarters half an hour away. Once inside the base, they were herded from the vehicle and taken inside the main office, where more soldiers met them.

Laurence was pleasantly surprised to see Joao, who was also in the office waiting like the other soldiers to meet with them. They were handed back their possessions – which were only the watches they had been wearing on the day of their capture. Laurence took hold of his Mortimer watch, the watch that he had begun his National Service with – and after turning it over a few times in his hand, he looked towards Joao. Making good on his promise that, if he were granted freedom, he would hand over his watch to him, he stretched out his arm. On the one hand, he had won his freedom, and on the other hand, Joao could now tell the time – ironically, in a dysfunctional country where very little ran on time.

'You three are now going home!' Joao said, through his broken English and with a hand firmly clasping his new watch.

They were now fully aware that they were on the road to freedom. As the vehicle bounced and jolted over the potholed tarmac, they thought about their freedom, and what the word meant. This word, which had been a stranger to their world for so long, seemed to become a reality as the vehicle sped across the Mozambican interior. After six hours of non-stop driving and six hours of standing, they eventually came to a stop at the Ressano Garcia border post. The back of the vehicle was opened up, and out of the cages the three South African soldiers crawled like three drugged animals, having been transported to a new game reserve.

'Where are we?' one of them asked nervously.

'Look over there!' another said. He pointed to a flag waving at them in the late afternoon breeze. A short walk from the guard post, they saw the unmistakable orange, white, and blue flying ever so proudly from a white flag pole, planted firmly in South African soil. The sheer sight of this flag, after the momentous turmoil of the last three months, brought a lump to their dry throats. The weak smiles in their sunken faces were a priceless picture, and they stood frozen like three statues – still not believing that they were about to be released.

'*Ek gaan hom bliksem!*' – I am going to hit him! – Sandor abruptly blurted, pointing at a FRELIMO soldier as they waited by the border gate, under the close scrutiny of the Mozambican soldiers.

Under armed escort, they began walking with excited and confident steps towards the South African border post, separated by a short stretch of roadway in no-man's-land. One of the FRELIMO guards followed the three, his AK-47 aimed at their backs, until they reached the South African side at Komatiepoort. Once safely back on South African soil, the three soldiers turned and directed their scowls of anger and hatred towards the guard and his FRELIMO government. Sandor turned with the agility of a rattlesnake and faced the guard, with three months of uncontrollable anger raging inside him. He began to push him backward, towards the corrupt government of Mozambique, and then, with the suddenness of a lighting strike, he lashed out at the soldier – connecting him square in the face and knocking him to the tarmac in a crumpled heap. Paul and Laurence walked up to Sandor and grabbed him on each arm, and together they turned and took the last few steps into their freedom. A South African policeman was quick to react, and also grabbed hold of Sandor, pulling him over to the safety of the South African side.

'It was right that you slapped him,' the Afrikaans border policeman said.

It was 12 December – exactly three months to the day of their fateful capture – that they walked away free men. When the border gate opened and they crossed back into South Africa, it felt like the gates of heaven had opened and welcomed them in, they sighed with relief – as if trying to shrug off the last three months.

Together they walked up to the three policemen standing at the border post and identified themselves as the captured soldiers.

'We know about you guys, and have been expecting you,' one of them said through a thick South African accent.

'You all look hungry. Do you want to eat?' the police sergeant asked.

'Yes, we are starving!'

Laurence was given a tin of corned beef, which he consumed in a couple of minutes, almost swallowing it whole. He was a lot faster than Paul and Sandor, who still were noisily scraping the sides of the tins when Laurence was licking his greasy and salty lips. After the meal, Laurence ran a steaming hot bath and began cleaning himself' as he sank into the soothing warmth, it washed away his mental torture and physical hardship. Now he had to face the aftermath of his trauma. Feeling like a king and looking like a new person, his eyes explored the base. The small camp was neat and tidy, like all South African bases, with a few bungalows and a well-stocked kitchen. It was ringed by a manicured lawn – so green from all the watering, in contrast to the burned, dry, dusty surface immediately surrounding the camp, looking like an oasis in the middle of an arid desert.

A major from the SADF welcomed Paul, Laurence, and Sandor home, casting a careful glance over them.

'Get ready to move out of the camp within the next few minutes,' he said to them, in an unusually polite fashion. They all climbed into the white Nissan Skyline and left the camp in a hurry, in the direction of Pretoria, to 1-Military Hospital in Voortrekkerhoogte. After six hours of mostly comatose sleep, they arrived at South Africa's main military hospital.

It was still 12 December when the weak soldiers walked into the hospital under the light of a new moon. This new moon shone a silver light of renewed hope towards a fresh start, casting a shadow upon them every now and then.

They were immediately placed under quarantine in separate rooms, in beds covered in starched, fresh, pearl-white sheets spread over a soft foam mattress. They glady exchanged their prison clothes for thin hospital gowns, and they climbed onto a bed for the first time in ages. They rested with peace of mind, safe and sound while the attentive and sympathetic young white nurses hovered over them, reacting to their beck and call. Within minutes the nurses hooked them up to an intravenous drip, feeding them the fluids they so badly needed. Then she took blood samples, which were quickly whisked away to the technicians in the laboratory. They also took urine samples' the three were forbidden to eat – they had to rely solely on the intravenous drips until the doctors had seen their blood tests. Friendly doctors in pure white lab coats entered each of their rooms and did a thorough examination of each of them. It was punishment enough for them to remain awake through the examination' they drifted in and out of sleep – making up for lost time over the past three months. When they woke they were startled with fear, wide eyed, and disoriented' and they fidgeted, trying to place themselves in their new surroundings, for their minds were still caged behind the dirty barred cells.

The doctors carried out more routine checks on them, they studied the printouts from the electrocardiograms, and the hourly blood pressure readings, and made a priority of restoring their health. When the laboratory results came back, they discovered that they were suffering from a severe lack of nutrition, as well as dehydration. On top of that, Paul had food poisoning.

While they passed the time, confined to their beds and waiting for their strength to return, a colonel from Intelligence stepped into their rooms. He had been sent by the head of the SADF to question Paul, Laurence, and Sandor on the set-up of army bases inside Mozambique. He probed and dug for answers to better explain its strengths and weaknesses. They answered the barrage of questions as best they could before they succumbed to sleep. The colonel sat before them in a chair, stared deep in to each set of drooping eyes, and instructed them to never retell their stories – not even to their fellow platoon soldiers at 4-SAI. In the eyes and ears of the tight-lipped SADF, it was to remain as if nothing ever happened during those three months in Mozambique. They were all quite sure that they had been involved in a top-secret prisoner exchange in order to buy their freedom. Nothing was ever said officially, but – knowing the brutality of FRELIMO – Paul, Laurence and Sandor's freedom could only have been granted at a high price.

After three days in the hospital, the soldiers gained weight and strength in body and mind. They had walked into the hospital having lost at least 20 kilograms, Laurence weighed 65 kilograms compared to the 85 kilograms he weighed while still inside the Kruger Park. Their rib cages showed through their pale skin, which was pulled tightly over the bumps of bone encasing their chests. Their faces, after being shaved clean, looked long, thin, and pointy, their eyes were sunken and seemed to droop down without a hint of expression. Their arms and legs were extremely thin, for the muscle had long ago wasted away. They looked more like three sticks than three well-trained and ultra-fit South African soldiers.

The nurses looked after them with keen interest and attention to their needs. With faces of sympathy and caring hands, they brought hearty meals of soup, jelly, and ice cream, and a smile of hope and encouragement.

Gleefully they dug into their first-class meals, armed with sparkling cutlery, they spooned warm soup into their drooling mouths and felt a million miles away from the blackened and dented aluminum plates filled with the sour-tasting rice.

In their beds of tangled tubes, and overtaken by a deep weariness, they briefly managed to see the faces of Lieutenant Bam and Grant, then sleep once again took them into a zone of warm comfort.

On the fourth day of their newly granted freedom, they were told that the SADF had arranged three flight tickets to Durban, East London, and Kimberley – to re-unite them with their families, who had already been notified of their release.

Still weak and overwhelmed at the ever-quickening pace of life in the outside world, they were transported by car to Jan Smuts Airport in Johannesburg, where they waited to be torn apart again – this time, however, in the opposite direction of home. The three of them stood together and watched the people rushing by, talking loudly, it somehow stunned them into withdrawal. They stood silenced by the agitating throngs of people, knowing that the pain and anguish was the same for the soldier on either side.

The closeness they shared had strengthened through each day behind bars, the three months had felt more like three years, and had forged an unwavering bond that would be impossible to break. They did not need to retell their stories to each other – they knew the deep-seated fears and mental scars that remained in their innermost being. Now all that mattered was that they had all survived, and were waiting for the next step in their journey of freedom – the most important one: to see family and home again.

They departed one by one, stepping onto their respective domestic flights, leaving behind two friends – the only ones to fully know and understand the living hell that they had made it through.

Walking onto the plane was a nerve-racking experience for Laurence, he felt the eyes of the strangers running over his vulnerable body, and he hunted anxiously for his seat – a place for him to hide from the self-conscious but curious stares. Finding his place, he threw himself down, withdrawing into himself, and fidgeting with his fingers as he scratched his head and arms in awkward movements – totally overwhelmed with the continual influx of people onto the aircraft. He felt trapped in his cushioned seat and sank deeper down, hiding behind the seat in front of him in an attempt to escape the piercing stares. It was as though he was back in his cell – only this time he was handcuffed to his seat – for the safety belt was locked tightly around his waist. Nervously he shifted his posture and tried to shake off this overwhelming feeling of helplessness.

With each noise, Laurence jolted, trying to place his whereabouts before sinking back into his seat. When the plane eventually touched down, his body was overwhelmed – his heart began to race and goosebumps spread rapidly over his skin.

I made it I am home! He said to himself, the words reverberated loudly through his mind. He wanted to scream with excitement at having finally reached the milestone that always seemed beyond him. He stared through the small window at the terminal building, knowing that his family waited eagerly inside – both nervous and excited to see him again, back in the safety of his hometown of East London.

Once inside the airport terminal, he caught sight of his family, standing in a tight group 30 metres away. His still-very-weak body began to shake, and he walked faster and faster towards his family, who in turn narrowed the gap and rushed towards him. They circled him like a cloak, shielding him from the inquisitive onlookers. Those who saw him could not have imagined in their wildest dreams what he had been freed from, or what nightmares lay in wait for him.

His legs became weak and he swayed like a drunken bum – overcome with the beautiful feeling of love that his family was showering upon him. He babbled and choked on words with tears and heartfelt emotion, as his blurry-eyed family led him out of the airport into the calm afternoon. The warm breeze helped to dry some of the joyful tears. Laurence's older brother Jan walked next to him, holding him up as they crossed the parking lot. Every now and then Laurence's legs buckled and when he suddenly sagged, Jan came to his rescue and fought to hold his lightheaded brother up. Once they reached the car, the true reality of his homecoming set in.

I am home, I have dreamed of this moment for three long months!

Like an excited old man, Laurence climbed into the car and they set off for Jan's place. He sat quietly and watched the countryside race by. The colours from the open terrain seemed so much richer as they jumped out at him – it had been more than five months since he had last been here. The simple beauty of neatly-ploughed fields, with mounds of fresh upturned earth, tall trees, and long, thick shoots of grass blowing in the breeze – the clear sky an ocean blue – held his mesmerized stare as Jan drove. Jan looked proudly back and forth between his younger brother and the smooth tarmac.

After a short drive from the city, they drove into the residential area and made their way to Jan's house. Laurence nearly collapsed at the sight of the table, covered from one end to the other with food and looking as though his family had prepared for Christmas a few weeks too early. They took their seats around this feast and bowed their heads in prayer – giving thanks to the Lord for sparing Laurence his life and returning him safely to them. His hands clenched tightly below the table, Laurence closed his eyes and said a prayer: 'I thank God, for giving me another chance to be with my family.'

He felt like a king, sitting at the head of the table, digging into the array of food – from cold meat, bread, and cheese to chicken and steak. He was overwhelmed, and had to leave the table. Standing on the front porch in the cool afternoon air, he broke down again.

After a satisfying meal, and one of the most memorable days in his 19 year life, he closed his eyes – with only a bright future beaming down on him, for life now would only be getting better with each passing day.

With the deepest and most rewarding sleep behind him, Laurence had breakfast with his family and after a few more laughs over hot coffee and eggs and bacon, he was driven back to the airport. In a new frame of mind, he hugged his family goodbye and boarded a domestic flight to Johannesburg for the next exciting reunion – with his friends from Bravo Company's Platoon 3.

Laurence met up with Paul and Sandor at the airport, and with a high-ranking officer they were escorted to a military car, and driven to Middelburg to serve out the remaining four days of their National Service. Happy to be together again, they all experienced the same overwhelming feeling when the gates of 4-SAI opened and allowed them in. Lieutenant Bam was summoned to lead his three troops back to their old bungalow filled with soldiers waiting eagerly to welcome them back.

It was 16 December 1985, and Platoon 3 was moments away from being complete again – a day that Paul, Laurence, Sandor, and the rest of the platoon, never dreamed we would still be in uniform to experience.

From a distance they saw Lieutenant Bam walking very quickly towards them. The father had come to welcome his lost sons and lead them back to their expectant brothers-in-arms.

The time had come to greet their fellow soldiers' and then it would soon be time to bid farewell, and turn their backs on their horror, and focus on their futures.

Paul, Laurence, and Sandor had been given a bright, new, second chance at life, and only they could fully comprehend the insanity that had nagged at them for three long months. No one else – unless they too have been through something similar – can come close.

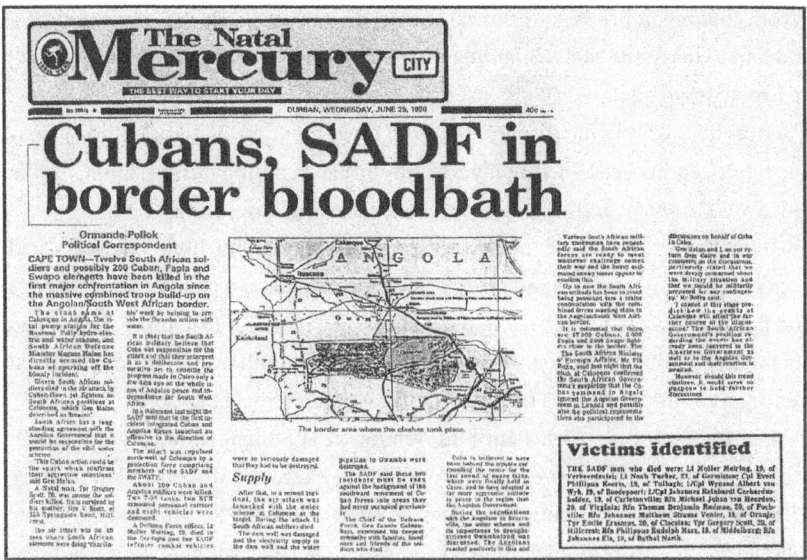

1988. The escalation in the war that triggered the author's last call-up.

27

Soldiering on
1988

In 1986 and again in 1987 I was called-up for Citizen Force service in Burgersfort and Tzaneen respectively. Both call-ups proved uneventful

On 30 June 1988, while at work at the OK Bazaars in Ladysmith, I picked up a copy of the *Daily News*. I scanned the front page, and saw the only picture, of passport size, of a young teenager's smiling face. Suddenly I froze I knew who that was – it was Greg from Hillcrest and I knew that something terrible had happened. I looked at the caption which confirmed it: 'Natal casualty of Angolan clash' and the main headline read: 'Stray Cuban bomb killed SA soldiers.'

I was in a state of shock and could hardly it was true, for I had only spoken to Greg a few weeks back at a drunken beer fest. I read through the list of the 11 victims which confirmed the horror of the bombing raid – the bombs supposedly had been aimed at the Calueque dam wall. Some had struck the target but others had overshot their mark. The troops were positioned by their vehicles, oblivious to the danger, as a Cuban MiG-23 fighter plane swooped down and dropped its bombs. One exploded between the vehicles and blew both it and them to smithereens.

Not for many years had so many South African soldiers been killed in a single day. Numbed, as if I had been there in the aftermath of this attack, I wandered away losing myself in the aisles of the store while I silently gathered my thoughts for a young soldier who could so easily have been me.

A few days after this unsettling news, I received a telegram from the SADF, calling me up for another two months. I thought about the timing, and knew for certain it was definitely connected in some way to the deaths. It seemed so odd to all of a sudden read about Angola in the newspapers – a subject, along with the ongoing border war in SWA – that had remained hidden from the South African public for decades. It seemed that the public, for the first time, was being allowed to read what was in fact happening in the operational area.

With my telegram in hand, I decided to phone Pretoria for the hell of it – to find out if I was destined for the border. I got hold of an Afrikaans man, who refused to tell me straight-out, but nevertheless asked me a telling question.

'Have you been watching the news?' he said.

'No,' I quickly replied.

'Start watching it,' he bluntly said, ending the conversation.

Back at my flat, I made a point of catching the news' and when I did, I realized what the man had meant. South Africans were dying in Angola, I knew for sure that I was also heading there, back to the place I had come to hate with such passion. My gut felt empty and my legs weakened – a feeling of catastrophic destruction came into my thoughts, together with the strange feeling that something really bad was about to happen to me.

I was quick to contact Wayne, who had also received a call-up, together with a few more Durban friends from Platoon 3. This news certainly perked me up, and made me feel slightly more secure about heading to the war zone.

I decided to move all my belongings out of my flat and into Alain's – a good friend, and a manager in the district team based in Ladysmith. Why I did this I don't know, unless I was acting on the fear of becoming a casualty of war. When I left Ladysmith for Hillcrest, I had that same feeling: that I most probably would not be returning' or, if I were lucky enough to, I would return a changed man. It was an odd feeling, and one that I could not place, but coming from my gut, I had to believe it.

In mid July I met Wayne at the Durban train station in uniform, quite drunk and with all my gear in my kit bag, ready to begin my third two month call-up. My beret sat awkwardly perched on top of my long-haired civilian head. I swayed slightly from a day of vodka, sun, and swimming at the Shongweni dam. There was lots of commotion on the platform, hundreds of troops milled about, all of them waiting to take the same ride to Pretoria. Steve, a good friend of mine from Hillcrest, had everyone in stitches as he paraded around with my beret on top of his blonde, curly mop of hair, shouting orders and volunteering to go in someone's place. It seemed to break the ice and the nervous smiles plastered across most of the troops faces' they forced a laugh at Steve and his crazy antics. It was also really good to have my brother John there to add moral support and wish me well with one of the firmest handshakes I had ever experienced – a sure testament to his iron-willed character. With no one seeing how sick I felt inside – even though the alcohol did wonders to lift my spirits – I waved farewell to my friends, and Wayne and I boarded the train.

'Tickets, tickets!' the conductor called.

'What do you mean tickets? We are going to a camp!' I shouted rudely – influenced by the alcohol.

'If you have not got a ticket, get off!' he said' and so we had no choice but to get off.

Back on the platform, I told Wayne: 'When the train starts moving, let's just run like mad and jump on!' which he agreed to.

27. Soldiering on 1988

The whistle blew and the train started to move in a chain reaction, while each carriage was pulled forward as if in slow motion. Our eyes waiting for the right moment, we watched it pick up speed.

'Now!' I shouted, and we launched ourselves towards the train, throwing our kit in and then following it with our bodies – we dived through open windows, helped on by fellow troops. Whistles instantly blew, and were followed up with shouts that brought the train to an abrupt halt. The conductor and platform guard entered the train and in a stern voice told Wayne and me to *'Klim uit!'* – Get off! which we obligingly did, finding ourselves back on the platform with no way of getting to camp.

Those on the platform and in the train were really enjoying the amusement, as if it were live entertainment. Wayne and I were like two clumsy clowns, running circles around the train personnel – who certainly did not see an ounce of humour in our antics.

Standing on the platform, we watched our fellow troops disappear with the train into the distance, leaving us unsure how we would go about reaching our camp in Pretoria.

'Just apologize, and then they will issue another ticket,' the platform guard told us. Wayne and I, along with my brother John, Steve, and a few other friends from Hillcrest, headed for the ticket office. Wayne and I had always looked at life as divided into plans – A, B, C. Having no tickets, Plan A had failed, getting thrown off the train, Plan B too had been a disaster. We had no choice but to go with Plan C, and so we dug deep within ourselves and apologized.

'No problem' here's two tickets. The next train leaves in two hours.' The guard spoke as if nothing had ever happened' and he had never met us before, and was genuinely happy to help us out. Plan C had worked very well, and had saved our skins. Not wanting to miss this train, we killed time for an hour and a half – until our train was destined to leave.

Two hours later we were finally on our way towards Pretoria and the camp at 1-RNT, wondering what this mechanized unit held in store for us. On arriving in Pretoria we boarded a Samil that was ferrying troops to the tent city of 1-RNT. We entered in a billow of dust, as the wind tore across the bare openness. Immediately we gave our names, numbers and rank – which were followed by the signing out of an R4 and any other military gear we required.

It was great to see familiar faces from the old Platoon 3. There were thousands of us milling around with rifles all wondering what this mass call-up meant.

'Do you think we are going up in Ratels?' we asked each other – a question that had to be answered in the affirmative, with all the rampant rumours that were spreading from troop to troop. Then an order was shouted to assemble into companies, and the rumours continued. The companies were broken down further into platoons, and then into sections. Latching onto our old friends, we formed a section with six of the originals from Platoon 3: Macky, John, Brian, Bolt, Van Rensburg, and me. We got to know Riaan, an Afrikaner, who wanted to join our section. He had previously been involved in Operation *Askari*. Upon learning this, we knew immediately what he had been through, and that he would not let us down. Vossie, who had been with me in Delta Coy in 1-SAI in 1984, became our Section Leader, old Nic became a rifleman, and Piet the driver. Grant and Wayne had opted to join up with Corporal Bean Platoon 1s corporal from our old Bravo Coy in 4-SAI and Paul, doing his first camp since the end of the two years, became the leader of the last fighting section in our new platoon.

All in all, there were nine of us who had seen National Service together, in a platoon that was clearly unbreakable. Our new platoon was now set, and my designated section would be operating under the new call sign of 11C One One Charlie – Alpha Company, Platoon 1, Charlie Section.

Again, I could not help but think that something really bad would soon happen and with this in mind, I was secretly glad that Wayne was in a different Ratel – because if mine got hit, he would be OK. One thing I was definitely going to miss was his superior working and the superb accuracy of his 20mm gun, which he had operated with such ease during countless practice attacks.

Once in organized sections and platoons, we wrote our names and army numbers on a sheet of paper, and then proceeded to the tent assigned to us. Somehow things started to feel a little better, now that we were with a section of men whom most of us not only knew but also could trust. From the tent, we were summoned to the 'sheep shearer,' who whipped our hair off in less than two minutes.

When all was done, we looked like cloned soldiers – with brush cuts and browns, and each of us carrying a rifle.

Soon after our haircut, it was confirmed that we were going up to the border as Ratel soldiers – which meant that in all probability we would be used in battle. Two days after arriving at 1-RNT, we were driven by Samil to the Waterkloof Air Force Base – leaving behind all gunners and drivers.

There was a civilian South African Boeing 767 waiting for us – which seemed odd, for we normally were flown up in the C-130 Hercules. But there was no reason to complain, the 767 was far more comfortable, and safer. Nervously we boarded the plane, taking our rifles with us as we stepped past a beautiful hostess, decked out in her blue uniform, her red lipstick enhancing a perfect smile that melted our fears away. Placing our rifles in the overhead bin, we took our seats, buckled up, and waited with all our uncertainties for the journey to begin. The flight was smooth and quite weird: having a meal served to us by the hostess, which gave us the carefree feeling that we were a bunch of tourists going on an adventurous safari into northern South-West Africa.

When the time came to buckle our seat belts, the plane immediately began its descent, banking heavily to one side and forcing me to stare down the length of the wing, which looked as though it might scrape the dry, scrubby land a few metres below it. I always hated flying, and this time was no different. I can remember thinking: I hope we crash, and then we won't have to go in – because something bad is going to happen anyway! This sense of paranoia was still stalking me, but I kept it to myself – even though my hands were sweating and my legs felt weak.

A few minutes later we landed at the J.H. Strydom Airport in Windhoek and while we filed down the corridor, the pilot, co-pilot, and hostess were there to wish us well. They had to know something was up, after all, it was unheard of to ferry troops to the border in a civilian plane – not to mention the urgency in getting us up to SWA. When I stepped out of the plane, my face was instantly hit with a scalding, dry slap of heat that threw me back as if I had been hit by a ton of bricks. In the distance, a heat haze hovered over the tarmac, blurring the aircraft and the emblem of SAA South African Airways – the flying springbok, painted proudly upon the plane's tail, over the orange background, with orange, white, and blue streaking above it to denote the colours of the South African flag. I had long ago forgotten the discomfort of this heat – but now it was back to haunt us, in full force.

Yes, we had certainly arrived back in this hellish land, with a climate capable of driving one totally insane. SWA had officially welcomed us back for the second time.

While we walked from the plane to the waiting Samils, back in Pretoria all our drivers and gunners were getting ready to be a part of one of the biggest – if not longest – military convoys in South African history. There were well over 80 Ratels, made up of Ratel 20s, Ratel 81s, and Ratel 90s' 15 to 20 low beds carrying Olifant tanks' dozens of Eland 90s Noddy cars' hundreds of Samil trucks, Kwevoels, diesel tankers, water bowsers, and Unimog ambulances. The attack force, along with all the logistics, were in place and began rumbling along the tarmac, heading northward for the uncertainties that lay ahead upon the soil of SWA and Angola.

According to Wayne, who manned the turret from one of the many vehicles, the convoy of armoury stretched over the flat plains as far as the naked eye could see, both forward and back. The convoy had been broken down into manageable sizes, with different groups of vehicles departing at different time intervals. The Military Police had been positioned along the route, and they maintained the convoy by halting all traffic and allowing the vehicles to rumble by undeterred – as if they were all part of a massive funeral procession. The civilians just switched their engines off – with no option but to sit back, watch, wave, and wonder what this sight of such strength was all about. One after the other, the sound of diesel engines whined past the stationary onlookers as they snaked their way towards the border line.

While the drivers drove and the gunners gave them moral support from the turrets, we set off in Samils from the Windhoek Airport, bound for northern Owamboland. After an eternity of driving, we eventually came to a stop in the middle of the bush – with darkness upon us, and none the wiser where we were. Quite normal army procedure, we were told very little of forthcoming events – leaving them up to our imagination' so we played the waiting game – which was nothing new to us.

In the morning we woke to some pandemonium, for a deadly two-metre cobra had slithered into our sleeping cluster and scared the hell out of one of the troops. In a side-winding movement, it shot across the dry, dusty scrub and took refuge in an unoccupied sleeping bag. Our sergeant grabbed the corner of the sleeping bag and shook it out, while still keeping a safe distance. Eventually the cobra appeared with its head sitting atop its coils. It raised its head, expanding the skin of its neck into a broad hood' upright and still, it was ready to strike and sink its fangs, with all its venom, into the nearest troop. The sergeant walked up to the cobra, and they faced each other as if they were in a duel – meanwhile we tightened the circle to witness the outcome. The sergeant drew his pistol from his holster, and the cobra swayed from side to side as if trying to provoke the sergeant' and then, suddenly, two shots ripped a hole into its head, splattering blood and snake over the unlucky troop's sleeping bag – a quick end to the duel. Grant and Paul, our two section leaders from National Service, posed for a photo with this deadly reptile. Grant opted for the tail' wincing and grimacing as he held it with two fingers' while Paul casually took the head, displaying the length to be two metres or more. Troops who were knowledgeable about snakes spoke of the possibility of more coming into our area after they smelled the dead one' the most vulnerable of all of the troops would be the one who slept in the bloodstained bag on which the cobra had just been killed. If this was true, we had to feel lucky – for our section was camped at least 20 metres away.

When all had settled down, we were summoned to an outside church service, during which an Afrikaans military priest took charge. He spoke in both

English and Afrikaans, and his sermon seemed to imply that some would soon die. Looking up at him, it seemed to us as though he were reading us our last rites, in preparation for the final hour – which had now come.

'Now is the time to make peace with your maker!' he told us – a reference to the heightened troop activity in northern Owamboland, as well as the battles that had recently raged in Angola. His words left emptiness in me, and I once again imagined us in the middle of the horrors of war. When he asked us to bow our heads in prayer, I closed my eyes tightly and repeated each word after him –he prayed for our lives and our families. When the Amen was uttered in chorus, we moved away from the service area, leaving the grass flattened by hundreds of troops. The feeling of impending death seemed to worsen as I replayed the message – most of us had the same feelings of the inevitable. There was nothing we could do, except wait with hope that we would remain strong and come through this in one piece.

Ration packs were issued to us, which stilled the pangs of hunger with a bland taste that none of us were too eager about, but nevertheless it was food. The long days dragged by as we waited for the Ratels to arrive, and did little more than rest. The evenings, as the sun was going down – and the mornings, before the sun rose, became bitterly cold. Layering ourselves with what army clothes we had, we bolstered our defence against the harsh cold. Grant pulled an extra bush jacket from his kitbag – which happened to be Gall's. His surname was printed in the material and sewn above his right pocket. Gall had always managed to have the last laugh, and we wondered what would transpire – in spite of the fact that he had been dead for over two years. Grant began to tear Gall's name from the jacket so that he could wear it nameless, rather than with a name that did not belong to him. It came off, and we greeted it with roars of laughter. To our disbelief, Angoose had managed once more to have the last laugh' underneath the nametag he had written his name in black marker – thus destroying all Grant's hopes of wearing it.

In the evening, we stood around a huge fire to gain warmth – which not only helped warm our bodies, but also helped warm our spirits. Grant acted out a battle comedy – which started off as a joke, wherein he was hobbling on one leg, the other had been blown off – and he also had a mangled arm, and dodging enemy fire. This comedy ended with the laughter dying down to silence – as reality once again returned to stalk our thoughts.

It certainly broke the ice – we laughed until our sides hurt, and hallucinated about the safety of home, so far away. It seemed so strange to have a fire at night on the border – for it threatened to reveal our position. But now we no longer cared' the threat of a mortar attack was trivial in comparison to a full-scale battle pitting Cuban manned T-54, T-55, and T-62 tanks against our Ratels.

When the fire burned down, we wandered back under the moonlight to our dew-soaked sleeping bags. Fully clothed and dirty, we climbed in and let the night take charge of our fears. Using my hands, cupped like a pillow under my neck and head' with my back firmly pressed to the hard ground' my eyes stared through the overhead of bush and trees – until I saw the stars. They twinkled, and sparkled messages of hope' I passed my dreams between star and mind, and clung to the safety of the dream over the shuddering reality of war – with my buddies and me in the middle of it. Here I lay, frozen with cold in one part of the bush, and this intense fear projected to another part, where the battle would supposedly be fought.

On the third day at our temporary bush camp, we were all loaded up into Samils and driven to a remote airstrip. Once on the ground, we were amazed to see our Ratels lined up in a straight, neat line, their V-shaped noses pointing towards the tarmac of the runway. It was here that I met a guy from Cape Town, who had a dislocated jaw and had been involved in Operation *Askari* in Angola. He was inside a Ratel when rockets from a RPG-7 rocket launcher bombarded it, incinerating all on board. Miraculously he survived, but was left to suffer alone through many months of rehabilitation in a military hospital. When I heard this, I said, 'How the fuck can they possibly call this guy up again for a possible repeat performance, after what he had already been through?'

Our good buddy Paul was another example. After what he had suffered in Mozambique, he too should have not been called up' but here he was, as his trauma began to replay itself. Did the army care, or was this an oversight? Who knows? I wondered.

Walking the line of Ratels, we eventually found our friends – enjoying the reunion with driver and gunner and sharing news and rumours. Standing next to our vehicles, we spoke of civilian life and what jobs we were in' but these things seemed to fall on deaf ears, for it really did not matter anymore. We were once again state property – being soldiers first and foremost, and every vestige of civilian thinking blotted from our minds. We concentrated upon the rumours of the Cuban and FAPLA Angolan army advancement to a mere stone's throw from the SWA/Namibian border line – just on the other side of Ruacana, where a month before 11 South Africans had been blown to pieces, Greg from Hillcrest being one of them.

Before darkness set in, we made sure we had finished our meals. We laid our sleeping bags out on the grass covering some uneven ground, next to each vehicle and close to the small airstrip. Fully clothed with a jersey and a bush jacket, we zipped ourselves up, our heads concealed against the chill within the bag' we lay still, wanting the night to fly quickly by. Looking over at a few unmoving troops, I could not help but think how similar these sleeping, unmoving bodies looked to dead soldiers zipped up in body bags. That night we froze, hardly able to sleep through the well-below-freezing temperatures, the semi-desert climate only adding another obstacle to our never-ending struggles in a land that I still despised as much as I did in 1985. The dew settled with the cold upon us' the clear sky had allowed any trapped heat to escape, leaving us to wait for the sun to chase the chill from our bones and replace it with another extreme – this time the blistering heat.

At first light, we emerged from our dew-soaked sleeping bags and tried to warm ourselves as best we could behind the running engine of the Ratel. We pressed our frozen hands to the engine block to thaw them out. Winter was upon us' we stood helpless in the cold, and the sweet smell of diesel hung like a cloud in the freezing air. We crowded for warmth at the back of the vehicle, our eyes streaming tears as the fumes burned penetrating holes into them, in between splutters of choking coughs – all to keep warm in this open wilderness of tree and bush. While we huddled together, in our new sections and platoons, a camouflaged Dakota droned overhead. Like a crowd at a concert, we all edged forward towards the airstrip and watched the plane land neatly and taxi down the runway, to the very far end.

'There's big brass on that plane,' someone said' we looked eagerly on from a distance, while our top officers met these generals and brigadiers, who had been flown in to brief them on our forthcoming moves. While we waited for this important meeting to end, we boiled a fire bucket of water and made coffee in an endeavor to warm ourselves.

When the coffee was consumed, the Dakota lined itself on the runway and sped by in front of us, disappearing into the blue sky. What was said had been shared with only a select few.

'Start your engines!' came the shout, a shout that echoed down the line. Suddenly the silence was filled with the diesel whine of at least 20 Ratels – an echelon of Samils and Buffels' the drum of engines awakened this sleeping part of bush, in the middle of nowhere.

One by one the vehicles peeled away into a long line, churning the dust into a windstorm of grit and cloud, with the grey plumes of smoke from the exhaust adding colour to the brown haze.

Where we were moving to was anyone's guess, but one thing was for sure, things were moving fast and furiously forward.

28

Operation Desert Fox

Sitting inside the vehicles, as opposed to riding on the roof, we shielded our freezing bodies from the cutting wind – which by no means had us sitting warmly, for the hull was as cold as a fridge.

After an hour of coughing on dust particles that had made their way inside, we surfaced for fresh air and into the burning heat of morning, staring into the back of a Buffel just ahead, with a Ratel just behind, emerging through a thick dust cloud. Maintaining the convoy, our vehicles stretched for miles across the flat and featureless, bone-dry terrain – far forward and back – until we could no longer see for grit and dust stung our watery eyes and forced us back into the dusty hull.

The convoy continued forward with nothing around us – not a building, a hut, a person' absolutely nothing – except dust and dry grass and a brown sky all around us.

'This is the Blue Route!' a troop shouted over the roar of the engine.

'Blue, black, what the fuck? Where are we?'

'In the middle of miles and miles of fuckall!' I said. 'Welcome back to South-West!'

We approached a dry saltpan that loomed massively through the dust cloud. The glare was too intense to stare at head on' it burned our eyes like the sun's reflection in a mirror. Once on the pan, I looked upon the hardened dry earth. The cracked, brown, solidified salt and sand curled up into puzzle-like shapes, looking more like broken pieces of chocolate Easter eggs.

The heat was unbearable – it beat on us, needling pinpricks of heat into our exposed skin with no let up. When it got too much on top of the Ratel, we sat inside and tried to sleep or talk' the dust swirled around us – only to be overcome by the heat and forced back onto the roof for more dust. A breeze was the only thing worth getting excited about. The extremes, in the matter of a few hours, were quite unbelievable' that one minute we could be freezing our nuts off in a Ratel as cold as a fridge, and the next sweating buckets and stripping off in the same vehicle, now as hot as an oven.

The dust that cloaked us was as fine as chalk, covering us in white from head to boot, and quite impossible to escape. Gradually we became unrecognizable to our buddies, for our hair had whitened, along with our faces, and the powdery dust and natural, bush makeup aged us. Our eyes burned itchy red, and our noses and ears became clogged, and our teeth began to grind on the dust particles as if we were chewing on sand paper' they left a dry, salty taste in our saliva-free mouths. We had no choice but to sit through it and wait for the journey to end. After hours of driving across this massive expanse of a saltpan, we eventually ground to a halt. The whole convoy stopped because of two vehicles, which had become bogged in just before they reached the other side of the pan. The harder the two logistical vehicles spun their wheels in four-wheel drive, the deeper they dug themselves in to the clay-like soil, which must have trapped water since the last rain. In Africa, as always, it pays to expect the unexpected – and as part of each Ratels tote, they were prepared for such an event. Out came a very thick, fifty centimetre wire cable, with one end fastened to the Ratel and the other to the first firmly-stuck Samil – the extremely important water bowser, its weight of liquid worth more than gold in this treacherous climate. The convoy started up, leaving the Ratel to free the two stranded vehicles' and as we drew in line, the Ratel easily pulled the first vehicle from the suctioning mud. Troops on the ground waved us by, and we left them choking on the last of our dust from the saltpan as we headed towards the dry grass, led on by the snaking convoy.

After a long and trying day on the 'Blue Route' – which I think should be renamed the 'White Route' – we finally emerged onto the less dusty soil of the open grassland. At least now we could pat ourselves down and shake off some of the fine powder that had settled over us. The drivers had been at the wheel the whole day, and we knew how their arms and legs must be aching, fighting the steering wheel and the brake pedal – the flat land being somewhat kinder to the manoeuvering of these heavy beasts.

To me it seemed as though we were driving in a northwesterly direction' the land slowly began to change, and hills appeared in the distance, still with the same dryness about them. Thankfully, and very gratefully, we eventually came to a stop – again in the middle of nowhere – with some of these hills now quite close to us. According to some troops, we were now just south of Ruacana in Kaokoland – just west of Owamboland' with miles and miles of untouched land all around us.

It was great to get out of the vehicles and stretch away all the aches and pains and breathe fresh air once again. Looking around at our new surroundings, we realized we had arrived at a bush camp set up for training purposes – with channels of trenches already excavated in the same way the terrorists were used to, and dug for the purpose of practising our mechanized warfare.

The Ratels parked in a long line, with all the noses pointed forward, towards the mounds of meandering earth that we would be storming and performing our drills upon. The rest of the day was spent milling around the vehicles, while all the rank were led away for orders in a secluded, shady part of the bush, below the canopy of a few thorn trees. There was urgency and tension in the air – the sudden call to orders heightened our anxious nerves. Rumours circulated like wildfire that the Cubans and FAPLA brigades were extremely close to the SWA/Namibian border, and that we had been sent here to defend the border. I felt as though I was standing on a sandy cliff, watching the sand trickle away from beneath my feet until I was falling forward into a black hole – with no way out except to float and be carried with the turbulent tide and follow through on my call of duty, in whatever capacity. I would never be able to live with myself if I showed cowardice, or left my buddies behind.

After a daylight fire to warm our rations, we wriggled into our sleeping bags and slept next to our Ratels in our different sections. With sleep coming fitfully, I once again used the stars as a comfort zone. I lay rigid and painfully stiff, holding my breath as I thought of the situation we had been placed in by our government – to serve and protect no matter what the cost. Here we were under the call of South Africa – 'At thy will to live or perish, O South Africa, dear land' – about to embark on a nail-biting challenge to gel together into a cohesive unit, so that we could emerge victorious through the ordeal – in whatever form – that lay ahead.

In the early morning we were once again shouted awake and after eating a quick meal we lined up, facing the trenches with our rifles drawn'and then on command, at our own time, we began to shoot them – we familiarized ourselves with the sights of the R4 once again. While we fired, shooting up specs of dust, the sun rose across the horizon rearing its ugly head to cast more punishment over our bodies. The heat wave reminded us that we were truly back in northern SWA.

While the riflemen shot their weapons at propped up targets, our gunners began readying themselves for their practice sessions with the 20mm cannons and 12.7mm Browning machine guns. The more we shot, the more comfortable we felt with our weapons – once our sights had been adjusted to our liking. We used the rest of the day to load our magazines for training on fire-and-movement – which involved all the riflemen and the machine gun group. One section at a time, we stormed the trenches, live ammo firing behind us and in front of us as we dashed in pairs, fell to the ground, rolled and crawled, and covered our buddies while they stormed past us – two of us firing forward while they advanced upon the trenches. Once we had arrived at the trenches, a grenade was thrown in, clearing an entrance through which, one by one, we made our way in, throwing a grenade at each bend and clearing it by firing two shots.

When our section had completed our drill, we waited at the side and watched as section after section rushed at these trenches' the noise and smell of burned gunpowder took me immediately back four years to the shit hole of De Brug.

While we watched, I saw a troop in the trenches, who had leaned his rifle against the wall of soft sand and fumbled with the grenade in his haste to remove the pin.

'Shit, I hope his barrel doesn't fill up with sand,' I said to the troop at my side. Expecting nothing to happen, we continued to watch.

The troop, as part of the drill, shouted 'grenade' and then threw it. There followed a slight shaking of the earth and a deep, muffled explosion. Grabbing at his rifle through the grey, sandy cloud that he had created, he pulled his weapon to his shoulder and fired. The bullet hit the sand, which had clogged his barrel – now, suddenly, it had nowhere to go. The 5.56mm round blew back down the barrel with immense force, exploding the working parts into the unsuspecting soldier's face in another loud bang.

Looking every bit like he had been shot, his head recoiled, forcing him to stumble a pace backwards while still remaining on his feet. His face was perplexed and frozen with fear – he still clutched his destroyed rifle while blood streamed down his deathly pale face in lines, smudging the dust and blackened gunpowder that had settled over him. Still paralyzed with shock, he lowered his rifle' troops rushed forward to his aid, catching him before he dropped to the ground. His bloody face began to swell – his mouth and nose having taking most of the impact – he sat blurry-eyed, gazing into oblivion with the million-mile stare. The troop was carried away to the medical facilities of the Unimog ambulance, where he was stitched up and given pills to kill the pain.

It was the first time that I had seen metal bent, broken, and sheared into sharp pieces with such devastating force. The body cover had shot clean off – the recoil spring was mangled and bent in half – the rotating bolt was sheared in two and the magazine clip had been forced open and all the bullets expelled through the bottom, leaving the spring exposed and hanging loosely from it. He was certainly very lucky to have escaped flying home in a body bag. Judging by the look of the rifle, the blood, the sound, and the confusion, he had to be thankful that someone was watching over him. He had never participated in mechanized warfare before, and looked more like he had been pulled from behind his office desk and thrown into the field to sink or swim – fortunately he learned the hard way and lived to swim with the rest of us.

Sitting in the Ratels, we careered over the flat, scrubby landscape – driver, gunner, and section leader linked by radio through their headsets. The gunners let fly with their cannons upon the trenches. The deafening noise and a hull filled with smoke had us perched on our seats, ready to disembark through the hydraulic doors at the order. Fossie, our section leader, told John to get us ready to 'Stop. *Stap uit*'.

'*Gereed!*' – Ready! 'Stop' *stap uit nou!* – Stop' get out now! And as one, we screamed: '*Stap uit nou*,' our adrenaline surging above the thudding noise. One by one we threw ourselves out of the moving vehicle. Immediately we formed a line on each side, and we broke automatically into fire-and-movement, and dashed, dived down into the ground, rolled, crawled, and shot like no tomorrow at the standup targets that we imagined were the 'Cubanie' – the Cubans. Fires sprang to life as we pummelled the targets with rifle grenades, 20mm rounds, and 12.7mm rounds – along with the small arms fire of R4 rifles and the LMG machine gun. The sound was deafening, with thud after thud kicking up a whirlwind of dust, and yellow and red smoke filling the air with a screen as we stormed in battle charge towards these excavated mounds. Once on top of the trenches, we broke in by throwing a highly explosive grenade and following it with two successive shots' and then the four of us entered the maze of tunnels. At each new tunnel leg, we took it in turns – throwing another grenade with more firepower, following the deep explosion' while the gunners gave us support from the side and we advanced through each branch of the trench. Our nostrils were filled with gunpowder and dust, and our eyes burned from the diesel – our hands shook from all the automatic firing, and from the adrenaline drug holding us dangerously on the edge and never feeling more alive.

Our training continued daily with these mock attacks, which we performed from morning into the blackness of night. Through it all we meshed into a tight unit of men, getting stronger with each new attack.

At night we would attack under the bright light of illumination flares, which were continuously shot into the dark night sky and would float back to earth on mini-parachutes – acting as bright floodlights and allowing us to see our way forward.

During one of these many fire-fights, John our gunner abandoned his post in the turret and joined us on the ground. He joined our line and remained closest to the moving Ratel. Brian was next to him, though he did not know it, followed by me, Macky, and Nic. We swept through the dark terrain towards the trenches. While we fired and moved two at a time, we began to shift to the left, leaving a gap between our Ratel and the first rifleman – that being Brian. When we realized that we were encroaching on the next section's light machine gun group, we began to tighten up the line, moving back towards our moving Ratel.

John, meanwhile, had advanced to a position ahead of the Ratel, but still to the left of it. Little did we know that he was now in our firing line – we closed the gap between Ratel and rifleman number one and continued to move forward, our rifles spitting out shell after shell. We tore the night apart with our weapons blazing on automatic fire. Just ahead I saw a shadow, and for a split second I thought it odd, but not suspecting anything I continued to fire. It seemed to move, but I thought it must have been the light creating a shadow and playing a trick on my strained vision. Brian and I continued to fire and with the shadow as a new target, I began shooting on rapid fire – expelling a single round at a time.

I took another step closer and screamed above the roar: *Staak vuur!* – Hold your fire! I could not even hear my own scream' the sound of the attack – the whistling and popping of flares – drowned out my words: the constant, deep thud of the gunnery' explosions dropping on the trenches' and the chattering of automatic fire – this attack of organized confusion in full swing. Totally deafened and hoarse from my shouts, I immediately turned to my right to see if Brian had heard my shouts. Whether he did or not, I don't know' but he had stopped firing when he realized that something was horribly wrong. Before us, as if this shadowy form had come alive, John sat cowering on the ground – with a face as pale as the segment of moon hanging out of the dark sky above us. When he saw us approaching, he tried to get up' but he could not hold his own weight and fell back down' his legs crumpled from beneath him.

Fuck, I just shot him! I thought. 'John, are you hurt?'

'I'm sorry, I'm sorry. I am OK' I am not hit!' John stuttered and stammered and gained the strength to stand up. Heavy-legged, he dragged himself forward with the support of a soldier under each arm. His face was sweaty and as expressionless as death – a strange smell was around him, which could only have been fear – for he waited for what he felt would be a certain execution before the firing squad of our barrage of bullets.

'Shit, I nearly shot you. What the hell were you thinking?' I shook my finger at him in anger and looked into his stunned face, and saw sheer terror. 'You fuckin' – I stopped my words in mid-sentence and shook my head in disbelief. I had wanted to say, 'You fuckin' idiot. Do you realize that I nearly fuckin' killed you, you stupid prick?' But what was the point? He knew that he had come within centimetres of death' and so I never bothered to express it.

It had been so surreal to see this close call played out, and my bullets flying through the shadow – only for a human form to emerge unscathed. How I missed him that awful night I will never know. The unwritten cardinal sin in our army was to take your own life, or that of a buddy' and even though I would have been in the clear, there would have been blood on my conscience for the rest of my life.

With this sobering thought, I took a deep breath and walked through the darkness, shaking from all the firing – as well as from what could have been. I made my way through the smoke-filled air, towards the silhouette of the Ratel. Back at the vehicle, I felt very unsettled at how close things had come – but I shook it off with a what-was-done-was-done attitude. Sitting in the Ratel, John recounted what happened when he left the turret to shoot his rifle. Having never done fire-and-movement before, he had gone too far ahead of the firing line – but when he realized it, it was too late. He stood frozen as the bullets whizzed past him, then dropped to the ground to become a smaller target. Sprawled in the dirt face down, he prayed while the bullets tore through the darkness right at him.

'I will never do it again' I promise!' he said in a solemn voice, though still gripped with fear – a voice we believed, and one to which he remained true' for he remained firmly planted in his gunner's turret from that eerie night onwards.

When we crawled into our sleeping bags after that attack, I once again looked at the stars for guidance, my chest tight, and tightening, as I lay unmoving as if at attention. This is for real, I thought and I thanked my lucky stars for sparing John his life. And, with the stars watching over me, I closed my eyes on another tense day.

It was quite amazing how we had transformed from civilians to soldiers within the first couple of weeks. Here I was, living as dirty as a wild animal, on the ground once again and working like crazy to hone my skills as a mechanized fighter. There were electricians, office clerks, managers, plumbers, salesmen, artists, farmers – and the list went on – but for now it did not matter what we were in civvie street – we were here to get ourselves ready for a big fight and the harder we trained and exercised our skills, the less would be our fatality rate.

The SADF had mustered a huge force of men. Rumour was there were as many as 15000 troops on the border. At least 2000 or more of us were from the 81st Armoured Brigade' many of us seasoned veterans had served on the border, and many had been involved in external operations into Angola. I met a guy in his thirties, who had been in Angola in 1975 and was part of a force that was going to take the capital of Luanda after the Portuguese abdicated their colonial rule. He recounted how close they were' they could actually see the lights of Luanda while they lay in wait to take the city on the command of the prime minister.

Most of us were between 22 and 40; we had left that shroud of invincibility behind in our National Service, for a new, more calculated approach. For many of us now had families to think about. A large percentage of the riflemen and the machine gun group within each vehicle had had no previous Ratel training in mechanized warfare. It was up to us, in each individual Ratel, to help train those soldiers who were not up to speed with these new drills.

Urgency was in the air – we mustered our strength from one day to the next, and grew in force from each sunrise to sunset – living with the hope of raising our chances of survival. Without speaking a word, we knew something big was about to happen' there was no way that we would be trained at this speed and intensity for a routine exercise. We were not here to play toy soldiers' we all knew this was for real.

Diesel and dust hung in the air as the morning cold awakened us. The heat of the bushveld was on its way, and we savoured our coffee, warmed over a fire' totally surrounded by bush, a small hill being the only reference point in an otherwise featureless landscape. For those of us who had been at 1-SAI, it revived memories of that hated desert De Brug, where we had lived for months and trained over terrain that spanned endless miles. Now here we were, in the same setting and temperate zone, but without tents' and training for combat with the unsettling fear of death. It made it harder to pull back from the future and remain grounded in the present.

The days became a blur – we lost track of dates, and only knew that Sunday had dawned when an outside church service was held to mark the Sabbath. The following day the attacks swung into full force – our heads swirled in burned gunpowder, and our minds raced blindly through the drills that had become so well ingrained. Each drill was executed with precision and accuracy, and every effort taken to grant each of us the highest rate of survival.

While we stood around after each attack, a few of us from our old platoon began to reminisce.

'Remember in De Brug,' Grant said, 'when Commandant Roetz made us use Alpha Company's Ratels to show them how an attack should be launched?' Instantly our blank faces filled with proud, glinting smiles, as we cast our minds back to the day that became the turning point for our superiority as a fighting platoon.

On that day in 1984, we waited our turn while our two sister platoons performed their mechanized attacks. When they had finished, we launched our assault, and performed a flawless mechanized attack in front of our company, as well as all three platoons from Alpha Company.

'Well done, manne. *Dit was uitstekend*' it was excellent, Commandant Roetz said with a broad smile.

It left me with a feeling of pride that I would never forget, because it seemed so out of character for any rank to give this sort of feedback. Sitting to the side, basking in our glory, we watched a platoon of Alpha Coy and wondered if they could do any better. Soon after they began to storm the terrain towards the trenches in the distance, one troop nearly shot another. The Commandant stopped the attack in mid-stream and called the platoon sheepishly back to where the rest of the companies were waiting.

Then he did something quite unheard of' he told the next platoon to vacate their vehicles and allow our platoon to resume control of their Ratels, with their full load of ammunition. Bitterly angry and disgruntled, they disembarked from their vehicles' and we filled their seats to show off our skill at mechanized warfare.

Under the watchful eyes of hundreds of troops, as well as high-ranking officers, Platoon 3 set off and proved its worth as a force to be reckoned with.

'Shit, we were good!' Wayne said. The handful of us nodded in agreement, still thinking about the good old days – which did not feel that long ago, even though it had been nearly three years.

If only we had Platoon 3 now, I would not be so worried about going into an op! I thought. What a team we had with that impeccable driver, gunner, and section leader – the sort of combination that could save lives!

'I want to go in and kill those black bastards!' Brian suddenly blurted, snapping out of his trance and leaping into the present.

In a sick kind of way, we had been robbed of an operation into Angola when we had felt our strongest. Now there were those of us who felt this would be our chance to go in and kill. Some of us were very eager for blood, and Brian led the way.

The prospect of killing the enemy did not bother me – after all, that was what we had been trained for – but what did was the calculated risk of always looking at both sides of a situation before weighing up the pros and cons. I knew only too well that battle casualties do not favour one side and with this thought in mind, I hoped we would be spared from the ordeal. There was no helping Brian through his tunnel vision of wanting African blood at whatever price – which came as no surprise to any of us, for we had seen him in National Service, living his life recklessly, with ox-like stubbornness.

Later that evening we had a fire in spite of the glow acting as a marker for our position. A few of our sections congregated around it for warmth, entertainment, and social camaraderie' we stared at the crackling logs as the flames licked around them. Grant, being the comedian that he was, again set in motion the fears that sat within us. We joked about death as if it was the furthest thing from our minds' meanwhile he spoke of body bags and returning as invalids – if we were that lucky. I looked around the group and again began to wonder if death would take one of us. Our laughter was forced' the nervous pangs of reality sat within each one of us.

This waiting in limbo was not healthy for any of us' in many ways, it would be easier to go in and face our fears head on. The mind is a very powerful machine, and it conjures up all sorts of paranoid feeling, further amplified by the constant, day-to-day swirl of rumours through the ranks.

If we did go into Angola, our vehicles and our kit would be written off and if they returned, it would be a bonus for the government and the taxpayer. We wondered if the same applied to our own lives.

Leaving the fire, we trod through the darkness to our sleeping area, our sleeping bags decked out on our groundsheets. There was the comfort of a section of men and a rifle close at hand. Bearded, dirty, and disgruntled, we marked off another day under the canopy of stars that radiated what peace it could through the tension and chilled silence of the night.

The morning brought further rumours with hidden truth to them.

'Our call-up is going to be extended to three months!' the troops started saying.

They had heard this from reliable sources, and relayed the new information from one to the other.

'Why?' we asked.

Most of us were not really sure what all this massing of force was about, for nothing had officially been told to us – even though we knew it was a very serious situation.

'Around 17000 Cubans, 5000 FAPLA, and 2000 PLAN members, the People's Liberation Army of Namibia are just over the border north of Ruacana – just north of our position right now!' one of the rank said.

We stared blankly ahead, not knowing quite what to believe.

For me, it just confirmed my fear that we would go in for the attack – we waited like inmates on death row for a last-minute reprieve – which seemed to us as unlikely as a white Christmas in Southern Africa.

Our civilian jobs had long been forgotten as we trained, burned, and sweated in the sun, surviving on our ration packs and not showering in four weeks. Our same stinking browns were now as brown as the terrain. Each day we walked into a designated arc of bush, with a roll of toilet paper and our rifle – which did not leave our sides for one moment, not even when nature called.

'Watch out for the minefield!' came the shouts as a troop made his way into the danger zone. Each excursion had to be taken with care and alertness, sidestepping our way into the stench of the open-air bush toilet – sand kicked over each mound with paper left as the only marker to flag the danger. Flies bigger than bees swarmed everywhere, settling on the half-covered crap and then flying at us. We fought the putrid smell by holding our breath, in a hurry to vacate this land sewer for cleaner air.

News reached us that a troop from our sister company, encamped 500 metres away, had been injured during one of its practice attacks. The severity was unknown, but it was severe enough for him to be evacuated by helicopter.

Gas masks were distributed to all of us, and we began to train with them on – due to the threat of chemical warfare from Cubans or FAPLA Brigades. Things seemed to be moving from bad to worse.

If the bullets don't get some of us, the gas will! I said to myself, and struggled to fit the mask over my dirty and sweaty face.

This life was tiring us out' we stared down a long, dark, never-ending tunnel with no exits. The grip of border-line insanity once more steered our minds towards breaking point.

We took each and every endless day in our stride as we stormed the trenches. The explosions flashed by and the dull thud of the cannons pierced our eardrums' the burned smell of gunpowder and the choking scent of diesel assaulted our noses' and the taste of grit and dripping sweat stuck in our dry, salty mouths. We rode the whining Ratels feeling charged and alive and on top of the world. For the moment, our fears were forgotten.

After nearly 30 days of intense training, we were ready for these bastards – our new band of buddies had been forged into a tight unit of men ready to kill when, and only if, the order was released.

Our section 11 Charlie decided to call our Ratel '*Madonna*,' as a good omen to protect us if the need arose. With a blue marker, Macky put his skills to good use and lettered out the word in bold, flowing cursive along both sides of the vehicle. Our Ratel now had a name – she was the graceful goddess with a dark side, housing a bunch of warriors ready to kill, and some wanting to far more than others. Here we were, forged together as brothers from varying backgrounds, with the same look of hardship and misery etched onto each dirty, streaked face' and the same dream set into each of us: to do what we had to do so we could return home.

Each Ratel bombed up in the morning with their usual fill of ammunition – the 20mm gun cases filled with belts, along with the 12.7mm Browning loaded to capacity – each rifleman had his six magazines loaded with 5.56mm rounds, and the LMG and MAG 2 had patrol bags filled with neatly-layered belts of 7.62mm rounds.

Late that afternoon the order flowed through the ranks to pack up and get ready to move which instantly triggered me to thinking: Angola, attack, destruction, and death. With enough ammo to take a small town, ration packs to last a week, and the diesel and water tanks filled and our kit stored within the hull, we waited nervously next to our vehicles.

'We are going in!' someone said – which stabbed me with a pang of anxiety. I am sure it did the others, too. I would face it head-on – I would not run and show cowardice to these my brothers in arms. If that's what the order is, so be it, I thought. Crazy with wait, we were eventually relieved of the tension as a shout echoed down the line – 'Start your engines,' which was again echoed by us in chorus, mainly through nervous tension.

Was this really D-Day? I wondered, and with this hollow thought, the vehicles started in unison, puffing out clouds of diesel, the noise amplified tenfold by all the vehicles revving at once. One after the other, we rumbled out in a long line, leaving a well-used piece of bush abandoned. We handed it back to the calming effect of nature. In convoy, we made our way northwards across the grasslands, with open savannah surrounding us as far as the eye could see.

It was not long after we left our camp that the light began to fade. We drove into the distance with the sun setting upon the strength of our armoury, and followed the lead towards an uncertain future. It was a soothing feeling to be in the midst of this picturesque beauty – the colours radiating across the horizon, allowing us to actually enjoy the sight. After the beauty had been absorbed into the darkness we continued on, following the dull glow of the red taillights in the absence of headlights. Slowly we drove, confined to the hull in the kind of darkness that swallows light and leaves not a spec to break the total blackness. It was as if I were sitting with my eyes closed and staring at my eyelids' but instead I was staring through the portholes, out into the open and into a wall of blackness.

My mind was racing a million miles an hour, with terror running through me as we sat silent, feeling every bump under the now-soft whine of the Ratel crawling through the darkness and Piet tailgating the vehicle in front of ours.

After what seemed an eternity, we came to a standstill. The Ratels were going in a circle and giving all-round protection, their noses and cannons pointed outwards. The troops filled up the spaces between every vehicle, each of us and our rifles pointing in the direction of the 20mm barrels. Thus we settled down for the night, totally oblivious of our surroundings within our sleeping laager. While I was lying on the ground, I remembered a story we had been told, about a Ratel in the darkness and a sleeping soldier. A Ratel driver had moved his vehicle in the night and had run over a fellow soldier's head, crushing it like a melon. Even though it had happened a few years ago, it just went to show that any freak accident was possible. Thank God we did not have to witness such a costly waste of life.

In the morning we woke, only to see that we were still in the open savannah. The only change was a few hills to the left of us, which meant that we were either in Kaokoland or on the border of Owamboland. After a hot coffee and some ultra-long-life milk to cool it down, and a quick ration pack mixed in the normal way in the thin plastic bags that we called FL's condoms, we were back in the vehicles, ready to move. In a convoy that looked scary in length, and extended like an endless snake across the landscape, Ratel after Ratel trailed each other, and the logistical echelon for support made up the rear. In our wake we left a dust cloud, and cut a path forward like deadly prehistoric beasts through the dry waving grass – with not a hut, water well, or any telltale signs of human presence in sight. There was just a beautiful, clear-blue sky, dust, tall grass, and hundreds of soldiers loaded to the tits. Under the drone of the diesel engines in the curving convoy, we moved forward, ready all the while, like a coiled snake, to unwind and take formation before being granted the order to unleash this pent-up tension as a strike on the enemy.

While Piet drove, John decided it was as good a time as any to smoke a joint and so, while we rocked around in the hull over every bump, we puffed casually on the crudely rolled marijuana cigarette, dulling the edge that constricted us. It was passed from one soldier to the next, clouds of smoke filling the inside with the soft, sweet smell and transforming our fighting vehicle into a hot box of very relaxed troops. Any tension we felt was abated for the moment.

After a long, dusty haul we came to a rest in an area, with a hill to the one side of us and a massive open vlei before us – which was a salt pan in the last rainy season but had now transformed into a dry, scrubby, hardened area of grey earth thirsting for the next rains. But the only water that was shed upon it was our own urine – which the ground quickly absorbed, as into a dry sponge.

Judging by the terrain and the sun, we were at a point just southeast of Ruacana – not far from the border line with Angola and the Calueque Dam, where the Cuban-piloted MiG-23s had killed Greg and ten other National Servicemen only a month ago. Our Ratels lined up, one parked next to another, their V–

28. Operation Desert Fox

shaped noses facing northwards in a spectacular show of force: the Ratel count being between 35 and 40.

On the far side of us, we saw the unmistakable Olifant tanks – which had also been developed in South Africa – mustering their powerful 105mm cannons. The Olifant had been modelled on the British Centurion, and had a far more sophisticated firing control system. Next to them were the Eland 90s, known to any troop as the 'Noddy Car' – with their long, 90mm cannons protruding oddly from their small, rounded, armoured shell set on four wheels. To our left, there was a group of Ratel 90s' capable of taking out enemy tanks and next to them were Ratels with their 81mm mortars.

Behind our line of armour, a battery of G5, 155mm cannons stood, capable of firing 42 kilometres away with deadly accuracy.

I passed my camera over to Grant to get a picture of our brigade. We waited in the middle of the savannah, looking out of place in this long line of brutal strength and enormous firepower. Unfortunately, the quality of my camera – along with the fact that I needed a panoramic lens to capture the full scene of vehicle and soldier in such massing' and the blistering heat of the midday sun – produced a picture that only told half a story and showed off only a portion of the vehicle strength that we had.

Standing idle on top of, next to, or inside these thick, armour-plated monsters, we waited a long time for the order that would set us in formation for a live practice attack – this time as a full brigade under the military unit of 81-Armoured Brigade.

'I hope we go in to attack I really want to kill those SWAPO bastards!' Brian exclaimed. Once again he spoke with meaning and belief. He wanted the black enemy's blood, and badly.

'Brian if we go in,' I said, 'some of us are going to die, or come back minus limbs!' But he wasn't the only one' there were quite a few soldiers who had such a deep, racial desire to fight for their country that they displayed not a trace of fear.

These hollow words really did not mean anything, however – we were all human, and deep within us, as scared as we were, we wanted to test our fighting skills. If we could kill, we would finally be able to release the hell-bent anger that had been plaguing us and shed the burden of suspense that was pulling tighter around us each day. For at the end of the day, it was the waiting game that was driving us stir crazy. Make a fuckin' decision! We were screaming silently every day – the scream getting louder as day followed day. We needed to know in order to brace ourselves and ready our minds; instead we sat in limbo, none the wiser to the plan for us. All we could do was assume, and allow time to tick slowly by.

Our lives were hanging in the balance awaiting that sought-after – for some – decision to send us steamrolling over the border at Ruacana and into war in Angola.

We were as ready as we could ever be – our fighting skills were as sharply honed as our training days back at 1-SAI, four years ago.

The silence was broken by a helicopter that flew over us and landed on a hill overlooking our staging area and from it, some extremely high-up brass got out and stood looking down over us and our military strength on the otherwise featureless grasslands.

We still did not know what the hell was going on, and we wondered if these generals and brigadiers were here to give us the nod to rumble into Angola and launch the attack that we had practised daily for a month.

'Start your engines', came the order, followed by an earth-shattering, ear-piercing sound that split the silence. Two Impala jet fighters came in low over us, breaking the sound barrier before becoming lost to the blue of the sky.

'What the fuck was that?' someone in our vehicle exclaimed. For a fleeting second my heart stopped, and I honestly thought we were under attack. Our adrenaline kicked in, and each vehicle lurched forward, throwing us about in the back of the hull. Every Ratel and Olifant tank moved onwards in a fire-and-movement charge, in the direction of the vanished jets, which were now only a telltale wisp of white smoke left in the sky.

The peace was turned upside down' empty shells rattled and rolled on the metal floor' the 20mm cannon thumped away, expelling round after round as the extractor fans pulled at the smoke-filled turret and hull. All the hatches firmly shut and sealed, leaving us to stare out of the bullet proof glass portholes and witness this battle charge. It felt as real as could be – all the sounds and smells were in place and our taut, expressionless faces and tense bodies were buckled into the seats, and our headgear firmly strapped around our chins. The vehicle bucked forward and lurched back with each deafening thud of the cannon, and we half expected to see Cuban tanks and FAPLA soldiers as we raced forward at full speed.

It was a military fact that a good gunner was worth at least ten infantrymen on a battlefield. I knew a few gunners, and in my eyes Wayne certainly stood ahead of the pack – he was certainly worthy of the ten-man count. He could swivel his turret with grace and speed, lining up the target in his sights and firing on it with such ease. I felt unlucky not to have him in my Ratel, as I had in '84 and '85' but I was very lucky to have him on my flank.

To our right, the Olifant tanks were blasting shells through the yellow smoke screens' they shook with each expelled charge, and the dust rose to mark its target, while mortar bombs rained down from the northwest side, pounding another invisible target. Thus we careered forward, the thrill of the adrenaline running thick through each of us. The intense noise had our ears ringing, and the smell of burned gunpowder itched its way into our nasal passages' we coughed, wanting to open the hatches for a breath of fresh air. Out of nowhere, a stray mortar bomb exploded with a deep crack, right next to our vehicle. Piet, the driver, swerved – allowing us to either feel the explosion or the sudden jerk of the wheel. The Ratel threw us around until he righted it, and then continued forward as if this were all part of the attack.

When the attack finished, we all jumped out of the vehicle and rushed to the side of the Ratel. Piet was last to join us. He was visibly shaken, having seen the detonation from his driver's window. Thankfully he was able to keep the vehicle grounded on its six massive wheels. The mirror had been blown clean off, and so too the wiper blade – leaving a shrapnel trail of white across his window. The side was peppered with lumps of roughed-up, sharp metal, dug out from the smooth surface. The thick rubber of the front tyre was also scuffed and deeply cut, but in spite of this we were all fine, and so was our powerful, protective beast – *Madonna*.

Having the hatches down, and us huddled in the hull, saved us from severe injury' for had it landed on our vehicle with the hatches open, the shrapnel would have bounced around the inside like ball bearings in a pinball machine, until the shards buried themselves in our flesh. Had we been standing like we normally did out of our hatches, the explosion would have risen at a 45° angle and taken pieces of us with its detonating force. It was a close call, and it illustrated how quickly something can go wrong' luckily, only the Ratel was scarred – instead of flesh lacerated and dismembered. It was an eye-opener how close soldiers can come to death in preparation for battle. Thank goodness someone was watching over us once again, sparing us from something that could have turned so ugly. We laughed, with that hint of nervousness and our shroud of protection to ward off any danger.

After the attack, all the riflemen were told to stand in a long line with rifles and chest webbings, and fire all their rounds into the wide openness before us. We each had six magazines loaded with 35 rounds' and on the command we let rip into the dry grass. The automatic fire chattered at the peace – we emptied one magazine after the next.

I was standing two troops away from Grant, who shouted over the barrage of noise: 'Look here!' He expelled automatic bursts with a huge smile set across his face. His barrel was smoking and glowing red-hot, like a poker pulled from a furnace. There was no rest for his rifle – his belt burned off and his barrel began to warp. Once he had shot through his last magazine, his rifle had become totally useless – the warp was visible to the naked eye. We had shot over 300 rounds in only a few minutes, and the heat rose from our barrels as though it were a smoking fire we held in our hands.

Operation Desert Fox was over and by the sound of things, was a huge success. While we made our way back to the Ratels, we caught sight of the helicopter ferrying those of high rank from the hilltop – they flew over us and out of sight – the answer to our future mission held amongst them.

'What now?' we asked, but it was an unanswerable question. We were as ready in body and mind as we would ever be for an operation into Angola.

1988-Oshigambo. Wayne and Grant in a dugout on the outside walls of the Oshigambo Base. This became our sleeping place for a month while the Cuban situation cooled.

29

On the outside in Oshigambo

Dirty, tired, and still slightly stiff from the drawn-out tension, we rode out in convoy into a glorious African sunset, marking the end of another sweltering day and the beginning of a long dark night.

Coming to a halt in the middle of nowhere, each Ratel was assigned ammunition and we all went to work loading up. The gunners always had the hardest task – of lugging the heavy belts from the ground to the turret, then lowering them down their tower and layering them into the metal boxes, then sliding the linked round into the cannon's chamber. Under the dancing flashes of light from torches, we completed our bombing up and waited, as usual, for the next order.

The darkness seemed to play cruel jokes upon us while we rested in the murkiness of the Ratels, or sat on top of them enjoying the cool night air that passed over our stinking bodies. I sat and watched dancing shadows in the silver moonlight – the starry night somehow made everything feel alright, and I too enjoyed the fresh cool air, hoping that it would take with it that lingering fear that something was soon to happen.

I wish I knew my fate, and those of my buddies' and then I would not have to worry! I kept saying to myself.

Rumours again began to circulate' our two-month call-up definitely was looking more like three. The thought that tonight would be the night we would go into Angola only fuelled the fire of our fears. Fear had to be faced, but it was not easy to keep our waiting minds clear of stories of incinerated troops sitting in Ratels, and Ratels disabled in minefields.

61-Mechanized Battalion, 4-SAI Battalion, and 32-Battalion – all Ratel units – had lost men in Angola in previous operations. The Buffalo soldiers, known as 32-Battalion, were a very well respected unit of men with an extremely high kill rate in comparison to their losses. Most of the African soldiers from this unit were Angolan soldiers who were trained into disciplined troops by white South Africans.

We imagined these units still to be in Angola, and wondered where we would fit into the puzzle. 61-Mech and 4-SAI were made up of National Servicemen serving out their mandatory two years. The Buffalo soldiers, on the other hand, were fulfilling their careers as fearless fighters – though with a meagre income to support their Angolan families, who were now living on the SWA/Namibian side of the border.

The darkness and the wait only added scare to our situation – we sat literally with our sanity and our lives swinging like a pendulum, and we wavered with each sway in and out of limbo. My chest felt tight, as if I were wearing a straight jacket and the buckles were tightening. Patiently we awaited the green light.

At around 22:00 our world was rocked by shouts of 'We are moving out' and so, sitting stony-faced, we took our places and went with the flow. The Ratel engines came alive, and with them the fear ran through me with hollowness in my gut, leaving my legs to dangle weakly. I was ready to get this started so it could be ended, one way or the other.

One Ratel behind the other, the driver navigated his way forward, following the set of round red convoy lights that guided us through the pitch-blackness.

'This must be it. I think we are going in tonight!' Brian exclaimed through the darkness of the hull, below the gunner's turret. The rest of us remained silent, and stared tense and wide-eyed into the darkness, without being able to see a hand in front of our shit-scared faces. After an hour's nerve-racking drive, we eventually halted and went into an all-round protective position for the night.

Sleep came surprisingly easily under the calming ceiling of a star-studded night – but before it did, that unanswerable question – how we could be on a mission of war in such a silent and peaceful atmosphere – nagged at my being. It seemed so out of place.

I said a prayer with my eyes tightly closed, praying for a protective hand over all of us – for I honestly felt this was the end. My gut had been telling me this for so long that I could not deny the overwhelming feeling that had suffocated me like a deathly illness for 30 days that felt more like a year. I was 23, and my life – along with those from Platoon 3 and everyone else from 81 Armoured Brigade – rested in the hands of our government in Pretoria.

If we went in, some of us would not come out' that was war – something we were ready for – but nevertheless it was a high price to pay. We were all too young to die, but obviously war does not select an age for death, it is random, and we all have an equal chance. It was like gambling at a casino: some would win and some would lose.

When the sun rose across the horizon, it brought with it a fresh new start to the day. The new day seemed so different from the night before, as if my prayer had been heard – changing all that was to be. Suddenly rumours swirled through the ranks that we were heading south, towards a base called Oshigambo, southeast of Ruacana and north of Ondangwa.

Is this true? I wondered. Because if it is, it looks as though our attack has been called off.

29. On the outside in Oshigambo

To celebrate this sudden change of luck, Wayne had us in hysterics' he stuffed Super-C tablets one after another into his mouth, stretching his cheeks to bursting point' but he maintained a straight face while we rolled around, holding our sides at his comical act.

'Nickol, you look just like a chipmunk!' Macky spluttered, consumed in laughter by Wayne's ballooning red face and sagging eyes – which held no emotion, for even a hint of a smile would release the mouthful of stuffed in tablets, like a barrage of bullets.

Scrounging for more, we tore our kit apart to add to his diminishing supply, adding it to his cupped hands as he squatted by the Ratel doorway. We rocked around in the hull, doubled over, our eyes streaming and our bodies hurting with laughter. Wayne had about 30 of these glucose tablets in his mouth – which was quite some feat in our eyes' and luckily for all of us, he did not choke on this huge mouthful.

What a great release it was to laugh – it did not matter at what, so long as we could forget where we were for a few minutes. Suddenly it felt like we had become new people, this heavy burden having shifted slightly from our shoulders – which still carried tension, but not to the degree of the day before.

To move south, we would be distancing ourselves from the danger of an all-out attack into Angola and away from the border line – allowing us to regroup our thoughts in a somewhat safer zone. Hours of driving had us squinting through thick clouds of dust, and getting rocked around while our bodies absorbed the impact of flesh on metal. Loud swearing followed laughter to numb our anger and frustration. Moving southward certainly helped lift our spirits, which had been at an all-time low only one day ago' and now here we were, riding a wave with a sudden blossoming of newfound energy.

Eventually our convoy of Alpha Company Ratels arrived at a South African base, fortified by high-heaped walls of rock-hard sand. The sandbanks added a further shield to our bunkers behind these walls. Our company had arrived at the Oshigambo base – a base that had been manned by 8-SAI, an infantry unit from Upington.

On entering the base, we automatically presumed that it would be our home for the last month of our camp. We were mortified to learn that this was not the case. Our beds would be next to our Ratels, on the outside of these high walls of sand and away from the protection of the deep bunkers. Beggars cannot be choosers' and we moved through the base and then lined up, one alongside the next, with the cannons pointing into the open. This was now our new home, and we had a stronger feeling of security than we had during our long and tedious first month living dirty in the middle of the wide-open bush – with not as much as a tent or a base in sight.

We were ordered to use our camouflage nets to cover our Ratels, which not only gave us a hiding place but added shade to our living area. In case of an air or ground attack, we were ordered to dig one to two metre deep trenches, and throw the excess sand around the sides for added height and protection. Our individual holes soon began to look like rows of graves, in which we had to lower ourselves for sleep every night.

'Knowing my luck,' Grant said, 'the mortar bomb will land right in my trench!'

'*Ja*, if we do get attacked it will be easy for them to bury us,' I said. 'All they have to do is put up a cross!'

We laughed together at the situation.

The sand was soft, like that from the beach – which made digging easier but sleep more or less impossible because of the constant trickle of this fine earth into our faces, hair, and sleeping bags. Lying still, as if we were literally dead, was the only way to escape the slow stream of these fine granules that drove us mad – the equivalent of water torture.

We lay below the earth with the stars looking down over us, trying to calm the turmoil that raged within us. I was surprised at how calm I felt below ground level, having always suffered from claustrophobia. I know it was the focus I had on the stars that steered me through, while my shoulders rubbed the sides of my trench and my head lay propped in my cupped hands, until sleep whisked me into a faraway place.

It felt good to have a place that we could call 'home,' with a canteen that we could visit between 18:00 and 19:00 to buy beer, and then return to the outside of the wall to consume it. To have a South African beer in our hands after such a long absence linked us back to our homeland, some 3000 kilometres away. We savoured each sip of an ice-cold tin of Castle in the desert heat, and in time to watch the sunset through the camouflaged nets. For the first time in a long while, we began to feel human again.

Time had abandoned us – our rubber-banded wristwatches spelled it out to us, but we still did not know what day it was. The only time we knew was army time – which had no boundaries' it ranged between routine patrols.

There was still lots of talk about the *Cubanie*, Cubans who – we had been led to believe – were very demoralized, for they felt abandoned by their leader, Fidel Castro, and their people, in this remote, dark part of Africa. We were also told by our rank that they were infected with AIDS and malaria and that was the main reason that Cuba did not want them back. Apparently they were manning

29. On the outside in Oshigambo

tanks that were in disrepair and urgent need of maintenance, and forced to fight in this war that they would rather not be a part of. Whether this was true or not, I have no idea. It could quite easily have been a propaganda ploy by our rank, to boost our confidence if we came head-to-head with them on the battlefront. Hearing their predicament did lift our spirits' and if the order came to attack, we felt we would have an edge over them.

Those ugly rumours of an extended call-up continued to swirl in light of the recent battles over the border, and the build-up of Cuban and FAPLA brigades within striking distance of the SWA/Namibian border line, and the continual Cuban disregard of the no-fly zones. Nevertheless it rattled us to live in this 50-50 balance with circumstances beyond our control, and the waiting eating away at us. By moving into Angola, we would at least have some control over it – as opposed to the limbo that enveloped us.

In 1988, in South-West Africa we experienced the largest massing of troops and armoury on foreign soil since the Second World War. Owamboland was crawling with thousands upon thousands of troops, waiting for that green light to steamroll into Angola. It was no wonder that we had been living out in the bush for a month and were now on the outside wall of a base' each base now overflowing with troop capacity, and each remaining on high alert.

Alpha Company had been lucky to be placed at the wall of the Oshigambo base, which housed an old decrepit fridge that chilled the beer, and had a shower that we could sneak into every few days – to scrub the filth from a dust-filled patrol, and ears and hair filled with fine grit after a night's sleep in our graves.

Our patrols took us towards the border with Angola' we randomly stopped at Cuca shops and kraals to look for SWAPO. An Owambo tracker and translator were assigned to two vehicles per platoon.

We had been informed by our captain that a Ratel from 4-SAI had been ambushed, and a few National Servicemen inside this vehicle had been killed by armour-piercing rounds that had been sprayed through the hull, killing them where they sat. When he finished telling the gruesome story, we were instructed to sit on top of the vehicle, and under no circumstances inside, using our elevated position to the advantage of seeing the enemy before they fired.

I always entered the kraals with caution on high alert and my rifle at the ready. This maze of a stockade was a great place for an ambush. A terrorist backed into a corner was always more wise to his surroundings than us. We made our way through the cooking areas, passing smoking fires and steaming clay pots, and pens for chickens and goats' and then proceeded into the living areas, on ground that was as smooth as a tiled floor – having being passed over constantly by the toughened feet of the local Owambo. We peered into each darkened hut, looking for any suspicious activity that could be attributed to SWAPO. At the sight of us, kids ran screaming and petrified to the shield of their elders, while we intimidating white soldiers scoured through their dwelling, barely uttering a greeting as we went. Our section usually left with the suspicion that weaponry was buried close by, awaiting SWAPO retrieval under cover of darkness. These kraals hardly ever had young men in them' they were fighting for or against us, leaving behind the old, the really young, and the mothers to hold their family units together. Some of these locals looked through us with scorn and hatred, while others saw us as protectors of their lives and their subsistence livelihood. Leaving the kraals, we almost always got a gut feeling who was on whose side and for those we felt were SWAPO sympathizers, there was little to nothing we could do about it.

Our patrols had taken on a different approach overnight, with a more relaxed feel as we sat on top of the vehicles, burning in the sun and enjoying the cool breeze passing over us – as if we had not a care in the world.

The drivers took to the sandy roads and we lazed on the roof, shirtless, scouring our surroundings, our rifles always in our hands. We ducked and dived as we passed under trees with low-hanging branches, which often whipped and lashed at our bodies and were followed with some vulgar cursing. I watched as the Ratel in front of us passed beneath a tree' its array of branching arms brushed a couple of troops, with the cleanest of sweeps, from the vehicle to the sandy road two metres below.

It looked funny for a few seconds, until we saw the discomfort of our fellow soldiers who had the wind knocked completely out of them. Lucky for them, they had been wearing their helmets strapped tightly around the chin – which had helped cushion their fall and a possible head injury.

With a little help from their fellow section buddies and us, they climbed aboard their Ratel and we continued over this meandering roadway, which was a mere path through the flat, open wilderness. Bouncing in a seated position, we stared through the dust as the Ratel raced at every bump. We were content to sit and stare, for the noise was too loud to talk. John interrupted my thought process as he thrust a lit joint into my hand and with nothing better to do, I sucked hard, taking my high before passing it to Riaan, Nic, and anyone else who wanted an escape route from this sweltering and unforgiving, dirty bush life. By the time it circled again, we were well and truly out of our trees' and we knew if we did hit a contact, we would be totally useless – our reaction time slowed to a crawl. Seeing the enemy was now the furthest thing from our minds, as we enjoyed our newfound relaxation.

29. On the outside in Oshigambo

Back at base, I decided to climb up a metal ladder to the top of a water tower – a height of at least 25 metres – in the middle of the Oshigambo camp. Once high into the air, I stood next to the glinting, silvery tin of the water tank and looked down onto the base, watching Ratels coming and going as they filled up with diesel and water. Meanwhile troops crossed the camp as small as ants emerging from tents, only to disappear behind more rows of tents and vehicles.

I felt like a bird in a tall tree as I gazed upon the nothingness, well beyond the graded walls of this camp, upon the flat heat haze of dry dusty land, which stretched for an eternity, and only a few green makalani palm trees breaking the endless drabness. The odd anthill stood as a statue, facing solidly north, surrounded by nothing but sand, with not a single stone on this land that was, for the most part, as flat as a tabletop.

The base is what gave life and location to an otherwise depopulated expanse beyond the four walls. On the eastern side of the base, I made out the unmistakable open graves, which had been neatly carved from the ground in a straight row at least 30 metres from the camp wall – waiting for our bodies to fill the void for our nightly sleeps.

Next to me, antennas reached skyward, connecting the base with valuable radio information – the important coordinates in a piece of rural land, where no other form of communication existed besides word of mouth.

Holding my gaze upon this wide-open landscape, with a slanted hand upon my brow as a shield to the penetrating rays of the sun, and sweat dripping from my face, I held my vision firmly upon this nothingness before me – a place I knew I could never find again on any given map, either with compass bearings or coordinates. It was a place I never wanted to find again' I despised every part of it.

'Fuck! I hate this torturous land!' I said, before hugging the metal ladder on my descent. Walking through the base, I caught a passing tune from a dusty and beaten-up radio – a tune that radiated hope and encouragement from the tiny, distorted speaker. It was the first time I had heard music in five weeks, and it felt good – but still nothing in comparison to that first full wash with soap, lathered over my itchy body that had been sandblasted with dirt. Our bearded faces had concealed some of the filth, and dried-on sweat, 35 days old, became the longest stretch I had ever gone without a wash. In the past, rivers, shallow *shonas*, or even rainwater had served as a shower or bath' but this time there were no rivers and the rainy season was months away. That first shower, as cold as it was, had been music to our ears and lightened our heavy feel' we danced to the music of water beneath the showerhead.

Back at the Ratels, everyone was under the shade' the afternoon sun powered its way down upon us. Wayne was up to his old tricks again, with a fire bucket of steaming tea and a teaspoon. Stealing his way behind an unsuspecting troop, his teaspoon simmering in the heat of his tea, he waited for the right moment before he withdrew the spoon and carefully touched it on a fellow soldier's inner arm.

'Fuck you, you bastard!' the soldier exclaimed, while we all fell into a ruckus of laughter on the sidelines.

Wayne was the fixer, and whenever a troop had a problem with a zipper, especially sleeping bags – Wayne was there with his needle and thread to fix the situation. We all had sewing kits, and attended to our needs with this brown pouch of emergency buttons, thread, and a variety of needles. There was only one button that mattered, and that was the waist button to hold up our cut-off browns.

While we laughed and joked, I caught sight of Paul sitting on top of his Ratel, staring out into nothing, his face serious and his thoughts a million miles from where the rest of his National Service buddies clowned around. The happy-go-lucky Paul, whom we had all grown to know so well during the early days of 1-SAI, had lapsed into a different person – confused, serious, and so out-of-reach from his old upbeat self. Gone were those fun days when he was Platoon 3s Alpha Section leader, having referred to everyone as 'Sakkie.'

'Those three months in Mozambique really fucked him up!' I said, turning to Wayne and Grant. We looked over at Paul, who was sitting in his own world of trauma, still walled in a dark, dingy cell, lost somewhere in the third world capital of Maputo.

'Bastards!' we thought, as we watched our buddy now greatly affected by his mental and emotional scars, sealed inside him like a curse.

None of us knew his story, but we knew it had to have been a living hell – a hell that had taken a good friend of ours and changed him into a person we no longer knew very well. It was sad to watch, but there was nothing we could do other than involve him as much as we could, and allow him to decide whether he wanted to join us or not. It was quite evident that Paul also wanted to go into Angola, to release some of the anger that was raging like an inferno inside him – as payback for the torture he had endured.

After a few beers next to our holes, ostracized from the comfort of the makeshift bar – which had an old television set and a video machine – we closed off another mindless day on the outside. When the beers were consumed and the talking had died down, we wriggled into our sleeping bags fully clothed, searching for a comfortable position between our sandy walls of safety.

29. On the outside in Oshigambo

In the morning we were projected back three and a half years' we embarked on our first foot patrol across this rugged land that gave us such a harsh backlash – we began a patrol with no end in sight, towards the furnace ball of glowing heat. Sweating and kicking at the dust, I could not help but think back to all our patrols, day in and day out, at the torturous hand of nature' we willed ourselves forward under the buckling loads of our gear.

After an hour's walk we stopped at a small bush shop known as a Cuca shop, which was always a great excuse for a warm bottle of beer or a soda drink. Sitting on a log positioned outside this weathered-looking tin shack, with a mismatch of painted sheets puzzled together, we sat with some local African people, who had all the time in the world to watch life pass them by. It was surprising to see some young men of fighting age, also congregated outside this shop. But since they had no uniform or rifle, we could only sit and speculate.

Our Owambo trackers and translators spoke to them for the length of time that it took us to finish our drinks. Back on our feet, and feeling slightly groggy, we continued through the bushveld – our patrol was intended not only as a show of strength, but also as a reaching-out to the local population, who could count on the soldiers for support and safety. The army called it the 'Hearts and Minds Campaign.'

The long, hot day took us into countless kraals, through many miles of wire strands acting as fences and barricading small, dry fields from scrawny, hungry cows and wandering goats, and past water wells bored into the hard ground. With a plastic bucket tied crudely to a frayed piece of rope, acting as the lifeline to draw the weight of water from below ground to the thirsting mouths at the surface, we watched their lives in action. The local Owambo people congregated around these ever-important sites with dirty metal drums, dented from years of use – they waited in line for their turn at pulling the rope up and over a log that sat in the fork of two V-shaped branches. Once their metal buckets were full, they ferried this vital source of life back to their dwellings – either on their heads or on the back of a docile donkey – and into the waiting clay cooking pots.

While we watched them threading their way through the bushes and trees, it did not bother us one bit, the tough life they had been dealt. We looked right through them and their burden of hardship, caring rather for our own well-being than their everyday lifestyle of fear and subsistence. We saw these underprivileged peoples for the most part as a cover backing for SWAPO and with this in mind, we viewed them as obstacles to our presence in this land. We had no sympathy or compassion for them. All we cared about was ourselves – serving out our time and returning to a normal life back in society, a million miles away. We were given only a mere glimpse of the hardship that these Owambo people lived through daily – one that we hopefully only had a few more weeks to endure ourselves.

After a long and very tiring day, we were thankfully reunited with our Ratels, and felt somewhat back to normal. Riding back into base, we were informed that between 2 August and 15 August, a total of 14 terrorists had been killed in northern Owamboland. It was weird to hear these statistics as we rode around and walked our patrols' knowing that the terrorists sidestepped our daily movements – so much so that we decided they were invisible, or a figment of our imaginations.

The sunset came in its usual way, and yet always so different from the last – it set about instilling that calm through one and all, and binding us with that true and very proud African feel. The magnificent scene was set with wild colours, contrasting and complementing each other with bright reds and fiery oranges streaking across a purplish grey backdrop. The sun had made its statement in all its glory, and the shadows began to erode the splashing of colour until it was finally replaced with darkness, ending another harsh day across the African plains and transforming the beauty into a dark coolness.

The next day we awoke to the sound of a bunch of roosters crowing out some very annoying tunes, forcing us up with the sun for an earlier-than-expected morning coffee. After some food, and orders for the day, we departed in our regular platoon convoys into the surrounding bush, for another day of driving while sitting on the roofs of the vehicles. While on the patrol, Grant found a stick with three prongs' and with his poncho already tied around his neck, catching the wind in the form of a cloak, he posed with his newfound fork as the devil himself.

This was our hell, and Grant had helped make a mockery of it – to the delight of everyone around, including the Owambo translators, who joined in with uncontrollable fits of laughter. By now they were convinced that many of us were quite crazy. Our joy and zest for life had been suppressed for so long, with all the uncertainties and insanities that swirled through our weary thoughts along this border line and it seemed to be coming out now. Just to express our amusement with hearty laughter once again made us feel normal, even if it only lasted a few measly seconds.

While on the patrol, a major joined our platoon and rode with Grant and Corporal Bean in the turret of their vehicle. Suddenly, out of nowhere, a springbok bolted from its cover and crossed our vehicles, leaping and springing through the air and overgrowth. The major gave orders to the driver to chase down the buck while he stood in the turret, ready to fire, his rifle set upon the frightened antelope that was trying to get away. The vehicle lurched over dips, rocking and swaying, rising and dropping, charging forward at an alarmingly fast speed. During the chase, Corporal Bean whacked his head against the metal in the turret, drawing blood, the Ratel almost rolling in the process while the driver fought to hold it upon its six wheels. Had it rolled, it almost definitely would have taken lives' the two in the turret would not have enough time to drop into the tower and those on the roof would have been flung like clothes pegs blown from a washing line. The major had used his rank in a very unprofessional way, and had come too close to causing death for us to let it pass quietly. Grant and Corporal Bean decided to push for charges against the major. That, in turn, was met with a big uproar and like most situations in the army involving big brass, nothing materialized and the charges were never laid. For the most part it was not worth the bother. Any military hearings that took place would mean that Grant and Corporal Bean would be called back to Pretoria. At the end of the day, when the anger subsided, it was not worth the effort.

We had little respect for this land. Ration pack wrappers were discarded in the wind or buried in the sand' Ratels ploughed through trees, half the time with the drivers egged on by excited troops. Fields were stepped through and crops destroyed by uncaring boots, along with looks of fatigue and anger, which were constantly written across our faces.

Being soldiers, we did not make it easy to win local support for our fight against these near-invisible terrorists. But for the most part we did our best to keep on the right side of the people – the 'Hearts and Minds Campaign' being at the forefront of the SADF's show of strength through Owamboland. The anger remained instilled in us, however, and our facial expressions showed our dissatisfaction with a predicament not of our own choosing. As a result we blamed the local people, and their godforsaken country.

Back in the base, on the outside of the wall, we were given a day to relax – which we spent washing our clothes with a bar of Sunlight soap under a cold tap in the toilet facility of the base. The rest of the day was spent in a hollowed-out hole, with a groundsheet covering it, filled with water to the brim. This was our makeshift swimming pool, which was barely deep enough to wet half our bodies' our feet stuck out into the sand, and we revelled in the beautiful coolness in a bid to temporarily escape the heat of the day. Time cast its shadow slowly across the scorching earth – we took it in turns throughout the day and when it became just too hot, we ran the gauntlet over the burning sand, back to the cover of coolness below the camouflaged netting.

While we laughed and joked, enjoying our time on the South-West African 'beach,' a bunch of locals came to the fence, trying to sell their round millet cakes for a few South African cents – which was always a nice change from the constipation of ration pack food.

'Mmmmbakumm!' Wayne sounded out, in comical reference to the Afrikaans word *bakgat* excellent. He bit into his yellowish brown cake with a satisfied smile across his face, and savoured every bite.

It was 26 August, and not a soul knew what this particular date meant – until the rank spelled it out for us. Our captain told us that it was the anniversary of the bush war – the first shots had been fired in a place almost impossible to find on the map – a small village called Ongulumbashe, in Owamboland, in 1966. It was hard to believe that this war had been going on for 22 years – death, both black and white, was just a part of this land's history.

The captain assured us that tonight we were going to be mortared by the terrorists. We looked at him as if to say: What the hell have you been smoking? What has brought this about so suddenly? Apparently this information had come from reliable intelligence in the field. It was common fact that bases had been bombed in the past – Okalango had been bombed in March 1988, and other bases had come under mortar attack – the worst being Katima Mulilo, where ten soldiers lost their lives in 1978.

We all knew anything was possible in this land' a mortar attack was not at all out of the question. It had happened before, and it would happen again. The question was: Would it be launched upon our base, with us hunkered down in our holes? Not taking the threat lightly, we dug our holes a little deeper, raising the sides with some sandbags for added protection, still not knowing what to expect, or whether to believe the warning or not.

In the evening we each bought a six-pack to chase away any lurking fears that the captain might have injected into us with his serious speech – which we could not help but believe. It was crazy how we joked about the attack' Grant, as sober as a judge, led the onslaught of comical antics.

'It was nice knowing you guys!' we sarcastically remarked to one another, and shook hands in mockery of a deathly farewell.

'You just watch, one of those bombs is going to land right in my trench!' Grant blurted out, to the drunken delight of all of us who sat in a circle of darkness in the sand. A generator from within the walls of the base fed our only light, and it cast shadows across the night and over the sand.

When the beer was finished, we felt our way through the blackness to the cut-out holes, before lowering ourselves carefully into our pits so as not to cause an avalanche of sand. With our rifles propped up in the holes – within easy reach in case we needed them in the night – we lay on our backs and gazed up at the show of stars, in their plentiful clusters, flickering and sparkling peace upon us, as they had done countless times before. There had been many times I had watched falling stars drop from the sky and fizzle out abruptly, like that of a light bulb. Captivated by the sight, I was left to wonder if anyone else had also seen it. Life seemed so peaceful at this moment as I lay rigid, staring upward past the sand walls of my trench, losing my thoughts to the heavens. Our fears always grew more meaningful at night' the calm and the darkness worked against us, especially on this anniversary. Finally our eyes grew weary, and I did not wake until the roosters drilled holes like a beeping alarm clock into my heavy head.

'Shut up!' someone shouted, hoping that the roosters would obey an English command from a weary troop.

'Skiet die foken ding!' – Shoot the fuckin' thing! – another screamed in Afrikaans. The death threat from the night before had gone by without another passing thought' the main focus was now shutting this bird up for good.

Unfortunately, the desire got the better of us, and had us all up early, for that annoying sound was much easier to handle in a wakened state with a warm fire bucket of coffee in hand.

It did not surprise us at all that the so-called promised attack had not materialized. This was part and parcel of life on the border: Bombs did rock bases, vehicles did hit landmines, and troops did die' but there was always that bulletproof shield of invincibility to ward off the inevitable.

Our last days in Oshigambo were spent riding patrols and drinking warm beer from Cuca shops – which made our Ratel patrols a little more exciting, and a little harder to endure, with a lot more unplanned toilet stops.

'Piss break!' came the shouts, bringing the vehicle to an emergency halt. We relieved our bladders on the sandy soil, leaving our mark next to the deep Ratel tracks.

Finally we got the news we had all been waiting for – the news of our departure southwards to Grootfontein. We met it with unbelievable jubilation mixed with sheer relief. We could now officially rule out all possibility of an attack into Angola. This news was the best we had heard in seven very long, drawn-out weeks – the catalyst for another drunken evening, for most of us needed at least a dozen beers to quench our dry thirsts. Laughing, and talking louder with each beer, we could not help but think of home, a hot shower, and a bed – and, best of all, our freedom to do as we pleased without the rifle, the uniform, and the threat of death.

The day had eventually dawned, and we massed up into another convoy, taking up a long stretch of white gravel road as we waited to move out, our open graves left to the wind. When the engines started, our hearts raced with them, beating with each rev as the air was filled with diesel and euphoria.

The first stage of the journey home had oh-so-thankfully begun. With smiles speaking volumes etched into our dirty faces, we looked eagerly forward' all with similar thoughts, returning us to the civilian world.

1988-1-RNT. 1-Regiment Northern Transvaal.

1988-Windhoek. Walking ecstatically towards two SAFAIR C-130s for our flights back to South Africa. The Cuban threat had faded with a settlement on Namibia's future reached in New York.

30
The frightening truth

Driving through the dust storm, we never realized that we were one of the first units to begin the historical withdrawal from SWA/Namibia. Never once had we dreamed of the idea, let alone being part of the actual pullout from this buffer zone – a sight we did not expect to see in our lifetimes.

We had no idea of the political side to our military presence in this country, which had striven for independence for decades from South Africa's rule. We were here to serve out our time and follow through on whatever was ordered' and so with the order being withdrawal, we only too gladly followed through.

Resolution 435 had been all the talk as the South Africans, Cubans, and Angolans brokered a deal to bring about peace with timely troop withdrawals, watched with keen interest by the United States and the Soviet Union. With South Africa keeping to its side of the deal, the last of the SADF troops drove out of Angola on 30 August. The withdrawal was already in motion within SWA/Namibia, as convoys of vehicles headed south towards Oshakati and Grootfontein. While the South Africans headed south, the Cubans were to head north towards set parallels within a specified time frame, until they were completely out of Angola.

Our convoy came to a halt at Okatope, where we lined our vehicles nose-to-tail in more parallel rows than I could count. The vehicles stretched for miles within this wide, sandy, open area and my guess was that there were at least 500 vehicles, comprising Samils, Kwevoels, Ratels, Casspirs, low-beds carrying tanks, recovery vehicles, and some vehicles that I had never seen the likes of before. To me, it seemed like this was a staging point – vehicles continued to roll in, filling up the sandy space with another long line of armoury and logistical strength. Sitting in clusters upon the vehicles, and standing next to them, were thousands of South African soldiers – all part of the massive troop pullout. We sat on the vehicles with shirts off, working on our tans until the next order came to roll out.

We waited our turn as one long row of vehicles moved out, leaving a timed gap between the next convoy as a safety precaution against the threat of an attack. We rumbled down the paved road as sitting targets to any SWAPO with an RPG-7. After a long wait, our Alpha Company was told to get ready to move out and with excitement we followed through on the order. Sitting on the top of the vehicle, we left behind the multitude waiting their turn to head south.

What a feeling it was to be sitting high and mighty on top of this glorious machine, which we knew would have done us proud had we gone into battle. Thankfully we were all sitting with our limbs intact, the war for us having been so miraculously averted. Our smiles were proof of the relief that we all shared.

The drive away from the border line was a pleasure in comparison to the drive across the Blue Route. Eight hours on the road was plain sailing, with no bumps or jarring and white dust, which we had sucked into our lungs only seven weeks ago. Tired and weary, we drove into the Grootfontein base in the late afternoon, again lining our vehicles up one behind the other. When each was accounted for, we handed them over. Stripping out all our kit, we made our way to some newly erected tents that awaited our entry into this camp.

Placing my kit bag in the tent, I decided to take a walk around the base, and made my way alone to the far corner, where I found a fenced-off area. I peered through and saw a graveyard of destroyed South African vehicles – some having hit land mines – some had been shelled by either RPG-7 rockets or by enemy tanks, and others looked as though they had been the victims of negligence. I surveyed the scene, my eyes darting over the destruction of these crippled and battered machines of war' but through all of it, I was looking at the death of young soldiers who had been snatched away suddenly – probably before they knew what hit them. It gave me chills to be staring at all of this, as if I were intruding on another soldier's space. While I stood and stared, with my hands clutching the open wire fence, a Samil recovery vehicle drove right by me towing a Ratel 20 – an exact replica of the vehicle I had been in. I could not believe what I saw when it drew level with my eyes. Where I would have sat, a huge opening had been blown through the solid hydraulic door, blowing out the interior and leaving the metal ballooned out and peeled back in charcoal black – in the same way as if one stabbed a knife into a tin can and then twisted it to enlarge the hole.

It seemed so surreal to have this vehicle pass before me, as if it were trying to make a statement to that dreaded feeling which had ebbed through me for so long. In my sleep, I had dreamed of one of our Ratels being taken out, and in my paranoid waking moments those visions continually flashed through my mind.

Was this what had been tormenting me all this time? I wondered. This vehicle had been recovered from the war in Angola – a place to which we had been destined. In typical South African battle honour – never to leave a vehicle behind unless it was unsalvageable – it was towed out, with the bodies having been flown home in body bags.

Here I was, a Ratel soldier who had believed that something bad was going to happen to me. Now, instead of being maimed or dead, I was alive, looking at a scene involving a less-fortunate section of men – if roles were reversed and circumstances were slightly changed, our section of men, and myself, could so easily have been incinerated in this tank blast, instead of them.

For too long I had felt I would see white South African blood shed and now to see with my own eyes, only a few feet away, the strength of this Ratel now crippled and a cloud of death within its hull, really hit me like a ton of bricks, deep into my gut where that feeling had lingered and plagued me like a sickness.

Shit, now I know how lucky I was. I took one last look at these military vehicles, with their open battle wounds and the invisible death of the young boys aboard. Quickly I turned, and started walking at a very brisk pace away from this destruction – so thankful to be the one able to walk away.

Back at the tent, I told a few of my friends what I had seen and left it at that – what had entered my mind at the time was best left untold. In spite of how I felt, I knew I would not have let my friends down had we been ordered into an operation, with the camaraderie built up amongst us overriding fear and taking care of our unit of men.

In the evening we were invited to attend a concert in a dome-covered stadium, with a few local South African bands performing. Taking in bottles of brandy and other hard spirits, we made our way through the terraced seating towards the back of the arena where we seated ourselves with a great view, looking down over the stage. Before the bands took to the floor, a man – holding the rank of a brigadier or general – took hold of the microphone and sincerely thanked us for our contribution to the war effort. He then began to brief us on the role we were to have played, which seemed so strange, for we were never put in the loop before.

Our training as a mechanized battalion, and then as an armoured brigade, was to penetrate into Angola and take a FAPLA/Cuban/SWAPO base at Xangango, 150 kilometres into Angola.

On hearing this, a hushed silence fell upon the stadium, as if a gunshot had suddenly been fired. We looked at each other with blank faces' the truth quite overwhelming on hearing it firsthand, even though we had sensed something of this magnitude all along.

Mention was made of the 11 National Servicemen who were killed by the bombing while they guarded the Calueque dam, and how angry the military was for this devastatingly high South African loss. He also said it was the first time that South Africa had to take a step back instead of a step forward in retaliation – so as to not upset the peace agreements that were in progress in Cairo. General Malan, back in South Africa, had described the act as 'treason,' the South African government interpreted it as a deliberate act by the Cubans to unsettle the peace process.

For the first time we got confirmation from a reliable source, which so captivated our attention that there was not even a whisper in the house. He went on to tell us how close the Cuban and FAPLA brigades had come to Ruacana. It was the furthest south they had ever been, and hence the biggest massing of South African troops on the SWA/Namibian side in the history of the border war – all to combat the situation if they continued south over the border.

Resolution 435 and the peace agreement had undoubtedly saved us from some gruesome losses, which would have been caused by flashes of fire from Soviet T-54, T-55 and T-62 tanks. I have no doubt that, had we gone in, we would have had far fewer casualties and would have won the battle thanks to our superior training and discipline.

It was unbelievable to hear that our lives were in the middle of all of this. Secrecy had long been the byword regarding South African operations against SWAPO, especially on Angolan soil. Most of us knew that deaths from the operational area hit the television sets back in the comfort of South African homes at staggered intervals – so as to not alarm the public of high casualties at any one time. Very little was known by the South African public about what had been going on for years in SWA/Namibia and Angola – censorship of press made sure the public was given only the basic story, and hardly any detail. In the same way, any information transferred to us was always short and sweet and never very elaborate. Military officials believed the less we knew, the better – after all, we were not paid to think but to follow through on orders. To hear this information only confirmed how close we had come to a full-scale attack, even though we knew something was up. But hearing it officially only amplified the vulnerable position we had been in for the past eight weeks. It was scary to know this now, and everyone took a few extra seconds to process all this information after the final word of thanks had been given for our efforts.

I took a deep breath and thanked my lucky stars for guiding my friends and me safely through this minefield of emotion and sparing us the horrors of war. The stadium erupted into loud cheering and clapping as the heavy-ranked military chief made his exit, passing the stage over to a young band of South African musicians. Twisting the tops off our half jacks of brandy, vodka, and whisky, we began to drink a toast to our lives and our anticipated reintegration into society. Swigging on our bottles and fire buckets of diluted alcohol, with ration pack cola crystals and water, we stood up and began to

30. The frightening truth

dance to the music – a sound we had hardly heard in the entire period of this camp' we celebrated and let loose with a feeling that we had been granted a second chance at life.

The first song that was played was *Our beds are burning*,' taken from that great Aussie band Midnight Oil. We all joined in' and it sounded as though the real Midnight Oil was playing before us. The second song was another from the same band, with the appropriate title *Put down that weapon*. Swaying from side to side, laughing and grinning from ear to ear, we enjoyed the moment, and mouthed the words until the chorus – and then the stadium erupted in what sounded like an emotional plea' we chanted the words in one loud, unified voice – 'Put down that weapon' – with more feeling and gut-wrenching emotion than I had ever seen or heard from a bunch of soldiers.

Goosebumps lined my arms with the hairs pushing straight up as my thoughts wandered and my body seemed to float and flow along with the current towards a burning bright light of freedom.

When those voices shouted and screamed: *Put down that weapon or we'll all be gone*, I was immediately torn from my trance and pulled into the chorus of drunken defiance with a rewarding feeling of having emerged unscathed on the other side. I looked around and could not help but wonder how few of us really wanted to have been a part of this mighty military force in a country we had little to no attachment for.

Again, we had followed through on our call of duty, ready to obey orders, unconditionally.

What a moving feeling it was to be integrated from all walks of life, with such varying professions under one roof, united in our stand for our country, prepared for whatever it took in the fight against Communism. The song and the voices reverberating around the arena moved a part of me, swelling my heart with pride for the first time in a very long time. The songs continued to pump out into the dimly lit stadium throughout the course of the evening, the drink drying up well before the music had ended. A couple of drunken soldiers left the stadium in a hunt for more of this intoxicating medicine. Macky was standing next to me, talking and laughing and half stumbling with the beat and then suddenly, without warning, he vomited right past me – spewing all over the seats in front of us.

'Who just shot a cat?' a troop shouted over the noise. Before anyone could answer, I followed suit, spilling my guts on the floor where I stood. Once I had regained my composure, I felt much better, and I continued to enjoy the music and the drunken atmosphere. Just before midnight, the concert came to an end and we stumbled, disoriented, back to our tents, where we dropped dead to the ground and passed out.

In the heat of the morning, we all suffered severe hangovers, and cursed each other and ourselves in one breath for drinking too much and in another laughing with joy at the fact that we would soon be flying far away from this way of life and these punishing conditions – which half the time we brought solely upon ourselves.

From Grootfontein we were driven in Samils, along with a convoy of Ratels that headed towards the main train station in Windhoek, where they would be loaded upon trains and transported back to Pretoria. According to one of the troops, an RPG-7 rocket had taken one of the Ratels out as it made the journey southward. It was quite believable, but whether it was true I have no idea.

In the small terminal at the J.H. Strydom Airport in Windhoek, we waited like civilians – eager to board and never letting go of our rifles for fear of losing them. It seemed so strange to be back at the same place where we had landed a full two months earlier. How much had happened, and how many fearful thoughts of battle had passed through our minds as we walked this thin tightrope of insanity. Things could have gone either way, and each person can only withstand the uncertainty of war and death for a certain period of time before it begins to wear mentally on actions and inactions. In our case, it had been two extremely long months, which felt like an eternity that had not only drained us but had also left behind tension and anxiety, with no words in our vocabulary to capture the full scarring.

Looking through the glass of the airport terminal on ground level, we spotted our two waiting C-130 Hercules aircrafts at the far end of the runway with, SAFAIR painted in black lettering. Finally we were told to walk onto the runway, and with a surge of energy we stepped proudly towards the aircrafts, our rifles either slung over our shoulders or hanging from one hand. Seeing these four-engine planes up close immediately brought an end to the flood of our uncertainties.

Excitedly we boarded these old cargo planes capable of carrying a maximum of 90 people. Luckily for us, we would be part of that magical number – this being our ticket out of this hellhole and away from a place that we had branded so many times as 'the arse end of the world.'

What became of this land after we left was someone else's worry – our duty had been done, and our time had been served. Now it was time for home, back to a country so rich in natural beauty, with an infrastructure and a climate so much subtler than SWA/Namibia – facts that we had taken so much for granted in the past.

30. The frightening truth

Sitting buckled into the hammock seating enclosed in the noisy cargo hold, with no windows, we sat back and stared at each other as the big bird began to groan its way slowly forward. When it straightened up, it stopped and then the noise began to bellow, as it thrust itself forward like a hippo in full charge, its belly full of nervous soldiers. Holding our breaths, we waited to feel that lift as it took to the air and began the long, almost vertical climb, with nervous cheers willing it up until it levelled out and began its journey home to South Africa.

'Home sweet home, here we come!' I said to myself, as I wiped my sweaty hands on the thighs of my clean brown uniform. Hating to fly, I tried to relax in the strapped seating as it swayed with each movement. The plane groaned and creaked as it lurched, hitting every air pocket – which raised and dropped my stomach, forcing me to clutch tighter onto my rifle as the tension took hold of me.

Shit, what if we crashed now after living on the edge for these past months? I wondered. This scare was further amplified by all the groaning and creaking along with droplets of moisture that dripped from the roof of this machine – which in my eyes had flown the skies ten years too many.

How old is it and how safe is it? I wondered as I closed my eyes, and tried again to relax myself.

'If we get through this flight, this shit hole has seen the last of me!' I said to the troop next to me. After at least three hours of flight, the wheels eventually made contact with the landing strip. My heart stopped, and then raced with the speed of this powerful cargo carrier as we headed down the runway, blinded by the enclosed sides. With smiles all around, shouts of 'We're home' immediately erupted through the hull – for below us lay the soil of the land we were so proud to live in – our home, South Africa.

When the plane came to a stop, we began to disembark onto the tarred runway of the Waterkloof Air Force Base in Pretoria. Placing my first step back onto home soil felt weird and very electric. Here I was, having side-stepped the war – with all thanks to the tense standoff during the peace process that concluded with the implementation of Resolution 435. It was this Resolution that would finally mark the end of more than two decades of border war with an independent country soon to be known as Namibia.

The heat seemed kinder on our skin, and the air seemed fresher, as we made our way towards a few Samils, which were there to transport us back to our camper unit at 1-RNT. We rode like the wind – as if the drivers sensed our haste to get home and out of these uniforms.

In the open campground of 1-RNT, we were amazed to see fellow soldiers ready to deal with us in the signing out from this camp. Our rifles were checked over and signed back with much relief, though we felt naked without them. It was the first time in two months that we were free of this lifeline, which had accompanied us through the journey from bush toilet to trench, and in sleep never more than a fingertip out of reach.

After our rifles were handed in, our rank grouped us together and told us that we had to go through each of seven tents – which they pointed out to us. In each tent there was a table and a few chairs, and a couple of military councillors, whom we called 'head doctors.' I made my way into the first tent and was met by a pleasant smile from a woman dressed in military step outs – a distinguishingly smart uniform worn by rank – and a red beret.

'Is everything OK?' she asked softly. I just looked blankly back at her, and wanted to say, Do you have any idea how fuckin' close we came to going into Angola and maybe losing our lives? You have no idea of the fear we lived under, blinded by the unknown, waiting for something big to happen. You ask is everything OK? Well, it is fuckin' not!

Opening my mouth, I instead said, 'Yes. Everything is OK.' I just wanted to get the hell out of this eerie tent and away from these people, who were freaking me out.

In each tent I had to sign a form to say I was alright and did not want any help – which was fine with me, placing me one step closer to home. I wondered why we were all going through this. Maybe they thought – with all the gearing up for an attack, culminated with the ongoing waiting – that it warranted some kind release' but now was the wrong time, with home the only thing that mattered.

Everything was a rush now, so contrasting to the last month of dragging time and numbing wait. Troops where whisked away in different directions for their homeward journeys. Shaking hands with those we could, we said our hasty farewells, knowing full well that we would never see these newfound friends ever again. It was as if these friendships had been lent for a time in dire need, and our differing backgrounds and hometowns not playing a part until now.

When the last of the signing was completed, Wayne and I, along with a small contingent of Durbanites, boarded another Samil and with train tickets firmly clutched in hand, we were driven to the station. Before the Samil even exited the camp, Eric and Raymond – two troops from our National Service in Alpha Company 1-SAI – smashed a bottle upon the metal seat and quickly stuffed the neck full of marijuana. It was lit and smoked, the plumes of smoke fanning out from under the sail and wafting out into the dust trail behind us, in total defiance of what had been, and in celebration for what lay ahead. Eric thrust the broken, smoking neck towards us in offering to the joyous end. The white toilet paper

30. The frightening truth

flapped in the wind, wrapped around the circular neck to prevent the burning heat from penetrating onto the holding fingers and touching mouth, which also served as a filter. Shaking our heads, we declined, seeing no reason to find an escape from the safe situation we were now in – we continued to sit, watch, and just think, with the Samil racing onwards.

Did those doctors in the tent really care, or were they just passing the day in their military jobs? I wondered as I sat gazing into the dust, while being rocked around over every bump, like so many times before.

'It's over! Thank fuck!' I said to Wayne, who turned his head and smiled back. 'Home, here we come!'

The driver of this Samil had done us proud, making it to the station within minutes of the departure time. Hurriedly we boarded the old reddish brown train of the South African Railways, shouldering our kitbags, our hearts pounding with pride, having reached the end and so often wondered whether we ever would. We found the closest unoccupied cabin, where we dumped our bags and ourselves. With a deep sigh, we sat back and waited for the whistle that would begin the final leg of this long journey.

After a drunken night on the train and a full day's travel, we finally pulled into the Durban station in the mid afternoon – all of our heads sticking out of the windows, adorned with broad smiles, revelling in the excitement at seeing the main city of our hometown once more, after what seemed like such a long absence. The train coasted the last few hundred metres before it came to a stop, at the very spot where it had all begun only two months ago – though it seemed like it had been a year.

Wayne's sister Sharon stood waiting on the platform to meet us, and after some final goodbyes with some fellow Durban troops, we followed her lead back to her car. Loading our kit into her Golf, we climbed with a strange feeling into the vehicle, which seemed so low to the ground after riding Ratels daily for almost ten weeks.

Sitting in the back, I suddenly had this overwhelming feeling that blanketed me' I watched in deathly silence as a new world opened up and rushed past, while we drove through the main streets of Durban. Tense and totally withdrawn, I looked through the window wide-eyed and dead still, and what I saw was spinning me out of control. Cars were closing in on me from all sides, hooting and jostling for position under flashing colours of traffic signals. People crossed the streets where they chose, rushing in urgency to their respective destinations. Foreign aromas wafted from street vendors, mixed with fumes from idling and revving engines. The chaotic noise of screeching cars and trucks, followed with backfiring and more hooting, and being cornered into dead-end lanes by trucks delivering goods, all began to push me lower into my seat. Throngs of people, mainly black, talked loudly – which sounded more like threatening shouts. The tall concrete buildings towered over me, the glass shop windows reflected a contrast of colours, not seen even in the wildest African sunset. It all began to feel too much. I sensed the panic of claustrophobia welling up, and this new jungle began to swallow and then drown me under the tall, cliff-like wall of brick and mortar.

I needed time to adjust from the sight of open bush, dust, the aroma of diesel, and the sound of silence – to pavement, concrete, and bustling noise. I felt trapped in the car – I just wanted to fling the door open and run – run to a safe place, where I could hide from all this clamour and havoc.

What the hell is going on with me? How can I feel this way? I've not seen action. I sank into a deep pit of silence, leaving Wayne in the front seat to catch up on news with his sister.

Maybe it was because I felt like I had fought the war. Maybe it was all the intense practice for the real thing, followed by the never-ending wait to go in! Maybe my nerves were frayed with all the swirling rumours of an attack, and the guessing of each other's fate. Maybe it was the continual not knowing whether I would live or die.

Whatever it was I do not know – but what I do know is that something up there in the solitude of open bush in northern Owamboland had stirred some strange feelings in me, and it was coming out now.

On arriving at Wayne's mother's house, we had a couple of beers to toast our homecoming before I made my way home to Hillcrest – feeling only slightly better about things, and yet abnormally out-of-place in the comfort of my home surroundings.

Taking stock over the two-and-a-half years that I had now served in the army, I realized that most of my time had been lived on the hard ground, at the mercy of the elements. I, along with my buddies, had journeyed through the bitter cold and into the scorching heat, through the soaking rains and across the dry powdery sands of dust, to have our bodies wrestled with fatigue for many hours' only to become bored out of our wits the next. We had been scared shitless many a time, only to have the feeling drowned away with heartfelt laughter – to be clean for a single day, after living with the stench of filth and the itchiness of grime and dried-on sweat for weeks on end.

Alcohol had strengthened our resolve and courage, and we used it to shake the feeling of insanity that lurked freely in us, so that we could feel human once

30. The frightening truth

again. Dagga had become a commonplace addiction for some and an escape for others, dulling our senses while passing idle time. Through all of these extremes, we had stood proud – only to have it shot down by the slightest ignorant, slanderous shout from the rank.

It had been hell through all the struggles, and yet our friendships brought us through, and our strength of character was built up on the sheer will to survive the ordeal and emerge as men on the other side.

Border-line insanity had, on too many occasions, steered our minds into a slow drifting into the past, only to speed them into the future in an effort to drown out the helplessness and depressing feeling of the present.

We had all come a long way, through the insane moments when we felt we were going to disintegrate under the hardship. But in the end, it had given me life-altering experiences and, in my eyes, the survival against many hard-to-overcome obstacles.

A long time ago – within the first six months of my service – I had said to myself: If I get through this, I can get through anything in life.

This vow became my motto, and I would use it time and again to conquer life's testing struggles.

The insanity that had lived with me on and off for two-and-a-half years along the border line had come close to pushing me over the edge.

Thankfully border-line insanity in uniform had finally ended.

2003-Ombalantu Base. Fifteen years after the end of the border war, a stark contrast to the picture perfect days of SADF control.

31

After the war was over
Revisiting Namibia fifteen years on

Here was I, a South African living in Canada and holding a British passport, sitting on a plane bound for Windhoek International Airport in Namibia. Under the calm of darkness and the coolness of night, I stepped off the plane and onto the runway, breaking that solemn army vow of never returning to that 'arse end of the world.'

Geographically I had broken this promise, but politically I had not' for the country I had served in was known then as South-West Africa, which no longer existed.

On clearing customs, I walked out of the small airport and stared into the darkness, looking up at the night sky. It had not changed one bit' the array of stars still shone as bright, unblemished by industrial pollution, with that same calming effect I had experienced all those years ago. Climbing into a taxi, I began to retrace my journey in the comfort of a civilian car, instead of one of those dreaded cattle trucks.

After a night in Windhoek, I rented a car and headed for the Etosha Park in the comfort of air conditioning – my protection from the dry, burning heat that rushed at me every time I got out of the car. I had not been in the Etosha Game Park more than five minutes before I spotted an impala grazing below a tree. Looking at the buck, my eyes caught sight of something above it in the tree' and to my shock, I realized it was a big martial eagle, perched like a statue on a branch, watching me. Immediately I was jolted back to that sad day when a small group of us had allowed Paul to shoot and kill one just like it. While I drove on, I reminisced about all our ambush positions, laid along the outskirts of the park, lying dirty in shallow dugouts and passing the many hours of boredom, in temperatures driving us stark-raving mad.

Driving through the park, I saw a wide variety of game – lion, buffalo, and elephant. The highlight of my drive along the dusty roads had to be a huge old lone elephant bull, as white as flour from all the rolling in the dry saltpans. He strolled majestically across the roadway, as if in slow motion three metres in front of my car – giving off the air of a king in this open savannah.

I exited the park at the Mpingana gate, and headed with relief towards the paved road, in the direction of Ondangwa and on passing it, I took in the all-too-familiar scenery. The makalani palm trees still towered over the primitive kraals, and the anthills still stood like statues, weathered by the heat and rains. The ground was still as flat as a tabletop and as dry and desolate as the day we had left it. After a long drive, I stopped in Ombalantu hoping to find the old SADF base and after asking a few locals, I eventually found it. It was no wonder that I had driven past it twice, for it no longer resembled a base. Back in 1985, I had spent some hellish nights here, battling the heavy rains, fatigue, and the weight of anger as we patrolled in the vicinity of this stronghold. I will never forget the march we took from our waterlogged positions, where no vehicles could reach us at the time, and we arrived at the base eight hell-bent hours later.

I can remember as clear as day, in the earlier weeks of our first border trip, lying asleep dead to the world, and yet aware of the slightest sound – only to be jolted awake by the harmless rustle of a bush or the breaking of a twig. Instantly our eyes would snap open and our thoughts would run wild. Our bodies remained frozen as we reached out, as if in slow motion, for our rifles, ready to ward off any lurking danger. This was border life, and we as soldiers were facing the real test head-on.

Stepping inside the base, I saw just the relic of its former glory – no longer recognizable as an SADF stronghold. The neatly kept, fortified walls had deteriorated with rain and neglect, and were now only half as high as they once were. The ash block mess hall, kitchen, and toilet area still stood with the black screen windows flapping in the wind like torn sails that had weathered the storm of all storms. It was this area that had served as a shield for many of us from the lashing rain and winds – the typical African downpours that we had experienced more often than we cared to remember. An old brown army canteen had been left behind in the building, just in front of a pile of stones that had been used, ironically, as a cooking fire on the very floor where we had sat – cold, but at least somewhat dry. The canteen was a stark reminder of the South African presence that had once occupied this area with such strength. Looking out of the flapping netting, I saw a sandbagged bunker – the bags solidified into hard bricks, crossing one another in neat layers over a half-moon metal covering, high enough off the ground for a person to walk upright into. At the entrance to the bunker, a green and yellow metal sign hung above the entrance, with the words 'BEV' in capital letters. This was short for *Bevelvoerder* Officer in Command, and these were his old sleeping quarters, now home to the locals who had laid claim to his old bomb shelter. The old signal tower still stood, which had linked the base to Sector 10 at Oshakati, along with some scaffolding that supported a water tower minus the water tank. The base was still marked by the giant baobab tree, which could fit 20 people inside. The old tree was the only thing that had not been affected by the elements. Ombalantu base now had a very desolate and eerie feel to it, having long ago been deserted by the strength and protection that the South African forces controlled, leaving it open for the locals to retake their land.

Getting back into the car, I turned around and left, leaving behind the scary stillness of the old camp and heading back to the tar road in the direction of Ruacana. On reaching Ruacana, I overlooked the Calueque Dam, where 11 National Servicemen had lost their young lives as the peace process was beginning to gain momentum. I drove up to the Angolan border post and saw a tattered red and black flag, fluttering in a way that resembled the predicament of the country. It marked the border with a decrepit and abandoned hut at the border post. This is where we would have crossed with Ratel after Ratel had we been given the order that many had wanted. I will always remember the anxiety, coupled with nervous tension, as we waited for that order that seemed so imminent. Living through this volatile situation definitely aged us, and geared us into a survival mode for future life challenges.

Before turning back, I took a look at the old Namibian power station, which had been totally destroyed and pockmarked by AK rounds as the terrorists crossed the border from Angola. Driving like crazy to beat the darkness which held the threat of hidden animal crossings upon this rural, single-lane 'highway' that had killed many, and would kill many more, I passed through Oshakati. I was able to see the regional headquarters of SWAPO, marked by a painted mural of a man holding his stance with a black-power salute, his right arm raised straight above the head, clenching a tight fist. The blue, red, and green of the ruling flag flew dominantly in the breeze – a sight that had never been seen by us soldiers, for this had been our enemy.

The more locals I met, the more I felt that the tension of the past had disappeared and been replaced with hope. I met quite a few ex-SWAPO fighters, who were unashamed to admit the role they had played in their past.

They had fought for what they believed in – or what they had been indoctrinated into believing – and we, on the other hand, had obeyed the orders for what our white government believed in. I looked at one particular Owambo man as he filled my car up with petrol. He had been a 'freedom fighter' in the independence struggle' his past was now buried, and replaced with a cheerful smile. He shook my hand after I told him that I had served in the South African army in his country' he harboured no hatred or resentment toward the drawn-out bush war, fought in Africa's very last colony.

I had heard first-hand horror stories from both sides, where the young and the innocent had met with untimely deaths, and those left behind were left to deal with the scars. I met an Angolan girl called Tuli, who was born in Luanda' and when life got bad there, she moved with her parents and settled in Ombalantu in northern Owamboland. Her father was a SWAPO delegate, so they were constantly in danger' and after the move they lived in Lusaka, the capital of Zambia, and Havana, Cuba. She went on to tell me how one of her relatives was killed by the Security Forces and dragged behind one of the army vehicles while the family watched. They were told if they shed a tear, they too would be killed.

Tuli went on to tell me about the battle at Cassinga, in Angola, in 1978, which was SWAPO's darkest day – over 1000 dead, which according to her account included many women and children. Her voice strained with emotion –she told me that when it was over, the sky was filled with red. She went silent after telling me this – I could see the horror in her eyes as she relived her side of the bush war.

She explained to me something I had heard about – but to hear it from someone who was a SWAPO supporter herself only added meaning to the story. SWAPO soldiers would dig holes and bury themselves beneath a piece of corrugated tin, which was covered with earth and brush, concealing them from patrolling South African soldiers. When nightfall came, they would reappear and continue their missions as insurgents, blending into the cover of night.

I left feeling the deep scars that had been inflicted on this Owambo woman of Angolan birth, whose life had been greatly affected by the bush war.

Driving northwards, I met two ex-Koevoet fighters – one out of work and the other living out an existence with part of his brain accidentally shot away by one of the soldiers in his Casspir. It was amazing how I had come to meet this fellow, known only as *Piesang* Banana. Passing through Tsumeb, I had a few beers at a local bar and got talking to two white men, who told me about this Koevoet soldier who had basically been left for dead. They told me he was now working as a guide, taking fishermen out along the Zambezi River. On arriving at the 'Hippo Lodge,' just a little way past Katima Mulilo, I met this man purely by chance. He sat quietly on a wooden bench, dribbling unnoticed as he stared over the calm and very peaceful waters of the Zambezi with a glass of neat spirits in his hand. The stillness was interrupted by a quick splash, followed with ripples spinning into circular rings around the disturbance.

'Tiger fish!' *Piesang* mumbled through his drawl, a slight smile pulled to one side of his mouth' he held a keen fisherman's glint in his eyes, firmly fixed upon the glassy waters. He was a big man with a round, suntanned face, who had begun soldiering in the early 70s with the Rhodesian African Rifles. He was one of the 'white' leaders who led the Mashona and Matabele regiments against the ZANLA and ZIPPRA terrorists in the Rhodesian bush war.

When Rhodesia became Zimbabwe, and any unfulfilled dreams were lost in the after effects of the long and costly drawn-out war, people mainly white moved south for the chance of a better and safer life. Soldiers who knew only one life chose the next war, and that was South Africa's war with SWAPO. Many of these hard-core Rhodesian warriors took up a new fight, bringing haunting images from one war into the next, leading many of the Casspir vehicles of Koevoet into countless skirmishes with SWAPO.

Piesang was just one of many forgotten soldiers, now just a shell of the man that he once was, with a bottle always close to his side. With sad eyes he raised his face and looked straight at me.

'I remember only two dates,' he said. 'The day I was born, and the day a bullet shot out a chunk of my brain.'

Then, like an old man, he pushed himself up with his well-used wooden stick, and once on his feet he held his balance for a couple of seconds before he shuffled away, dragging his paralyzed right leg, which trailed grotesquely behind him. I remained seated, wallowing selfishly in the mesmerizing beauty, watching helplessly as this old bush war veteran disappeared along with his silent and lonely tangle of thoughts. The drink helped, but when it wore off he would once again be swallowed by the inner darkness that consumed him.

Sitting alone, the carnage of butchered bodies that had met my eyes in Angola all those years ago popped back into my head as clear as yesterday – the rotten flesh again creeping into the back of my throat. A clean death – if there could be such a thing – would have been easier to bear than the bloody massacre of women and children left to rot in the sun.

Taking a mouthful of beer, I quickly washed away the scene and reconnected with the tranquility all around me.

Leaving the Caprivi Strip, I drove down to Grootfontein, staying one night there, with such a different feeling to that first night in the Grootfontein base on our arrival in 1985.

Certain songs from the 80s still bring me back to that time and place. Our fear of the unknown had burdened us, and when we did catch a wave of a tune, it was in a futile attempt to escape reality. One particular song, which will stick with me forever, is Cyndi Lauper's *Time After Time*:

31. After the war was over: Revisiting Namibia fifteen years on

Caught up in circles, confusion
Is nothing new.
Flashback – warm nights
Almost left behind
Suitcases of memories,
Time after time
Then you say – go slow
I fall behind
The second hand unwinds
The drum beats out of time
Time after time.

Our lives had not only been governed religiously around time, but our minds had become muddled as we travelled back in time to our civilian lives, away from the pressures and strains of keeping up on the patrols when very little ever made any sense to us. Having lived through our army world under tough conditions, and far too many absurd orders, was most certainly a constant challenge – time after time. I think I can speak for most of the platoon when I say that not for any sum of money would we ever consider doing this again. Being young and stupid at times, this experience had taught us valuable lessons in life, which could not be bought but only acquired through struggle and hardship. Out of this mind-altering passage we had emerged as young men from a lasting human experience, rooted deep within our souls.

Standing in Namibia and gazing out upon nothing, as we had done so many times before, I realized deep down what a tremendously proud South African I had become. Staring into the hazy heat, I thought about Angoose, Kort Beentjies, and Sakkie – Gall, Brian and Paul – all of whom had died soon after our service. Their untimely deaths really struck a chord in me – it left me with thoughts of good young people, who would not have thought twice about safeguarding their fellow troops in a life-or-death situation, and now they were dead before they reached their late twenties. It did not seem right or fair.

When Wayne told me about Paul's death, it really shocked me. His passing was by far the saddest of the three. He had been my leader, and a good one at that, surviving three months in the hell of a third world Mozambican jail cell, only to die on the road when his vehicle struck a horse while passing through the Transkei. He had died taking his horrific ordeal with him – having never been able to disclose his bottled-up secrets to any of us. Those who knew him well knew how the episode had come to haunt him.

Gall had also died in a car accident, but Brian on the other hand had died sitting in a car while an African man held a gun to his head. As he fumbled for his gun hidden under the seat, he was executed in cold blood, right in front of his girlfriend. Brian had lived his army life on a dangerous edge, and unfortunately had died by the same headstrong principles. His death, nevertheless, came as a shocking blow to those of Platoon 3, leaving us with the memory of a cheerful character and a tenacious but happy-go-lucky attitude towards army life.

A few years ago I found out that Sax, our medic had sadly died of kidney failure.

And then there was Sandor who had survived hell in the Machava prison, and tragically committed suicide. He had not been able to shake off the ghosts from his capture and suffering with PTSD had turned to alcohol to deal with those demons that haunted him daily since 1985. After numerous attempts to become sober, he sadly ended his life at 3am, on 2 October 2013. Sandor shot himself.

Looking back at Platoon 3, Sandor was the last person who I would have thought would take his life. He was fearless, had a carefree attitude and his strength and stamina was second to none, and he could lug his heavy mag around like a child would wrestle with a toy.

His suffering with PTSD had terminated his life before he reached 50 years of age.

After all we had been through, it seemed so senseless and out of place that their eager lives had been snuffed out so suddenly. It just went to show that those days of being invincible were now long gone.

Even though it had taken 19 years to look back on my life, I felt I had discarded a burden of tension and anxiety, bitterness and subdued anger, in the very place where most of it was insanely born in me.

Leaving Namibia, I saw my life as having come full circle. Never before had I seen things in my character so clearly. I was now ready to take the last step and reflect on myself – where my mind had conquered the physical and hauled me through the insanities day by day and week by week, into the months and the years ahead – until the end eventually came.

Today I can honestly say I am glad I did it, and I feel proud to have been a part of those good old army days – days that cannot be taken away, changed or ever forgotten.

I had no idea how I would feel to tell this story. The more I wrote, the more I felt my army anger and aggravations dwindle – to a point where I felt I had performed a catharsis upon myself.

31. After the war was over: Revisiting Namibia fifteen years on

I now believe I have emerged as a new person – a whole lot lighter and far more energized, with much of my tension and anxiety abandoned within these pages rather than left to fester inside of me, in the way it had for many silent years.

Life is all about the journey and how we as people – or in our case soldiers weather the ups and downs along the way. The desination is only the end of the journey, the building of character having already been unconsciously groomed along the way, within us.

Border-line insanity had certainly strengthened my character and all those with whom I served.

2005-Machava Prison, Mozambique. The hell-hole where Laurence, Sandor and Paul had been imprisoned after capture by FRELIMO troops.

Glossary

Balsak	kitbag
1-SAI	1-South African Infantry Battalion
4-SAI	4-South African Infantry Battalion
1-RNT	1-Regiment Northern Transvaal
61-Mech	61-Mechanized Infantry Battalion
Basics	basic military training lasting three months
Bivi	groundsheet
Bombed up	replenishing ammunition etc
Browns	South African army uniform
Buffel Buffalo	mine protected infantry fighting vehicle, carries a section of troops
Canteen	metal drinking cup/pot/shaving dish. Called a fire bucket in army slang
Camps	one to three-month call-ups over a ten year period that began after completion of National Service.
Campers	slang for Citizen Force soldiers attending camps.
Casspir	mine-protected infantry fighting vehicle, carries a section. Used mainly by Koevoet
Cattle truck	army slang for Samil 100 troop carrier
CB	Confined to barracks
Chopper tent	tent with a metal frame that sleeps five to six troops
Citizen Force	reserve force comprising civilians who had completed National Service
Cuca shop	African shop in SWA named after an Angolan beer
Dagga	marijuana
DB	detention barracks
Dixie	two aluminum rectangular boxes, that fitted into each other and were used in the bush to eat from
Extra days	time added to the mandatory two years National Service.
FAPLA	Angolan army
Flossie	C-130 Hercules cargo aircraft
FRELIMO	Mozambican Liberation Front
Fuel tablet	white flat round tablet used to heat food and water
Go-cart	army slang for fibreglass toilet shells placed over a hole in the ground

Glossary

Grootsak	backpack
Gunship	Alouette helicopter armed with a 20mm cannon
Kas	metal cupboard
Klaar	out leaving on completion of two years National Service or a Citizen Force camp
Koevoet	South-West Africa Police Counter Insurgency Unit
Kwevoel Grey Lourie bird	mine-protected logistical vehicle
Locals or PBs	black people resident in an area
Loot or lieutie	lieutenant
Mahangu	millet
Makalani palm	palm tree in Owamboland, which produces vegetable ivory
MPLA	Popular Movement for the Liberation of Angola
NAAFI	no ambition and fuck-all interest
National Service	two years' mandatory military service
Olifant(Elephant)	medium battle tank with a 105mm tank gun
Opfok	punishment and training
Oshanas	pans that fill with water during the rainy season.
Ou manne	soldiers serving the second year of their National Service
Owambo	tribes-people of Owamboland, pronounced Ovambo
Owamboland	region in northern South-West Africa/Namibia
Panga	long, broad and heavy bladed knife, machete
Paraat	prepared and ready to follow each and every order
PB	*plaaslike bevolking* local population
PF	Permanent Force of the SADF
Pikstel	army issue cutlery set
PLAN	Peoples Liberation Army of Namibia SWAPO's military wing
Puma helicopter	used for transportation, lifting of casualties, search and rescue
Rank	soldier's slang for an NCO or officer.
Ratel 20 honey badger	armoured infantry fighting vehicle armed with a 20mm cannon, carries a section comprising a driver, gunner, commander, tail gunner, and seven riflemen
RENAMO	Mozambique National Resistance

Rondfok	being messed around by [people of] rank
Rower	new recruit
RP	Regimental Police
SADF	South African Defence Force
Samil 50, 100, 120	Mine protected vehicles used for logistics and troop carrying
Siff	very dirty
Soutie	English speaker
Spoor	tracks
Staaldak	steel helmet
States	serviceman's slang name for South Africa
Stove	tin with holes used to warm food with the aid of a fuel tablet
SWAPO	South-West Africa Peoples Organization
Takkies	lace-up running shoes
TB	temporary base.
Terr	Terrorist/insurgent, guerrilla
Trommel	metal trunk
UNITA	National Union for the Total Independence of Angola
Vark	stupid/pig
Varkpan	stainless steel eating tray
Vasbyt	perseverance and showing willpower to stick it out
Yati	boundary line that separates South-West Africa and Angola

Bibliography

South Africa's Border War 1966-89 Willem Steenkamp
Illustrated Guide to Southern Africa Reader's Digest
Illustrated History of South Africa Reader's Digest
Lonely Planet Namibia Deanna Swaney
The Buffalo Soldiers Col Jan Breytenbach
Guerrilla Warfare John Pimlott
Peoples of Africa from Afrikaner to Zulu J. Middleton
Communist Military Machine General Editor: Ian Beckett
Death of Dignity Angola's Civil War Victoria Brittain
The Natal Mercury archives, Don Africana Library, Durban RSA

Credits

*Page 289
"Major Tom (Coming Home)"
by Peter Schilling and David Lodge.
©1982 by Peer Musikverlag GmbH.
Copyright Renewed. International Copyright Secured.
Used by Permission. All Rights Reserved.
Administered by Peermusic Canada Inc.

*Page 494 & Page 495
"Time After Time"
(Hyman/Lauper)
Published by Dub Notes Music & Rellla Music Corp.
Rellla Music Corp. Administered by Sony/ATV Music Publishing Canada.
1670 Bayview Avenue, Suite 408, Toronto, Ontario, M4G 3C2
All Rights Reserved – Used by Permission.

"Time After Time"
Words and Music by Cyndi Lauper and Rob Hyman.
©1983 Dub Notes and Rellla Music Corp.
All Rights on Behalf of Dub Notes. Administered by WB Music Corp.
All rights Reserved. Used by Permission of Alfred Publishing Co., Inc.

Made in the USA
Monee, IL
28 April 2026